Event Management & Event Tourism
2nd Edition

Donald Getz, Ph.D.
Professor, Tourism and Hospitality Management
Haskayne School of Business
University of Calgary
2500 University Drive N.W.
Calgary, Alberta, Canada T2N 1N4

i

COGNIZANT COMMUNICATION CORPORATION
New York • Sydney • Tokyo
www.cognizantcommunication.com

Event Management & Event Tourism
2nd Edition

Cognizant Communication Office:

U.S.A.   3 Hartsdale Road, Elmsford, New York 10523-3701

Library of Congress Cataloging-in-Publication Data

Getz, Donald, 1949-
  Event management and event tourism / by Donald Getz.– 2nd ed.
     p. cm.
  Includes bibliographical references and index.
  ISBN 1-882345-46-0 (softboound)
  1. Tourism. 2. Special events. I. Title.
  G155.A1G438 2005
  910'.68–dc22

                              2005020409

Printed in the United States of America

Printing: 1 2 3 4 5 6 7 8 9 10 Year: 1 2 3 4 5 6 7 8 9 10

Contents

List of Photos

List of Tables

Cover photos: Fireworks display (with permission from ZAMBELLI Fireworks Internationale); Stampede site, Calgary (credit: Calgary Exhibition and Stampede); Volvo Ocean Race, Gothenburg Stopover (credit: Volvo Ocean Race/Rick Tomlinson); East Timor handover ceremony (credit: William J. O'Toole); Start of the 2003 Gold Coast Airport Marathon (credit: courtesy of the *Gold Coast Bulletin*); 2003 Rotary International Convention.

Acknowledgements

Many people provided information and ideas for this book; however, I take full responsibility for any errors or misinterpretation of the facts.

General thanks go to all the researchers and authors cited in this book, and the entire research community that continues to develop the event management field and event studies.

Special thanks are given to the following persons and organizations who made specific contributions to this book, particularly in writing sections and granting permission to use material.

> Bethlehem Musikfest (Jo Pritchett)
> Betsy Wiersma (Wiersma Experience Marketing and Creative Event Development)
> Calgary Exhibition and Stampede (Leslie Stang, Brenda Hanchar)
> Canadian Tulip Festival (Michel Gauthier)
> Cherry Creek Arts Festival (Tony Smith)
> Chicago Mayor's Office of Special Events (Cindy Gatziolis)
> Concepts Worldwide (Theresa Breining)
> e=mc2 event management (Ken Christofferson and Jocelyn Flanagan)
> ESPN (Melissa Gullotti)
> Gold Coast Events (Cameron Hart)
> Goran Lindhal
> Got Event, Gothenburg, Sweden (Toralf Nilsson)
> International Association for Exhibition Management (Cathy Breden)
> International Association of Fairs and Exhibitions (Rachel Stutesmun)
> International Festivals and Events Association (Steve Schmader)
> International Special Events Society (Kevin Hacke)
> Meeting Professionals International (Kelly Schulz)
> Orange County Convention Center (Shannon Cooper, Julie Snith)
> Portland Rose Festival (Adrian McCarthy)
> Queensland Events Corporation (Sharyn Sawyer, Fiona Lammie)
> Tourism Ottawa (Martin Winges)
> Volvo Event Management (Sven Osterberg)
> William O'Toole, Event Project Management System Pty Ltd.
> The *Journal of Travel Research* has granted permission to use two diagrams published in Vol. 39(4). 2001.

Preface

The fields of event management and event tourism have grown dramatically since I wrote *Festivals, Special Events and Tourism* in 1991, and even since 1997 when the first edition of *Event Management & Event Tourism* was published. Many new career paths have emerged, and the publication of relevant books and papers has mushroomed. Academic programs in event management are now well established in many institutions around the globe. Both the academic study of event management and the profession are maturing.

It is also now possible to talk seriously about a new academic field called "Event Studies." In 1991 there was very little literature, and only a few subjects taught, about events, generally within tourism, recreation, or sports programs. Now it is possible to get graduate degrees specific to event studies. Event Studies is a field of inquiry drawing on many other sources of theory, knowledge, and methods. Creation of *Festival Management & Event Tourism* (now called *Event Management*) as the first research journal devoted to this field (in 1993), cofounded by myself and Dr. Bruce Wicks, gave impetus to the academic study of events.

Event Studies subsumes event management and event tourism. To become a professional in event management or event tourism requires foundation knowledge concerning the nature of events and their importance in society. If they were not such important phenomena why would we invest so much in their production and marketing?

This book is the second edition of *Event Management & Event Tourism* (Cognizant Communication, 1997), but it has a somewhat broader role to play, both in providing an overview of Event Studies and providing a foundation for professional event management. I have deliberately expanded the discussion of research, theory, and the contributions of other fields and disciplines, as well as updated and expanded all the management-specific material.

Key Objectives of the Book

1. To define and explain the field of Event Studies as an academic foundation to the professions and practice of event management and event tourism.
2. To provide a comprehensive, systematic study of events as social, economic, and environmental phenomena.
3. To provide students with the knowledge and skills for event management careers.
4. To explain the nature and importance of event tourism, and how to employ events in destination planning and marketing.
5. To interpret and apply principles of business, public, and not-for-profit management to the special needs of events and event organizations.
3. To use case studies of successful events in demonstrating how managers can improve their effectiveness and efficiency in producing successful events and meeting their organization's wider goals.

4. To demonstrate how different perspectives on events (i.e., economics, community, visitors, organizations, sponsors, the environment) require different management approaches, and how recognition of the interrelatedness of all these perspectives can enhance event production, marketing, and goal attainment.
5. To foster professionalism in event management, covering the knowledge base, theory, methodologies, and ethics.

This book is specifically intended to be a college and university level text. Compared with the majority of event-related books, it places less emphasis on how to produce events and more on the following:

- underlying theory and knowledge from contributing disciplines and related fields,
- the value and specific contributions of research,
- integrative themes and methods,
- discussion of important issues,
- the necessity and nature of ethics in professionalism,
- application of fundamental management theories and practices.

I decided to keep the Event Tourism theme, in part because none of the other books on event management include it. Events are of profound importance in tourism and hospitality and the tourism market is important to many event producers, so it makes sense to combine the two.

In addition to a separate chapter on event tourism planning for destinations, I have also integrated this theme throughout the book. Look for specific event tourism topics in the overall chapter outline, as well as in the chapter-specific learning objectives.

Revisions Made for the Second Edition

In addition to the emphasis placed on establishing Event Studies as a legitimate field of inquiry, and Event Management as a profession, other changes have been made to the format and contents of the book:

- chapters begin with learning objectives (which encompass pertinent management competencies);
- chapters end with basic and advanced study questions (the advanced questions are more suitable for assignments and essays);
- Internet addresses and sources are provided throughout the text, especially with regard to organizations and events that are profiled;
- expanded sections on risk management, project planning, sponsorship, legal issues including contracts, and logistics;
- "research notes" provide important findings from published sources on many topics discussed in the chapters; these should encourage students and practitioners to consult the research literature;
- more comprehensive coverage of the diversity of event careers and settings;
- many examples have been kept, but updated and expanded, while some have been replaced with new ones.

New for Instructors

Instructors using this text now have online access to an Instructor's Manual including a full set of PowerPoint slides (both summary points from the text and all the line draw-ings). The manual provides lecture outlines and advice on how to use the case studies, profiles, and research notes.

Disclaimer

Although this book has been carefully researched and is very comprehensive in its examination of event management, the event producer and manager must take ultimate responsibility for ensuring that proper care is taken to operate a safe, financially sound, and enjoyable event. The contents of this book are intended to inform and stimulate the event manager and are not to be interpreted as firm advice that can be applied to any specific situation.

Chapter 1

Introduction to Event Studies, Event Management, and Event Tourism

Learning Objectives

- Be able to explain the field of "event studies."
- Understand the essential elements and foundations of event management as a profession.
- Understand the nature and importance of event tourism, including the five main economic roles of events.
- Know the key disciplinary perspectives on the study of events and how they contribute to event management.
- Know where events fit into closely related professional fields.
- Learn about the nature and importance of events in society, the economy, and the environment, and how research is essential to support both event studies and event management.
- Learn key terminology for the events field and the typology of planned events.
- Understand what makes some events "special."

Do You Want to be a Professional Event Manager?

The profession of event management is exciting, fast growing, and global. It presents a kaleidoscope of opportunities for careers in public, private, and not-for-profit organizations, and for personal challenges and artistic creativity. You can apply your skills to all types of events in many different event facilities and settings, or concentrate on sports, festivals, meetings, exhibitions, or other specific types. The scope for invention and mobility is almost limitless.

Or you could start an event-related business, being a party or meeting planner, a sport marketing consultant, a festival or entertainment producer, or a trade show designer. Knowledge of how events are produced, managed, and marketed will give you countless opportunities to provide the industry with services and products for profit.

Events are also very important as social services and for fund raising to support a large number of causes, giving you scope to contribute to society and the environment. Whatever your motives and interests, there is something for you in the world of events.

To start thinking seriously about event-related career paths, read the profiles of professionals in this text. Also read the profiles of event-producing organizations, each of which provides a number of career paths related to events.

What Is Event Management?

"Event management" encompasses the planning and production of all types of events, including meetings and conventions, exhibitions, festivals and other cultural celebrations, sport competitions, entertainment spectaculars, private functions, and numerous other special events. Event managers might also be required to form and administer the organizations that produce or govern events. Skills in event management will also be useful for careers in related fields such as tourism, hospitality, arts, culture, sports, recreation, and leisure.

Event management used to be a sideline to other occupations, something one did because events were required. Or people became event planners and managers because their particular skills were needed, and they could adapt. All that has changed, and within the last 15 years event management has been given formal academic status in many colleges and universities. Today's event manager is better educated, much more sophisticated in terms of the fundamental management skills, and more versatile. In addition, there are numerous other professionals, such as in sport, recreation, or arts management, who need to study event management in order to fulfill their responsibilities.

At the same time, the event "industry" has surged ahead in terms of the number and size of events, their economic, cultural, and social significance, and media coverage. There is no room for unprofessional conduct, and demands for professional accountability are ever-increasing. Today's professional event manager has skills and experience that can adapt to all types of events in many different settings; it is no longer desirable or necessary to be confined to one specific event-related job within a company, facility, or organization.

In this book all the fundamentals of event management are provided for the student interested in a professional career, or interested in adding event management to other professional skill sets. Readers will first be presented in this chapter with the academic context for their profession—a field I have termed Event Studies. You will see how it is necessary to draw on many other disciplines and fields, plus the basics of management, before specializing in one or more aspects of event management. Readers will also be informed of the ways in which events are produced and managed as part of sports, arts, hospitality, and other professional management careers.

Chapter 2 gets to the heart of event management careers and professionalism. A number of professionals are profiled, as well as professional associations representing the key specializations within event management. Certification and ethics are discussed in this context.

In the subsequent chapters key management functions are covered in detail, including planning, organizing, marketing, and evaluation. Special attention is given to a number of topics of crucial significance within the world of events, such as risk management, project planning, sponsorship, and logistics. Throughout the book the connections between events and tourism are stressed. Tourism is not covered in depth in most event management texts, but I believe it is important for students of tourism to understand how events are managed, and for event managers to know more about the important tourism market and the tourism-related roles and impacts of events.

Event Studies

Not only are events produced increasingly by professional event managers, but a field of study and research has recently developed to support this profession and its industry. Professionals calling themselves "event manager" should be able to explain what is unique about events, why they are important to society and the economy, and how they are evolving. If your career or job involves the production, coordination, marketing, or evaluation of events, you want to know that your efforts are important and valued.

"Event studies" is a field of research and teaching focused on the nature and importance of events in society, the economy, and the environment. Learning more about events directly contributes to increased professionalism in event management. Event studies borrows from other fields and academic disciplines, including anthropology, history, sociology, psychology, leisure studies, sport and business management, art administration, geography, planning, design, and economics. Event managers, to the extent that they learn from their experiences and communicate that knowledge to others, also contribute to developing the filed.

Much of what has been written about event management, marketing, and impacts makes a contribution to greater understanding of the phenomenon of events. While event management necessarily focuses on planned events with a social or economic purpose, event studies has a somewhat broader scope of concern. There are many unplanned events to be studied. Consider the protests and riots that increasingly accompany gatherings of political or business leaders. Are they planned or spontaneous? Do they reflect in any way our approach to festival production or publicity stunts? What is the boundary between what Boorstin (1961) called "pseudo events" and real news? In the modern world, are the distinctions slipping or important?

Figure 1.1 illustrates a conceptual framework for connecting event studies, management fundamentals, and event management. The model was first published in the research journal *Event Management*, Volume 6(1), 2000, and revised in 2002 (Getz 2002a), in large part to mark the changing of the journal's name from *Festival Management & Event Tourism* to *Event Management*. This change specifically recognized the facts that event man-

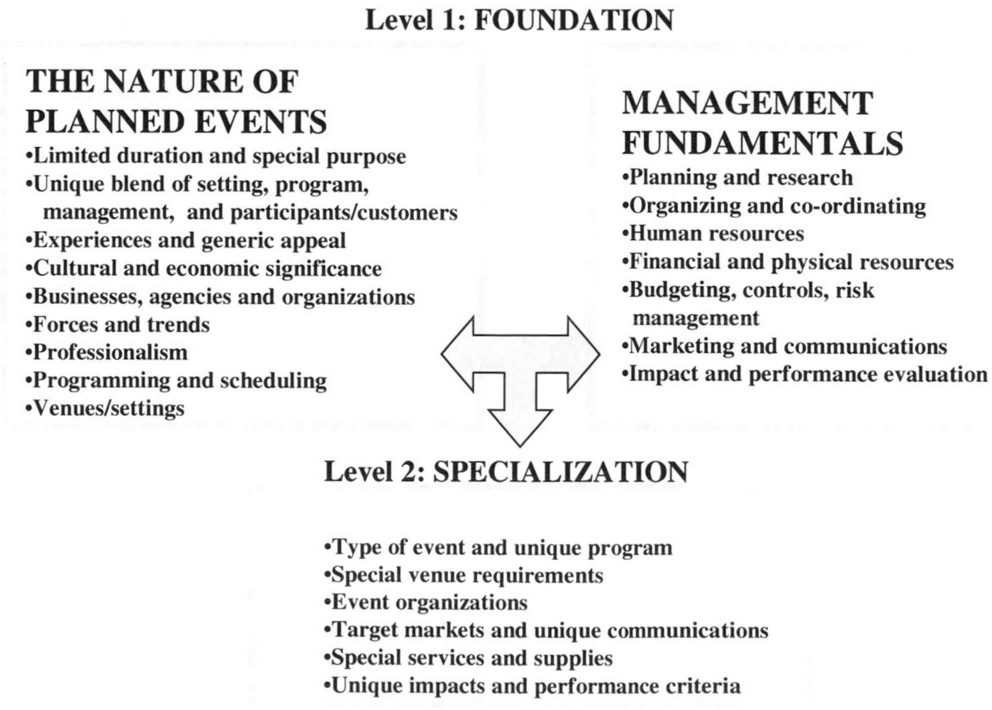

Level 1: FOUNDATION

THE NATURE OF PLANNED EVENTS
- Limited duration and special purpose
- Unique blend of setting, program, management, and participants/customers
- Experiences and generic appeal
- Cultural and economic significance
- Businesses, agencies and organizations
- Forces and trends
- Professionalism
- Programming and scheduling
- Venues/settings

MANAGEMENT FUNDAMENTALS
- Planning and research
- Organizing and co-ordinating
- Human resources
- Financial and physical resources
- Budgeting, controls, risk management
- Marketing and communications
- Impact and performance evaluation

Level 2: SPECIALIZATION

- Type of event and unique program
- Special venue requirements
- Event organizations
- Target markets and unique communications
- Special services and supplies
- Unique impacts and performance criteria

Figure 1.1. Studying event management.

agement was becoming an accepted field of study and that its contents applied to all types of event and event settings.

Interest in defining the body of knowledge associated with event management is growing. Julia Silvers (CSEP) has a website dealing with this subject (www.juliasilvers.com/embok.htm). She defines types of events and a "knowledge domain structure" in which the basic "domains" are administration, operations, marketing, and risk management. Similarly, the International Association of Assembly Managers has a Body of Knowledge website that explicitly includes many elements of event management (www.iaam.org/ProfDev/BOK/BOKcore.htm).

The basic premise is that a profession must be founded on a distinct body of theory and knowledge, and we have to blend management with event studies. The management fundamentals are all covered in this book, although a greater level of detail in one or all of the management functions will be required for anyone seeking a specialized or senior management position.

Another premise of the model is that "specialization" should occur only after a firm foundation has been attained. Traditionally, the field of event management has been fragmented by type of event, with little if any overlap or transfer. For example, "meeting planners" are well established but largely confined to the meeting and convention business, while festival managers and sport event professionals have also specialized on certain types of events. There is no good reason why this should be the case in the future.

Specialization has also occurred over time according to "setting." Those who manage specific types of facilities, including hotel/resort manager, arts/exhibition centers, or sport halls, and those involved with parks, attractions (such as zoos), or destination marketing, all have somewhat unique perspectives on events. Again, there is no good reason why event professionals cannot work well in all these settings. Other forms of specialization can occur by reference to program (the types of activities or experiences created by the event) or target market (e.g., events for seniors, spectator versus participant sports, etc.).

Where does event tourism fit? It is a large and economically important specialization, but there are two ways of looking at it. The first is that event tourism is specialization based on setting: those who market destinations are very interested in bidding on, producing, and facilitating events for their tourism and economic benefits. The other perspective is that of target market: tourists have different needs from residents, and that fact helps shape event programming at attractions and event-specific venues. The type of event is not so important in a tourism context, nor is the program of greatest concern. In other words, event tourism is primarily a specialization based on marketing.

Research

Thought has been given to developing a research agenda for event studies and event management. At a conference held in Sydney in 2000, researchers, academics, and practitioners considered where the field and the profession were heading and how research would support these changes. The paper by Getz explicitly laid out a research agenda, and in a subsequent presentation in Ireland (Getz, 2003) expanded the paper to include advice on how various stakeholders should be brought together to reach consensus on research needs.

Australians were probably the first to develop a national research agenda, linked to the Cooperative Research Centres for Sustainable Tourism initiative (see Harris, Jago, Allen, & Huyskens, 2001).

Research Note

Harris, R., Jago, L., Allen, J., & Huyskens, M. (2001). Towards an Australian event research agenda: First steps. *Event Management, 6*(4), 213-221.

Three groups in Australia (academics, practitioners, and government officials) were asked to rank the importance of research needs. Practitioners, as expected, were more concerned with management topics, the top ones being related to learning more about sponsorship, identifying needs and motivations of attendees, market segmentation, and determining why events fail. Government officials picked reasons for event failure as their top research agenda item, followed by identification of risk management factors and developing standardized research tools and methods. Academics chose risk management strategy formulation as the number one research need, followed by valuing the events industry and reasons for event failure.

Disciplinary Perspectives on Events

The major disciplines within social sciences and the humanities all make important contributions to event studies and event management. Business, public, and not-for-profit management studies are increasingly bringing new insights, and even engineering makes its contribution through project management techniques. There is no room in a single book for detailed examination of all these connections, but a brief introduction to the main contributing disciplines will benefit the student by providing academic context and showing where additional insights can be discovered. Research notes accompany each disciplinary perspective, to draw your attention to important contributions.

History and Events

Planned events of all kinds have been an integral part of civilization for thousands of years, from political assemblies to sport competitions, feasts, and revelry to religious celebrations. What explains the vast history of events? Some would suggest that people are simply gregarious, social creatures, but that in itself does not explain the economic and cultural importance attached to planned events, the formalization of related professions, or creation of specialist venues. It could easily be argued that events are a fundamental and essential human experience, both rooted in culture and at the same time helping to define our civilizations. The evolution and life cycle of events is an important historical topic with management implications, as examined by Sofield and Li (1998).

Research Note

Sofield, T., & Li, F. (1998). Historical methodology and sustainability: An 800-year-old festival from China. *Journal of Sustainable Tourism, 6*(4), 267-292.

These researchers took an historical perspective on an 800-year-old festival in China, seeking an understanding of its survival and evolution in the context of political, sociocultural, and economic forces. The Chrysanthemum Festival of Xiaolan traditionally took place only every 60 years, and before the Communist regime took control of China in 1949 it was last held in 1934. However, it was held three times before its next 60th anniversary, when Communist Party officials used it to demonstrate aspects of leadership, authority, and power in 1953, 1973, and 1979. In 1994 it was promoted as a leading cultural tourist attraction. Analysis of the historical records was conducted, plus participant observation by the researchers at the 1994 event and interviews with event personnel provided contemporary insights. Sofield and Li concluded that tourism was playing an important role in the dynamics of change in China, particularly because heritage events that were once banned are now officially viewed as tourism "products." The cultural authenticity of this ancient event is beyond doubt, and it meets the definition of a sustainable event because of this authenticity, its obvious longevity, and a high level of official and community support.

Geography and Events

The main traditions of "human geography" research are all applicable to the study of events. Geographers have concentrated on human–resource interactions, especially spatial and temporal patterns of human activity and including impacts on the environment. "Event geography" would therefore, at a minimum, consist of these major themes: the spatial patterns of events and related resource dependencies (such as a connection to agricultural products or community ethnicity); the temporal dimension (the annual calendar of festivals); and the impacts of events on the environment and community.

Supply–demand interactions are fertile ground for event geographers. Analysis and forecasting of demand for a particular event or a region's events will in part depend on population distribution, competition, and intervening opportunities. Along these lines, Bohlin (2000) used a traditional tool of geographers, the distance-decay function, to exam festival-related travel in Sweden. He found that attendance decreased with distance, although recurring and well-established events have greater drawing power. The difficulties of forecasting event attendance have been well noted in the literature (Mules & McDonald, 1994; Spilling, 1998; Teigland, 1996). Demand mapping (e.g., Verhoven, Wall, & Cottrell, 1998) has also been used as an event marketing tool.

Getz (1991) illustrated several models of potential event tourism patterns in a region. One option is clustering events in service centers, as opposed to dispersing them over a large, rural area. These are related to the concept of "attractiveness" and also have implications for the distribution of benefits and costs. Analysis of the zones of influence of events has been undertaken by Teigland (1996) specific to the Lillehammer (Norway) Winter Olympics, and this method has implications for event planning, especially regarding mega-events with multiple venues. The elements of these zones of influence are the gateways, venue locations, tourist flows, transport management, and displacement of other activities.

Robert Janiskee's many contributions to the geography of events deserve special recognition (see the Bibliography for a full listing), including development of a huge database of American festivals.

Research Note

Janiskee's 1980 paper examined the themes, locations, timing, program of activities, reported attendance, and benefits of rural festivals in South Carolina. His 1991 paper looked more carefully at festival history in the state, including when they were established, and their spatial distribution over time. Janiskee's huge database of over 12,000 American "community festivals" is a unique research tool, not duplicated anywhere else. He has used it to analyze the spatial and temporal patterns of festivals in general, as well as to examine specific types of festivals.

Janiskee's 1994 paper documented how his "Fest List" database was compiled from various published sources and interviews and presented analysis of growth in festival numbers. We can clearly see in graphical format an almost exponential growth rate, with exploding numbers after 1970. In the 1996a paper Janiskee examined the monthly and seasonal patterns of community festivals in the US, making it clear that their numbers are relatively low in winter, late autumn, and early spring. Although regional patterns are different, across the country a huge number occur on the July 4th weekend. In the conclusions to this paper the researcher raised the issue of saturation and asked how many festivals can be held at any one time?

Cultural Anthropology and Events

Cultural anthropologists have long held an interest in the many forms and cultural meanings of performances and celebrations, including carnivals and festivals. Anthropologists and sociologists (e.g., Manning, 1983) have long been interested in the nature of celebration and how it both stems from, and helps define, culture. This viewpoint includes a focus the annual calendar of celebrations related to factors such as the harvest and changing seasons.

Farber (1983) argued that the study of festivals and events can reveal much about a community's symbolic, economic, social, and political life, as events create links between people and groups in a community and between the community and the world. For example, drawing on the seminal writings of Turner (1982), Tomlinson (1986) examined the small-town festival as a "performance." The parades are full of imagery and symbolism reflecting local or nationally held values: purity, beauty, humor, religion, and politics. The townfolk are provided with a stage on which to perform for themselves, for the community, and as representatives of the community. Roles can be reversed, a persons' status temporarily abandoned, and all kinds of behavior tolerated that would otherwise be socially unacceptable.

Many authors have worried about the negative influence of tourism on traditional cultures. Often these effects are most visible in the area of cultural productions such as rituals, music, dance, and festivals, and particularly those that incorporate traditional costumes. Residents of destination areas quickly learn that culture can be a commodity for which tourists will pay a great amount, resulting in either the transformation of occasional, sometimes sacred events into regular performances, or the modification of rituals into forms of entertainment that are easier to perform or please the audiences more. In both cases, the rewards become monetary and divorced from their cultural meanings. This process has been called the "commercialization" or "commodification" of culture (for examples and related discussions see: Greenwood, 1972; Jordan, 1980; Wilson & Udall, 1982).

However, there is little agreement on tourism being bad for cultural events, or on how and why negative impacts occur (see, for example, Getz, 1993a; Macnaught, 1982; Noronha, 1977). Some authors have argued that tourism actually helps to preserve or revive traditions and strengthen indigenous cultures (e.g., Boissevan, 1979; Cheska, 1981), and events are one of the most common mechanisms. Sofield (1991) examined a successful, traditional event in the South Pacific and drew conclusions regarding the analysis and attainment of sustainability for indigenous cultural tourism developments.

See Cavalcanti (2001) for a contemporary, anthropological study of a Brazilian festival.

Research Note

Cavalcanti, M. (2001). The Amazonian Ox Dance Festival: An anthropological account. *Cultural Analysis, 2* (available on the www).

An anthropological perspective was taken by this researcher to analyze and interpret this spectacular folk festival in Brazil. Cavalcanti interprets the event as a contemporary cultural movement, exploring its historical roots and how it helps create a regional identity. The event's authenticity might be challenged because of its substantial growth in response to political and tourism forces, but the author concludes that it is indeed authentic and shows the capacity of folk culture to transform and update itself. As well, she argues that this festival succeeds in integrating popular culture and elite cultural realms. Anthropological research on events generally emphasizes symbolism and rituals, and Cavalcanti observed that the Ox Dance Festival is a powerful ritual process with the aim of displaying the community to Brazil and the world. In addition to a review of historical documents, the ethnographic research tradition was followed. Ethnography requires observation and evaluation of social groups in their native habitat, usually involving participant observation. In this article is a detailed account of the origins and evolution of the event in its social and cultural context.

Sociology and Events

Sociologists study social institutions and relationships, including organizations such as events, and the demographics of populations. Lifestyles and the life cycle of individuals and families is an important sociological topic with implications for event studies. Age and gender roles, and host–guest relationships, can be studied with implications for event management. Studies of population and demographics are important, and these are forces shaping the events sector.

The sociological perspective has been applied to events mostly in the context of event impacts, frequently including cultural effects. B. Ritchie (1984) suggested that the socio-cultural impacts of hallmark events could include the benefits of an increase in activities associated with the event (e.g., arts or sports) and strengthening of regional values or traditions. But events and event tourism programs also have potential to introduce social and cultural costs to the host community. Host–guest interactions, while hopefully improved through joint participation in festivals and events, can also be strained by events and tourism in general.

A fascinating account of a special event gone wrong was provided by Cunneen and Lynch (1988). They described how the annual Australian Grand Prix Motorcycle Races had become the scene for institutionalized rioting, despite, or perhaps because of, the efforts of organizers and police to control crowd behavior. Hall (1992) also noted that major events, particularly those with global media coverage, tend to attract potentially violent protests and political demonstrations. Recent attention has concentrated on measuring resident perceptions and attitudes towards events (see, for example, Fredline, Jago, & Deery, 2003).

Research Note

Fredline, L., Jago, L., & Deery, M. (2003). The development of a generic scale to measure the social impacts of events. *Event Management, 8*(1), 23–37.

The authors argued that more effort is needed to develop consistent measures of social impacts. The concept of "social capital" is relevant (i.e., what citizens, organizations, corporations and government agencies "invest" in making more livable, safe, and healthy communities). Anything that impacts on "quality of life" is part of the social impact concept developed by these authors, and so that include economic factors like jobs and income. While some impact studies are "extrinsic," applying frameworks or models to the study of social impacts [e.g., Doxey's Irridex (1975), which suggests an evolution of attitudes towards tourism as its negative effects become increasingly obvious and annoying to residents], these authors use an "intrinsic" approach based on determining resident perceptions and attitudes. Residents are asked to self-assess changes attributable to events and how their quality of life is affected (positively or negatively).

The Psychology of Events

Psychology helps us understand personal motives to attend and participate in events of all kinds. Even in the case of business-related events, such as trade shows and conventions where attendance is work related, event marketers realize they have to maximize personal and social benefits to attract those who have other options. Later in this book we examine in great detail various motives to attend, and benefits derived from events, as this knowledge is essential for event marketing. The book chapter by Getz and Cheyne (2002) reviews the motivational literature regarding events.

The event experience demands greater attention from researchers. The psychological dimensions of the event experience have not been well researched, and other disciplines can also make a vital contribution—particularly because attendance at most events is either for social reasons or involves social interaction. Environmental psychology has an important role to play in helping to examine how people interact with the setting, and how event atmosphere can be modified to maximize enjoyment and prevent social problems.

Research Note

Getz, D., & Cheyne, J. (2002). Special event motives and behaviour.

In C. Ryan (Ed.), *The tourist experience* (2d ed., pp. 137–155). London and New York: Continuum.

This book chapter provides a review of the literature on leisure and travel motives and research to date specific to motivation for attending events. The authors develop a conceptual model for exploring and explaining event motives consisting of three intersecting dimensions: generic leisure and travel motives (needs satisfaction, seeking and escaping); extrinsic motives (business reasons, obligation, and incentives to attend); event-specific motives (benefits targeted at special interests). For any person or group attending an event some combination of these motives might apply. In addition, the authors suggest that resident motives and tourist motives are often overlapping when it comes to seeking novelty, having fun, and pursuing their special interests, but that for residents many events offer routine leisure choices on par with other forms of local entertainment. Tourists, on the other hand, might be pursuing general travel motives in which the event is not a major determinant, or might be searching for an authentic experience that only the event can provide. As well, researchers will find tourists who are accompanying friends and relatives to a local event (whether they want to or not!) and some who are "casual" visitors because they happened to be in the area and followed the crowd.

The Political Science of Events

There are many political reasons for staging events, and politics often influence their management and marketing. Ideological reasons lie behind many mega-events, wherein the dominant power in society seeks to demonstrate and reinforce its values, or to win support (Hall, 1994a). As observed by the Canadian Task Force on Federal Sport Policy (cited by Chernushenko, 1994, p. 57), community bids for sport events are usually promoted by influential community members, which leads to intense pressure at political levels to give support. Events, given their image-making potential, present attractive opportunities for propagandizing and blatant political messages. At its worst, this can lead to manipulation or control over media coverage—either to hide elements or to highlight others. Event boycotts have occasionally been used as political tools, especially at the Olympics.

Hall (1992) argued that "Emphasis should be placed on the allocation of resources for events and the manner in which interests influence this process, particularly through the interaction of power, values, interests, place, and the processes of capital accumulation" (p. 99) While this is a critical issue for mega-events, political controversy often surrounds the funding of events or bidding on events at the community level. To succeed in gaining support and resources from the host community, event managers must pay attention to local benefits and costs, the various cultural meanings of their event, and related political factors.

In his examination of tourism and politics, Hall (1994a) pointed out the negative side of using events to achieve political goals. Events can not only be used as an excuse for overriding normal planning and consultation processes, but can displace powerless groups—especially in the inner city—in the name of urban renewal and economic development. He rightly argued that mega-events are almost always sought after by the community's elite who stand to benefit the most, whereas ordinary residents are seldom consulted. Hall noted that proponents of the successful Sydney, Australia, bid for the 2000 Summer Olympic Games regarded opponents as "unpatriotic" or "un-Australian" and that the public was consulted only be means of polls. Research by Hiller (2000) provides a look at the politics of Olympic bidding.

Research Note

Hiller, H. (2000). Mega-events, urban boosterism and growth strategies: An analysis of the objectives and legitimations of the Cape Town 2004 Olympic bid. *International Journal of Urban and Regional Research, 24*(2), 439–458.

Hiller analyzed the Cape Town bid for the Olympics in the context of government policy, specifically how it was legitimized as a tool in urban transformation. Nine specific developmental roles of the mega-event were identified, including that of a catalyst to accelerate change. Facilities were to be built in disadvantaged areas, leading to economic and social improvements—especially new housing and sport venues. The greatest expectation was that the Games would bring many new jobs. The original bid group, led by a prominent businessman, was replaced by national government as the driving force, so the politics were elevated from local to national level. Social gains were therefore added to the intended economic gains to justify such a huge investment. There was certainly opposition to the bid, but it received widespread political and public support.

The Economics of Events

Economists have been active in studying the economic impacts of events, especially in a tourism context. The most obvious economic impact stems from the role events play in attracting to an area visitors who would not otherwise travel there, but there can be other positive economic effects. For example, several authors have examined the "leveraging" of events in order to improve local businesses (e.g., Chalip & Leyns, 2002) or trade (Brown, 2002). The concepts and methods of economic impact assessment for events are covered in detail in Chapter 14, and comprehensive advice, together with research findings on event impacts, has been published by Dwyer, Mellor, Mistillis, and Mules (2000a, 2000b).

Costs and benefits have been scrutinized, starting with the landmark assessment of the first Australian Grand Prix held in Adelaide (Burns, Hatch, & Mules, 1986). The "multiplier" or "input–output" tables to estimate impacts of events are purely economic tools. Some economists have examined the economics of why governments should be involved with events, especially if they require a subsidy (Mules & Faulkner, 1996).

Research Note

Dwyer, L., Mellor, R., Mistilis, N., & Mules, T. (2000). A framework for assessing "tangible" and "intangible" impacts of events and conventions. *Event Management, 6*(3), 175–189.

Dwyer, L., Mellor, R., Mistilis, N., & Mules, T. (2000). Forecasting the economic impacts of events and conventions. *Event Management, 6*(3), 191–204.

Their first article in this issue of *Event Management* develops a comprehensive framework for assessing event impacts, both tangibles and intangibles, while this second article shows how to make impact forecasts. Both were derived from research completed to enable Tourism New South Wales to make better event support decisions. Results from previous impact studies of a number of sport events and festivals were compared, with the conclusion that their methodologies and quality were inconsistent. Also, very few studies in Australia had included media and fiscal impacts. Similarly, published reports on convention impacts were compared, with the observation that they differed in methodology, scope of analysis, data collection, and accuracy. Results of this major review led to recommendations for standardized impact assessments and forecast, and in particular the need for consistency so that reliable trends can be measured. Results also indicated that economic benefits were likely to be highest from sports events and medical and business conventions because (in Australia) they tended to attract the most high-yield tourists.

Event Management Within Closely Related Fields

There are several closely related fields of management that involve events and contribute to event studies. Although professionals in these fields might not call themselves "event manager," the coordination, production, or marketing of events is sometimes an important part of their work.

Sport Management

Graham, Goldblatt, and Delpy (1995), in their book *The Ultimate Guide to Sport Event Management and Marketing*, described this sector in detail, including types of careers and specific sport event issues. In the book *Profiles of Sport Industry Professionals* (Robinson, Hums, Crow, & Philips, 2001), contributors described their career paths and jobs, many of which involve events. Because sports by nature involve competitions, both regularly scheduled and one-time, the coordination, production, or marketing of events is usually an essential part of the job. This generally applies in athletics departments of educational institutions, international sport federations, professional sport clubs and leagues, sport facility and fitness club management, recreational sports (for parks and recreation departments or associations), sports commissions (city-based agencies active in event tourism development), and sport marketing firms. Professional management firms, such as the international IMG, create events as marketing tools, manage sport celebrities, and develop corporate sponsorship platforms involving events.

Venue Management

The International Association of Assembly Managers (IAAM; www.iaam.org) represents public assembly facilities from around the globe. IAAM members include managers and senior executives from auditoria, arenas, convention centers, exhibit halls, stadiums, performing arts theaters, and amphitheaters. They attract millions of patrons to a large variety of events from football to rock concerts, conventions, and performing arts.

Clubs fall into several major categories, including sports (e.g., golf and country), clubs owned by not-for-profit associations (e.g., ethnic), fitness and health, and a wide range of private, member-based clubs. The common element is that members and other users have access to a facility or facilities that can be used for regular programs and activities and for special events. The magazine *Club Management* is aimed at professional club managers, and their association is Club Managers Association of America (www.cmaa.org).

Entertainment and catered events are common at clubs, requiring a certain amount of investment in a stage, sound and light systems, kitchens, decorations, and security. Some clubs employ professional special event directors to create events that interest members, promote the club, raise money for charity, or participate in the community. Some clubs are also dependent on generating revenue through events. The events director might therefore have responsibility for booking entertainment, arranging caterers, or hiring decorators. It helps to have a talent for creating a party atmosphere.

Event Management in Parks and Recreation Agencies

Leisure and recreation management is a field of study with an established body of literature and ideas on the motives for participation in many activities, the nature of experiences that we call fun, entertaining, stimulating, or fulfilling, and the benefits of events.
Recreation, sport, and art administration all offer specific material on types of events and
event settings. Most towns and cities run sport facilities that host numerous events and
parks that provide spaces for festivals and other public gatherings. Increasingly, they employ professional event managers to produce their own events, or event coordinators to
oversee the events strategy and portfolio. Many are also explicitly involved in event tourism.

Hospitality Management (Hotels, Catering, and Resorts)

Events are a core hospitality subject, embodying catering, service quality, and experiential dimensions. More specifically, hotel and restaurant managers are responsible for the
events or "functions" markets in their properties, while many resorts specialize in events
suited to their recreational amenities and beautiful settings. The most common "functions"
held in hotels, restaurants, and other hospitality venues are:

- weddings and banquets;
- private parties (graduations, bar and bat mitzvahs);
- meetings and conventions;
- consumer and trade shows;
- entertainment events (as opposed to regular entertainers);
- corporate functions like product launches.

For hospitality establishments to enter the conventions or exhibitions market they must
have special-purpose facilities, equipment, and services above and beyond the usual catering competencies. An important trend is the use of unique, nontraditional venues for meetings and conventions, such as museums, historic houses, or even zoos.

What Is Event Tourism?

"Event Tourism" is a term used mostly in the tourism literature to describe a destination development and marketing strategy to realize all the potential economic benefits
of events. From the perspective of an event manager, tourists are potential customers
(and in many events the main customers), so knowledge of their characteristics is important. In this section the main tourism and economic roles of events are discussed,
while Chapter 4 is devoted to destination planning and marketing of event tourism.
Tourist markets for events are discussed in later chapters, and the economic impacts of
event tourism are thoroughly covered in the final chapter.

Event Tourism: The Economic Roles

Figure 1.2 illustrates the main tourism and economic roles of events, each of which are
discussed below. Any one or all of these roles can be important for a community or destination, and event managers should evaluate how their events can make a positive contribution or tap into tourist markets.

Events as Attractions

Although many tourism organizations stress international tourism, there is no doubt that
most festivals and events are dependent on local and regional audiences. But whether events

PLACE MARKETING
-create positive images
-improve quality of life
-attract residents and
investors

TOURIST ATTRACTION
-attract quality tourists
-spread demand
-increase visitor spending
and length of stay

IMAGE MAKER
-for attractions, resorts,
destinations
-create and enhance themes
-combat negative imagery

CATALYST
-stimulate infrastructure
-assist urban renewal
-stimulate business/trade
-support other attractions

ANIMATOR
-encourage first and
repeat visits at facilities,
resorts, attractions

Figure 1.2. Economic and tourism roles of events.

are true tourist attractions (i.e., motivating overnight or nonlocal travel), or a reason for visitors already in an area to stay longer, they can have tourism value. Events can also have the effect of keeping people and their money at home, rather than traveling outside the region. Event "drawing power" or "attractiveness" to tourists is discussed in detail in Chapter 4. A particular concern is the spreading of tourist demand over time (to overcome the tourist seasonality problem) and space (to spread demand throughout a country or region).

Events as Animators

Resorts, museums, historic districts, heritage sites, archaeological sites, markets and shopping centers, sports stadia, convention centers, and theme parks all develop programs of special events. Built attractions and facilities have everywhere realized the advantages of "animation"—the process of programming interpretive features and/or special events that make the place come alive with sensory stimulation and appealing atmosphere.

The potential benefits of animation through events are of major importance to facility and attraction managers:

- to attract people who might otherwise not make a visit because they perceive the facility or attraction itself to be uninteresting;
- to encourage repeat visits by people who might otherwise think that one visit is enough;
- to encourage people to bring visiting friends or relatives who might otherwise not include certain attractions on their list of things to do;

- to attract publicity for the site or facility, including the highlighting of historical events associated with the site;
- to encourage longer stays and greater spending;
- to target groups for special functions.

It is a rule of theme park marketing that new attractions must be brought on stream periodically to attract repeat visits. Similar success can be achieved through regular entertainment programs, especially when "big names" are featured, and with festivals and other special events. Theme parks are, in fact, typically designed with appropriate facilities for indoor and outdoor entertainment at a large scale, as well as more intimate viewing and seating areas for minor performances. Kelly (1985) described the Six Flags philosophy on events at their theme parks: "Special events are employed to attract local repeat trade" (p. 281). The events are mostly entertainment in nature, and this element, combined with new rides and site amenities, is designed to help extend the life cycle of the product.

Baxter (2001) looked at how waterparks employed entertainment and special events, finding that some of them view it as a way to increase attendance and revenues while others want to increase consumer awareness among target segments and reinforce branding. Operators are well advised to experiment and evaluate to see what types of events generate specific benefits.

Events as Image Makers

It is apparent that major events can have the effect of shaping an image of the host community or country, leading to its favorable perception as a potential travel destination. With global media attention focused on the host city, even for a relatively short duration, the publicity value is enormous, and some destinations will use this fact alone to justify great expenditures on attracting events. For example, Wang and Gitelson (1988) observed that the annual Spoleto Festival in Charleston, South Carolina, does not appear to be economically justifiable, "but the city holds it every year to maintain a desirable image" (p. 5). Cameron (1989) noted the role of festivals and events, and cultural tourism in general, in altering the image of the Lehigh Valley in Pennsylvania.

Longitudinal studies of the impact of hosting the 1988 Winter Olympic Games on Calgary (B. Ritchie & Smith, 1991) showed how a definite positive image boost grew, peaked, and started to decline afterwards, so there is a life cycle to image enhancement related to one-time events. But additional gains in tourism infrastructure and the legacy of enhanced tourism marketing and organization can potentially sustain the effect.

What happens when negative publicity strikes a destination? To a degree, bad news events can be managed: both to minimize the negative impact and to fight back. Ahmed (1991) argued that negative images can be turned into positive ones by organizing festivals and commemorations of the event, although this is restricted mostly to natural disasters and entails the risk of stirring up unhappy or controversial memories.

Events and Place Marketing

Kotler, Haider, and Rein (1993), in their book *Marketing Places*, identified the value of events in enhancing the image of communities and in attracting tourists. They demonstrated how places compete for investments, quality people, and tourists, all in pursuit of more livable and prosperous communities. Place marketing provides a framework within which events and event tourism find multiple roles, as image makers, quality of life enhancers, and tourist attractions. More traditional approaches to economic development stressed industrialization, provision of physical rather than cultural infrastructure, and downplayed the economic value of tourism.

One key feature of place marketing is its attention to cultivating a positive image. Thus, events produced or assisted by economic development departments, mayor's offices, tourist agencies, or convention and visitor bureaus all must attract media attention, portray the place in the best possible light, and be tangibly linked to other promotional campaigns. This can, of course, distort event goals and lead their managers into potentially difficult political territory.

Events as Catalysts

Mega-events, such as world's fairs and Olympics, have been supported by host governments in large part because of their role as catalysts in major redevelopment schemes. The Knoxville World's Fair was conceived as a catalyst for urban renewal through image enhancement and physical redevelopment, and left a legacy of infrastructure, a convention center, private investments, a better tax base, and new jobs for the Tennessee city (Mendell, MacBeth, & Solomon, 1983). Dungan (1984) gave a number of examples of the indirect and direct physical legacies of major events, including improvements to the Los Angeles airport, Montreal's subway system, Knoxville's freeways, fairground renovations in Oklahoma City, parks in Chicago, and various urban renewal schemes. He also pointed out that physical structures, particularly those created for world's fairs, such as the Eiffel Tower in Paris or Seattle's Space Needle, have become valuable permanent symbols for their cities.

Atlanta's 1996 Summer Olympic Games generated $2 billion in construction projects in Georgia, including sport facilities, an urban park in central Atlanta, housing improvements, and educational facilities (Mihalik, 1994). In particular, the Games were a catalyst for achieving a $42 million federal housing grant to revitalize a low-income housing project next to the Olympic village. The Olympic Park, funded privately, was said to be valuable in restoring a blighted area next to the city's convention center.

Major events tend to attract investment into the hospitality sector, especially hotels and restaurants. Sometimes these additions have been brought forward in time, while others represent new infrastructure related to expected longer term increases in demand. Sport events generally lead to new or improved facilities that can be used to attract events in the future, and improvements to convention or arts centers can have a similar effect. In this way a community can use the event to realize a "quantum leap" in its tourism development, accelerating growth or jumping into a higher competitive category.

Event Terminology

This section begins by defining "event" itself, plus a number of somewhat ambiguous terms that are used in event management. Another useful source is *The International Dictionary of Event Management* by Goldblatt and Nelson (2001).

Event

From the dictionary, synonyms include "occurrence," "happening," "incident," or "experience." "Event" is also commonly used in sports to describe a specific type of competition, as in "three different running events constitute today's sport meet." The basic criterion defining all types of "event" is that they are temporary. A "news event" is an incident that attracts media attention. A "sport event" is fixed in time and space by its rules and venue. For the purpose of event management, however, we focus on "planned events," the kind that involve professional managers.

Planned Event

All events have a finite length, and for planned events this is usually fixed and publicized in advance. People know and expect that events end, and this fact generates a major part of their appeal. When they are over, you cannot experience them again. True, many events are periodic, but each one has a unique ambience created by the combination of its setting, program, management, and people. So this definition applies to all planned events: *Planned events are temporary occurrences with a predetermined beginning and end. Every such event is unique, stemming from the blend of management, program, setting and people.*

Special Event

The word "eventful" implies something important or momentous, which to many people also suggests "special." Goldblatt and Nelson (2001) define special event as "A unique moment in time celebrated with ceremony and ritual to satisfy specific needs" (p. 181). But it will never be possible to come up with a universal, standardized definition, nor a classification of what types of events are "special." It is clearly a matter of perspective or preference.

Context makes some events special to their organizers or guests, and it is quite possible that organizer and customer will not agree on the "specialness" of an event. Consequently, we need two definitions: 1) *A special event is a one-time, or infrequently occurring event outside the normal program or activities of the sponsoring or organizing body.* 2) *To the customer or guest, a special event is an opportunity for an experience outside the normal range of choices or beyond everyday experience.*

These are good working definitions, but they do not do full justice to the meaning of "specialness." A synthesis of many pertinent themes contained in this book provides a subjective list of factors that create or heighten the quality of "specialness" (Table 1.1), and additional insights were provided through consumer research by Jago and Shaw (1999).

Research Note

Jago, L., & Shaw, R. (1999). Consumer perceptions of special events: A multi-stimulus validation. *Journal of Travel and Tourism Marketing, 8*(4), 1-24.

These Australian researchers asked 500 randomly selected adults to identify the attributes of special events that they believe are important. Respondents identified these key determinants of "specialness": number of attendees; international attention due to the event; the improvement to the image and pride of host regions as a result of hosting the event; and the exciting experience associated with the event. These findings shed light on how people might decide if an event is more attractive to attend than others, and gives clues to event marketers about how to promote "special" events.

Hallmark Event

This term can hold a variety of connotations. Graham et al. (1995, p. 69) referred to hallmark sport events as being those that mark an important historical anniversary. B. Ritchie (1984) defined them this way: "Major one-time or recurring events of limited duration, developed primarily to enhance the awareness, appeal and profitability of a tourism destination in the short and/or long term. Such events rely for their success on uniqueness, status, or timely significance to create interest and attract attention" (p. 2).

If we look to a dictionary, "hallmark" refers to a symbol of quality or authenticity that distinguishes some goods from others, or pertains to a distinctive feature. An event, therefore, can aspire to be the hallmark of its organizers, venue or location. In other words, "hallmark" describes an event that possesses such significance, in terms of tradition, at-

Table 1.1 What Makes Events "Special"?

Uniqueness	Every event offers a unique experience through the blending of management, setting and people; many events rely on a "must-see," "once-in-a-lifetime" uniqueness to attract visitors.
A multiplicity of goals	Specialness is related to the diversity of goals that events successfully pursue.
Festive spirit	Specialness increases with the ability of events to create a true festive spirit. The ambience can encourage joyfulness (even revelry), freedom from routine constraints, and inversion of normal roles and functions.
Satisfying basic needs	All the basic human needs, and related leisure and travel motivations, can be satisfied in part through events. Specialness increases as the number of needs and related motives are better satisfied.
Quality	Poor quality will destroy any pretence of being special; high-quality events will go beyond customer expectations and generate high levels of satisfaction.
Authenticity	This is related to uniqueness, in that events based on indigenous cultural values and attributes will be inherently unique. To the tourist, specialness will be heightened by a feeling of participation in an authentic community celebration.
Tradition	Many events have become traditions, rooted in the community, and attractive to visitors because of the associated mystique. "Hallmark events," which are closely associated with the host community so that event and destination images are mutually reinforcing, are traditional by nature.
Flexibility	Events can be developed with minimal infrastructure, can be moved in space and time, and adapted to changing markets and organizational needs. This fact makes them special products for organizations and destinations.
Hospitality	The essence of hospitality is to make every event-goer feel like an honored guest. In destinations, the tourist is provided with community hospitality and the resident is proud to be a host. Some events and communities are recognized for the special welcome they give to visitors.
Tangibility	The event-goer can experience the "specialness" of a destination theme, and its ambient resources, through its events. This applies to culture, hospitality, and natural resources.
Theming	All elements of the event can be themed to maximize festive spirit, authenticity, tradition, interactions, and customer service. Theming adds to the feeling of specialness.
Symbolism	The use of rituals and symbols together adds to the festive atmosphere, and can also give an event special significance above and beyond its immediate purpose and theme.
Affordability	Events providing affordable leisure, educational, social and cultural experiences will be special to large segments of the population without the means to pay for alternatives.
Convenience	Events can be special opportunities for spontaneous, unplanned leisure and social opportunities. This is of increasing importance in a hectic, work-oriented world, and especially in urban environments.

tractiveness, quality, or publicity, that the event provides the host venue, community, or destination with a competitive advantage. Over time, the event and destination can become inextricably linked, such as Mardi Gras and New Orleans.

Mega-Event

"Mega" means large or huge, or more precisely "1 million" in the metric system. Certainly world's fairs and the Olympics are big enough to earn the prefix "mega," but what about an annual festival or political happening? Marris (1987), summarizing a conference of the International Association of Tourism Experts that was themed on the subject of mega-events and mega-attractions, noted that mega-events can be defined by reference to their volume of visitors, their cost, or by psychological criteria. Their volume should exceed 1 million visits, their capital cost should be at least $500 million, and their reputation should be that of a "must see" event. Marris thought the key to getting mega-events through the political approval process was the prestige factor. Others might prefer a definition that stresses the economic impacts of the event, rather than its costs, size, or image. Vanhove and Witt (1987), in the same conference, stressed that a mega-event must be able to attract worldwide publicity. So an event can be a "mega" success if it generates exceptional levels of coverage or fosters a strong positive image among key target segments.

The definition of mega-events will therefore always remain subjective. It is really more a question of the relative significance of an event, rather than any particular measure of size. To summarize: *Mega-events, by way of their size or significance, are those that yield extraordinarily high levels of tourism, media coverage, prestige, or economic impact for the host community, venue, or organization.*

Media Events

Some events might never attract large numbers, but still generate enormous exposure through media coverage. These "media events" are gaining in popularity, based especially on the power of television and Internet coverage to reach global or very targeted audiences. Examples are sport events in which spectating is impractical but television appeal is high, such as cross-country eco-challenges. Media events are created primarily for live and/or delayed broadcast (television and Internet) as opposed to those held for large spectator audiences.

Corporate Event

"Corporate events" are those produced by corporations. According to O'Toole and Mikolaitis (2002), authors of *Corporate Event Project Management*, the corporate event planner or manager might reside in marketing, corporate communications, or human resources departments. These professionals must understand how their events fit with corporate culture and are affected by corporate politics.

There is another possible interpretation. Some events are hugely popular with corporate sponsors who lavish hospitality on their business associates and sometimes their employees. For example, the Honda Indy 300, the annual CART motorsport race held in Gold Coast, Australia, is reported to draw 25,000 "corporates," including 2500 from the US to Australia. Its organizers claim this makes it the country's largest "corporate event."

Cause-Related Event

This term refers to any event produced for the financial or political benefit of a charity or other social or political cause. Many charitable and even governmental organizations hold events to raise money or generate support for a social or political cause. In classifying an event as "cause related," the program is less important than the intended outcomes. In this context events are potential tools of "social marketing" or "propaganda." Social marketing seeks to change people's attitudes and behavior, such as to quit smoking or give more to charity, while political propaganda has more sinister aims—to convert people to a particular political philosophy.

Publicity Event (or "Stunt")

Any type of event can be exploited for publicity; it is one major reason why many corporations sponsor events. The so-called "publicity stunt" is usually not a major event but a contradiction in terms—a "planned news event." In other words, it is intended to attract media attention like a news story, despite its apparent or sometimes hidden orchestration.

Periodic Event

Periodic events occur regularly, as with festivals held every year in the same place, or events that are held regularly but in different locations each time. Later we look at the "pulsating event organization," which is the group responsible for producing periodic events that require temporary expansion in staff and volunteer numbers as well as management capacity.

One-Time Events

These events are completely unique, such as a never-to-be-repeated exhibition. But the term is also used to describe events that move around and seldom if ever return to the same place. Countries, tourist organizations, and venues systematically bid on such events, including meetings, exhibitions, world's fairs, and sport competitions, and they are considered to be one-time events from the perspective of the hosts.

Typology of Planned Events

The universe of events is amazingly diverse, and any classification is bound to be incomplete. Figure 1.3 makes an attempt to sort out major categories, distinguishing between those in the public domain and those of primary interest to individuals and small, private groups. Depending on the purpose and circumstances, events can fall into more than one category.

Any of these events can be considered "special," considering the previously mentioned criteria, but "mega" and "hallmark" are terms that usually can only be applied to public events. Any of these events can also become "news," depending on media coverage and other factors such as relative uniqueness, but other news events such as war, disaster, or crime are not "managed" in the ways we discuss in this book. Unplanned news events,

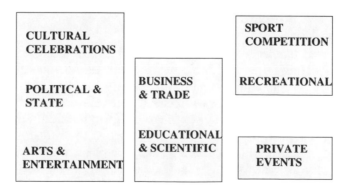

Figure 1.3. Typology of planned events.

however, can impact on planned events and on the image of destinations, organizations, and sponsors.

The seven categories of planned events can be found in virtually every culture and community. They can be linked by way of economic development and tourism policy, through cultural strategies or by professional event managers, yet they are often produced and managed in complete isolation from each other. A great exercise for students and researchers is to attempt an inventory of all these types of events—an exercise that is bound to result in frustration owing to the large number of events, the usual absence of up-to-date information, and problems of classification.

Cultural Celebrations

"Celebrate" has multiple meanings: to observe a day or event with ceremonies of respect, festivity or rejoicing (such as Thanksgiving celebrations); to perform a religious sacrament or ceremony (such as to celebrate mass or a marriage); to extol, praise, or acclaim; to make widely known. Synonyms include: to commemorate, honor, or distinguish.

"Culture" pertains to the many and diverse ways that identifiable human societies and groups live their lives (i.e., their "lifestyle"), organize their affairs (e.g., forms of government and social conventions), and distinguish themselves from others (e.g., through rituals, celebrations, and traditions). In the 21st century there is growing opposition to economic globalization and the formation of a "global culture," in favor of retaining and celebrating cultural differences.

"Popular culture" refers to the cultural preferences and activities that individuals most immediately associate with, such as their entertainment and sport preferences, foods and beverages, tastes in art or music. By contrast, the term "high culture" is usually reserved for more classical and often state-supported forms of art and music. However, many people find that distinction to be irrelevant or elitist.

Cultural celebrations, therefore, take many forms. In the following paragraphs we more closely examine some of the most common forms, especially those that typically involve professional management. Most religious events, by contrast, involve religious institutions. However, religious festivals are highlighted, and many private ceremonies involve both religious and secular elements, such as bar mitzvah or wedding parties.

Commemorations

Festivals can be themed around an historic event that is to be remembered, but generally we would call this type of event a commemoration. The celebrations of D-Day or of Remembrance Day are well-known commemorations, but most countries and communities have some form of historical or heritage commemoration in their annual calendar. Occasionally a major anniversary comes along, resulting in a whole year of celebrations, such as centennials or the Bicentennial of Independence.

Carnival and Mardi Gras

The word "carnival" stems from the practice of feasting on meat and the associated revelry before the fasting required during the period of Lent, which precedes Easter. Carnivals became periods of merriment and revelry, often including dressing up in costumes and the wearing of masks (hence the association with masquerade balls). In Europe, the Association of European Carnival Cities exists to maintain the traditions and foster better events. In the Americas, a special carnival day has become "Mardi Gras" (literally, fat Tuesday), and a host of "winter carnivals" has developed to bring a little fun and warmth into the coldest time of year. "Carnival" is sometimes used synonymously with festival, or to describe a traveling amusement show with rides and games.

Festival

Festivals are one of the most common forms of cultural celebration, and while many are traditional, with long histories, the majority have been created in recent decades. Parades and processions are common elements in festivals, but those that are held on their own also display many celebratory elements. Many of the other major types of event, especially art and entertainment, are frequently found within or as the theme of festivals, and sport and recreational events are also common festival elements.

Falassi (1987) has summarized contemporary English language definitions of "festival," of which the most pertinent is "a sacred or profane time of celebration, marked by special observances" (p. 2). While traditional festivals often retain religious or mystical roots, contemporary festivals are primarily "profane," or secular. And although many traditional festival themes have been retained, including those related to the harvest, countless new themes have been established.

For a working definition that is concise and simple, the following is offered: *a festival is a public, themed celebration.*

Unless the public is invited to participate, the event is a private party. Merely selling tickets to the public might not be sufficient to qualify as a festival, as the celebration should be by and for the public. The object of celebration, which can be called the theme, is often explicitly recognized in the name, as in Festival of Music, or Tulip Festival. But many festivals with diverse programming are actually celebrations of the community itself. Falassi (1987) noted: "Both the social function and the symbolic meaning of the festival are closely related to a series of overt values that the community recognizes as essential to its ideology and worldview, to its social identity, its historical continuity, and to its physical survival, which is ultimately what festival celebrates" (p. 2).

Photo 1.1. Ukranian Fest on Chicago's west-side Smith Park (credit: City of Chicago).

Festivals and other "cultural performances" in which cultural elements are displayed are rich in meaning and provide a "text"—the "reading" of which can educate an observer about the host culture and community. As explained by Manning (1983), celebration is performance: "it is, or entails, the dramatic presentation of cultural symbols" (p. 4). Celebration is public, with no social exclusion, is entertainment for the fun of it, and is participatory—actively involving the celebrant who takes time out of ordinary routine, and "does so openly, consciously and with the general aim of aesthetic, sensual and social gratification."

It is common to label events as "community festivals" if their purpose is primarily to celebrate civic identity, pride, or sharing. This type, generally represented by International Festivals & Events Association (IFEA) and similar national festivals and event associations, often encompasses a broad program of events appealing to the whole community (e.g., parades, sports, fireworks, concerts, food) and increasingly many of them are also tourism oriented. One of the main justifications for local government to get involved in producing or assisting such events, at least in the New World, is the absence of traditional events to mark the seasons and bring everyone together. As well, modern life involves so much moving about that communities typically lack a stable population and so the government (or some other organization) has to create a means of identity.

The Arts Festivals network in the UK (www.artsfestivals.co.uk) describes the following thematic types: opera; literature; early music; dance; new festivals; anniversaries and celebrations; festival commissions and premieres; family and children's events; classical music; theater and performance; jazz and music world; community and street arts.

Religious Events

Many religious festivals occur around the world, although many appear to have been secularized to some degree. Religious or spiritual symbols and rites are also frequently incorporated into otherwise secular events, ranging from prayers at public assemblies to the blessing of ships before sailing. One generic type of religious event is the "pilgrimage" to holy places. Shackley (2001, p. 102) identifies them as "linear events" in which the journey might be as important as the destination in terms of visitor motivations and experiences. Quite possibly the world's largest regular event (of any type)—in terms of attendance—is the annual religious pilgrimage of members of the Islamic faith to Mecca where the specific Ka'bah shrine is the focus of attention. Perhaps 2 million attend each year, from over 100 countries, imposing enormous logistical challenges for local authorities and occasionally resulting in serious mass accidents.

Tours by the Pope and other religious leaders often include huge assemblies for mass or other celebrations. Many religious festivals are purely local and sacred in nature, held by and for the community, but numerous such festivals are popular with tourists as well. Shackley (2001) described the host—tourist interactions and problems related to Buddhist festivals in the Himalayas. Some, like Mexico's Feast of the Dead, have become national holidays (literally, holy days). The Japanese "Matsui" are a type of religious event, generally community based, produced by volunteers, and celebrating a variety of religious or spiritual themes.

Parades and Processions

These are linear forms of event, with the entertainment, spectacle, or religious celebration moving past the viewer. In rare cases, such as certain carnival parades, everyone participates! Some are primarily media events, but in general parades are extremely popular forms of special event appealing to the whole family. Parades can be a part of many other types of event, or stand on their own as a form of cultural celebration. A real risk is that parades increasingly tend to rely on spectacle and entertainment, downplaying their cultural significance. Military parades, whether the marching of troops, display of equipment, performance of drills, or playing of the bands, have always marked victories, going to war, or the celebration of public holidays. They are full of symbolism and definitely stir the emotions, especially during times of civic or international strife.

A "flotilla" consists of boats in procession, while a "cavalcade" features horse riding.

Art and Entertainment

"Art and entertainment" events are often celebrations, but performances and exhibits also occur frequently on their own, and often in a for-profit environment.

Art festivals are universal, but with considerable diversity in form and types of art featured. By way of classification, the following categories of art are important:

- visual (e.g., painting, sculpture, handicraft);
- performing (e.g., music, dance, drama, cinema, story telling, poetry; usually involve performers in front of audiences);
- participatory (no separation of performer and audience).

More specific criteria for classifying art events include:

- professional versus amateur artists;
- competitive versus festive;
- mixed or single genre (e.g., just jazz, or many music types);
- single or multicultural;
- paid or free performances;
- regularly scheduled, periodic, or one-time;
- temporary (i.e., visual art created with a limited life expectancy, or a one-time only performance) versus permanent.

Almost by definition, "temporary art" is a special event. A building or island draped in material is intended to attract attention and engender celebration. An original, one-time performance is another type. This is a potential high-growth area in the events world.

"Concerts" are musical performances, usually of more than one artist or multiple numbers by an artist, and can be regularly scheduled performances or one-time and periodic special events. Uniqueness can stem from unusual locations, assembling special talent, or creating a festive atmosphere.

The Oscars or Grammies come to mind as special events with huge media audiences, but even the smallest town's annual sport awards banquet qualifies as a special event.

Art Exhibits

Galleries, museums, and other art facilities are formally in the exhibition business, but their normal displays of art are sometimes replaced by "touring exhibitions" or one-time-only exhibits. These can have major drawing power, generating substantial income for the producers and hosts, and for destinations.

Business and Trade Events

The broad category of "business and trade" covers meetings, conferences, fairs, sales and markets, consumer and trade shows, expositions, fund-raising, and publicity events. They are held either in the course of private business and association management, or as retail and trade opportunities.

Fairs

This is another word with multiple, and often confusing meanings. Dictionaries recognize the following:

- A gathering held at a specified time and place for the buying and selling of goods (i.e., a market).
- An exhibition (e.g., of farm products or manufactured goods, usually accompanied by various competitions and entertainments, as in a state fair); exhibitors may be in competition for prizes.
- An exhibition intended to inform people about a product or business opportunity.
- An event, usually for the benefit of a charity or public institution, including entertainment and the sale of goods (also called a bazaar).

The term "festival" is sometimes used as a synonym of "fair," but fairs have a long tradition of their own, as periodic exhibitions and markets. Waters (1939) traced the history of fairs from the earliest days of human barter and trade. Although North Americans associate the word "market" with a place to do shopping, fairs were originally occasional markets. Every society had to have fairs, where goods were sold and traded at specific times, and usually in specific places that became markets or fairgrounds. The Latin word *feriae*, meaning holy day (which evolved into holiday), is the origin of the English word "fair." They were often scheduled on church-sanctioned holy days.

Although fairs were often associated with religious celebrations, and now usually contain entertainment and amusements, fairs have more to do with productivity and business than with themed public celebrations. Indeed, Abrahams (1987) argued that fairs and festivals are like mirror images. But he also suggested that in modern, urban society they have become almost synonymous because the old ways of production, as celebrated in fairs, have faded.

The most traditional fairs in North America are the numerous county and state fairs that are held annually on the same site, most of which continue to reflect rural and agricultural themes. Some are called "exhibitions" or "expositions," reflecting their educational orientation. Most fairs are operated by independent boards or agricultural societies, though many have close links with the host municipality. Typical elements of agricultural fairs and exhibitions include agricultural demonstrations and contests, sales and trade shows (farm machinery, etc.), amusements of all kinds, eating and drinking, parades and a variety of entertainment. Education is also a vital program element, with close ties to 4H clubs as an example. This type of fair is often called a "show" in the UK, Australia, and New Zealand.

The website of International Association of Fairs and Expositions (IAFE, profiled in Chapter 2) gives a brief history of fairs. It notes that the first North American fairs were held in French Canada in the early 1700s, while in British North America the first was held in 1765 in Windsor, Nova Scotia, and it continues today! In 1807 the first fair was held in Massachusetts, in the form of an exhibit of sheep. IAFE says there are approximately 3250 fairs held annually in Canada and the US, attracting an attendance of about 150 million. The largest is the State fair of Texas in Dallas, hosting about 3.5 million visitors (*Amusement Business*). The Calgary Stampede (profiled in Chapter 12) has attendance of about 1.1 million, although total attendance figures reported can greatly exceed paid attendance at many of these events.

World's Fair

"World's fair" has a very specific meaning, derived from an international agreement in 1928 and regulated by the Bureau International des Expositions (BIE) in Paris. BIE sets the policies for bidding on and holding world's fairs, which are often called Expos. Their nominal purpose has always been educational, with particular attention paid to technological progress, but some authors have described them as glorified trade fairs (Benedict, 1983) and political tools (Hall, 1992).

There is a large body of literature on world's fairs, reflecting both their significance in economic and social terms and their popularity among expo lovers. Competition to host them is often fierce, as cities and countries see them as an opportunity to attract attention and tourists, typically in concert with urban renewal or other development schemes.

Exhibitions (Trade and Consumer Shows)

Sandra Morrow (1997), in the book *The Art of the Show* (produced for the International Association for Exposition Management, IAEM), highlighted the core purpose of "trade" and "consumer" shows, saying they "provide a time sensitive, temporary marketing environment where the buyer comes to the seller" (p. 3).

"Consumer shows" are open to the public, often with an admission fee, and popular themes are linked to automobiles, travel and recreation, pets, electronics, gardening, arts and crafts, or other hobbies. The producer, usually a private company, moves the show from place to place so that it is typically annual in any community. Venue owners might also produce their own. Manufacturers test new products at shows, retailers try to sell, and the consumer is searching for both ideas and entertainment.

"Trade shows" are usually for invitees only, based on specific business needs or association membership. Manufacturers or suppliers exhibiting at these events are trying to sell their products and services, or at least trying to inform potential customers. Common types are industrial, scientific and engineering, or health care. Many include educational presentations or seminars. Frequently they are attached to association conventions, such as when suppliers to the events industry exhibit at a trade show attached to professional association meetings. "International trade fairs" are a special class. Typically they are at the large end and targeted at a global or multicountry audience, and therefore are usually held in cities with major airports and exhibition halls.

Photo 1.2. Expo Expo: The annual IAEM meeting and exhibition, 2003 (credit: IAEM).

The Center for Exhibition Industry Research (CEIR) (www.ceir.org) exists to provide data to the industry. According to CEIR, "Attendees rate exhibitions as the number one most useful source of information with which to make a buying decision." Professionals attend trade shows to learn about new products and meet face to face with suppliers. Often competitive products can be evaluated side by side, which helps explain why people go to consumer shows where many manufacturers exhibit side by side. And the entertainment and social aspects of shows must not be underestimated—attendees should have fun while learning.

In 2000 there were 12,188 exhibitions held in over 2000 venues, but *Tradeshow Week* magazine (www.tradeshowweek.com) documented major declines in attendance at shows in the aftermath of September 11, 2001. Terrorism and market recession were given as the main reasons.

Sixteen North American cities host 46% of all exhibitions, each with over 200 events in 2000 (CEIR Direct 2002: www.ceir.org). The top three were Orlando (hosted 625), Las Vegas (589), and Toronto (582). Total gross revenue generated by exhibitions in North America was estimated to be $10.4 billion, generating $120 billion in total economic impact.

Exhibitions have a seasonal rhythm, with the lowest month for show-starts being December and the peak 2 months being (almost equally) October and March. Summer (July and August) constitutes the second low season. Part of the growth in venues is attributable to the shortfall of space during the two peak exhibition seasons.

Meetings and Conventions

People assemble for many reasons, and have always done so, but according to Spiller (2002) the modern convention industry grew in concert with industrialization and trade in the late 19th and through the 20th centuries. A parallel movement was the growth of trade, professional, and affinity associations of all kinds. The first convention bureau in the US was established in 1896 in Detroit, and at that time hotels were the main suppliers of venues.

The Professional Convention Management Association (PCMA) and the Convention Industry Council reported that the annual US convention and meeting market is worth $83 billion, and "b-there.com" claimed there were 1.7 million meetings of 10 or more people annually, generating expenditures of $121 billion (cited in *The 2002 Travel and Leisure Market Research Handbook*, p. 304).

Corporations and associations employ meeting or convention managers to handle their business get-togethers. Numerous meeting-planner firms exist, some of which have expanded into the special events field. Hotels, resorts, and convention centers also employ professionals whose jobs cover the marketing and hosting of meetings and other events. Meeting Professionals International (MPI) distinguishes between association, corporate, scientific, and incentive meetings, but "meeting" is a generic term applicable to an assembly of people for any purpose. However, it usually connotes a small, private business affair.

The term "conclave" is sometimes used to describe a secret or very private meeting. An "institute" refers to continuous training programs (e.g., an institute for sport development). "Retreats" are short getaway meetings, or a period of group withdrawal for prayer, meditation, study, and instruction under a director. "Seminars" are small-group discussions (e.g., a graduate seminar on event studies) while at a "workshop" participants get hands-on training (e.g., how to construct a float). At a "forum" a moderator oversees discussion on a topic by experts, or it is a public presentation with questions from the audience. Academics might hold a "colloquium" for presentation of scientific papers plus

Photo 1.3. 2003 Rotary International Convention.

questions and answers. "Symposium" describes a social gathering at which there is free interchange of ideas, or a formal meeting at which several specialists deliver short addresses on specified topics

"Conferences" are assemblies for the purpose of conferring and discussion, and should be small enough to facilitate interaction. Rogers (1998) said that conferences are often one-time only, with no tradition necessary. Academics hold numerous, themed conferences on specified topics or themes of broad interest within a field of study. "Conventions" are generally large assemblies of people from associations, political parties, clubs, or religious groups. Often convention delegates must go through a screening process. In Europe the term "congress" is generally used instead of convention, although it typically connotes an international meeting.

The market for meetings and conventions is usually separated into those held by associations and by corporations. The largest are typically held by associations, such as professional groups (medicine being one of the mainstays), religious organizations, educational and scientific bodies, or political groups. The Rotary International annual convention, for example, regularly pulls 20,000 or more delegates and other participants to the host city. According to the International Congress and Convention Association (ICCA) (www.icca.nl), association conventions are usually 4 to 5 days in length, and utilize a single venue if possible. ICCA estimates there are approximately 10,000 meetings organized on a regular basis, and they have information on more than 80% of them!

A trend has been noticeable in the increasing number of trade shows held in concert with association conventions, and it is an interesting fact that most such trade shows are produced under contract by a very few exhibition companies. Trade shows broaden the appeal of the convention and make the association some money. Regular exhibitors are likely to join the association as affiliates and to financially sponsor the convention or host receptions.

The "Corporate" segment is different in a number of ways. Companies hosting large numbers of meetings and conventions are likely to employ their own event managers or meeting planners, although large associations also do this. Corporate events are also likely to be more diverse than those initiated by associations, including training, hospitality, product launches, motivational assemblies, retreats, publicity events, grand openings, and team-building exercises. There is a strong tendency for corporate clients to repeatedly use the same venues, and strong links have been forged between corporations and specific hotel and resort chains for this purpose.

Profile: The Orange County Convention Center-Orlando, Florida (www:orlandoconvention.com)

Tom Ackert is the Executive Director of this impressive facility, one of the largest in North America. In 2003 a major expansion was completed (funded by a hotel tax and bonds). The center now boasts over 7 million square feet in total, with 2.1 million square feet of exhibition space. There are also 74 meeting rooms with 232 breakout spaces, and a state-of-the-art auditorium. Events requiring 1 million square feet are no longer unusual, although five or more shows can be held simultaneously in the available space.

Although it is called a convention center, most of its business consists of exhibitions: trade shows (65%) and consumer shows (11%). There are 380 full-time and 575 part-time staff. The convention center also maximizes its use of on-call staff. Because the technique of staggering events is highly implemented, it also allows for the staggering of staff. This has made the convention center operate smarter and take full advantage of the increase in event activity.

The main purpose of the expansion was not to accommodate larger events, although this is a benefit, but to allow the staggering of major shows. Different start and finish dates for shows (using the two facilities) will greatly increase the flow of visitors to Orlando and the area, thereby improving hotel occupancy rates and smoothing out demand. A major trade event like the annual Shot Show (everything to do with hunting and guns!) takes 11 to 14 days including set-up and take-down. As most guests arrive by air (80%) only for the open days, there is little traffic at either end of the show. Additionally, while a larger show is moving into one building, other shows can be taking place in the other building.

Peak seasons for events in Orlando are January through April and mid-September through mid-December. In the summer (which is off season for pleasure travelers to Florida), more price-sensitive meetings by associations, religious, and fraternal organizations are attracted to the convention center.

Annual repeat visits by shows to the center account for 38% of their business, while other events come there on a 2- or 3-year rotation that includes other cities. Accordingly, staff develop strong relationships with clients, and that results in smoother event production.

Reed International, a major exhibition producer, has entered into a contractual arrangement with the center. It is not an exclusive deal, but does result in Reed bringing a number of shows to the facility. For example, Reed manages the huge annual Shot Show.

Sport Events

In their book *The Ultimate Guide to Sport Event Management and Marketing*, Graham et al. (1995) noted there were literally millions of jobs in sports in the US, including a growing number specific to the production, managing, and marketing of events. These authors argued (p. 8) that sport events and other special events share commonalities, including their service orientation, the incorporation of celebration and drama, media coverage, and similarities in organizing and operations. Motivations of customers and travelers might also be similar, especially with regard to the ritual of attendance and related traditions. Traditional sport events like the Olympics always incorporate ceremonies and festivals, and it has now become commonplace to build a program of special events around a sport meet to create a "festival" or special event with heightened appeal.

The authors of *The Ultimate Guide* described indoor and outdoor sport events, subdivided by types of sport. Clearly this is an important typology for sport events as the facilities and conditions affecting the event will be quite different. This and other important criteria are:

- indoor versus outdoor;
- land versus water based (or airborne);
- regularly scheduled versus periodic or one-time only;
- public (spectators sought) or private;
- professional versus amateur (or pro-am combinations);
- events that must be bid on versus those that stem from league play.

Another classification approach is to look at the format of sport events:

- the regularly scheduled game, race, or competition (in a league);
- scheduled tournaments and championships (for leagues or invitationals);
- One-off sport "spectaculars" (media or spectator oriented);
- exhibition games with touring or invited teams;
- sport festival (emphasis on celebration and usually youth);
- multisport events (e.g., Olympics; Masters Games).

The term "meet" can be applied to any sports event, but the usual connotation is a meeting for the purpose of competition. A "tournament" is a sport meet organized to select a winner from participating players or teams through various rounds of competition; they are sometimes by invitation only. The Royal Tournament in London, England, is a special military display with historical connections to medieval jousting tournaments. A degree of pageantry accompanies this type of tournament.

"Championships" are play-offs within league play to select the winning team, or can be athlete focused and designed to select the top performers from members in a sport category. The term "grand prix," or top prize, is often used to describe the premier events in a type of sport or among top athletes. The International Amateur Athletics Federation (IAAF) brings together all the national-level sport associations and sanctions most international athletic events. IAAF manages a series of grand prix events to encourage athletic excellence and attract attention to the sports.

The term "Olympic Games" is restricted to uses sanctioned by the International Olympic Committee (IOC), based in Switzerland, and is applied to the Summer Olympic Games and Winter Olympic Games. Associated with these are the Paralympic Games for persons with special challenges.

Educational and Scientific

Events in this category are held for educational purposes, such as training workshops or seminars, or for scientific collaboration. They are frequently handled as meetings and conventions, but their goals lead to different requirements. Interpretive events are held to educate visitors by way of the event program. It could be an historical reenactment or a celebration of nature.

Recreational

Most communities and many organizations host numerous recreational events such sport games (rather than formal competitions), social outings, and not-for-profit amusements. The essential difference from related events is in the total orientation to having fun. Games and sports for fun are marked by participation (not spectating), are typically noncompetitive, or at least winning is downplayed, and might feature skills development or team building. Amusement events will likely feature rides or games of chance.

Political/State

"Political and state occasions" are perhaps the smallest category, but nonetheless usually make a big impact. Visits by very important people (VIP) always attract lots of attention, as do political rallies (demonstrations to support a specific cause) and conventions for political parties. Less frequent, but often more colorful, are the spectacle and pageantry surrounding inaugurations (e.g., the President takes his vows), coronations/investitures (the Prince receives a crown), and the like. Governments and political parties host conventions, ceremonies, and state visits.

Private Events

Although "private events" are held for individuals, families, and social groups, they often require professional event managers and specialist venues. Hotels, resorts, restaurants, private clubs, and catering facilities might refer to these as "functions." One universal example is that of weddings. Shone and Parry (2001), in their book *Successful Event Management*, gave details on the UK wedding industry, as it is coveted by hotels, clubs, and other function centers. About 2.5 million couples get married every year in the US, averaging 12 people in the party and 150 guests (Rebecca Grinnals, Engaging Concepts Inc., cited in *The 2002 Travel and Leisure Market Research Handbook*, p. 333).

There are about 10,000 reunion meetings held every year in the US (see The Reunion Network: www.reunionfriendly.com). They average fewer than 200 attendees but last an average of 4.6 nights. Military, school, family, religious, and other affinity groups regularly produce these private special events.

Study Questions

- What are the main elements in the field of "event studies," and how does it support event management?
- What disciplines contribute the most to event studies and event management?
- How are "event geography" and "event psychology" useful in event marketing?
- Where does event management fit into sport management, arts administrations, parks and recreation services, and the hospitality industry?
- Distinguish between fairs and festivals, and between exhibitions and meetings, from the perspectives of their purposes, venues, and reasons for attending.
- Discuss what makes some events "special."
- Why are many sport events combined with celebrations?
- Define "event tourism" from the points of view of consumers and tourist organizations.
- Give examples to illustrate each of the five main economic and tourism roles of events.

Advanced Study Questions

- Explain each of the economic roles of events and find specific examples in your community. Who is responsible for each role? Do they coordinate their efforts?
- Research one of the disciplines or fields contributing theory, research, and methods to event studies and event management. What are the main specific applications to a specific type of event?
- Does your area/city have a "hallmark event"? How could it get one, and what would be the implications?
- Discuss the social, cultural, economic, and political significance of all types of planned events in your area/community.

Chapter 2

Event Management:
Practice and Professionalism

Learning Objectives

- Learn how event management can be conceptualized as a system, and how to use the systems model for diagnosing problems.
- Understand the meaning and foundations of professionalism and the importance of ethical conduct.
- Know the major career options and paths associated with event venues and types of event.
- Understand the roles of professional associations related to event management.
- Appreciate the roles of various stakeholders in event management, and learn how to manage those relationships.
- Know what it takes to be an effective "manager."

Professionalism

Event practitioners belong to a relatively new and rapidly growing career field, complete with professional associations, certification, and formal educational programs. No overt barriers exist to entry or advancement at present, however, and it is safe to say that the majority of event professionals came into their careers from some other background— not an event-specific college diploma or university degree. Energy, experience, and ambition are the current keys to success, not credentials. But that is changing, just as it has in other emerging professions.

Are There Grounds for Professional Status?

Issues pertaining to event professionals have been discussed by Getz and Wicks (1994), with reference to earlier debates in the parks and recreation field. Generally accepted criteria pertaining to the delimitation of a profession are not met by most groups calling themselves "professional," including those in parks, recreation, tourism, and event management. These criteria include:

- government sanction, normally through licensing (i.e., the exclusion of those not licensed);
- accreditation by the professional governing body of educational delivery programs or institutions;

- a set body of theory, technical skills, and occupational values or ethics;
- self-regulation, normally through certification.

Governmental licensing is not found in the event field, nor is it likely to occur. Accreditation of educational institutions by professional bodies has begun, but is currently uncommon (see the International Special Events Society profile, later in this chapter). The relationship between professional event associations and educational institutions will have to evolve as more and more formal programs of study are developed. Self-regulation or certification has been institutionalized by a number of professional associations, and also is a growing trend within the tourism industry.

It is obvious that there are clear technical skills for event managers, but are there theories? This book seeks to at least identify the appropriate theoretical and methodological knowledge required by practitioners, and to demonstrate that many are rather unique to the events field. It goes without saying that management theory and skills are essential, but their application to events requires adaptation. Generic management and marketing concepts are covered in this book, plus facts, concepts, and methods specific to the events field.

Certification

Certification is one of the important roles in each of the major professional associations profiled later in this chapter. The IFEA made a good case for this process:

> Professional Certification is an important step in the career track of leaders in all industries. It enhances professional stature among one's peers; recognizes those who have gone beyond expectations to be the best that they can be; makes a statement to those with whom we do business; provides a leveraged position from which to negotiate and build career success; and sets higher standards for our industry.

Roles of Professional Associations

Several major professional associations are profiled in this chapter, related to the main event management career paths. But Arcodia and Reid (2003) found 147 professional associations worldwide that were involved with event management, and their major goals and objectives were examined. In descending order of frequency, those associations sought the following:

- act as an information exchange;
- provide education and training;
- achieve identity and recognition for the profession;
- ensure ethical standards are met;
- forge networks and friendships;
- enhance business management (consultations, etc.);
- provide membership benefits;
- provide leadership and be the premier voice in the field;
- product development;
- be a change agency (advocacy, etc.).

Ethics

An essential element of professionalism is that of personal and profession-wide ethics. In the profiles of major event associations that follow, their codes of conduct are summarized, and these should all be studied by students and practitioners because all these per-spectives provide importance guidance.

In her book *Event Planning Ethics and Etiquette: A Principled Approach to the Business of Special Event Management*, Judy Allen (2003) says there is a quiet revolution taking place in this industry. "Planners are assessing how and with whom they will do business" (p. 227). The book asks readers to set high standards and takes readers through a number of business issues that reflect on ethics, especially working relationships and fair competition.

Goldblatt (2002, p. 316) also highlighted some typical ethical issues facing event professionals, such as:

- breach of confidentiality (thereby giving some party an advantage, or violating a contract);
- taking or offering bribes;
- sexual harassment;
- theft of intellectual property (stealing other people's ideas; violating copyright laws).

Perhaps the big question is how you will personally cope with ethical issues? Take this self-quiz to see how you will deal with ethical issues.

- Have you all the facts (not just opinions and rumors)?
- What is the law (do not violate it willingly or out of ignorance)?
- Do you have a corporate or organizational policy or code of ethics to guide you?
- What can you do about it (what is feasible)?
- How will you feel about the various possible decisions you can make?
- Have you a personal moral code to draw upon?
- Who will gain or lose depending on your decision or actions?
- Is "just following orders" good enough for you? Can you make up your own mind on difficult ethical issues?
- Will you be held accountable for your decision or actions on this issue?
- Is the customer always right, or should you draw the line sometimes?
- What is in it for you? Assess your own ulterior motives.
- Is there a higher power to consult?

The nature of ethical issues requires contemplation and referral to the law, a higher power, or you own values and standards. Many ethical problems have no clear or right solution.

Specialized Career Paths in Event Management

Events occur in diverse settings, and there is increasing interdependence among types of events, so professionals have to be adaptable. The traditional event management break-down by type of event is employed here, because each of the following has one or more professional associations devoted to it. Some are also closely associated with specific types of facility, and we start with them.

Exhibition Management

Trade and consumer shows are typically produced in hotels or special-purpose exhibi-tion and convention centers. Some facilities are privately owned, and many are publicly financed. Private exhibition centers will stress events that generate profit, while public facilities might equally be interested in attracting and hosting events that generate tourism benefits for the area. Many exhibitions and shows are produced by private exhibition companies who hire professional managers. They not only produce the expo but sell it to exhibitors and attendees and deal with service contractors.

Job Profile: Exhibition or Show Manager

Typically works for an exhibition production company, association, or an exhibition venue. This work can involve a lot of travel and show managers might have to do any or all of the following tasks:

- set goals and objectives for the show;
- target marketing and related promotions (to exhibitors and/or attendees);
- design the program and hospitality for guests, exhibitors, speakers, entertainers, the media, VIPs, etc.;
- create a budget; manage finances;
- select the venue;
- manage the logistics of people, materials, exhibit, and equipment movement;
- negotiate contracts;
- engage in necessary liaison with the venue and other stakeholders;
- develop the marketing plan;
- hire subcontractors;
- design the exhibit space including food and entertainment; maximize accessibility for all users;
- undertake comprehensive security, health, safety, and risk management (working with the venue managers);
- supervise staff;
- produce a "green event"'
- arrange for evaluative research; final reporting.

The website www.exhibitornet.com contains classified job postings. Professionals looking for work also post ads on this site. Some examples illustrate the types of careers available:

- A health education and communications firm seeks an Exhibits Manager responsible for planning and implementing an annual exhibit program of over 20 events (tasks: market research; formulating exhibit plans; logistics; transport and onsite management).
- Major professional sport organization requires a manager of events and attractions to manage the planning and execution of several tour programs (tasks: planning, budgeting, and managing third-party performance).
- Large corporation seeks a director of trade shows (tasks: negotiation with vendors; marketing).

The International Association for Exhibition Management (www.iaem.org)

Organized in 1928 as the National Association of Exhibition Managers (IAEM) to represent the interests of tradeshow and exposition managers, the IAEM is the premier association for anyone with business interests in the exhibition industry. Today IAEM represents over 3600 individuals and companies who conduct and support exhibitions around the world.

The Mission of IAEM is to promote the expansion of the exhibition industry by providing unique and essential education, services, and resources to its members around the world. IAEM's primary objectives are geared toward individual and industry growth:

- Promoting the trade show and exposition industry throughout the world.
- Educating all persons who are involved in the industry by providing regular opportunities for education and skills enhancement.
- Distributing information and statistical data about the show industry.
- Providing opportunities for individuals in the exhibition industry to meet and exchange ideas and information, providing advocacy for its members.

Activities and Services. Meetings and education, along with networking events, are the major benefits of IAEM membership. Throughout the year, several meetings and educational programs are offered both at the chapter and international levels.

Expo! Expo! Is IAEM's annual meeting and exhibition, dedicated to providing education and networking opportunities to foster and build relationships. The "Professional Development Conference & Supplier Showcase" is a regional meeting held twice per year in locations that compliment the Annual Meeting. IAEM Services, Inc. is a wholly owned subsidiary of IAEM. This for-profit corporation provides the exhibition industry with a variety of relevant products and services. The buying power of IAEM members enables IAEM Services Inc. to form marketing partnerships with companies that in turn offer their products and services to IAEM members at reduced prices.

TradeshowStore.com is the IAEM's virtual shopping center, offering:

- products, such as badge holders, lanyards, and ribbons;
- publications such as *The Art of the Show*, and *Hotel Contracts: A Roadmap to Successful Negotiations*;
- IAEM/Amazon.com bookstore features topics specifically related to the exhibition industry;
- learn about IAEM's affinity programs;
- links to IAEM Services Partners.

Certification. IAEM has a comprehensive learning program leading to designation as Certified in Exhibition Management (CEM).

The *CEM Learning Program* is the cutting-edge educational opportunity designed for exhibition industry professionals to succeed. The CEM curricula, a dependable source of specific knowledge for all individuals, emphasize direct application to daily challenges. Because of the emphasis on practical knowledge, the *CEM Learning Program* is first, an educational program, and second, a certification program.

To earn the CEM certification, individuals must:

- Successfully complete all nine parts, including passing the appropriate examinations within 3 years beginning the year following their first pass.
- Have at least 3 years of full-time experience as a practitioner in exhibition management.

In 2003, CEM Europe, CEM Singapore, and CEM China were launched through licenses issued to organizations in those countries.

Code of Ethics. "IAEM members pledge to conduct themselves professionally with honesty and integrity in their business practices. We will carefully monitor conduct by asking:

- Is this legal?

- Is there sufficient disclosure of essential facts so that the parties can make informed choices?
- How will it make me feel about myself, my organization, and my industry?

In the conduct of our business we will aim to treat others as we would expect others to treat us."

Exhibition Industry Foundation. IAEM and CEIR have combined their foundations, creating the new Exhibition Industry Foundation to focus on supporting the exhibition industry. The consolidation of the two existing foundations does not create a new entity; rather it creates a stronger foundation to promote the exhibition industry. Leaders of CEIR and IAEM believe that one foundation representing the interests of the exhibition industry as a whole will have a greater ability to garner the resources needed to promote the continued growth and expansion of the exhibition industry.

Profile: Julie Smith, CMP, Supervisor of Event Coordination, Orlando Orange County Convention Center

Julie works in the Event Services Division at the Orlando Orange County Convention Center. She was an "Event Coordinator" in the center for 6 years before being promoted to the "Supervisor" position with responsibility for 15 coordinators. This division is responsible for setting up exhibitions and event coordination in one of the nation's largest convention and exhibition venues.

A team of "account executives" markets the facility and sells the space, with event coordinators taking over up to 18 months from the date of the event. Julie assigns coordinators to individual events, but uses a team approach with three to a show, generally. She also manages the overall event schedule for the facility. They do not develop the trade or consumer show concept, and their clients—the event owners—hire decorators and other contractors to design the exhibition. The floor plan is checked and approved by Julie, plus a fire marshal is on site to ensure compliance with regulations. The event manager educates clients as to what is possible, informs them of regulations, and pinpoints logistics challenges to help produce a successful show. Certain proposals by clients can be vetoed, and regular visits to the events help identify specific challenges

Certified Meeting Planner (CMP) is one of the preferred professional designations in the convention center, although there is one person who is a Certified Exhibition Manager. Several internships for 6-month periods are normally available in this division. Some of these are filled by students from the nearby Rosen School of Hospitality Management (part of the University of Central Florida). Two permanent job descriptions follow.

Event Coordinator
General Functions: Responsible for the coordination of all events within the Orange County Convention Center.

Distinguishing Characteristics of Work: This is responsible administrative work concerning all aspects of events coordination. An employee assigned to a position allocated to this class of work is responsible for the coordination of all events within the Orange County Convention Center to include event outlines, equipment coordination, monitoring events in progress, event billings, customer service and relations, and contractual matters. The employee is expected to exercise independent judgment in all activities with clients, event patrons, and the general public. General supervision is received from the Operations Manager and is reviewed through activity reports, conferences, and results achieved.

Representative Duties/Assignments:

- Maintains liaison between users of the Orange County Convention Center and the Center's staff.

- Attends preevent meetings with clients.
- Supervises the overall coordination of events.
- Reviews contracts and operational schedules to make certain that the dates, times, facilities, and equipment provided are correct and that provisions made have been fulfilled.
- Prepares and issues set-up and service requests and schedules for events to the Building Operations staff and other affected staff members.
- Works hours as required to include evenings, weekends, and holidays.
- Perform other related duties as assigned.

Minimum Qualifications: Requires a bachelor's degree in Business, Public Administration, Recreation, or Hospitality Management and 2 years of experience in Convention/Event Coordination, or an equivalent combination of education, training, and experience.

Account Executive

General Functions: Performs sales-related work in support of the marketing program for the Orange County Convention Center. This is responsible professional sales and marketing work with extensive public and professional contact. An employee in a position allocated to this class of work is responsible for assisting the Sales Manager in conducting the day-to-day activities of the Marketing Department to include initial customer contact and account follow-up, contract preparation, and scheduling. Work is reviewed under the direct supervision of the Sales Manager.
Minimum Qualifications: Graduation from an accredited college or university with a Bachelor's degree and one year of experience in marketing or sales with a convention center, convention bureau or a convention hotel; or graduation from high school or equivalent and five years of experience in marketing or sales with a convention center, convention bureau or convention hotel.

Meeting and Convention Management

Hotels and other facilities host numerous meetings and conventions, and cities build dedicated convention and meeting centers specifically to attract major conventions that the private sector cannot necessarily handle. For the most part the venues do not produce the events, but concentrate on selling their space and bidding on events. However, some convention centers do produce events themselves in order to make money, especially in otherwise slow-demand periods.

Meeting Professionals International (www.mpiweb.org)

Established in 1972, MPI is the leading global community committed to shaping and defining the future of the meeting and event industry. As the largest trade association for the $102.3 billion meeting industry, MPI defines the return on investment and strategic value meetings bring to individuals, organizations, and the global economy. MPI helps its members enhance their professional value by providing them with best practices, superior education, the latest research and trends, professional development, and networking opportunities.

MPI has grown from 159 members in 1972 to 19,000 members in 60 countries today. Its membership spans the globe from North and South America, Mexico, Europe to Asia. Seventy-one Fortune 100 companies are represented in the MPI membership. There are currently 61 chapters, and an additional four in formation. MPI's current membership ratio is 46% planners and 54% suppliers.

There are three membership categories: planners (who orchestrate and manage meetings); suppliers (provide industry goods and services); students (enrolled full-time in a postsecondary program).

MPI Strategic Plan. Launched in 2003, the Pathways to Excellence plan aims to guide the association's future and prepare the industry for change. It calls for creation of "defined career pathing" for meeting planners, increasing influence with corporate, association, and other senior-level decision makers, and intensifying business opportunities for industry suppliers.

MPI Vision. "MPI will be the pivotal force in positioning meetings and events as a key strategic component of an organization's success."

MPI Mission. "MPI will be recognized as the leading global membership community that is committed to shaping and defining the meeting and event industry."

Activities and Services. MPI offers its members a variety of services and benefits including:

- Affiliation with one of 61 chapters or one of 4 chapters in formation.
- Volunteer leadership opportunities.
- Two annual adult education and networking conferences featuring industry trade shows.
- Annual European adult education conference.
- Canadian administration with an office in Ontario.
- European administration with an office in Luxembourg.
- The Certification in Meeting Management (CMM) designation, a strategic senior meeting management education and certification program.
- Full access to MPIWcb, an interactive technological tool featuring online learning and networking forums, a job bank, and other online resources.
- Monthly magazine, *The Meeting Professional.*
- Annual membership directory.
- Extensive recognition and awards programs, including Chapters of the Year, the Meeting Professional Awards, and the Global Paragon Awards.
- Discounted business services.

MPI hosts the meeting industry's most dynamic gatherings of meeting professionals, including the World Education Congress (WEC), the Professional Education Conference-North America (PEC-NA), and the Professional Education Conference-Europe (PEC-Europe). "MPI's award-winning monthly, *The Meeting Professional*, underwent a complete redesign in January 2002. This content-rich publication is one of the industry's leading resources. In addition, Community NetNews is MPI's weekly member care e-mail blast delivering association, chapter, industry and workplace-related news."

Certification. "Institutes I&II" is an intensive meeting management certificate program offering Continuing Education Units (CEUs). MPI's CMM program is the first university co-developed global professional designation for senior-level meeting professionals, which focuses on strategic issues that are critical to advancement in the meeting industry. Throughout the residency and postresidency portions, attendees are led through exercises designed to promote strategic thinking, leadership, and executive decision-making skills. In 2003, 250 meeting professionals worldwide had obtained this acclaimed certification.

MPI is one of 25 member organizations of the Convention Industry Council (CIC), which sponsors the Certified Meeting Professional (CMP) program based on professional experience and academic examination.

MPI Foundation. Founded in 1984, the MPI Foundation conducts research and develops projects annually to ensure growth and recognition for meeting professionals and the industry. A self-sustaining, self-governed organization operating solely on voluntary contributions from individuals, corporate suppliers, MPI chapters, and other affiliated organizations, the Foundation's focus is ongoing research and development of new ways to improve meeting planning process, function, and management. The Foundation also directs the research and development of the Women's Leadership and Multicultural Initiatives.

Ethics. "Meeting Professionals International's (MPI) Principles of Professionalism provide guidelines recommended for the business behavior of its members that impacts their perceived character and thus the overall image of MPI. Commitment to these principles is implicit to membership and is essential to instilling public confidence, engaging in fair and equitable practices and building professional relationships with meeting industry colleagues. As members of Meeting Professionals International, we are responsible for ensuring that the meeting industry is held in the highest public regard throughout the world. Our conduct directly impacts this result."

Maintaining Professional Integrity:
- Honestly REPRESENT AND ACT within one's areas of professional competency and authority without exaggeration, misrepresentation or concealment.
- AVOID actions which are or could be perceived as a conflict of interest or for individual gain.
- OFFER OR ACCEPT only appropriate incentives, goods and services in business transactions.

Utilizing Professional Business Practices:
- HONOR written and oral contracts, striving for clarity and mutual understanding through complete, accurate and timely communications, while respecting legal and contractual rights of others.
- ENSURE rights to privacy and protect confidentiality of privileged information received verbally, in writing, or electronically.
- REFRAIN from misusing solicited information, proposals or concepts.
- COMMIT to the protection of the environment by responsible use of resources in the production of meetings.
- ACTIVELY PURSUE educational growth through training, sharing of knowledge, expertise and skills, to advance the meeting industry.

Respecting Diversity:
- EMBRACE AND FOSTER an inclusive business climate of respect for all peoples regardless of national origin, race, religion, sex, marital status, age, sexual orientation, physical or mental impairment. *Encompasses oneself, the association, fellow members, meeting attendees, clients and customers, suppliers and planners, employers and the general public.*
- Adherence to these Principles of Professionalism signifies professionalism, competence, fair dealing and high integrity. Failure to abide by these principles may subject a member to disciplinary action, as set forth in the Bylaws of Meeting Professionals International.

Awards. MPI has a number of awards for individuals (e.g. International Planner, International Supplier) and chapters. Global Paragon Awards are designated for meetings with budgets up to US$1,000 per attendee and those with budgets more than US$1,000 per attendee (excluding transportation costs). In addition to the Category I and II award categories, MPI has three additional awards of excellence:

- Best Themed Event
- Best Promotion for a Meeting or Event
- Best Product Launch Event

Job Profile: Meeting Planner or Conference Organizer

These professionals can be independent consultants (see, for example: Concepts Worldwide Inc., www.conceptsworldwide.com), work for specialized event companies, or are employed by associations and corporations. A number of unique tasks are associated with this field:

- working with clients to plan the event and find the location and venue (usually associations and corporations);
- negotiating and working with venue managers (such as hotels, convention centers, retreats);
- negotiating and working with production companies (who set up the stages, exhibits, equipment) and caterers;
- registration (managing the area for receiving and registering delegates or guests; the computer software; collecting fees);
- program planning; designing and printing the program;
- distribution of material to delegates;
- production of conference proceedings (all the papers in one volume);
- accommodation booking and catering arrangements;
- organizing a social program including pre- and postevent tours.

Additional insights are available from research on the meeting planner. Bryant and Gaiko (1999) looked at necessary skills, while Sheehan, Hubbard, and Popovich (2000) profiled the hotel and conference center meeting planner. O'Brien and Shaw (2002) profiled independent meeting planners in Canada.

Research Note

Bryant, S., & Gaiko, S. (1999). Determining skills necessary for meeting planners. In W. Roehl (Ed.), *Proceedings, The Convention/Expo Summit VII*, Las Vegas, Department of Tourism and Convention Administration, William F. Harrah College of Hotel Administration, University of Nevada at Las Vegas.

Bryant and Gaiko (1999) conducted research on the skills necessary for being a professional meeting planner, based on responses from MPI members in the US. Perhaps surprisingly, the number one skill deemed necessary was that of negotiation. Other important skills included: listening; time management; and crisis management. Knowledge of the industry came fifth in that survey, but obviously professionals have to know the basics before they start work. What the survey reveals, in fact, is that practitioners have to have generic skills (like negotiation) and personal skills (like time management) that are not specific to event management.

According to the 1998 Meetings Outlook Survey (conducted by the magazine *Association Management*), the most significant change for meeting planners is likely to come about through technological progress. Such changes affect the ways in which meetings are conducted and the planning and marketing activities of the planners. But it is worth remembering that technological changes are now a fact of life—every year the industry is confronted with something new that can be used for better events and better event management, so the professional has to be constantly scanning for innovations and deciding which ones to use.

What are the hot technological changes affecting the industry? Computer-enhancement of meetings will continue to develop, with instant data sourcing and analysis as needed. Satellite conferencing is already well established, but convention centers are becoming "info-ports" that enable global conferencing and education without travel. The "virtual meeting" promises to become more and more important, especially during times when travel is perceived to be unsafe or too expensive. Universal accessibility to the Internet, and wireless communications, makes it increasingly possible to work anywhere, even when on retreat.

The meeting, therefore, might very well cease to be an escape from work—a time out for contemplation and refreshment—and become another dimension of group work. Reflection, discussion, and action can be merged. It is possible to contemplate the role of meeting planners evolving from that of purely event management to one of business facilitator. At the same time, other meetings and conventions will maximize their global educational reach, requiring meeting planners to become learning facilitators.

"Special Event" Management

The term "special event" is generic and rather ambiguous, but The International Special Events Society (ISES) has a focus on the production of events and the industry that supplies them. As delimited by ISES, their industry consists of a number of interrelated sectors, each with their own sets of skills and professional concerns:

Photo 2.1. Terri Breining of Concepts Worldwide leads an event planning session (credit: Concepts Worldwide).

Profile: Concepts Worldwide Inc.(www.conceptsworldwide.com)

Theresa Breining (CMP, CMM) is owner and president of this successful, San Diego-based meeting management company. She started it in 1988 after working since 1976 in association management, hotel sales and catering, and conducting volunteer training for the fundraising events produced by a social service agency. All that experience served as confirmation of her desire to set up her own business in event management.

At first the business looked shaky—no business plan, few clients (whatever she could get), and little revenue. Theresa, as a new owner, worked at home for 2 years before getting a part-time assistant and later an office. She managed to get by with periodic paydays, but there was no regular salary for 5 years! Having a dream, and persevering, eventually paid off. She got involved with MPI right away in 1988 and the networking and learning environment helped her a great deal.

Theresa now devotes a lot of her time to MPI, in which she has been International Chairwoman of the Board for 2003–2004. She also teaches and coordinates a meeting planning program at San Diego State University. The General Manager of Concepts Worldwide now handles day-to-day operations of the company. Her advice to students: have a passion for working in events, take satisfaction more from the challenge than the monetary rewards, and get involved as soon as possible. And keep learning!

Concepts Worldwide concentrates on corporate meetings and conventions, some of which require trade show planning as well. They offer a full service approach to the planning and organization, including logistics, of meetings, conferences, trade shows and events worldwide. A set of "core values" has been formulated to foster a creative, supportive, and ethical environment. They created C.A.R.E.S. (Concepts Acting Responsibly for the Environment and Society) as a community involvement and "green" management program. Clients are encouraged and assisted in holding environmentally responsible events.

The staff of Concepts Worldwide is divided into three departments. They are Administration, which includes a General Manager, Director of Finance, Accounting Manager, manager of Internet Technologies, Executive Assistant/Office Manager, and Receptionist. The Sales Department is comprised of a Director of Sales and three account executives, who are responsible for identifying and maintaining relationships with clients. They work closely with the program development group of three, who focus on the costing and proposals, to ensure that the programs are priced right internally and presented appropriately to clients or potential clients.

The "product" of Concepts Worldwide is delivered by the Operations Department, which consists of Meeting Managers, who are responsible for the overall success of meetings once the contract is signed, and the meeting coordinators, who work side-by-side with the meeting managers on everything from registration management to a variety of other tasks. In addition to the regular, full-time staff, Concepts Worldwide utilizes a pool of contractors, who have been trained to the Concepts' standards, and take on individual projects. This combination of staff and contractors allows Concepts Worldwide to take on a lot of projects without adding unnecessarily to the overhead costs.

Concepts Worldwide belongs to and participates actively in a number of professional associations: Meeting Professionals International, Society of Incentive and Travel Executives, International Franchise Association, and the Professional Convention Management Association, and is a committed supporter of APEX, an initiative sponsored by the Convention Industry Council that is developing standards for the meeting industry.

- special events producers (e.g., festivals and trade shows);
- party and convention coordinators;
- destination management companies;
- caterers, decorators, florists;

- corporate event planners;
- special effects experts;
- tent suppliers and rental companies;
- specialty entertainers and balloon artists;
- convention center managers and hotel sales managers.

There is obviously some overlap here with other professional groupings, especially the producers and the convention-related professionals.

International Special Events Society (www.ises.com)

ISES was founded in 1987 "to foster enlightened performance through education while promoting ethical conduct." It works to join professionals to focus on the "event as a whole." "The solid peer network ISES provides helps special events professionals produce outstanding results for clients while establishing positive working relationships with other event colleagues."

ISES consists of over 3600 professional members in 38 active chapters worldwide. Its membership covers special event producers (from festivals to trade shows), caterers, decorators, florists, destination management companies, and suppliers of rentals, special effects, and tents. It includes balloon artists, audio-visual technicians, party and convention coordinators, educators, journalists, hotel sales managers, specialty entertainers, and even convention center managers. As delimited by ISES, their industry consists of a number of interrelated sectors, each with their own sets of skills and professional concerns.

For an example of ISES members, see Betsy Wiersma, CSEP (Wiersma Experience Marketing and Creative Event Development: www.betsywiersma.com). e=mc² event management (www.emc2events.com) is an event management company involved with ISES.

Ethics. Principles of Professional Conduct and Ethics have been adopted. Each member is to adhere to the following:

- Promote and encourage the highest level of ethics within the profession of the special events industry while maintaining the highest standards of professional conduct.

Profile: Betsy Wiersma, CSEP (Wiersma Experience Marketing and Creative Event Development)

Betsy is founder and president of Wiersma Experience Marketing, her own training, consulting, and event marketing company based in Denver, Colorado. Betsy is the author (with Kari Strolberg) of the book *Exceptional Events, Concept to Completion*, and the Creative Event Development workbook.

She is one of a growing number of Certified Special Event Professionals and recently served on the President's Council for ISES and the Advisory Board for *Special Events Magazine*. She has won a number of prestigious awards for her work in the events industry, including three Esprit awards from ISES. She also served for 5 years as the Events Director for "The Special Event" annual convention hosted by *Special Events Magazine*.

Betsy is recognized internationally as a leader in "BIG IDEA" thinking. She creates results-oriented events and has helped numerous clients, both cities and corporations, to use events as strategic marketing tools. Betsy's innovative thinking is reflected in her involvement with the first privatization of an urban festival, Kroger Circlefest, which resulted in a 700% increase in corporate sponsorship and charity funds raised.

Betsy graduated from Purdue University with a degree in Liberal Arts. Purdue honored Ms. Wiersma in 1996 as Distinguished Alumni and their youngest-ever Purdue Old Master.

Betsy's email newsletter is available free on request. See her website: www.betsywiersma.com.

- Strive for excellence in all aspects of our profession consistently at or above acceptable industry standards.
- Use only legal and ethical means in all industry negotiations and activities.
- Protect the public against fraud and unfair practices, and promote all practices which bring respect and credit to the profession.
- Provide truthful and accurate information with respect to the performance of duties. Use a written contract clearly stating all charges, services, products, performance expectations and other essential information.
- Maintain the industry-accepted standards of safety and sanitation.
- Commit to increase professional growth and knowledge, to attend educational programs and to personally contribute expertise to meetings and journals.
- Strive to cooperate with colleagues, suppliers, employees, employers and all persons supervised, in order to provide the highest quality service at every level.
- Subscribe to the ISES Principles of Professional Conduct and Ethics, and abide by the ISES Bylaws and policies.

Professional Development. "Eventworld" is the annual international educational conference, and other ISES-sponsored classes are offered to members. Affiliation with local chapters facilitates idea exchanges and educational opportunities, including Regional Educational Conferences. Online web courses are available only to members.

Certification. ISES created an educational foundation (ISEF) with the specific mandate to establish an educational program and certification process, leading to the designation "Certified Special Events Professional" (CSEP). Applicants must register for the program,

Photo 2.2. Calgary Cares, annual fundraiser (credit: e = mc2 event management).

and it is open to members and nonmembers of ISES (with different fee structures applying).

Certification is based on a combination of education, performance, experience, service to the industry, portfolio presentation, and examination.

Once professionals enroll in CSEP they start a program of self-study using materials provided by ISES, and they begin to accumulate points for specified activities. Knowledge of technical terms is required for the exam, based on the *Dictionary of Event Management*. An Exam Blueprint helps prepare applicants for the required exam by detailing all the competencies of event management. Mentors are aligned with candidates to provide wisdom from experience. Recertification is required every 5 years.

The ISES Education Foundation also provides scholarships to individuals seeking certification or other education in the field, and grants for projects advancing special event education.

Excellence Awards. The "Esprit Awards" are an industry recognition program. The "Spirit of Excellence" awards are internal, given by the society to current members for exemplary service to ISES, or to a particular chapter or region.

ISES recognizes *Special Events Magazine* (www.specialevents.com/) as the official magazine of the industry in North America, and The Special Event as the official trade show.

Profile: e=mc2 event management (www.emc2events.com)

This award-winning event management company in Calgary has been rapidly expanding in size and scope. They received a prestigious GALA award from *Special Events Magazine* in 2004 for the Best Theatrical Entertainment Production, for their Calgary Cares event (an AIDS fundraiser) and have also received an award for Most Outstanding Event Over $300,000 in Canada from the Canadian Event Industry at its 2003 Awards Gala.

Co-owners Ken Christofferson and Jocelyn Flanagan jointly started the company in 2001. They are both members in the Canadian Special Events Society, ISES, and MPI.

Ken's previous experience includes operations and marketing as well as special event production with a variety of companies. Jocelyn's background includes competitive figure skating, and she began organizing skating and other sport events in Europe.

Both teach event management at Mount Royal College in Calgary, and are involved in setting up local ISES chapter.

The company organizes industry conferences, official openings, product launches, fund-raising events for associations, galas, awards banquets, incentive travel, and other special occasions. They are sometimes asked by corporate clients to do weddings. In 2003 they grew from 3 to 11 full-time staff, expanded their downtown office space, and added destination management services (e.g., delegate activities, programming, and transportation built around conventions).

Festival Management

Festivals tend to organize by type, so that children's festivals will meet with each other and jazz festivals will stick together. This is necessary to a point, as they all have specific programming needs, but unhealthy if not accompanied by exposure to the whole range of festivals and the world of event management in general. Several factors are instrumental in shaping festival management as a career:

- Most are operated by not-for-profit organizations (many of which are charities).

- They tend to stress the program, and have been slow to adopt a marketing orientation.
- Many are dependent on a few public grant-giving agencies, although corporate sponsorship is increasing in importance.
- They rely heavily on volunteers.
- Although many have clear themes (the type of music, an art form, or an object of celebration/commemoration), a large proportion—in North America in particular—are "community festivals" with very broad mandates and programs.

International Festivals and Events Association (IFEA) (www.ifea.com)

The International Festivals and Events Association (IFEA) is the industry's premiere professional association serving events and related professionals and organizations (in 36 countries) whose common purpose is the successful production and presentation of festivals, events, and civic and private celebrations. More than 2700 professionals are currently members of the association, covering a broad spectrum of organizations and professional interests (i.e., events and suppliers, sponsors, media, tourism, municipalities, facilities, parks & recreation, education, etc.). The IFEA has regional directors throughout the US and enjoys the support of affiliated chapters in the USA, Canada, Europe, Asia, and Australia. IFEA celebrated its 50th anniversary in 2005.

Five major goals guide the IFEA:

- furtherance of industry image and value;
- professional recognition for the industry;
- member awareness and knowledge of industry issues and trends;
- promotion of professional standards and ethics;
- availability of valuable and useful benefits for members.

Networking among members is a key benefit, facilitated by several publications and regular events. The IFEA Expo Experience, featured at the annual convention, is the only trade show of its kind devoted to the festivals and events industry. The Expo Experience markets top-of-the-line festival products and services, including props, entertainment, financial services, attractions and displays, decorations and signage, food and beverage products, bleachers and seating, carnivals, communications, technology, security and crowd management, educational programs, rental equipment, operational supplies and support services, fireworks/laser shows, parade floats and inflatables, sponsorship, graphics/printing, insurance, merchandise, media and syndication services, photography, portable restrooms, power, stage/lights/sound, ticketing and wristbands, transportation, video production, and more. Focused regional and Behind-the-Scenes seminars are also offered throughout the year. Held in conjunction with member events, such as the Pasadena Tournament of Roses Parade, Macy's Thanksgiving Day Parade, Fiesta San Antonio, SunFest of Palm Beach County, the Kentucky Derby, and the Pro Football Hall of Fame Festival, seminars offer first-hand educational opportunities.

IFEA offers its members a plethora of valuable benefits, including access to the largest professional network in the industry, conventions and seminars, regional and local programming, music licensing discounts, credit card processing programs, directors and officers insurance, top-quality publications and resources, IEG publication and service discounts, economic impact estimates, and group buying discounts. Many publications specific to festivals and events are available through the IFEA's online bookstore, some of which are produced directly by IFEA. *ie: the business of international events*, the IFEA's industry leading quarterly magazine, is received by all members. Online, at www.ifea.com, members have 24/7 access to "Affiliate Connection," an electronic newsletter with the latest event news and trends from around the world. The website also includes access to job banks, member forums, event and calendar links, IFEA Marketplace suppliers, current new updates, benefit information, and much more. The IFEA Foundation provides convention scholarships, and funds other IFEA educational programs. Donations are tax-deductible.

Awards. IFEA partners with key sponsors to produce the Miller Brewing Company/IFEA Hall of Fame, the Zambelli Fireworks Internationale/IFEA Volunteer of the Year Award, and the Haas and Wilkerson Insurance/IFEA Pinnacle Awards, presented for event promotional materials and creative initiatives.

Certification. In 2003 IFEA somewhat changed their certification, renaming their designation "Certified Festival Executive" to "Certified Festival and Event Executive" (CFEE). This not only reflects the IFEA name better but avoids duplication of acronyms, especially Certified Fair Executive (offered by the IAFE). A new IFEA Academy of Event Education was established to oversee the process.

A core curriculum has been identified, covering the following major competences:

- Sponsorship and sponsor service;
- Administration and management (strategic planning; feasibility studies; financial and budgeting; internal auditing; effective management models; systems and procedures; standards and ethics; quality control);
- Human resources (staffing issues; employee manuals; volunteer programs; board relations; motivation; legal issues; compensation and benefits);
- Marketing and media relations (promotional materials and campaigns; public relations; media partnerships; media interview techniques; effective issue and crisis management; web marketing);
- Operations and risk management (programming, entertainment booking; technology; logistics; evaluation; creating an environment; venue selection; stage, lighting, and sound; permits; working with the city and other agencies; safety and security; insurance; emergency plans);
- Nonsponsorship revenue programs (merchandise; food and beverage; foundations; fund-raising event).

Electives will also be offered (at least four will be required), including: writing and presentation skills; creativity and innovation; time management; leadership; economic impact; current industry issues and trends.

At least 5 years of paid employment experience in events is also required to get certified as CFEE, including at least 3 years in a management position. Candidates must also attend at least two IFEA conferences, make a verbal presentation, and write an article for publication. The final step is a formal assessment of the candidate's "capstone portfolio," which is to include case studies showing how he/she has applied the required knowledge. Recertification will be required every 5 years.

Ethics. The IFEA Code of Professional Conduct and Ethics has been established to encourage, promote, and ensure that its members and the industry itself represent and project the highest standards of ethical and professional conduct in the promotion and presentation of festivals and special events. The following principles and guidelines are a general guide adopted by the membership of the IFEA and intended provide a framework for professional behavior, ethical conduct, and conflict resolution. The following are excerpts:

Members should aggressively seek to acquire for themselves and their colleagues professional development and training, and support the like development of others within the industry.

Members should take such action as necessary to ensure that their relationships with sponsors, vendors, employees, volunteers, media, and the public at large are made with the highest professional quality and ethical standards in mind.

Event professionals and organizations should engage in enterprises for which they are qualified, and avoid undertakings that require a competency which they do not have, or cannot reasonably acquire.

No member shall in performance of professional duties engage in any wrongdoing, corruption, financial impropriety or illegal act. Similarly, members should seek to avoid all acts of wrongdoing, impropriety, or illegality, whether in the course of business or in private life, which if disclosed, would serve to embarrass, impair or jeopardize the event or organization he/she represents or serves. Because of the "public" mission and nature of our industry and our dependence, in part on public trust and support, Members, like members of the legal profession, are charged with the responsibility to "avoid the perception of wrongdoing."

The activities of members and their organizations shall be conducted in accordance with all applicable laws.

Members shall embrace and promote the highest standards of human resource training and management . . . members should take such action as necessary to ensure that they, as individuals and organizations, establish and practice ethical hiring, termination and discipline practices for employees and associates; avoid the practice and tolerance of discrimination based on race, creed, national origin, age, handicap, political affiliation, sex, sexual orientation, religion, parental or military status, veteran status, or disability.

Members and Member organizations shall engage in and embrace plans of education and professional training and development that improves and empowers the professional abilities and performance of its employees and members.

Members and their organizations should constantly make event and participant safety a primary concern in the performance of services and the conduct of business affairs.

Members shall at all times have in place or cause their business organization to have in place and full force adequate policies of insurance and protection from injury, liability, fraud, and misconduct and harm caused by its events and activities or by its board of directors, staff, volunteers or organization.

Members should avoid conflicts of interest that undermine the generally accepted business practices and ethical business conduct.

Members shall make every reasonable effort to resolve business disputes with clients, other Members, sponsors and others in a fair and professional manner.

Fair Management

International Association of Fairs and Expositions (www.fairsandexpos.com)

The International Association of Fairs and Expositions (IAFE) is a voluntary, nonprofit corporation organizing state, district, and county agricultural fairs, state and provincial associations of fairs, expositions, associations, corporations, and individuals into one large association interested in the improvement of fairs and allied fields. In 1885, the IAFE began with a half dozen fairs and a commitment to service for all of its members. Today, the IAFE represents more than 1400 fairs in North America and around the world, as well as more than 1500 members from allied fields. Throughout the years, the IAFE has remained true to its purpose of promoting and encouraging the development and improvement of fairs and expositions.

The IAFE functions through a Board of Directors that consists of 19 elected members plus a President elected by the Board as an ex-officio director. The directors include a chair, two immediate past chairs, two vice chairs, a treasurer, a representative of the Federation of State and Provincial Associations of Fairs, a representative of the Canadian Association of Fairs and Exhibitions, a representative of the National Association of Fairs and Festivals of Mexico, two directors-at-large from associate members, and eight directors elected from and representing each of the eight zones in the US and Canada.

Activities and Services. The Annual Convention and Trade Show, held in Las Vegas, is the largest event serving fairs and expositions. Published 10 times a year, *Fairs & Expos* magazine is the source for information for fair trends, innovative ideas, and association activities. The magazine is designed to assist members in sharing their success and learning from the experiences of others.

IAFE members enjoy special discounts, such as one $5,000 AD&D insurance policy.

Members can access information about the association by visiting the IAFE's website at www.fairsandexpos.com. An updated calendar, member website directory, and product and service information are just a few of the numerous offerings currently available. In addition, members are able to register for meetings, update information, and search the resource library in the Members Only Area.

A variety of professional improvement and networking opportunities are available for members, including an annual management conference, special seminars, zone conferences, and state- or provincial-level meetings.

Certification Program. The IAFE created the Certified Fair Executive (CFE) Program to provide incentive for professional improvement in fair executives, to recognize those who achieve the specific standards, and to develop professional status in the field of fair management. Certification is an individual accomplishment that honors members who have demonstrated their abilities through years of service to their fairs, communities, and the IAFE.

Contests. Each year, the IAFE conducts contests for its fair members, which recognize and reward excellence. All contests are judged by IAFE member representatives and professionals from respective fields. The Agricultural Awards Program has three main goals: to improve the agricultural education of fairs; to help fairs determine ways to be of service to both fair exhibitors and the fair-going public; and to give recognition to fairs that provide outstanding agricultural education. Established in 1988, the Competitive Exhibits Contest recognizes excellence in competitive exhibit display methods and supplements the IAFE resource library by increasing the amount of helpful information available for members. Member fairs can also submit their promotional campaigns in the Communications Awards Program.

Recognition Programs. The Hall of Fame award, the highest honor bestowed by the IAFE, is presented annually in recognition of an individual's distinguished achievement in, or contribution to, the fair industry. The Heritage Awards program was launched in 1994 to honor the work of volunteer fair managers.

Education Department Offerings. The IAFE Library is designed to provide members with the information and research tools they need to succeed. These free resources have generally been obtained through donations from members and cover topics such as contracts, employee handbooks, job descriptions, media packets, agriculture education ideas, policy and operations manuals, and surveys.

In addition, the IAFE has a number of products available, including the Fair Management Reference and the Sponsorship Proposals Handbook. Other products include the Advertising Packet, the Color the Fair coloring books, Farmer for a Day and Milk Maker traveling educational exhibit displays, and the Read & Win program.

Levels of Management and Managerial Knowledge and Skills

Managers work at different levels that are often referred to as senior and middle management, and a lower level of supervisors. For events, this hierarchy can be applied as follows:

- Senior: The "general manager," and perhaps a second-in-command, can be considered "senior." The terms chief executive officer (CEO) and executive director are often used when the manager reports to a Board of Directors.
- Middle: Managers of functional areas often have titles such as "marketing manager," "volunteer coordinator," or "program director." They might head or liaise with a standing committee.
- Supervisory: Those persons acting as hands-on supervisors of various aspects of event production might also be called task managers. For example, "stage manager" is a term used to describe the person responsible for the physical stage setup, but this person usually does not manage the overall program.

As staff or volunteers rise in this hierarchy, gaining responsibility and exercising more leadership, their knowledge and skills base must change. Senior managers must possess some of the technical skills associated with hands-on event production—indeed, they often progress from the technical jobs to the management level. But they must also acquire more human management knowledge and skills, becoming people managers. As well, senior managers need conceptual knowledge and skills—the concepts, methods, and problem-solving aptitudes presented in this book—that can be applied to many different challenges. And they must have a vision and the ability to plan for the future.

Leadership

Some management experts argue that leadership is the pivotal role of managers, and the central task of the strategic plan (Mintzberg, 1994). Leadership in this context means creating a vision, establishing related strategies and goals, and inspiring the rest of the organization to pursue the vision. But leadership must also be present every business day and throughout the event.

Different styles of leadership exist, based in part on personality and in part on management theory (see, for example, Boella, 1992, p. 256). Building on these, some modifications pertinent to the events sector can be suggested, and some or all of the following event leadership styles will be familiar:

- Charismatic: staff and volunteers want to do whatever this attractive leader says (when this leader falters or leaves, the organization can collapse).

- Autocratic: expects orders to be obeyed; makes all the important decisions (bound to inspire a revolt!).
- Democratic: wants a vote on everything (fine, but where does the leadership come from?).
- Bureaucratic: nothing gets done without a subcommittee being struck for a thorough study of all implications and options, followed by rules and regulations (often, nothing gets done!).
- Inspirational: inspires others to get things done; not concerned with knowing all the details or having the last word (well-liked, often effective, but risks poor coordination).
- Artistic: wants to be creative with the program; leaves operations to everyone else (needs a partner with management skills!).
- Technocratic: concentrates on the details; no creativity (efficient, but dull; hook up with "artistic" for balance).
- Entrepreneurial: knows how to make money; wants all decisions to reflect the "bottom line" (great, but sometimes the bottom line gets in the way of successful events).
- Visionary: sees only the future, in glorious technicolor; might have trouble finding a way to get there (needs a multitalented team to plan the route).

To Oakley and Krug (1991, p. 223), creative leaders empower people to make decisions, but take responsibility for them; they focus on goals and results, but are both current and future oriented; they seek opportunities and are change oriented. Leadership style obviously affects the organization and event in many ways, from short-term planning to long-term survival. The events sector is more prone to idiosyncratic leadership than many other management fields, because of its great scope for creativity, its reliance on so many volunteers, and the fact that it must cater to many diverse interests.

Within nonprofit organizations the chief elected officer (i.e., chairperson or president) is usually expected to be the leader. According to Fidler (1995), this person "must transcend day-to-day focus and lead the organization toward its future by maintaining:

- a framework of meaning in the form of mission and goals;
- a delicate balance of dynamic relationships among various components—members, volunteer leaders, staff, and the outside public;
- a healthy environment in which the organization may explore its future in a spirit of civility" (p. L-41).

The leader must also be a role model, inspire a strong group process, and be supportive of staff and volunteers. Leaders make important decisions on behalf of their organizations, or to impose their will, but managers and supervisors must also make decisions. With the modern emphasis on "empowerment," staff and volunteers at all levels might be given responsibility to make decisions, especially—and this is crucial for events—when attempting to satisfy customers and ensure high quality.

A Model of the Event Management System

No event takes place in isolation, and every management task impinges on others, hence managers must learn to think and act systematically. Figure 2.1 is a model of the event management system. Essentially, a system is a set of interdependent or interacting elements. Any change in key environmental factors will affect the event and its management, while the event's impacts on the community, economy, and environment are equally important. Managers must understand the dynamics of the interdependencies, anticipate change, and adapt through various strategies. Specifically, we are talking about an "open system" that depends on and influences the environment around it.

Outcomes

The organization and the event have the task of creating certain outcomes such as economic and social benefits, or profits. The event and its organization are really vehicles for attaining goals. Outcomes can also include unintended and negative impacts, which should be identified through research. The model also serves to draw attention to the fact that competitors and other organizations—including allies—are also creating similar opportunities for consumers. Marketing is introduced this way, as attention to competitors and complementary groups is an essential ingredient in assuring the survival of the organization. This interconnection also suggests the need for networking and forging alliances so as to avoid duplication or needless competition in the public service and voluntary sectors. Later we deal specifically with stakeholders and their management.

Inputs

Inputs consist of all those things needed to operate the organization and produce the event, including: tangible resources, such as money, equipment, and facilities; human resources, both volunteers and staff; political and moral support; information, including feedback from evaluation processes and market research. A key input to the organization might also be the mandate or goals, if they come from a higher level or authority. This situation can occur within a government agency, such as a parks and recreation department, where the event production or coordination staff receive their goals from the department's general mandate and strategy.

Acquiring adequate resources is a major management function, and for many events it is a preoccupation. But managers should remember that a resource is not an input until means are found to actually use it. It is also desirable to monitor the flow and outcomes of

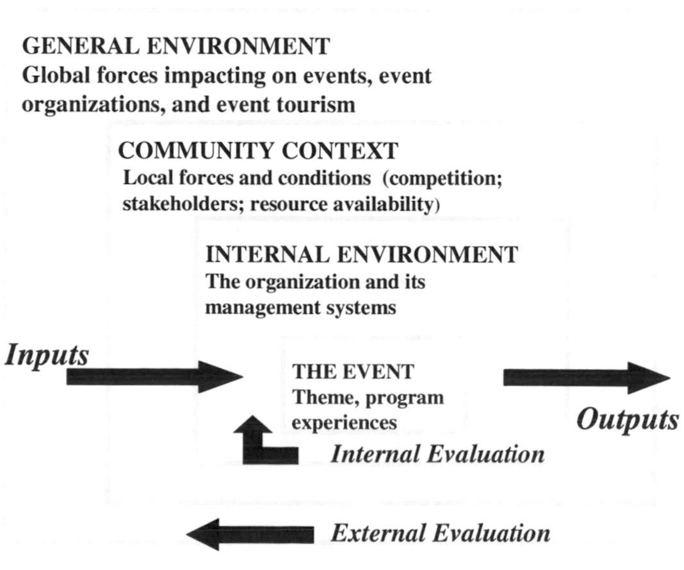

GENERAL ENVIRONMENT
Global forces impacting on events, event organizations, and event tourism

COMMUNITY CONTEXT
Local forces and conditions (competition; stakeholders; resource availability)

INTERNAL ENVIRONMENT
The organization and its management systems

Inputs → **THE EVENT** Theme, program experiences → *Outputs*

Internal Evaluation

External Evaluation

Figure 2.1. Event management system.

resources to ensure that management itself does not consume a disproportionate amount. In fledgling events most tangible resources will go directly into the production, but as management sophistication increases, more and more resources are required for staff, office, and related activities. Unchecked, this natural tendency can subvert the event and lead to a situation in which the event becomes the mechanism to perpetuate the bureaucracy.

Tangible resources are obtained from the community and general environment within which the event organization operates. Acquisition cannot be left to chance, so formal strategies and mechanisms have to be developed for this purpose. These tasks are normally called "development," "grant acquisition," "sponsorship," "fund-raising," and "merchandizing." They must be closely related to general public relations strategies, as resource acquisition will often depend on developing a strong image and network in the community. Another way to look at this linkage is to say that tangible resources and political/community support are two sides of the same coin.

Information resources can be acquired casually, through reliance on staff/volunteer expertise and external data sources. But as an event matures (and for major one-time events) it has to develop its own information system suited to specific needs. Market research is essential to determine demand, customer satisfaction, and competitor factors. Information exchange with stakeholders and partners or sponsors is important. Feedback from the evaluation process must be formalized.

Transforming Processes

All the basic management functions are intended to transform inputs into outputs. These transforming processes include staff actions such as spending money on needed supplies, land and facilities adapted for use as the event setting, and information used in such a way as to increase the event's marketing efforts.

The event itself is one of the transforming processes. Corporations and agencies that produce events as part of their marketing or profit-generating efforts know this implicitly, as the events are a means to an end. When managers focus on event production to the exclusion of its multiple possible outcomes we say that they are product oriented or inward looking. Today, no event can afford to ignore its stakeholders and all the possible outcomes.

Evaluation and Feedback

The model shows internal evaluation, which pertains to management's collective responsibility to ensure that all functions and programs are meeting goals and that operations are as efficient as possible. External evaluation covers both the organization's linkages with other agencies and stakeholders and the impacts of its actions.

Ongoing evaluation helps steer the organization towards meeting its goals. The event can always be improved, marketing enhanced, and benefits increased. As well, evaluation can help avoid, and suggest ways to eliminate or ameliorate, negative consequences. Evaluation means, literally, assigning a value or worth to something, and it inherently involves subjective judgment as well as technical analysis.

The management system model is more than a theoretical framework—it can be used to systematically evaluate the organization or an event, and to diagnose specific problems. A leading cause of event failure, for example, is overdependency on a single source of external funding. The model helps identify the flows and uses of resources, including money and information that are the lifeblood of all events. It helps identify key stakeholders who have to be brought into decision making. And systematic evaluation helps the manager keep the whole picture in mind, whereas the natural tendency is to get lost in daily problem solving.

The General and Community Environments

In the event management system there are continuous interactions between the organization and its environment. The bigger picture is a giant system consisting of many events related to the economy, society, politics, and ecology, all interdependent and influencing each other. Making sense of the big picture is difficult, as in trying to predict demand or second-guess legislators. The basic strategy for coping with all this uncertainty and complexity is to develop networks and alliances with government agencies, professional associations, tourist industry groups, or other special interests. Each event can deal with its own community context, but few are large enough to master all the general factors that can influence the event.

The "community context" (or immediate environment) is that which impacts directly on the event and its organization. As already mentioned, specific strategies and mechanisms have to be created to acquire resources and foster good public relations. Every event will have to do its own research (although events within one community will benefit from cooperative research) to determine local market conditions. Networks and alliances, especially among volunteer groups, will often be crucial. Competitors must be considered, as well as complementary events and organizations.

Stakeholder Theory Applied to Event Management

"Stakeholders" are people or organizations that can influence your event or event organization, or are affected by you. The degree to which they are consulted and supportive can determine your success, so "stakeholder management" is a vital part of event management. Consider a possible list of key stakeholders:

- your volunteers and staff;
- suppliers, performers, and other participants;
- agencies providing grants;
- corporate sponsors;
- participating organizations (i.e., partners and allies);
- the media;
- the local community/residents;
- social and environmental lobby groups;
- your customers and potential customers;
- governmental agencies at all levels.

Internal stakeholders include staff, volunteers, and participants. External stakeholders might have power to influence you, or can become allies, while others will be impacted by your actions. These groups have to be managed differently. For general references on stakeholder theory see Freeman (1984) and Jawahar and McLaughlin (2001).

"Legitimacy" is a term of importance in stakeholder theory. Some persons or groups will want to be consulted or will seek to influence your actions, but you do not see them as being "legitimate." What is to be done with them? In some cases, it is wise to accept their self-defined legitimacy, in others to ignore them. There are no hard and fast rules about this, but perhaps it is wise to be as inclusive as possible and not shut out too many potential stakeholders.

Managers are advised to give serious thought to their stakeholders and how each is to be managed. A useful tool is the stakeholder map. Place your event at the center, then identify each important agency, group, company, or person you obtain resources or approvals from, as they are certainly key stakeholders. Which of these linkages are crucial for your survival, as those stakeholders have power over your operations. Are any dependent on your event for resources? Are there linkages between your stakeholders that you should understand, such as collaboration or legal ties between levels of government? You can indicate these on the map by connecting the stakeholders.

Now consider those who are likely to be impacted by your event, and those who will want a say in how it is operated. These stakeholders should be consulted, although perhaps they do not require permanent, formal links of the kind you need with those on whom you are dependent. For issues such as environmental quality or community support you might have to deal with elected officials and special-interest groups that feel they represent those perspectives, so stakeholder management can be a very political process.

The map will suggest where your stakeholder management priorities lie, then you need to formulate appropriate strategies. A proactive approach is recommended for all those having high priority—in other words, you go to them to ensure you have good relations. Formal links and regular meetings will likely be needed. If you depend on their resources, you will want to be accountable in a regular manner. The ensuing discussion of resource dependency suggest more detailed strategies For a look at research on event stakeholders see Larson (2002).

Research Note

Larson, M. (2002). A political approach to relationship marketing: Case study of the Storsjoyran Festival. *International Journal of Tourism Research, 4*, 119–143.

With a Swedish festival as her case study, Mia Larson examined stakeholder interests, conflicts, and power in a "project network" (i.e., the actors coming together to produce the event). She used the term "political market square" to describe the project network, and looked at interactions that were cooperative or characterized as "power games." In terms of organizing and marketing this festival, she identified critical stakeholders as the media, artists, associations and clubs, public authorities, sponsors, local trades and industry, and characterized each as having diminishing or strengthening power. Actors participated in various political processes called "gatekeeping" (controlling entries into the event), "negotiation" (making agreements), "coalition building" (for purposes of creating power), "building trust" (a strategy to increase one's power), and "identity building" (to maintain the image and position of the event.) The dynamics of these interrelationships helps shape the event and its meaning for the participants and the community. One set of changes in the power structure of the event resulted from "turbulence" among the stakeholders, but led to innovation and product development.

Collaboration and Partnerships

Increasingly event organizations are involved in external relations that require collaboration (where each actor must give up some autonomy for the good of the whole), partnership (where equals work closely together on the same project), or some other form of alliance (which might be a permanent or temporary organization, such as a professional association). Partnerships and collaborations often stem from funding initiatives in specific political jurisdictions, wherein money is available that individual events cannot otherwise access. Examples include theme years (usually tourism promotions) and culture or arts development funds aimed at increasing audiences.

In collaboration theory (see Gray, 1989; Jamal & Getz, 1995), development of "cultural tourism" or "festival tourism" is called a policy domain. It exists only to the extent that collaborating parties can make it work, because it has no life of its own outside the bounds of the collaboration. If a government agency wants an arts tourism plan, it has no choice but to involve all the key stakeholders. Getting and keeping them involved and effective will require resources, management, and possibly a new organization. Individual members will likely contribute and stay involved only if they see real benefits for them or the policy domain overall, and to the extent that the benefits outweigh any costs or perceived sacrifices. Research by Long (2000) sheds light on a specific partnership initiative affecting festivals.

Research Note

Long, P. (2000). After the event: Perspectives on organizational partnerships in the management of a themed festival year. *Event Management, 6*(1), 45–59.

Although the contribution of arts and festivals to tourism is well recognized internationally, different agencies, cultures, goals, and priorities often make for uneasy partnerships. Arts people often fear that tourism goals might supplant their own, or that needed resources come with too many strings attached. Tourism people sometimes think that arts organizations and particularly festivals do not make sufficient efforts to become tourist attractions or even tourist friendly. Long examined the themed festival year in the UK called Year of Visual Arts, and initiative that required cooperation between arts organizations such as festivals and tourism organizations. Partnerships of this type are contractual and short-lived, normally in pursuit of a specific objective. More "federational" partnerships, according to Long, include local tourism initiatives in which whole industry sectors or groups work together—potentially on a permanent basis. Partnership can also form for broad, system-wide policy development in the arts and tourism. Long's conclusion was that some lessons from this particular partnership are transferable, particularly the need for clear objectives combined with flexibility in implementation and local ownership of program delivery. Long also identified a number of typical interorganizational relationships facing festivals and events that can benefit from knowledge of partnerships and collaboration theory: securing sponsorships; reconciling goals among partners in any program or contract; ensuring economic efficiencies in all relationships; dealing with political influences.

Resource Dependency Theory Applied to Event Management

Pfeffer and Salanick (1978) examined organizational interdependence by looking at an organization's needs (e.g., the importance of specific resources to make an event happen) and another's control of those critical resources. Additional considerations relate to the scarcity of resources (are there plenty of volunteers in a community?), alternatives for obtaining the resources (are sponsors and grant-givers substitutable?), the nature of the operational environment (are events competitors or cooperative in seeking resources?), certainty (do grants fluctuate from year to year? can you obtain permanent funding?), and variability (do your resource needs change or stay constant?). The greater the need and uncertainty, the more vulnerable is the event to those who control the resources.

Many events are quite dependent and cannot generate sufficient funds on their own to become self-sufficient. That is not necessarily bad, but it presents managers with a major challenge. The first implication is that every event manager should address the question of whether or not independence is desirable and/or feasible. Is it a goal to work towards? If so, strategic planning is required. If not, several other issues present themselves. First, is there a serious threat to the event? If external support is terminated, does the event cease to exist or are their back-up plans to keep it going? Second, how can the dependency be managed to ensure the event continues and prospers?

The event manager can take a number of actions to manage dependency:

- spread dependency more widely (i.e., get more sponsors and grants);
- reduce dependency absolutely (e.g., generate more internal revenue sources);

- foster stronger alliances and partnerships so that the threat of termination is reduced (e.g., with the sponsors and grant-givers);
- restructure the event to make it an integral part of a parent organization's mandate rather than an optional activity.

Population Ecology Applied to Event Management

This theory looks at whole "populations" of organizations, such as the festival sector in general (Hannan & Freeman, 1977). Why some succeed and others fail might be due in large part to the dynamics of the population rather than the individual festival organization. In this way, population ecology is opposed to "adaptive" theories wherein the organization deliberately shapes its own change process.

Baum (1996) said that all ecological theories of the organization begin with three observations. First, diversity is a property of aggregates of organizations. Second, organizations often have difficulty changing fast enough to meet the demands of uncertain environmental conditions. Third, and perhaps the most germane, is the observation that organizations arise and disappear continually.

The "selection" of organizations that fail is basically attributable to competition for scarce resources. By biological analogy the number of organizations (e.g., events) is likely to increase to a point where demand for resources exceeds supply. Survivors demonstrate the best "fit" by occupying a "niche" for which they are especially suited and by adaptation to environmental changes.

The concept of "structural inertia" suggests why some festivals cannot adequately adapt to changes in their environment. If they are highly specialized (i.e., have no alternative resources to obtain or products to offer), if they are unable to monitor and assess change (i.e., they are not a "learning organization"), or if there are severe political/legal constraints on their actions, these festivals might be unable to change. The "core" values or processes of an organization, especially its fundamental goals, have a high degree of inertia. Marketing strategies, on the other hand, are much more flexible.

Population ecology suggests that in a dynamic environment, where change is constant, highly specialized organizations are less able to adapt and therefore more likely to fail. Older, more generalized organizations have a better chance of survival because the reliability of their performance encourages others to supply resources. New festival organizations, therefore, will often have a difficult time getting adequate resources and learning how to survive. However, Baum (1996) argued that research does not confirm that failure rates decline with organizational age.

Without doing too much research it should be possible to evaluate a community's or region's "population" of events. This exercise helps the manager to determine potential competitors or allies, and to see if gaps exist in the area's "portfolio" of events (by type, location, season, target market). Where does any given event fit into the total population of events? Can the size or composition of the whole population affect individual events? Yes, it can.

Human organizations and events are able to adapt and to plan ahead, so there is no "law" saying that any particular one will perish or prosper. But it is easy to see that events often fail to grow or prosper, that many never get off the drawing board, and others disappear completely. Therefore, the challenge to managers is twofold:

- how to ensure your event prospers;
- where appropriate, how to plan for the event's timely demise (i.e., predetermine its life cycle).

Some event managers think they have no competitors. Their event is unique, or so popular that there are no competitive threats. So they think! The first lesson of "population ecology" is that every event is competing for resources, if not audiences. As the number of events in an area grows, whether they are similar or not, demand for sponsors, grants, volunteers, good dates, venues, consumers, and community or political support also intensifies. Events without a "competitive advantage," or those without a good niche to occupy (i.e., a good fit with their environment), might perish or not even get going.

Event Failure

"Failure" can be absolute, as in the disappearance of the event or bankruptcy of the event organization, or relative, as in failure to grow or to attain its goals. Failure is sometimes averted but the event experiences a major crisis that threatens its viability.

Events can fail for many reasons, not the least of which is bad management or corruption. In my exploratory research on event failure (Getz, 2002b) I surveyed festival professionals to obtain information on the incidence and types of failure they knew about as well as their opinions on why festivals fail. The largest category of potential causes of failure they identified, based on personal experience, related to marketing and planning: the two highest were "inadequate marketing or promotion" and "lack of advance or strategic planning." "Inattention to program or service quality" was also a potential cause.

External factors were thought to be fairly important potential causes of failure, especially the weather and competition ("competition from similar events in the area" and "competition from events at the same time as ours"). Because weather is such a universal issue for event planners, it has to be asked if dependence on good weather is not a management failure. However, for some events there are few choices other than an outdoor venue. The serious competition problem raises the issue of target marketing and choice of dates, which are controllable by management, but also raises the theoretical issues of capacity and life cycle discussed later in this book.

Human resource problems were not highly important, as a group, but "incompetent event managers or staff" and "volunteer burnout" appear to be a threat to some festivals. If managers are incompetent, management systems will be inadequate, but whose responsibility is that? This raises the matter of festival governance, which, in not-for-profit festival organizations relying on volunteers, can itself be inadequate.

Two resource-related problems are believed by respondents to be highly likely to lead to festival failure: "lack of corporate sponsorship" and "overreliance on one source of money." Other resource-related problems were also thought to be important: "not enough attention to making money or profit," "cash-flow problems," and "poor control of costs." Of the causes related to organizational culture, only one was thought to be important, namely "lack of strong leadership."

Although these problems provide useful insights into the causes of festival failure, each problem on its own might very well relate to, or stem from others. Overdependence on good weather or a single funding source is clearly a weakness, but why does it occur? Should managers prevent it? Other problems do not seem to threaten failure very often (e.g., corruption), but in specific cases they could be devastating. And some problems might be very difficult to detect and prediction of their consequences might be uncertain, such as marketing research. Is there every enough research done? Can it not always be improved? Predicting failure, therefore, is not merely a matter of correcting one or more identifiable problems. Rather, it will require a more systematic effort to improve the quality of management in all its dimensions. With this in mind, see the research paper by Beverland, Hoffman, and Rasmussen (2001), who took a strategic look at event crises.

Research Note

Beverland, M., Hoffman, D., & Rasmussen, M. (2001). The evolution of events in the Australasian wine sector. *Tourism Recreation Research, 26*(2), 35–44.

These authors examined a number of New Zealand and Australian wine festivals that had operated from 4 to 27 years, from the perspective of their place in the hypothetical organizational life cycle. Each event had undergone changes either in their structure, program, strategy, or consumers, and reasons were sought for these adaptations. Each stage, according to the analysts, was marked by a crisis, such as gaining support, media awareness, or legitimacy, achieving critical mass (of consumers and involved wineries), achieving focus, retaining loyal customers, or developing a brand. It was concluded that events might have to reinvent themselves to ward off decline. This could be a new "unique selling proposition" or brand. Close relationships with the key industry stakeholders (wineries, in this sample) was viewed as being critical to sustaining the event.

Study Questions

- Define the main elements of the event management system and explain how inputsbecome either desired outcomes or unintended impacts.
- Why is event management an emerging profession?
- What is the importance of ethics in professional practice?
- Compare major career paths in event management with regard to the types of jobs performed, typical employment opportunities, and related professional associations.
- Why do events fail? Refer to stakeholders, collaboration/partnerships, resource dependency, and population ecology.
- How do required skills and responsibilities change as one becomes a senior event manager?
- What are the various leadership styles found in event management?

Advanced Study Questions

- Use the event management system model to conduct a diagnostic audit of an event, focusing on stakeholder relations and the flow of resources.
- Interview and profile event professionals in different organizations, with the purpose of comparing them on the skills and knowledge required, their career paths or business development, and challenges they have faced.
- Through interviews with professionals, analyze one or more ethical issues in event management. Describe the issue and how it was resolved. Discuss the implications and lessons learned.

Chapter 3

Planning Events

Learning Objectives

- Understand the nature and principles of planning.
- Be able to employ project planning methods for planning a one-time event, including critical path analysis.
- Be able to conduct feasibility studies and prepare winning bids.
- Be able to formulate and implement a strategic plan.
- Be able to undertake analysis of forces and trends.
- Be able to prepare and utilize a business plan.

What Is Planning?

Planning is always future oriented, focusing on the formulation of goals and the means to achieve them. Goals can be expression of things that are desired, or to be avoided. While organizations engage in planning as a continuous process, one-time event organizations work towards a specific target completion. Planning is also political in nature, involving various stakeholders in public or private decision-making processes. Because of its political nature, the exercise of leadership is very important, and leadership is generally based on values and includes a vision of the desired future. Although a specific type of plan is often the end product, the planning process itself is often more important. After all, the future cannot be predicted nor can its shape be guaranteed. Whatever plans humans formulate, adaptation and revisions are always going to be needed.

Planning and leadership are closely related. The leader, often the event founder, senior manager, or perhaps a board chairperson, seeks to influence the actions of others to meet the vision and goals. This requires the ability to motivate others, and good communications skills. As noted by Oakley and Krug (19913),"An enlightened leader has the ability to get the members of an organization to accept ownership for a vision as their own" (p. 23).

Decision making cannot be unregulated and unaccountable; a framework is needed through organizational structure, policies and procedures, and evaluation. Careful attention to organizational structure will help ensure that decisions are carefully made and fully implemented. The committee structure should be designed to allow easy flow of information top to bottom, and among committees. Responsibilities must be carefully defined, so job descriptions become important.

"Policies" are normally formal rules governing the activities of all members of the organization, and as such are usually developed and voted on by the board of directors. Or they may be unwritten guidelines understood by everyone—with the proviso that while this approach allows flexibility it also risks abuse. Indeed, many organizations formulate their policies in response to problems, rather than as part of their planning and management systems. Policies implement the mission and goals of the organization by showing what actions are desirable, permissible, or forbidden. Within each policy field, procedures will be formulated to regulate routine actions.

When first organizing, one of the critical steps is to develop a set of policies and procedures (perhaps informally) to get the event produced. The organizers must also formulate policies and procedures for the governance of the organization, sometimes before its work begins, and sometimes as it evolves. Over time, many organizations develop thick policy and procedures manuals. Managers have the responsibility to establish and enforce policies and procedures, but with the proviso that they cannot become so detailed and rigid that the organization becomes bureaucratic and reactive. There is always a balance to be achieved between policies and procedures that keep everyone honest, on target, and satisfied, and those that get in the way of attaining goals or fostering innovation.

Ultimately, all decisions must be evaluated and the decision maker held accountable. Where poor decisions were made, but in the proper context, the object is to learn and do better next time. Decisions made outside one's authority or without regard to proper procedures can lead to disciplinary action.

Crisis Management

Some event managers work in an environment that seems like a permanent crisis! Some leaders like to foster an occasional crisis atmosphere to get the most out of their workers. But a true "crisis" is unplanned, dangerous, and unpredictable, so leadership and wise decision making are required. One approach to crisis management is to establish a team to deal with it. Another is to assign exceptional and temporary authority to a group or a leader to enable rapid response. Every organization should have a procedure in place, and should rehearse the response mechanisms.

Because many risks are associated with events, and often their likelihood and severity can be estimated, it is possible to deal with many crises from a position of strength. "Contingency planning" is therefore required: it is the process of formulating strategies or detailed plans to deal with possible and unanticipated problems. The more severe and probable the risk, the more important it is to have a contingency plan in place.

Key elements in any crisis management situation are the following:

- Who has the responsibility and authority to deal with crises?
- Do officers and managers have exceptional powers to deal with problems?
- What procedures should be followed? (e.g., is there a contingency plan? who to notify or consult; what are the limits of actions available?)

Project Planning and Management

"Project planning" can be defined as the design and implementation of a plan to create a new event, on time and within established parameters pertaining to resources, venues, and impacts. A project planning model for one-time events is illustrated in Figure 3.1 and the key components are discussed below.

William O'Toole (2000) stresses that events are projects, and that project planning and management techniques and concepts should be part of the event manager's skill set. O'Toole pointed out that many projects fail, or overrun their schedule and budget, so identification of the reasons and consequences of failures should be a concern. Another

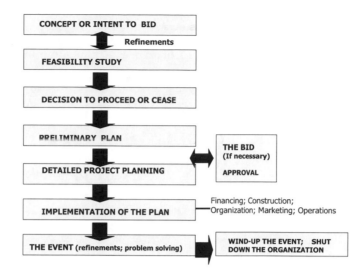

Figure 3.1. Project planning process.

issue is that of finding a common language so that everyone involved in event projects can communicate clearly.

Projects, including those designed to implement a one-time event, have a definite start and end date. Sometimes the event, as in the case of the Olympics, gives rise to a permanent organization with responsibility to manage the financial and physical legacy, but many event organizations end shortly after the event itself. Project planning and management methods can also be used to create and launch a new periodic event, or a program within an existing event. Unfortunately, many event organizations struggle from year to year, and their planning ends up being very much like a one-time project, when what they really need is strategic planning for the long term.

Many small events are planned and produced within months, but the project planning process can be lengthy. For Olympics or world's fairs several years will likely be spent on feasibility studies and making the bid. If won, the Olympics provide for a period of 6 years to make the detailed plans and get all the venues and management systems in place. World's fair projects can easily take over 10 years. With increased competition for conventions and sport events, the bidding and planning period is increasing, and many bidders find they have to try two or three times to be successful.

Projects always entail uncertainty and a variety of risks. While flexibility and adaptability are necessary, in response to changing environmental forces, project planning and management employs a variety of tools to assess and minimize risks.

Concept or Intent to Bid

The process can begin with an idea for a new event, a call for proposals from a corporation or association, or an interest in bidding on an event that can be "won" for the community or a venue. Most "biddable" events are "owned" and the bidders must abide by specifications set in advance, perhaps with some leeway for innovation in the concept. This generally applies to major sport events, and to meetings and conventions. When a request for proposals (RFP) is sent out, the company or organization responding to it will have to decide of they can meet the specifications and add any value that would give them a competitive advantage.

Coming up with a completely new concept for an event is a rather different process, involving more creativity and requiring more testing and refinement to make it work. Lots of event ideas never get off the drawing board, or an organization commits to them only to find they cannot get enough support to make it work.

Mega-events like the Olympics and world's fairs will require the establishment of new organizations, sometimes becoming permanent if real property assets or a financial legacy have to be managed. When professional event management companies are retained, the organization for project planning does not have to be created from scratch.

Project Scope and Definition

"Scope creep," as defined by O'Toole and Mikolaitis (2002) in their book *Corporate Event Project Management*, is a "gradual expansion of the amount of work to be done." What starts out looking like a simple task can later become a complex nightmare for those charged with its implementation. Only experienced event managers can fully anticipate this kind of work inflation. If each project is viewed as a learning experience, project planners and managers will get more accurate over time.

"Scope creep" can also occur when the client, sponsors, or other influential parties start making requests for changes to the event concept or its specific elements without due consideration of the implications. This is probably the bigger risk, especially when the event is being planned in a highly political environment. The best protection against this common project management problem is the detailed work plan and related schedule and budget. Planners and managers should be able to use the documentation to show exactly how any deviation would add delays, costs, or new risks. This is a kind of "sensitivity analysis," the purpose of which is to always be able to demonstrate the magnitude and direction of changes in a budget forecast or a schedule that will be caused by alterations

Feasibility Study

A "feasibility study" for an event (or new program idea) has a number of possible purposes:

- determination of ability to get funding and/or approvals;
- refinement of the concept through market tests and demand forecasts;
- assessment of affordability or profitability;
- determining if it can physically be produced (including climatic and weather considerations, venues, accessibility, accommodation);
- evaluation of potential impacts;
- evaluation of the desirability and suitability of the event.

When an event management company considers a job they must determine if it will be a profitable venture for them, and sometimes must show that it will meet the potential client's budget and goals.

Major events should not only play a role in the destination's tourism plan, but be acceptable and supportable by the host community. It must not only be financially sound, but its full costs and benefits should be evaluated. The politics of attracting events, especially mega-events, is sometimes bizarre and frightening. Several authors have noted how irrationality, rather than sound planning, tends to accompany the pursuit of events (Armstrong, 1985; Butler & Grigg, 1987). In such cases there is likely to be tension or outright hostility between proponents and those who insist on detailed feasibility studies and cost–benefit evaluations.

Proponents of major events should demonstrate that the venue, host community, and destination area all have the capacity to absorb the event and its impacts. This requires a detailed forecasting and evaluation of the potential impacts, generally based on experience with other events, and consideration of how positive effects can be maximized and how negative effects or costs can be avoided or ameliorated. Will the event "fit" the proposed venue and area? This matter of suitability is too often ignored, but can be vital in determining the success of the event, as well as its impacts. A number of points can be considered, although every situation is unique:

- is there a track record of hosting successful events?
- the nature of the population (cosmopolitanism; wealth; interests; receptiveness to new ideas);
- availability of volunteers and leaders, sponsors and supporters;
- politics and ideology;
- sophistication in organizing events.

At this stage it should be possible to estimate the likely costs and revenues, and thereby calculate financial feasibility. In other words, can we afford it? The more adventuresome might ask: "if we commit ourselves, can we raise the money?" In fact, this is how many bids proceeded. Even so, a risk assessment is vital. What happens if the grants or revenues fail to materialize, or costs escalate? Who pays? It would be wise to consider the potential for political disruption, the effects of bad weather, and possible organizational failure.

A formal environmental impact assessment (EIA) might be required during the feasibility stage, or perhaps after the decision has been made to proceed. Social and cultural impacts are generally included. EIA legislation varies among jurisdictions, but generally will consist of the following elements:

- specification of all actions likely to have environmental and community impacts (on land, water, and air resources; on the built environment; on social/cultural process and ecological systems);
- determination or forecasting of the likely nature of impacts and related uncertainties and risks;
- determination or forecasting of the likely direction (positive or negative) and severity of impacts;
- plans for avoiding and reducing potential negative impacts, achieving positive impacts, and ameliorating any resultant problems;
- evaluation of costs and benefits of the project in light of impact forecasts and plans.

Economic feasibility is slightly different, and pertains more to the community or destination as a whole. Opportunity costs must be considered, as well as the possibility of adverse economic impacts. Long-term gains and losses must be assessed. The tangible economic costs and benefits to the destination area and host community must be compared, and intangibles considered subjectively. Financial or economic considerations should not predominate, as equal consideration must be given to social, cultural, and environmental factors. If the benefit-to-cost ratio is favorable, that is still not sufficient grounds to proceed. It might very well be that some costs are not acceptable under any circumstances (such as destruction of heritage or ecological damage). It will also be possible to conclude that the potential benefits, however much in excess of costs, do not justify the effort required, or that the benefits are too concentrated in a few hands to warrant public investment.

Decision to Proceed

The feasibility study leads to a decision to proceed/bid or not, or to proceed with a modified concept. Numerous events are produced following routine business decisions by clients and event management companies. Sometimes there is negotiation between a client and one company, with no bidding process involved. Once a deal is struck, a contract is required and event planning begins in earnest.

For larger, public events, politics and public input are often involved in the decision. There might have to be a "prefeasibility" study undertaken to determine if it is even worth making the effort to start a detailed feasibility study! Money might have to be raised from government agencies and corporate sponsors, perhaps millions of dollars, before a serious bid for a mega-event can be contemplated.

Preliminary Plan

Following concept refinement and feasibility evaluation, a preliminary or draft event project plan might be needed, especially where a formal bid process is involved. This plan gets reviewed by the owners/clients and after a decision is made to award the event more detailed project planning can commence. It will have to have a certain level of detail on the following points:

- feasibility in terms of: venues, target marks, costs and revenues, impacts, necessary approvals;
- program for the event;
- a workable budget;
- construction schedules (if new facilities and infrastructure are required);
- a marketing plan;
- human resources (staffing, volunteers);
- organization and management systems;
- meeting any other specifications.

Detailed Project Planning

When the detailed event project planning begins, a task analysis and work plan must be developed, leading to precise scheduling and a final budget. Readily available software includes Microsoft's Project, and a number of websites provide detailed advice on project planning including the various scheduling tools, Critical Path Analysis, and PERT (e.g., www.mindtools.com). Be sure to visit William O'Toole's website, which is specific to events (www-personal.usyd.edu.au/~wotoole/).

Task Analysis and the Work Plan

One of the most difficult aspects of project planning is the detailed breakdown of work into discrete but interdependent "tasks." Later, a critical path analysis will determine the sequencing of these tasks. A work plan can proceed from two starting points:

1. An a priori description of the event, where its detailed elements are known in advance (e.g., a sport event or function that has a standard structure).
2. A statement of goals and objectives leading to development of the final structure of the event (e.g., planning a celebration with a known theme but yet-to-be-developed program and setting).

The basic unit in the work plan, called a "task," must be a discrete activity that can be performed by one or more people with known resources, preferably within a defined period of time. For events, a specified place is also often part of a task. From the onset of this procedure it must be remembered that eventually all tasks have to be integrated and scheduled, and resources and costs will have to be assigned to each.

Tasks will have to be assigned to various managers, subcontractors, or work groups, so some form of geographical clusters (e.g., the stage, the exhibition floor, the food court), technical (audio-visual, lighting), or functional groupings (marketing, human resources) have to be established at the beginning. Computer software available for project planning/management makes it possible to start with a general definition of work clusters and then proceed to more and more detailed tasks under each heading. Where uncertainty exists on any of these points, as it often will, project planners have to consult with experienced event managers to determine the details and their interconnections.

The nature of an event will largely determine the shape of the task breakdown. Venues are a good starting point, because there are huge differences between, for example, sport venues and convention centers. Programming is the next big factor. In Chapter 6 the various "elements of style" are discussed. Advice is given in that chapter on how these can be used for event project planning, essentially by first conceptualizing the event as a package of programming elements such as education, entertainment, and spectacle. Third, the people element has to be considered in more detail: will there be large audiences, many participants, or a few party-goers? Then management systems have to be examined. What are the staffing and volunteer requirements, will subcontractors be involved, etc.? In some events the essential services such as food and beverages are a lesser consideration, being standardized within a facility, while in others they are of primary importance—as in a food or wine festival. These considerations help shape the task analysis and scheduling.

Figure 3.2 illustrates task analysis for an event. It shows six functional groupings that have to be planned in detail, with the focus on No. 6, logistics (see the next chapter for more discussion of logistics). The first level of logistic tasks to consider includes ticketing/cash, performers and participants, supplies, public transport, and parking for guests. Focusing on 6.1, parking, the next level of tasks includes the police presence (necessary for highway traffic control), staffing (probably a volunteer crew to be trained), signs and

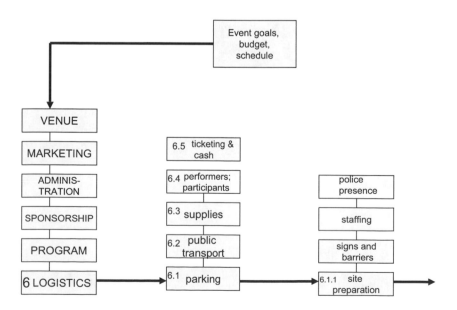

Figure 3.2. Task Analysis.

barriers (what types, where to get them, and where to place them), and site preparation (are there suitable spaces, do they need grading or paving). And so it goes, with ever-more detail. This task analysis is also vital for human resource planning (how many staff, volunteers, contractors, etc., are needed to complete each task, and to manage the function when the event is held).

Scheduling

Even while task analysis proceeds to greater levels of detail, scheduling can begin. The crucial point about timing in project planning is the fact that in most cases the date is fixed and there is no choice but to meet the deadline! Critical path analysis is therefore vital, and for major events will require computer software. A small meeting or function can be handled on paper.

Critical Path Analysis (CPA)

CPA is a planning and scheduling tool that can help streamline the process and avoid costly miscalculations. It examines interrelationships among all the players and activities needed to deliver the event as and when intended. All tasks are arranged in chronological order, working BACK from the event dates so that each prerequisite activity gets scheduled in proper sequence. The resultant schedule is a network of interconnected tasks and the actual "critical path" in the network is the shortest possible sequence of events needed to get the job accomplished. When all the tasks are linked and critical dates established (i.e., those dates by which tasks must be finished), a line can be drawn to make it clear how long at a minimum the process will take and how various pieces fit together.

Steps in CPA are as follows:

1. Identify all crucial tasks and the ultimate shape of the project (i.e., venues, facilities, infrastructure, management systems).
2. Set and prioritize goals and objectives (consider if all tasks are equally important).
3. Determine time lines and critical dates (how long does each task take? by when must each be completed? by whom?).
4. Establish the critical path (in what sequence must tasks be completed? what is the shortest path connecting all the critical tasks?).
5. Control the process to stay on schedule.

Separate exercises could be undertaken for the different program areas, venues, or specific activities related to the event, and then brought together at key points in the network diagram. Computerized scheduling will be essential for tasks this complex.

Program Evaluation and Review Technique (PERT)

PERT is similar to CPA, but instead of working back from a fixed date it is based on identification of minimum, most likely, and maximum projected time lines. This approach is obviously suited to events that do not have to be produced on a specific schedule. It allows estimation of the final completion date, or of milestones along the way to a fixed event date.

Both CPA and PERT have several crucial planning applications. The first is to impose logic on the planning process, as drawing the network will quickly reveal gaps and illogical thinking. The question: "how do we get there from here?" requires a detailed task analysis. Second, scheduling follows from the plan—especially identification of the absolutely critical steps and sequencing. The next section covers other scheduling issues. Third, resource allocation is partially based on knowing the project's sequencing and when the really big tasks have to start and finish. For mega-events this often means the large facility construction projects.

Control also follows the CPA or PERT. Progress is checked continuously against the schedule and network, as well as the costs. Variances will become clear sooner, and corrective action is therefore more effective. Also, if the project is lagging (i.e., behind schedule) some activities might be identified as "compressible" to make up time. Lastly, communications are improved by using CPA and PERT networks. Everyone sees the project in its entirety and can monitor progress or shortfalls. Teamwork should be greatly enhanced, as even the value of the smallest unit or task can be seen by all.

Drawing the Network

Figure 3.3 is a simple illustration of a critical path network. Computer software is available, but a basic diagram for a small project can be done manually. It starts with identification of activities necessary to plan and produce the event, and each activity is given a discrete code letter or number. Interdependencies are determined, showing what activity must be completed first. When the network is finalized, the software can calculate the estimated minimum completion time for each activity (in units of hours, days, weeks, months, or years).

There are a number of rules to follow:

- Every network diagram has a single start and finish point, and the sequencing flows only from left to right.
- Each activity is shown by an arrow; activities require time and resources to complete.
- Circles are called "events" or "nodes" and have three compartments; they record start and finish dates (the left- and right-side numbers), and each event itself is numbered at the top.

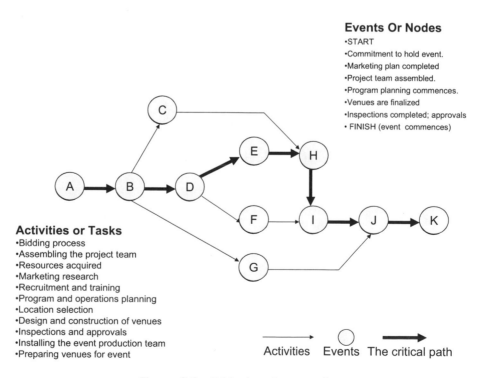

Events Or Nodes
•START
•Commitment to hold event.
•Marketing plan completed
•Project team assembled.
•Program planning commences.
•Venues are finalized
•Inspections completed; approvals
• FINISH (event commences)

Activities or Tasks
•Bidding process
•Assembling the project team
•Resources acquired
•Marketing research
•Recruitment and training
•Program and operations planning
•Location selection
•Design and construction of venues
•Inspections and approvals
•Installing the event production team
•Preparing venues for event

Activities   Events   The critical path

Figure 3.3. Critical path network.

- Start events points have to have lower numbers than finish events (initially use multiples of five, thereby allowing insertion of new activities and events later).
- A "logic dummy" (shown by a dotted line) is used when an activity is dependent on another, but they are in different paths and not otherwise linked.
- An "identity dummy" (also a dotted line) is used to distinguish between two or more activities that otherwise would have received the same event numbers because of sequencing.
- One problem to avoid in complex networks is "looping," where an activity appears to depend on a later one.
- "Dangling" occurs when an activity (other than the finish) is not followed by another; this violates the dependency rule, namely that all activities depend on a preceding one.

Overlapping can occur in critical path sequencing, when activities can be started before the previous one actual ends. For example, the interior finishing of a building can start before all aspects of the exterior work are completed, but only an expert can plan this. The network diagram can handle this by showing parallel activities and using "real-time dummies" to indicate the overlap.

Time Analysis

Once the network is complete and tested for sequencing and dependency logic, the schedule and critical path can be determined. A second diagram is developed, showing the following:

- The "duration" of each activity is indicated by a number alongside the arrow (use constant units: days, years, etc.); estimating duration might require considerable analysis or judgment, and even negotiation with those responsible for its completion.
- The "earliest time" for each event has to be indicated in the left-side of the event circle (the start point is zero, and each event after that is zero plus the duration of intervening activities—using the longest cumulative duration for calculating "earliest time"; this is called the "forward pass" calculation).
- The "latest time" for each event is recorded on the right side of the circle; it is the latest date by which all activities arriving at the event can be completed before delaying the project; by implication it is also the latest possible date for starting subsequent, dependent activities (use the "backward pass" calculation, starting with the earliest possible date for the end event and subtracting duration times for each activity from its latest finishing time).
- By calculating earliest and latest start and finish times for each activity, the existence of potential spare time—called the "float;;—can be assessed (of course, its existence depends on the accuracy of all previous estimates).

The "critical path" emerges from this timing exercise. It is the earliest possible date for the completion, given the cumulative durations of all necessary activities and taking into account the "float" (i.e., the critical path is the one taken where there is no spare time in the connecting activities). Following this analysis the truly critical activities become clear, as these must be completed on time or the entire project suffers a delay. Knowing those activities allows the manager to decide if it is worth extra money to accelerate them or to overcome forecast delays. There might also be political and legal implications arising, such as imposition of no-strike rules on workers or severe penalties on subcontractors.

Resource Analysis

A third diagram can be developed showing the costs of each activity in dollars or hours of labor. Daily, weekly, or other periodic estimates of resource commitment can be calculated from this information and it can be used to amend the start or finish dates of non-critical activities by assigning more or fewer resources. And if one assumes that the entire critical path leads to an unacceptable completion date (for an event, this means to miss the scheduled date!), the analysis can be used to determine how much it will cost to reach the deadline—assuming that extra resources will be able to accelerate the project. In some instances, no amount of money or planning will overcome some of the obstacles.

Calendars

Most working people use calendars or date books to record important meetings and to jot down reminders of things to do. The operations of an event organization over the year, or the actions for each program committee or operational area, can also be written down on a calendar. The appropriate unit of time must first be specified: weeks or months for all-year schedules; days, hours, or minutes for event programming. Within each cell can be written specific to-do actions, some of which will run across a number of cells. Start and end points can be specified with symbols, as can other critical dates. One benefit of calendars is that they can be designed at a large scale and posted for everyone to see at meetings, and reduced so that everyone has a personal copy.

Gantt Charts

These graphs are a simple, visual way to schedule event planning over any period of time, or to schedule the event program when it contains multiple, nonsequential elements. The unit of time must be specified, and a decision must also be taken on whether the scheduling applies to individual persons, programs, or team/committee work.

Figure 3.4 is an example which shows that program elements or assignments are sometimes sequential (e.g., one can only begin when another is finished), while others are overlapping (e.g., at different venues). Some program elements or management actions are intermittent. The entire planning period or event must be scheduled, so some activities must start at the beginning and some must run until the end. These start and end points

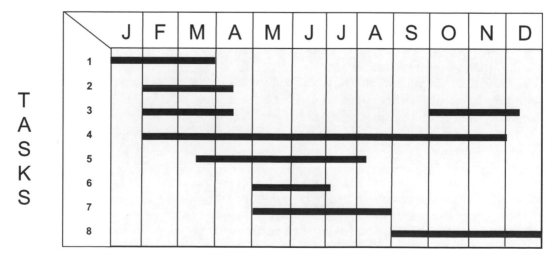

Figure 3.4. Gantt chart.

can be determined in advance, or be determined after all the activities have been scheduled.

Gantt charts are also very useful in scheduling an event program, at least at the general level.

Decision Points and "Decision Trees"

Where uncertainty exists over the feasibility of the project, whether or not a bid will be won, or a political decision is needed, specific decision points should be predetermined to force "go, no-go decisions." Unless these are scheduled, work might plod on without appropriate reference to the project's ultimate viability. In the case of committed events, the decision points might apply to specific elements such as programs or facilities, with the event itself being a given.

Some events and projects will incorporate a "drop-dead" point in the planning schedule at which time certain predefined conditions must be fulfilled or the event is cancelled. These criteria could be:

- financial commitments in place (money is in the bank);
- political support is committed (letters are in hand);
- attendance thresholds are guaranteed (through advance sales);
- facilities or other resources are committed (contracts signed).

In other circumstances critical decisions will have to be made in the absence of predetermined criteria. In such cases the use of a "decision tree" is helpful. For each key decision that has to be made along the way to producing an event, ask the following questions:

- What are the immediate known, and possible implications of making this decision? (e.g., does this decision to proceed commit us to more spending?)
- If we decide against this course of action, what will or might happen?
- In what order do the critical decisions have to be made, by whom, and when?
- Are the potential consequences of the decision too risky, or is the risk acceptable?

The "decision tree" combines elements of critical path analysis, feasibility and impact evaluation, risk assessment, and scheduling. Advice on their construction and use is available online (www.mindtools.com).

Working Under Time Pressure

For one-time events it might prove difficult to anticipate the full number of tasks and the likely schedule. PERT can then be used to estimate project time lines and determine if the event even looks feasible. In most cases, however, once a commitment has been given the project team must get it done on time, no matter what. This pressure leads to several possible issues:

- the need for "fast tracking," in which governments agree to suspend or modify various regulations to ensure completion;
- increased expenditure (e.g., as the deadline looms, more money might have to be spent than was budgeted, such as for overtime payments to workers);
- quality sacrifices (e.g., to produce the event on time plans might have to be modified and quality reduced);
- plan revisions might be required frequently, and without adequate assessment of impacts;

- increased susceptibility to external forces, such as protests or suppliers, or to internal forces, such as labor disputes;
- public relations problems, especially if it appears that the project is behind schedule or is being reduced in quality or scope.

Scheduling and controlling of the project are therefore critical management responsibilities, and no doubt many project managers have worked under considerable stress to deliver the event as planned.

Implementation of the Plan

Producing the event is the target, and all planning and implementation processes work back from the event's set dates. If the dates are flexible, so too can be the planning process. However, much of the infrastructure, financing, staffing, and other actions must be in place before the event, so a great deal of scheduling and controlling are necessary.

For major events, financing the planning and construction can become a major issue, especially if money has to be raised along the way. The construction of new infrastructure, such as public transport, and the event venues, can easily be delayed. Marketing must gear up potentially years before the mega-event. Finally, a new organization will have to be established to manage the event, and a lengthy transition period will be needed. This organization will have to test venues, programs, and systems, including the recruitment and training of numerous staff and volunteers.

Vital systems that must be put in place prior to the event opening in order to facilitate problem solving and refinements:

- risk analysis (anticipate the potential problems);
- contingency plans (for all eventualities, including budget shortfalls);
- emergency procedures (for security, health, and safety);
- training (staff and volunteers are prepared, confident, and empowered);
- information and marketing (to inform everyone of changes).

Producing and Terminating the Event

During the event, refinements and problem solving are usually necessary, but the manager's ability to act depends in part on the effectiveness of planning and on the event's duration. Also, can its program and scheduling be altered if, at the last minute, the preparations are incomplete? Afterwards, the event and its organization must be terminated or adapted.

Catherwood and Van Kirk (1992, p. 185) noted that it can take years to wind down a major event. Major investments have been made, infrastructure has been built, numerous staff and volunteers have been employed, and the sponsors and various authorities expect accounting and reports to be completed. The main wind-down tasks are:

- paying bills and obtaining all promised and owed revenues;
- auditing the accounts;
- filing and processing insurance claims;
- settling any lawsuits;
- cleaning and closing venues; some venues might be turned over or back to different organizations;
- disposal of lands and other accumulated resources;
- thanking, rewarding, and, if necessary, "outplacing" (i.e., help get jobs) staff and volunteers;

- completing evaluations and impact assessments; making reports to sponsors and authorities;
- checking and terminating all contracts;
- filing necessary tax returns;
- terminating the organization (e.g., corporate papers and other legal documents, bank accounts, closing offices).

The Project Management Team and Organization

Given the nature of one-time event projects, a number of special circumstances apply. First and foremost is the highly political nature of mega-event projects, usually resulting in some form of direct governmental representation on a specially created governing board. It might also prove desirable to separate the political processes, especially the lobbying that goes on during the bid stage, from the project management team. Hence, a spokesperson, champion, or "ambassador" can be appointed to handle political tasks.

The project management team itself will consist of a general manager (or executive director) and a range of professions and functional area managers reflecting the nature of the project. For a world's fair or the Olympics, the need for infrastructural development will figure prominently in shaping the team. For less ambitious events, programmers and marketers might dominate.

Huffadine (1993) suggested that project management teams must maximize internal communications and flexibility, making a bureaucratic hierarchy inappropriate. Rather, a "flat" structure will work best, in which the project manager is very close to the professionals. This structure must also incorporate quality control mechanisms, especially when construction is planned. The project manager will require skills and experience in event or general project management. The manager's ability to organize, motivate, and manage a team of experts and volunteers is also a primary qualification. This person might very well be the one to determine the exact composition of the team of professionals and managers needed to complete the mandate.

Special considerations apply to project management. The first stage is dominated by team building and planning, but thereafter control is the main management task. Production of the event often requires an entirely different set of skills from the early stages. The team, therefore, will usually have a built-in transition of people with the appropriate skills of planning, control, and production.

Mega-events are often racked by political problems that tend to result in high turnover among top staff people. As well, staff tend to be highly motivated at the beginning, but this might fade near the end of the project. For events, the staff who engaged in most of the hard work up front should be able to enjoy the fruits of their labor. Burnout is another serious risk, as working to an inflexible deadline can impose considerable stress and fatigue on the key workers. Outplacement services will also be necessary for staff at the end of the project, and perhaps special counseling to overcome personal problems.

Case Study: Handover Ceremony and Celebrations in East Timor From a Project Management Perspective (written by William O'Toole)

We would like to thank Ray Johnson of the AFP and Lt. Colonel Grant Johansen, United Nations Transitional Administration Peacekeeping Force Operations Officer, upon whose work this study was based.

The Event

East Timor is a tiny island of 800,000 people in the Indonesian Archipelago. On midnight of May 20, 2002, it became the first new nation of the new millennium. To celebrate the handover

Photo 3.1. East Timor handover ceremony (credit: William J. O'Toole).

of the government event, the United Nations and an event team made up of representees of many countries organized a ceremony for the handover of the administration of East Timor from the UN to the newly elected government.

The East Timor handover ceremony and celebrations took place at a number of sites on the island. The event marked the end of 24 years of Indonesian rule over East Timor and the 500 years of colonial occupation of the Portugal.

The only recent celebration events of such magnitude and world significance in this region were the handover of Macau and Hong Kong to the Chinese Peoples Republic. This celebration marked the beginning of a new nation. The planned program included:

- The formal handover ceremony, the raising of the new flag and the swearing in of the new president occurring at midnight on the Sunday. Similar ceremonies were conducted, on a smaller scale, concurrently in a number of the districts.
- Independence Day Street Parade.
- Independence Day Music Concert.
- Dinner co-hosted by the Government of East Timor and the World Bank.
- Missa Campal—Mass held for the people of East Timor (including communion).
- Religious pilgrimage across the 13 districts of East Timor.
- Business Expo.
- Official reception for visiting delegation.
- Various cultural and religious events.
- Fireworks Grand Finale.
- Some of the heads of government used the opportunity to inaugurate the various capitol works such as the national Community and Exhibition Centre in Dilli.

Some of the characteristics of this event that contributed to its complexity included:

- Huge number of VIPs, heads of governments, and their staff—all of whom had to be welcomed, transported, accommodated, farewelled, while ensuring their security. All of this using the correct international protocol.
- Scale of activities required logistic support to be provided by international sources.
- World media interest and their logistic requirements.
- Lack of infrastructure on the island including roads, airfields, port facilities, and communications.
- Limited national security forces.
- Intense political interest by surrounding countries.
- Lack of suitable accommodation for the numerous guests.
- Limited planning duration, January to May 2002.
- Uncertain funding.

The guest list included thousands of VIPs and heads of government of 25 countries including:

- United Nations Secretary-General Kofi Annan.
- Former US president Bill Clinton.
- Indonesian President Megawati Sukarnoputri.
- Australian Prime Minister John Howard.
- East Timor independence activist Jose Ramos Horta.
- President-elect Xanana Gusmao.

The complexities of the actual celebration event illustrated by the words of Ignatius Jones—the celebrations event director—in an interview on ABC radio:

> [T]here's 13 districts in Timor because of the mountainous nature of the country, they're extremely diverse. There's 15 indigenous languages, not counting Tetum Prasa or Tetum Dili which is the lingua franca. Or Portuguese, which everyone over 35 speaks. Or Bahasa, which everyone under 35 speaks. So there's been enormous pressure from the districts that each of them be represented. So to do this it's been very, very difficult to do this in such a way.

> There's 13 districts and a sub-district; if I give every one of them 2 minutes, we're up at half an hour. And half an hour out of a 2-hour ceremony is an enormous amount of time when you consider you've also got to pay tribute to the traditional law, the elders of Timor are very, very important there. The youth of Timor, the resistance itself, and then of course the formal hand-over.

The Management

The evolution of the tools and techniques that make up project management has been one of constant improvement through its use in the civil engineering industry. It is not surprising that traditional project management emphasizes a stable planning environment and a highly defined scope and asset. For this reason the greatest success in the application of project management in the past has been in annual or repeated events and festivals. Many large sporting events, such as the Olympics and the Masters Games, employ project management. The East Timor event is unusual because it was unique and therefore there was not a management model to draw upon. Instead of a rigid project planning model for this event, a model of progressive development is perhaps more apt. The program for the event was evolving as all the other areas of management progressed.

The traditional tools of project management such as the work breakdown structure, risk management plan, and stakeholder management plan had to be modified to use for this event. The characteristics of this event that reduced their applicability were:

1. Short period of planning.
2. The number and importance of the stakeholders.
3. The lack of a communication infrastructure in the host country.

4. The lack of logistic support (i.e., equipment such as scaffolding, lighting, seating, tentage and power generation), available in the host country.
5. Uncertain and/or untimely funding from other countries and international organizations.
6. A lack of personnel with event management experience.
7. Major changes occurring right up until the day of the event.

The solution to this situation was to use a committee system and delegate as much authority to the committees as possible. These semiautonomous groups produced "situations reports" at the meetings. The meetings (schedule shown below) agreed on the milestones and the responsibilities of the committees. An area identified early on in the planning was the lack of suitable accommodation. An accommodation committee was set up to solve this with the authority to act and report back regularly to the meetings. The meetings were held three times a week and included:

- Security (UN Police).
- United Nations Transitional Administration, Department of Administration (DOA).
- Special Representative to Secretary General (SRSG) Advisor on Independence Day.
- Peace Keeping Force, Independence Day Celebrations Operations Officer.
- East Timor Public Administration Representative (ETPA).
- Ceremony organizers such as Ignatius Jones and his key staff.
- Other stakeholders as required.

Reports were sent to the other stakeholders. At the meetings the tasks were assigned and the millstones identified. The frequency of the meetings increased as the events drew closer. The week prior to the events the various representatives met as often as twice a day to ensure activities and issues were coordinated or creative solutions to problems were found in a local and timely manner.

From a project management point of view a large part of the management of this event concerned the management of the stakeholders. A sample of the stakeholder management table as prepared by Johnson is show below.

East Timor (ET) Handover Ceremony: Sample of Stakeholder Management Table

ET Constituent Assembly	• Independence day is the day that they take full responsibility for Government. They wish for ET to be viewed Internationally on this day as a fledgling democracy in need of assistance. • They need the event to be peaceful and attended by many international representatives.	• There is some friction between the current Prime Minister and the likely President. This friction is increasing as the election approaches. • As the succeeding government of ET they state that they feel pressured by the UN regarding aspects of the Event. • The Government wants the event to focus on the people of ET not as entertainment for the international community • Limited, if any, capability to assist in funding the events.
ET President elect	• As for constituent assembly. • Needs his first appearance of the international stage to be well received.	• There is some friction between the current Prime Minister and the likely President. This friction is increasing as the election approaches.
Catholic Church	• Proper respect is paid to the Catholic faith during the celebrations. • All ET have a chance to take part	• With 90% plus of the population being Catholic the influence of the church is significant. • Decision-making in the Catholic Church in ET was very centralized

		though religious events were being conducted throughout the country at various stages. This created a dilemma between centralized control and decentralized execution.
Pro Integration Militias	• Are very much against independence. It if from this quarter that delivers the highest threat to security.	• The UNHCR Returnee activities have returned a large number of low level militia to ET, many of whom now will attend in the events and it is difficult to get a feel for their expectations of Independence day. • UN cannot engage them in the process for obvious political reasons. Therefore knowing their intentions is difficult.

This stakeholder management table was used by the Event Operations Group to identify risks. In particular, as Johnson points out, "it had extensive downstream effect" and assisted when there were major changes.

Many of the project management tools were used by the Event Operations Unit. The manual became a "consulting document," rather than a controlling document. The manual contained:

- Event Summary
- Order of Service
- Event Execution
- Event Operations Management Structure
- Venue Operations Management
- Communications Plan
- Logistic Support Plans
- Media Plan
- Aviation Management Plan
- Catering Plan
- Infrastructure Development
- Reporting Requirements including UN, ET, PKF and nations.
- Dignitary Liaison
- Security reporting
- Communications Logistics
- Radio Communications
- Protocol/Ceremonies
- Security/Public Safety
- Traffic Coordination Plan
- Medical Plan
- Pass Identification
- Risk Management

According to Johnson, the stakeholder management and the creation of the manual resulted in the Event Operations Unit taking on more of a coordinating role. This was fundamental to the success of the events as the many changes, of various magnitudes, could be coordinated and integrated with the other activities and support plans.

One of the most important applications of project management for this event was as common communication for the key management team. Most of the team came from a military logistics or security background. The languages of project management used in this area of the military included: mission, objectives, tasks, milestones, deliverables, and specified any coordination requirements. The physical communication systems depended on mobile phones and military radios provided by the PKF. The mobile phone network required supplementation in the form of mobile towers thereby boosting network capabilities and expanding the range of coverage to specific locations. Key communication staff were provided by the PKF who conducted training, established networks, and provided support staff throughout the activities.

The risk management had to be a very active. The many changes are illustrated by two incidents

Indonesian warships. The Indonesian government sent a number of warships as advance security for their President, Megawati Sukarnoputri. As the independence of East Timor occurred after a protracted insurgency campaign against Indonesia, the arrival of warships caused a great deal of concern.

Accommodation. The accommodation problem was solved by sourcing a boat, the *Dolphin*, from Thailand. However, the facilities for docking the *Dolphin* were inadequate. On the Sunday of the event, while the dignitaries were arriving at the airport, the *Dolphin* finally became accessible from the shore. This meant that some of the dignitaries had to be kept busy while the boat docked.

In such an event environment, the formal risk management process needs to be adapted to the level of autonomous teams solving the problems as they arise while keeping the central event operations unit informed.

From a project management perspective, the event team successfully adapted their management to the situation in order to create the asset (i.e., the event) to the satisfaction of the stakeholders. This did not mean slavishly following a series of steps or a process as set out in a system. It meant devolving authority and managing by exception. In this way the tools and techniques of project management did not become a source of inertia for the management team. The scheduling, tasks, and scope were able to respond to changing conditions. The coordination of devolved responsibilities was the key to the success of the East Timor Independence Ceremonies.

The Business Plan

The most common reason for preparing a business plan is to obtain financing. Banks usually require proof of management competency, including detailed plans to generate revenue and pay back the borrowed money. But there are a number of very good reasons for preparing and periodically updating the business plan:

- to obtain financing from sponsors, lenders, grant-givers, memberships;
- to demonstrate management competency to all stakeholders, including staff and volunteers (i.e., credibility);
- to facilitate partnerships and alliances;
- to make clear the organization's mission, goals, and priorities (i.e., direction);
- to get started on a project; attract key people;
- to establish sound financial planning and control mechanisms (i.e., discipline).

The format of the business plan can be important:

- most business plans are short; up to 40 pages in length plus appendices;
- the format should be professional and easy to use;
- provide detailed contents, executive summary, and useful support material;
- state the intended use(s) and distribution of the plan; is it confidential?

Background on the organization and event must be provided:

- outline the origin and development highlights;
- describe the organization as a legal entity;
- describe the management team;

- profile key leaders and key staff;
- document volunteer support;
- stress the partners and sponsors;
- provide an organizational chart;
- highlight the existence of a strategic or marketing plan;
- state the mission, vision, key goals;
- note the existence of human resource or operations plans, strategic and site plans;
- give evidence of sound management, especially successes to date;
- append a fact sheet, including contact names and addresses.

For the event itself:

- explain the event's purpose, program, and benefits;
- stress its uniqueness and tourist appeal, if applicable;
- mention any competitors;
- describe plans for developing and improving the event;
- outline quality control measures;
- provide tangible evidence of attendance and growth; append photographs.

Marketing strengths should be demonstrated:

- state marketing and communications goals and objectives;
- highlight the marketing budget and innovations;
- summarize positioning and marketing mix strategies, especially as they relate to revenue generation;
- highlight research efforts and results of past market research;
- profile the audience;
- forecast demand/growth in attendance;
- stress key target market segments and their financial importance to the event (e.g., income levels, willingness to pay);
- describe integrated marketing with sponsors;
- show tourist-oriented promotions and packaging; mention the distribution system (of tickets, etc.).

Financial issues are the most important:

- explain cost and revenue management efforts and successes;
- explain financial control systems;
- note cash flow issues (e.g., do you earn all your revenue at the event?);
- document the organization's assets and available collateral;
- give financial forecasts and risks;
- provide: the current budget, cash flow statement, income/loss statement, balance sheet (assets and liabilities), key performance ratios;
- state financial needs;
- explain plans and methods for repayment of any desired loans.

In a summary, make the case for financial assistance, if applicable. Appendices may be desirable:

- photos and other tangible evidence of the event and the organization; highlight successes and uniqueness;
- research highlights;
- organizational chart;
- examples of media coverage (or summary of its value);

- endorsements and testimonials;
- resumes of key leaders and staff.

All event managers should consider the fact that business plans will prove very useful in strategic planning and budgeting. The exercise of developing and updating the business plan will tend to force higher levels of management competency on the organization and lead to better cost—revenue management. It will also prove useful on that "rainy day" when you have no choice but to head to the bank, business plan in hand.

The Strategic Plan

"Strategic planning" is a future-oriented process that seeks to attain goals through the formulation and implementation of broad, long-term strategies. A "strategy" is an integrated set of policies and programs intended to achieve the vision and goals of the organization or destination. Strategy is rooted in a vision of the future and it outlines general ways to get there; it often leads to more detailed plans, policies, and programs. Many event managers get by without such a strategy, but they succeed because of their vision and managerial skills. Most events would benefit from going through a strategic planning exercise, even if they did not prepare a formal plan.

Figure 3.5 illustrates a seven-stage strategic planning process. Its logic is straightforward, although developing the process can be quite complex. It does not have to be linear, but can combine and repeat elements of the various stages, as appropriate.

Mandate, or Mission

Why does the event exist? Most organizations have a clear enough mandate, such as service, profit making, economic development, or fostering a cause. It is helpful to express this in terms applicable to the event itself, such as the following two examples:

Calgary Exhibition and Stampede: The basic purpose of the Calgary Exhibition and Stampede is to preserve and enhance the agricultural and historical legacy of Alberta and to fulfill appropriate aspects of the agricultural trade, entertainment, sports, recreational, and educational needs of Calgary and Southern Alberta, in particular, and where appropriate, those of Alberta and Western Canada.

Texas Folklife Festival: The primary purpose of the Texas Folklife Festival is to provide an educational setting where traditional folklife activities of Texans from all over the state can be demonstrated to impart knowledge to the public and encourage the preservation of these activities. . . . A secondary but very important purpose of the Festival is teaching through entertainment. . . . The Festival will continue to be organized and managed so that it will be financially self-supporting and provide some operating funds for other Institute programs.

A good statement of purpose will provide event organizers and managers with a firm foundation upon which vision and strategies can be built. There must be clarity about the basic roles, such as service versus profit making, and some direction given on key points such as programming, marketing, or setting, if these are crucial. On the other hand, it must be general enough to allow for creativity and flexibility on the part of staff and volunteers.

Depending on the context, some events will have to work out their own statement of purpose, while others will have a mandate imposed upon them from the parent organization. It is also possible that the mandate or purpose will be developed at the same time as visioning and goal setting.

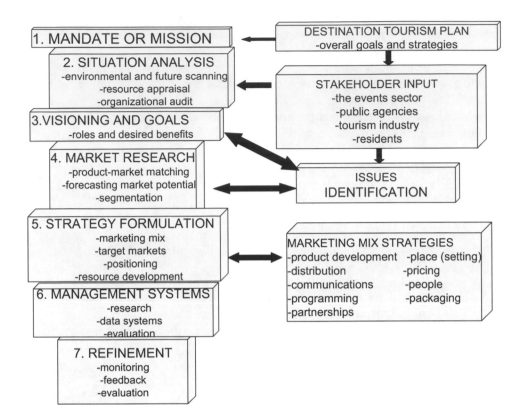

Figure 3.5. Strategic planning process.

Situation Analysis

A "situation analysis" is equivalent to taking stock of the organization and its environment. It has several major components. "Environmental scanning" seeks to identify conditions and underlying forces shaping events and event tourism. Existing and potential markets must be identified, and competitors and complimentary events and event tourism products evaluated, leading to identification of threats and opportunities. "Future scanning" extends trends into the future to assess the probability and potential impacts of future conditions. "Resource appraisals" examine the availability of human, financial, political, and material support to meet the event's goals. An "organizational audit" should be part of this scanning, to ask where have we been and where are we headed? What are our organizational strengths and weaknesses?

Environmental Scanning

Every manager has to conduct ongoing "environmental scanning" to stay current, but especially when engaged in strategic planning. The basic elements and methods of environmental scanning include the following:

- Determine what information is needed for ongoing event management or event tourism and for related strategic planning.
- Locate the best sources and obtain the information regularly (e.g., from magazines and journals) or periodically (e.g., new census data).
- Establish relationships with other organizations and experts (such as consultants or academics) to ensure you learn from them.

- Establish a system suitable to your style and the organization's capabilities to acquire and use appropriate information.
- Become a "learning organization" devoted to continuous improvement.

Distinguishing trends from fads is one challenge, and applying global forces to local and event-specific planning is another. Obviously, the more experience managers have the better they should be at obtaining and using the most important information. Professional associations, conferences, and publications can be a big help in this process.

This stage should ideally involve a great deal of research, but at a minimum can be done through expert consultations and discussion among the leaders or planners. Stakeholder input is vital. Consider that the most knowledgeable people are often already on top of trends and issues. Sharing information and research among events, professional associations, and with educational establishments is desirable. Also, tourism and economic development agencies will have pertinent data that they can provide and interpret.

Public input, either through formal surveys, focus groups, or public forums, will be useful. Consult the public on their attitudes towards the organization and towards events and tourism in general; also measure the current and potential market for events.

The manager has ongoing responsibility for ensuring effective and efficient operations, but sometimes it pays to have an external expert do an organizational audit, just the way the accounts are audited. Each functional area will be examined, as well as the organizational structure and leadership. Recommendations will be made to improve the organization and the way in which it conducts its business.

Force-Field Analysis

The acronym PEST is sometimes used to describe the main forces to be reviewed: political, economic, social, and technological. Social is the broadest, including population and demographic forces, cultural and value changes. Major forces and trends affecting events are assessed at the end of this chapter.

SWOT Analysis

Analysis of strengths, weaknesses, opportunities, and threats (SWOT) is a standard evaluation and planning tool. It can be done internally, based on how the organization perceives itself, or by external consultants who will make comparisons to other organizations. The SWOT analysis is also an excellent way to assess the competitive position of the organization or its events. When tied to "benchmarking," it can help the organization make specific changes for improvement.

Visioning and Goal Setting

Mintzburg (1994, p. 209) proclaimed that "visioning" is at the heart of strategic planning. It is a process of setting the broad outline of a strategy, or identifying elements of a desired future. Every event organization should have not only have a mandate, or statement of its purpose, but a vision statement that can motivate and foster unity of purpose among all stakeholders. At the heart of visioning is consideration of ideal future state of the event and/ or its organization. For example, the vision might be to become the largest and best event of its kind within a given area. This vision can then be translated into goals pertaining to:

- desired size (e.g., attendance, volume, revenues, staff, volunteers);
- desired setting (e.g., the best venues, location);
- desired reputation and market position (e.g., the best and biggest event of its kind within a defined area);

- desired market mix (e.g., dominant and secondary segments attracted);
- desired financial state (e.g., profit or surplus revenue and its uses, debt elimination, self-sufficiency for continuance or growth).

A good vision statement is one that reflects the organization's mandate or mission, is broad and general enough to attract widespread support, and sufficiently inspired and forward-looking to stimulate innovation in its pursuit. Consultations with stakeholders will be important in shaping the vision, especially if they will be asked to support the strategies and goals which flow from it.

The following is a hypothetical statement that stresses what the organization believes is its mission and desired future state of its event: *This fair is dedicated to the entertainment and education of our community, to the preservation and development of the agricultural industry, and the attraction of visitors to support our tourism and hospitality sectors. Our vision is to become the best midsize fair in the state, noted for its family-oriented entertainment, highly competitive prizes, and excellent customer service. We aim to be a top-100 tourist attraction in the country.*

Statements of mission or vision provide general direction for the organization, but not for specific programs or management functions. Goal statements are needed to help translate the general direction of the organization into more tangible, results-oriented efforts. Goals can be of three general types. "Input goals" concentrate on what is required to get the job done, including resource acquisition, organizational structure, and processes that convert inputs into outcomes.

These can be thought of the means to achieve desired outcomes. An example is: *Maximize sponsorship revenue without compromising our mission.*

"Outcome goals focus on desired outcomes, or what the event or event tourism is supposed to achieve. For example: *Generate surplus revenues to support community arts projects.*

"Avoidance" goals specify problems or costs to be avoided or ameliorated: *Minimize waste and prevent any damage to the environment.*

Goal statements should ideally comprehensively cover all aspects of the organization's management, the event, and all impacts, but broad policy statements can accomplish much the same thing, such as: *It is our policy to be an environmentally responsible event, avoiding waste and environmental damage while pursuing "green" practices that benefit the environment.*

Once goals are formulated they must usually be translated into specific objectives that provide measurable targets and time frames. Objectives must be realistic and attainable, and it is generally useful to build in measures by which results will be evaluated (i.e., "performance criteria" or "key results"). For example, an objective to implement the environmental goal/policy stated above could be: *To reduce waste packaging and serving material at the event by 50%, as measured by weight, relative to the previous year's.*

Note that this objective is precise and direct in commanding specific actions and in showing how the intended outcome will be evaluated. Bear in mind that just as one goal might have a number of objectives, one objective might have several performance measures associated with it.

Case Study: Canadian Tulip Festival (www.tulipfestival.ca)

In 2002 The Canadian Tulip Festival, located in Ottawa, the nation's capital, celebrated its 50th anniversary. It is the world's largest tulip-themed event, and its age makes it a real success story—although not one without failure and rebirth along the way.

The event began in 1953 when the Dutch royal family donated bulbs to thank Canada for hosting them during World War II. Over the years the festival grew in size and popularity but was plagued by underfinancing. Volunteers who operated the festival also felt there was a lack of community support, with the perception being that it was a federal government responsibility. It also did not have enough attractions, other than the weather-dependent flowers, to hold tourists overnight. In 1975 a reorganization occurred and it was renamed Festival of Spring.

Festival of Spring had a mandate to become a tourist attraction and become a community-based event for the entire National Capital Region, so a series of free events was initiated. Originally a number of local municipalities in both Ontario and Quebec provinces were involved, but after their withdrawal the City of Ottawa became the festival's main backer. The National Capital Commission is also involved of necessity because the flowers are on its lands. Occasional provincial grants and some corporate sponsorships were important sources of revenue.

From 1974 through 1986 professional management was obtained under contract, after which the first full-time employees were hired. The City of Ottawa had insisted on greater professionalism and accountability after repeated financial losses. A city-sponsored consultant's report recommended a number of important changes in 1986, including a return to the original floral theme. After this transformation, festival staff aggressively pursued innovative programming and sponsors.

The 2002 festival was an 18-day program of activities and flowers in bloom, and although the weather does not always cooperate, the organizers, under the direction of Michel Gauthier, make certain that all visitors have a memorable, festive experience. Some highlights:

Photo 3.2. Tulip artist at Canadian Tulip Festival (credit: Canadian Tulip Festival).

- based on a telephone survey, 28.3% of area residents attended, an estimated 268,000;
- average number of visits by residents was 1.63 (lower than normal owing to inclement weather);
- 148 group packages were sold to tourists visiting the festival, plus 769 individual packages;
- 26% of the sampled population said they had visiting friends or relatives come at least in part because of the festival;
- a "conservative" estimate was made that over 400,000 tourists came, for 672,000 person-nights;
- estimated gross economic impact from tourism was over $28 million (Can.);
- within the gated Major's Hill Park venue, paid attendance was 86,320;
- Tulipass sales increased 36% to 14,475, bringing advance sales revenue to $446,493;
- 1400 volunteers participated (700 had applied online).

Five-Year Vision 2004–2008

Mission Statement: "The Canadian Tulip Festival is a celebration of the tulip as a symbol of spring, of international friendship and of the national Capital Commission."

Goals
1. To showcase tulips through artistic and horticultural means.
2. To promote international friendship.
3. To be one of Canada's finest festivals and a major tourist attraction.
4. To be representative of the National Capital Region's cultural and linguistic diversity.
5. To produce a Main Stage Concert Series that is a showcase for Canadian talent and a box office success.
6. To operate at all levels in a professional business manner, with integrity.

Branding: "The 'brand' of the Canadian Tulip Festival is tulips. The marketing statement reinforces the expectations of the Festival's audiences that our tulips will be special, different—Wow. This is the promise of the Canadian Tulip Festival branding."

Five-Year Vision: For each year, 2004–2008, the major theme is identified (e.g., for 2005: World Tulip Rendezvous) plus specific goals (e.g., in 2005 to host the World Tulip Summit). Each major venue is also described as to its program and experiences. New projects are identified.

SWOT Analysis, Canadian Tulip Festival (From the Five-Year Vision 2004–2008)

STRENGTHS	THREATS
Tulip-symbol of the Capital	Weather
Activities in Ottawa and Gatineau	Cash flow
50 year tradition	Growth without revenue
Ongoing growth	Volunteer leadership dependent
Credibility—goodwill	National Capital Commission—landlord of
Bilingual event	sites and tulip beds
International flavour	Same level of tulip beds
Internet friendly	Departure of experienced staff
Full time staff	Positioning of festival as a tourist product
Preferred suppliers	Economic downturn
Tourism product—generating important	Withdrawal of key supporters
economic impact	Fragile support in Quebec
Volunteer commitment	Risk that sponsorship will diminish
Active and high profile board	
National and international recognition	
Ongoing partner support	
Financial stability	
Experienced executive director and	
industry leader	
Community support	

Uniqueness
Well respected by all levels of government

WEAKNESSES	OPPORTUNITIES
Too many protocol special events	Development of tulip WOW factor
Lack of strategic development plan	Development of a five-year vision
Lack of research data	Pursue international tulip networking
Lack of succession planning at staff and board level	Quebec office and program elements
	Development of new sites
Too many fundraising programs	New human resources department
Too many special events	New fund-raising department
Sell our soul for $	Networking with Ottawa and Gatineau Festival Networks
Lack of active commitment from official sites Overstate revenues/understate expenses	New program elements—launched for the 50th anniversary
Staff bulge/ongoing new staff	Increase in Tulipass sales
Last minute execution	Review existing sponsorship approach
Too many elements not related to tulips	New board members
Try to be all things to all people	
Weather dependent	

Market Research

Research is necessary to identify and answer these crucial questions:

- Who are our potential customers? What trends are noticeable?
- What factors are affecting interest in and demand for our event and the destination?
- What are their needs and motives?
- How can we best reach them and influence their decisions?
- What is the role of events in creating/enhancing our destination theme, and in increasing the attractiveness of our other tourism resources?
- How can we gain a competitive advantage?
- Are customers satisfied with our products and information?

Events cannot appeal to everyone—each has its natural interest groups and each can be modified to attract others. The "product–marketing matching" process is used by managers to ensure that the event offers what target consumers want. To be marketing oriented requires market research, segmentation, and identification of target groups, and ongoing modification of the marketing mix. This is not to say that some events cannot remain forever popular using the tried and true formula, but this strategy will become harder and harder as competition grows and consumer interests change. Even the best traditional events must continuously adapt and try new approaches.

Market research and marketing strategies must be focused. Not all potential markets can or should be targeted. "Segmentation" means the identification of relatively homogeneous groups that can be targeted for competitive advantage and to meet destination goals. Increasingly, destinations are concentrating on finding competitive advantage through niche marketing, and this helps explain the growing interest in event tourism. The search for quality tourists is a segmentation issue.

Issues Identification

Arising from the background research and analysis any number of issues will be identified. Public and stakeholder input will always lead to generation of issues, some stated as goals to achieve, and others as problems. Arising from this stage are issues that must be dealt with, and others that are set aside because the organization cannot or does not want to deal with them. Of those requiring action, some can be handled by immediate decisions while others lead into the strategy formulation stage for resolution.

Strategy Formulation

Remember that a strategy is an integrated set of policies and programs intended to achieve the vision and goals of the event. Strategies will be required for each of the management functions and so will require input from the staff or volunteers and committees that oversee finance, marketing, human resources, and the rest. In some ways the formulation of strategies is like budgeting. Ideas come from the various committees, implications, and alternatives are evaluated, and the directors or owners make final decisions. But strategies are seldom blueprints to be followed slavishly—they should be viewed as adaptable approaches to achieving goals.

The full marketing mix is affected by, and shapes, all strategies. If marketing is thought of as the set of communications, exchanges, and other connections between the event and its stakeholders, including customers, it is clear that each element in the marketing mix must have a strategic direction. And how they all work together is vital.

Implementation

Numerous plans and strategies have found their ultimate role to be that of dust collector on a shelf. To avoid this fate requires early attention to implementation methods, the viability of the strategy, and action plans that will motivate the key people. Failure to involve all stakeholders will also affect implementation. Feasibility studies and cost–benefit evaluations should be used to determine the viability of a strategy, especially if it requires a great deal of resources and advance planning.

To ensure that plans will be implemented, the following principles should be followed:

- develop a shared vision that all stakeholders can accept;
- maximize shareholder involvement in the entire process;
- develop strategies, rather than detailed blueprints;
- focus on results and how to attain and evaluate them;
- develop action plans with time lines and assigned responsibilities.

Management Systems

In addition to the crucial research efforts mentioned above, a comprehensive evaluation system must be established. Are goals being reached? At what costs? Can the strategy be made more effective or efficient? What unexpected outcomes or impacts have been generated? This analysis is fed back into the system for purposes of both accountability and improving the strategies.

A number of management support systems are required to implement the strategies:

- technological support: computer and communication systems;
- databases (accounting and finance; customers; stakeholders; resources and inventories; events and competitors);
- ongoing research and evaluation instruments and standardized measures of performance;
- external audits and evaluations (e.g., by experts and stakeholders);
- training and professional development.

Strategic choices often require modification to the organization, such as its committee structure or leadership roles, to ensure implementation. There is little point in changing the structure unless it will serve a broader strategy or solve a specific, serious problem.

Refinement

Strategic planning is an ongoing process. Indeed, some people believe it is a waste of time to actual write a plan because it will either get out of date quickly or it will serve to stagnate the organization. When too much effort is expended on implementing the plan, opportunities and threats might be missed. Nevertheless, managers have to at least think strategically, and they must have the planning, research, and evaluation tools at their disposal.

All plans have to be refined and adapted as environmental forces change. This can be done formally, every year or two, or through ongoing changes in direction. "Emergent" strategies are those that evolve out of the day-to-day operations of the organization and at some point will have to be evaluated and possibly abandoned or formalized.

Forces and Trends Affecting Events

Political Forces

This force field encompasses political and legal matters that could influence events. By its very nature political forces will vary a lot between countries and at different levels (e.g., national, state, and local governments). How much public money and effort is spent on events or event tourism is, of course, a political issue. Many communities are aggressive in their support, while many politicians have other spending priorities and the event sector is left to its own.

The world has generally become a safer place in terms of reduced superpower tensions, but terrorism has emerged as the new enemy of peace, safety, and travel security. Since September 11, 2001, planned events have been forced to pay much closer attention to the threat of a terrorist attack, resulting in heightened security at all events and event venues. The presence or even the threat of communicable diseases quickly takes on political dimensions, as observed with regard to the SARS scare in 2002. Travel in particular is disrupted and reduced, causing governments to react. Events are likely to be cancelled, as they present the opportunity for dispersal of germs, but ironically are also used to help a country or city fight back. For example, Toronto held a Rolling Stones superconcert to attract favorable publicity after its tourism industry was decimated by SARS.

Not only are major events always potential targets for terrorism and political protests, but protests themselves have become a category of planned special events. Visit www.protest.net to enter the world of protest events. They are orchestrated to achieve very specific goals, mostly media oriented to get publicity for the diverse causes being represented. They are hardly ever spontaneous, are usually peaceful and legal, but occasionally erupt (or are nudged) into violence. With the Internet providing a sense of community, and enabling the scheduling of protests, they continue to spread and achieve greater impacts.

Economic Forces

It appears that in North America polarization of the rich and the poor is increasing. Consequently, we witness a set of festivals and events for the rich and another for the poor. Arts events in particular are susceptible to escalating production costs, and even with government subsidies they are sometimes priced beyond the reach of lower and even middle income groups. This problem has forced them to become more interested in tourist markets. Government agencies, particularly those involved in community sports and recreation, community development, and popular culture, are most involved in creating free and inexpensive special events for the public. Their role in this respect will become more important. The big challenge is to somehow blend the best of free, public celebration with the best of professional or other high-quality performances so that no group is excluded by reason of income alone.

Event managers are now definitely bottom-line oriented. Many have been hit by cutbacks in government grants or subsidies, rising operating costs, more value-conscious clients, and more competition for sponsorship revenue. They have been forced to become more professional and aggressive in finding resources and more efficient in their use. Those who manage money best are likely to prosper, while others face increased uncertainty and possible decline. One of the more important consequences is the trend for event organizations to hire full-time "development" or fund-raising professionals.

By 2003 most economists believed that the economy was bouncing back and growth could again be sustained. Then SARS hit, particularly damaging tourism and events in Canada and parts of Asia. Again, everyone was forced to adjust to a shock to the economic system. Accordingly, we should all be cautious about overoptimism, and we need to be prepared for the possibility of more nasty surprises. What recent events should have taught us all is that the worst case scenario can happen—so how can you be prepared?

The changing nature of work is an economic force to consider. Cetron and Davies (2001), writing in *The Futurist* magazine, predicted that by 2005, 83% of American management personnel will be "knowledge workers" (many more people will be choosing home or part-at-home work arrangements). A greater proportion of the workforce has flexible conditions, including hours of work, working at home, and seasonal jobs. Some of these are not by choice, but many flex-workers will take nontraditional times for business and entertainment events. They are used to shopping on line and will be aggressive in looking for information about event options.

Education is the best predictor of participation in the arts (discussed later) and many other cultural pursuits. Education levels have continued to rise, so that all around the world there is an educated population willing and able to participate in leisure and travel. Online programs make it possible for everyone with access to a computer to receive the education and training they need. The Internet is also a major source of empowerment because of the ready available of information and opinion.

Cetron and Davies (2001) spoke of the increasing proportion of people engaged in retraining at any time. Consequently, more adult education and lifelong learning are necessary. But the rising cost and speed of education and specialist training is an issue, with implications for meeting and exhibition planners in particular. Demand for these events is spurred by the need for quicker and more efficient dissemination of products and ideas, leading to competition between events and electronic communications.

We have entered the era of The Experience Economy, according to Pine and Gilmore (1999). Retailers have discovered what event managers knew all along—that people will pay for fulfilling and unique experiences that engage not only all the senses but challenge the mind as well. One implication is that event producers can presumably get more work in the retail sector. Another possible effect is that consumers in general will become much more demanding of events of all kinds, expecting more unique and engaging experiences.

Population and Demographic Forces

The US population will likely be 350 million in 2025, and it will be a country in which no one racial or ethnic group dominates (Wellner, 2003). In particular, the number of Asians and Hispanics will have doubled. Increasing political power comes with population growth, and increasing economic power comes from rising living standards among visible groups. Leisure and travel preferences are in part culturally determined and marketers are increasingly sensitive to the differences. The Travel Industry of America report on minority travelers (2001) found a significant increase in travel by minority Americans. Non-Hispanic whites have the highest participation in the arts (National Endowment for the Arts, 2002). This topic is also discussed later.

Many demographic forecasts made in the 1980s and 1990s were accurate: that over half of all married couples would be dual income in the year 2000, families headed by women would continue to grow, and the average household would be smaller than ever (U.S. Travel Data Center 1989). The majority of American families now have no children at home, and a significant decline in married couples occurred.

Gender-specific differences apply to many of the leisure and tourism trends discussed in this chapter. Importantly, women in general are more likely to be interested in arts and cultural events (National Endowment for the Arts, 2002) and men are more interested in sport, although overgeneralizations have to be avoided. More men travel to business events, but the female business traveler is an important and growing segment. Cleanliness, safety, and appearance are more important to women when selecting accommodations, and these preferences might apply to other purchases and activities.

Gender-specific events are a small minority (e.g., bridal shows, female and male sports, women's investment conferences, gay and lesbian events) but are likely to increase in number and significance. Gay and lesbian travel is already accepted as an important tourist segment in many destinations, and some of the events generate major economic impacts (e.g., Sydney;s annual Gay and Lesbian Mardi Gras).

Age is obviously important to all forms of leisure and travel consumption. European, North American, and many other countries are getting older! The median age of adult Americans increased from 42 to 45 years of age between 1992 and 2002. The proportion of the adult population aged 25–34 declined 5% (National Endowment for the Arts, 2002). This aging of the population has profound implications that event managers have to take into account.

A "life stage" approach focuses on how the interests and activities of individuals and families change as they go through distinct life stages, namely childhood, young single adult, family, empty nesters (the kids have left home), and the elderly (these can all be subdivided). A generational approach looks at similarities of age "cohorts" with names like Generation Y and the Baby Boomers. In this section we will combine elements of both.

Analysis made in "Discover America 2000" (U.S. Travel Data Center, 1989) related to generational groups thought to be important for shaping trends into the next century (Table 3.1). Other good sources on demographic forces and trends are the books *American Generations* by Susan Mitchell (2000) and *Kidfluence* by Anne Sutherland and Beth Thompson (2003).

Today's Children

Children have more money than ever, and are permitted to spend it on their own preferences (Sutherland & Thompson, 2003). Marketers know that kids and youth respond well to popular brands, such as running shoes, soft drinks, and equipment. Television shows and entertainment are specifically aimed at youth to capture their immediate spending and longer term loyalty. They are media savvy, but skeptical, so advertisers must gain credibility (such as through celebrity endorsements).

Youth today are more technologically sophisticated than their parents, and are more connected to the whole world. Because technology changes constantly, many new opportunities exist for communications, learning, and entertainment targeted at their interests

Table 3.1. American Generations

Generation	Born	Age in 2005	Formative Years
World War 1	pre-1924	82+	pre-1936
Depression	1924–1934	71–81	1936–1946
World War II babies	1935–1945	60–70	1947–1957
Early Baby Boomers	1946–1954	51–59	1958–1966
Late Boomers	1955–1964	41–50	1967–1976
Baby Bust (Gen X)	1965–1976	29–40	1977–1988
Echo Boom (Gen Y)	1977–1994	12–28	1989–2000

Source: U.S. Travel Data Center (1989) (updated to 2005).

and needs. They spend a great deal of time plus their money (and their parents') on this technology for home entertainment. On the other hand, they tend to be overscheduled by their school obligations and parents who want their kids to be involved in sports and cultural pursuits, so kids are out of the home more than ever.

The "Echo Boom" or Generation Y

- Born: 1977–1994; aged 12–28 in 2005.
- Three times the size of Generation X.
- Almost one quarter of the US population.

These are the children of Baby Boomers, hence the Echo Baby Boom label, but Mitchell (2000) called this cohort "Millenial Generation" because they were growing up around the turn of the century. This generation is as large as the original boom generation (see below), although a substantial portion of this younger cohort are recent immigrants. According to Mitchell they are opinionated consumers and already exert an influence on music, sports, computers, and video games. Whereas most "boomers" had comfortable postwar upbringings, the "echo boomers" face a tougher economic challenge. Well-paying, secure jobs with good career prospects are much harder to get and hold, and the cost of education is ever-increasing. Socially, this generation must wrestle with the specter of aids, high divorce rates, crime, and violence. Nontraditional families are much more common. Many have been raised by single parents and women who work.

Mitchell (2000) observed that they share many of the same values as their Boomer parents, but are more liberal than Generation X. They are culturally and racially diverse and are a highly segmented market. Sport participation, health-related activity, and advanced education for females, as well as political activism, have all increased with this cohort. Martin and Tulgan (2001) examined Generation Y in detail, finding that they differed substantially from the previous generation. Generation Y youth were depicted as upbeat and full of positive self-esteem, valuing tolerance, education, and diversity. They are socially conscious and are likely to become volunteers.

Teens are mostly in school, which defines their peer group, and at home, which results in the usual intergenerational conflicts. Because these are difficult, stressful years, the rates of rebellion and depression are both high. Engaging social programs, rewarding educational events, and challenging physical activities are needed but not always available in communities. This is a major social challenge for events professionals.

Teenagers were the subject of an internationally comparative study by Elissa Moses (2000). Six value segments were identified, each with marketing implications. "Thrills-and-

Chills" teens were described as hedonist, sensualists, and free spenders who value music and love to attend concerts. In contrast, the "Resigned" have low expectations for their futures, are alienated, prefer heavy metal and grunge music, and do little in the way of attending cultural events. When it comes to entertainment and event preferences, it is clearly wrong to think of teenagers (or any other age-defined segment) as an undifferentiated group.

Young singles in higher education will be acquiring knowledge and preferences to last a lifetime. Participation in many types of sports is directly correlated with sport experiences at college, and educational attainment is directly correlated with participation in the arts. However, there is often a lag between educational completion and arts attendance. Arts participation rises gradually between the ages of mid-30s and mid-60s, then falls off sharply (National Endowment for the Arts, 2002). Working singles have money, are independent minded, and most likely to travel for fun rather than business. This is often translated into event attendance and event tourism.

The "Baby Bust" or Generation X

- Born: 1965–1976.
- About 16% of the US population in 2002.

This generation of young adults has been raised, for the most part, with considerable materialism, technology, and expensive tastes; it is a generation that loves to shop for designer clothes and high-tech items. On the other hand, many of this generation were raised in single-parent families and had to work hard to get money. Many of them lived at home a long time because it was too expensive to go out on their own. It is also a very multicultural generation, at least in North America, with a large proportion coming from immigration.

"Gen X" are mostly well educated in terms of the length of time spent in school and college, but there has been criticism of the quality of their education. Mitchell (2000) described Gen Xers as being well educated, media savvy, cynical, and self-reliant. This cohort also stayed at home longer, but they are not as well off economically because of the shift from manufacturing to lower-paid service jobs. Marriage comes later than for previous generations, if at all, and both partners will likely be working—with children delayed a long time.

Cetron and Davies (2001) said that for Generation X, the post-Baby Boom generation, "work is only a means to their ends: money, fun, and leisure." They also suggested that Generation Xers and the younger "dot.com" generation (a term that already seems dated, giving the collapse of the dot.com bubble at the turn of the century) thrive on challenge, opportunity, training, and whatever else will prepare them for their next career move. They are not loyal to specific employers.

Generation X is very comfortable making bookings online, so web-based marketing will reach them. They are in the peak years for taking business trips and adding short family vacations to them.

Baby Boomers

- Born: 1946–1954 (early boomers); 1955– 1965 (late boomers).
- 28% of US population in 2002.

"Early" Baby Boomers, born between 1946 and 1954 in the US, will be aged 51–59 and in their peak earning years by 2005. Most boomers are married, with two-income families, but soon the children of early boomers will have moved on, the parents will have time and energy for leisure and travel. Late boomers, born between 1955 and 1964, are now well into the family and career establishment years. As this combined "big generation" ages, the whole pattern of family, work, and leisure shifts with it.

A high percentage of Baby Boomers are well educated, career oriented, and upwardly mobile. In the 1980s and 1990s this phenomenon was associated with smaller families, more women in the labor force (especially in the professions and nontraditional jobs), and more single-parent families. Nevertheless, boomers are predominantly family oriented and are responsible for the large "echo boom."

The "boomers" tastes are different from past generations, and they demand more for their investment of time and money. Parents with only one or two children tend to pamper the kids, take them traveling, and teach them their tastes in higher culture. A whole new leisure industry responded, with dance, music, and art classes, with computer and drama camps, with the best in athletic equipment and training.

Baby Boomers are the biggest and most affluent part of the North American travel market (Travel Industry Association of America, 2003), and while they travel more than other cohorts for business purposes, they are also likely to have at least one child along on a household trip. Favorite travel activities include shopping, outdoor pursuits, visiting heritage sites or museums, going to the beach, attending cultural events, and visiting national and state parks. Married-couple households are the most likely to take vacations. Those with children will likely have much different travel (e.g., more likely to travel by car) and event-going behavior, as kids are often a primary factor when selecting destinations, trip styles, and activities. Childless couples are a major travel and leisure segment, and have more choices and probably more disposable income. They fly more than families do.

As they age, older "boomers" will desire upscale resorts combining less strenuous recreation (such as golf), second homes, and cultural events. "Late boomers" will be very active in business travel, travel with children, weekend getaways, winter trips, and city destinations. Specialty travel linked to hobbies and avocations are popular. All these trends bode well for festivals and events, particularly in the cultural field, off-season, and at resorts.

The "Empty Nesters" stage occurs when the last child has left home, and this is already happening for early boomers. Couples suddenly have less parental responsibility, they have pent-up demand for their own leisure and travel preferences, and probably have more disposable income. Mature travelers (aged 55+) are more likely to attend cultural events or festivals, visit friends and relatives, and drive themselves. Business travel is much less for this age group (The 2002 Travel and Leisure Market Research Handbook, p. 93). Arts participation peaks between the ages of 45 and 64 (National Endowment for the Arts, 2002).

The Elderly

- Persons aged 65+ constituted about 12% of US population, some 36 million in 2002.
- Wellner (2003) predicted that by 2025 the US will have 70 million seniors aged 65+.

The first "boomers" turned 50 in the late 1990s, and they will be retiring in huge numbers by 2010. This will be the fastest growing cohort in North American populations right up to 2025, so there will be many more than today. But truly spectacular growth is occurring in the older age categories past retirement. Those aged 65 and up constituted 12.4% of the American population in 2000, but will become 16% by 2020. The proportion of elderly will be even higher in Europe (e.g., 20% in Germany) and Japan (27%) by 2020.

The elderly of today are different from previous generations. They are much more likely to be:

- healthy enough for travel and many recreational activities;
- wealthy enough to spend on whatever they want, including entertainment;
- demanding of high-quality services;
- nostalgic, preferring familiar things.

The elderly are living longer and healthier lives, resulting in increased demand for all kinds of leisure and travel experiences. On the other hand, many will want to keep working, but on their terms (perhaps at home, or seasonally). Health and security are much more important issues to the elderly, so events have to create both the reality and perception of being elderly friendly. As various disabilities and frailties increase with age, attention to many different special needs is required.

Grandparents play a special role in the events field, as they will often be the ones to provide the money or baby-sitting necessary for kids and families to get out of the house. More specifically, it has been shown that grandparents are especially instrumental in sport event tourism (discussed later).

Influence of the Media

Special-interest audiences are large enough, and many are rich enough, to warrant programming or magazines aimed specifically at narrow interests (called "narrow-casting"). This is especially true in sports, hobbies, and entertainment, and it has helped to generate demand for new special events: tournaments for every sport; shows for every hobby; conventions on every conceivable topic; festivals to package all forms of art and entertainment.

More and more "media events" will become desirable and feasible within event tourism and place marketing strategies. People do not have to travel to a destination to be interested in the events it produces, but watching those events on television is bound to influence decisions regarding travel—to see the event in person perhaps, or to see the destination because event coverage makes it look appealing. According to Gratton and Kokolakakis (1997), the biggest single change in sports has been the dramatic rise in revenues from television broadcast rights, and this in part reflects the increase in dedicated sport channels on television. Global live coverage of events helps fuel interest and increases audience numbers for advertisers, while the elevation of athletes to superstar status generates even more media coverage and merchandising.

Technology Forces

New technology leads to new leisure pursuits, and has created the entire computer-based game sector. Technological innovations affect managers directly, especially to increase productivity and competitive advantages. In the events sector, technology also affects consumers—both in terms of their expectations for high-tech services and their interest in technology itself. For example, ticketing at events is increasingly becoming computerized, enabling better control and detailed accounting of sales. Use of "smart cards" (similar to direct debit cards from banks) is being introduced, potentially resulting in the cashless event. Consumers expect to be able to make bookings online.

By the turn of the century the world was already accustomed to the Internet and experiencing a revolution in integrated, wireless communications. Access to the Internet increased dramatically throughout North America and other wealthy nations during the 1990s, and is approaching saturation levels; it will soon be as common as television, and often part of an integrated home entertainment and information system. Cetron and Davies (2001) forecast that 80% of US homes will have computers by 2005.

Observers such as Laermer (2002) believe that television, home entertainment in general, and computers with Internet in particular, are resulting in less and less interaction among people and thereby causing social and psychological disfunctioning. People need to interact at the micro and macro scales; events are ways in which people have always gotten together to share, and that is more important now than ever.

Marketing with the aid of computer databases is now commonplace. Desktop publishing means that any event can prepare and mass produce its own communications, or have them faxed in batches overnight. Technological advances also make it possible to ensure higher levels of safety and health standards, and consumers expect fewer and less serious problems as a result. Event consumer surveys are being conducted using hand-held computers with wireless connections to a central computer where analysis can be completed almost instantly.

Technological themes should be expanded in the event sector. Trade fairs and exhibitions with technology themes are common enough, but technology-themed festivals are few and far between. Nostalgia for old cars and trains is fine, but what about celebrating leading-edge technologies?

There is a risk in using technology only for spectacular effects, as seems to be the trend at many events. The combination of lasers, huge sound systems, and other techniques always attracts attention, but what else does it accomplish? Gregson (1992) had these thoughts on the subject: "I must not lose sight of how high-tech elements focus the purpose of an event rather than hide its lack of content" (p. 31). Technology can overwhelm events and keep people from participating or feeling ownership.

Two other considerations for managers are related to technology. Information databases are essential tools for management and marketing, but how secure are they? Information and communications must be protected against theft or unauthorized use, and the privacy of personal information must be respected.

"Virtual meetings" are not only technological feasible in all parts of the world, but rising costs and fears about travel and security have brought renewed interest in alternative delivery systems (Testa, 2002) such as teleconferencing and videoconferencing. Convention centers are increasingly viewed as "information ports" with satellite and Internet broadcasts of meetings in order to extend their reach. Clients are increasingly concerned about the "cost of proficiency" regarding education and training, so Internet-based delivery systems look appealing. Webcasts can be live presentations to a group, video presentations, or include varying degrees of interactivity.

Will these forces put the meeting planners and convention/exhibition centers of the world out of business? A Center for Exhibition Industry Research news release (March 26, 2003) proclaimed "nothing could be further from the truth." Their research confirmed that face-to-face interaction was vital in the marketing process. But professionals and venues will have to adapt. Increasingly, the event manager has to be competent in technological solutions to a variety of problems.

Cultural Forces

Many communities, regions, and nations have become increasingly multicultural through immigration, differential birth rates, and changing values, which have resulted in greater emphasis on heritage. For events, these shifts present numerous challenges and opportunities, especially as they are linked with other important segmentation variables like age, family composition, education, and income. Cultural diversity is increasingly accepted as being the norm in North America. The future is certainly one in which no one group dominates, and the term "minority" will be obsolete. People will be identified more by their interests.

Growing cultural diversity means that organizations have to examine their composition, values, and activities—in short, do a cultural sensitivity audit. Events must be proactive to meet the needs of economically and physically disadvantaged persons, and to ensure cultural or racial equality. It is now expected that serious efforts will be made to correct imbalances and avoid any degree of discrimination. Prevailing values now require that all events be environmentally friendly, and hopefully proactive about "green" management and operations. More environmentally themed events can be expected, linked perhaps to ecotourism, conservation areas, and special-interest groups devoted to nature conservation. Sponsors want to be associated with "green" products and can help provide the cash or technology to improve environmental practices.

The family is alive and well, and will continue to be a force shaping entertainment and participatory events. Corporations still want to reach the family through event marketing. Two-income families are the norm, so finding "quality time" is still a challenge. Many college-leavers return home for a time, as do children experiencing lifestyle and relationship changes, so families are more fluid than ever. Same-sex and single-parent families are no longer unusual.

Cetron and Davies (2001) believed that societal values are changing rapidly. This is in response to changing demographics, technological advances, and educational attainment. As the Baby Boom generation ages, there has to be more emphasis placed on the values and preferences of younger adults and youth, so that will also hasten value shifts. What should we expect?

Cetron and Davies (2001) also argued that consumerism is on the increase, especially because of networking and communication advances. As well, young people are motivated to become financially secure and wealthy. Gender issues have not disappeared, but considerable progress has been made in realizing equality between males and females. Women are much more of a force in shaping entertainment trends and in selecting travel destinations. Women are well connected on the web and in the workforce.

Trends in Leisure and Recreation

Has leisure time decreased? James Gleick (2000), author of the influential book *Faster: The Acceleration of Just About Everything*, argued that because things can get done very quickly, especially with instant, global communications, everyone now expects everything to be done at once. That puts a lot of time pressure on organizations and individuals, leading to stress in both.

People need to slow down—a lot. But multitasking or "polyphasing" has become the norm for active people. Mobile telephones and Internet connections, home and portable computers, and wireless "hotspots" all make it easy—too easy—to combine work with everything, or to bring one's private life into the work environment.

The World Tourism Organization (1999) report, *Changes in Leisure Time*, noted that workers everywhere are putting in more hours, while increases in the proportion of women who work meant less family leisure time was available. In many countries the time required for commuting has been increasing significantly, resulting in even further erosion of time for preferred activities.

Cetron and Davies (2001) reported that American workers are spending 10% more time on the job than a decade previously, contributing to a high-pressure environment. Time-pressured people want more simplification in their lives, and an occasional taste of luxury. "Wellness" has become a big policy issue. In fact, leisure is more and more viewed as a health-related field (Kraus, 2000).

In Canada, the "National Work-Life Conflict Study for Health Canada" (Higgins & Duxbury, 2001) reported that almost 60% of Canadians who are employed outside the home cannot balance work and family demands. Technology has not freed us but enslaved us, resulting in longer working hours—even though some of it is outside the place of employment. The average work week for professionals is up to 50 hours! The 25–44 age cohort feels they have the least amount of leisure time.

Jacobs and Gerson (2001) concluded from their analysis that it has not been a change in work hours but the trend toward two-income families and single-parent households that is most responsible for problems in balancing work and family. Employed couples, professionals in particular, put in very long workweeks. Women are increasingly finding it difficult to juggle career and family obligations. One solution is a more flexible workplace.

One effect of all the time pressures we face will be to enhance the value of events that maximize social and family togetherness, fun, learning, and consumption all at once. For harried people, time is the most important asset and event managers must not waste it. As well, a taste of luxury has great appeal. Events catering to the occasional need to splurge will find a ready market.

Trends in Leisure and Cultural Pursuits

The impact of technology on leisure habits is amazing. Between 1996 and 2001, spending by Americans on video and audio goods, along with computers and software for home uses, grew to dominate recreation spending. They accounted for 23.7% of total recreation spending, a gain of over 18%. Spending on tickets to performing arts declined from 1.9% to 1.3% of total recreation spending. Over the same 6-year period spending on spectator sport events declined from 1.6% to 1.3% (National Endowment for the Arts, 2002).

The Bureau of Economic Analysis reported that American consumers spent $10.6 billion on performing arts events in 2001. That was almost $2 billion more than on movie tickets and $500 million more than on spectator-sport events (reported by the National Endowment for the Arts, 2002).

The National Endowment for the Arts conducts regular research, and of particular interests are results of its 2002 Survey of Public Participation in the Arts (http://www.arts.gov/pub/ResearchNotes.html):

- Nearly one third of American adults reported going to at least one jazz, classical music, opera, musical, play or ballet performance during the 12 months preceding August 2002 (not including elementary or high school performances).
- One quarter said they had visited an art gallery or art museum.
- Growth in attendance since 1992 had been considerable, but largely due to population growth rather than an increase in the participation rate.
- Counting all forms of participation, 76% of American adults made the arts a part of their lives.
- Art/craft fairs and festivals attracted 33.4% of adults, 7% below 1992 (possibly due to September 11th and a decline in travel).
- Wmen had higher attendance rates except for jazz, which is about equal; females accounted for almost 70% of ballet goers and 60% of attendees at musicals, plays, and arts/craft fairs.
- "Non-Hispanic whites" had the highest participation rates.

- Non-Hispanic African Americans had the highest attendance at jazz concerts.
- Age, income, and particularly education are better predictors than race/ethnicity when it comes to arts attendance.
- Higher incomes do translate into higher participation, but education is actually more important.
- Those with incomes below $30,000 (in 2002) were underrepresented at art events.
- In keeping with the aging of the population overall, arts attendees grew older between 1992 and 2002; the median age of adults attending classical music was highest, at 49 years; for jazz it was the lowest, at 43 years of age; the proportion of young attending arts was lower.
- Participation rates are highest for those with college and graduate school education (e.g., graduates had 5 times the participation at classical music concerts than high school graduates); jazz has a higher appeal than the other art forms for those with only high school education.

Sport Participation Trends

A surge in female sport participation (especially in soccer) is one of the most notable trends documented by The Association of the Sports Product Industry in their major 2002 study called "U.S., Trends in Team Sports" (see: www.sgma.com). Girls represented 41.5% of all high school varsity athletes. The study also revealed a number of impediments to participation in organized sports, including substantial growth in informal action sports, a loss of free time to scheduled activities, more electronic diversions, and the decline of physical education in schools.

American Sports Data, Inc. (www.americansportsdata.com) in 2002 also reported the impressive growth of action or extreme sports over the previous several years. Their "Superstudy of Sports Participation" nevertheless found that participation rates in team sports are still dominant, including the trendy ones like soccer, lacrosse, and fast-pitch softball. Generation Y is fuelling the action-sport surge, with a notable propensity for thrills and risk taking. These Generation Y action sports are often solitary and encompass a freedom from regimentation and authority. "Coolness" is all.

Additional sport trends are covered under Tourism Trends, and physical fitness is covered under Health Issues, below.

Health Issues

Worry about disease and personal safety while attending events and traveling has increased dramatically in recent years. Consequently, events must be made safer and customers must perceive them to be refuges from the troubling world of everyday life. Places that offer safe events will become more attractive.

Events will have to offer healthier choices and be wary of alcohol consumption. There is a growing antialcohol movement, linked to events by way of corporate sponsorship as well as the abuses of alcohol observed at many events. In the case of Cinco de Mayo it also has a strong cultural connection, and has engendered considerable debate. "Since 1997, Latinos & Latinas for Health Justice (formerly California Latino Leadership United for Healthy Communities) has been involved in the 'Cinco de Mayo Con Orgullo' (With Pride) statewide campaign to combat the abuses of the alcohol industry in relation to this important cultural holiday" (quoted from: www.cal-lluhc.org/cinco/index.html).

The Centers for Disease Control in 2001 determined that 21% of the US population is obese and the percentage of overweight children had nearly doubled since the early 1980s (reported by American Sports Data). The American Obesity Association (www.obesity.org)

reported that diabetes, hypertension, and other obesity-related chronic diseases that are prevalent among adults have now become more common in youngsters. The percentage of children and adolescents who are overweight and obese is now higher than ever before. Poor dietary habits and inactivity are reported to contribute to the increase of obesity in youth. Today's youth are considered the most inactive generation in history caused in part by reductions in school physical education programs and unavailable or unsafe community recreational facilities.

According to the 1998/99 National Population Health Survey (Statistics Canada), 58% of Canadian youth aged 12–19 were physically inactive in the 3 months prior to the survey. However, as many as 84% may not have been active enough to meet international guidelines for optimal growth and development. Girls are significantly less active than boys, with 64% of girls and 52% of boys being considered physically inactive. In addition, youth living in higher income families are the least likely to be physically inactive (44% versus between 57% and 67% for other income levels).

As Baby Boomers age there is great demand for health and fitness programs and clubs, not to mention plastic surgery. But American Sports Data, Inc. reports that frequent fitness activity peaked in 1990 and has remained level in terms of numbers, so that on a per capita basis there has been an actual decline of 15%—but a decline of 41% for children aged 6–17! (www.americansportsdata.com/pr_10-01-03.asp).

What is needed, clearly, is more emphasis on physical fitness and health by governments and the educational establishment. Events can do their part by getting people active and eating/drinking responsibly. Overconsumption is one factor that has to be dealt with, yet how many special events educate patrons about the quality and quantity of food? Corporations are now adapting to public demand for healthier foods, so events can expect to be able to negotiate with food and beverage sponsors to further this important cause.

Laermer (2002) believed that spirituality in many forms is on the increase. Sadness and stress lead to anxiety and an inability to cope with the modern world, so people turn to religion or other forms of metaphysical support. They also turn to mind and body-oriented programs and facilities (from yoga and the martial arts to spas and detoxification clinics) that can nurture the whole person. Self-fulfilling leisure and travel emerge from this force, so that many people are searching for experiences that satisfy the needs of mind and body.

Urban Conditions

Most people in the industrialized world live in cities or may be considered urbanized in their outlook and lifestyles. Over 80% of Americans live in metropolitan areas; what happens to and within cities affects most people directly, and the rest indirectly. The range of urban lifestyles is great, but there are commonalities that affect everyone: increasing congestion and commuting times, pollution, crime, social tension, and a declining sense of community on the negative side; enhanced arts, cultural, leisure and entertainment opportunities, and new forms of relationships and economic possibilities on the positive side.

In America the flight to the suburbs, out into the country, and into the sunbelt and "lifestyle resort zones" has continued, leaving many inner cities poor. Rich enclaves and gated communities are commonplace. This movement is in part attributable to lower costs, to antiurban attitudes, and to retirement communities. It has the effect, especially in the US, of reinforcing social divisions based on race and wealth.

The majority of neighborhood and community festivals or events are celebrations of the special character of urban life. Some are intended to strengthen community pride or a sense of place; others are linked to ethnicity and special interests. Larger, city-wide events usually have multiple purposes. They are flourishing in cities active in urban renewal and redevelopment schemes. They are more obvious tourist attractions, and tourism is generally viewed as a means to help revitalize decayed or underutilized inner areas. Many are linked directly to major arts, cultural, sporting, and shopping facilities, which in themselves are attractions, but are static without festivals and events.

Throughout the 1980s and 1990s, American cities in particular engaged in urban redevelopment schemes that "put a heavy emphasis on sports, entertainment and tourism as a source of revenue for the cities" (Sports Business Market Research, Inc., 2000, p. 167). And according to Gratton and Kokolakakis (1997), in the UK "sports events are currently the main platform for economic regeneration in many cities." Whitson and Macintosh (1996) argued that countries and major cities compete for mega sport events in order to demonstrate to the world their "modernity and economic dynamism." To those authors, international sport "has become one of the most powerful and effective vehicles for the showcasing of place and for the creation of what the industry calls 'destination image' " (p. 279). This force reflects the growing integration of news, entertainment and promotion. Cities have to "position" themselves as service centers, places for entertainment and shopping, because their manufacturing sectors are no longer vital.

Indianapolis is widely acknowledged as being a sport tourism success story. Rozin (2000) termed it a "classic case" of civic turnaround, based first on the efforts of a newly established Indiana Sports Corporation to attract amateur sport governing bodies after 1978. Massive infrastructure development followed, aided by the private Lilly Endowment, pumping $884 million into sport facilities between 1979 and 1984. This helped make the city attractive for other corporate headquarters. Indianapolis expected to gain some $304 million from sport events in the year 2000.

Environmental Forces

Although people are more environmentally aware than ever, it is clear that industrialized societies are not engaging in sustainable development. All too often we equate "development" with growth indicators like jobs, wealth, and trade instead of quality of life, equity among all people, and environmental integrity. Continued population growth, and urbanization, means that resource scarcity and conflicts will increase. The costs and benefits of growth will have to be scrutinized more carefully (Wellner, 2003). One implication is that major events will have to justify themselves in terms of resource consumption and conduct environmental impact assessments.

All events must become environmentally responsible and practice "green management." One example of how the momentum is growing is that of Green Festivals (www.greenfestivals.com). "This two-day event that brings together green entrepreneurs, environmental community organizations, and the growing sector of the general public that is interested in creating an alternative to the corporate-dominated, profit-at-all-costs economy. The Green Festival will bring and connect groups and individuals who share a desire to build an alternative economy, but may not have had the forum to work together."

Study Questions

- What are all the ways that planning occurs in event management?
- How is planning related to leadership, decision making, and policies?
- Explain the project planning process.
- Show how to conduct a detailed work breakdown for an event.
- What and how are feasibility studies completed?
- When do you use PERT instead of CPA?
- How and why is a SWOT analysis done?

- What is project creep?
- What is a Gantt chart used for?
- Why is a business plan useful for all events?
- Outline a strategic planning process, including definitions of mission/mandate, visioning, and goals.
- What are the main PEST forces acting on the events sector?

Advanced Study Questions

- Select one or more key forces affecting the events sector and show how they will impact on demand, marketing, organization, or other management functions. Provide local evidence of trends in the events world that are related to global forces.
- Discuss some of the issues that arise when planning an event under time pressure, with particular reference to resources, costs, and quality. Find real-world examples.
- Prepare an outline business plan for a proposed event, including the concept and a tentative budget.
- Analyze an existing, long-established event, from the perspectives of its life cycle, organizational culture, and strategic planning, to explain its success.

Chapter 4

Site Planning, Operations, and Logistics

Learning Objectives

- Be able to develop an attractive and effective site or venue plan appropriate to the event and its environment.
- Be able to understand the processes and management systems necessary to produce the desired event program and experience, according to schedule and within budget.
- Be able to use logistics to ensure that all people and materials are delivered to the right place, on time, according to plan.
- Be able to use appropriate techniques to schedule the event.
- Be able to make all events sustainable, in part by implementing "green operations."

Planning the Venue or Site

This chapter is concerned with actual design and production of the event: how the site will look and function (i.e., site planning), how management systems will directly affect the event program and customer's experience (operations), and how people and materials—everything needed for event production—will be delivered on time at the right place (logistics). The final section covers sustainable events and "green" operations.

Generic Types of Event Settings

There are a number of generic event settings related to the nature of the event.

Assembly

Conventions, concerts, festivals, and spectator sports—any event bringing together large numbers of people—require facilities or outdoor settings suitable for viewing and listening. The event manager can often rent venues that have their own management systems, including convention centers, hotel ballrooms, exposition halls, concert halls, auditoria, and arenas. Later we look at "festival places" as a special case of assembly.

Procession

Parades, flotillas, cavalcades marches, and other similar events are linear, mobile forms of entertainment, spectacle, or ritual with special design and management requirements. The audience might be standing, seated, or moving along with the procession. The most common linear setting, however, is a street with a static audience along the route. Some processions pass through seating areas and even stadia, where they take on the form of theater.

Linear-Nodal

Many sport events involve races or other linear forms of activity, including long-distance multisport events, which combine procession with nodes of activity. Usually the audience congregates at the nodes, such as start, finish, and transition points.

Open Space

Frequently events make use of parks, plazas, and closed-off streets. Free movement is a feature of these settings, but they usually also contain subareas for assembly, procession, and exhibition/sales. Gregson (1992) gave advice on using sidewalks, streets, and buildings to stage events, noting that architects generally fail to take account of seasonal changes and the needs of public gatherings.

Exhibition/Sales

These settings are designed to entice entry and circulation, browsing, and sales. Sometimes the audience merely views the exhibits, at others sales are made. Food and beverage concessions are often in this form.

Activities

Sports and other activities often require purpose-built facilities, although many can be integrated within other settings.

Most events require a range of support spaces and facilities, and the need for any of these (based on Korza & Magie, 1989) will in part determine the appropriateness of the setting:

- entrances and exits, ticketing, greeting, waiting;
- storage, utilities, security, lost and found;
- cooking, eating, concessions;
- communications and media, information;
- dressing and rehearsal;
- hospitality, comfort;
- washrooms, toilets, showers;
- first aid, emergency crews, emergency access/egress;
- repairs and equipment;
- waste storage and disposal, recycling;
- administration;
- parking, drop-off zone, shuttle routes.

Whatever the setting, it must be planned with many or all of the above functions integrated or nearby. The manger cannot assume that all venues provide or are capable of providing all the spaces and services needed by a given type of event.

Location

A number of important locational factors must be considered, starting with "visibility." For attracting customers, high visibility might be a key factor in choosing the event location. This is more important for open air events and parades, whereas indoor events rely more on consumer knowledge of the venue and its accessibility (including parking). Certain types of events want high visibility for the media, rather than on-site audiences. Choosing a parade route, for example, involves determination of the photogenic backdrops and optimal broadcasting viewpoints. Many races require special types of beginning, ending, and transition points.

The more spontaneous the decision to attend, the more likely it is that visibility will influence customers. Passers-by, or even those planning to attend, should not be able to observe something that might dissuade them from attending. Rather, they should get easy visibility of some of the event's ambience and attractions.

Accessibility

How customers reach the event (e.g., by car, bus or train), and the volume and timing of each type, will help determine suitable locations. As well, the location should be capable of handling surplus demand, such as through the provision of back-up parking areas. Large sport and entertainment facilities usually have adequate parking and public transport, but many parks and street settings do not. If accessibility is anticipated to be a problem, events will have to provide their own shuttle services from parking areas or public transport stations. If tourists are targeted, easy connections to airports, freeways, and public transport terminals are essential.

Centrality

Organizers often prefer a central location within the community to maximize accessibility, visibility, and other factors. Geographic analysis could be performed to determine just how central and accessible various locations are, relative to target markets. Other considerations are political and symbolic. Central locations, close to or using civic facilities, might be favored by politicians, whereas the business community might prefer main streets or shopping centers.

Clustering

Centrality usually leads to clustering, which is the association of events with other attractions and services. Events on a city's waterfront or within the tourist business district will likely maximize clustering and therefore offer the customer more to see and do in the area. This is more important for tourist markets than locals, especially because many visitors might not know about the event in advance and will gravitate to areas where attractions, services, and events are concentrated.

Appropriateness

Streets are often used for parades and community festivals, but the manager must ask how appropriate it is to close off and divert traffic. Will a safety hazard be created? Will businesses on the street suffer? These issues can quickly become political. Public parks are easy choices, but are certain activities appropriate for all parks? An environmental, social, and economic impact analysis should be undertaken when evaluating potential locations and venues. Some events by their nature result in noise, congestion, trampling, unruly behavior, litter, bright lights, etc.

Cost

Many event locational decisions are made on the basis of cost, especially if rental fees must be paid. Some related costs, such as security, communications, or utilities, could be impacted by locational decisions. Also, the cost to consumers in terms of driving time, transport, or parking charges should be considered.

Support Services

Are all necessary services and functions in place or must the event provide them? A location with all the utilities and services at hand will be less expensive and easier to use than a site without them.

Atmosphere and Image

Historic districts, waterfronts, natural areas, and gardens all have an ambience suitable for certain events, whereas streets, stadia, and other buildings provide the right atmosphere for others. The way in which people perceive an area (i.e., its image) might greatly influence attendance, although events are often used to help change negative images.

Site Planning Principles

There is much more to site planning than having someone prepare a hand-drawn sketch of the location. Many authorities will require a site plan for any outdoor event, even building permits for temporary structures. Beyond the purely legal considerations, the setting plays a very important part in creating the right atmosphere, and can be instrumental in maximizing sales by vendors and publicity for sponsors. Crowd behavior will also be determined in large part by design and related management systems.

Citrine (n.d.) suggested that site planning is as important to the event as programming, with customer reactions to the site being critical in determining success. To Citrine, the "wow factor" is a guiding principle: visitors should be dazzled when they arrive and leave. Site layout can also help generate revenues, such as through the channeling of people past and through food, beverage, and merchandizing areas.

Below, we look at legibility, capacity, traffic, crowd management and control, and special needs/accessibility.

Legibility

Event customers and guests should find the site to be "legible" (i.e., clear in its organization and meaning). This term has significance in the design of any service environment (Bateson, 1989), as customers usually arrive with an expectation of how the site should function. They develop such expectations through past experience at the event or other events and attractions, as certain conventions are followed. These conventions, such as the siting of information booths at entrances and meeting places in the center, differ from culture to culture.

Based on the pioneering work of Kevin Lynch (1960), a number of principles for maximizing legibility at events can be stated:

- use landmarks to improve orientation (e.g., world's fairs usually incorporate towers or tall, memorable buildings at the core);
- pathways (separate pedestrians from vehicles and connect paths in a logical pattern; avoid the maze effect; use signposting or other directional indicators like color-coded pavement; ensure visibility from paths towards landmarks);
- nodes (important assembly and activity points will naturally result in movement towards and through the node; ensure that key program areas are easily reached and that traffic can flow easily through or around them);
- edges (people understand that a site has limits, and these can be fixed barriers or more subtle but clear edges marked by signs, decoration, landscaping, or even activities; internal districts also need edges);
- districts (event settings are often easily subdivided into functional districts, such as amusements, different kinds of entertainment and activities, consumption, etc.); districts need edges (sometimes "hard," as in sound-proofed barriers, and sometimes "soft," as in visual cues; also use paths, nodes, and secondary landmarks to make districts unique but legible within the overall design).

Capacity

The term "design capacity" is used when the event managers consciously plan for a certain experience that requires limits to be imposed on the number of attendees. Events that permit, or even encourage, unlimited attendance invite serious problems. Congestion can lead to accidents and injury, stress, crowd problems, and even riots or stampedes. This is more a problem for outdoor festivals with no gates, as indoor venues will almost always have fixed capacities determined by fire and/or building codes. Some events must worry about catering to peak versus average attendance—sites that can comfortably handle 10,000 visitors over the day might be terribly congested if half of them show up all at once. There is a natural tendency to want to plan for the biggest possible crowd, but this strategy has higher costs and risks a substantial loss if the forecasts are not met.

Peak-time congestion at events is very common, usually because leisure activities are concentrated (especially on sunny, Sunday afternoons). If the site can handle only so many at peak times, efforts must be made through marketing to disperse attendance in time and/or space. Failing that, limits might have to be imposed. A sound strategy is to sell tickets or restrict attendance at gates (through line-ups or queuing), rather than risk disaster through overcrowding. Yet some events manage year after year with enormous crowds and everyone seems happy! Their managers obviously have the site and program well under control.

Generic capacity management strategies involving site design and other techniques were identified by Mowen, Vogelsong, and Graefe (2003):

- ticketing for the most popular activities (either to ration or regulate the timing of their use);
- spacing of activities and attractions (leave lots of room);
- ropes or gates around popular areas (physical barriers to use);
- informing people in line of the length of wait;
- refreshment sales for people in lines;
- entertainment for people in lines.

The importance and practice of capacity management was researched by Preda and Watts (2003) for an event venue.

Research Note

Preda, P., & Watts, T. (2003). Improving the efficiency of sporting venues through capacity management: The case of the Sydney (Australia) Cricket Ground Trust. *Event Management*, *8*(2), 83–89.

Surplus and constrained resources have to be identified and the implications managed. The amount of space available for event goers or activities is a capacity management issue, as is the lack of crucial resources or equipment to effectively produce the entertainment. A constraint might be external or internal, and it can be an absolute shortage or a "bottleneck" that impedes flow/shipment. At event venues a common bottleneck is the entry point, especially when combined with ticketing and the necessity for waiting (as opposed to unrestricted entry). When patrons prepurchase tickets there is a different entry flow. Other potential bottlenecks are: entry to seating time; seating to exiting; time spent at concessions, because these involve most or all guests. Some on-site measurements can determine the theoretical capacity of various parts of the venue, staff/volunteers, and subsystems, to be followed by measurements of actual efficiency during events. Solutions to bottlenecks include technological improvements (especially ticketing and food/beverage provision), staffing, and other management systems.

Crowd Management and Control

Why do some events lead to unruly behavior, and how can it be prevented? The site and venue have a large part to play in controlling or shaping behavior. Rutley (n.d.) distinguished between crowd management and crowd control. "Crowd control" entails directing or constraining and at events should normally be the function of police or trained security forces. More desirable are various forms of "crowd management," which include security measures and a number of site design and operational factors that do not entail force, and that enhance customer service and the overall event experience.

Two special event hazards are that of panic, leading to stampedes and possibly crushes against barriers. Berlonghi (1991) stated that panic stems from perceived or real threats, and can be attributed to communications problems or other management failures. Sometimes an act of violence leads to panic, and certainly fear of fire can do so. Berlonghi identified eight types of crowd and related characteristics to help managers identify potential problems and related management and security needs.

One key design factor is the difference in behavior that results from requiring crowds to sit, as opposed to standing and moving about. The combination of seating and separation of fans from different teams/cities, or separation of distinct user groups, can prevent problems. Avoiding barriers to panic or emergency movement is essential, or crushes can occur. Clear marking of emergency exits is crucial. Events that do not use reserved seating run the risk of crushes as people attempt to get the best spots. Thus, "festival seating" is increasingly being banned or more tightly controlled. Types of performers and their reputation are also factors to consider.

When designing the site/venue consider the following measures to enhance visitor experience and help prevent misbehavior or other crowd-related problems:

- provide ample space at access and egress points and through circular movement corridors;
- avoid dead-ends, clutter, and bottlenecks that will lead to congestion or movement against the flow; consider a one-way pedestrian system;
- provide adequate directional signage to services and attractions;
- disperse vital services over the site;
- ensure that all staff, including security, are customer oriented; visitors often require assistance;
- screen and block off no-go areas where risks are high;
- separate vehicular and pedestrian movements;
- use signs and public announcements to advise patrons of rules, problems, and opportunities;
- use trial runs to test all systems against the possibility of creating a hazard or crowd irritant;
- provide visible, on-site security facilities and services install security devices (cameras, locks, etc.,);
- use lighting to avoid hazards and maximize security;
- segregate potentially incompatible activities and user segments;
- maximize staff communications through use of cellular phones and radios;
- provide, test, and adequately mark emergency exits;
- avoid common crowd stressors, such as: excessive waiting; overcrowding; subjection to excessive sensory stimulation (e.g., loud noise, smoke, bright lights, strong odors); overwhelming security, regulations, or threats; fencing that prevents escape or is illogical; restricted movement (i.e., bottlenecks).

Research into event crowding has been undertaken by H. Lee, Kerstetter, Graefe, and Confer (1997), Wickham and Kerstetter (2000), and Mowen et al. (2003).

Research Note

Mowen, A., Vogelsong, H., & Graefe, A. (2003). Perceived crowding and its relationship to crowd management practices at park and recreation events. *Event Management, 8*(2), 63–72.

This research confirmed the contention that crowding can be a positive influence on the satisfaction of event-goers, but it also demonstrated that perceptions of crowding and preferences for related crowd management techniques will vary by activity and zone. The researchers questioned attendees at three park events in Cleveland, using a sampling technique to ensure that all places on the sites were covered, over the entire duration of the events. The authors concluded that "people perceive that something is wrong with the product if there is not a critical mass of customers/visitors." Respondents to the surveys were more favorably inclined toward crowding at the main stage areas, and most negative about it at food concessions where line-ups occurred.

Queuing

People hate waiting in line, which is why its best to avoid queuing if at all possible. If line-ups are necessary, then event managers have an obligation to make that experience as brief and comfortable as possible. Theme parks provide shade, entertainment, refreshment sales, information about the length of wait, and even special exemptions for purchase that allow the lucky ones to skip the wait altogether. And just when you get into the building or exhibit you realize that part of the experience is further waiting!

Queuing is often a key element in capacity management. A ride, theater, or area can only hold so many people and the rest have to wait outside. The line-up can serve to discourage some people (who might come back later), as well as to build anticipation for the experience to follow. At free-entry events, forced queuing might be the only way to prevent serious overcrowding.

There are clearly both physical and psychological dimensions to managing queues. On the physical side, safety and security issues must be evaluated. The tradition of allowing crowds to rush into a concert hall or festival site all at once has proven to be dangerous and probably illegal. Some form of controlled entry is required, often associated with security checks (for weapons, drugs, alcohol, food, etc.). Where long line-ups are anticipated, a system of fencing or other barriers will be needed, in part to prevent interference with other on-site movements. But remember that once a crowd is placed inside a barrier, safety and health problems can occur. There must be outlets and personnel in attendance, for constant surveillance.

The perception of time is a tricky matter—a few minutes in a crowd can seem like forever. Waiting for an experience detracts from its enjoyment for some, but adds to the excitement for others. Consult an environmental psychologist (or theme park designer) about how to make it more positive.

Scheduling solutions are available for queuing management. Sport events and concerts often require everyone to arrive and depart at the same time, whereas a staggered program of activities can spread out demand and avoid peaks. Multiple sites can also be used to reduce congestion, such as where entertainment is offered in different locations at the same time.

There is another concept worth mentioning, that of "batch" processing. Instead of allowing a constant flow of arrivals or departures, have all attendees assembled in one or several staging places for simultaneous transport to the venue. That will work best for relatively small groups, such as at private parties or limited-number concerts. The assembly and arrival can be choreographed as part of the experience.

Traffic and Flow

Special attention has to be given to the needs of bus tours, the long-distance traveler who is unlikely to be familiar with the setting, and the passing tourist who might be lured to the event. If tourist and local traffic can be separated, both groups are going to be happy. Running shuttle busses from parking areas and arranging for special transportation from major regional markets will solve some problems. Signs and information should be posted for the traveler's convenience, and written and designed for the person totally unfamiliar with the area.

Other concerns include the provision of access for emergency vehicles and service equipment, parking for vendors and suppliers, and security routes. On-site movement is usually a problem of pedestrian flow, but large or congested events benefit from people-mover transport. Allowing pedestrians and normal traffic to mix could be disastrous, so clear, physical separation is essential. Pedestrians coming to, and leaving, the site can also cause problems, particularly if the crowd arrives or leaves all at once. Police control will be necessary for these situations. Parades are particularly troublesome and require considerable planning with emergency services and police requirements specified in minute detail. The needs of tourists are different from residents, mainly with respect to their lack of knowledge, so signs and information sources must be designed and situated to maximize their value to the stranger.

Citrine (1995) argued for circular flows of pedestrians within the event site, as this both reflects natural preferences and avoids dead-ends where congestion can occur. Clutter must be avoided, both to maximize flow and prevent hazards. Signs are essential in advising and steering people to desired attractions and services.

Special Needs and Accessibility

Many countries have legislated equal access to events and facilities, and many events cater specifically to those with special needs, including the Paralympics. Some of the legal issues that arise (Darcy & Harris, 2003):

- lack of wheelchair access to the event venue and its functions;
- charging fees to both handicapped person and their attendants;
- lack of information suitable for the blind or deaf;
- diminished quality of experience (e.g., poor viewing for those in wheelchairs).

Accommodating guests with special needs is a challenge, and usually a pleasant one, for event managers. Fleck (1996) gave advice on how events can meet the requirements of the Americans With Disabilities Act, and these site planning and operational principles should be globally applied:

- provide specific signs and information regarding the special-need services (in large print, and in Braille);
- provide special communications devices (i.e., TDD: telephones for the hearing impaired; closed-captioning TV and video; audio rather than printed information, with ALS-assisted listening devices);
- remove physical barriers to wheelchairs in order to ensure access to all buildings, activities, and concessions; consider the width of aisles, the need for ramps and elevators;
- install accessible toilets and rest areas;
- add handicapped parking spots with easy access to the site.

Research Note

Darcy, S., & Harris, R. (2003). Inclusive and accessible special events planning: An Australian perspective. *Event Management, 8*(1), 39-47.

The authors examine how disability and access issues can and should be incorporated into special events planning and production. In Australia the National Folk Festival has prepared a Disability Action Plan that provides for the following:

- appointment of an access coordinator;
- use of disability liaison officers;
- consultations with persons and organizations;
- annual updates of the access plan;
- access information posted on their website;
- disability awareness training to all staff and volunteers.

To be comprehensive, an access plan has to consider:

- consultations and evaluation/feedback;
- information provision;
- ticketing and pricing policies;
- transportation;
- physical access and comfort;
- amenities;
- the nature and quality of the event experience;
- training;
- handling inquiries, complaints, and special needs;
- affordability;
- integration (not segregation of certain groups);
- exposure to risks;
- special equipment needed (e.g., for Braille);
- requirements imposed on concessions and other participants in the event;
- preventing delays/inconveniences due to any of the access provisions.

Festival Places

Festival Places are physical settings in which festivals and other public celebrations are held. They become special cultural and tourism resources for cities when purpose built, or when their popularity and ambiance gains them recognition as places in which celebration is expected.

Historic cities, especially those in Europe, contain many public squares or plazas that have traditionally been used for festivals and other celebrations. These are often complemented by theaters and halls that accommodate concerts and meetings. One of the best examples is that of Salzburg, Austria, which proudly features its historic "festival district" and renowned venues on its website (www.salzburg.info/festspiele).

Getz (2001) compared European and North American festival places. North American cities generally have fewer heritage resources and many have deliberately created festival and event places in or near their central business district or along a waterfront. Urban festival spaces are important from several perspectives, including the arts and cultural life of the community, preservation of built heritage, tourism and place marketing, and frequently for their role in facilitating urban renewal. Event districts are being created, combining sports, culture, outdoor performance spaces, and convention/exhibition venues.

According to Falassi (1987), some form of "valorization" ritual is used to temporarily set festival places apart from normal use, in terms of function and emotional significance. The opening ceremony, for example, valorizes the setting and "modifies the usual and daily functions and meaning of time and space." During festivals, a number of rituals or rites reinforce the differences from normal, including rites of reversal (especially at carnivals), conspicuous display (exhibitions and parades) and consumption (food and drink), games and competition, exchanges (buying and selling), and dramas.

Table 4.1 provides a starting point for planning and designing festival places, and can be applied to other event settings and types. It specifies major considerations under the headings of setting, management systems, and people. This is also a starting point for developing our site operations checklist.

Research Note

Getz, D. (2001). Festival places: A comparison of Europe and North America. *Tourism, 49*(1), 3–18.

This exploratory study drew on responses from tourism marketing organizations in European cities and festival professionals (members of IFEA) in North American cities, with the purposes of documenting and comparing the use and management of festival places. Both groups mentioned parks, open spaces, and outdoor amphitheatres most frequently as types of places used by festivals in their cities, but this category was much more predominant in the North American sample. Streets were the second-most frequent type of festival place in North America, but in Europe it was squares or plazas. The high number of European mentions of indoor facilities (theaters, concert halls, and auditoria), compared to none in North America, suggests a major difference in types of festivals. A higher proportion of European cities apparently have constructed special-purpose festival places. In terms of respondents' opinions on the importance of factors in creating excellent festival places, there were some important similarities and differences between the two samples. Five factors were rated very important by both samples (means greater than 4 out of 5), two of which are locational factors, two pertain to accessibility, and the fifth to infrastructure.

The Operations Plan and Logistics

When it gets to actual production of the event we are at the stage of "operations and logistics." "Operations planning" consists of three subsystems, each of which involves the logistics of moving people, equipment, and materials to the right place at the right time.

1. Customer-oriented systems include accessibility, parking, queuing, information and assistance, ticketing, and provision of essential services including food and beverages, comfort, and safety. Crowd management and controls are involved, as well as customer service provided by staff and volunteers.
2. Producer- and supplier-oriented systems involve building and maintaining the infrastructure (utilities, tents, stages, audio-visuals, control centers, gates, etc.) and contingency planning and management; managing performers, VIPs, the media, and participants.
3. Communications systems encompass the equipment used, procedures, accrediting and hosting the media, and performance scheduling.

Figure 4.1 illustrates the elements of operational planning and logistics that synergistically combine to produce the event experience. The model shows that operational goals and policies flow from the interaction of programming and management factors, including experiential factors, with the realities of the venues/settings plus other constraints. Sometimes the venues will suggest programming, experiential or management improvements, rather than act as constraints.

Table 4.1. Factors Affecting the Planning and Design of Festival Places

Setting	Management Systems	People
Location	**The festival program**	**Staff and volunteers**
Accessibility	Rituals (e.g., site valori-	Uniforms/designations
Parking	zation)	Customer orientation
Visibility	Celebration	(host–guest contacts)
Centrality	Games, competitions,	Service quality
Clustering	amusements	**Participants**
Appropriateness to the	Entertainment; art	Performers
festival theme	Spectacle	Vendors
Cost of use/rental	Commerce	Suppliers
Site characteristics	Education	Sponsors
Infrastructure	Other sensory stimula-	**Audience**
Support services	tion (e.g., smell)	Numbers
Size/shape	**Amenities/services**	Demographics
Aesthetics	Comfort; seating	Origins (tourists, resi-
Capacity	Food and beverages	dents)
Acoustics/noise	Welcome and hospitality	Expectations
Ventilation/wind	Temporary services	Behavior
Surface texture (grass,	(communications and	
pavement)	media, light, sound,	
Social–cultural context	etc.)	
Heritage value (authen-	Special needs (e.g.,	
ticity)	disabled guests)	
Community significance	**Controls**	
Symbolism (e.g., land-	Ticketing	
mark, monument)	Security/safety/risk	
Generic event settings	management	
Assembly (e.g., plaza,	Traffic flow	
amphitheater)	Environmental (green	
Procession (street)	operations)	
Open space (park)	**Design**	
Exhibition/sales (conven-	Decorations; costumes	
tion or exhibition	Theming	
facility)	Atmosphere	
Activities (sport field)	**Site planning**	
Concert hall	Legibility (entrance	
	statement, pathways,	
	districts, nodes and	
	landmarks, edges)	
	Design capacity (desired	
	maximum attendance)	

A checklist covering many of the elements to be considered in operational planning and logistics is presented in Table 4.2. Every manager should develop event-specific checklists based on unique program, setting, and management factors, kept current through evaluations.

Programming Factors

The generic nature of the event (i.e., assembly, procession, sport, etc.) and the specific elements of style (see Chapter 6) in large part dictate operations and logistics. A simple

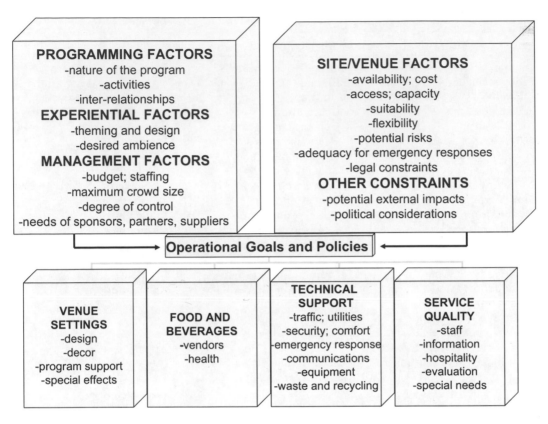

Figure 4.1. Operations planning process and elements.

sport event, involving one competition in one venue, is quite a different challenge than a multicountry yacht race like the Volvo Ocean Race. Often it is the interrelationships between venues and activities that cause the most difficulties, because these necessitate moving people, equipment, and goods.

Experiential Factors

The desired ambience and other theme-related goals will have a major impact on operations and logistics. For example, guests might be left to find their own way at some large, outdoor events, but at meetings and theme parties they might be handled like royalty.

Management Factors

The budget will have to provide for all aspects of venue preparation, programming, and logistical support or the event will not work. Staffing is therefore a key element in operations, as the volunteers and paid staff must be able to implement the plan effectively and with confidence. Specific capacity and crowd management systems will impact on the event experience and must be implemented with sensitivity to the guest. Other stakeholders' needs, including sponsors, partners, and suppliers, will also shape the operations plan.

Site/Venue Factors

Ideally the venue or site is selected and developed (or decorated) specifically to meet the organization's goals and create the perfect atmosphere. But in some cases it is a con-

Table 4.2. Operations Checklist

Activity requirements; Setting types

Stages and assembly; dressing rooms; trailers; rehearsal area

Special technicians; seating arrangements; viewing quality; acoustics

Processions: parade marshals; crowd controls; seating; staging and activity area requirements; viewing

Open spaces: paths versus free movement

Exhibition and sales: optimal site arrangement for viewing and line-ups (floor plan)

Theming; decorations; design elements

Permission and special provision for fireworks, loud music, lasers, balloon releases, oversize balloons, or equipment

Special provisions for animals

Infrastructure

Power needs (generators and dedicated lines; amperage for special equipment; protection from weather; outlets; heat or air conditioning; lighting and sound systems; backup and contingency plans)

Consultations with suppliers; electricians or permits needed; covers to protect people and lines

Water: for drinking; food and beverage preparation; washrooms; participants; check legislation; backup supply

Sewerage: existing lines and capacity; toilet requirements

Gas availability

Equipment, tools, and supplies for

Ticketing and financial control

Merchandizing; food and beverage

Command and communications functions

Program activities

Suppliers and participants

Customer services and information

Volunteers

Accessibility and flow

Number and arrangement of entrances and exits; gate controls

Direction and signs

Parking: number of spaces for cars, buses, trucks, bicycles; loading zones; reserved spots; special needs; emergency vehicles; parking permits or fees; collection and control

Personnel; directions and signage; vehicle repair and emergency

Services; barriers; check appropriate legislation; overflow and other contingency plans; entrance and exit segregation; avoiding congestion

Shuttles and public transit (special or extra services; schedules posted)

Special needs (wheelchair access; others)

Crowd control devices (barricades, signs)

Fire regulations; capacity (persons, vehicles, etc.)

On-site vehicles for staff (and identification of)

Accreditation

For: media, VIPs, staff and volunteers, officials (police, fire, etc.)

Types: badges; tickets; uniforms; wrist bands

Authority to issue; controls (e.g., preapproved lists, photo ID)

Safety, security, comfort, and health

First aid; lost children; lost and found

Emergency response and accessibility; evacuation procedures

Comfort stations; toilets; water; sewerage

Shelters from weather

Police or security presence

Waste disposal and recycling; green solutions; hazardous substances and the law

Safe storage spaces

Table 4.2 continued.

Merchandizing and financial control
  Special equipment (booths, cash registers, computers, kitchens, ice, refrigeration, storage, carts, canopies, seating, etc.)
  Security guards and vehicles; special accessibility and identification
  Supervision or electronic monitoring
  Safe money counting, storage, and removal
  Deposit slips and receipts
  Foreign exchange rates posted and accounted for
  Credit card validation machines and computer linkups; validation slips
  Alarms and emergency signals
  Bonding of key personnel
  Cashiers and cash registers
Hospitality
  Facilities for VIPs, sponsors, officials, and performers
  Separation from other activities
  Special viewing requirements
  Special transport to, from, and on site
  Protocol for VIPs
  Food, beverages, gifts
  Hosts/servers; any tour guides needed?
Command and operations facilities
  Office and communications center
  Visibility in and out
  Centrality and accessibility
  Links to staff, emergency response teams
  Refreshments and rest areas for staff, volunteers, participants
Communications
  Needs assessment (users, types of use, especially security, media, suppliers)
  Types: telephones; radios; computers; pagers; photocopiers; signs; notice boards; maps; audio-visual
  Special needs (e.g., telecommunications device for the deaf)
  Emergencies
  Translation services
Quality control, supervision, and evaluation
  Rehearsals
  Supervision
  Evaluation
Cancellation or venue change procedures
  Weather forecasting and monitoring
  Crowd and vehicle counts; observation to identify problems
  Ways of instantly communicating changes (e.g., loud speaker system; signs)
  Policy and procedures for reissuing tickets, rain checks, etc.

straint on what can be done. The various site/venue factors have already been discussed, but it has to be stressed again that the event experience is a product of people, program, management systems, and the setting.

Other Constraints

Environmental forces, including the weather, and political considerations, might impact on event operations. It might be desirable to have an outdoor ceremony, for example, but weather and security issues might prevent it.

Table 4.2 continued.

Storage and movement
  Tools, equipment, and vehicle storage
  On-site movement
  Structures needed (permanent or temporary)
Technicians needed (and related equipment)
  Electrical; lasers and special effects
  Sound systems
  Fireworks
  Plumbing (water and gas)
  Audio-visual equipment
  Communications equipment
  Computing
  Video and photo; audio recording
  Broadcasting
  Timing and scoring
  Registration and ticketing
  Emergency response; police; fire; ambulance; first-aid; medical/dental
  Vending machines
  Cooking/heating
  Mechanics

This checklist is merely a starting point for operations. Each point is simply a reminder of possible needs or actions.

Operational Goals and Policies

When it is time to implement the plan, the decorators, technicians, caterers, other staff, and volunteers have to know their specific goals and tasks as well as the policies and procedures covering their actions. Service and program quality specifications have to be in place. Supervision is required, plus evaluation and instant problem solving.

Detailed Logistical Considerations

Logistics is the detailed and precise management of movement, specifically the flow of goods, services, information, and people necessary to make the event work. The logistics manager is responsible for a plan, closely liked to the critical path, site planning, and other systems, to ensure that the event is staged as intended and problems are overcome.

People Movement

Many events employ the services of destination management companies (not to be confused with destination marketing organizations) to provide transportation and tours. Some event management companies include these services in order to integrate operations and logistics.

According to MPI, these experts have to have detailed knowledge of their city/destination: airports, busses, shopping hours, restaurants, caterers, hotels, event venues, local culture and protocol, social and recreational activities.

Registration

When a conference or trade show gets going, people arrive already registered (increasingly this is done online) or in need of registration and information. Numerous computer software programs are available for registration tasks, and they can be customized. MPI's (2003) textbook *Meetings and Conventions: A Planning Guide* provides advice on physical layout of the registration area, as well as procedures and materials needed.

Ticketing and Admission

Whether the event decides to sell in advance or (rarely) at the event only, or use distributors such as Ticketmaster versus selling directly, a number of security and logistical issues are raised. There are also a number of alternatives to tickets that have an impact.

Increasingly the Internet is being used for advance sales, while many events are abandoning tickets in favor of "smart cards" that contain a lot of information and are prepaid to permit entry and on-site purchases. At many events customers wear wrist-bands or badges that are coded to indicate the exact privileges each patron has paid for (e.g., day use versus a season's pass). Wine festivals tend to sell wine glasses for repeated samplings, and some events use "scrip" or funny money instead of cash.

Technology is increasingly counted on to solve logistics problems, such as by utilizing real-time ticketing to ensure that customers get the best seats available for a concert. That is the big advantage of using a distributor, along with the inherent control of revenue that distributors provide to the event. Logistical solutions must also be found to the problems of physically moving tickets—will they be mailed or picked up? Purely electronic ticketing is possible, as used by some discount airlines. Security and queuing come into play at the gates when tickets, cards, etc., have to be issued or checked. Ticketing is also used to inform the customer (times, places, privileges) and to waive liability (the customers' rights to sue the event, for example).

Procurement and Supply Chain Management

Task analysis and detailed programming generate procurement needs—the lists of supplies needed to construct and produce the event. The range of materials used by events can be enormous, including food and beverages, tents and stages, audio-visual and special effects equipment, communications, etc. An "order sheet" can be formulated to specify all requisitions and where they are to be installed or delivered.

What are the possible sources of supply for each item needed? Consider the basic choices:

- purchase or build it yourself (potentially very cost-effective when amortized over a number of years, but requires a capital budget);
- borrow (from other events, a government agency, individuals);
- donations from sponsors (ideal!);
- rent from commercial suppliers.

Rentals require contracts to be negotiated, but so might borrowed items. For example, the event will likely have to assume responsibility for losses, thereby requiring insurance coverage for all valuable materials and equipment.

"Supply chain" refers to the distribution channel of a product, from its sourcing, to its delivery to the end consumer. The supply chain is typically comprised of multiple companies who must be coordinated. "Supply chain management" refers to the process of identifying all necessary supplies, then assuring they are delivered and used as needed, within budget and according to established technical specifications.

It will often make sense for permanent events to share in supply procurement, or to use a government agency. This can save administration and perhaps reduce the cost. Beware of "switching costs," which limit or impose a fee on changing your orders or switching to new suppliers.

Communications

At small events staff and volunteers can communicate effectively by way of internal systems, mobile phones, pagers, or walky-talkies. The office probably needs fax and email links, and maybe live television and radio. Larger events—especially outdoors—might require the installation of a temporary, high-tech system.

Live media coverage in particular will necessitate a sophisticated communications center with lots of electric power or generators, satellite uplinks, special trucks, and camera platforms. Security and emergency personnel need their own system, including a control center and outposts. A public address system will be essential at many events. Traffic control must be able to interact with police. One of the main logistical problems is ensuring that all communications systems work without interfering with each other, while maintaining a central control to override all subsystems in case of emergency.

Don't forget low-tech solutions either. Signs, the kind that can be written on by staff, might be effective in informing patrons. Notice boards to leave messages can be useful. A large, flashing electric sign will certainly catch the attention of everyone. Where signs are to be placed is a part of the site planning, service quality, and emergency processes. Consider the special needs of those with visual or hearing disabilities, and those speaking other languages. Can sponsors be found to provide the special services and equipment needed?

Traffic Management

Events small and large often create traffic problems for the organizers, patrons, other road users, police, and emergency services. Of necessity, an important part of applying for an event permit (especially parades) or developing an event venue will be the traffic management plan, complete with contingency plans for the (almost) inevitable problems that occur.

Advice is readily available, such as the National Outdoor Events Association (UK) guidance note on traffic management, available online at www.noea.org.uk. This document covers traffic directions and marshals, vehicles and parking, and has a companion advisory note on barriers, fencing, and temporary roadways. Another useful guide is the document "Traffic Management for Special Events," produced in 1999 for events in Sydney Australia and available online at their roads and Traffic Authority site (www.rta.nsw.gov.au). It is a companion piece to the document "Major and Special Events Planning: A Guide for Promoters and Councils" (see: www.dig.nsw.gov.au/97-65.pdf).

The Sydney plan template includes the following main headings:

- Cover sheet (who is applying for what authority; space for signatures).
- Contact details (the event and pertinent officials).
- Situation analysis (background and overview of the event).
- Mission and goals of the event's traffic management plan.
- Execution: in general terms, the key aspects of the plan, followed by details including identification of responsibilities (i.e., who must do what).

Some of the key issues that have to be considered:

- efficient and comfortable entry and exit from the site;
- signs and direction systems (such as color-coded parking);
- identification of needs and application for policing or emergency services;
- potential disruption of general traffic;
- potential disruption of businesses and residents;

- parking on and off the site; parking fees, ticketing, and cash control;
- provisions for regular and special-service public transport;
- shuttle services from remote parking or other staging places;
- indemnification of authorities freeing them from claims arising from the event;
- informing patrons, the general public, and other stakeholders of the plans;
- segregation of pedestrians and vehicles;
- security for parked vehicles and patrons moving to and from vehicles;
- separation of patrons from organizers and suppliers; arrangements for VIPs and the media;
- safety, first aid, provision for emergency vehicles (emergency lanes, helicopter landing area, boat access);
- cleanliness, removal of litter, and any necessary repairs;
- noise and pollution control; waste receptacles;
- services for automobiles (break-down, fuel);
- traffic and parking direction by staff and volunteers (training, safety, comfort clothing/identification);
- special vehicles requiring additional attention (e.g., tow trucks, race cars, water trucks, fuel trucks);
- customers with special privileges (e.g., preferred parking and valet services);
- special transport to prevent drunk driving;
- transport for the handicapped or feeble;
- taxis and limousine services;
- contingency plans for any of a thousand possible problems!

A traffic management plan will also likely have to include one or more maps showing access and egress points, parking areas, etc. A route map is a necessity for parades and processions. Periodic events can obviously refine the basic traffic plan in response to evaluations, whereas one-time event planners might have to go to experienced event organizers for initial advice. Venues that host regular sport events should be able to provide sound advice.

When developing a traffic plan tie it directly to risk, environmental, health, and safety management. Traffic problems are a potential source of customer dissatisfaction, so it links to service quality as well. A wise policy is to promote public transport as much as possible, thereby reducing pollution and energy waste while making it easier for patrons to reach the event.

Permits

The City of San Diego has issued a Special Event Permit Application (http://www.sannet.gov/specialevents/permit.shtml) that provides forms for making all the necessary applications. Most cities and venues have a similar system in place to facilitate the event manager's legal tasks. More and more authorities are putting their requirements and forms on the Internet.

Applications often require basic information about the event, its legal status, structure, personnel, and contacts. The payment of application and rental fees is normal, as is the requirement for providing certificates of insurance. Many authorities want to know the event's tax status (must certain taxes be collected and paid?). Site plans, parade routes, security, health, traffic, emergency, and environmental management schemes might be obligatory. Meeting requirements for special needs (e.g., wheelchair accessibility) is a must in the US and other countries.

What types of permission might be required?

- alcohol use (many jurisdictions require a special event permit);
- permission for use or closure of streets;
- permission to use or install waste, sanitation, water, and other systems;
- food preparation and meeting the health inspection requirements;
- building permits (including permanent and temporary structures);
- approval of the fire department and other emergency services;
- application for police services to be provided;
- permission to install signage on and off the site.

It would be ideal if all required notifications and applications went to one place, but frequently the applicant has to search out all the requirements and pay multiple visits to various agencies.

Case Study: The Volvo Ocean Race—Stopover Göteborg 2002 (Written by Göran Lindahl, Site Manager)

The Volvo Ocean Race, Stopover Göteborg 2002 took place on the Swedish west coast in the city of Gothenburg (Göteborg), home of Volvo (see Chapter 9 for a case study of Volvo sponsorship including the Volvo Ocean Race). The Stopover event took place between May 31 and June 8. However, that was only the public dates. The event actually used the site for about 6 weeks, from May 5 to June 18.

The site location was an old shipyard about 3 kilometers from the city center. The area had a commuter ferry and buses stopping in adjacent areas. The site consisted of two large open spaces and the sides of the former dry-dock.

Setting up the event required a large amount of material and crew transportation both related to the race activities as well as the public event activities. The main actors in this process were the race organization, the stopover organizer, the seven race syndicates, and the main sponsors/exhibitors.

The race organization brought with them equipment and two exhibitions to the site. The equipment was promotional material, office equipment, press and media center equipment, signs, and miscellaneous equipment that was needed to keep their organization of some 20 people going. The goods was transported in four 20-foot containers arriving a week ahead of the boats. Pallets and flight transport containers were also used. The containers came from the previous stopover in La Rochelle, France, via truck or plane, as a boat trip would have taken too long. The containers were managed by the local branch of Volvo Logistics and handled, by fork lift and crane, by the Stopover organizer. One of the exhibitions was managed by Volvo and one by the official logistics sponsors, Peters & May. Both exhibitions were built into containers, a total of six, and handled on site by the Stopover organizer.

The race organization staff arrived 3–5 days before the boats arrived. They stayed at a hotel within walking distance. Their personal transports were carried out by themselves in their sponsor cars, Volvos, or by the Volvo VIP shuttle service. This service was housed in the Stopover organization's offices and was the same temporary setup as used by Volvo for the Scandinavian Masters golf tournament. Volvo's local transport organization was not used for these transports.

The Stopover organizer was responsible for setting up the event site. This included building structures, tents, adding jetties in the dock, building a sewer system, and setting up a temporary electrical infrastructure handling in total over 1000 amps. The Stopover organizer also built an office complex consisting of 17 porta-cabins/containers as well placing 19 porta-cabins used for the race syndicates' service/shore crews in the service area. Additionally, there was a digital telephone system and Ethernet/ISDN cabling that served the site. There was a Kayam structure, used for public events, covering 7000 square meters, which had to be built to allow transports entering the site during setup. Once it was finished the site had to be accessed through public walkways, a fact that during the hasty finishing days caused intensive traffic in the areas left open.

The first structure that was built was the main restaurant. During the setup and take down there were two large Lulls (a type of forklift) and a fork lift used continuously. There were also mobile cranes and trucks used for transports and lifts within the site. During the event the Stopover organizers provided the race syndicates with mobile cranes to lift the boats. There were also divers, electricians, and welders supplying services. During the event, transports within the event area were only allowed before 10 AM. Each night there was cleaning and emptying of garbage containers, an overnight operation including some 20 people with trucks and special vehicles.

The Stopover staff consisted of 4 people during set up, and 25 during the running of the event. In addition to this, approximately 100 other persons were working on site during set up and take down. During the event itself, some 500 people worked on the site.

The Stopover organizer was also responsible for cooperation with the municipal public transport company. Thus, a complete bus stop for four buses was organized on site. Bus lanes were prepared and unauthorized traffic was stopped at strategic streets in order to avoid traffic difficulties. Large parking places were also possible to arrange on adjacent former shipyard areas. The commuter ferry (which connects to downtown Gothenburg) got a whole new arrival/departure structure to cope with the increase in travelers. This meant ramps, stairs, barricades, fences, and signage. The bus was planned for a maximum of 6000 people per hour and the ferries 3000 people per hour. Due to the heavy publicity encouraging event patrons to not take private cars to the site, as it would have created a traffic jam, we found that we had too many parking spaces! The bus system with a large bus stop with feeding bus lanes managed to handle the 10,000 to 20,000 visitors each night.

The race syndicates arrived a few days before the boats and their shore crews. Each syndicate had one 20-foot container provided by the Stopover organizer and brought with them another two to three containers of equipment. These containers were managed by either the syndicates themselves or various logistics operators. On site they were handled by the Stopover organizer, mostly by mobile crane. The syndicates also used forklift and mobile cranes for services during the Stopover.

Some of the race syndicates also had an exhibition and commercial activity on site. SEB, ASSA-ABLOY, and TYCO were the largest ones. They had their own structures and exhibitions. Sponsors, exhibitors, and restaurants all contributed to the event and to the transportation around it. The largest exhibitor was Volvo, followed by Musto—which provided the race merchandise—and TYCO. Volvo had a customized exhibit that took 2 weeks to build. The exhibition structure used in previous Stopover ports was not used in Göteborg. Main sponsors utilized tent structures for their purposes. Minor sponsors and exhibitors had the same type of 5×5-meter tent modules in order to give the site a coherent design. One exhibitor did not get their exhibit from a previous stopover, so a new exhibit was produced on site together with the Stopover organizer. New pictures were mailed to the Stopover organizer and local suppliers printed new material.

The event was characterized by an intensive work process from day 1 to the last day of cleaning the site. As the site had not been used before for this type of activity, a whole new infrastructure needed to be put in place. Accordingly, there was always something happening on site that required logistics of some kind—from the predriving and drilling of stakes for the Kayam structure done before the material had arrived, to the welding and take-down of a fence by the dock during the event in order to widen a walkway. This widening was done in the midst of a busy afternoon.

The logistical situation for this large, one-time event was characterized by multiple logistics agents that mainly used the same handling equipment brought to the site by the Stopover organizer. This did work well due to a flexible and cooperative atmosphere during the event. The logistical situation can therefore be described as separate operators merging their activities under the Stopover organizer. One could ask if there were many conflicts, and the answer is that as most logistical activities were well defined they were clear and easy to prioritize. But we could have used two more fork lifts!

Planning for "Green" and Sustainable Events

Event producers, sponsors, managers, and hosts have an ethical—and often legal—responsibility to make events socially, culturally, and environmentally responsible. This means that events must not merely produce a profit or avoid major negative impacts, they must also maximize benefits to the community and become environmentally responsible. Environmental initiatives can also save a lot of money. Garbage disposal costs can be greatly reduced, and recycling can generate some income or be tied into sponsorship.

The principles of "sustainable development" require consideration of economic, environmental, social, and cultural processes. Sustainable events are those that maximize benefits in each of these categories while minimizing negative impacts; sustainable events are those that can endure indefinitely without consuming or spoiling the resources upon which they depend, including the vital resource base of community goodwill and support. This implies that "sustainable organizations" create sustainable events.

All the key stakeholders must be involved in creating sustainable events. Event producers and managers have to work with those affected by events, including agencies and groups who represent special interests such as the environment or heritage preservation. The bigger and more public the event, the more stakeholders there will be and the more complex the challenge.

Larger, public events will have to prepare, enforce, and evaluate a more comprehensive code of conduct regarding all the principles of sustainable events. In the following sections we examine the essentials of environmental management, followed by principles of social and cultural responsibility.

A Systems Approach

Figure 4.2 views the event as part of a system that uses resources in order to produce a number of desired outcomes. But there are other outcomes that might not be desirable (e.g., social disruption) and "externalities" such as pollution that are imposed on the community at large. A sustainable event will take care to minimize resource uses (e.g., water, energy, material supplies) and to avoid or minimize negative impacts. Because people are involved in all events, there is an opportunity to educate guests on sustainability issues, and to manage the audience in ways that will achieve sustainability objectives—such as by preventing litter or environmentally destructive behavior.

In terms of costs and benefits the event can be seen as an equation: do the positive outcomes (e.g., profit, economic impact, entertainment, community spirit) equal or exceed the value of resources consumed and taking into account the costs of waste and negative impacts?

Green Festivals

Organizers of smaller events should also be striving to become more "green." For example, an award-winning environmental program was created by the Cherry Creek Arts Festival in Denver, Colorado. Their Environmental Blueprint won the award for Best Environmental Program by the International Festivals and Events Association in 1993 and 1994, yielding good publicity for the festival and for Conoco, the program's sponsor.

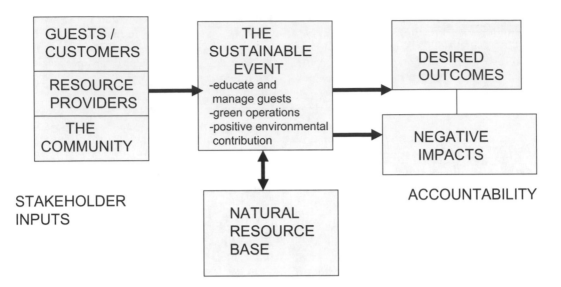

Figure 4.2. Environmental system for events.

Profile: Cherry Creek Arts Festival, Environmental Blueprint

The festival began in 1991, attracting an attendance of 150,000 over 2 days, and grew very quickly to a current attendance of around 350,000 over 3 days and a considerably expanded site. CCAF is a year-round, nonprofit, arts services organization that presents that annual festival during the July 4th holiday weekend in Denver. The festival has been ranked Number 1 outdoor arts festival by a number of industry publications. Since 1991 CCAF has won over 85 IFEA awards including Winner, International Festivals and Events Association's Best Environmental Program, 1993–1995.

Admission to the festival is free, thanks to the support of the Janus Capital Group, Cherry Creek North Business Improvement District, City and County of Denver, the Scientific and Cultural Facilities District, and many corporate sponsors. Merchandise sales are an important source of revenue as well. CCAF sustains a year-round program of arts education programming aimed at young people. Other nonprofit community groups benefit from revenue generated by the festival, such as by selling beverages—which account for a substantial profit.

Mission Statement

The mission of the Cherry Creek Arts Festival is to create access to a broad array of arts experiences, nurture the development and understanding of diverse art forms and cultures, and encourage the expanding depth and breadth of cultural life in Colorado.

Environmental Blueprint

In 1991 the organizers set up a committee that conducted a "waste audit" and found that most waste was in the form of packaging and serving containers. Waste management and recycling firms were approached to see what could be done, leading to an initial on-site program to sort and recycle waste as well as efforts to reduce it. Major sponsorship for the program was provided by Conoco.

Production and presentation of the Cherry Creek Arts Festival is governed by high environmental standards. This program, created and refined annually by the Arts Festival, adhered to these standards and achieved a remarkable success rate for recovering recyclable materials from Arts Festival waste. The Cherry Creek Arts Festival informed and educated the community and other special events about the benefits of recycling.

The emphasis of the program was education of the public through demonstration of practical environmental steps to be implemented in their own lives. The Arts Festival promoted precycling, self-sorting of waste, efficient use of transportation, and reuse of materials in creative ways. Each effort demonstrated to the public effective, proactive methods that individuals may undertake in their homes.

The Cherry Creek Arts Festival was named Colorado's Recycler of the Year. Still, the Arts Festival understood the need for improvement and change of the environmental program. In 1999 the state of Colorado enacted stringent alterations to the rules and regulations regarding recycling. As a result, the Arts Festival implemented a logical system that made it easier to identify recyclable products and encouraged continual public participation. The program emphasized and demonstrated practical steps the individual household could undertake.

The Arts Festival encouraged the public to separate their recyclables through superior signage and by differentiating between trash cans used for trash only and those for recyclables. The Arts Festival facilitated public participation by using specific signage and by placing lids on trash cans for recyclables with holes designed to fit only cans, plastic, and glass bottles. Sorting stations were placed in 140 locations around the festival grounds. To avoid confusion, the sanitation company used color-coded trash bags to indicate trash versus recyclables.

Cardboard recycling was an area in which vendors, especially participating restaurants, greatly contributed. Culinary arts volunteers regularly monitored the restaurants to ensure that cardboard items reached the designated dumpsters and to assure low contamination levels in the cardboard rolloffs. Approximately 120 cubic yards of corrugated cardboard was recycled on site.

Many beverages served from Arts Festival soda booths were in PET bottles rather than plastic cups. A program in the Arts Festival's Pepsi Oasis location served only PET bottled products. Conversion to the PET program created funding opportunities, resulting in a $12,000 grant to underwrite recycling costs.

On-Site Recycling Education Program

Various methods were used to educate the public about recycling:

- Festival Guide Magazine: Upon entering the Arts Festival, visitors received a Festival Guide Magazine. This magazine had a section about the recycling program and explained how the public can involve recycling both at the Arts Festival and at home.
- Volunteers and Education: "The Green Team" was the group of volunteers that made up the Arts Festival's Environmental team. They also acted as public information liaisons. Volunteers were stationed around the Arts Festival grounds at the various sorting stations. Here they informed the public about the new programs and how they could recycle materials at the Arts Festival and at home. Volunteers also distributed educational materials at two on-site information booths.
- Art Activities: On-site activities reinforced the importance of recycling and the environment. In Creation Station and ArtZone, the interactive education areas for children and adults, numerous projects made use of recycled or reused materials.

The Arts Festival had a partnership with a nonprofit company, Creative Exchange, a Denver-based recycler. Creative Exchange collected waste materials (extra wire, paper scraps, and unused Styrofoam pieces, etc.) from corporations and donated them to various nonprofit organizations and institutions within the community to be reused as art projects. These supplies were used in various on-site interactive projects.

Activities also promoted use of a circulator bus system, the B-line. Festival patrons were invited to decorate buses in a colorful design or to contribute their own creative design in a competition for bus bench decor, creating knowledge and investment in the new system

CCAF also sold reusable canvas bags in its merchandise program. These bags were made from recycled materials and encouraged festival attendees to participate in recycling each time they visited the grocery store.

The key elements in the "blueprint" included:

- "Precycling" by dealing with suppliers and vendors who helped reduce packaging and nonrecyclable materials; the festival required all beverages to be poured from fountains, rather than serving bottles or cans; food was served with few required utensils, using recyclable #6 polystyrene; recyclable cups were used; all paper products were made from recycled material; propane was used for cooking, not charcoal.
- Primary sorting of waste was done by consumers who placed material in different labeled containers.
- Secondary sorting into nine categories of waste was done by nonprofit groups that received remuneration; volunteers were called the "Green Team" and worked in two shifts to cover the entire day.
- Nonrecyclable waste was compacted into one compostable product.
- Leftover nonperishables were donated to local food banks.

In 1995 the event saw a 17% increase in attendance, but total waste generated by attendees decreased 13%. The Green Team ensured that 92% of waste would be recycled. Conoco introduced "Recyclasaurus Max," a costumed character, to help educate children about recycling.

More recently, demand for recycled materials has diminished, and the City of Denver implemented recycling, making it less valuable for recycling companies and sponsors to be involved at the festival. Volunteers became harder to recruit for sorting through trash that got thrown in with the recyclables. Finding a company to do all the work would have been very expensive. The festival now does what it can with its volunteers and staff to assist the City in its efforts. They are always investigating new solutions. In this way the festival has been a leader in both Denver and the world of events in encouraging recycling and waste reduction.

Green Meetings, Conventions, and Exhibitions

Several organizations have provided advice on how to produce green meetings and conventions. For online material, see: www.bluegreenmeetings.org.

Major areas of concern include:

- Registration: use electronic, not paper forms; recycled or reusable name tags.
- Conference materials: minimize paper use; recycled and reusable materials favored.
- Catering: healthy choices; small portions; no disposable utensils; no throw-away containers; suppliers to minimize packaging and ensure they meet your green standards.
- Equipment and furniture: ensure equipment is energy efficient and does not generate waste.
- Landscaping: use indigenous, lasting plants.
- Transportation: minimize travel through locational choices; favor public transport and alternative-energy vehicles.
- Exhibits: place restrictions on materials, paper, energy consumption.
- Venues and hotels: do they have their own environmental management certification?
- Energy and water: reduce consumption.
- Waste: reduce, reuse, recycle! Get all participants to buy in; ensure all hazardous materials are avoided or properly utilized.
- Entertainment: avoid pollution (noise levels, smoke, needless energy waste).
- Education: provide information about environmental issues and management.

The Greening of Sport Events

In his book *Greening Our Games*, Chernushenko (1994) argued that sports events must become more environmentally responsible. He pointed to Montreal's 1976 Summer Olympic Games and others as being symbolic of wasteful, grandiose projects with little thought given to post-Games legacies. And the 1992 Winter Olympic Games in France were said to exemplify inappropriate, destructive, and unfeasible developments, including the creation of hazards for residents, increasing air pollution, wetland destruction, and erosion. More recently, the Olympics in particular have attempted to become environmental showcases. A Sport and Environment Commission was set up in 1996 to advise the IOC on environment-related policy.

An excellent source is available online: Environmental Management and Monitoring for Sport Events and Facilities, by Green and Gold Inc., 1999, for the Department of Canadian Heritage, Sport Canada (www.greengold.on.ca/). Managers are encouraged to develop an environmental action plan, and all the elements are outlined. Some valuable implementation principles are stated:

- identify all stakeholders;
- set targets appropriate to the event's size;
- make all staff and volunteers responsible, but provide them with adequate information and training; keep them involved;
- set ambitious but feasible targets, then build on successes;
- measure results and monitor progress;
- identify needed improvements.

A number of case studies are presented from past sport events. Specific "Environmental Performance Indicators" (EPIs) are suggested, encompassing those related to policy (is it approved?), objectives and targets (measurable and achieved?), having a green office (measure its waste reduction), waste reduction at venues, progress with involving suppliers and sponsors, transportation (e.g., use of public transport to venues), health conditions (pollution levels), resource conservation (energy consumption levels), habitat protection (trees cut or replanted), and education (audience reached).

The Main Environmental Management Concerns for Sport Events

- Air quality for participants; air pollution caused by the event or related activity.
- Water quality for participants; avoid pollution.
- Land and water use: not all activities or development is sustainable.
- Waste management: waste cause by supplies, materials, food, and beverages.
- Energy Management: reduce consumption.
- Transportation services: reduce the need to travel; use public transport.
- Accommodation services: their construction and "green" management.
- Facilities construction: are new ones needed? their sustainability.

Waste Wise Events Program (www.ecorecycle.vic.gov.au)

Research conducted for this Australian organization, EcoRecycle Victoria, determined that 87% of people support the introduction of recycling at public events and are willing to pay a 5% surcharge on a $20 ticket to support the initiative. Fully 67% said they would use recycling bins on site. Almost everyone (95%) agreed that event caterers should be encouraged to use environmentally friendly packaging, and 50% believed that action should be required of them. Armed with this kind of public support, event managers should have no trouble in justifying a waste-wise event.

EcoRecycle Victoria's Waste Wise Event Program helps event organizers integrate simple and cost-effective waste, recycling, and litter management systems into their event. The Seven Steps to a Waste Wise Event Manual, available online, provides details and worksheets to implement an effective waste reduction program. It covers planning ideas, information on packaging materials, sample do-it-yourself audit sheets, and recommendations for equipment. Purpose-built event recycling equipment and standard signage are available to organizers following the Waste Wise Event Program. Organizers are advised to introduce the Waste Wise Events Program as early as possible. Waste minimization policies should be adopted and suppliers should be required to adhere through contracts and agreements. Specific policies and actions are needed on packaging to reduce waste material, reuse or recycling, and composting.

Study Questions

- Describe each generic type of event setting and types of events that illustrate each.
- What is the best location for an event? Discuss the various locational considerations.
- When designing an event site, what are the main design criteria?
- Is site capacity determined just be the size of a venue?
- How are crowd management and crowd control different?
- What are the main factors affecting the design and management of a festival place?
- Outline an operations plan for an event.
- Define logistics and show how it applies to event management with specific examples.
- Explain how a traffic management plan would be developed, and describe its main elements.
- Describe the environmental management system for an event.
- What are green events? What has to be done to become environmentally responsible?

Advanced Study Questions

- Show how to use the multistakeholder approach to develop an operational and logistics plan for an event.
- Audit an existing event with regard to its logistical systems including traffic, supplies, equipment, people movement, and environmental management.
- Compare several festival places as to their design, management systems, programs, and the resultant visitor experience.
- Discuss how the nature of certain types of events results in crowd control problems, and suggest solutions.

Chapter 5

Destination Planning and Marketing for Event Tourism

Learning Objectives

- Be able to formulate and implement an event tourism strategy for a destination, including a vision, goals, and strategies.
- Be able to develop an event tourism portfolio for a destination.
- Be able to undertake a resource and supply appraisal including an inventory and evaluation of strengths, weaknesses, opportunities, and threats (SWOT analysis).
- Be able to classify events from both a supply and demand perspective.
- Be able to evaluate the destination's capacity to host events, including the fit between events and host communities.
- Be able to formulate an event tourism policy, including criteria for assistance to events, sponsorship, equity, and direct production of events.
- Be able to manage the media coverage of events for optimum promotion of the venue, community, or destination.
- Be able to bid effectively on events.
- Be able to leverage events for maximum benefits to the community and destination.

Tourism Trends That Influence the Events Sector

Global travel continued to increase throughout the 1990s, with the biggest surge occurring in the Asia-Pacific region. Long-distance travel was increasing, and at a rate faster than the global average. After September 11, 2001, travel declined sharply and many events were cancelled or postponed, all around the world. Through 2003, economic recession, the wars in Afghanistan and Iraq, and SARS disease further hurt the travel and hospitality industry.

The new realty of tourism, as it affects events, includes the following:

- All providers must now adapt to stay alive, given the serious downturn in tourism since September 11, 2001. Meetings and conventions are particularly challenging. Technology might be making many meetings unnecessary, hastened by the crisis in travel.
- Last-minute planning and booking has become the norm, making forecasts of attendance or occupancy very difficult. Sport events and entertainment are now more subject to last-minute decision making.

- A focus on "core customers" is more important than ever, and shotgun marketing is a waste. Consumers are looking for value and making active comparisons among providers. Safety and personal comfort must be assured.
- Leisure travel is predicted to experience slow growth, with an emphasis on closer to home travel and weekends. Family travel seems to have experienced a resurgence, in part due to the otherwise negative travel-related events of 2001–2003. Families and married couples want to share their quality time, precious as it is.

Many tourism trends remain strongly influenced but the habits of the Baby Boom generation. According to the Travel Industry Association (TIA) of America's Domestic Travel Market Report 2003 Edition, those aged 35–54 generated more travel than any other age group in the country, resulting in more than 241 million household trips in 2002. They are more likely to stay in hotels, travel for business, and fly to their destinations. As well, TIA reported that families accounted for 74% of all vacation travel in the US.

The duration of pleasure trips has, on average, shortened. The strong trend toward weekend pleasure trips is even stronger in dual-career families where short breaks are easier to coordinate. And more short-break trips are being taken outside the traditional summer vacation periods. Urban centers and their numerous services, amenities and attractions, are increasingly popular destinations for vacations, business meetings, and day or weekend pleasure trips.

Demand is growing in four-season resorts, especially as places for second homes, retirement, or investment properties. Most resorts are well-established event producers and coordinators, with some of them using events prominently in their branding strategies.

Business Travel

MPI and American Express teamed up to produce a report called "Futurewatch 2003," which highlighted that relationships were changed by the events of September 11, 2001, and the subsequent fall-off in meeting demand and travel. Some of the key findings:

- increased emphasis on having planners and suppliers demonstrate the value (a return on investment) of meetings; traditionally planners and suppliers have focused on the value of location and venue;
- suppliers taking a larger share of the risk in case of event losses (cancellation and attrition clauses are negotiable);
- increasing reliance on the Internet for information distribution and bookings;
- emerging, nontraditional meeting locations due to the high cost of many venues and cities.

Sport Event Tourism

Numerous cities or regions have established sport commissions or event development corporations that have the mandate to create, bid on, and facilitate sport events, plus most destination marketing organizations also engage in bidding. In the US, the Cincinnati-based National Association of Sports Commissions was established in 1992 and pulls together commissions that had their roots in chambers of commerce or visitor and convention bureaus. Their Executive Director, Don Schumacher, explained the rationale: "Increasingly, the value of the sports event industry in terms of tourism, economic development and image enhancement is being recognized. In response, communities are forming sports commissions whose purpose is to attract sports events" (personal communication, 2000). The national association provides a forum for exchange between commissions, and with national sport governing bodies, event rights holders (i.e., the owners of events), sport marketing firms, and service or equipment suppliers.

One of the best sources on domestic sport event tourists comes from the TIA 1999 report, "Profile of Travelers Who Attend Sports Events," using 1997 survey data that examined travel over the previous 5 years. Sport event tourism has been increasing in popularity in the US, alongside other forms of special-interest travel. Thirty-eight percent of US adults had been sport event travelers (defined as those attending a sport event while traveling at least fifty miles from home), either as event participants or spectators, within the previous 5 years. Seventy-six percent of these travelers listed the sport event as their primary purpose for their most recent such trip. Fully 84% of the most recent sport event trips were to spectate, rather than participate, and one quarter were to watch children or grandchildren play in the event. Sixteen percent of sport event travelers participated in the event (most recent such trip), including a minor portion who both participated and spectated. In total 6% of all resident trips (amounting to 60 million person-trips) in 1997 included a sport event, making it the 10th most popular travel activity.

In the US, 45% of men and 31% of women attended sport events while traveling over the previous 5 years. The dominant segment consists of parents, especially among those on trips made specifically for a sport event, so there is a very large family market to tap. The average age of the sport event traveler was 45 years, but compared to all US travelers they were more likely to be younger, have children, and be employed full-time. The percentage of sport event parties having children was 30%, compared to 21% overall, but party size was comparable.

The most popular sport events attracting tourists were baseball/softball (17% of adults had done so over the previous 5 years), followed by football (15%), basketball (9%), auto/truck racing (8%), golf tournament (6%), skiing/snowboarding (5%), soccer (5%), and ice hockey (4%), while all other sports events attracted 13% of adults. Professional and amateur sports were attended equally on respondents' most recent trips. Professional sports attracted 50% of the travelers, with the most popular amateur events being high school (14%) and college-level sports (13%). The other categories of amateur sport event were amateur athletic (12%), little league (5%), church/intramural (4%), and other (6%). Summer is the peak season, followed by autumn. It is very interesting to note that men and women identically ranked the top for types of sport events attended, although females were less interested in golf and hockey. Men definitely traveled more for professional sport events (54% of males compared to 45% of females). Mothers (the infamous "soccer moms"!) do support their children's sporting activities.

Data from the Canadian Travel Survey indicated that "active sport tourists" (all related to events) were both males and females, aged primarily 20–34, university educated, and with higher incomes. In contrast, Gibson (1998) determined the "active sport tourist" to be primarily male, but also college educated with higher incomes. Gibson said these active sport tourists are likely to travel for participation in favorite pursuits well into retirement.

There are many clearly identifiable, special sport event tourism segments, each with their own events. Pitts (1999) reported on the gay and lesbian sport tourism industry, finding this target segment to be large and affluent, with its own sport travel industry, media, and events. The Gay Games are an annual, international participation event with substantial economic impact, and many smaller, sport-specific events are growing in popularity. A number of professional groups hold major sport events at the international, national, and regional levels, such as the World Police and Fire Games. This event is won through competitive bidding by cities, and the 1998 event in Calgary, Canada, attracted over 7000 participants. Masters Games have become a global phenomenon, involving older adult competitors, as have paralympic games for persons with disabilities.

Sport event trips involve about the same amount of spending as all types of trips, although the TIA research determined that this segment tended to purchase sport-related equipment or clothes for their trips. Travel is mostly done by car, although some use air transport. Overnight travel for sport events is high, with 84% of trips being overnight, compared to 82% for all US trips. Just over half (52%) stayed in commercial accommodation, but their overnight trips were shorter than the average US overnight trip (3 nights versus 3.3). Overall, sport event trips were the same average length (3.3 nights) as all trips. Group tours accounted for only 4% of the total person-trips among sport event travelers, which is the same proportion as for all US travelers. Party size for sport event trips was found to be slightly higher (2.1 compared to 1.9 persons).

Cultural Tourism

A definition of cultural tourism was offered by Lord Cultural Resources Planning and Management (1993): "Visits by persons from outside the host community motivated wholly or in part by interest in the historical, artistic, scientific or lifestyle/heritage of a community, region, group or institution."

The World Tourism Organization defines cultural tourism as "covering all aspects of travel whereby people lean about each other's way of life and thought." Much of cultural tourism focuses on historic sites and other heritage attractions, many of which produce interpretive events. Another integral dimension of cultural tourism is all forms of cultural festivals and celebrations that give visitors access to local traditions and lifestyles. A third major component is that of performing and visual arts, with theaters, museums, and galleries being the pertinent objects of tourist interest. Native or aboriginal tourism fits into the cultural tourism definition, encompassing events like powwows in North America, or Maori entertainment in New Zealand.

Even sports can be considered as a cultural product, especially when combined with festival programming.

Cultural and heritage attractions are expanding in popularity, and there is more interest in authentic experiences, as opposed to traditional resort holidays. "Discover America 2000" reported that an explosion in arts has occurred since the 1960s, leading to an ever-increasing demand for cultural tourism. A study by TIA and the *Smithsonian Magazine*, called "The Historic/Cultural Traveler 2003," found that 81% of adult Americans who had traveled in the past year could be considered "historic/cultural tourists" based on their activities and interests.

They are high-yield tourists, in terms of lengths of stay and spending, and for 30% their choice of destination was influenced by a specific historic or cultural event or activity. Over half of them had a hobby or interest that influenced their travel. This is not a passing fad, as cultural tourism in general has been leading the way over the past decade. Older, better educated, and more sophisticated, tomorrow's tourists will be even more interested in cultural/historic sites and events.

A distinct profile sets cultural tourists apart from other leisure travelers and makes them an appealing market (Vancouver's Cultural Tourism Initiative, 2001). These tourists tend to have the following features:

- 45 to 64 years old (especially baby boomers);
- female;
- some postsecondary education;

- higher income level;
- spends between 8% and 10% more per day when traveling;
- stays almost an entire day longer at a destination;
- uses more commercial accommodation;
- spends more on consumer products such as souvenirs, arts, crafts, clothing, etc.

Nearly 93 million Americans say they included at least one cultural, arts, heritage, or historic activity or event while traveling in 2001, according to a survey conducted by TIA. About one in five (21%) of total domestic person-trips (business and pleasure) includes an historic/cultural activity. In fact, historic/cultural travel volume is up 10% from 1996, increasing from 192.4 million person-trips to 212.0 million person-trips in 2000. Art and music festivals are the most popular type of festivals attended while traveling.

Environmentally Friendly Tourism

Geotourism is "tourism that sustains or enhances the geographical character of the place being visited, including its environment, culture, aesthetics, heritage and the well-being of its residents." In the report "Geotourism: The New Trend in Travel" (Travel Industry Association of America, 2003), sponsored by the magazine *National Geographic Traveler*, a growing awareness and interest in sustainable tourism practices was documented. Most want authentic experiences. This movement will likely gain momentum, requiring tourism operators and event producers to adopt green practices and promote themselves as being environmentally friendly. Look for some kind of environment-friendly event certification covering all types of events in the future.

Event Tourism Planning and Policy

Vision, Goals, and Objectives

Without a clear vision and goals, event tourism initiatives are likely to become ad hoc and ineffective. B. Ritchie and Crouch (2003) explained how a vision statement should reflect the philosophy and values of tourism development in a destination, and establish "the more functional and the more inspirational portrait of the ideal future that the destination hopes to bring about" (p. 154). Regarding event tourism, the big question is the importance or centrality of events: are they a supporting element or one of the major platforms of tourism development and marketing? In the case of Calgary, documented by Ritchie and Crouch, events figured prominently in helping to achieve the central concept of the city becoming "host, consultant and educator to the world." Specific facilities and types of events were identified as means to help realize the vision, including world-class sports events and winter sport facilities. Recent discussions in Calgary have focused on how to sustain the city's reputation as a world-class, winter sports capital.

Event tourism goals for a destination should address the following general issues:

- the extent to which existing events are to be developed and promoted as tourist attractions;
- the extent to which support will be given to develop or assist the creation of new events and bidding for events;
- the roles events are to play in extending tourist seasons and the geographic spread of tourism;
- the role events are to play in creating and enhancing images, particularly a desti-

nation area or attraction theme, and in correcting negative imagery;
- the roles events are to play in fostering the arts, cultural goals, sports, fitness, recreation, nature and heritage conservation, and community development;
- the acceptable costs associated with development, and who is to pay for them;
- the means to identify, prevent, ameliorate, or remove negative impacts;
- the need for organizational development at the level of interest groups, communities, destination areas, and government agencies/departments to support event tourism.

Sample event tourism goals and objectives are provided in Table 5.1. The goals are general, and while most are worded to focus on intended benefits, some are expressed as negatives to be avoided. The sample objectives are more specific statements of how the goal is to be implemented, and each of them should include measurable key results or performance criteria.

Surprisingly, few communities and destinations have event tourism strategies or policies. Probably the most progressive country in this regard is Australia, with event development corporations or units in every state. The case of Queensland Events Corporation

Table 5.1. Sample Goals and Objectives for Event Tourism

Goals	Objectives
Create a favorable image	Attract and create high-profile events to maximize positive media exposure. Key results: bid and win one mega-event each decade; achieve television coverage of major existing events; increase awareness of destination by 50% in key market segments.
Attract foreign visitors and increase their yield	Favor events that attract foreign visitors. Key results: increase foreign tourist attendance at events by 10% within 3 years.
Expand the tourism season and spread demand throughout the area	Attract or create new events during winter and autumn, especially where none exist.
Use events as a catalyst to expand and improve tourism infrastructure	Achieve a new multipurpose event facility within 5 years.
Stimulate repeat visits	Produce and market a program of events at all attractions and facilities.
Develop and improve the infrastructure and management necessary to create, attract, and sustain events.	Provide assistance and advice; foster the pooling of resources; create cooperative marketing and promotions.
Foster development of the arts, sports, culture, heritage, and leisure.	Assist all types of events; link events to other policy areas.
Ensure maximum benefits to the host community.	Conduct cost–benefit studies; follow community-based planning process.
Avoid negative environmental foster conservation.	Stimulate nature tourism impacts through events; require impact assessments.

concludes this chapter, demonstrating major elements of their strategy and policy. The profile of Gothenburg, Sweden, illustrates how a city can become an "event capital."

The policy formulation process described in this section is a way to refine and implement strategies through consideration of the following:

- What roles should events play in tourism and economic development, social/cultural development, and environmental quality? How is the event sector to be integrated with other tourism, cultural, social, leisure, and environmental policy fields?
- What are the appropriate goals for: creating new events and venues? attracting (bidding on) events? assisting existing events and organizations?
- How can goals best be achieved (e.g., through funding programs, bidding, training, and marketing)? What are the appropriate roles for destination organizations, local and senior governmental authorities?
- What management support systems are required (i.e., research, information systems, planning processes)?
- Do we need an event development organization or unit?
- Are licensing, regulations, or other controls on events needed?
- What evaluation and accountability measures are desired?

The initiative to do a plan or set policies does not have to be made by tourism agencies. Events might wish to consider how they can convince the authorities or tourism bodies to formulate event-supportive policies for economic, cultural, and social reasons.

Potential Roles

There are four tangible roles that an agency can play in the development of the events sector, and it is likely that some combination of these will be implemented (Figure 5.1).

Producer

Many municipal agencies and some tourism organizations directly produce events (see the case of Chicago Mayor's Office of Special Events). Advantages of direct involvement include:
- control of the theme, timing, program, and setting;
- relieving the burden from community groups;
- raising money; controlling admission prices;
- enhancing the agency's image;
- ensuring professionalism and quality.

Equity

A degree of ownership, or equity, can be taken in events while still leaving the production and management mostly or entirely to the partner. This kind of joint venture most likely will arise when either the agency or event organizers lack the resources to produce an event on their own, and where the agency believes its own goals can be met without exercising total control. A contract should stipulate exact obligations, risks, and potential benefits (especially of costs and revenues) accruing to each party.

Sponsor

Sponsorship is not restricted to the private sector. Tourist agencies and local authorities can realize substantial benefits through selected sponsorship in events by helping organizers financially. A tourist organization can exhibit at events, boost its profile through promotions and imagery, and capture the event database for future targeted promotions.

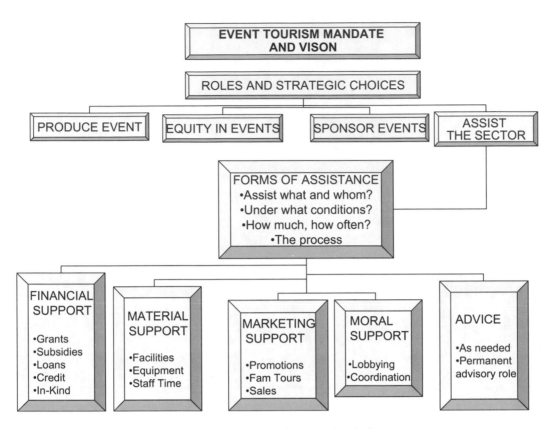

Figure 5.1. Roles and strategic choices.

Assistance

A number of forms of direct and indirect assistance can be provided to the events sector: financial, material, marketing, moral, and advice. Research in the Province of Ontario, Canada (Getz & Frisby, 1990) provided insights on what event organizations need. In descending order of frequency, organizers wanted help with: services and facilities; financial support; labor; advice/administrative support; and ideas on how to improve events. They also look to their municipality to enhance the event's image and gain political support. "Red tape" and delays in getting assistance are major concerns of organizers, and they want municipalities to have a better understanding of the needs and value of festivals and events. It was generally felt that a firm policy on events would be beneficial to the long-term survival and stability of the event.

Financial assistance, beyond ownership and sponsorship, can include grants, subsidies (e.g., free use of facilities), loans, lines of credit, and in-kind donations. Other forms of material assistance can include the provision of equipment, staff persons (as volunteers, or seconded to events), and the use of offices.

Marketing support can take the form of joint or free promotions and assistance with the marketing plan. Market research and the provision of timely, useful reports will help managers a great deal. Moral support should, at a minimum, extend to lobbying on behalf of events and the event tourism sector. The giving of professional advice will also be appreciated by many event managers and the tour industry. Tourist agencies or local authorities can also aid the events sector through coordination, ranging from the production of event schedules to the overseeing or creation of an event association.

Criteria for Giving Assistance

To whom, or to what organizations, should assistance be given? It might seem wise to support only experienced groups with good track records, but this would not encourage the development of new groups and ideas. Other criteria might include: the degree of community support of the event; the size or tourist attractiveness of the event; the degree of risk or potential benefits involved; and the demonstrated need of organizing groups.

Another consideration is an assessment of how the assistance will be used. Unconditional operating grants and subsidies to event organizers used to be common, but are fast disappearing. Alternatively, aid can be given for specific purposes such as feasibility and marketing studies, economic impact research, promotions, or specific elements of events (such as local artistic performers or public entertainment).

Different situations affecting events must also be considered. "Seed money" can be provided to help new events get established, or the assistance can be provided on a continuing basis to support operations of established events. Ad hoc aid in emergencies, or to support new initiatives, is also an option. Along with these choices is the necessity to impose some restrictions on financial assistance, including maximum amounts available yearly, and the criteria and application process by which the limits can be attained. The duration of assistance is also a major consideration. Variable amounts of funds can be given, for example, depending on annual needs and success of the events. Alternatively, a long-term, fixed grant commitment could be used to achieve stability in event production. Increasing amounts are used to reward performance (according to defined criteria), while decreasing annual grants could be employed to foster self-sufficiency in the event organization. There is no correct or optimal strategy in this regard, so some experimentation might be desirable.

Procedures must be put in place to obtain and review applications, and this can be done by staff who are identified as the contact. If applications are judged on merit, then specific criteria have to be publicized. Standard application and evaluation forms promote fairness, although there should be some flexibility due to the "once a year" characteristic of most events (e.g., organizers of summer events may find fall application deadlines difficult to meet).

Event Tourism Strategies and Tactics

Developing a Portfolio of Events

Start by thinking of a portfolio of events, each contributing to achieving the vision, and then developing and managing this portfolio for sustainable competitive advantages. A variety of strategies and tactics will be required. Every community and region has an existing "portfolio" of events that can be classified by type, season, size, and impacts, and event tourism planning has to be concerned with developing and sustaining the ideal portfolio to achieve its vision. A good starting point in event tourism planning is to evaluate the current supply (discussion in detail later in this chapter) and assess how it can be developed and managed to achieve tourism goals.

Full portfolio evaluation cannot occur without market intelligence and environmental scanning, but it can be commenced alongside the resource appraisal. The first step is to thoroughly assess resources and the supply of events, then measure demand and consider market trends. Although profit-seeking businesses will stress criteria such as market share, demand trends, profitability, and costs, these are not so relevant to destinations and event tourism. Many events, after all, are not seeking profits, while goals other than profitability are more crucial to the destination. Therefore, a somewhat different type of portfolio evaluation is required.

Figure 5.2 provides a starting point that can be adapted to various destinations' needs. Events within the area can be grouped according to two criteria: demand (measured by trends in the number of tourists attracted) and value in meeting other tourism goals (e.g., media coverage, image enhancement, theme development, sustainability). Sustainability of events should be a primary factor when examining value, as events with long-term community support, financial self-sufficiency (which will stem in part form ability to make surplus revenue), and which are environmentally "green" will have more strategic significance.

One key underlying principle shapes this approach: almost all events have tourism and community value, but only some are capable of generating major tourism demand. Within any destination there is likely to be evident a hierarchy of events, with the majority having little direct tourist attractiveness, whatever the type. They nevertheless have value in the various roles discussed earlier, and some of them might have potential to become attractions. A smaller number of events will have medium tourism attractiveness and value, which usually means regional in scope. Some will have medium attractiveness but with low value in terms of other criteria, or vice versa.

The smallest number will be those events with high tourism attractiveness and high value in other roles, such as image enhancement. Mega-events and hallmark events are those that display the greatest value and attractiveness. Mega-events are likely to be occasional, while hallmark events are periodic.

Events as Core Attractions

Events can be used as primary attractions, around which theming, image building, and packaging are created. This will likely be most appropriate at the community level, as

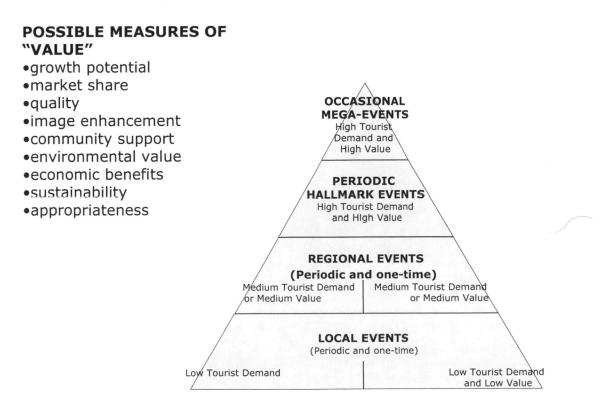

POSSIBLE MEASURES OF "VALUE"
- growth potential
- market share
- quality
- image enhancement
- community support
- environmental value
- economic benefits
- sustainability
- appropriateness

OCCASIONAL MEGA-EVENTS
High Tourist Demand and High Value

PERIODIC HALLMARK EVENTS
High Tourist Demand and High Value

REGIONAL EVENTS
(Periodic and one-time)
Medium Tourist Demand or Medium Value | Medium Tourist Demand or Medium Value

LOCAL EVENTS
(Periodic and one-time)
Low Tourist Demand | Low Tourist Demand and Low Value

Figure 5.2. Event tourism portfolio.

many towns and cities have fashioned themselves as "tournament capitals" or "festival cities." It can also be a good strategy for rural areas lacking major tourist infrastructure. In effect, the destination's positioning strategy is shaped by one or more event attractions and the theming that surrounds them.

One or more hallmark events will be desirable (i.e., events with such profile that the image of event and destination become inseparable and mutually reinforcing). At a minimum, the destination will require media-oriented events to attract substantial publicity. Substantial event venues are also desirable, and might be a prerequisite for hosting major events and bidding on others. However, even the smallest community can adapt its recreational and cultural facilities for events.

"Attractiveness" is a measure of the relative strength of attractions, in terms of the number of people drawn, the geographic spread of the market area, or its appeal compared to the competition. Mill and Morrison (1985) used the term "drawing power" and linked it to the distance people are willing to travel to experience the attraction. They distinguished between local, regional, and national or international market areas. Event tourism must therefore seek to enhance the attractiveness of individual events and festivals and to use them to enhance destination attractiveness. S. Lee and Crompton (2003) researched the drawing power of three events in Maryland.

Research Note

Lee, S., & Crompton, J. (2003). The attraction power and spending impact of three festivals in Ocean City, Maryland. *Event Management, 8*(2), 109–112.

Three festivals in one city in 1 year (held in May, late September, and November–January) were compared in terms of drawing power. This was measured by the number of tourists attracted specifically because of the event, and the distances traveled (i.e., the market areas). All three proved to be valuable in drawing tourists (41–55% of attendance) and generating economic benefits, although attendance was much higher at the September event. The "return on investment" to the city in each case was judged to be positive.

Mega-Events

For destinations pursuing a strategy of awareness and large-scale tourism growth, a number of mega-events in the same year or in sequence can be effective in attracting attention and boosting visitor numbers. Olympics, world's fairs, and other major sports events have proved to be most popular for achieving these goals.

The cost will be enormous and big government involvement is essential, as the private sector might be able to produce one major event but not several. Consequently, the decision to employ this strategy will likely be made at the highest level of government—either proactively, to achieve set goals, or in response to unique opportunities.

Big events always have big impacts, both good and bad. While citizens generally support one-time mega-events, people are more likely to sustain support for occasional mega-events and a variety of periodic community events. Controversy can be expected.

Theme Years

While many countries and regions have employed special promotions like "Visit India Year" or "The Year of Tourism," theme years featuring events are of growing importance. Events either provide the focus of the promotion, as events are excellent ways to manifest cultural and other themes, or provide added value to a tour.

Theme years can be used to spread demand seasonally and geographically. These were major goals in planning the John Cabot 500th Celebrations in Newfoundland, Canada, for

1997. Many new events were to be created in communities across the province, and held throughout the year, to mark the famous explorer's journeys to and around Newfoundland.

Variety in Community Events

This strategy builds on existing and new community events, rather than attracting or creating new and/or big events. It relies on authenticity, variety, and strong community support to attract and satisfy tourists. The cost advantages can be great, although extra effort will be required to generate publicity and involve the tour industry, and to mobilize and facilitate communities and interest groups to pursue tourism marketing.

Adding Value to Attractions and Resorts

Even if events are not a major part of the destination's portfolio, they can still be significant as animators of resorts and attractions. Added value comes from packaging events within tours, adding events to meetings and conventions, and from enlivening public places.

This strategy might incidentally generate events with tourist appeal and lead to greater recognition of the event sector. While it might happen through individual initiatives at resorts and attractions, it would be more effective to encourage the process through education, advice, and financial assistance. Small amounts of investment could go a long way to get the event sector mobilized.

Bidding on Events

Numerous events, particularly sports, can be won through a formal bidding process. Who regularly bids on events? Tourist organizations bid on events that are expected to attract tourists and favorable publicity to a destination. Convention centers, exhibition venues, and hotels all bid on events to fill their facilities. Private event-producing companies bid on events that are tendered by corporations, associations, or individuals.

Catherwood and Van Kirk (1992) wrote from experience about bidding on special events, particularly in the sports sector. Most sports have governing bodies responsible for sending out requests for proposals to host their events. For the coveted Superbowl, huge lists of specifications and demands are made, and typical bids are 100 pages long. Site selection committees are typical, and this group visits competing destinations or venues. Escalating competition to obtain events in the US has led to the offering of cash guarantees by destinations. In other words, regardless of event attendance or sales, the organizers are guaranteed a certain amount of money. This practice tends to overcome some of the risks of holding an event in unproven locations.

The highest bids in monetary terms are not always winners. According to Catherwood and Van Kirk, international governing bodies also want tangible benefits and excellent treatment for athletes, trouble-free management, and the best venues and hospitality. The potential for popularizing and expanding the influence of their sport is another important bid determinant. These authors provided a seven-point list of rules to follow in making bids, including the making of a unique selling proposition.

McCabe et al. (2000), in their book on the convention business, provided a case study on event bidding by the Sydney, Australia, Convention and Visitor Bureau. Sydney is ranked as the world's top international convention city, and no doubt the 2000 Summer Olympics helped to secure that enviable position by adding to the city's already attractive image. The Sydney CVB makes bids on behalf of the city, competing internationally. The bureau "promotes itself as a not-for-profit organization which provides a free and unbiased service to put conference organizers in touch with the best Sydney has to offer" (p. 168).

They develop customized bids, obtain written endorsements from key political and industry representatives, locate appropriate venues and support facilities, prepare preliminary event budgets, and plan and host site selection teams. The bureau can also help event organizers apply for state or Commonwealth funding to assist an event to come to Sydney. They will make bids themselves or assist associations in doing so. They will also assist in selecting local professional conference organizers for events needing that service.

To compete at the global level a destination will require one of the biggest and best facilities (sports stadia, convention centers, exhibition halls, arts complexes, etc.). Most destinations will seek to host a variety of events within a hierarchy determined by the event's tourist attractiveness (i.e., international, national, regional) or its economic impacts, as well as by type of event (as each type has different needs, seasonality, and impacts). This leads to a portfolio approach in which the destination seeks to balance its resources and needs with different types and sizes of event.

Destinations can also gain competitive advantage by improving the quality of services offered to event owners and by improving the events. This requires improvement of event management and marketing, fostering a hospitable resident population, and investment in staff and services aimed at both event owners and managers. Getz (2004a) sought to determine critical success factors for winning events by surveying experts.

Research Note

Getz, D. (2004). Bidding on events: Critical success factors. *Journal of Convention and Exhibition Management*, 5(2).

This research obtained information on event bidding from Canadian visitor and convention bureaus. A variety of goals were identified pertaining to both intended outcomes (e.g., economic impacts) and the process of event bidding. Goals pertaining to economic impact dominated, including maximizing economic impacts, filling beds, and increasing tourist numbers. Overcoming seasonality problems and enhancing destination exposure or branding are also important goals. Of the "process" goals, the most frequently mentioned were concerned with winning events (e.g., the success rate) and making better bids. Critical success factors for event bidding were also identified:

- have strong partners in the bid process,
- make excellent presentations to the decision makers,
- treat every bid as a unique process,
- promote the track record of the community in hosting events,
- assist other organizations to make better bids.

Emery (2001) described the process of bidding through local, national, and international sport governing bodies and examined why cities in the UK bid on major sport events. It was concluded that cities needed to develop relevant professional credibility, know their strengths and weaknesses compared to the competition, learn about the decision-making processes, and not assume that rational criteria are always employed in awarding events.

Figure 5.3 illustrates the bidding process. The destination pursues events that "fit" its goals, while the event owners pursue destinations and venues that will best meet their needs. Managing stakeholder relationships is obviously very important in this process.

If a formal bidding process is required, the major components of the bid document should include the following;

- personalized letter to the client, or sanctioning body;
- letters of invitation/support from all important local organizations and officials (be careful of order, considering proper protocol);

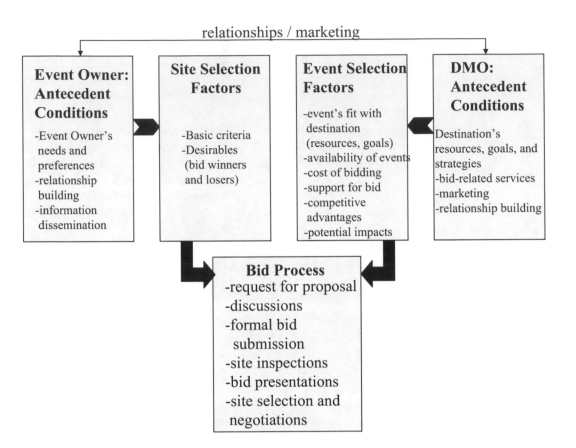

Figure 5.3. Event bidding process (from Getz, 2004a).

- executive summary;
- profile of the group making the bid and accepting responsibility for the event and its financing;
- support already obtained for the bid;
- summary of the event concept (as it conforms to specifications plus additional, proposed features);
- details of the plan: venue, facilities, investments, timing, scheduling, programming, meeting all the criteria;
- forecast of attendance; marketing plan;
- assertion of financial and economic feasibility; financial plan and budget;
- forecast of impacts; contingency plans;
- highlights of the legacy;
- advantages over competitors for the event.

Combating Seasonality

The tourism industry is in many places preoccupied with overcoming traditional "seasonality problems" (i.e., demand is concentrated in one or more "peak seasons" rather than being spread uniformly over the year). Events have unique advantages in overcoming seasonality. They can capitalize on whatever natural appeal the off-season presents, such as winter as opposed to summer sports, seasonal food and produce, and scenery or wildlife viewed in different places and under changing conditions. Or events can ignore the climatic differences altogether and concentrate on indoor activities. Also, in many destinations the residents prefer the off-season for their own celebrations, and these provide more authentic events for visitors. Of course, if this strategy is too successful, there will be no off-season

Advantages of Peak Season Events

- Competitive advantage can be gained over destinations without events
- Themes are easier to establish when large numbers of visitors are exposed quickly to the images and events.
- The local tourist industry is already geared up for crowds, and promotions are already in place.
- The weather is generally better and more predictable; main-street festivals and other outdoor events are best held in dry, warm weather (not the hottest or coldest or wettest times of year).
- Volunteers can use vacations to help out.
- In resort areas with many second homes, the seasonal visitors may feel a part of the community and want to participate.

Advantages of Off-Peak Events

- Creates tourist demand when spare capacity is high.
- Can encourage a four-season destination image.
- Provides entertainment for residents when other opportunities are limited.
- It might be easier to attract performers or displayers who are normally busy in the peak season.
- Certain sports competitions are seasonal by nature.
- Organizational capability might be highest, as most local groups will be meeting regularly and members will be at home.
- Funding might be easier to obtain if an expanded tourist season can be created.

Certain tourist segments have a natural preference for off-peak travel, either because of potential cost reductions or a desire to avoid crowds of other tourists. Retired persons and upper-income segments with more than one holiday opportunity a year are the key targets. Events can pull them for short breaks or even main holidays. Dedicated music lovers, athletes, sports fans, and other special-interest travelers will potentially attend events at any time of the year to satisfy their desire for special experiences. These target markets might be smaller, but also more loyal and easily reached through targeted promotions. Meeting and convention travel often favors off-peak seasons, both to secure lower costs for participants and to ensure sufficient space in facilities.

Despite the advantages events have in creating off-peak demand, festivals and sports events tend to adhere to the tourism peak season—generally summer. Janiskee (1996a) examined a large database of American community festivals and determined that January was the least popular month and July the most popular. He concluded:"The first weekend in May can be regarded as the unofficial start of the high season for festivals" (p. 131). The numbers dropped dramatically after mid-October. Regional variations related to climate were observed, and it became clear that certain periods of time were congested with events.

A study of event demand in the American Midwest (Wicks & Fesenmaier, 1995) proved that summer was most popular, followed by fall, for attending events. The dearth of participation in spring and winter could, of course, reflect supply, but it also suggests the need for caution when planning off-peak events. Wicks and Fesenmaier recommended identification of a market niche that was prepared to travel at off-peak times for specific events.

Leveraging Events and the Legacy

Destinations want to "leverage" events for broader, and longer term benefits by generating nontourism benefits (e.g., business and trade), promoting the destination (branding, image enhancement, media management), and developing a permanent legacy (money, facilities, other infrastructure, enhanced capabilities, etc.). The research evidence on the effectiveness of such strategies is mixed, at best. A lot of money and effort is spent to justify bidding on and hosting major events, and often it seems that the supposed long-term benefits are highly exaggerated.

Faulkner et al. (2000) discussed mega-event impacts and the legacy, describing the research done in Australia to measure the effects of its leveraging program surrounding the Sydney Olympics of 2000. Generic leveraging strategies included the following:

- using the event to build or enhance destination "positioning";
- enhancing visitor spending at the event;
- fostering longer stays and add-on trips/activities;
- building new relationships.

Leveraging the Games requires stakeholder commitment and coordination among many partners. B. Ritchie (2000) looked at the Calgary and Salt Lake City Winter Olympics and drew 10 lessons for event legacy planning.

1. Involve all stakeholders (costs and benefits).
2. Understand and build upon local values.
3. Include cultural, educational, and commercial components, not just athletics.
4. Involve and get support from the wider region.
5. Because enthusiasm wanes after the event, plans must be solidified in advance.
6. Residents have to be "trained" in providing hospitality.
7. Develop "satellite" festivals and conferences.
8. Use the event to foster social and cultural understanding and cohesion.
9. Achievement and impacts of the event have to be preserved and publicized for younger generations.
10. Tangibly connect the event to other local events or characteristics for synergy.

Induced Demand

As shown in Figure 5.4, events can generate "direct demand" in the form of attendance at the event, and "induced demand" before and after the event. Induced demand is heavily influenced by media coverage, and this can begin well in advance and afterwards. Before the event a destination can attract media preparing stories, officials checking preparations, curiosity seekers looking at new facilities being built, and teams for training sessions. Mega sporting events like the Olympics generate a lot of pre-Olympic events designed to test management systems and the facilities. After the event a "halo effect" might attract repeat visitors who enjoyed the event itself, those who received positive word-of-mouth recommendations from event-goers, and others who were favorably impressed by what they saw or read about the event and the host destination. To a degree, induced

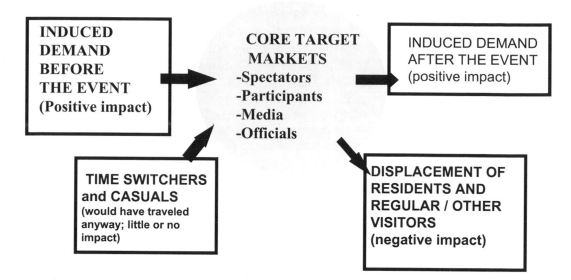

Figure 5.4. Tourist segments associated with events.

demand can be manipulated and leveraged, such as through pre- and postevent tours, maximizing media coverage of the destination, and providing inducements to visit.

Kang and Perdue (1994) examined the long-term impact of the 1988 Seoul Olympics on tourism flows to Korea and drew several important conclusions. These researchers felt that any increase in Korea's global tourism market share could not be estimated, but that the mega-event did have a positive effect in increasing long-term visitation to Korea. Because the host country was an emerging destination, the impact might be greater than for mature destinations. Consumer reaction to the image enhancement created by the event was judged to be lagged and protracted, or what others have called the "halo effect." It was apparently greatest the year following the Olympics and might extend as long as 10 years.

It is a major mistake to assume that the "halo effect" will result in a huge increase in tourist demand. Many other factors can quickly neutralize positive destination promotion, which is exactly what happened to Australia after the 2000 Summer Olympics. And even if there is a lasting effect, what will constitute proof? Unfortunately, in bidding on the Olympics the Australians had to justify the enormous expense somehow, and they latched onto the supposed tourist value of 10 years' worth of "induced demand" to offset the costs. Many experts believe this is unjustified (there is little research evidence) and misleading (real costs balanced by hypothetical and largely uncontrollable future gains).

Generating Nontourism Benefits

Will hosting a mega-event contribute to long-term economic development? Spilling (1998), a Norwegian researcher, concluded that the Winter Olympic Games of 1994 in Lillehammer had "rather marginal" long-term impacts in the context of the overall economic activity of the region. The benefits that were created included an increased capacity to host events and better tourism infrastructure. No long-term impact on unemployment could be detected, and overall business growth was minimal. Thus, the Games could not be justified in terms of economics, and this is likely true in all lightly populated regions where infrastructure costs will be high and business growth opportunities small. Event tourism was the real winner!

Leveraging Events for Local Business Advantages

Chalip and Leyns (2002) reported on how local businesses could get the most out of a major sport event. These authors noted that the uneven distribution of benefits from events is an important issue, because if local businesses feel little direct benefit they might oppose or fail to support events. Standard marketing practices can be employed (e.g., promotions, theming areas in line with the event, adding entertainment, extending hours), but the key is working collaboratively as a business community. A study by Pennington-Gray and Holdnak (2002) examined the potential for event leveraging in Florida.

Research Note

Pennington-Gray, L., & Holdnak, A. (2002). Out of the stands and into the community: Using sports events to promote a destination. *Event Management,* 7(3), 177–186.

Spectators to a drag race event in Florida were examined within the context of tourism impacts and place marketing. In this case it was found that a majority of the sport tourists participated only in that event, while most others spent money in the county only on one activity: dining out. The researchers found this to be disappointing and recommended that the county should work specifically to overcome the "disconnect" between the event (which attracted lots of tourists) and the attractiveness of the area (which had been largely overlooked by the visitors). Destinations employing events as place marketers and wealth creators have to learn how to better leverage their events.

Leveraging Events for Urban Renewal and Social Development

Carlsen and Taylor (2003) observed that major events in the UK are seen as an integral part of urban renewal and economic development. Specific to Manchester and the Commonwealth Games, goals included:

- heighten the city's profile;
- give impetus to urban renewal through creation of major sporting and commercial development;
- create a social legacy of benefits through culture and educational programs associated with the games.

Between 1999 and 2004 an economic and social program was established in concert with preparations for the Games, to improve skills and education, especially among young people; improve community health; enhance business competitiveness. The volunteer component of the Games involved training 3000 disadvantaged people from the region. As well, the "Let's Celebrate" program aimed to foster increased intercultural understanding around the multicountry Games. The city invested little in infrastructure, relying on UK grants and private investment, thereby allowing it to concentrate on social, cultural, and environmental legacies.

The Built Legacy

Dimanche (1996) provided a graphical model of how the New Orleans World's Fair or other major events might generate lasting impacts, especially in terms of increased visitor travel to a city. The main initiators of change are:

- leisure visits and other participation in the event, leading directly to repeat visits in the future;

- infrastructure improvements (hotels, transport, other facilities) leading first to increased capacity and visitor satisfaction, then to more tourist demand;
- community benefits leading first to resident satisfaction and word-of-mouth recommendations;
- increased media coverage leading first to increased awareness and improved tourist image;
- increased tourist promotion leading first to increased awareness and improved tourist image

Branding Through Events

Images associated with events can be transferred to the host community or destination, leading tourism agencies to increasingly include events explicitly in their destination positioning or branding strategies. Branding strategies for destinations usually aim to create a single, positive, and unique image that will create lasting competitive advantages. Some events will help create brand "equity" and others might detract from it. "Hallmark events," as defined in Chapter 1, become closely associated with the destination and therefore form a critical part of its branding. For example, it is difficult to change Calgary's brand image to anything that conflicts with the Calgary Stampede's western theme.

A "brand" originally was a mark or symbol that signified the maker or owner of a product (or cow). In modern marketing parlance it has a much broader meaning. Brands have both functional and symbolic dimensions that communicate what the product (or destination) has to offer and the quality or uniqueness associated with that offer. Strong, positive brands attract loyalty, which can be crucial for tourist destinations as they are typically perceived by consumers to be highly substitutable. In this context, a strong destination brand might have greater impact on attracting events, leading to a "golden spiral" wherein success with events generates more demand for events.

Strong brands might also help strengthen stakeholder relationships within a destination, to the degree that the brand is widely supported and shows sustainable benefits. By the same token, conflict over branding can erupt when some industry segments perceive that the brand does not help them sell their product or it favors others. Having a strong brand might help in dealing with tour companies and other product distributors, as they might come to believe that consumers are happier with "brand name" destinations.

A key problem with branding is that it tends to throw all the destination's eggs into one basket. After the main brand image and slogan are selected the destination risks being perceived as unidimensional. The brand therefore has to be broad and flexible enough to support positioning strategies aimed at all the important target markets. For example, how does a region branded as a tropical paradise "sell" itself for anything other than fun in the sun? It is a considerable challenge to the marketers.

"Co-branding" refers to the efforts of two or more partners to associate their individual brands for mutual gain. Events with their own image and appeal can be 'co-branded" with the destination, assuming they are both positive. Researchers in Australia have paid particular attention to these relationships (Brown, Chalip, Jago, & Mules, 2001; Jago, Chalip, Brown, Mules, & Shameem, 2003). Workshops with tourism marketers and event managers were held in several Australian cities, revealing a number of important themes that both stakeholder groups must collaborate on. Community support for events was viewed as being the most important criterion for successful co-branding, as the absence of strong support will hurt the event and its image. A closely related factor is the event's "fit" with the destination, n terms of values, culture, and use of infrastructure, as this will affect local support.

In repositioning a destination, the way in which the community wants to be perceived must be taken into account. Recurring events probably have a better chance of a close fit than do one-time events, leading to the next theme: longevity or tradition. On the other hand, hosting a once-only mega-event can help develop a profile and establish new traditions. Participants in the workshops also believed that uniqueness was important, to the degree that events help differentiate the destination. If all places host the same kinds of events, or events providing the same benefits sought by consumers, little is gained.

Having an attractive and diverse portfolio of events was perceived to be important in destination branding (Jago et al., 2003). Large events might attract the greatest media attention, but small events can help support larger ones while developing community support and event management skills. The researchers concluded that hosting quality events is a necessary condition for effective co-branding, but there is also the need for integrating events into destination marketing and communications.

Media Management to Promote the Destination

Many destination marketing organizations (DMOs) seek to obtain specific promotional and image-building benefits from media coverage of events. To make this work requires an understanding of consumer decision making, how destination images are formed, and of managing the media to ensure that they communicate desired images and messages to their audiences.

Getz and Fairley (2004) examined the media management of a number of sport events in Gold Coast, Australia. While there were some notable efforts being made to promote the destination, it was concluded that a lot more could be achieved through better planning and in particular through coordination of all the stakeholder actions. Table 5.2 lists the major actions that can be taken by event organizers, DMSs, corporate sponsors, the travel trade, media, and sport organizations for the joint goal of promoting the destination as a tourist attraction.

Postcards

Destinations want to get these short, visual features inserted into broadcasts and rebroadcasts of events, but they often cannot control their use. They are designed to showcase the attractiveness of the host destination—its people, culture, scenery, or attractions. If the event is owned by a destination, the inclusion of postcards can be a requirement.

Simon Shibli provided a good description of a "postcard" used in the 2002 Embassy World Snooker Championship held in Sheffield, England. One feature shown on television included Steve Davis, seven-time world snooker champion, starting the 2002 Sheffield Marathon and included images of the Don Valley Stadium. The idea was to promote the city as a National Center of Sport.

Research for Event Tourism Planning

Resource and Supply Appraisal

"Resources," in this context, are the human, financial, physical, political, and technological factors that can be used in developing and marketing event tourism. It is useful to think of resources as having potential, while "supply" defines the existing infrastructure of the tourism industry. Many events have the potential to become tourist attractions, but are viewed as "resources" until they are actually developed or marketed for tourist consumption.

Not all resources should be exploited. It is not legitimate, and might actually be counterproductive, to attempt to promote all events as attractions, or to encourage all commu-

Table 5.2. Stakeholder Roles in Media Management to Promote the Destination

Stakeholders	Actions
Event organizers	Utilize media relations professionals, photographers, and videographers
	Develop long-term media relationships
	Secure media sponsorship
	Use the event website to feature the destination and link to tourism sites; incorporate potential visitor experiences (stories and packages)
	Employ imagery consistent with the destination
	Co-brand through use of the destination name (e.g., Gold Coast Airport Marathon)
	Place destination signs at event
	Provide destination information to all participants and visitors
Destination marketing organizations	Require assisted events to adopt destination promotional goals and actions
	Prepare video "postcards" and feature stories
	Build an integrated branding campaign around major events
	Develop and assist events that reinforce desired images or help repositioning (i.e., co-branding)
	Arrange "fam" tours for events
Corporate sponsors	Co-marketing should include destination imagery
	Sponsors should use event and destination-related material (e.g., videos) in their own promotions and B to B contacts
Travel trade	Create packages for events to sell in target countries/regions
	Sponsor events and incorporate destination imagery in all promotions
	Travel agents to promote the event and destination together
Media	Sponsorship deals with media should specify destination promotion goals and methods
	Media will sell advertising spaces to DMOs
	Media will purchase coverage in some cases
	News coverage can be improved through cultivation of media (e.g., "fam" tours; hospitality)
Sport organizations	Participating sport organizations should promote the destination as well as the event
	Sports and their governing bodies should be long-term allies of the DMO

nities and organizations to produce events. Accordingly, there is much more to resource and supply appraisal than simply listing and classifying events. Judgment and stakeholder input is called for when assessing such issues as classifying events as to their tourism potential.

Figure 5.5 illustrates an event tourism resource and supply appraisal process. It is both a technical and evaluative process, as judgment is required in a number of areas:

- what to include or exclude (e.g., all events? all venues?);
- evaluation of resource potential (e.g., what can be done with existing human resources?);

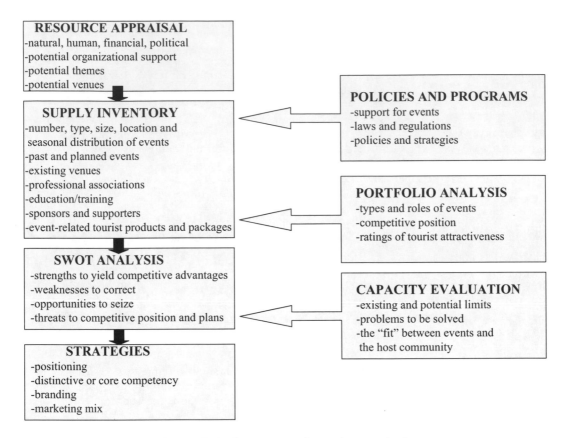

Figure 5.5. Resource and supply appraisal.

- obtaining quality input from research and stakeholders;
- assessing the data in meaningful ways;
- developing rating systems of tourist attractiveness;
- conducting portfolio, capacity, and SWOT evaluations;
- formulating strategies.

Resource Analysis

Financial Resources

Financial resources include the means to plan, bid on, and produce events, including development of event venues. Much of the capital for events comes from the private sector, especially sponsors, and from nonprofit organizations.

Natural Resources

Events can be used to interpret, protect, and enhance parks and protected areas, so a general resource inventory should be evaluated to determine existing and potential linkages. The natural resource base can also suggest themes, such as agricultural or other resource-based industries, and the community's interdependence with other environmental factors (such as wildlife, scenery, climate). Potential venues should be considered, including parks and open spaces. An activity analysis can be formed using a natural resource inventory and database of maps. All recreational activities, including wildlife viewing and nature interpretation, are potential event themes. Questions of capacity and compatibility will have to be evaluated.

Cultural Resources

Many event themes are derived from the cultural makeup of communities, including their history, ethnicity, traditions, and folklore. Built heritage is also important in suggesting event venues (like historic districts). Arts and crafts activities will be included, as will entertainment and performing arts. Consideration of cultural uniqueness and authenticity is important. Religious and educational institutions should be covered, as they are both sources of events and potential stakeholders or supporters of events.

Human Resources

Organizations and their memberships should be covered, leading to identification of event producers, potential facilitators, and volunteer pools. Who are the community leaders? What groups are most involved in activities that could become event attractions? What are current levels and patterns of volunteering? Who has the expertise to bid on events or produce them? An assessment of training and education needs for events might be important, but should be covered under general tourism and hospitality labor evaluations. Are there any event-specific training opportunities in the area? What institutions or associations could provide them? If there is little event management experience in the area some outside advice and assistance will be required.

Physical Resources

This category covers the built environment, particularly venues for events. All attractions and public facilities should be examined as to their potential for hosting various types of events, and their management invited to suggest ideas and state requirements for developing the events sector.

Political Resources

Is there support for tourism and events? Is there a bias towards one type of event, or one event in particular? Who can exert leadership in favor of an event funding policy? Examine interorganizational linkages, the degree of cooperation among organizations, and the roles of various political persons or parties in getting things done. In other words, allying with "movers and shakers" in a community is a good way to initiate event tourism plans. Also consider political events and the ability to attract them to the destination. This might involve direct lobbying of political parties, marketing by convention centers, or more subtle forms of getting heard.

Technological Resources

Are there technological themes that could be developed through events, such as inventions, transportation heritage, or communications innovations? What technological resources exist to help produce or market events? Is there a computerized ticket reservation system in place? What is the state of local and regional media, especially in terms of covering and promoting events?

Supply Analysis

Supply is tangible and can be measured. How many events, venues, and sponsors are there in the destination? What are the trends in numbers, size, location, seasonality, and demand? It is useful to examine past events as well, and failed bids. Event organizations and sponsors should also be counted and scrutinized for possible contributions to an expanded events sector. Tourism services, including event-related packages, should also be inventoried and assessed.

The inventory is a quantitative exercise intended to accurately describe the nature and size of the event sector. Many destinations and communities do not have adequate data, and even if there is a directory or calendar of events it will likely be reliant on voluntary submission of information—and therefore incomplete. Research will be needed to complete the inventory and to assemble a permanent database useful in planning and impact assessment. The usual starting point will be whatever calendar or listing is available, followed by telephone calls and interviews to update and refine the database. It cannot be done without first establishing a classification system, as well as criteria to determine what exactly constitutes a "festival" as opposed to, say, a "fair" or "party." A degree of interpretation will likely prove necessary, so it is best to acquire information on the event program and goals to assist in classification. The scope and detail of the inventory will depend on resources available to do the job, and the ultimate uses of data. Enlisting the help of the events themselves is a wise tactic, especially if they have an association or other means of regular communication.

Components of an Event Inventory

- Name or description of the event
- Main theme(s)
- The organizers (a profile or cross-reference to another inventory)
- Dates, times, venues, locations
- Frequency or periodicity
- Indicators of professionalism (e.g., business plan, budget, staff)
- Key contact persons and addresses
- Visitor/guest profile; target market segments
- Estimated attendance; growth; percent local versus tourist
- Tourist orientation (e.g., reflected in goals, marketing, attendance)
- Activities (i.e., the program)
- Goals and objectives of the organizers
- Historical background (e.g., date of origin; development)
- Major sponsors (any "title" sponsor?)
- Staff and volunteer numbers; staff positions; full- or part-time?
- Total operating budget
- Economic impact
- Operating surplus or loss
- Grants or other support received (amounts; sources)
- Sponsorship revenue (amounts; in-kind)
- Other revenue (amounts; sources)
- Any strategic plan? marketing strategy?
- Support requested or needed (link to SWOT evaluation)

Policies and Programs

Particular attention should be paid to government policies and programs at all levels. What is the current and potential future level of support for tourism in general, and for events? Do policies stress one type of event, such as the arts or sports, over others? What regulations, such as licensing, apply specifically to events? Are the tax, labor, and safety laws a deterrent to events tourism development? More subjectively, is the political mood favorable?

This latter question raises the need for compiling a database of all stakeholders, including groups and individuals that could support or threaten event tourism. The planning process must involve all these stakeholders to identify problems and opportunities, and to ensure collection of all pertinent information.

Classification

Within a resource and supply appraisal, classification is a useful tool, whether for types of event, themes, programs, activities, venues, organizations, or services available. In the

Netherlands (Bos, 1994) events are classified by the Board of Tourism by reference to the scale of tourist attractiveness: local events; small regional; regional events with above-regional importance; national events with only domestic importance; major events with a truly international level of attraction.

In a study for the Province of Ontario, consultants (Economic Planning Group and Lord Cultural Services, 1992) recommended a six-level classification based on five criteria: size and scale of the event; uniqueness of the product; quality of the experiences offered; image established in the marketplace; reputation in the marketplace. Although such classifications (they are really rating systems) are useful, there are many potential problems in determining where any given event fits, and the more important issues of whether existing conditions or the event's potential should form the basis of the evaluation. As all events have tourism potential, focusing on one or more of these five criteria could impair future development of the sector, especially if financial assistance is linked to a high rating. Would it not be better to use the criteria in a self-diagnosis or marketing audit to look for ways to improve each event?

As noted by Jago (1994), most attraction and event typologies are from the supply perspective, whereas a marketing orientation suggests a consumer or demand-side classification should be developed. How do potential customers of events view them? What criteria do they use? As noted earlier, securing the opinions of the tour industry is one important step. Researching consumers is another. To a limited extent this has been done by Getz and Cheyne (1996) through focus groups, which covered event trip motivations, benefits sought, and related behavior and experiences.

Results suggested that a number of factors were important when people consider an event-related purchase or trip, and these can be utilized in a classification system:

- uniqueness: opportunities to experience something different (e.g., major entertainers or international sports celebrities);
- socializing: opportunities for family outings; meeting and seeing people; party atmosphere;
- learning: opportunities for authentic experiences; interpretation provided;
- packaging the event with a wider social and travel experience;
- participating in an event; viewing friends and relatives who are participating.

The demand-side classification could therefore include the types of events shown below, with dichotomies or ranges possible within each:

- once-in-a-lifetime opportunities (as opposed to periodic);
- celebrity events (see/meet the stars or VIPs);
- participatory events (versus spectator);
- public, festive events (as opposed to private parties);
- learning events (including authentic cultural experiences);
- leisure events (featuring relaxation, fun, health);
- family- or friend-oriented event outings;
- event-related tour packages (self-assembled or all-inclusive).

Once such a system is established—and more research is required to determine its applicability to different consumer segments under varying circumstances—communications could stress the relevant messages in a variety of media. While supply-side classifications might be of value in planning, demand-side typologies will have greater applicability in marketing.

SWOT Analysis

A "SWOT" analysis consists of a summary of the destination's strengths, weaknesses, opportunities, and threats pertaining to event tourism. Strengths, in the context of resource and supply evaluations, are resources, events, or related services and packages considered to be of high quality, high attractiveness, or strong in terms of numbers and/or variety. Tourism strengths are likely to consist of:

- unique theme or setting;
- large and diverse program or activities;
- existing large audiences, many of whom are regulars;
- a good reputation outside the area;
- specialized appeal;
- high quality of program and service;
- a captive tourism audience (at resorts, convention centers, staying with friends and relatives, at second homes);
- a range of complementary attractions and services in the area;
- widespread promotion through media coverage;
- sponsors with national or international interests;
- existing packages and services for tour groups;
- solid support from the community, including volunteers and political support;
- organizational and management capability (to expand, improve, and innovate);
- a high ratio of benefits to costs.

Tourism opportunities are anything that can be taken advantage of to enhance tourist attractiveness, such as:

- new/developing tourist attractions in the area;
- newly emerging target markets;
- opportunities for joint promotions and packages;
- potential addition or improvement of new event activities/attractions.

Tourism threats are emerging or potential obstacles to achieving goals, including the following examples:

- competition;
- markets are changing to favor other types of event or attraction;
- declining quality of the event product due to age or poor management;
- inability of event management/volunteers to adapt and innovate;
- loss of community and volunteer support if benefits are not obvious or costs/ problems grow;
- lack or support and promotion from tourist organizations.

SWOT Criteria

When conducting a SWOT evaluation several important criteria should be considered: variety, quality, drawing power (attractiveness), image, and reputation.

"Variety" is a measure of the breadth of resources such as events, by type, size, location, or whatever. There can be no measure of variety without an inventory and classification of all events in the area. Are certain types over-or underrepresented?

Some resources display higher quality or potential than others. How this is determined is open to debate and experimentation, but quality can be evaluated in three general ways:

by reference to external conditions; through customer feedback and consumer research; and by expert evaluators. For example, determining whether the destination has high-quality human or cultural resources for event tourism is likely to be answered by experts and through input from many stakeholders. To determine if the area has high-quality events requires a different approach. Almost everyone has experienced a variety of events and can apply that experience to the evaluation. Input from event managers and sponsors will add a great deal to the evaluation. Comparing local events with external ones will be improved by obtaining an outside expert's judgment.

Are events currently drawing tourists? From what distance and for what length of time? Strengths derive from existing events with tourist drawing power, from organizations that produce or sponsor these events, and from high-quality event venues that appeal to tourists. There might be high-quality events in the area that, for lack of promotions, do not have current drawing power. This conclusion leads to an "opportunity" to be exploited. Threats are likely to come from competitors, but also from internal factors that could, for example, change domestic demand for local events.

Is size a factor in determining attractiveness? There is little doubt that large events generate publicity, excitement, and repeat visits, but small events can be just as important for particular market segments. In fact, it may be that many consumers will seek out the small events, associating them more with authentic cultural experiences.

Image and reputation are also key criteria. Surveys of the tour industry and media can determine if events have a good reputation. However, it is more important to find out reasons and to use this knowledge for improving events.

Core Competency (What Do We Do Best?)

Arising from the forgoing evaluation should be a statement on "core competency." This statement identifies what the destination does best in the events sector. In part this is a direct output of the portfolio and SWOT exercises. One school of thought holds that a business should stick to what it does best, shunning temptations to continuously add new products or cater to different markets. Hence, a community that has a strong base of sports venues, clubs, and related events would not stray into arts festivals even if potential demand and local interest existed. A contrary strategy would be to hold onto and develop the core competency while at the same time expanding the variety or market appeal of its events.

Capacity and Fit

When appraising the resource base certain limitations will become evident. For example, there is likely to be a limit to the number of volunteers a community can muster, or to the number of event venues. And each venue will also likely have a fixed capacity in terms of crowd size or the range of activities it can support.

As much as possible, the analysis should identify these limits and translate them into strengths, weaknesses, opportunities, or threats. Each should be quantified, such as by making an estimate of the maximum number and types of sports events an area can accommodate by fully utilizing its existing supply. A resultant statement of strengths might be: "This destination can accommodate a wide range of high-quality sporting events," with a directly related weakness being: "but only at the scale of local and regional competitions."

A more difficult issue is that of determining the community's or destination's capacity to absorb tourism, or a specific type of tourism like events. "Fit" is a related concept. An area might be able to host a major sporting event, but is there compatibility (or good "fit") between the community's capabilities, strengths, and weaknesses and the needs of the event or the potential impacts of the event? Part of the evaluation will be the issue of capacity, and part concerns other factors such as management capabilities and goodwill towards events and tourists.

Planning Implications

A host of planning implications follow from the above analyses and evaluations. Before formulating strategies, these implications should be listed and studied. Some might suggest additional research and analyses; others might be answerable only through a political debate. The major types of implications arising from the material presented in this chapter are stated below; these are a starting point only:

- What explains the pattern and types of events held in this area? Is it the result of policy, unplanned cultural factors, or economic conditions?
- How best can the events be influenced towards achieving tourism goals?
- How can the identified resources for event tourism be mobilized? At what cost?
- Do we have the interest and capacity for hosting major events? for creating many new events? to bid on events?

Case Study of Gothenburg, Event Capital of Sweden

Gothenburg is Sweden's second-largest city (about 500,000 population), the home of Volvo, and an events capital. A lead role is taken by "Gothenburg and Co.," a unique destination marketing and management company that has been quite successful in bidding on and hosting major events. Their media management skills also ensure that the city, and Sweden, are front and center when it comes to promoting the destination through events.

"Got Event" is the company established by the city to manage its major sport venues, namely Ullevi Stadium (Scandinavia's largest outdoor stadium), Valhalla Swimming Hall, and Scandinavium Indoor Arena (home of an ice hockey team). As well, the city boasts the Swedish Exhibition and Congress Center, and outdoor sport venues. Because all the major event venues are in close proximity to each other and the central city, a highly attractive events district has been created.

"Gothenburg and Co." functions as the city's visitor and convention bureau, but it is unique in a number of important ways. It is an incorporated private company, but its ownership brings together all the key stakeholders. The city is a major shareholder, as well as other local authorities in the region, the West Sweden Chamber of Commerce, the Swedish Exhibition and Congress Centre, and major companies in the tourism business and hotel and restaurant associations. Got Event, the sport event management company, is also an important shareholder. Shareholders have entered into long-term agreements to develop and market Gothenburg and the region. Its vision is: *Gothenburg is to be a preferred choice among cities in Europe by being one of Europe's most pleasant and attractive urban regions to visits and in which to live and work.*

Second, its four operational areas include business travel, private travel, events, and trade and industry, with support functions including research and development through the independent but affiliated Swedish Research Institute of Tourism. They are a member of the European Cities' Tourism association and in 2003 hosted their annual conference.

The events function within Gothenburg and Co. is directed by a Steering Committee that generally includes representatives from events, the sport venues (i.e., Got Event), arts venues (e.g., the Opera House), hotels, and other private business. Their mission is: *to ensure a richly varied range of events in Gothenburg. This is achieved by attracting new events, supporting existing and returning events, aiding and working with arenas and institutions on their event initiatives and being responsible for project management and implementation.*

2006 European Athletics Championship

Toralf Nilsson is employed by Got Event and is General Secretary and in charge of preparing for the 2006 European Athletics Championship, to be held in Gothenburg. The city, through Gothenburg and Co., bears the financial risk for this event, and it is in part this willingness of local politicians to accept such risks that makes Gothenburg unique and successful. To win the event, and produce it, Gothenburg and Co. has partnered with Got Event, the Swedish Athletic Association, the Gothenburg Athletic Federation, and Swedish Television.

While this event is not in the same league as the World Championships, held there in 1995 (which attracted 592,000 spectators), it is certainly a mega-event for a city of this size. Much was learned from the 1995 event, including how to manage the media to promote a destination. Also, the organizers learned that while income was adequate, high costs and taxes became a financial problem. Nevertheless, while the city could afford to take a financial loss, it is harder to develop and sustain a positive image.

Beginning in January of 2003, some 600 media people in Europe received the first of four annual bulletins to prepare them for the event and to encourage advance publicity. Ticket sales were to begin in the fall of 2004, so major advertising and promotions are to begin coincidentally.

Media management surrounding the event will be provided by the media management group within Gothenburg and Co. Although Swedish television is the official host broadcaster, Toralf does not feel they have any interest in tourism promotions, only sports. And the National Tourism Authority does not usually use sports in its promotions, although its new strategy in 2003 recognized the importance of event development. Ironically, Toralf wants to promote it as an event of national Swedish significance, in order to attract sponsors. A further complication is that the governing body (i.e., the event owner, the European Athletic Association) controls 85% of the marketing rights and they have their own sponsors.

Case Study of Queensland Events Corporation

Queensland Events Corporation Pty Ltd was created in 1989 following the success of Brisbane's World Expo '88. Queensland Events was given the mission "to develop and support events that are capable of generating substantial economic activity and that lift the profile of Queensland both within Australia and overseas."

World Expo '88—and earlier, the 1982 Commonwealth Games (the most financially successful games of their time)—had increased awareness of the major economic and social benefits that can be derived from events. The Queensland state government felt that event professionalism had increased substantially as a result of Expo '88 and that a formally established organization could help the state maintain that level of progress. As a result, Queensland Events was established to continue attracting world-class events to the state.

Queensland Events is a limited liability company wholly owned by the state government and forms part of the portfolio of the head of state, the Premier of Queensland. Queensland Events also owns and operates the Gold Coast Airport Marathon and the Pan Pacific Masters Games through a wholly owned subsidiary company on Queensland's Gold Coast.

Queensland Events' major objectives were at first devoted to the following:

- identify and bid on major international events;
- review and develop existing events with the potential to achieve national or international profile;
- develop new events of all kinds that have the potential to promote the state.

The following early priorities for Queensland Events were established:

- identify Queensland's strategic assets;

- identify major events that could be held in Queensland;
- continue liaison on existing proposed events;
- identify existing events with potential to develop a national or international profile;
- develop criteria for funding assistance;
- develop a database of international events;
- establish priorities for developing new event concepts;
- conduct feasibility studies;
- establish a computer model for evaluating economic impacts of proposed events;
- develop a standardized list of financial criteria to assist event organizers in preparation of their business plans and budgets;
- prepare guidelines to assist event organizers in their submissions to Queensland Events;
- review marketing strategies and tools used by Australian cities in event bidding;
- identify agencies and organizations that can contribute expertise and resources to future bids;
- brief the major companies in the state on Queensland Events role, and determine their sponsorship and marketing policies;
- provide advice to event organizers and introductions to potential sponsors;
- conduct meetings with relevant government departments aimed at offering assistance with their representation at international events;
- upgrade marketing support material;
- produce a brochure outlining the role of Queensland Events;
- assess the viability of a special event newsletter;
- produce a brochure offering advice of use to event organizers;
- produce a high-quality publication to promote Queensland's natural attractions and competitive advantages to event organizers, international sanctioning bodies, and potential sponsors;
- update a database on event marketers and sponsors;
- identify relevant overseas trade exhibitions and events at which the state should be represented.

Their earliest major triumph was attracting the first IndyCar race to be held outside North America. This was held on the Gold Coast in 1991, leading to the annual Lexmark Indy 300, Gold Coast. Queensland Events established a new company to operate the race, which took a 5-year contract with CART (the owners of IndyCar racing) plus an option for 5 more. The event is now run by Gold Coast Motor Events Company (a joint venture between the Queensland government and International Management Group) under a contract with Open Wheel Racing Series LLC (formerly Cart) until 2008. This event gives very high international profile to the state's premier tourist destination and provides it with a new peak season in late October. In 2004 it attracted a record 309,583 people. The economic impact is calculated at A$50.4 million with an international promotional value of A$15.5 million.

Since Queensland Events' inception, more than 200 major events have been staged in Queensland with the corporation's support, returning an estimated A$1 billion in additional revenue to the state. Successes include hosting the 1994 World Masters Games, 1994 World Gymnastic Championships, the 1998, 1999, and 2000 Davis Cup, 2000 Olympic Football, 2001 Goodwill Games, and the 2001 WAVA World Veterans Athletics Championships.

In 2001, the state introduced an events policy and the strategy of investing in major and regional events. The Queensland Events Regional Development Program supports events outside the state capital of Brisbane, taking event tourism throughout the state (see details below).

The year 2003 was a big year for events in Queensland, as 22 major events were supported by Queensland Events resulting in the "highest level of event-driven visitation from interstate and international markets in the state's history" (Queensland Events the Year in Review, 2003, p. 10). Biggest of these was the Rugby World Cup, an Australia-wide event in which Queensland hosted 12 matches involving 14 national teams that attracted over 400,000 spectators. The

Photo 5.1. Dirver Mario Dominquez in the Lexmark Indy 300, Champ Car race, Gold Coast, Queensland (credit: Mark Horsburgh, Edge Photographics).

state's Premier described the media coverage obtained by this globally televised event as "priceless."

Although most major events are sports (see the profiles following), 2003 also brought the Rotary International Convention, which attracted over 17,000 delegates from 114 countries and generated over 120,000 room nights in the state. Delegates were surveyed and it was determined that the average spending per person, per night was A$295.68. It was the first convention to win the Queensland Tourism Award for Major Festivals and Events. Rotary International declared the 2003 event "the best convention in Rotary's 94-year history," stating the assistance the city and state provided with logistical support, venue, city hospitality, transport, and generally its attitude is no doubt the reason behind its success.

Queensland Events Regional Development Program (QERDP)

By the end of 2004 almost A$2.5 million had been invested in support for more than 125 events since this program's inception in 2001. The QERDP is administered through the program secretariat in Townsville, North Queensland.

The program involves a partnership with local councils and regional tourist organizations, which endorse projects before assessment. Any financial support under the QERDP is based on the potential for the event to grow and develop for the benefit of the region in which it is staged. It supports events that:

- increase local economic activity and development;
- enhance the appeal of the destination in which they are held; and
- enhance the visitor experience.

Applications will only be accepted from a formally constituted organization, or any group that has a written agreement with a formally constituted organization to provide an auspice. Priority is given to applications that clearly demonstrate local government support. New and existing events can apply for funding under the program. Organizations intending to bid for an event to bring to their region may also apply. Funding will only be available once the event is secured. Funding is for the event only and is not available for the bid process.

Some examples of funding uses are:

- the employment of personnel to further develop and market the event;
- operational costs where it can be demonstrated that the funding will contribute to improving the visitor experience (i.e., visitor facilities such as temporary toilets, improved access);
- strategic marketing campaigns to increase awareness and visitations.

Funding is not provided for capital or equipment costs. The amount of funding requested cannot be greater than 25% of the total event budget. There is no upper funding limit; however, it is expected that most proposals will be funded in the vicinity of A$20,000–25,000. The minimum amount that can be applied for is A$5,000.

Hailed by the state government as an outstanding success, in 2004 the program was expanded to include additional funding under the Core Program and two new schemes: the Significant Regional Event Scheme and the Regional Events Innovations Scheme.

Profiles of Major Periodic Queensland Events

Gold Coast Airport Marathon: The year 2004 marked the 26th running of this event, newly named through a major title sponsorship by the city's airport authority in 2003, attracting over 2000 marathoners, while all the events involved a record 11,000+ participants from 20 countries. The Gold Coast Airport Marathon is an annual, 1-day event. The event includes a full marathon, half marathon, 10k run, 7.5 km walk, and a 2.25km and 4km Junior Dash. Given the nature of the sport of marathon, the main focus is on attracting event participants rather than spectators.

Media relations are primarily maintained through the employment of a professional media relations officer whose role is to create media interest in the event and ensure a continuous feed of stories to the media. Newspapers are the predominant communication media utilized to attract event participants, specifically Australian East Coast regional papers using editorial supported by advertising. The event website has demonstrated its success as a key marketing tool. Radio, television, and the Internet and, to a lesser extent, magazine advertising, are used. The official Gold Coast Airport Marathon website is designed to attract event participants in part by promoting the general attractiveness of the area. Extensive destination information is accessible via an included link to Tourism Queensland's website. A media monitoring service is used to archive the national media coverage of the event; however, this information is not subjected to detailed analysis.

The Marathon has international links with sport organizations, sports travel specialists, and general travel agents in New Zealand, Japan, Hong Kong, and South Korea. The Marathon utilizes these contacts to attract overseas attention and increase interest in the event. This activity, supported by targeted advertising in international running magazines, attracts participants from over 20 countries (including more than 500 from Japan, 400 from New Zealand, and growing numbers from the US).

Photo 5.2. Start of the 2003 Gold Coast Airport Marathon (credit: courtesy of the *Gold Coast Bulletin*).

The event was named the state's best major event at the 2004 Queensland Tourism Awards.

The Pan Pacific Masters Games: This event was previously named the Asia-Pacific Masters Games and is a biennial, 9-day-long, multisport event. In 2003 it was renamed to the Pan Pacific Masters Games and will be held every year alternating between the cities of Sacramento, California, and the Gold Coast in Queensland. This alliance has been formed between Queensland Events and the Sacramento Sports Commission.

Being a complex event encompassing approximately 45 sports, the operation of individual competitions is contracted out to pertinent sport organizations, and acts only as an umbrella organization providing infrastructure and marketing activities. Similar to the Marathon, the Masters Games focuses on attracting participants. Coverage of the event at a local level includes print, radio, and some television. Until recently, national coverage of the event has been limited to regional Australian newspapers featuring human interest stories (e.g., profiling "home town" participants). It is therefore positioned primarily as a lifestyle event. For the 2000 event a professional camera crew was hired to produce a 30-minute broadcast highlights package.

The 2004 event staged on the Gold Coast attracted close to 10,000 participants from 30 countries.

Study Questions

- Why do destinations so aggressively pursue event tourism? Discuss their main goals.
- What roles and specific actions can a community or tourism agency take in developing event tourism?

- Explain the event portfolio model, including major criteria for determining the tourism value of events.
- What are the generic event tourism strategies?
- What are the "resources" used in developing event tourism?
- Give criteria for evaluating the strengths and weaknesses of events in a tourism context.
- How can the media be "managed" to promote a destination through events?
- What research and planning is needed to bid on and win an event?
- Explain "leveraging" and explain three specific ways events can be "leveraged" for tourism and nontourism benefits.
- What is "induced" and "direct demand" for events?

Advanced Study Questions

- Find evidence to support or counter the commonly made proposition that a major event can generate many years of "induced demand."
- Use the event bidding process model to examine an actual bid for an event, with emphasis on the concept of destination/event "fit."
- With regard to the various possible measures of event "value," develop an event tourism portfolio for your area. Show how tourism and other community goals can be mutually supportive.

Chapter 6

The Event Experience, Programming, and Quality

Learning Objectives

- Be able to create attractive and satisfying event experiences, appropriate to the nature and purpose of the event.
- Develop an attractive program of activities using the key elements of style.
- Employ portfolio analysis to ensure program balance and the meeting of diverse goals.
- Recognize implications of the program life cycle and implement life cycle program planning.
- Understand the meaning of "quality" and be able to produce high-quality events.
- Understand how service quality gaps affect consumers' perceptions of the event.
- Formulate and implement service quality measures.
- Employ the concept of interactive marketing to enhance the event experience.

Program Planning

How do guests or customers experience an event? How do interactions among people, setting, program, and management systems shape the experience? What does "quality" mean in this context, and how can the event manager ensure that visitors are satisfied?

In their book *The Experience Economy*, Pine and Gilmour (1999) argued that in the world of retailing and service provision it is the creation of customer-engaging experiences that provides competitive advantages. They talked about "experience realms": entertainment, education, escapism, and aesthetics, combined with passive or active participation by customers, and immersion or absorption. Entertainment, for example, is passively absorbed through the senses. With education, customers or guests "absorb" the experience through active participation—you must be part of an educational experience. In an escapist experience the guest actively participates in an immersive environment (being physically or virtually part of it), such as taking part in a fantasy camp. Aesthetics refers to the appreciation of art or beauty.

The Pine and Gilmore approach surely appeals to event producers who, after all, have been creating quality, memorable experiences all along. In this chapter we look at programming, creativity, and the "elements of style" that can go into the creation of event experiences. Then we examine both program and service quality as well as its management.

Often events start with the program concept and then consider how to manage and market it. This is not necessarily wrong, especially from the perspective of creativity, but it can pose problems if the organization cannot produce the concept or potential customers do not like it. Ideally, programming ideas and decisions form part of ongoing strategic planning in the organization, including constant evaluation and improvement.

A set of "foundation issues" must be considered, including location, venue, and the opportunities and constraints imposed by the setting such as capacity and the feasibility of certain activities. Sometimes decisions on setting will be made prior to the event programmer or planner becoming involved, while in other circumstances the program can be planned and an appropriate setting later found. In most cases the programmer will have to shape or modify plans because of location and venue considerations, not to mention the proposed budget.

All events must provide a number of essential services, and these can both shape the program and suggest creative themes. For example, while food and beverages are generally required, they can also be the purpose of an event (as in a food festival), provide minor themes (as in theme parties), or be of such quality as to elevate a basic function to a memorable occasion.

"Theming" is a vital part of event planning. Often this is left completely to the creative imaginations of programmers and setting designers, but usually the basic concept suggests appropriate themes. Theming involves the integration and consistent communication of a number of elements including the event name, logo, mascots or other symbols, design of the setting, and the specific activities and tangible products available to the guests. Because events are experiential, theming is important in communicating the goals and benefits of the event. Furthermore, theming is often essential in creating the right ambience for celebration or learning.

Program and service quality management are essential to satisfying guests and customers and to meeting the event's goals. Specifications for quality programs and services must be formulated, and staff and volunteers trained to implement them correctly. Constant improvement and innovation is part of this process, as is the identification and prevention of problems.

Stakeholders and Programming

Someone with a clear artistic, educational, or entertainment concept might want complete control over an event program, but this is usually not practical. There will likely be many stakeholder "voices" to take into account. If you have major sponsors, those corporations want specific benefits that will influence the program—such as maximizing television audiences. Local government might want greater diversity in the program, with emphasis on meeting the needs of the disadvantaged. The tourism marketing agency might very well ask that more consideration be given to elements of the event that can be attractively packaged for visitors. In short, it is often difficult to meet everyone's expectations.

A "multistakeholder" approach to event planning is clearly the answer. This can be formalized through membership in the board of directors or a steering committee, or undertaken in an informal manner through open program planning and event evaluation sessions.

The Elements of Style

At the core of event programming are the activities and other program elements that can be thought of as "elements of style," and they give considerable power to the programmer. These elements can be mixed and matched in unlimited, creative ways, giving rise to a "portfolio" of programs and activities. They are not mutually exclusive, and many program activities can fall into several categories at once. In fact, the last element—entertainment—is really a way of looking at the other elements, any of which can be considered as entertainment by the guest or customer.

"Style" has three general meanings of relevance to events. The first and most important is that of a characteristic manner of expression or design. A certain combination of elements leads to an identifiable "style" of event that sets it apart from others, and within these characteristic styles there will be subcategories. Within the style of event called a parade, for example, there are subforms like military and carnival parades, religious processions, and others. Festivals in particular take on many different substyles, which, for example, distinguish children's festivals from food festivals. Fairs also come in different styles, notably agricultural, world's, and arts and craft fairs. Although many elements of style and their associated activities are suitable for different forms of events, not all are common or appropriate for all forms. For example, religious processions are uncommon at fairs, while carnival floats and costumes are inappropriate at religious festivals.

The second definition of style is "excellence of artistic expression." No matter how the elements and activities are combined and presented, there will always be differences between events, and between each edition of a regular event. This is due to artistic excellence, quality control, or subtle variations that escape analysis. In part this is an area of concern for organizers who pursue excellence and develop quality control mechanisms. In part it is inevitable and not altogether undesirable. For reasons stated earlier, events are expected to be unique, and variations can become delightful surprises.

A third definition of style is that of "fashion." Cultures change, albeit slowly, while tastes and preferences in leisure, tourism, and events can change more quickly. Some styles of event, such as folk festivals, go through cycles of popularity.

The elements of styles discussed below are all potentially important when designing or programming an event and the event setting. There is no specific number of elements, nor are they all mutually exclusive. Rather, this is a way of looking at programming.

Aesthetics and the Senses

Anything appealing to your senses of vision, smell, hearing, taste, or touch can be considered an aesthetic experience, although most people think of it in terms of beauty. The senses can all be stimulated for multiple purposes, including making people thirsty or hungry, encouraging quiet or celebration, and even to manage crowds. But aesthetic appreciation through any or all of the senses is generally a mental process. An art exhibit is the obvious kind of event for pure aesthetic appreciation, but aesthetics are also important in the design of event venues, costumes and uniforms, souvenirs, food and beverages. An aesthetic theme or themes can run through an entire event program or can be the highlight. Creativity comes to the fore in this element of style.

Escapism

Events offer many possibilities for people to escape their normal lives and environments, either to be stimulated or to relax. Escapism is a powerful motive for leisure and travel pursuits and can be facilitated in a number of ways. The event theme can be pure fantasy, or an exotic setting used. Entertainment can carry away the audience to another place or time—remember that nostalgia is always popular. Anything that makes people forget their worries is escapist.

Celebration

Celebration is at the core of festivals, and it is the spirit that organizers want to encourage in many types of special event. The essence of celebration, commemoration, and carnival is public sharing of themes having common cultural significance to participants. Belonging and contributing to the cause is also an important motivator for the volunteers and organizers. Once the atmosphere or mood is established, merry-making can become infectious. For more solemn ceremonies, the festivities are usually separated in setting or time.

Other emotional responses can be fostered at events, especially patriotism, pride, revelry, or religious fervor. At some events risk-taking can be fostered, perhaps unintentionally. How are these feelings created? The event programmer basically employs all the other elements of style in a way that leads the audience to an emotional response. It is in large part a matter of ambience, within which the most effective elements can be ritual (including speeches), stirring music, and spectacle. The Olympics are a classic example, although Olympic ceremonies contain emotional elements that other events might find difficult to emulate (e.g., being broadcast to the world, global competition, mega-event magnitude, powerful symbols—the Olympic rings, a celebration of youth, and connotations of goodwill and peaceful coexistence).

Ritual

A ritual is a set form or system of rites, religious or otherwise, and a rite is a ceremonial, often solemn, act. Most traditional, enduring festivals have a strong ritual component or are derived from religious or pagan rituals, all appealing to some higher principle, deity, or religious meaning. It is also present in most contemporary events, regardless of their tradition, in forms such as opening and closing ceremonies, the singing of national anthems, and the inclusion of symbols like flags and banners. Ritual can also be incorporated thematically in special events, through the employment of coordinated and mutually reinforcing symbols, ceremonies, colors, and visitor activities, so that the whole event becomes a ritualistic endorsement of community values, nationalism, or even political philosophy.

It is useful to look at specific types of rite and ritual. Rites of valorization and devalorization mark out the setting for temporary special purposes—what Falassi (1987) called a "time out of time." Contemporary events employ these rites in the form of opening and closing ceremonies, usually with speeches, national anthems, or other symbols of power and authority. Rites of purification often accompany the valorization of special settings, particularly in the form of prayers.

More secular events, especially carnivals, employ rites of reversal in which people take on fantasy roles or switch places with others; costumes and masks mark these occasions. Rites of conspicuous display and consumption are the hallmark of feasts, now expressed as food and beverage festivals, and also trade fairs and merchandizing-oriented events. Displays often reveal power while consumption shows wealth.

Ritual dramas are ancient elements of celebration, and are still found in contemporary events through several formats. Parades and processions encompass drama through floats that tell stories, although this time-honored tradition is now reduced mostly to superficial spectacle—especially in television-oriented parades. Festivals often incorporate historical reenactments that can be thought of as ritual drama.

Rites of passage, marking the progress of people, places, or institutions, are frequently celebrated through personal events, including the birthday and anniversary party, and for corporations the grand opening. For many people, their first participation in a special event is tied to a "rite de passage" such as birthday, entering high school or college, or getting married. Because many events are considered to be community and cultural traditions, attendance can take on personal significance.

Finally, rites of competition dominate the sport event sector. Viewed as ritual, competitions are substitutes for more violent conflict or warfare, symbolize but ameliorate intergroup rivalries, and demonstrate the individual's or group's skills, accomplishments, or aspirations.

Protocol

How people are handled, especially officials and dignitaries, is the subject of protocol. There may be formal protocols that have to be enforced, such as how opening and closing ceremonies are conducted, who sits next to whom, what flags and national anthems are to be played, or how awards are announced. Other protocol can be situation specific, following general rules of etiquette and hospitality. The more formal the event, and the more attention it commands from the media and government, the more necessary it is to check all aspects of protocol with appropriate authorities. Start with governing bodies (e.g., sports), previous hosts of the event, and government departments.

Lynn van der Wagen (2001) discussed the following protocol issues:

- titles,
- order of appearance or precedence,
- styles of address (sir, your honor, etc.),
- dress,
- timing and length of speeches,
- seating plans,
- religious and cultural considerations,
- awards,
- media activities (e.g., when can pictures be taken?),
- flags.

Spectacle

MacAloon (1984) noted how the Olympics epitomize the spectacle associated with many special events. Spectacle is visually oriented, incorporating larger-than-life displays and performances, parades and ceremonies, ritual and action. It can be both a strength and a weakness, for while there is no doubt that spectacle has universal appeal, and is especially suitable for television, it can also overpower the more fundamental meanings of festival, ritual, and games.

Media-oriented events, and sports in particular, emphasize spectacle and even fabricate it when desirable. The Super Bowl is a football game, but the Super Bowl media event is a hyped-up spectacle. This might not matter in the realm of professional sports, but it can harm amateur sports and community or cultural festivals.

Spectacle is also, by definition, a spectator activity. Fireworks, parades, colorful displays, and ceremonies add vibrancy to any event, and serve to attract attention. But this type of spectator activity will not directly help to meet community or cultural goals. Event organizers must be cautious with this element of the mix, employing it for its publicity value and mass appeal but not relying on it to the point where the remaining elements are diminished.

Other Sensory Stimulation

While visual stimulation tends to dominate at events, great potential exists to excite the other senses in order to achieve emotional responses, to educate, and to entertain. As noted by Goldblatt (1990), "a special event should first elicit a sensory response and then create an opportunity for physical participation, ensuring a level of active involvement" (p. 3).

The hospitality industry in general knows the value of olfactory stimulation (i.e., smell) when it comes to attracting customers to eat, and many attractions rely on sounds, like music or laughter, to entice customers. Touch is particularly important in an educational context, with interactive, "hands-on displays" being especially important to children. Finally, taste comes into play through the all-important food and beverage opportunities found at most events.

Programmers also know that combinations of sensory stimulation can have tremendous emotional impact. The recall of many special events includes not just their list of attractions and activities, but the essence of the events as captured in sights, sounds, smells, tastes, and feelings. Smells in particular can stimulate recall of long-lost memories, so they clearly have a powerful mental impact.

Authenticity

Authenticity means genuine, unadulterated, or "the real thing." It is much debated in the literature, both as to its meaning for tourism and events and with respect to whether or not tourists seek or can even recognize authenticity. The problem is that tourism often leads to the commercialization of events and places, and even the tourists who seek out unspoiled settings and cultures can contribute to alteration or destruction of these things.

MacCannell (1976), in his book *The Tourist: A New Theory of the Leisure Class*, suggested that modern tourists seek authenticity precisely because it has become so scarce. The tourist wants a spontaneous experience that reveals, or better yet allows the sharing of, some aspect of the daily life of a different culture or community. He used the term "backstage" to describe the physical setting in which a visitor could observe, meet, or share something authentic. "Backstage" is an obvious analogy to theater, where everyone knows that the visible action is a play, not real life, and that meeting the actors or seeing the activity backstage is a totally different experience.

Given that the essence of authenticity is its cultural meaning, the bottom line must be that host communities determine what is meaningful to them. In this perspective, authenticity is not so much the ritual, games, spectacle, or celebration itself as it is the degree to which these components have been manufactured, modified, or exploited just for tourists, the media, or financial success. In other words, has the event any cultural meaning for the host community and the participants, or is it merely a commodity to be sold? Do the hosts and performers think of the event as having importance in their lives, or are they cynically involved in a tourist rip-off?

Authenticity of festivals and events will be maximized when they:

- reflect indigenous themes;
- are controlled by the host community;
- are valued and well attended by residents;
- offer culturally genuine goods and performances, such as local foods, costumes, dances, crafts;
- do not exploit tourists through profit maximization at the expense of quality.

Hospitality

Programming hospitality is a key ingredient in successful events. Making guests, and especially tourists, feel welcomed, informed, and satisfied must be a major goal of every event programmer. Visitors should be greeted, and this is really important for tour groups who expect and often require extra attention. Information must be offered, and readily available. High-quality, "high-touch" service will please the guest, and this can be assisted through the use of guides and interpreters, little extras that exceed customer expectations, and prompt, effective response to needs and complaints.

Connecting hosts with guests will maximize the enjoyment of many visitors, especially the cultural tourist. Those seeking authentic cultural experiences want to experience what its like to be part of your culture or community, and meeting residents is the best way to accomplish this. Try connecting tour groups with local families who escort their guests to the event and share the experience with them.

Socializing

People-watching is a universal pursuit, and events provide ample opportunity for it. But programmers can also facilitate the kinds of social interactions sought by families (e.g., activities they can do together), meeting like-minded people (guests can be prescreened for specific interests), and even for matchmaking. Events heavy on spectacle and entertainment will probably offer less opportunity for socializing than events offering a variety of activities in different social settings.

Physical Activity

Spectator events result in static guests, whereas participatory sport events require physical activity from everyone. Those are the extremes, with plenty of scope for movement in between. As an element of style, physical activity is closely related to games and competition.

Competition

This is the essence of many sport events, but is also found in fairs (e.g., judging of livestock or wine), association conventions (awards to members), and many festivals with diverse programs. Numerous competition sport events add festival programming to broaden their appeal. The book *An Insider's Guide to Managing Sporting Events*, by Jerry Solomon (2002), documents a variety of sport event formats. Also see *Event Management for Sport Directors* (American Sport Education Program, 1996) for programming ideas and competition management.

Games

People expect to have fun at most special events. It is part of the social meaning of public festivities, and it is expressed most directly through the myriad form of games. Games are more than sports and physical recreation. Also popular at special events are games of skill and chance, competitions, and humor.

This last element, humor, is often ignored or misunderstood. Humor can be created by entertainers, such as by clowns and costumed characters, comedians, and masters of ceremony. But what of humorous sights, sounds, smells, tastes, and situations, all of which can be created or facilitated throughout the event setting and a full range of activities? Sociologists suggest that part of the attraction of carnivals and other festivals is role reversal and the elimination of behavioral norms. Celebrities and political figures become objects of ridicule (the water-dunking event!), and normally reserved settings become playgrounds (the civic square or street). Mardi Gras and traditional carnivals probably embody this humorous flavor the most.

Programmers should also incorporate elements of surprise into events. This is an excellent way to differentiate the event, even if its program is similar to many others. What would surprise the event visitor? Try:

- pulling the guest into a street performance (buskers are great at doing this);
- confronting the patron with performers acting as other guests, but displaying eccentric behavior;
- encouraging role reversals (dressing up or down, costuming, wearing masks);
- changing the announced program (do not try this for name-brand entertainers!)

- incorporating unexpected sensory stimulators into the site (e.g., sudden aromas, sounds).

Because surprise can also engender some degree of risk, the programmer must always consider the impacts of activities on individuals and crowds. Some surprises will be too unnerving or confusing to guests and are not worth the risk.

Education

Business and scientific events are usually devoted to learning, but all events can be educational in some way. Certainly any event associated with a cause must seek to inform and educate, and possibly persuade, but all events will benefit by heightening the educational experience. Mature, educated consumers and travelers are looking for attractions and events with substance. Even if the theme is not educational, displays of all kinds can easily be incorporated.

There are different forms of learning that can shape the program. Information or knowledge can be communicated to people in many ways, but levels of comprehension will vary (Are they paying attention? Do they have time to think about it or test it?). In workshops, participants apply new knowledge to solve problems or learn techniques. Meeting planners and exhibition managers in particular need an understanding of communications theory to make sure the important messages within the event program are effectively reaching the target audiences.

According to the MPI (2003, p. 62) textbook, *Meetings and Conventions: A Planning Guide*, the meeting planner must be knowledgeable of adult learning characteristics. Physical aspects of the setting can influence learning, as can socializing, emotional stimulation, real-life experiences, and avoidance of distractions. Different types of learning sessions can be created, from participatory workshops to small-group discussions. Instructors have to be versed in a variety of styles, including case studies, lectures, panel discussions, poster sessions, product demonstrations, round-table discussions, and talk shows.

Commerce

Many events are created to sell, such as art and craft shows, or to exhibit with the hope of future trade (e.g., world's fairs). With the rise in corporate sponsorship, demand for on-site samplings, exhibitions, demonstrations, and sales is high and should be recognized as a legitimate program planning element. What do the sponsors bring to the event, it should be asked, that will improve or expand its programming?

On-site merchandizing is not something to relegate to the fringe—it should be a production! People associate leisure with shopping, and spend much more freely at attractions and while traveling. It should not be dominating, of course, nor garish and intrusive. But a good merchandizing program must be planned and designed like all the other elements. Is the commercial element of the event program entertaining, educational, and attractive? If not, the programmer must do more to integrate and highlight it.

Entertainment

Any element or combination of elements of style can be entertainment. This is a function of the expectations and reactions of the customer, but can also be influenced by the program and the context. People will expect entertainment to be publicized and often to have a price attached. "Free entertainment" will usually consist of performances in well-marked settings. Street performers take the entertainment to the audience, but they are usually easily identifiable. When entertainment is more subtly blended into the overall experience, surprise and extra enjoyment can result.

In some instances clues will have to be provided as to what is not entertainment. Solemn ceremonies might be entertaining, but certain audience reactions such as clapping might be inappropriate. Cultural differences will occur, especially between residents and uninformed tourists as to what is entertainment, so visitors should always be informed of the meaning and appropriate related behavior attached to certain rituals or activities.

Like spectacle, entertainment can easily overwhelm other important elements of style. To protect against narrow programming, the entire set of elements and related activities should be explicitly considered. Some elements are bound to be more important than others, given the nature and orientation of the event, but balance is a highly desired goal.

Combining Elements of Style

One tool used by programmers is to cluster activities and other program elements by reference to how they meet the event's goals or provide similar benefits to patrons. For example, a combination of seminars, exhibits, and hands-on interpretation are all good ways to teach about new products or communicate new ideas. Programmers also have to consider the age, gender, and abilities of participants. Is there a risk or cost involved? Obviously a children's festival differs considerably from a music concert aimed at teenagers.

In Figure 6.1 several elements of style are applied to the programming of a heritage event. Note that while each type of event is closely identified with at least one element of style (e.g., sports with competition; festivals with celebration; conventions with education; trade shows with commerce) there are unlimited possibilities for programming a unique, memorable event using the various elements in creative ways.

Developing a Program Portfolio

Just as a destination wants a portfolio of events and event-related products, event organizers should seek to sustain a range of program elements that meet key goals. Some activities will make money, some will cost a lot but maximize service to the community; others will attract target segments or generate great publicity.

In for-profit situations the traditional portfolio evaluation can be employed (i.e., Boston Consulting Group Matrix), based on demand and market share factors. "Stars" are programs that capture a high share of a growing market, such as an activity that is becoming more popular each year and is not available at competitive events. The organizers will naturally consider developing this activity for maximum growth and profit, turning it into a "cash

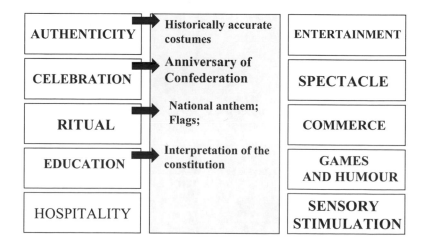

Figure 6.1. Elements of style (combining elements for a heritage event).

cow." This latter category is well established, showing competitive advantage and high market share, but little or no growth. It can be sustained as long as possible for maximum profit, but major investment is not warranted. At some point it will likely start to decline.

In contrast, "dogs" are programs with declining demand and low market share or little competitive advantage; perhaps they cost more to put on than they are worth. In a strictly bottom-line situation they would be terminated at once. Other programs or activities might reveal uncertainty about their future performance. Demand might be growing fast, but the event currently only captures a small share of the market. These "problem children" must be monitored carefully.

However, many nonprofit organizations will not want to base program decisions solely on considerations of demand, profitability, and growth prospects. Consequently, other variables must be considered. One approach was suggested by MacMillan (1983) in which competitive position, program attractiveness, and alternative coverage are considered. An event might run an attractive (i.e., high-demand) program for children, which has strong competitive position, but there are many others like it in the area. Should the event continue to offer it? For nonprofits, especially charitable organizations, it is reasonable to suggest that resources ought to be directed where they are most needed, and oversupply should be avoided.

For many events, a range of factors must be considered when evaluating program strengths, weaknesses, opportunities, and threats. Certainly it is desirable to possess some programs that generate surplus revenue, as they are needed to sustain others the have little revenue potential but are considered to have value in meeting the organization's mandate. Some programs might be required because of sponsorship considerations even though they do little to increase demand or meet overall target marketing objectives. How can all these variables be sorted out?

Figure 6.2 provides an illustration of how to develop a balanced portfolio. Just as elements of style should be balanced, types of programs and activities should not be skewed entirely towards pure service (i.e., costing money) nor towards profit. Popular events must be balanced against those that meet very specific needs for minorities. There will be no one right or optimal portfolio for the nonprofit event organization, even assuming that the organizers can correctly determine demand, market share, and profitability.

In short, the manager or programmer can use portfolio evaluations to assist decision making, but these methods will not do away with difficult decisions. It must also be realized that such analyses tend to be static, whereas a strategic perspective should always be taken.

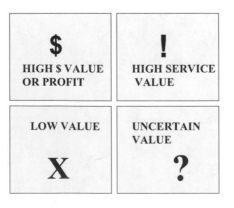

Figure 6.2. Program portfolio.

The Program Life Cycle

Programs should be planned to have a life expectancy, and if it is not a planned process there is a real risk that the event will lose popularity or money. As everyone knows, if only from visiting amusement parks, new attractions must constantly be added to stay fresh or competitive. If some programs are added, some might have to be cancelled.

The standard measure of growth and change is demand, and a program can be said to have a beginning, a period of growth, a peak, and decline in terms of attendance. However, this cycle is often not smooth and there are likely to be multiple peaks. In some cases revenue or profit might be a better measure of the life cycle, particularly where increased "yield" can be obtained by attracting fewer but high-spending visitors. Certainly all event organizers should be concerned about demand and revenue factors, but in service-oriented events it is not as important. It is therefore legitimate to apply other measures of "value" as discussed earlier, although measuring and monitoring nonquantitative values over a long period of time might prove to be difficult.

Do programs (and, indeed, whole events) have a natural life cycle in which decline is inevitable? Kotler, Bowen, and Makens (1996, p. 302) said that the life cycle concept can apply to a product class (e.g., food festivals in general), product form (e.g., chili cook-offs), and brands (a specific event or event company). A product class should have the longest life cycle, and in fact it seems logical that there will always be food festivals. A specific type of food festival, on the other hand, can be expected to rise and fall in popularity, and any given event will either follow the life cycle of that type of event or will be subjected to specific forces that give it a different life expectancy. There is no certainty about the life cycle, only the general principle that the likelihood of decline exists for any event and any program element. The act of recognizing and planning for the life cycle ensures that management is in charge, not external forces.

The program life cycle model (Figure 6.3) can be used as a planning tool leading to informed decisions concerning the introduction, development, and/or replacement of programs, or as a warning as to what might happen if programs are simply allowed to continue indefinitely. A generic strategy for periodic events (see the case study of the Calgary Stampede) is to continue traditional program elements while constantly innovating through the introduction of short-term programs or features. This can be described as planned redundancy, and the strategic mix of new and traditional programs should succeed in attracting repeat and new visitors each year while maximizing the event's ability to promote and sell its programs well in advance.

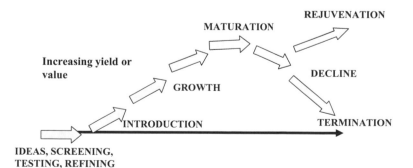

Figure 6.3. Program life cycle.

The following sections look more closely at the program planning process within the context of the life cycle.

Ideas Generation

New program ideas could emerge from any number of informal sources, like a sponsor's request or volunteer's suggestion, or from more formal studies. For-profit event companies will naturally undertake market research looking for a match between good program ideas and potential target segments. This might very well include the adoption of ideas from other events. Many nonprofit event managers do the same. "Needs assessments" might be more pertinent to service organizations, however, involving a search for community needs not being adequately met elsewhere. In this context, whole events or specific programs might be suggested, such as in the case of a community lacking a children's festival—a new event could be created, or an existing event could add children's programming.

The ongoing evaluation of the event's existing portfolio will likely suggest new ideas. If "stars" or "high-value" programs are identified, others like them should be contemplated; if none exist, the event organizers had better create some! Similarly, the presence of "low-value" activities should suggest alternatives.

Creative programming is one of the essential success factors for festival and special event producers, especially for their artistic directors. But in general, how does an organization foster the kind of creativity that will keep every event fresh and competitive and make it a memorable experience? The learning organization is more likely to be an innovative organization. Not only does the learning organization generate and retain knowledge better, because it institutionalizes research and evaluation, but it fosters a culture of continuous improvement and therefore innovation. It is also less dependent on individuals who might leave and take their creativity with them.

It should be stressed that copying ideas is not always bad. Event professionals go to conferences where ideas are freely shared and copying seems to be encouraged. The risk is that all events begin to look and feel the same, while the benefit is that "best practices" are diffused widely throughout the events sector. Just make sure that copying is not a substitute for learning and innovation in your own organization.

There are several well-known techniques that can help with creativity.

Brainstorming

Brainstorming sessions are used for generating new ideas, not for analysis and planning. Carefully define the problem or task, or you risk going in too many directions; this will require a moderator. It might be best to not have participants prepare in advance, otherwise they might simply regurgitate someone else's ideas. And under no circumstances should ideas be criticized or dismissed during a brainstorming session. One useful technique is to have each participant write down one or more ideas, then have the moderator read them out anonymously. This can overcome the shyness or fear factor.

An example is to hold a program planning session, inviting a mix of staff, volunteers, experts, and other stakeholders, so many points of view will be represented. The moderator can state the challenge and invite participants to each write down one or more ideas, or verbally express them, going to each participant in turn. No one's ideas are criticized or rejected. Subsequent rounds can be used to exhaust all ideas, then to go back and elaborate on those for which some enthusiasm or consensus has been expressed. When the session is over the moderator has the task of summarizing the results and getting back to all the participants with a full list of ideas and an explanation of why some of them are worth pursuing. A good tip is to never throw out ideas, but to invite people to champion them.

Storyboarding

When an event program or site is to be designed, "storyboarding" can be an effective source of new ideas as well as a test of them. It is a visual expression of everything that will be contained in the program and what it will look like. Can an event program be conceptualized as a story? Or an experience consisting of different but orchestrated program elements? Each of these can be depicted in words or pictures until the entire event has been portrayed. This process allows participants to have some fun, generate a lot of ideas and see if they fit, and ultimately to produce a very detailed program.

Also storyboard the event venue or site. Imagine the different views and experiences that patrons will have and describe or sketch them. Combine this technique with "service blueprinting" (discussed later in this chapter) by plotting out the visitor's entire experience: approach, entry and orientation, activities, and departure.

Mind Mapping

This popular technique was pioneered by Tony Buzan (www.mind-map.com), who has placed a lot of useful information on his website. The goal is to draw your thoughts in pictures and words, all connected to a central concept or problem. The resulting sketch should give you both the big picture and the details. Applied to event creativity, try this:

- Write the central concept or goal in the middle of a page (e.g., its party time!).
- Draw a line out from the center for each major thought about the party (this can be group brainstorming—have some fun with it!); for example, one branch of your thinking will be "music," another "eats and drinks," another "surprises and tricks."
- Now develop each of these themes with other, cascading ideas that flow from the first ones—you can get real detailed before a visual mess forces you back to reality and a simplification of the map.
- Use words, numbers, little pictures to help conceptualize the party (see the resemblance to a story board?).
- Finally, when it looks like a creative masterpiece, convert the map to a program (or use the sketch as a visual brand for the party).

Screening, Testing, and Refining

Screening occurs internally as staff and volunteers critically examine new ideas, and externally as sponsors, other stakeholders, and the public are invited to participate. Formal research through market area surveys and focus groups can greatly assist in screening new ideas, but care must be taken to specify in advance what criteria are being used. Keeping the portfolio analysis in mind will help in setting evaluation criteria.

Those ideas that look promising, if they involve major commitments, should be subjected to a feasibility study. Costs and revenue-generating potential must be considered, as well as the likely effectiveness of the program in meeting its goals. Comparison to other events and their existing programs is desirable.

Comparisons will give some indication of likely success, but no two event circumstances are ever identical—other ways of testing new "products" must be found. One method is to develop a small-scale version of the program. This "sampler" will look and feel like the real thing, but be small enough to minimize financial and other risks. Structured evaluation of this experiment is essential. Another testing procedure is to take a well-articulated concept to the target markets through focus groups and/or surveys.

Introduction

Following screening and testing, program concepts are refined and scheduled for introduction. If the program is significant, considerable effort should be put into the "launch," complete with media coverage, ceremony, and special promotions to attract customers. The public relations and revenue-enhancing potential value of the launch might be heightened by scheduling it prior to the main event. Scheduling several program introductions simultaneously will lessen the impact, and quite possibly make evaluation of effectiveness difficult or impossible.

Consideration should also be given to the question of who is most likely to try new products first. The target market might very well consist of those who always want to be the first to experience something new (innovators or risk-takers), the majority who will try something only when it has been demonstrated to be safe, affordable, high quality, or popular, and others—the laggards—who never try something until everyone else is moving on to new things. This principle of "diffusion" applies to many products and must be considered when doing market research and feasibility studies.

Even though a new program might be aimed at young adults in general, it is likely that only certain segments will be quick to give it a try. Their experience, carried through word of mouth and media coverage, will directly influence the majority. This diffusion process can therefore be managed, starting with making certain that the launch is well attended, provides an excellent experience, and gets lots of media coverage. Early customers can be provided with price incentives to try it once, coupons for cheaper repeat visits, and other incentives for bringing new customers. In the case of "free" programs, a variety of incentives can still be used to maximize early attendance and word-of-mouth recommendations. But pricing should also reflect the true costs of the new program. If it is first offered "free" or at below-cost prices, it might be difficult to ever realize surplus revenues.

Growth

If the launch was successful and the program well received, growth in demand and/or revenue should follow. This period of growth is unpredictable as to duration and speed, and will obviously vary from product to product and place to place. Monitoring attendance, costs, and revenues is essential so that growth can be quantified and the program evaluated.

Of course, it is possible that the program is an instant success and further growth is not possible. This can occur because of site capacity, financial restrictions, or other limitations. If this happens it strongly suggests reconsideration of the program with a view to expansion. In other cases the organizers might not want to expand or grow, in which case the life cycle is artificially controlled.

It is also possible to experience an instant failure. The launch might be evidently successful, but follow-up growth fails to materialize. Abandonment of the program should not be seriously considered, however, until effort has been expended on investigating the reasons for slow demand and on remarketing the program.

Maturity

After some time has passed and that first period of growth has ended or substantially slowed, it can be said that the event or program element has entered "maturity." This stage will also be marked by peak levels of attendance, value, or revenue, low costs per customer and resultant high profits, the broadest possible market appeal, and possibly lots of imitators. The marketing strategy for a program is to defend its profitability and market share, price to match or beat that of competitors, intensify the distribution system to maximize tourist demand, and advertise to stress the benefits of the program. Sales promotions can be used to encourage switching from competitors.

Programs in the mature stage have to be monitored carefully to avoid making mistakes about their ultimate fate. It cannot be assumed that growth will not return, nor that decline is inevitable. At this stage the organizers must start to make contingency plans for phasing out or rejuvenating the program, subject to the above considerations.

Decline

It can be seen that planned termination of programs is a strategic option for organizers, but in other cases a decline in attendance or value might be a slow process. Nevertheless, at some point the organizers must face the prospect of terminating or rejuvenating the program. The following considerations will be important:

- gradual reduction resulting in poorer quality, as opposed to quick elimination, might anger loyal users;
- quick elimination allows a more efficient transfer of resources to new programs;
- terminations can be celebrated in the same way as launches, assuming that it will not arouse protests;
- where an important service is being delivered, the old program can be phased out as its replacement is gradually introduced; a transition will likely please most users, and will avoid confusion.

Rejuvenation

Some programs can be rejuvenated when they show signs of reduced value. In fact, it is a good idea to be proactive and plan the rejuvenation of important programs on a cyclical basis. Each year one or more programs can be selected for renewal, employing these principles:

- rejuvenation involves the entire marketing mix; do not tinker, but fully renew the program and communicate this to target markets;
- change should be in keeping with quality management guidelines discussed later in this chapter; in other words, do not change a program unless it can be improved;
- do not change programs without doing market research; remember that programs provide benefits to guests, and these benefits must be sustained, transferred, or increased—not eliminated.

The Quality of Events

"Quality" has many connotations. To some it is a mark of excellence, or being the best, and does not necessarily mean expensive. To others it means reliability, with experience always equaling or exceeding expectations. It can mean "getting it right the first time," or conformance to specifications. To Edosomwan (1993, p. 16) it includes:

- error-free performance; no defects in goods sold;
- safe performances, activities, services, and setting;
- promptness of service and on-time programming;
- efficient and effective performance of all services;
- the correct solution of problems;
- courteous, reliable, and trustworthy behavior.

Swarbrooke (1995) advised that quality means "offering a product of the right grade for the chosen market or markets, at the appropriate price" (p. 295). So event managers must know their audience and consider their target segments before setting quality standards. And because quality is a tradeoff between that which is possible and what the event can afford and the customer is willing to pay for, it is a dynamic concept.

Event "quality" can be conceptualized as the amalgam of program and service delivery as presented to consumers. It requires skillful management of the interactions among the setting (venues, decoration, atmosphere), people (guests, staff, volunteers, and participants), management systems (such as health, security, and communications), and the event program (whether a competition, celebration, entertainment, education, or business). To a large degree event quality is dependent upon organizational and personnel quality, as it is difficult to imagine a high-quality event being produced by incompetent organizers. These interactions are illustrated in Figure 6.4.

Program Quality

Program quality from the consumer's perspective is certainly implicit in designations like the annual Top 100 Events in North America (by the American Bus Association). However, other criteria might apply, such as judgments regarding the event's tourist attractiveness or recognition for long-term success. "Program quality" refers to the event as performance. It is more difficult to judge, especially if artistic or cultural in nature.

Consumer satisfaction measures are useful (e.g., what was your overall level of satisfaction with this event?), as are the evaluations of other stakeholders including the tourism industry (e.g., how would you assess this event in terms of its tourist appeal and satisfaction of visitor needs?), professional artists or cultural interpreters (e.g., how would you rate this event's artistic program in terms of cultural authenticity and artistic merit?), and those who fund the event (e.g., did it meet your expectations and requirements?).

Organizational Quality

Generic quality assurance programs, such as the widely employed ISO 9000 series, focus upon the organization itself by prescribing standard processes and management systems. ISO 9000 places the emphasis on adoption of policies, procedures, and management

Figure 6.4. Interactions shaping event quality.

systems, and documenting everything to do with provision of quality products or services.

Event managers are increasingly required to be certified by professional associations. Unfortunately, many small event organizations cannot afford to help their managers get formal, event-related education or certification, and many people in the industry have migrated into it from other backgrounds. The main challenge, therefore, is to ensure that all event staff and volunteers are well trained and competent in fulfilling their specific, assigned tasks.

Organizational quality standards should begin with philosophy and values, and cover all management systems including human resources. For tourism-oriented events, a separate set of "tourism readiness" standards will apply, such as procedures for greeting and orienting visitors and policies covering price and packaging.

Service Quality

The best-known approach to service quality is the "Servqual" model (Zeithaml, Parasuraman, & Berry, 1990). They argued that quality in services can only be defined by considering the customer's expectations, experiences, and satisfaction. Based on their research, a number of generic dimensions used by customers to evaluate service quality were identified, and these have been grouped into five categories. These dimensions will influence how event customers compare their perceptions of the experience with their expectations and derive satisfaction or dissatisfaction.

Tangibles

- the "hygiene" factors (safety, health, comfort, convenience);
- appearance and cleanliness of all venues and equipment;
- appearance of symbols, logos, and other representations of the event;
- hours of operation;
- physical accessibility (including for special needs);
- waiting times and conditions (queuing).

Reliability

- absence of problems (getting it right the first time);
- accuracy (e.g., of information, money handling, food service);
- running programs on time;
- honoring promises;
- consistent treatment of all guests;
- different standards of service are clear to all patrons.

Responsiveness

- prompt service when needed and asked for;
- returning calls; following up on all requests;
- readiness of staff and volunteers to give service (empowerment!);
- accessibility of staff and assistance when needed by guests;
- coordination of efforts (teamwork).

Assurance

- competence of staff and volunteers; display of knowledge and skills;
- courteous service to all;
- security (absence of real and perceived threats; confidentiality);
- credibility (honest and trustworthy staff and volunteers; reputation of the organization and the event);

- communication (listening to customers; accurate, understandable and on-time information; assuring guests that problems and queries will be handled in a timely, effective manner).

Empathy

- caring (customers feel they are cared about);
- individualized attention (e.g., for tour groups and special needs or requests);
- approachability (guests feel comfortable asking for help).

Bowdin and Church (2000) equated quality at events with meeting customer needs and measures of customer satisfaction. They argued that quality programs have costs, but they are quickly recovered by the event organization—first by reducing waste and failures, and second by reducing quality inspections and evaluations over time.

Impacts and Quality

Events are globally valued for their economic benefits, and event managers might be tempted to stress their success in attracting tourists and generating favorable publicity for the destination or host community. This is a legitimate measure of event quality, but should be carefully balanced through conducting benefit–cost evaluations that also consider the often intangible social, cultural, and environmental impacts. More and more events are becoming "green" through recycling, reducing, and reusing practices, and this introduces a whole new set of quality standards. — fairtrade. — Charities —

Quality Management

Quality control is a fundamental responsibility of event managers and should consist of the setting of quality standards, customer and market research, evaluation and control mechanisms, and continuous improvement systems (including benchmarking, and staff and volunteer training), all within a customer-oriented culture. Each event and event-producing organization must consider the meaning and importance of quality as applied to their specific type of event and its key goals. To the owners and managers of events, adopting quality standards and management should lead to continuous improvement, better performance in terms of achieving the event's goals, and fewer problems. Tourism-oriented events will gain from heightened appeal, as the tourism industry wants better events to attract and satisfy specific market segments. Quality standards can also provide assurance to customers that basic services will be provided at least to a reasonable standard, and that they do not have to fear for their safety or health.

Those who fund events (government agencies at various levels), or sponsor them commercially, will associate quality standards with risks. In other words, top-ranked or certified events should be better able to use the money wisely and therefore provide the desired return on investment. Governments at all levels have an important stake in many festivals and events, both directly (when funded or produced by an agency) or indirectly (because events reflect upon the place in which they are held). When the perspective of external stakeholder groups is taken, event impacts become a measure of quality.

Although each event must ensure its own quality, increasingly there are collective efforts to improve quality across all events. For example, Carlsen (2000) reported on the approach taken by the event industry in Western Australia. The Canadian province of Quebec has adopted quality standards for event organizations, and a collaboration between the tourism ministry in the province of Ontario and Festivals and Events Ontario is developing even more comprehensive standards (see Getz & Carlsen, 2005).

Credit crunch

Government Support waning

Numerous events conduct visitor studies, but very few academic studies of event quality have been published. A notable exception is that of the Dickens on the Strand Festival in Galveston, Texas, which has been studied systematically. The early research (Ralston & Crompton, 1988a, 1988b) examined service quality within the context of reliability, tangibility, responsiveness, assurance, and empathy and identified high- and low-ranked items through a series of statements presented to visitors. In a paper published in 1995, Crompton and Love concluded that the tangible dimension was most important at Dickens On The Strand, specifically ambiance, sources of information at the site, comfort amenities, parking, and interaction with vendors. Actual performance measures were found to be substantially better predictors of quality than importance assigned by customers to various service attributes and various disconfirmation operationalizations, which incorporated expectations of service quality. They concluded (Crompton & Love, 1995): "It appears that respondents either did not form meaningful expectations or, if they ever formed, did not use them as criteria against which they measured performance to determine quality" (p. 19). The authors recommended that different measures of quality be employed in event evaluations. Also, they suggested that importance measures were of practical value to managers.

Crompton (2003) also used research at the Dickens festival to test the hypothesis, based on the works of Herzberg (1966), that some event elements are "dissatisfiers" that can undermine the visitor experience, while others are "satisfiers" that provide benefits. "Dissatisfiers" are like Herzberg's "maintenance" factors—they must be provided to expected levels of quality, but in themselves do not satisfy visitors. Crompton argued that most of the physical factors at events, such as parking, rest rooms, and information, are dissatisfiers, while ambiance, fantasy, excitement, relaxation, escape, and social involvement are satisfiers. High-quality events must meet expectations in both categories, but they are noncompensatory in that a single or small number of attributes can determine perception of overall quality. Tentative support for this model was confirmed, and the researcher believed that certain attributes were perceived to be of so poor or high quality that visitors disregarded or discounted other attributes in giving their overall appraisal.

Baker and Crompton (2000) argued that "quality" is an output of the event management system (i.e., the opportunity provided to event guests), whereas "satisfaction" is an "outcome" equated to "quality of experience." The satisfaction or experiential outcome is not fully controllable by event producers because of external influences. From the responses of a sample of 524 festival-goers they identified four "quality of opportunity domains": generic features of the event; specific entertainment features; information; and comfort amenities. Information and comfort amenities were called "hygiene" factors, and they can provoke dissatisfaction if poor, but do not add to overall satisfaction if exceptionally good. Generic and entertainment features of the event were found to be more likely to generate increased satisfaction and motivate return visits or positive word-of-mouth recommendations. The authors recommend that event organizers evaluate both the quality of the performance and visitor satisfaction.

Saleh and Ryan (1993) found that quality of the music program is the most important service factor in attracting people to jazz festivals. Overall satisfaction levels affected the intention for repeat visits. Similarly, Thrane (2002) explored the link between satisfaction and future intentions of festival-goers. The study took place in Norway. He and students conducted interviews asking for performance ratings concerning music quality, plus an overall satisfaction rating and future intentions regarding repeat visits and giving positive recommendations about the event. Analysis of results suggested that music quality affected overall satisfaction, which in turn affected the intention for repeat visits. However, regarding the potential for recommending the festival to others, music quality had both a direct and indirect effect (as mediated by overall satisfaction). The most important conclusion is that event managers must try to improve program quality (in this case music) AND be concerned with other factors that shape overall satisfaction.

Stiernstrand (1997), in Sweden, determined that high perceived quality of "essential services" (i.e., hygiene factors) did not translate into repeat visit intentions, but low perceived quality of essential services would result in lower repeat visitation. For tourists, who often seek novelty, low satisfaction ratings would definitely result in low repeat visits, but high ratings did not necessarily translate into repeat visits. Price, accessibility, and weather were also found to be important factors—in addition to perceived service quality—in explaining satisfaction with events.

Quality Management Methods

"Quality assurance" guidelines and procedures should be put in place to ensure that everyone does their job to standards, and therefore problems are prevented. This obviously requires specialized training, not only in doing the job but in identifying and avoiding potential flaws.

"Total quality management", or TQM, is a more complex management system aimed at constant improvement. Appropriate goals and standards must be set, the entire organization must be committed, and everyone imbued with both the philosophy and the responsibility for achieving ever-more-stringent goals. But as discussed by Swarbrooke (1995, p. 304) in the context of attractions in general, many different perspectives on quality can be found among staff. Managers might be most interested in minimizing complaints, while front-line volunteers might tend to stress total customer experience. In fact, the whole process could get bogged down in technical details, so the customer's perspective should always be at the fore.

The core of TQM (Edosomwan, 1993; Morrison, 1995) is a set of measurable goals and objectives for continuous improvements in service quality, productivity, and customer satisfaction. Formulating a TQM vision is important, and this can be done within a strategic or business plan. Baseline data should also be available on how the organization has done in the past, its control and evaluation systems, and areas in need of improvement. Having tangible problems to contemplate might focus everyone on the goals and benefits of the TQM process.

Managers of the process must work as hard on changing attitudes and behaviors of staff and volunteers as they do on matters of technical improvement. It will accomplish little if the venue is top quality but the staff are surly. Objections and problems will be encountered, so the process must include methods of channeling them into productive sessions. Action teams, or quality circles, can be established to ensure that all such obstacles are identified and discussed. Innovation and creativity must be nourished.

Integrated training at all levels in the organization is necessary. Quality improvements will rest on both technical competence (e.g., how to develop a better food-service system) and the empowerment of personnel to satisfy customers. Staff and volunteers will have to understand how performance criteria are established and evaluated. Constant measurement of problems and improvements will have to be institutionalized.

Ongoing research into customer needs, wants, and experiences is essential, with the results being used to set and achieve new targets for improvement. Market research that identifies noncustomers and past customers will also be valuable. Finally, the reward system will have to be reoriented to recognize achievements and new ideas for creating an excellent event experience.

TQM is not without its critics. To some it is just another buzzword. Others believe it fails to fully take into account the human factor, as people tend to want to know how any given program will benefit them, and will not buy into a process that does not increase their own short-term satisfaction.

Service Mapping and Service Blueprinting

"Service mapping," as illustrated in Figures 6.5 and 6.6 (from Getz, O'Neill, & Carlsen, 2001), is a quality evaluation method. But it also provides the basis for "blueprinting" the entire event experience for visitors from beginning to end. The blueprint literally shows what event managers have to do to produce the event and satisfy the customers.

Visitor flows and actions are first assessed. The sequence can be interpreted in the context of anticipation, arrival, and orientation that mark all visits to attractions or new areas. Event mangers can enhance their customers' experiences by maximizing anticipation of an enjoyable experience (through communications), facilitating an efficient and smooth arrival, and providing a user-friendly orientation through information, signage, or greeters. The design of the site can also contribute by providing an obvious and attractive entrance (both physical, as in a gateway, and symbolic as with signs, greeters, decorations, or other visual cues). Of critical importance is the direction of visitors to important areas, in this case viewing, vendors' and sponsors' facilities, the stage with scoreboard, and the VIP area.

Figure 6.6 details the customer actions associated with on-site experiences. These are nonsequential because visitors were free to come and go from the site, choose their viewing spots, and make use of toilets, vendors, sponsors' booths, and promotions. Physical evidence of service quality must be evaluated, revealing good points, problems or potential problems, and suggestions for improvements. Specific observations are shown on the map, covering such topics as: signage and access; entrance; information and signage on-

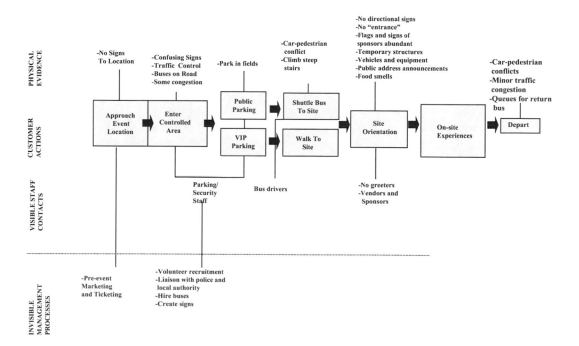

Figure 6.5. Service mapping for 1998 Margaret River Surfing Masters. Stage one: approach and orientation.

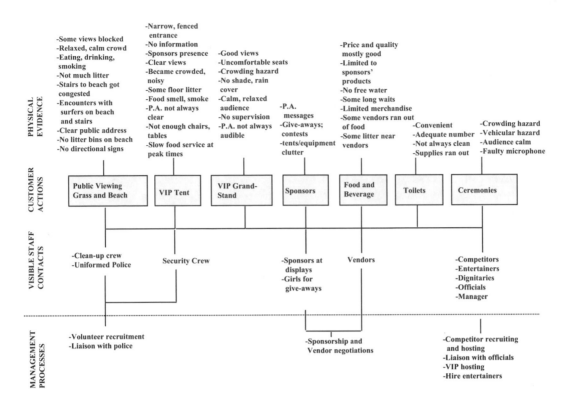

Figure 6.6. Service mapping for 1998 Margaret River Surfing Masters. Stage two: on-site experiences.

site; site layout and aesthetics; seating and viewing; toilets; cleanliness; public safety; communications with audience; food and beverages; other vendors; officials and police; parking; security; information; announcers; sponsors; and staff contacts.

Service mapping is an audit tool and should therefore lead to event improvements and, ideally, detailed specifications for desired service quality. This second stage is called "blueprinting." The blueprint will have the same structure and components of the service map, except that it becomes a map of what must happen, in sequence, to deliver the event and satisfy the customer. Because it can be quite complex to develop, blueprints might be used only for the most important areas of customer experiences. To use it this way requires knowledge of what guests think is most important.

Research Note

Getz, D., O'Neil, M., & Carlsen, J. (2001). Service quality evaluation at events through service mapping. *Journal of Travel Research, 39*(4), 380–390.

The researchers evaluated service quality at a surfing competition using three methods. A visitor survey was employed to gain feedback on program and service quality issues, including measures of satisfaction. Direct observation involved checklists covering observations of attendance, crowd behavior, and visitor characteristics. Thirdly, log books were also kept by nine participant observers, generating written notes that were afterwards transcribed by each observer into a narrative of their experience and assembled into a composite. Then a service map (based on Bitner, 1993) was prepared from the composite notes. Because of the detail involved, the map was subdivided into two sections covering: a) approach, site orientation, and departure, and b) on-site experiences. Analyses of the map, narratives, and composite notes are complementary. On its own, the map provides a clear picture of the sequence of visitor movements surrounding the event, including the range of on-site experiences, together with interactions with setting and staff or volunteers. But it does not provide essential details such as notes on quality, problems observed, or even potential areas of improvement.

Importance–Performance Measurement

Importance–performance (IP) measures are an extremely useful part of quality management and should be included in event visitor surveys. The basic principle is that there is little point in knowing how customers rate event program and service elements unless you also know how important the various elements are. IP measures can be used to determine:

- how important various aspects of the event are in attracting guests, and how well these benefits were realized;
- how well the event did in satisfying all the program and service elements, and how important each was to the customers' satisfaction levels.

Customer input should first be obtained, or the literature consulted, to prepare a list of the program, setting, and service elements to be included in the IP measurement. Then ask respondents to indicate on a scale of 5 or 7 how important each of the items was in attracting them, or in creating a good experience. You cannot ask for both in the same question or it will be very confusing. Next, for the same list, ask how satisfied the respondent was with each item (basically satisfaction is a postexperience rating of quality).

Specifications and performance criteria for every program element and service encounter should be formulated and communicated to all staff and volunteers to ensure that delivery meets the specifications. For events, the following sources are useful.

- customer reports on satisfaction (e.g., rating scales); complaints; likes and dislikes;
- peer evaluations of staff and volunteers;
- self-reporting by staff and volunteers;
- objective measures of conformity to service procedures (by supervisors);
- objective measures of defects and problems and the number resolved effectively;
- subjective measures (e.g., of personal conduct and attitudes);
- deviation from average, minimum, or maximum delivery and response times.

The five groups of service quality dimensions, described previously, can be turned into more refined criteria and measures.

Ryan and Lockyer (2002) used IP in their study of Masters Games, while Baloglu and Love (2003) used it to assess the perceived performance of Las Vegas by association meeting planners, drawing implications for marketing and making event bids.

Research Note

Ryan, C., & Lockyer, T. (2002). Masters' Games—the nature of competitors' involvement and requirements. *Event Management, 7*(4), 259-270.

Ryan and Lockyer studied satisfaction levels of participants in the South Pacific Masters games in New Zealand—a friendly, multisport event for older athletes. Respondents indicated their level of satisfaction with various items on a 7-point Likert scale, plus the level of importance of each. The items to be rated covered the entire event experience, including various administrative procedures, site conditions, and the competitions. Results were analyzed in two ways, first by examining the differences between the means of satisfaction and importance scores (large gaps could indicate potential problems) and secondly by plotting means on an importance–performance (IP) matrix divided into quadrants. Managers need to pay particular attention to improving items of high importance but low satisfaction. In this sample the prime motivators—seeking challenge and fun—were found to be satisfied by the event. A factor analysis was also used to identify five components of importance to participants, namely: social (social events plus meeting people); registration (good communications); challenge; after-event communication; and that the competition is both fun and serious.

Critical Incidents in Service Encounters

Because many elements of service quality are subjective, staff and volunteers might have difficulty understanding what kinds of behavior are expected, discouraged, or empowered. "Critical incident analysis" is a useful training and evaluation tool in this context. Bitner, Booms, and Tereault (1990) identified three groups of incidents in which the service staff react to customer complaints or disappointments, respond to customer needs and requests, and take unprompted or unsolicited actions related to guests. In each of these groups satisfactory and dissatisfactory behaviors or responses can be identified—preferably by observing real event situations, but also through role playing.

For example, how do event volunteers serving food respond to a complaint about poor service, quality, or the price? By rehearsing possible responses, and having positive ones reinforced by managers, staff and volunteers will learn how to cope. In the case of complaints that are justified, customers should receive an apology and replacement, or other compensation. If the complaint is unjustified, staff might be advised to refer the situation to a supervisor who is empowered to take other action. In all cases, it is preferable to take time for explanations and dialogue instead of either dismissing the customer or starting an argument.

What happens when the stage manager receives a request from a guest to go into a restricted backstage area? Empowerment does not mean that good rules can be broken, so the manager must politely decline—with explanation. In other circumstances, a variety of special needs requests should be met—it does not hurt to bend some rules and provide extras, but staff and volunteers must have a reasonable idea of the limits.

The third category involves incidents where service delivery people take initiatives to enhance the quality of the event experience, or to prevent a problem. In order to accomplish this laudable activity they must first be trained and empowered to use discretion—again, within limits. Behaviors that would have the opposite effect must be discouraged, through examples.

Critical incident analysis is also an excellent way to train security people for events, as they often encounter unusual and sometimes risky situations. As the organizers gain experience they should catalogue various real incidents for use in training.

Analysis of Quality Gaps

In attempting to deliver high-quality programs and service the event manager faces a number of planning, marketing, and operational challenges. No event or service can ever be truly perfected, so constant innovation and improvement are essential. The main problems that arise can be viewed as "gaps," as shown in Figure 6.7 (based on Parasuraman, Zeithaml, & Berry, 1985). The gaps can be summarized as follows:

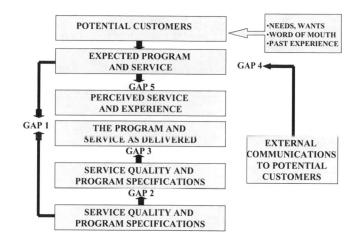

Figure 6.7. Quality gaps (adapted from Parasuraman et al., 1985).

Gap 1: We do not fully understand what potential and actual customers/guests need and expect from our event. How are their expectations formed? What exactly will satisfy or dissatisfy them?

The only way to meet this challenge is through continuous market research and evaluation of customer experiences. Research must include both current and potential customers.

Gap 2: We cannot adequately translate our understanding of customer expectations into program and service quality specifications.

Event organizers might be overwhelmed by the results of market research, or confused by many contradictory ideas and demands on the event program from various publics and stakeholders. In these cases, focusing on key target segments might overcome the problem. When it is known what needs and expectations the event should meet there still remains the difficulty of matching the program and service elements to that ideal. Constant experimentation, evaluation, and refinement of the program and other service elements are needed.

Gap 3: We have a good program and clear service quality specifications, but they do not get put into practice; something always goes wrong; our implementation system is flawed.

Probably the most common reason for failures is training, or its absence. The best program and service plan cannot succeed unless all staff and volunteers understand what must be done and are fully competent to execute their duties. They must also be trained and empowered to cope with unexpected problems as they arise.

Gap 4: We have achieved an excellent program and service delivery system but do not adequately communicate this to our markets.

Event communications often fail to fully inform potential guests of what exactly they can expect, so customer expectations will not match the event reality. As well, managers should educate customers and other stakeholders of all the efforts made to ensure a high-quality program and experience—sometimes these efforts are not visible or understood.

Gap 5: Deriving from any or all of the previous four gaps, our customers do not get what they expect and many are dissatisfied.

To determine if this is true requires skilled research. Asking customers superficial questions about their likes and dislikes, or their overall level of satisfaction, might not reveal the presence of problems. On the other hand, it is likely that most event-goers will not expect perfection, and the presence of some problems will not necessarily detract from their enjoyment and overall satisfaction with the experience.

Study Questions

- What are the elements of style used in event programming?
- How do you evaluate the value of a program or program element?
- Explain the life cycle concept as it applies to event programs and to events over-all.
- How can you foster creativity in event programming?
- How are event blueprints derived from service maps?
- What are the five service quality dimensions?
- Give an example of each quality gap and show how it can be closed.

Advanced Study Questions

- Examine and compare several different types of event with regard to their elements of style and how they result in unique event experiences.
- Use the service mapping technique to evaluate an event and make suggestions for improvements. Develop a blueprint for the visitor experience.
- For each of the five quality gaps develop appropriate management systems integrating with planning, organizing, human resources, marketing, and evaluation.

Chapter 7

Organization and Coordination

Learning Objectives

- Be able to understand basic principles of organization as applicable to events.
- Be able to develop a structure suitable to the purpose, resources, and culture of the organization.
- Be able to eestablish and effectively manage committees.
- Be able to work with the Board of Directors to govern the organization through vision, leadership, and policy.
- Be able to manage the relationship between boards and chief executives.
- Be able to evaluate the effectiveness of organizational structure and operations.
- Be able to understand the meaning and implications of organizational culture for professionalization, planning, and management.
- Be able to create and manage a "learning organization."

Perspectives on Organizations

"Organization" encompasses the creation, structuring, and internal coordination of the management system, all with the purpose of fulfilling the organization's mandate. In this chapter we begin with a discussion of multiple stakeholder perspectives on events, including the differences between governmental, not-for-profit, and for-profit event management.

A major organizational issue is to determine how stakeholders should be represented in the event organization and its planning. Some will opt for a broad-based advisory board, while others like to get key stakeholders represented formally on the board of directors. This is partly a matter of organizational culture, as giving stakeholders power can certainly change the organization and its events. No doubt many event managers think the best partners are those who give money with no strings attached, but that is seldom realistic.

Event Mandate and Goals

Figure 7.1 depicts major perspectives on events and their impacts within a stakeholder environment. The event has its own mandate and goals: given to it by a parent organization; internally negotiated (such as by accommodating grant-giver and sponsorship demands); negotiated by accommodating diverse interest groups in the community and industry; or taking into account various political agendas. There is also the necessity for ensuring that consumers or guests are always part of the process.

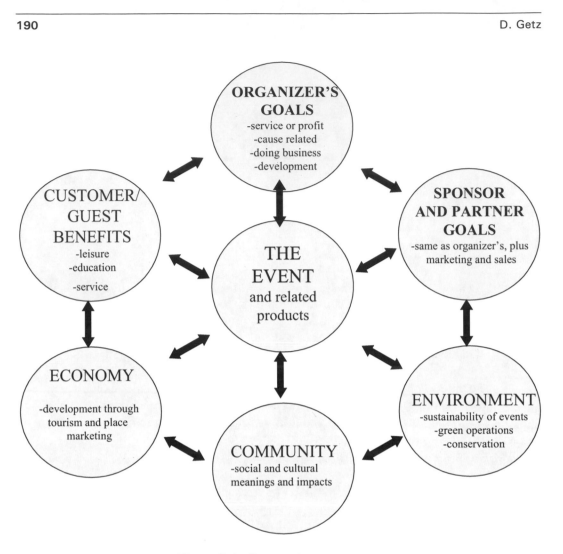

Figure 7.1. Perspectives on events.

Three Types of Event Organizer

In Figure 7.2 different mandates and goals are indicated for governmental, not-for-profit, and private for-profit event organizations. This is an oversimplification, because a governmental agency or even a charitable organization could create a separate, for-profit event. Also, it does not show the role of professional event management and production companies that exist for profit regardless of the type of event and its owners.

Government agencies usually pursue public-oriented goals, whether social, health related, cultural, environmental, or economic. Governments at all levels justify the production and ownership of events by pointing out these public benefits, but the question always remains if some other group could do a better job achieving the desired benefits. Indeed, many cities and agencies have outsourced events to professional, for-profit companies. Public–private partnerships, most notably tourism organizations, are heavily involved with events to meet the specific needs of their members (i.e., generating tourism demand) while also contributing to general economic prosperity and jobs in the community.

Numerous not-for-profit organizations produce events, and many of these are also registered charities (i.e., donations to them are usually tax deductible). Sometimes the event is

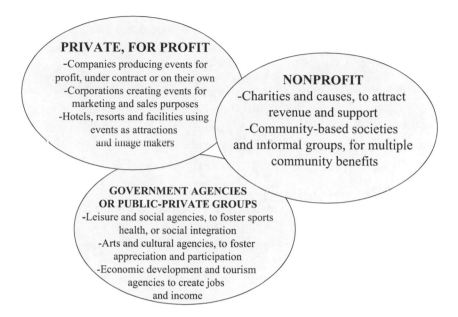

Figure 7.2. Organizations producing events and their main goals.

intended to raise money for its owners, to promote a cause, or simply to give the community entertainment. Probably a majority of festivals are produced by this type of organization, and often the organizations are set up to produce just one event.

A growing number of for-profit companies are in the events business. They provide many supplies and services, produce and manage events on contract, or produce their own for sheer profit. A noticeable trend is for companies that sponsor events in a big way to also produce and own events, such as the case study of Volvo in Chapter 9.

The Community

The community has a major interest in the social, cultural, environmental, and economic costs and benefits of events and event tourism. For the most part the normal political decision-making process is in control, but for major events and when controversies occur, special interest groups will insist on being heard and the public in general should be consulted. Working effectively with the community is an essential event management skill, and will pay off in terms of support.

Customers/Guests

Identifying and cultivating groups that support events will also lead to marketing and servicing customers and guests. Although a "marketing orientation" places customer needs and desires foremost, many events also have a responsibility to the wider community or a special mandate, such as fostering the arts or a sport. Regular public and guest surveys are essential for understanding community and customer concerns.

The Economy

A number of agencies exist in most communities that will work toward maximizing the economic benefits of events, including destination marketing organizations and economic development offices. Event managers should find these to be natural allies, but there might also be tension in terms of goals and operations, particularly with regard to the different orientation required to attract and satisfy tourists.

The Environment

Although there are environmental agencies and "watchdog" groups in most communities, sometimes the natural environment is ignored until a problem occurs. Instead of letting that happen and possibly facing fines or negative publicity, event organizations should be proactive in their environmental planning and implementing green operations.

Sponsors, Grant Givers, and Other Partners

Sponsors and grant givers have a financial interest in the event, and they increasingly impose conditions on events to ensure a favorable return on investment or the meeting of specific social/cultural objectives. They are also partners in marketing the event and potentially in supplying volunteers. Where possible, important resource suppliers should be invited to become long-term partners with event organizations, although this brings the risk of goals displacement and changes to the organization.

Organizational Structures for Events

There is no one, best way to structure an event organization, as much depends on the environment and unique circumstances facing the organizers. As well, structures evolve over time, with a tendency to become more complicated and bureaucratic. Consequently, this section illustrates and discusses a number of basic structures and options that can be used as the starting point for creating and developing event organizations.

Setting Up an Event Organization

Events are being created all the time, and many of these require new organizations. While it is natural for organizers to initially concentrate on the event production, care must be taken to establish an organizational foundation for the future. The first challenge is that of "inclusion," or who wants in and who gets in? The founders normally decide the basic inclusion principles: is an investment of time or money required? A fee-paying membership can serve events well.

Founders can also influence whether power (i.e., the ability to control the organization and its actions) is "centralized" within a tight circle of leaders or owners, or "decentralized" among the membership or a large board of directors. A third factor to consider is the motivation behind the organization and behind decisions to join. These "founding principles" might be based on service to the community, self-enrichment, or the furthering of specific causes. Structures and management style should reflect these principles, but there are no hard and fast rules.

Informal, Founding Committees

Unless there is an existing organization or agency to provide the start-up structure and initial resources, a person or group will have to take responsibility to create a "founding," "steering," or "interim" committee. These devices have limited duration and lack sanction or structure; they exist for the sole purpose of stimulating a permanent organization, or perhaps getting an event produced in a hurry.

Their credibility might be directly related to the influence of the people on them, so some thought has to be given, even at this early stage, to alliances, networking, and power structures in the community. Some events spring from existing community networks, others from individuals with a great idea, and still others from special interest groups. Public agencies or business-related agencies increasingly have staff with a responsibility to generate and facilitate events. In all cases, the people with the idea have to persuade others to support it, then establish an organization appropriate to achieving the goal.

Start With a Plan

Without formulation of a vision, goals, and strategies, an inappropriate organizational structure might be created. Groups expecting large numbers of volunteers will more likely need a well-structured organization, whereas if the plan is to stay small and lean, a flexible team structure might suffice. Similarly, starting with a business plan, including a sound budget and cash flow projections, will get the organization off on firmer footing.

Organizational Culture

As discussed in detail later, the organizational culture will be an important factor in strategic planning. Consider the current leaders or founders and their commitment to the organization. If their leadership exists only for the short term, then the structure will have to cope with changes in the near future. Consider also that a structure, once in place, can be an impediment to innovation.

Determining what type of organization is appropriate, and getting it formally organized, is a matter of forward planning, consultation with experts, and possibly trial and error. Voluntary event organizations sometimes go through several spurts of formalization, each followed by failure or reorganization.

At the critical stage of formalization, the facilitative efforts of networks and agencies can be most effective. Reliance on supporters, including sponsors and local authorities, tourism agencies, and other events, can translate into long-term stability and strength.

Multiorganizational Structures

Events can be produced by one group working alone, or by a number of independent organizations. Figure 7.3 depicts options in which more than one organization can coop-

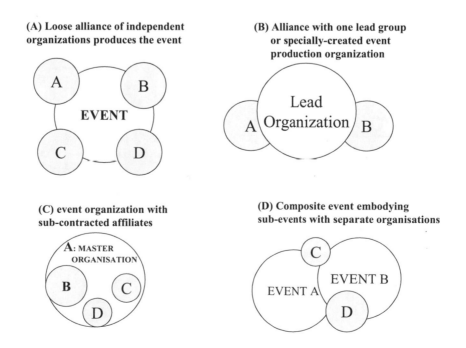

Figure 7.3. Multiorganizational event structures.

erate or partner to produce an event. The first is a loose, temporary alliance of equal partners who come together to create an event, while (B) is a grouping in which one existing
organization acts as coordinator or a new organization is established just to produce the
event. An example might be a multicultural festival produced by several ethnic clubs. If
none of the participants can, or wants to, take the lead, a third party such as an event
development agency or municipal culture department might have to coordinate the event.

Some event organizations take on affiliates only for the event itself (C). The core group
manages and produces the event, but the affiliates are assigned, or subcontracted, elements of it. In this way a small, permanent event organization can expand its scope without taking on the burden of a much larger structure. An entrepreneur who owns an event
product might use this structure.

In model (D) a large event with its own permanent organization joins with smaller
events with their own organizations—none of which are necessarily permanent. Community festivals sometimes grow this way, taking on other events and packaging them as a
larger attraction. The main organization must manage the overall event and sanction the
subevents, but each subevent has its own management system. With this approach coordination can become a problem.

Sport Events

Numerous sport events are produced by existing organizations, but many require new
and often temporary structures. In Figure 7.4 two models are illustrated (based on Klop,
1994). The first depicts a common situation in which a volunteer committee, perhaps
elected or appointed by various sport groups, oversees the event. A paid or volunteer
event coordinator supervises or coordinates various functional committees. This type usually dissolves quickly following the event wrap-up.

In the second type a sport governing body sanctions an event to be produced by a local
group, normally with a special event organizing committee. Control and coordination can

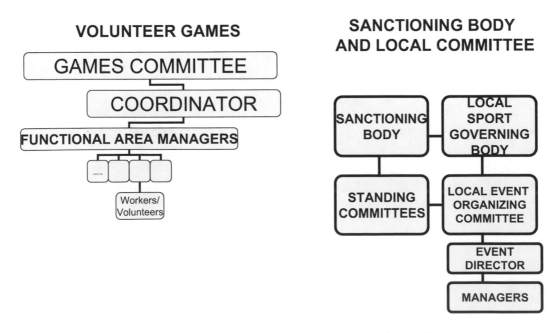

Figure 7.4. Typical sport event organizational models.

be strained because the sanctioning body might seek to closely supervise the organizers, but the local group can also benefit greatly by using the resources of the governing body. Linkages between standing committees of the superior body and committees or staff of the local body will be important.

Not-for-Profit Associations

Probably the majority of festivals and community-based events are organized and legally constituted as not-for-profit organizations, and many are also registered charities. The entire organization exists to produce the event, but must also manage its internal operations throughout the year. In other cases, not-for-profits spin off a committee to produce their events.

A typical association structure with a membership base is illustrated in Figure 7.5 (from Perry & Kelly, 1988). Members are usually required to pay fees, but not always. Directors will be elected from the membership at Annual General Meetings (AGMs), along with the officers. Alternatively, some associations allow their directors to internally select an executive committee and/or officers. Some associations also have an advisory board, and there is a trade-off to be made between large, very representative boards and a smaller, more manageable board plus an advisory body. The board will constitute standing committees with officers as chairpersons; members and other volunteers might serve on these committees.

The staff are organized under the supervision of the chief executive officer (or general manager or executive director) who reports to the board as a whole. Staff might also have their own standing committees.

Volunteers are a special issue for most not-for-profit events. It is likely that all the members and directors are volunteers, so they are fully integrated in the structure described above. When volunteers serve as directors of the organization, they are the governors and staff report to them.

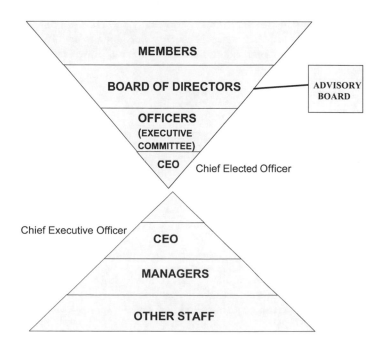

Figure 7.5. Not-for profit event organization with board of directors and paid staff.

Profile of a Not-for-Profit Event Organization: The Portland Rose Festival Association

The Portland Rose Festival, Oregon's premier civic celebration, has been a Northwest tradition for 97 years. This unique festival bursts into bloom each spring to celebrate the City of Roses with events, excitement, and entertainment for all ages. The Portland Rose Festival is Oregon's largest civic celebration, attracting 2 million people every year to its more than 80 events.

The International Festival & Events Association (IFEA) ranks the Rose Festival as one of the top 10 festivals in the world. IFEA recognized the quality of the Rose Festival by awarding it 14 Pinnacle Awards in 2002, one of the most honored organizations among 2500 festivals and events in the Association. The Grand Floral Parade is ranked as the second largest all-floral parade and the fourth best parade overall in the US, according to *USA TODAY*.

The Rose Festival is made possible by the efforts of thousands of volunteers, including a 100-member board of directors. The Portland Rose Festival Association is a nonprofit civic organization composed of professional businesses and individuals whose mission is to promote Portland and the entire state culturally, socially, and economically by presenting this annual celebration of our community.

The Board of Directors consists of 100 members, plus honorary directors including all past presidents. The Portland Rose Festival Association is entirely self-supporting and derives most of its income from admission to events, Association membership contributions, and corporate sponsorships. Any individual or business may join the Association by paying annual dues. This broad-based civic support makes it possible for the Association to present a full month of events every year—most of them free to the public. Members are entitled to gifts, events, and discounts, and membership comes in different levels (for different fees).

A full 28 days of events are produced annually, including 60 sanctioned events and over 20 produced by the Association itself. Most events are free to the public, but some are substantial revenue generators. Sufficient income is generated to support over $30,000 in scholarship donations each year.

Economic impacts to the area are estimated to be over $65 million annually through event tourism, retail sales, media sales, and facility use. Hundreds of thousands of dollars are returned to participating not-for-profit groups. Since 1984 nearly $3 million has been paid to the city for improvements at festival venues, especially the raceway and waterfront park. Over $200,000 in fees is paid each year for parade permits and facility/park use. At least 36,000 hotel/motel room nights are generated from tourists drawn from around the continent and abroad.

Portland Rose Festival Charitable Foundation

The Portland Rose Festival Charitable Foundation was created to support certain Rose Festival events that concentrate on education, youth, arts, and the environment. Contributions support the community and ensure that Foundation events remain available to spectators, participants, and recipients. Tax-deductible contributions to the Foundation ensure that Rose Festival events and programs remain available to all.

The Rose Festival Family Club helps hundreds of low-income and specially identified Portland-area children and their families to enjoy round-trip transportation to events, reserved seats at the Southwest Airlines Grand Floral Parade, free rides, and lunch at the Pepsi Waterfront Village.

Rose Festival Kids Helping the Community (presented by Parr Lumber Company)

is a noncompetitive program designed by the Portland Rose Festival Association to involve children in community service projects. Over 500 students participate in community service projects that include beautifying neighborhood parks, maintaining watersheds, volunteering at hospitals, and painting trash receptacles.

The Court Scholarship Program promotes education among the 14 Rose Festival court members. Each court member receives a $3,000 scholarship courtesy of Randall Realty Corp.

Project Management

Another common structure in the festival and events field is that of the one-time project team (Figure 7.6). Sometimes the team is attached to an existing organization, while for other events a new structure must be created. Specialist professionals within organizations can be assigned to the project team temporarily, but many volunteers are also usually required. A critical path dictates the pace of the work, while the looming deadline shapes the style and degree of structure within the organization. Sustaining control and accountability are often difficult in these organizations, especially for large-scale projects like the Olympics or a world's fair.

It is possible that multiyear projects can take on a function-based structure, but the essence of project management is that it should be more flexible than standard structures. Staff and volunteers might have to be moved around to many unrelated tasks, while subelements in the development process, such as construction of facilities, have individual termination dates.

Another factor in project-based organizations is the difference between the development and operational stages. Getting an Olympics or world's fair planned and developed is quite different from running them. Different teams and management structures are likely required, with some overlap and continuity of key personnel and tasks, particularly financing and marketing.

Project structures, according to Huffadine (1993), should be "flat," not hierarchical, and ensure that professionals and area managers are close to the general manager.

Informal Organization and Coordination

Whatever the structure looks like on paper, it might very well operate quite differently. The lines of authority indicated on an organizational chart might not in the least reflect the way managers and staff deal with each other. This can be good or bad, of course. In a bureaucracy, informal structure (e.g., getting things done according to who knows whom, or by cutting through the red tape and going directly to the top) can speed things up considerably. In small, team-oriented structures, the kind volunteer festival groups might like to have, it can subvert policy and control processes. In such cases, little cliques actually run things, while the nominal manager or board becomes ineffectual.

The Committee System

Almost all events will establish a committee system, given that the complexity of event management and production requires multiple talents and division of labor. Many small

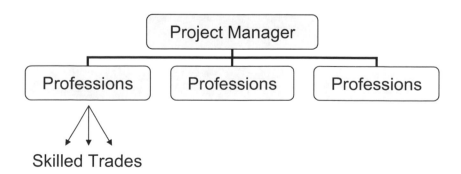

Figure 7.6. Project management organization.

events are structured entirely by their committee system, without much regard for boards of directors, officers, or other elements of the formal systems described above.

Function-Based Structure

These are the most common, simplest to organize and understand, and are often best for voluntary organizations. They are based on "departmentalization" (i.e., the grouping of related tasks), and thereby encourage clear specialization of labor. Overlapping responsibility can be avoided through careful structuring, with committees given precise mandates. A few basic committees with broad responsibility can be created first, with increasing differentiation (i.e., more committees) set up as the organization matures.

Figure 7.7 is the organizational chart for a hypothetical event association incorporating a functional committee structure. It is an all-volunteer group, without paid staff. Some or all of the board members (perhaps just the officers or executive committee) chair the standing committees. Subcommittees may exist under the main standing committees, and occasional "ad hoc committees" (i.e., established for a specific, temporary task) can also be established.

A more complicated variation is shown in Figure 7.8 for an event association with governing committees (including only directors), professional event manager, and function-based committees for volunteers. Obviously many variations can be created, but the principle of organizing by reference to management functions is widespread in the events field.

There is the possibility that teamwork will suffer as committees and individual volunteers become isolated from each other. Maintaining control and accountability in a highly departmentalized structure can also become difficult, requiring a strong board or CEO. One way to combat these problems is to periodically transfer volunteers, and particularly committee chairpersons, among the committees. This will build cohesion and potentially train people for assuming higher positions in the organization.

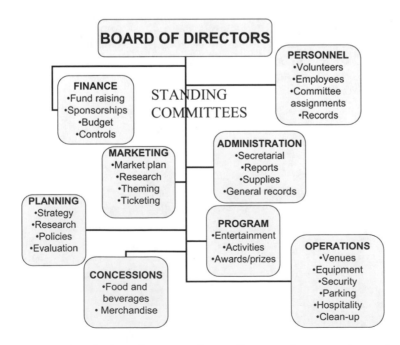

Figure 7.7. Organizational chart for a not-for-profit event incorporating a function-based committee system (no paid staff).

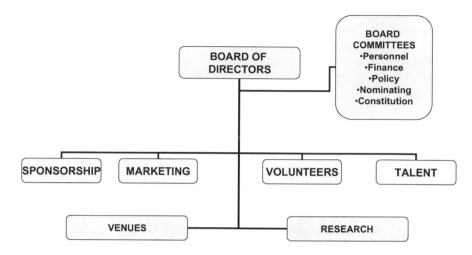

Figure 7.8. Function-based committee system for event associations with paid staff.

Program-Based, Matrix Structure

A program-based structure might be preferred. Committees or working groups are established to deliver a specific program element. For example, an arts festival might want separate committees for dance and music, while a sport event might find it easiest to have separate committees for each venue. An example is shown in Figure 7.9. A challenge is to ensure that a preoccupation with programming or venues does not result in operational, coordination, and authority problems. Accordingly, basic services like security, communications, and technical support must be organized to cut across all the program or venue areas, thereby forming a matrix structure.

Either the support workers must be assigned to each program area or they are expected to go where needed during the event. Either way, the essential support services must have their own committees, or at least supervisors, separate from the program committees.

Team Structure and Teamwork

Teamwork is a notable feature of many event organizations, Sometimes there is only one team, constituted as the board of directors, and sometimes each committee functions as a team. Alternatively, the manager can set up impermanent teams to deal with projects or tasks on an as-needed basis. The essence of teamwork is reflected in the following principles:

- internal flexibility: team members do what is necessary to complete their assignments without regard for formal structure;
- malleability: managers can create and shape teams as needed;
- unity of purpose: fostering a spirit of cooperation and a focus on the job at hand.

Making teams work together effectively is often a challenge. Rogers and Slinn (1993) advised that cohesion can be fostered by defining roles within the team, reconciling differences, and setting rules and procedures. Team leaders can be assigned, or allowed to evolve internally. Short-term, task-oriented teams might not require formal structuring or leaders, but longer-term teams will require assistance in solving problems and developing.

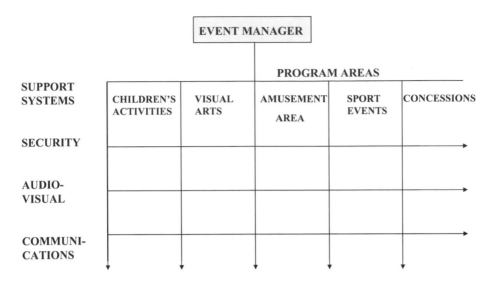

Figure 7.9. Program-based matrix structure.

Managing Not-for-Profit Associations

Organizational and management issues are quite complex for not-for-profit event associations. This section focuses on details of their structuring and management, including governance by the board of directors, roles of the chief elected officer and chief executive, and other technical matters affecting good management. Many of these principles can also be applied to other organizational types. See Exhibit 6-1 for a profile of a not-for-profit festival organization.

Legal Foundation and Bylaws

Most associations are based on a constitution or charter, depending on the pertinent laws governing not-for-profit corporations, charities, and societies. Changes can usually only be made through membership votes, and normally this is done at the Annual General Meeting (the AGM). The charter or constitution will establish mandate and perhaps goals, but often the details of organizational structure are left to bylaws, which can be modified more readily. Bylaws will cover many or all of the following critical items (based on Perry & Kelly, 1988):

- name and official corporate seal;
- location of head office (which specifies the jurisdiction governing the organization);
- membership criteria and categories; eligibility to belong and to vote; membership dues or other responsibilities;
- meetings of members (e.g., an annual AGM); numbers needed to petition for special meeting, and the process;
- quorums for voting; the use of proxy votes;
- size, composition, terms, and election of the board of directors; naming the officer positions;
- eligibility to hold board or officer positions;
- filling vacancies on the board;

- authority and responsibility of the board (e.g., elect or appoint officers and committees; authorize expenditure; make contracts; borrow money; establish bank accounts; appoint signing officers or agents);
- board meetings (frequency; giving notice; quorum; who calls the meetings; minority rights);
- removal of directors;
- remuneration and reimbursement for expenses;
- indemnity against legal action;
- standing committees (names, composition, etc.);
- the fiscal year;
- use of rules of order at meetings;
- a code of ethics;
- formula for amending the bylaws.

The Board of Directors

Boards exist to govern; they must take complete, collective responsibility for fulfilling the organization's mandate, vision, and strategies. Depending on applicable laws, board members—called "directors"—assume legal and financial responsibility for the actions of the organization, its staff, and volunteers, and can be held liable for losses or illegal activities. Webster (1995) described these "fiduciary responsibilities" and instructed board members to manage with care, diligence, and prudence to the benefit of the organization.

Organizations constituted as charities and not-for-profit societies or associations are often exempt or somewhat protected from such liability, so their directors do not assume major risks. This is a rather crucial point of law to be determined when creating an organization, or when agreeing to sit on a board of directors. Many associations carry liability insurance specifically to protect directors from legal actions (see J. Black, 1995).

Boards normally elect their "officers" who assume specific responsibilities and areas of authority, as defined by the constitution or bylaws. Carver (1990, p. 150) calls for the minimum number of officers permitted by law, usually a chairperson (or president) and secretary. Because the CEO has overall responsibility for financial management, the role of "treasurer" is usually redundant. Nevertheless, many boards opt for the positions of president, vice president(s), secretary, and treasurer.

The president or chairperson is responsible for the functioning of the board, and represents the organization to the public and stakeholders. Vice-Chairs or VPs might be desired, but are not necessary. VPs essentially take over when the president/chair is unable to function, or are assumed to be presidents-in-waiting. Some organizations require service as a VP prior to being eligible for chair.

The "secretary" is often relegated to the position of minute taker, but should function as that of record keeper for the board. The secretary's most important job is to certify the authenticity of board documents, especially the policies (Carver, 1990).

Boards Without Staff

Many event organizations do not have staff, in which case the directors constitute the main source of leadership AND performance, at least until the core of on-site volunteers gears up. In such cases, directors must usually assume specific functions, including the chairing of volunteer committees. Without a staff to do many tasks, the "working board" has to manage itself as well as the event operations, and often it is board-related tasks that suffer.

Should it become possible to hire a staff person, even a part-timer, serious problems can arise. The lone staff person cannot really function as a CEO, but is often held accountable for the success or failure of the event. These awkward situations must be resolved through board policies that stipulate the performance expected and related criteria for evaluation, plus the relationship between staff and board. Who exactly is the staff person responsible to?

Governance and Policy

While it is common for small event boards to actually manage and produce events, this approach is neither practical nor desirable for larger events, those that have formal structures, and particularly for events with paid staff. The board's primary function is governance, not management (Carver, 1990; Charney, n.d., c).

To Carver, all not-for-profit boards should concentrate on the following elements of governance:

- vision-setting (but not the actual strategic planning);
- addressing values, setting goals, and specifying desired results;
- developing fundamental policies, not detailed procedures;
- enabling an outcome-driven system (not managing it);
- dealing with large issues, not trivial operational matters;
- speaking with one voice.

The main tool of board governance is policy making. To Carver (1990), "Policy leadership clarifies, inspires, and sets a tone of discourse that stimulates leadership in followers" (p. 24). The key policy fields for board attention are as follows:

- ends to be achieved (goals, desired outcomes, or impacts);
- means to the end (empowerment of staff to make decisions; specification of staff ethics and principles for efficient and prudent resource use);
- board–staff relations;
- the process of governance (functions, roles, and responsibilities within the organization).

A set of concise, available, and understood policies, according to Carver (1999, p. 38) can replace most of the usual board documents, except for articles of incorporation, bylaws, and minutes. Board policies, being concerned exclusively with governance, are quite separate from staff or volunteer policies and procedures pertaining to operations.

Board Membership

What is the ideal board of directors for an event? The only qualification for being on many working boards is dedication or the act of volunteering. Over time, this situation tends to evolve into something more formal, or collapses from exhaustion.

When an event is well enough established to actually have the luxury of recruiting ideal directors, or in the case of a new event commencing on a fully professional foundation, board members should be sought to meet specific needs. These might include:

- professionals who can oversee important functions like budgeting, accounting, marketing, law, planning;
- well-connected people who can help secure support and resources, such as politicians and corporate leaders;
- experienced business managers with a skill for cost and revenue management;

- community leaders and experienced volunteers who know the public, the volunteer base, and the politics;
- representatives of key stakeholder groups and constituencies, such as sponsors, suppliers, community associations, public agencies, tourism industry, arts.

If a large board is desired, the executive committee will actually do most of the work. An alternative to large boards is the creation of an advisory board with no real responsibility but that can otherwise meet the criteria stated above.

Succession and Continuity

In many event organizations there is a problem with recruiting both volunteers and board members, resulting in succession problems and weak continuity. Ideally, the board positions, and especially those of officers, are subject to bylaw provisions setting terms of office and prescribing the method of election and succession.

One common practice is to have staggered terms of office so that each year one or more positions are replaced through election or appointment. Many associations prefer to have their officers elected from the membership directly, thereby maximizing democratic involvement and hopefully ensuring a larger pool to draw upon. On the other hand, this procedure leaves the organization vulnerable to a "takeover" by any group able to stack the AGM with its supporters. Alternatively, the association can require its members to first serve on the board of directors for a specified period before being eligible for an officer position. This builds a more experienced board and resists takeovers, but can also have the effect of creating a club-like atmosphere.

Stipulating the terms of office is important. For example, the bylaws can specify a 2-year term for officers or directors, with starting dates staggered so that the entire group does not turn over at once. Some associations also like to sequence their officers, so that, for example, someone elected to the position of vice-president automatically becomes the next president and eventually is moved into the position of past-president. This ensures continuity but might discourage some people who do not want to make such a lengthy commitment of time.

The Chief Executive Officer (CEO)

Selecting the top staff position and managing the relationships between CEO and the board is the collective responsibility of the board. Schmader (n.d., p. 7) advised that the CEO of an event organization must be:

- a strong administrator with "hands-on" abilities;
- dedicated to the event and willing to work outside normal hours;
- excellent on people skills, including leadership and motivation abilities;
- creative, and able to ensure quality control in all operations;
- forceful, with a strong personality.

To Schmader, the CEO "provides the focus for the organization, working with the day to day operations, assessing past successes and problems, looking down the road and keeping the event on track with its defined mission." The main responsibilities of the event CEO, subject to policy approval from the board, include:

- prepare and implement the budget(s);
- supervise all staff;
- strategic planning;
- evaluation;

- operating policies and procedures;
- dealing with the board and outside agencies or sponsors;
- serving the various committees.

The CEO reports to the board as a whole, and not to individual directors. Equally important, directors deal with staff only through the CEO. Deviation from these rules of good governance will cause severe problems.

Some boards prefer to give the CEO a vote, perhaps exclusively to break ties, so they appoint the CEO to a directorship. In some cases the CEO and President functions are combined, resulting in a very powerful position, but one that can entail conflicts of interest over such matters as salary and performance evaluation.

Relationships between event boards and CEOs are often strained and inefficient (Charney, n.d., c, p. 51). Event settings present a number of special challenges, which Charney describes as follows:

- diversity is desired on event boards;
- people attracted to festivals in particular might want to take a "hands-on" role, but this is usually inappropriate;
- there might be a perception that event staff are not professional, because it is such a new management field.

How can these problems be avoided? Carver (1995, p. 88) advised that boards should establish a distinct policy called "executive limitations" in which certain undesirable activities and practices are proscribed and limits set on other activities. Specific executive limitations could govern:

- minimum standards of behavior and ethics;
- unacceptable risks;
- debt limitations;
- limits on spending;
- equitable treatment of staff and others.

More important than limitations is empowerment. The CEO and staff should be empowered and motivated by the board's policies to achieve the desired results. If boards try to specify exactly what is to be done, innovation will be stifled and relationships will become tense. Boards are to govern, not operate events.

Charney (n.d., c) illustrated this governance model as applied to the Cherry Creek Arts Festival in Denver, Colorado. He acknowledged that "Getting an organization . . . to move into a new method of governance is no easy task . . . it requires a sense of commitment on the part of both staff and board leadership to want to improve organizational effectiveness" (p. 52).

Committee and Meeting Management

In organizations with staff and governing boards, the role of standing committees is to serve the board. In working event boards, committees often do all the work, with each committee assigned management or operational functions. Staff too can establish committees, or teams, and these are all accountable to the CEO.

To function properly committees need clear terms of reference and effective chairpersons. Intercommittee coordination is vital, and is the responsibility of their chairs. Committees performing the governance role should not engage in work that duplicates that of staff, or which might be interpreted as giving direction to staff. If staff sit on, or advise these committees the relationship must not interfere with the CEO's responsibility to direct staff.

Committees of working boards are generally structured to perform the main functions of event production, as shown in Figure 7.7. These standing committees do all the work, and the directors (who might chair the committees) must work together at the level of executive committee or full board to ensure that all committees are coordinated.

Schlegel (1995a, 1995b) gave advice on conducting board meetings. The chair must "craft the agenda" to start and end with unifying, not divisive, topics. Controversial items should be spaced out, and the number of items restricted to ensure they all receive adequate attention. Background material should be provided on topics requiring detailed consideration, and the chair can ask different people to make presentations. When items are complete, responsibilities for action and follow-up should be assigned.

According to Schlegel (1995b), the chair should ensure that everyone has a say during meetings. Circular tables are best to establish eye contact, thereby permitting the chair to keep everyone involved. The chair should aim to "guide, mediate, probe, and stimulate discussion" (Schlegel, 1995b, p. L46) and, when necessary deal (preferably at a break) with anyone engaging in dysfunctional behavior. The chair also ensures that meetings start on time and keep to schedule.

Issues should be put to a vote when a decision must be made. Complicated motions and amendments might have to be sorted (see the following section), but consensus should first be sought. Unanimous support for a motion, however, is seldom required.

Rules of Procedure

To avoid chaos and inefficiency around the board or committee table, most organizations rely on published rules of procedure, such as Robert's Rules (see Simonson, 1995). Whatever the system, it should provide for the following:

- calling meetings (by whom? what advance notice and to whom?);
- determining the quorum (how many are needed to validate decisions?);
- setting and following the agenda (normally the chair's role; who performs this task in the chair's absence?);
- determining who can speak or table motions (normally the chair's role, subject to points of order);
- procedures of debate and voting (entitlement to make motions and vote; requiring a "seconder" and discussion on all motions; "tabling" motions rather than voting on them);
- closing the meeting (at specific times? requiring a formal motion?);
- requirement for the secretary to record all motions; must motions be made in advance in writing?).

In the absence of agreed-upon rules of procedure the chair must be authorized to run meetings. This can create problems, of course, particularly if certain people feel cut off from influence.

Organizational Culture

Why do some organizations remain all-volunteer and informal in nature, while others evolve into more professional and formal groups? Why do leadership crises occur within events? Why are some events more strategic and marketing oriented then others? The concept of "organizational culture" can help explain these differences and can have important implications for strategic planning. Schein (1985) defined "corporate culture" as: "the deeper level of basic assumptions and beliefs that are shared by members of an organization, that operate unconsciously, and that define in a basic 'taken-for-granted fashion' an organization's view of itself and its environment" (p. 6).

The assumptions and beliefs are "learned responses to a group's problems of survival in its external environment and its problems of internal integration." A distinct corporate culture will take time to evolve, depending on sufficient shared experience to develop patterned and largely unconscious ways of doing things, including the teaching or indoctrination of new members. Where such conditions are not present, cultures can be in the process of forming, or a number of subcultures can be at work within a given organization.

Organizational Culture and Change Processes

Katz (1981) suggested five stages of organizational growth: origin, informal organization, emergence of leadership, formalization, and professionalism. However, he noted that voluntary groups might avoid the last two stages through a desire to maintain community involvement. Sigelman (1981) said that organizations might initially lose effectiveness as they become more structured, but this can be reversed by replacing ad hoc management with rational management. Overbureaucratization, however, could eventually destroy gains in effectiveness as it can cause "goal displacement" (i.e., the deliberate or gradual changing of goals), rigidity, and dehumanization.

Within the specific context of assessing the role of corporate culture in organizational change, Schein (1985, p. 271) described a staged process. The early stage of an organization's evolution is likely to be dominated by the founder, with culture being an integrative and identifying force. Socialization of group members will be stressed. A possible crisis occurs with leadership succession, and then culture can become a battleground between conservatives and those favoring radical change. "Midlife" spawns subcultures, so that integration declines within the organization. A crisis of identity might accompany the loss of key values and goals, but there is an opportunity to manage cultural change. During "maturity" internal stability might emerge, or stagnation sets in; there is likely to be little interest in change. In this context, culture can be a constraint on innovation and is used as a defense or source of esteem. "Transformation" can occur through identification of essential cultural elements to be preserved, or "destruction" might occur through massive changes in key people, or other fundamental cultural changes such as takeovers.

Getz and Frisby (1988) assessed 52 festival organizations in Ontario, followed by three more detailed case studies (Frisby & Getz, 1989), with a view to determining factors influencing the change process. These studies concluded that management sophistication in festival organizations was more related to the size of the community (a probable indicator of resources available) than to the age of the organization. As well, the evolution of festivals is more likely to reflect a program life cycle, with periodic decline and rejuvenation, than the linear model suggested by Katz (1981) in which increasing sophistication comes with age. Festivals were found to be operating in a highly uncertain environment, especially with regard to acquiring resources.

Some organizers in the Getz and Frisby sample wanted to keep their group small and informal, knowing that formality and professionalism can engender higher costs, more work, and less enjoyment. Others seemed to be concerned only with producing a good event and gave little thought to organizational matters. Still other festivals can be observed to progress through all the stages, or even to start life in a fully professionalized mode, complete with staff, office, and marketing plan.

Research by Mayfield and Crompton (1995) revealed substantial differences between event organizations in their marketing orientation. They tested the concept by creating three scales on the topics of visitor orientation, strategy development, and strategy implementation. Their self-completion questionnaire was administered to 706 festival organizers in Texas, excluding events of only 1 day in length or a single activity, and achieved a response rate of 44%. They found that as the number of years of operation increased, marketing orientation tended to decrease; it tended to increase with the population size of the community, the amount of sponsorship support the events received, and the presence of professional staff. Newer events seemed to feel a greater need for marketing, and perhaps older events were more complacent about "knowing" their customers.

The importance of resource availability on professionalism and organizational change is clear, but much of the variance among event organizations can only be explained by intangibles such as leadership, community context, the backgrounds of organizational members, and underlying values and attitudes.

Figure 7.10 is an evolutionary model of organizational change in events as related to the key factors of time (i.e., organizational age) and resources available (which is often a function of community size). It hypothesizes that as the organization ages, and as resources increase (generally these must go together), professionalism will increase. "Professionalism" can be measured first through increasing formality and bureaucracy, and, for events, by the presence of paid staff, a marketing orientation, and strategic planning. As mentioned earlier, many event organizations are being created in a fully professionalized mode, complete with office, staff, and large budget, so this model does not apply except to suggest that any event can fall back to a lesser professionalized state if its resources or leadership fail.

There is no inevitability to increasing formality or professionalization, just as there is no certainty that events or organizations will grow, prosper, or decline. To incorporate the elements of planned choice and uncertainty, we need a different framework, as shown in Table 7.1. This model, adapted from Schein (1985), hypothesizes a founda-

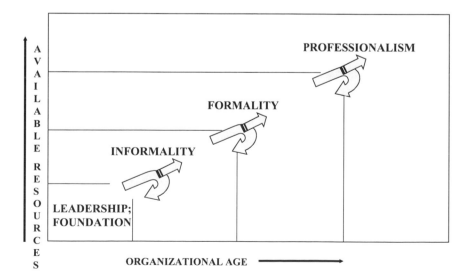

Figure 7.10. Life cycle and professionalism.

tion stage in which the founders are dominant in leadership roles and the vision is shared and clear. This might not occur, of course, as some event organizations might have to go through a period of informality and groping before any kind of leadership or structure emerges. In the hypothetical mature stage the organization and event(s) are well established but problems can occur. If these problems and the change process are not effectively managed, either through preservation or transformation, decline and destruction can occur.

Consider too that decline might be inevitable for some events, and their life expectancy can possibly be predicted. As well, events can fail as resources disappear, and that might be beyond the control of organizers.

Table 7.1. Organizational Culture, Evolution, and Strategic Planning In Event Organizations (Adapted From Schein, 1985)

1. The Foundation Years
Original founders are the true leaders.
Founding "culture" holds the group together; it is marked by a shared vision of the event and its roles.
Socialization of new members is important (i.e., they must be integrated into the founding culture).
Formality emerges over time and as resources are accumulated.
Planning Implications:
Make the vision explicit; develop clear goals.
Introspection is needed to evaluate the culture and its impact on the organization and its event(s).
Guarding against goal displacement might be important.
Prepare for the possibility of succession crisis as founders leave.
Plan for (or against) increasing formality.

2. Maturity
Formality and professionalism will peak.
Bureaucracy might impede progress.
Subcultures might be created
Values and the vision are possibly challenged.
A succession crisis might occur as founders leave.
The imbedded culture can be an impediment for innovation and necessary adaptation, or a source of pride and cohesion.
Planning Implications:
One option is to deliberately renew the organization with new members, new vision and new event ideas.
Another option is to reassert the founding culture.
A compromise is to plan for some renewal while preserving the elements that have made the organization/event a success.
Changes in leadership, volunteers, and staff, if not managed, can wreak havoc on the organization and threaten the event.
Conducting an organizational audit (using outside experts) can help focus the issues and options more clearly than incessant internal debate.

3. Transformation Possibility
Planned transformation into a new or renewed organization.
Planned transformation of the event(s).

4. Destruction Possibility
Unplanned obsolescence and decline (loss of leadership and/or resources for the organization; loss of demand for the event).

Links to Planning

All organizations undertake some form of operational planning, while long-term, strategic planning tends to occur once the organization attains (or is created with) a degree of professionalism. Understanding the theory and applications of culture to organizational change can greatly facilitate strategic thinking.

First, recognition of the existence of organizational culture and its potential influence can be a revelation to the founders and organizers, leading to introspection on goals and managerial style. It is likely that in many event organizations the culture is shaped by founders, so a conscious addressing of the beliefs, attitudes, and values of members, as well as their values-in-use, can have potentially dramatic impacts on how the festival itself is conceived, executed, and changed over time.

The hypothetical stages of culture development might have some predictive value. Organizers, or outside advisors, might draw attention to the possibility of cultural change over time, and use this to shape strategic planning. For example, anticipation of the possibility of a crisis precipitated by the departure of key founders could allow the organization to prepare transition strategies and mechanisms. Similarly, anticipation of a mature stage in which an imbedded culture becomes a constraint on growth or adaptation could lead to the formulation of policies governing the length of term for officers and the planned recruitment of new directors. Of course, strategic planning in itself might not prevent conflict when imbedded cultures resist change, but it can at least make the issues and options clear to all concerned.

The Learning Organization

The value placed on learning and sharing is part of an organization's culture. According to Schein (1985), the organization's assumptions and beliefs are "learned responses to a group's problems of survival in its external environment and its problems of internal integration" (p. 6). Learning occurs over time, and is not necessarily a structured process. To develop patterned and largely unconscious ways of doing things, a certain amount of stability or continuity of personnel is required, or the organization must have a built-in mechanism for passing on the learned responses to new members (i.e., indoctrination and/or socialization). So while learning helps form the organizational culture, the learning process is itself a function of that culture.

Culture can be manifested in a number of tangible and intangible ways, including indicators of status, professionalism, decision making, leadership styles, language, structure, and formality in planning. With regard to evaluating the learning process in festivals, some key indicators would be:

- Is there a formal evaluation and planning process?
- Is research valued and adequately supported?
- Are staff and volunteers encouraged to seek knowledge and new skills?
- Are innovations encouraged and rewarded?
- Does the festival have a mission, vision, or strategic plan that stresses learning and adapting, as opposed to protecting the status quo?
- Are professionals utilized for their expertise?
- Does the organization belong to professional associations?
- Does networking take place?

According to Senge (1990), learning organizations are those in which "people continually expand their capacity to create the results they truly desire, where new and expansive patterns of thinking are nurtured, where collective aspiration is set free, and where people are continually learning to learn together" (p. 3). Organizations must learn in order to adapt to changing conditions, and to enhance their ability to create, or be innovative. In a competitive environment, organizations must learn in order to prosper and survive, while in the governmental and nonprofit sectors organizations might place more emphasis on the role of learning in leading to higher service levels.

It goes without saying that individuals learn, which can in turn advance the organization's goals, but systems can be established to ensure that the organization benefits more from the learning and memory processes of its workers. Indeed, it is legitimate to say that organizations must develop institutional memories that survive individuals, and this in turn relates to the organization's culture. As Senge (1990) noted, "building learning organizations entails profound cultural shifts" (p. xv).

Redding (1997, p. 85), drawing on the work of Argyris and Schon (1978), proposed that three levels of learning within an organization that must be considered, each defined by the speed, depth and breadth of learning processes. Level 1 learning "provides simple solutions to the problems and roadblocks encountered, resolving obvious symptoms." Level 2 learning "provides deeper, systemic solutions to the problems and roadblocks encountered, often resulting in the need to modify the fundamental norms, management practices, procedures, structures, and processes of the organization." The third level is learning that "serves to identify weaknesses with and improve the learning process itself." In this schema, levels 2 and 3 learning affects organizational culture and the major management systems.

At a basic level, organizations learn through the knowledge of their employees and can accelerate the process through continuous education/training of staff and bringing in staff with new knowledge. As well, a number of intervention techniques have been developed to facilitate and speed up learning within organizations. For example, Redding (1997) compared "future search conferences," the "conference model," "action learning," and "action science" as to the speed, depth, and breath of their impacts.

The "learning organization," one that adapts and sustains its competitiveness (or ability to meet its mandate), must incorporate research and evaluation in all its management functions. Referring back to the system model of the organization (in Chapter 2), research and evaluation should facilitate learning by:

- continuously scanning the external environment and bringing new information into the decision-making process (i.e., situation analysis, environmental scanning);
- monitoring and evaluating all management processes (i.e., measures of efficiency of operations and effectiveness in producing desired outputs);
- searching for and evaluating unintended outcomes, or impacts on the environment;
- ensuring that the results of evaluation are fully incorporated into the decision-making process (e.g., through planning and/or budgeting).

A "learning organization" not only formalizes the evaluation and planning processes but consciously changes, or adapts, in response to internal and external forces. As noted by Steers (1991), "When stability and continuity are threatened, organizations must adapt their structure or behavior to ensure long-term growth and survival" (p. 616). But learning and adaptation should not be restricted to crisis situations; indeed, the object is to prevent a crisis.

Whose responsibility is evaluation and learning? In large corporations there might very well be professionals and units for research, planning, training, etc., but in small, not-for-profit organizations the responsibility is in the hands of the board of directors and through them to the executive director or manager. Where volunteers are important, as in most festivals and special events, the culture must be constructed specifically to ensure that staff and volunteers understand the importance of evaluation and learning, and make effective contributions.

Senge, Roberts, Ross, Smith, and Kleiner (1994:7) wrote: "Learning in organizations means the continuous testing of experience, and the transformation of that experience into knowledge— accessible to the whole organization, and relevant to its core purpose" (p. 7). Knowledge, in this sense, provides capacity for effective action.

Benchmarking

Benchmarking can be defined as a learning process through formal comparisons with industry leaders, resulting in quality improvements and competitive advantages (Watson, 1993). Essentially, one company is scrutinized carefully by another wishing to learn how to do things better. Not only are the best practices to be discovered, but the benchmarking must reveal how to enable the process to work.

Why would one company agree to allow another to learn about its successes? Either the process is reciprocal, giving advantages to both parties, or there is a belief that no competition exists between the firms. There might also be a belief, particularly in the nonprofit sector, that an overall improvement of the organizations in one field can benefit the position of all. For example, better quality in the events sector can potentially benefit all events through heightened customer satisfaction and cooperative marketing.

An essential ingredient in benchmarking is the ability to identify best practices within a field, as the value stems from learning from winners and leaders. Thus, a certain amount of sharing is required in advance, or some measure of a company's performance (e.g., profit, growth, market share) can be used to evaluate the field. In the festivals sector this kind of comparison might be more difficult, given the absence of profit and frequent inability to provide reliable attendance figures or other concrete measures of performance. As a consequence, festival managers might have to rely on the general reputation of an event or its manager, or attend events in order to determine which ones are worth studying.

A certain amount of comparison can be accomplished informally, and even without permission or knowledge of the company or event being studied. Anyone can buy another's product and study it, and in the festival field there is little legal protection for outright copying of good ideas. Certainly copyright protection can be obtained for names, logos, designs, etc., but not for the numerous programming or management ideas that can be readily observed and copied or adapted. While this can result in events becoming more similar, the fact is that most festivals and events have unique circumstances that lead to divergence.

Benchmarking is not without its critics. On the subject of making comparisons based on "best practices," Senge (1990) said: "While interesting, I believe such descriptions can often do more harm than good, leading to piecemeal copying and playing catch-up" (p. 11). From this perceptive, benchmarking should clearly be used with caution, and in a context with other learning methods.

A typology of event cultures can be constructed in part on the basis of sharing and searching patterns revealed in a study by Getz (1998b):

- inward-looking versus outward-looking (the degree of internal versus external searching might be based on profound conservatism or a product, rather than consumer-oriented focus);

- formal versus informal (how searches are conducted might reflect the degree of professionalism of managers and staff, or an overall emphasis on creativity rather than rational planning);
- local versus regional or international outlook (parochialism versus global perspectives);
- generic versus genre-specific outlook (reflecting a tight focus on one art form versus a feeling of belonging to a wider culture of festivals and events);
- experiential versus theoretical (reliance on theory as obtained through publications, formal study at institutions, or through seminars, as opposed to reliance on the collective experience of staff, volunteers, and other stakeholders).

To become better learning organizations, festivals should consider adoption of formal methods such as those listed below, as well as more systematic approaches to comparisons such as benchmarking. This might very well require a major shift in organizational culture, so that a shift to greater professionalism, strategic planning, and formal comparisons (like benchmarking) might be accompanied by, and dependent upon, a realignment of power, change in mandate or goals, and replacement of key personnel. On the basis of this research, it seems unlikely that most festival managers would pursue formal learning processes if it caused major disruption; the opposite seems more likely to occur, such as where shifts in core values (e.g., greater professionalism) lead inevitably to a greater emphasis on learning.

Selected Mechanisms to Formalize Organizational Learning

- planned research program;
- subscribe to publications;
- create archives;
- do strategic planning;
- networking/informal sharing;
- share tangible assets;
- hire and develop professional staff;
- benchmarking;
- retain experts/consultants;
- encourage volunteer continuity.

Implications for benchmarking are also suggested by this research, arising from increased knowledge of how reputations for excellence are earned, communicated, and utilized among festival managers. To be worthwhile, benchmarking must involve successful events, and in the minds of festival managers the reputation of success appears to be based primarily on programmatic or artistic quality. While this attitude likely translates into higher quality performances, it tends to ignore the fundamental importance of organizations and sound management practices that are necessary for mounting a quality event production. Reputation is also determined primarily by word of mouth and personal observations of other events, rather than any system of comparison or quality evaluation, so managers could easily make mistakes.

Several points can be suggested for facilitating more formal comparisons and learning among festivals, regardless of whether or not benchmarking studies are conducted:

- Professional associations giving awards are in fact suggesting models for emulation or comparison; therefore, it is essential that awards be based on comprehensive and systematic criteria that are made known to potential learners.

- Awards should be applied separately to programming/artistic quality, various management systems, and service quality as experienced by consumers, in order to guide potential comparisons.
- To facilitate direct comparisons and benchmarking, successful events can institute formal seminars and hands-on, experiential learning.
- To encourage formal benchmarking professional associations or other facilitators, such as city agencies, could match requests from learners to successful events willing to share information and ideas; as well, partnership arrangements could be brokered between events wanting to learn equally from each other this exchange would work best if both events possessed different areas of excellence and were noncompetitive for resources or customers.
- Festival managers prefer to learn through direct observation of other events, so formal study tours can be organized to visit multiple events.

Case Study of the Chicago Mayor's Office of Special Events (MOSE) and "Taste of Chicago"

Mission and History of MOSE

The Mayor's Office of Special Events (MOSE) provides Chicagoans and visitors with 12 months a year of family-style entertainment, by producing and promoting free festivals and city-wide holiday celebrations. Major downtown festivals such as Taste of Chicago, the Air and Water Show, Venetian Night, and six music festivals draw millions of people each year to the lakefront, contributing significantly to tourism and economic development for Chicago. MOSE assists city-wide community development by providing grants and technical assistance to over 80 community-based organizations for neighborhood festivals, and facilitation of over a dozen ethnic parades.

MOSE is unique in the US. The office began as a "one-man show" with Colonel Jack Reilly serving as an aide for then Mayor, Richard J. Daley. Reilly arranged ticker-tape parades for visiting dignitaries and heroes, ceremonial dinners, and receptions for visiting heads of state. Over time, and with each new mayor, the Office of Special Events grew in size and responsibility. In particular, the office broadened from serving primarily as a protocol branch to becoming a major tourism promoter and events organizer for Chicago. This evolution was spurred, in part, by the rapid growth of local events that began to put increasing pressure on city government in terms of police, sanitation, fire, and traffic services.

It was slowly recognized that the city might best cope with the challenges and demands being placed on it various departments by directly providing funding, technical assistance, marketing advice, and organizational suggestions for local events organizers. Many of the festivals were also seen as a way of promoting harmony and understanding among various ethnic groups in this highly multicultural city. By 1994, the number of neighborhood and ethnic events supported or run by MOSE had grown to over 80 annually—in addition to the larger city-wide events they are best known for.

The city-wide events began to be developed in the late 1970s and have grown since then. They include Venetian Night (started in 1958), Air and Water Show (1959), Chicago Jazz Festival, Chicago Blues Festival, Chicago Gospel Music Festival, Viva! Chicago (a Latin music festival), and the Chicago Country Music Festival. MOSE also became coproducer of the Taste of Chicago (described below) in 1980. "Taste" has grown to become the second largest tourist draw in the state of Illinois.

MOSE continues its role in protocol support, especially through arranging visits and receptions for dignitaries and heads of state and serves as a liaison with the Consular Corps of Chicago. MOSE also oversees the operation of the Office of Sports Development and the Chicago Film Office, which promotes the city as a venue for film production. The Office of Special Events was a major player in coordinating the opening ceremonies of World Cup '94.

Financing the Office

Funding for MOSE comes from the following sources:

- a room tax on all hotel and motel rooms within the city generates $4.2 million (2003 data);
- revenue from food, beverage, and souvenir sales at major festivals plus sponsorships generates $19.5 million;
- grants provide $158,000.

The operating budget is almost $24 million. Salaries consume $3.9 million; another $6.3 million is paid to restaurants participating in the Taste of Chicago. Operations require the largest portion, about $10 million, with programming and marketing consuming $2.5 million, sports development activities taking $0.5 million, and neighbourhood programs costing $0.65 million.

Staff

In 2003 MOSE had a staff compliment of 70 salaried positions, and at any given time there were student interns, seasonal temporary workers, and volunteers. Staff of MOSE provide a wide range of skills including public relations, finance, and programming. Sponsorship alone employees six full-time people. MOSE is increasingly used as an advocate to promote better liaison among city departments and between community groups and City Hall. This agency necessarily works closely with a wide range of other municipal departments to ensure that all city ordinances, regulations, and community needs (such as traffic control and sanitation) are met during festivals. These other departments include Police, Health, Streets and Sanitation, and Fire.

Corporate Sponsorship

The MOSE Corporate Sponsorship Department offers a variety of sponsorship packages designed to reach any marketing goal and accommodate any budget. By partnering with one or more of their events, companies have a tremendous opportunity to enhance any promotional campaign, from building brand awareness, attracting consumer sign ups, driving store traffic, or product sampling. Many levels of sponsorship packages are available and each includes complete marketing and promotional benefits. Some benefits may include: on-site promotional booths, media exposure, VIP concert/seating tickets, and corporate hospitality tents. (By way of example, see the sponsorship benefits offered for Taste of Chicago in the ensuing profile.)

Event Operations Department

The MOSE Operations Department is responsible for coordinating the logistical needs of the city of Chicago's internationally renowned downtown lakefront events and music festivals. The Operations Department is also responsible for overseeing and troubleshooting the logistical needs of newer events.

Neighborhood Festivals

The Neighborhood Festivals staff works with Chicago's community-based organizations in the production of summertime festivals designed to celebrate Chicago's many neighborhoods. Cultural programs, ethnic customs, music programs, and/or local businesses are showcased.

Assistance is provided primarily for local community groups and nonprofit agencies involved in promoting their service areas economically, artistically, and culturally. Neighborhood festival producers are local agencies defined as a community organization that fosters the development of quality activities in the community.

The Neighborhood Festival Program is designed to provide grants and technical assistance in obtaining the necessary food and liquor vending permits, street closures, and required special permitting. This area also works closely with all city departments to ensure proper staffing and event awareness.

Event Programming Department

MOSE is a city office designed to present public programs all year round. The calendar year begins in January with a 9-week Winter Delights program that includes a special kids' weekend, blues weekend, and jazz weekend. The second quarter follows with a special program titled, "Bloomin' Terrific." The summer features free outdoor music festivals and the year concludes with a special Kids and Kites festival and the Chicago promotion, which includes holiday festivities beginning with Chicagoween, Holiday parades, the tree lighting, and concludes with a spectacular New Year's Eve fireworks display.

Each program is coordinated by a staff member. The office produces the programs by utilizing the resources available to the office via marketing and operations. The programming coordinates all efforts related to the event or festival, including booking performances, organizing operations, facilitating sponsor partner participation, and assisting in promotion. The coordinator collaborates within the office as well as brings an interagency team together. The team consists of other city departments as well as bringing in many civic groups together to access all community interests in the production of the city-run events.

Sports Development Department

The Sports Development Office (SDO) was created in 1994 to support existing sports programs and foster the development of new sports activity in the Chicagoland area. SDO coordinates and produces annual events, including Mayor Daley's Holiday Sports Festival, the Race to Taste 5K Run and Walk, the Mayor's Cup Youth Soccer Tournament, Bike Chicago, and many more sports-related events geared toward youth and families. SDO serves as a liaison between the city and outside sports promoters and organizations, supports existing sports events and activities in the Chicago area, and provides professional management counseling to local sports organizations. It also evaluates and bids for national and international amateur sports programs, sports conventions, and sports congresses. By developing and maintaining relationships with sports organizations, creating new sports activities and events, and serving as the link between Chicago and the global sports communities, the SDO hopes to become the focal point of sports activity and support within the greater Chicago area.

Public Relations

The MOSE public relations staff produces and distributes pertinent information to all media outlets including print, radio, television, and the Internet, which, in turn, generates news items, programming, and images. Events encompassed are all public music festivals, sporting events, tournaments, and holiday celebrations.

The public relations staff is responsible for gathering event information and writing press materials, fact sheets, media alerts, public service announcements, photo captions, speeches, and speaking points. In addition, they handle choreographing press preview events, photo opportunities, and the pitching of story ideas to local, national, and international press. They also field incoming press inquiries. Marketing responsibilities include writing and editing copy for collateral materials, which include brochures, flyers, program books, display ads, and bus and train advertisements.

E works in tandem with other city, state, national, and international entities, including but not limited to, Department of Cultural Affairs, Navy Pier, McCormick Place, Chicago Park District, Chicago Public Schools, Chicago Public Libraries, and the various tourism offices around the country.

Taste of Chicago

The Taste of Chicago began in 1980 when Arnie Morton, a local restaurateur, elicited support from several fellow restaurateurs to ask MOSE to hold a food festival to celebrate the American Independence Holiday (July 4). The motives for the festival were a combination of civic celebration and advertising for the participating restaurants. The plan was approved, with a budget of $150,000 and a target of 75,000 visitors for a 1-day event. The first "Taste" far surpassed the targets: 250,000 attended, with gross revenues for the city exceeding $330,000.

Photo 7.1. The multicolored tents of the many Taste of Chicago restaurants draw millions of visitors each year (credit: City of Chicago).

The initial event was held as a 1-day, three-block party on Michigan Avenue, but its success caused the event to be moved in the second year to Grant Park, which is also the location of the Chicago Art Institute, Adler Planetarium and Shedd Oceanarium, the Field Museum, the Chicago Cultural Center, and a music shell. Grant Park is also easily accessible by public transportation and provides a stage, dressing rooms, and showers for performers as well as ample seating for concerts. Grant Park continues to be the location of the festival, although the size of the crowds is such that the city closes streets surrounding the park as well.

For the first 8 years, the festival was mostly adult oriented. Major features included food, public concerts, and fireworks, plus a small circus and a "Family Oasis" (an area for quiet times with kids). A new Director of Special Events, Kathy Osterman, was appointed in 1989, and she decided to push for a reorientation of the festival to a family-centered event. The festival was rethemed as "America's City Picnic," and the "Not for Kids Only" stage presentation was added.

Today, the Illinois Restaurant Association (IRA) is a partner in producing Taste of Chicago, and food, of course, continues to be an important attraction. Over 10 days in 2002 an estimated 3.5 million visitors enjoyed food served at 65 food tents. Interest among restaurants in participating is keen. The IRA determines which restaurants can participate, through an application process, based in part on an evaluation of health and food safety and whether or not the applicant can sustain its presence over 10 days. There are also 12 "sponsor restaurants" who pay a fee of $25,000 to be in the festival.

The festival is marketed through packages and cooperative advertising with United Airlines, local hotels, major retailers, and restaurants. Festival-goers purchase food tickets valued at $1 to $4.50 each. They then trade the tickets for food items ranging in price from $0.50 to $4.

Although a visitor could create an entire meal at an individual tent, most visitors prefer to "graze," by visiting numerous tents and sampling a wide variety of cuisines. Restaurants pay a fee to participate; food tickets are sold by MOSE. Revenues are then shared with individual food tents, based on the number of tickets they collect.

Because of the location of the festival in the very heart of the city, a large number of visitors are downtown workers. However, many visitors also come from the suburbs and even further away. The festival draws heavy media coverage. Several local radio stations broadcast daily from Grant Park, and a number of local television stations have regular news reports from the festival. Local papers run stories and daily schedules highlighting events.

Taste of Chicago festival has recruited hundreds of sponsors over its 15 years, in order to keep the concerts and other attractions free to the public. For example, Dominick's Food Stores sell tickets in advance that are discounted $1.50 from the regular Taste price. Patrons can pick up the tickets and the Taste booklet at grocery stores until opening day, thereby promoting the event. This sponsor also owns the Chef's Cooking Corner on the Taste site, providing a daily feature of national and local chefs preparing dishes in a designer kitchen.

23rd Annual Taste of Chicago Sponsorship Opportunities

- Sponsorship packages begin at $25,000.
- Benefits may include: Signage Opportunities, Food/Beverage Vending, Sampling/Promotional Booths, VIP Concert Tickets, Hospitality Tents, Name/Logo on Brochures.
- Media exposure: Considered a marketing manager's dream, Taste of Chicago appeals to a broad spectrum of people. This event is one of the top tourist attractions in Illinois drawing over 3.5 million people annually. It is the largest free-admission food and music festival in the US generating over $10 million on food and beverage purchases. This favorite Chicago tradition offers cuisine from more than 70 restaurants, plus entertainment and activities for young and old alike. Listed as the main reason for visiting Chicago by 70% of those attending from outside the city, the Taste is your ticket to reaching a young, well-educated, upper middle class audience with 40% of those attending bringing their children. Nearly 90% of those surveyed agreed that sponsorship of an event like Taste leaves a positive image of the company.
- Unique promotional opportunities include sponsorship of the Gourmet Dining Pavilion, Chicago Living Pavilion, Water Slide, or the Extreme Team High Divers.

Critical Success Factors

The success of Taste of Chicago is due to a number of factors:

- Chicago has a tradition of hearty dining, with a wide range of ethnic cuisines.
- The event is basically free to the public. Although participants must pay for food and drinks, there are numerous free concerts, attractions, and displays as well as free admission to the grounds.
- The event is held during high summer, when the weather in Chicago is generally good.
- The venue is centrally located in the downtown core, with good access to the suburbs via public transportation and nearby expressways and good parking.
- A wide diversity of high-quality musical events is offered, ranging from rock through classical to ethnic. Nationally known artists are featured every year.
- New events and attractions are added virtually every year. A country music "satellite" festival was added; during the 2 days of that festival, many "Taste" restaurants feature country or western-theme food items.
- A wide variety of well-prepared foods, from hamburgers and pizza to exotic foreign cuisine, ensure satisfaction of every taste.
- A substantial administrative structure facilitates cooperation of other city departments.

- The professional staff in MOSE includes marketing experts, financial officers, purchasing and contracts staff, and sponsorship representatives.

The Taste of Chicago and MOSE operates at a level that is beyond the scope of all but the largest cities. However, many of the "secrets" of their success can be adapted to medium and even small-sized towns. These include the need for increasing professionalism in management, a continuing focus on customer demands, product innovation, imaginative packaging and marketing, and a commitment to the highest quality possible in whatever event or attraction is being planned.

Study Questions

- Why are multiple stakeholder perspectives important to the organization of an event?
- Explain the fundamental differences in mandates and goals between the three generic types of event organizations.
- What is organizational culture and why is it an important consideration when setting up an event organization?
- Why do some events rely on several organizations to produce them? How do they coordinate?
- In not-for-profit organizations what are the key roles of the Board of Directors and Chief Executive Officer?: explain governance in this context.
- What is a standing committee and what types are generally needed for events?
- How does a matrix structure differ from a function-based committee structure?
- What can be done to create a learning organization? Why is this important?
- Define benchmarking and illustrate how it works.
- What is unusual about the Chicago Mayor's Office of Special Events?

Advanced Study Questions

- Compare several event organizations from the perspectives of their culture, structure, and effectiveness. Is effectiveness linked to how they are organized?
- Trace the evolution of one or more events in terms of structure and professionalism. Is the Getz/Frisby model confirmed?
- Can you find examples of events that have faced a crisis or failed? What aspects of their culture might explain the problem?
- Analyze the ways in which an event learns in practice, and make recommendations for becoming a better learning organization. Use the event management model as a systems diagnostic tool.

Chapter 8

Human Resources Management

Learning Objectives

- Know the unique human resource challenges facing events.
- Be able to plan the human resource management system, including staff and volunteers.
- Be able to conduct needs assessments and job analyses, make forecasts, and prepare job descriptions.
- Be able to formulate policies and procedures to formalize the staffing process.
- Be able to recruit, screen, hire, and orient new employees and volunteers.
- Be able to initiate training and professional development programs; work to enlarge the jobs of staff and volunteers.
- Be able to supervise and evaluate staff and volunteers using performance criteria; use rewards and discipline as appropriate; resolve conflicts; manage the termination, outplacement, and reenlistment functions.
- Be able to manage the essential functions of pay and benefits, working conditions, labor relations, and employee records.
- Be able to use motivation theory relevant to the specific needs of staff and volunteers.

What Is Human Resources Management

Human resource management is the process of organizing and effectively employing people in pursuit of organizational goals. Generic human resource functions (adapted from Stone & Meltz, 1988) include:

- planning (needs assessments, forecasts);
- job analysis (resulting in job descriptions);
- recruiting and hiring (including screening and evaluation of candidates);
- orientation, training, and staff development;
- compensation and benefits; discipline and termination;
- health and safety; working conditions;
- labor relations;
- counseling and outplacement assistance;
- organizational change programs.

Tanke (1990), writing on human resources management for the hospitality industry, added coaching and team building. These are also particularly relevant to the events sector. Not all these functions will be pertinent to every event, and in many cases it is the CEO rather than a professional personnel manager who has these responsibilities. Yet every organization must formally or informally ensure that these functions are met. Some events will not want to be bothered with job descriptions, but that does not mean people will be working in a vacuum—someone still has to supervise, and that supervisor must have at least a mental plan.

As well, the specifics of each function and the balance between them will change through the stages of an event's life cycle. When a new event is created, recruitment and training tend to dominate, while a mature event will have to place more emphasis on evaluations and job analysis in order to improve efficiency and effectiveness.

Unique Human Resource Elements of Events

The human resources manager for events faces a number of unique challenges:

- most are dependent upon volunteers;
- they are often organized and produced by volunteers in informal organizations;
- some workers are required all year round, but most are needed only during and around the event itself;
- professional staff are often part-time and have risen through volunteer ranks;
- staff and volunteers are often part of the product (as the Disney Corporation puts it, they are all "cast members");
- relationships with stakeholders and the community are vital for recruitment of volunteers;
- managers must often work directly with staff of other organizations, such as parent agencies, sponsorship companies, suppliers, and regulatory bodies;
- leadership and control is often expressed through direct, interpersonal methods, rather than formal personnel systems;
- cultural diversity is frequently an issue, to ensure the event fairly represents the community it serves and to manage diversity among the staff and volunteers.

The Human Resources Planning Process

Figure 8.1 presents planning process for managing the event's human resources. The human resource system takes its basic direction from the mission, vision, and strategic plan of the organization. Fundamental issues must be addressed, namely:

- Is it to be a volunteer-only organization?
- Do we want to professionalize?
- Must we recruit in any specific manner (e.g., local community; from certain supportive groups)?
- Do we have a budget for hiring and rewarding?
- Are we growth oriented?
- Will certain aspects of the event or organization be handled by other groups, such as sponsors or parent agencies?
- Is there a need or desire for a permanent organization, versus a project using short-term volunteer efforts?

Needs Assessment

Many event managers will be forced by circumstances into taking whatever human resources they can get. However, as the event matures, more emphasis should be placed on

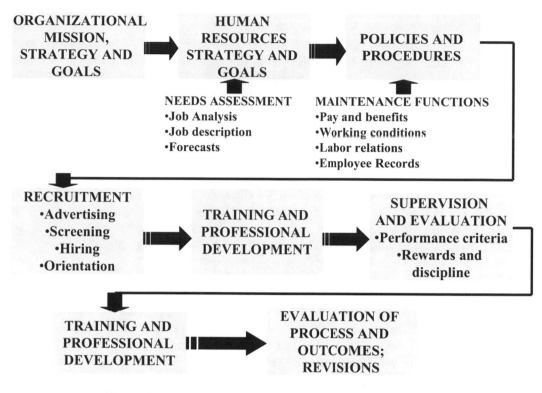

Figure 8.1. Human resource planning process for events.

evaluating current and future personnel requirements. For a large, one-time event, human resource needs will figure prominently in the feasibility study and early planning, as too much is at stake to risk inadequate staffing or overstaffing. A generic needs assessment results in forecasting of future staffing needs by:

- examining turnover (e.g., how many volunteers leave each year? are assignments regularly rotated?);
- projecting growth or changes in the organization that will result in the need for different levels of staffing or different types of staff;
- identifying likely gaps between what is needed and what is likely to occur, or any surplus that might arise;
- developing programs to recruit or downsize, train or counsel, in order to ensure staffing meets needs; consider alternatives and select the best course(s) of action;
- evaluate outcomes using preestablished criteria; revise the projections and programs as necessary.

This assessment should lead to specific forecasts of:

- numbers of staff and volunteers required, by time period;
- types of skills and knowledge needed.

To make more refined forecasts of needs, and to help with supervision of personnel, it is desirable to conduct job analyses and prepare job descriptions.

Job Analysis

Within the organization a "job" is a position or group of positions with common duties and tasks. For example, there will be security jobs, parking control jobs, and various management jobs. A "position" is a place occupied by one person, usually with a title like "director of marketing." Each position must fulfill "duties," which are the major required activities or responsibilities. More specifically, "tasks" must be defined as subsets of duties, or lists of specific actions the position entails.

Remember that each person must know their responsibilities and the lines of authority, or confusion and stress will follow. Sometimes a systematic process is not possible, or not desirable—organizers might want to keep the event small and informal. In such cases a simple "task–interest matching" process can be followed, in which each volunteer is asked to state their interests and given a choice of possible matching tasks. Of course, as much as possible volunteer and staff interests should be matched to their jobs, but there are usually other criteria to consider, such as experience, seniority, unfilled positions, and aptitudes. Job analysis can be undertaken in several ways:

- direct observation leading to a description of what the person does and related performance standards (this works best for simple or repetitive work);
- "critical incident" methods (captures nonroutine behavior, such as dealing with a crisis, but is difficult to translate into job descriptions);
- interviewing and self-description, resulting in customized job descriptions (time consuming; perhaps best suited for key volunteers and professionals);
- classification of types of jobs (each worker in each type gets a similar or identical job description; requires an expert comparison of tasks and workers).

Determining the Minimum Number of People Needed

Perhaps the most basic example of human resource needs assessment is that of determining the minimum number of people needed to produce the event. In this case the starting point is not the organizational chart, but the event program or operational plan.

Step 1: Break down the program or operational plan into discrete tasks (things that people must do to produce the event). For example, to prepare the site:

- set up fencing according to site plan;
- erect tents, portable toilets, stage, signs;
- clean up the site; dispose of waste in approved manner;
- return equipment to specific sites/owners.

Step 2: Determine through experience or estimation how many people are needed to complete the various tasks. For example, do all the actions have to be done in sequence, by the same crew, or all together by a larger crew? How much supervision is required?

Step 3: Make a list of the ideal work crew in terms of its numbers, supervisor(s), and skills needed.

Policies and Procedures

Strategy and needs assessment leads to formulation of policies and procedures for human resource management. Principally these must cover the elements shown in Figure 8.1, namely: recruitment and selection; training and professional development; supervision and evaluation; termination; outplacement; reenlistment; maintenance functions; and evaluation.

A governing board sets the general policies within which the CEO makes human resource decisions, whereas a working board (i.e., without paid staff) gets intimately involved with all volunteer matters. How detailed and restrictive these policies and procedures should be is a matter for debate. Many event organizations will be bound by higher authorities (i.e., their company or agency policies), and all organizations are bound to obey laws, especially those pertaining to discrimination, health and safety, compensation, and dismissal. Having an experienced human resource manager on the board is a good idea.

Job Descriptions

Event managers often do not have the time or resources to prepare sophisticated job descriptions, but it is important to know what should go into their preparation under ideal circumstances. As events professionalize, the job description becomes a more important management tool.

As noted above, analysis of duties and tasks does not necessarily lead to job descriptions. One person might be able (or have to) perform many tasks in various functional areas. In small organizations this is the norm, whereas in larger organizations job differentiation increases and workers are more restricted.

"Overspecialization," in which workers are restricted to doing narrowly defined tasks, carries the risk of fostering inflexibility and bureaucracy, with all its impediments to creativity and adaptability. As a general rule, it is likely that most events will benefit from avoiding overspecialization. For many volunteers, however, this principle will not be realistic nor desirable. They will want the comfort and protection of a very narrowly defined job description; they fear overcommitment. In these cases, the manager should encourage volunteers to try different jobs, and eventually they might become comfortable with a broader job description.

Various detailed elements that might go into a job description are discussed below. Job descriptions should indicate the effective date and dates of revisions in order to demonstrate they are current.

> **Position Title:** Managers and supervisors generally need specific titles that reflect their position in the organization and their functional areas, such as Marketing Manager, or Supervisor of Security and Parking. It might be pointless to try to give a unique title to each and every volunteer, however, so a general job description might suffice (e.g., "Assistants to the security and parking supervisor").
>
> **Responsibility and Duties:** Managers and supervisors have responsibilities, whereas most workers have only duties. When a responsibility is assigned, the person must have a description of its limits (e.g., "Responsible for ensuring that the site is secure from unwanted intrusion, that safety and risk management procedures are effectively implemented, and parking is adequately controlled"). Duties will be given as a list of things to do, such as: "ensure that parking attendants are in place one hour prior to the opening time."
>
> **Authority:** This defines who the person reports to, and who reports to the person. For example, "The Supervisor of Security and Parking has general on-site authority to ensure security; reports to the General Manager and takes direction from the GM on matters of policy; all security and parking personnel on site report directly to, and take instructions from, the Supervisor."
>
> **Tasks:** Specific tasks generally do not need to be listed for supervisors and managers—their duties are broad enough, and the tasks of their workers define their

responsibilities. Most workers, however, will want a detailed list of tasks, along with a clear-cut line of authority (i.e., who they take orders from and report to).

Key Results, Performance Criteria, and Job Specifications: For purposes of evaluation, and to assist in human resource needs assessments, it is helpful to list the criteria by which persons will have their work evaluated. They can be expressed as "key results" (statements of the most important outcomes of the work), "performance criteria" (measures of effectiveness in attaining goals and measures of efficiency in using resources), or both. Performance criteria follow from designation of key results. If detailed performance criteria are specified, they will be harder to achieve; failures to perform might result in human resource problems. It is generally a good principle to set high standards of performance, but only if they are realistic. Instead of "failures," evaluation can focus on learning and planned improvements.

Personal Attributes: It can be useful to include a statement of what is expected from each worker in terms of behavior and attitudes. This is particularly important at events because many staff and volunteers are highly visible and important elements of the product and contribute directly to service quality and ultimate customer satisfaction. Behavioral criteria cover the visible actions of workers, including performance of duties and overall deportment, dress, words, and expressiveness. For example, "parking attendants will behave professionally, according to the operational plan; will respond to inquiries politely and informatively; will dress smartly and suitably for the weather and other conditions; will smile and be friendly!"

Knowledge and Skills Needed: Many volunteers can be slotted into a variety of tasks without related knowledge or skills, and training can overcome many deficiencies. But for professional staff and key volunteer managers and supervisors the job description should specify the knowledge base (what they need to know to do the job) and necessary skills (what tasks they must be able to do). For example, "the artistic director must be experienced in developing entertainment programs and be able to negotiate contracts with performers and agents."

Commitment: How much effort and time is required of personnel? The job description can state the job duration (all year, over 1-year, or part-time over 3 months?), time commitment (3 hours a week, all year; 10 hours on date of the event), and effort required (e.g., the tasks are highly physical and demanding in nature). If appropriate, risks (of physical danger, financial loss, unexpected time demands, etc.) should be stated. No one, least of all a volunteer, should be exposed unknowingly to hazards or be subjected to unreasonable changes in their duties or working environment.

Resources Available: What resources will be supplied to permit the person to achieve the desired results? Managers need office resources, supervisors must have crews and equipment, some jobs need a line-item budget, and others need only the instructions of supervisors. Some volunteers might be reluctant to accept a position if they fear they will not be given adequate resources.

Rewards or Incentives: Most events provide some rewards in the form of souvenirs, parties, awards, or food. It can be helpful to specify what the volunteer can expect if they adequately perform their duties.

Recruitment and Selection

Given the newness of the events field, experienced and appropriately trained professionals are scarce, while the competition for good volunteers has never been greater. With so many events and other worthwhile causes as competition, recruitment cannot be left to chance, nor to the traditional networking that constitutes the basis of most recruitment strategies. The adage "if you don't ask, they won't volunteer" holds true, but reliance on just asking is no longer good enough—there is a good chance that most people asked will already be volunteering!

The recruitment and selection process might consist of the following elements, with the caution that certain questions and lines of inquiry might be illegal in your area. Always check antidiscrimination and labor laws, and as a general rule avoid any situation that would tend to discriminate against people on grounds not specifically related to the job requirements. The health and safety of your guests is critically important, so be certain to determine what details of an applicant's or recruit's background can legitimately be examined or challenged.

> **Applications:** Obtain information about the recruit, such as competencies, interests, experience, and references to contact.
>
> **Screening:** Check references, and where appropriate use professional or police security checks for critical positions. Assess specific qualifications and short-list the most desirable recruits.
>
> **Interviews:** It might be best to use professional recruiters, to avoid bias and ensure thorough screening. Use prepared and standard questions, to permit comparison, but allow for personalities to come through. Personality or skill tests might be useful.
>
> **Offers:** Make them in person and in writing, to avoid misunderstanding; specify the job description and working conditions.
>
> **Negotiations and Contracts:** These are not usual for volunteers, but might be necessary for staff positions.
>
> **Notifications:** Thank-you notes should be sent to successful and other candidates.

Targeting specific people known to have desired skills, contacts, or resources is common practice. Sometimes professional recruitment (or "headhunter") firms are employed to select key professionals. For voluntary directorships, use senior people in the organization, or in key stakeholder groups. Many event organizers recruit mature professionals to occupy the vital officer positions (especially finance and law), or ask professionals from various backgrounds to sit on planning or advisory committees.

Many companies support community volunteering on the part of their employees, with the lead given by senior executives. Some even give time off for volunteers. Sponsors can be a primary source of temporary professional help. Consider making the provision of key volunteers, or internal recruitment, part of sponsorship deals. Other partners, including grant-givers, receivers of donations, suppliers, and other stakeholders, should be approached.

Cities usually have central community volunteer bureaus to process volunteers and match them to groups looking for help. Private and government employment agencies are sources for paid staff. Schools and colleges are a great source of workers. Create internships and projects for students to get involved in the event. Similarly, recruit from affinity groups and clubs to get volunteers in larger numbers; their cohesion might make them better for certain functions.

The event itself can be a powerful recruitment vehicle. Why not have a booth available for information, including how to volunteer? Social events can be used to invite the community at large, or for staff and volunteers to bring potential candidates. Advertising will sometimes be needed. Pay for ads, but preferably only when other techniques are failing.

Also, incorporate volunteer requests in other communications such as newsletters and public service announcements.

Orientation and Socialization (Induction)

It can be terrifying to be thrown into a new job or assignment without proper orientation. New recruits have certain needs, and the organization also wants to ensure that their investment is properly handled, so the following actions should be taken with new staff and volunteers:

- provide basic information about the organization and event (e.g., use your business plan);
- tours of venues, offices, suppliers, or whatever fits their potential jobs;
- meeting staff and other volunteers;
- indoctrination to organizational culture, mission, work styles, if appropriate;
- testing and screening, if needed for specific assignments;
- introduction to the training program.

"Indoctrination" is potentially controversial. Low-keyed orientations can use personal testimonials of leaders and other volunteers to demonstrate the values and goals of the group. In some organizations, more formal methods are desired, including team-building sessions and coverage of rules and regulations. The danger is that recruits will be intimidated and then drop out. The potential benefit is a more cohesive group committed to the same vision.

According to Hanlon and Cuskelly (2002), generic "induction" of new personnel includes:

- providing an organizational framework (vision, goals, and expectations are discussed);
- establishing relationships that include team training;
- providing resources, such as a manual;
- evaluating effectiveness.

Induction will be required for seasonal and outsourced managers as well as those volunteers who show up year after year for the event itself. Hanlon and Cuskelly concluded that on-site manuals were necessary for events. Role playing and dealing with various scenarios might be effective. Induction processes can generate higher morale (less anxiety), increase volunteer retention, and improve productivity.

Training and Professional Development

Training seeks to ensure that all recruits and existing personnel can fulfill their assignments, grow within the organization, and develop their potential. It might also constitute a reward, as many people are seeking new skills, while the training process itself can be made fun and desirable. A volunteer's level of interest might also determine whether a basic or intensive training program is required.

The most basic training is "on-the-job," incorporating showing (by those who know how to do the job) and doing. "Positive reinforcement" is the key, as most people respond better to encouragement of desired behavior than to criticism of mistakes. This approach costs little, and might only require minimal supervision, but is not appropriate for sensitive and difficult jobs.

Training is necessary for those taking up responsible positions and doing jobs requiring specific skills. Options include:

- using existing staff or volunteers, as trainers or more informal "mentors" (i.e., advice givers and confidants);
- team approaches (mutual responsibility for all team members' training);
- bringing in experts for formal sessions and courses;
- using formal education programs, or correspondence courses;
- attending conferences;
- enrolling in professional association programs;
- apprenticeships and internships.

An "apprenticeship" places the trainee with a skilled worker for a prescribed period in which all skills are passed along and practiced until competence is achieved. "Internships" involve a placement within the organization that will usually involve exposure to more than one job, and with no specific skill to master. They are great ways to introduce students to the organization and to event management.

Managers in particular must have training and ongoing professional development. This applies to both volunteers and professionals. The effectiveness and efficiency of training should be evaluated, not assumed. In part this can be accomplished through regular and systematic performance appraisals, which are discussed later.

Volunteer training programs can be established well in advance of major events with multiyear planning periods, but for annual and ad-hoc events there are usually severe time constraints. Periodic events rely heavily on repeat volunteering, so experienced volunteers can be invaluable in helping to train new recruits. As well, the core of dedicated, repeat volunteers should be fertile ground for identifying those with strong leadership, and managerial and mentoring potential.

Leadership training is important for key personnel, whether permanent staff or volunteers. The main elements to cover would include (from Tzelepi & Quick, 2002):

- challenges facing leaders;
- skills and attributes for effective leadership;
- the supervisor's role at the event;
- composition and motivations of the workforce;
- planning and decision making for the event;
- the event environment.

Research Note

Tzelepi, M., & Quick, S. (2002). The Sydney Organizing Committee for the Olympic Games (SOCOG) "Event Leadership" training course—an effectiveness evaluation. *Event Management, 7*(1), 245–257.

The researchers measured participants' expectations and satisfactions with the training they received. Conclusions were:

- event leadership courses should be adjusted to the needs and special characteristics of participants (flexibility) (e.g., form subgroups of similar attendees);
- content should highlight the practical, not theoretical, as participants want to acquire skills (use real-life scenarios, role playing, and knowledge practice);
- adjust training to participants' roles (not generic).

Supervision and Evaluation

In the most informal of event organizations there is little or no supervision, and sometimes this works well. But the bigger and more complex the event, it will become more

necessary that all staff and volunteers receive appropriate supervision to ensure job performance and satisfaction.Although some good workers prefer to be left alone, many flourish
only when someone more experienced or with authority is available to give instructions,
solve problems, and reinforce excellence. Supervision should therefore not be viewed as
unnecessary or intrusive.

Supervisory tasks and methods will be different for ongoing management of the organization and for the event itself. Those who occupy directorships or who chair standing
committees might not be qualified for, nor interested in, on-site supervision. Often a completely different set of skills, and attitudes, must be brought to bear. For example, the
accountant who chairs the finance committee might not be a good choice to supervise
money-takers and counters in the beer tent. That job is probably best handled by someone
more used to handling cash, solving customer-related problems, and ensuring a secure
environment. It is therefore a task of all managers to prepare supervisory job descriptions
for event operations, or to have the Operations Manager do so.

If a team approach is taken, the need for supervision is not eliminated. Rather, its form
changes. More emphasis is placed on consensus building and constant improvement through
mutual criticism and reinforcement. But someone must still make difficult decisions and
take responsibility for team actions.

Conflict Resolution

When interpersonal conflicts occur, the manager has a number of choices:

- denial (refuse to acknowledge a conflict exists);
- avoidance (ignore it and hope it goes away; give the problem to somebody else);
- informal resolution;
- formal resolution.

Denial and avoidance are common, but not responsible strategies. Informal resolution is
often preferred, and here the interpersonal skills, experience, and attitudes of the manager
can be crucial. The essence of informal resolution is that paperwork is not required, the
conflict is kept close to the affected parties, and no coercion or appeal to higher authorities is exercised. The manager's role will usually be to listen and then encourage a mutually acceptable solution. Compromise will often be required, but sometimes the manager
can suggest that one solution is preferable to others.

Of the formal conflict resolution mechanisms, managers must find the ones that work
best in their situation. Informal organizations will tend to avoid these approaches altogether, while events with parent organizations will likely rely on established mechanisms.
The key options are:

- edict (the manager listens, then determines what will happen);
- arbitration (a third party is asked to resolve the problem, either in a binding or
  nonbinding format);
- hearings (all affected parties state their positions, discuss possible resolutions,
  and work out the acceptable solution; the manager can act as consensus builder
  or in the end make a final decision).

A focus on behavior, not personality, is the best approach. Personality conflicts are common, and when they cannot be resolved, someone has to be shifted. Stress future improvement and learning from mistakes, not fixing of blame.

Performance Appraisal

Evaluation of staff and volunteers is an important human resource function, forming the basis of advancement within the organization and hopefully leading to a better event and workers. Without ongoing performance appraisal, disciplinary action or termination of staff and volunteers is made extremely difficult, and training effectiveness cannot be determined.

The most common form of performance appraisal in the events field is probably informal observation by supervisors, but this system has potential problems, and is often ineffective. Common appraisal methods used in the hospitality industry (Tanke, 1990, p. 230) can be adapted to events, including: the critical incident method; behaviorally anchored rating scales; management by objectives.

A number of variables must first be considered (from Stone & Meltz, 1988, p. 337), and these can be used as guidelines to implement an open, positive, and reinforcing approach—rather than a secretive and possibly counterproductive method:

- Is there a relevant job description for each person?
- Has the subject been adequately trained and informed of the criteria to be used in evaluation?
- Will the person be involved in the appraisal? Is it open?
- Who does the appraisal? What degree of self-reporting is used? Will there be an honest and open exchange?
- How frequently is evaluation conducted? Are the results used to help the person improve their work?
- When are appraisals done? Before, during, and after the event? If before, something can be done to improve performance at the event.
- What methods and measures are used to evaluate performance? They must be systematic, fair, reliable, and valid for each case.
- Will both appraiser and staff member or volunteer be adequately prepared? What material and analysis is required from each?
- Personal circumstances: is the person paid or volunteer; committed or uninterested?
- How will the results be used: to help the employee or volunteer achieve organizational and personal goals or just for reward or disciplinary action?

Managers must remember that evaluation is related to power and politics, effective leadership, human rights, and personal well-being—it is not just a routine tool. Be aware that if it is not done well, it could create worse problems.

Critical Incident Method

Positive or negative behavior can be documented in the employee's or volunteer's confidential file. "Incidents" might include problems that were faced or initiatives taken, based on feedback from supervisors and customers/guests or the worker's own reports. Each incident can display behavior to be encouraged, discouraged, or assessed.

Little is to be gained from such documentation if it is not openly discussed with the worker, leading to mutually agreed behavior in the future. As well, it is better to deal with serious incidents right away, and not wait until a periodic performance appraisal.

Self-Appraisal and Management by Objectives

Some form of self-appraisal should be part of everyone's job. Who knows better what was done and what could be improved? The process can be formal, involving prepared and detailed forms, or informal.

One of the most formal and systematic methods is "Management by Objectives" (MBO). In this approach the manager works with each employee or volunteer to prepare annual or longer term objectives for the person, criteria by which they will be evaluated, and mutual appraisal of results. Because both parties know exactly what was planned and how performance is judged, the process can be smooth and positive. However, it will also take a lot of time and paperwork, and must be done in the context of detailed job descriptions and operations plans.

Behaviorally Anchored Rating Scales

This type of evaluation is feasible only if a detailed job analysis and description have been completed so that appropriate or necessary behaviors are already identified. The worker's performance is then compared directly to the quantitative and qualitative criteria previously set forth.

Quality of work can be broken down into a number of components, some of which are inputs (what you need to do the job) and some outcomes (direct evidence of job performance). Evaluation based mostly on inputs, such as the preparedness of the worker to do the task, is only of partial value because it raises questions of who is responsible for ensuring the employee or volunteer has what is needed, and ignores whether or not the job was done to standards. Furthermore, even an unskilled and untrained person can do well in some jobs.

The following lists present useful input and outcome criteria for performance appraisals.

Input criteria:
- knowledge essential for the job;
- verbal and written skills;
- attitudes and personality traits;
- motivation;
- experience.

Outcome criteria:
- completion of assigned tasks; quality of that work;
- behavior, appearance, interpersonal relations;
- reliability and punctuality on the job;
- judgment in the face of crises or the unexpected;
- leadership displayed; effectiveness of those supervised;
- innovation demonstrated; creativity;
- problem solving, planning, and organizing demonstrated.

Measurement problems increase as evaluation moves from a simple determination of whether or not the assigned tasks were satisfactorily completed to more intangible qualities like leadership. How are the evaluation data to be obtained? A number of basic sources can be used:

- verbal self-reporting by the employee/volunteer;
- written reports by supervisors based on observations;
- customer feedback (through surveys or complaints);
- feedback from other workers, especially team members;
- measurement of task completion and quality (as determined by at least two perspectives, employee and supervisor; team reports can also be used).

Table 8.1 illustrates useful scaling techniques, beginning with simple checklists of whether or not tasks were satisfactorily performed. Often this is enough, and the checklist itself can be the work plan for both worker and supervisor. Qualitative grading scales are useful instruments, wherein the quality of tasks performed is ranked from high to low. Supervisors and teammates are best placed to make these judgments, but customer input can be valuable in certain jobs. The workers should also be asked to grade their performance.

Objective measurement of key results is the most powerful technique. Many event positions are appropriate for development of technical specifications pertaining to accuracy (like cash handling and information dissemination), completeness (e.g., work meets all health requirements), or problem avoidance and solution. Other jobs must be evaluated more qualitatively, including customer satisfaction for service providers or performers.

Whatever the level of sophistication in evaluations, it must be remembered that effective preparation and supervision are going to produce better results. For more complex evaluations, such as those to be completed for managers, different methods will be used. Self-reporting will be very important, and the person might be asked to submit actual work completed, go through a formal interview, or provide an entire portfolio to support the MBO approach.

Corporations use "secret shoppers" to assess staff, product, and service quality, and event managers can use the same system. This involves sending evaluators (volunteers can be trained) to the event, with specific items to check. For ethical reasons, on-site staff and volunteers should be informed in advance that evaluators will be present, and what they are looking for. Only the identity of the evaluators remains secret, not the process.

Rewards

Reward systems used in the private sector could be adapted to staff or volunteers in event organizations, such as:

- salaries, bonuses, or profit sharing;
- equity (a share of ownership), which in many events means increased formal responsibility;
- promotion to other jobs or events;
- perks (use of cars, equipment, trips, etc.).

Table 8.1. Types of Measurement for Performance Appraisals

a. Checklist of tasks:
satisfactorily completed or not satisfactory

b. Subjective grading of the quality of work:
1 = high quality, 2 = medium, 3 = low quality

c. Objective measurement in key result areas, such as:
cash handling (e.g., amount of losses)
food preparation (e.g., measure wastage, violations of health regulations, orders taken accurately)
information (e.g., all questions answered accurately)
security (e.g., no site intrusions; incidents dealt with according to policy and law)

d. Customer satisfaction (e.g., number and types of complaints; compliments received)

e. Customer satisfaction scales (e.g., How satisfied are you with the service provided by. . .?)

Range of 1–10 where 1 = not at all and 10 = completely

When it comes to rewarding volunteers, events have proven to be very creative and effective. While we discuss volunteer motivation in a later section, here are a number of common ways that event volunteers are rewarded for their efforts:

- free admission to the event; free food and beverages;
- souvenirs of the event (especially pins and clothing);
- social occasions, such as closing-day parties;
- certificates of appreciation;
- public acknowledgement through the media and at the event;
- added responsibility and moving up the volunteer hierarchy;
- meeting celebrities, performers, and other VIPs;
- personal thanks by managers, directors, sponsors, and VIPs.

Discipline

Traditional forms of discipline can work with staff (e.g., pay penalties, failure to promote, formal warnings leading to eventual dismissal) but will not work for volunteers. Forms of discipline potentially appropriate for events include:

- admonition from supervisor (don't do it again; do it right the next time);
- peer pressure (especially useful in team situations);
- example (show exactly what is expected, without recourse to seriously embarrassing the person);
- reassignment (it is often best just to move the person);
- withholding of rewards;
- asking the person to suggest possible solutions.

If the disciplinary action is inappropriate, the volunteer will usually withdraw. This can be the easiest solution for everyone, but can also lead to bad publicity, poor morale, and future recruitment difficulties. To avoid serious problems, managers should establish a clear system of policies and procedures, which must be known by all. A reporting system will help, especially to document performance problems.

Termination, Outplacement, and Reenlistment

Paid employees in events are often under definite term contracts, so they anticipate termination. For periodic events, seasonal staff must hope for reappointment. Other staff are subject to probationary periods of employment and their permanence depends on successful completion of the performance appraisal. CEOs can and do get fired; this requires a board decision and should be regulated by a process specified in a contract or board policies.

But how do you fire a volunteer? If other human resource management practices work well, this unpleasant task can be avoided. A number of possible approaches can be suggested:

- make all volunteer appointments for definite terms; each year they must reapply and go through another screening process;
- use job descriptions and performance appraisals to provide evidence for taking appropriate action;
- use other volunteers to exert peer pressure for a resignation;
- find them positions somewhere else (move the problem);
- move them into positions of little value and hope for a resignation.

The last three approaches to volunteer termination are somewhat "backhanded" and present both ethical and public relations issues. Peer pressure can certainly be made to work, but only if the other volunteers agree that someone should leave. Moving a person to another event or venue can solve one problem, but might simply move it. Reassigning a volunteer into a lesser position, presumably where they can do little damage, might lead to their resignation but might also lead to disgruntlement and damaging behavior.

Outplacement, Reenlistment, and Membership Services

When a position is made redundant or the worker chooses to leave, they should be offered assistance in finding other opportunities and meeting transition problems. When events work together through a volunteer bureau, outplacement can lead directly to recruitment for another event.

Effective volunteers should never be allowed to simply resign and disappear—unless there is no alternative. Member-based organizations, and any that use volunteers, need a system to recruit, receive, retain, renew, and recover (Perry & Kelly 1988, p. 79). "Membership services" can become the full-time responsibility of a staff position in large event organizations, with the following possible tasks:

- sending newsletters to all former volunteers;
- inviting them to social occasions and to the event itself;
- calling them once a year; make them feel needed;
- offering an incentive to reenlist;
- support and counseling;
- database development (mailing lists, task–volunteer matching).

Maintenance Functions

Every human resource system needs technical support. The important "maintenance functions" require record keeping and managers' attention to the pay and rewards structure, working conditions, labor relations, and employee tracking. Human resource managers must keep lots of personnel records, preferably on computer files for each staff member and volunteer. The following types of records are usually needed:

- application forms;
- resumes;
- letters of reference;
- contracts;
- annual reports;
- timesheets; vacations and leaves;
- wages and benefits;
- health and safety;
- task analysis;
- job description;
- incidents;
- performance evaluations;
- insurance.

Motivation Theory

What motivates staff and volunteers? How can they be encouraged to pursue excellence? What style of leadership works best? These questions occur to all managers, and while there are theories to employ, there will always be an element of uncertainty and subjectivity involved in human resource management. A necessary starting place is motivational theory, upon which managers can base their own distinctive leadership style.

Human Needs

Almost all motivational theory rests on the belief that humans have basic needs that motivate behavior. Probably the best known theory of this type was formulated by Abraham Maslow (1954), and his "hierarchy of needs" is important both to work motivation and, in a marketing context, for motivation to travel and to attend events. The theory postulates that only when a person's basic needs are met can higher order needs be met. So basic physiological and security needs must be met before social needs. At the top of Maslow's hierarchy is the need for self-actualization, or realizing one's potential, and this motivates learning, setting and meeting challenges for intrinsic rewards, and the search for new and aesthetic experiences.

This hierarchical model is by no means proven. Many researchers believe that people are often simultaneously motivated by several levels of need. Furthermore, in many wealthy countries where most people's basic needs are met, they are usually pursuing higher order needs.

Two-Factor Theory

Hertzberg (1966) developed a "two-factor theory" that has wide applicability and develops the Maslow concept. Things like pay levels, policies and procedures, job security, and working conditions in themselves do not motivate or satisfy people, according to Hertzberg, but their absence or perceived diminishment can stimulate considerable dissatisfaction or even hostility. Employees and volunteers are more likely to be motivated and satisfied by achievement, recognition, advancement or growth, responsibility, and interesting work.

Theory X and Theory Y

Influenced by Maslow's work, McGregor (1960) suggested that there were two contrasting management theories and styles. Those favoring "Theory X" believe that people basically hate work and therefore must be coerced and controlled to get desired results. On the other hand, "Theory Y" stresses that humans always strive for self-actualization (i.e., higher order needs) and can be motivated accordingly. Therefore, managers using "Theory Y" would rely more on incentives than on punishment and control, and would motivate workers by providing opportunities for individual goal attainment.

Because most events rely heavily on volunteers, and most staff persons are event lovers by their nature, "Theory Y" is clearly more appropriate. This does not mean, however, that managers can ignore evaluation, discipline, training, and the other human resource management elements.

Behavior Modification

"Behavior modification," as advocated by Skinner (1938, 1974), is widely employed in all sectors, even though it is controversial in some respects. Skinner stressed the use of positive reinforcement to ensure that people did what was expected or required of them. Punishment is often unproductive, so people should be rewarded for doing good. Personality is not at issue, merely observable behavior. Managers should give valuable feedback and promote the self-esteem of workers. Clear, solid personal goals are desired. Rosenbaum (1982) stressed that interaction between managers and staff can foster self-esteem, with staff engaged in problem solving rather than simply being told what to do. Successful behavior modes can be defined and regular behavioral patterns encouraged.

Expectancy Theory

Money on its own does not necessarily motivate people, but it is clear that rewards should be linked to effort. According to Vroom's (1964) "Expectancy Theory" the worker must perceive that their efforts will be rewarded, and that greater effort or competency achieves higher rewards. In the hospitality industry it is common to offer workers incentives for higher productivity and quality, and this can be especially important with part-time employees (Tanke, 1990).

Motivating and Managing the Volunteer

There is no research evidence to suggest that event volunteers differ substantially from other types of volunteer, but casual observation, and the author's own direct volunteer experiences, suggest there might be some unique event volunteer traits:

- most are usually very enthusiastic about the event itself, but not always about the organization responsible for it; others are very supportive of the cause behind the event;
- they often lack experience and need specific training;
- many want to have fun—they know how to throw and enjoy a party;
- many prefer short-term responsibilities, especially at the event itself;
- many are artistically creative, rather than technically oriented.

Generalizations are dangerous, so the above list should not be taken as a given. Events will attract different types of volunteers depending on many variables. To complement the following discussion, see the detailed profile of elements of volunteer management at the Bethlehem, Pennsylvania, Musikfest.

Defining the Volunteer

A "volunteer" is one who enlists or offers their services to the organization of their own free will, and usually without expecting to be paid. But volunteers have personal goals they want to attain through the act of volunteering. In practice, many so-called volunteers are actively recruited in a manner that suggests bribery or subtle coercion, such as through the application of social pressure or the promise of rewards. It is, in fact, increasingly common to find volunteers receiving tangible benefits from their positions.

Who Volunteers?

The organization Independent Sector (www.independentsector.org) reports periodically on voluntarism and charitable giving in the US. From its 2001 survey came the following facts:

- 44% of American adults over age 21 volunteered with a formal organization in 2000;
- the average time spent volunteering was about 24 hours a month;
- women volunteer more than men (46% to 42%);
- volunteers need to be asked: 50% of volunteers were asked, and of those asked to volunteer, 71% did so.

Why People Volunteer

There is a common mythology surrounding volunteers that paints them as "altruistic" do-gooders, thoughtful only of the needs of others. There is some truth in this, of course, but the event manager must be more sophisticated in understanding what is likely to motivate and satisfy volunteers. A number of research findings and theories follow, each of which sheds some valuable light on this complex issue.

Smith (1981; cited in Bharadia, 1986, p. 21) argued that there is no such thing as pure or absolute altruism and that multiple factors explain the act of volunteering. To Smith, three types of incentives interact: material rewards (goods or money), interpersonal rewards (prestige or friendship), and purposive incentives (achievement or self-fulfillment). "Social exchange theory" suggests that volunteers might start out with altruistic motives but will tend to evaluate their continued service by reference to specific rewards. The dynamics of giving and receiving must therefore be considered together. An example would be the volunteer who thinks it is the right thing to do, at first, but later insists that there be "something in it" to induce reenlistment. Both the organization and the volunteer must be involved in mutually satisfying behavior.

This argues for a volunteer system that pays attention to changing needs over time. The system should offer different kinds of rewards that evolve alongside the individual volunteer. Periodic consultation and reassignment of duties might be needed for some, while others could be content to do the same thing. The volunteer system should include different ways to recruit, recognizing that what some people seek out, others stumble into. As well, acknowledging the stages of a volunteer career can be used in conjunction with the notion of evolving rewards to anticipate and provide for the eventual withdrawal of volunteers, and subsequent efforts to reenlist the dropout.

Volunteering can also be viewed, in many instances, as "serious leisure" (Stebbins, 1982). Many volunteers view the act as leisure, in the same way that others value regular participation in sports. Less serious forms of play, however, offer less opportunity for potential career development (e.g., learning new skills through volunteering), status, ego enhancement, or self-fulfillment. The volunteer pursuing "serious leisure" will be more committed and persevering, sharing in the event's culture and values, and strongly identifying with the event or the organization.

Why People Volunteer for Events

Only a handful of researchers have examined the event volunteer. Taking part in something really special is viewed by many volunteers as a "chance in a lifetime" (Farrell, Johnston, & Twynan, 1998). Green and Chalip (1998) found that the prestige of the event influenced some volunteers, including "bragging rights," and the celebrity atmosphere. Elstad (1996) determined that excitement and meeting people were powerful motivators, as is "being part of the action" (Williams, Dossa, & Tompkins, 1995).

Williams et al. (1995) examined volunteers for the 1994 Men's World Cup of Skiing at Whistler, British Columbia. They were mostly males (75%) aged 15–44, and came from both within and outside the resort community. The primary motives were socializing with those holding common interests (especially for nonresidents), and enthusiasm for skiing and the Canadian team. Resident volunteers, and especially the females, were more interested in building the community's image and spirit.

Williams and Harrison (1988) found that an important factor in attracting event volunteers was the extent to which events are perceived to be supporting local community development goals. Residents are more likely to support events that fit the community's needs, as well as those of the individual.

Ryan and Bates (1995) studied the motivations of a unique type of volunteer for the Manawatu (New Zealand) Rose and Garden Festival. Four typical leisure motivations were found to apply: relaxation; social interaction, intellectual challenge, and showing competency. The evidence suggested that festivals provided a means of creating a strong sense of community and pride in one's accomplishments.

Coyne and Coyne (2001) learned through research that 79% of volunteers at a golf event had volunteered at previous events and most were golfers themselves. It seems logical that those holding a special interest in an event theme or sport, as evidenced by their own participation, will be the primary target group for volunteer recruitment. Farrell et al. (1998) found something similar for a curling event.

Research Note

Farrell, J., Johnston, M., & Twynam, D. (1998). Volunteer motivation, satisfaction, and management at an elite sporting competition. *Journal of Sport Management, 12*, 288-300.

This article reports on a study of (60% female) volunteers at a women's championship curling event. Results showed that the dominant motives were "purposive," related to doing something useful and making a contribution—in particular to make the event a success. Partly this stemmed from the fact that 66% were participating in curling that season. The second most important category of motives pertained to socializing, group identification, and networking. A very interesting finding was that participation in this major event increased the likelihood that volunteers would volunteer for other sport events. In terms of satisfaction, most were satisfied overall but "hygiene" factors (in this case air quality and parking, food, and toilet availability) were major sources of dissatisfaction.

Recruitment

The Institute for Volunteering Research (IVR) in the UK (2003) (www.ivr.org.uk) studied what volunteers want from the organization and drew implications for recruitment and management. Volunteers want flexibility and well-organized but informal volunteer management. Demands on their time should not be onerous, and while they do not expect to get paid they do not want to incur private expenses. A welcoming atmosphere is desired, and the whole organizational culture should be volunteer oriented.

To get people involved for the fist time they recommended highlighting the variety of volunteering roles, emphasizing the benefits to the volunteer, and providing more and better information about how to volunteer. Word-of-mouth recruitment is crucial, so each volunteer should be a recruiter. Clear descriptions of roles, rights, and responsibilities have to be presented to those who make an inquiry. Individuals should be given choices and carefully matched to the opportunities. An informal but efficient interviewing process is recommended by the IVR. If an appropriate placement cannot be found, referral to other organizations should be made.

Inclusiveness is an issue when recruiting. Does everyone feel welcomed and valued or do certain groups dominate in the organization and its volunteers. In part this is a matter of image, requiring good public relations, and in part it is a serious matter for introspection and a possible change in the organizational culture.

Specific to recruitment of young volunteers (aged 16-24), IVR recommended the following:

- improve the image of volunteering to be relevant to young people; more positive imagery is needed, especially so that volunteering is cool for boys;
- maximize flexibility in terms of working hours and times;
- more information and more entry points to volunteering are needed; stress the education system;
- offer new skills, challenges, and interesting experiences that can help with personal and career development;

- offer incentives and rewards, as well as full payment for any expenses incurred;
- make the experience relaxed, fun, and satisfying.

Induction, Training, and Supervision of Volunteers

"Induction" is the process of bringing volunteers into the organization and getting them involved. It generally requires a formal orientation and some training. In terms of organizational culture theory, a certain amount of indoctrination into the philosophy, values, and style of the organization takes place—possibly leading to some rejection by one party or the other when they see a poor fit.

Training should aim to provide the volunteer with confidence and the skills to do the required tasks. IVR also recommended that some form of certification should be offered so that volunteers have something tangible to aim for. This is important for young people desiring to learn or improve their skills and others who want to improve their employment chances.

A combination of on-the-job training and special training courses is common for volunteers. Some events start with special courses for their volunteer board of directors, then for their core, all-year volunteers.

Commitment and Continuance

Event organizations need to work hard to keep their core volunteers, not just because it is more efficient than recruiting and training new ones all the time, but also because the retained volunteers can recruit and train others, and can even become board members or hold staff positions.

IVR argued that volunteers should not be treated as paid staff, even though their research determined it was the dominant model applied to volunteering in the UK. Personal and professional support has to be given, including "light-touch" supervision. Volunteers also need to be consulted and to feel appreciated. A variety of other actions can help with retention, including counseling on personal and business matters, offering insurance, and tangible rewards.

Green and Chalip (2004) studied volunteers for the Sydney Olympics and concluded that their satisfaction was derived from obtaining desired benefits and a sense of community, which then led to commitment. The experience of being a volunteer at the event was determined to be more important than the specific rewards, however, leading these researchers to recommend that event managers concentrate on fostering camaraderie, shared purpose, and pulling together. As well, volunteers want to learn how the event works, and doing so is exciting and satisfying. Elstad (2003) also studied commitment and continuance among volunteers.

Developing "careers" for dedicated volunteers is an excellent idea. These will vary from event to event, and might have to be implemented by a volunteer sharing system (see, for example, Sydney's Major Event Volunteers: www.volunteering.com.au/set/). The idea is to recruit, retain, and develop the commitment of the best volunteers. Their involvement could lead to more responsible positions, membership in the organization, a position on the board of directors, or even to paid employment.

Research Note

Elstad, B. (2003). Continuance commitment and reasons to quit: A study of volunteers at a jazz festival. *Event Management, 8*(2), 99–108.

Why had 30% of the volunteers surveyed by Elstad at a major Norwegian jazz festival considered quitting? The management issue is simple—how can the event increase the commitment of its volunteers to continue in the future? Elstad theorized that commitment stems in part from event-specific considerations (job challenge; feedback from managers; cooperation among volunteers; rewards and volunteer welfare systems) and in part from volunteer motivations (opportunity to specialize; material rewards; altruism; impact or status in the local community; connection to hobbies and interests). Before and after surveys of volunteers were undertaken, with several important findings. The main reason volunteers gave for considering quitting was workload, and the best predictors of continuance were feedback from managers and food (from the event-specific factors) and altruism and hobby/interest (a love of jazz) from the motivational factors. Commitment was also found to increase with length of service to the festival. Managers in each event function have to learn how to give proper feedback and express gratitude to volunteers, as well as to ensure they do not burn out. And volunteers most interested in tangible rewards seem to be the least likely to persevere.

Integrating Paid Staff and Volunteers

What are the attitudes of paid staff towards event volunteers? Do they automatically get along and work effectively together? Do many volunteers actually want to get a paid job with the event? Clearly, these questions show that staff–volunteer relationships have to be managed.

Given the motivations of volunteers, as discussed above, it is quite possible that many of them will want an enriching experience of the event itself, while others will be seeking new skills and interpersonal contacts with a view to building a career. In these cases, where strong motives drive volunteers, there might easily be a clash with staff in terms of their desired to use volunteers effectively to get specific jobs done. Staff might even feel that their own credibility and job security might be adversely affected if "their" volunteers do not perform well at assigned tasks. In these cases, conflicts can arise.

Several strategies can be employed. To start, maintaining a core of experienced volunteers from event to event will have tremendous advantages. Not only should they get better with experience, but they can be expected to establish working relationships with staff based on trust. As well, the experienced volunteers can become trainers and mentors for the new volunteers. If some of these long-term volunteers eventually get paid staff positions, they may be more sympathetic to incoming volunteers.

A second strategy is to identify as soon as possible those volunteers interested in developing a career so that they can be provided with the right opportunities. Volunteers with a greater interest in the event as an experience or in "doing good" can be motivated and rewarded in different ways. Knowledge of volunteer motives should make staff–volunteer relationships smoother.

Legal Issues

Are your volunteers protected by workplace legislation covering their health, safety, and comfort? Are they included in your insurance, because sooner or later there will be accidents. Are the volunteers serving on your board of directors protected by insurance against lawsuits arising from the event or the board's activities?

Just as laws protect against discrimination in hiring employees, are there similar laws (or perhaps civic policies) that prevent discrimination in volunteer recruitment? Are certain groups to be given special consideration? And risk management for volunteers is necessary, as they might be exposed to particular kinds of hazards. This is covered in Chapter 10.

The Politics of Volunteering (Discrimination)

In 1971 the National Organization for Women in the US "denounced the lack of power and prestige associated with women's volunteer work, and the exploitation of women in the non profit sector" (cited in Harvie, 1986a). In the subsequent decades the participation rate of females (i.e., the proportion active in the workforce) has risen substantially, and women now have more choice about work and volunteering. Nevertheless, it is likely that men still gravitate towards sports, recreation, and prestigious community groups, and to positions of authority, while women occupy more service positions. This was confirmed in the Calgary research by Harvie as recently as 1986.

Managers should ask if women in their organization hold positions of power or responsibility, or only positions of servitude. How is recruitment done? Is there systematic bias or is it from personal choice and preference that one gender dominates. The same questions should be raised regarding any minority group or persons with a disability. In the 1990s, most professionals were sensitive to the different needs of genders, minorities, and the differently challenged. As well, many countries have specific legislation to prevent discrimination and to provide equitable services.

Volunteer Burnout

Events can generate a large number of "stressors" for staff and volunteers, some of which are unique to this field. The following are potential causes of burnout:

- intense time and energy commitment immediately before, during, and after the event;
- too few qualified or dedicated people trying to do all the work; workloads too high or too demanding;
- tension between staff and volunteers, and within groups, usually owing to a lack of effective leadership or management systems;
- large crowds and the resultant risks and pressures;
- media coverage, political interest, and open public scrutiny;
- lack of financial support and the constant need to secure resources;
- the absence of tangible rewards for volunteers;
- insecurity over one's appointment or volunteer position;
- lack of direction;
- boring or unfulfilling labor.

Howell (1986) observed that the most deeply involved and highly productive volunteers are the ones most likely to burn out, generally from the stress of doing too much and having excessive responsibility. Unfortunately, it is the event leaders and key managers who often fit this description, resulting in potential crises for the organization. Three symptoms of volunteer burnout, according to Dean (1985), are:

- emotional exhaustion (e.g., "I have no more to give!");
- depersonalization (reflected in poor opinions of others);
- feeling of reduced personal accomplishment (perhaps accompanied by depression or loss of self-esteem).

Managers should learn to identify these symptoms and deal with affected persons directly.

"Rustout" is another term for dying from boredom. Staff and volunteers must be given meaningful and challenging tasks, variety, and social stimulation. Planned mobility within the organization and among tasks is a good strategy to avoid boredom. Regular objective-setting exercises will also help. Feeling that one's services are no longer required is another source of volunteer withdrawal (Howell, 1986). Managers must always acknowledge the contributions of volunteers and ensure them of their continuing value.

Conflicts and unresolved problems will turn off volunteers and staff alike. Managers adopting a "let-things-lie" approach will find that volunteers in particular will simply walk away from the problem, whereas intervention could potentially solve it permanently. Other factors leading to volunteer frustration (Howell, 1986) include: lack of training; criticism of the paid staff; bureaucracy; lack of communications; feeling underutilized; lack of influence; disagreement with how the organization reaches its goals.

Profile: Bethlehem Musikfest (Bethlehem, Pennsylvania) (www.musikfest.org)

Musikfest is a 9.5-day celebration held each year in August. The 2003 festival was the 20th, and in that special year Musikfest attracted just over 1 million visits. A 1-day attendance record of 180,000 was set. More than 650 musical performances were held (mostly free) at 124 outdoor and 6 indoor venues, all within the historic downtown of Bethlehem. The festival program is much more than music: activities include fireworks, plus day-long showcases aimed at lovers of country and reggae music.

Musikfest and the annual Christkindlmarkt is produced by ArtsQuest (formerly Bethlehem Musikfest Association), a volunteer-managed, not-for-profit organization. Its mission statement: "Musikfest provides a celebration of music to entertain and educate a diverse community and to promote the quality of life, tourism and economic development in the Lehigh Valley."

The all-volunteer board of directors of ArtsQuest retains the services of professional staff, including a President. The Vice President has direct responsibility for Musikfest, and operational directors (e.g., marketing, development, sponsorship, community, visual arts) report to the VP. About 10 standing committees provide liaison between staff and volunteer directors.

Finances and Budget

Total revenue from 25 ticketed concerts reached $1.3 million—a new record—while food and beverage sales generated $2.75 million gross sales and netted about $1 million for the organizer. Additional revenue is secured from sponsorships ($1.4 million), merchandise, transport, and miscellaneous sources ($0.5 million), and from grants and Club Musikfest memberships. It cost approximately $5.2 million to produce the event. In-kind donations of services, supplies, and media support is valued at an additional $1 million. Surplus revenues benefit ArtsQuest's Banana Factory—an arts center and gallery located in Bethlehem. In addition, a dozen area community groups raised more than $28,000 to benefit their organizations through their volunteer efforts during the festival.

Volunteer Management at Musikfest

The Musikfest volunteer mission statement:

As Musikfest Volunteers:

- We take pride in our event and community.
- We provide enthusiastic, efficient and caring service.
- We extend courtesy to everyone.
- We provide a safe and comfortable atmosphere for all.
- We take responsibility for our actions.
- We make volunteering a fun and satisfying experience.

Volunteers are responsible for the success of Musikfest, a 9.5-day festival featuring more than 650 free performances. Volunteers serve on committees that plan each year's event. They set up and take down the sites located in downtown Bethlehem. During the festival, nearly 2000 volunteers sell tickets and souvenirs, serve beverages, run the stages and provide performer hospitality, deliver supplies, keep the sites clean, handle recycling, survey visitors, assist media personnel, help with children's activities, serve as trolley hosts, and help out in other ways. In all, there are 86 categories or functions at which volunteers assist in the festival.

Photo 8.1. Musikfest volunteers at work (credit: Christopher Christian).

Volunteers choose the areas where they want to be involved and are each asked to spend at least 18 hours during the 2 weeks of setup, the festival, and 4 days of takedown. Nearly 80% of volunteers return each year, and in 2003 they had 51 volunteers celebrating 20 years and 55 who had put in 10 years of service.

Potential volunteers receive a Volunteer Information and Registration Form listing all the volunteer positions available. ArtsQuest (formerly the Bethlehem Musikfest Association) is concerned about the safety of its guests and volunteers, and volunteers are asked if they have been convicted of a felony. Each individual situation is considered and answering yes to this question does not automatically disqualify a person from volunteering.

A volunteer must be at least 12 years old and first-time volunteers under the age of 15 must volunteer with an adult who knows them. Parents of volunteers under 17 must sign a parental release form. All first-time teen volunteers attend a mandatory orientation in addition to the training sessions for all volunteers.

Approximately 60% of the annual volunteers are female; almost half live in Bethlehem and most of the rest from elsewhere in Lehigh Valley, but some volunteers travel from as far a way as California and Florida.

The Musikfest volunteer experience begins with training and all volunteers must attend a session where general orientation information about the festival and specific training about the volunteer functions is given. Volunteers also pick up their volunteer appreciation packages at these sessions. The package includes a golf shirt (the uniform for the volunteers), a name badge, a souvenir pin, and a souvenir program book. During the festival, volunteers receive free transportation from off-site parking areas, food and beverage tickets, and air-conditioned volunteer hospitality areas with indoor plumbing.

The Commonwealth of Pennsylvania laws regarding use and service of alcohol are strictly obeyed. A volunteer must be 21 or over to serve beer or wine and must not consume alcohol while on duty.

About 200 volunteers serve in supervisory roles and have responsibility for providing leadership and supervision. They play an extremely valuable role in making sure each site and function runs efficiently and smoothly. LEAP (Leadership, Education, and Preparedness) is a 2-year program that provides volunteers with additional training and assignments in many different functions to give them a total picture of festival management. Ten volunteers are chosen each year and the goal is for them to assume leadership roles in the future.

Volunteers' opinions are extremely important and they are asked to fill out an evaluation form following the event. Many improvements have been made based on their suggestions. Their opinions are valued and their comments are not criticism but come from the deep sense of ownership and pride that they feel.

In 1993, because of the efforts of volunteers, Musikfest received The Pennsylvanian's With Disabilities Day Award in appreciation of its awareness and sensitivity to the needs of people with disabilities. Since 1985, volunteers have held the responsibility and joy of hosting and assisting guests who are elderly or disabled.

Volunteer nurture and recognition is very important. Each year, during Musikfest, volunteers who are participating in their 20th or 10th festival are honored at the opening ceremonies. They are given pins and shirts, and their names are featured on our "Volunteer Walk of Fame," which is posted in a highly traveled area of the festival. FEST NOTES is a quarterly newsletter, written for and by volunteers to inform and spotlight them. A volunteer appreciation event is held each year and volunteers have an opportunity to spend an entertaining evening together with the chance to win prizes donated by sponsors, area merchants, and the BMA.

Musikfest is an innovator. The LEAP program was perhaps the first of its kind and has been widely emulated. Musikfest developed the EMOS (Event Volunteer Organization System) computer software to professionally track and monitor their volunteer efforts. This system has been sold or shared with numerous other events, but has been replaced with new software called VolunteerWorks.

Study Questions

- What are the main human resource management challenges facing events? Are they unique to events?
- Outline a human resource planning process for events, and be sure to feature the roles of volunteers.
- Explain how to forecast human resource needs for an event.
- What motivates people more: discipline or rewards? Refer to the motivational theories for your answer.
- Explain why people would volunteer for a particular type of event.
- In what ways should volunteers be trained for their work?
- Where does teamwork fit into the human resource system for events?
- What is burnout and how can it be prevented? And rustout?
- What elements of the Musikfest volunteer system relate to motivation, legal issues, and training?

Advanced Study Questions

- Show exactly how needs assessment and job descriptions relate to project planning task analysis and critical path networks.
- Evaluate an event volunteer system from the perspective of how volunteers are motivated and their commitment sustained. Make recommendations for improvement.

- Outline an induction and orientation process for both a one-time and a pulsating event, with specific reference to the role of organizational culture and motivational theory.

Chapter 9

Acquiring Resources, Sponsorship, and Financial Management

Learning Objectives

- Be able to develop and implement a comprehensive and ethical strategy for acquiring financial and other necessary resources.
- Be able to manage grants, merchandizing, food and beverage sales, and sponsorships.
- Be able to develop a pricing strategy for admission to the event.
- Be able to use break-even analysis.
- Be able to create events as sponsorship platforms.
- Be able to develop effective sponsorship campaigns, proposals, and sales techniques.
- Be able to understand the potential costs and benefits of sponsorship to event organizers and sponsors.
- Be able to develop methods to be accountable for grants, investments, and sponsorship received.
- Be able to implement financial planning and control mechanisms, including capital and operating budgets.
- Be able to analyze cost and revenue centers to help improve organizational efficiency; employ cost–revenue management techniques.
- Be able to prepare and use essential financial statements: the balance sheet, income (profit and loss), cash flow, and retained earnings.
- Be able to know how to evaluate and document the solvency and worth of the event/organization.
- Be able to implement standard accounting practices for all financial operations, and establish other controls as needed.

Where's the Money?

Although for many special events the budget is fixed and event managers work within known limits, many managers of permanent and one-time events do not have the luxury of guaranteed and sustained revenue. Inability to secure sufficient resources is a leading cause of event failure, so competency in generating revenue and in financial management is extremely important.

Responsibility for revenue in not-for-profit organizations starts with the Board of Directors. In fact, being well connected and willing to give money as well as go out and get it is often a leading criterion for being asked to sit on a board. Many events have learned that a full-time sponsorship manager or "resource development officer" is vital to their survival and growth. These professionals might come from a fund-raising background rather than out of the events field. There duties will typically include the following:

- generating leads (requires background research);
- making sponsorship and grant proposals;
- managing the relationships with sponsors and grant givers;
- evaluation and reporting of results (accountability).

When the organization does not have a development professional the general manager or executive director will carry much of the burden to generate revenue. This person is crucial in all cases, however, because many sponsors will want a personal relationship with senior people at the event.

Fund-Raising

Events are frequently created specifically as fund-raisers, while festival organizations often produce smaller events to generate revenue. Common fund-raiser actions include:

- telethons,
- auctions,
- door-to-door sales,
- awards ceremonies,
- banquets, galas,
- corporate challenges,
- coupon books,
- donations,
- raffles.

Wyman (1989) classified fund-raiser events as follows. "Extravaganzas" consist of major events, are costly, exclusive, memorable, and base their appeal on meeting the right crowd. They can generate large amounts, but are risky. "Bargain hunters and gamblers" describes events where good deals are sought, such as auctions, or where good luck plays a part, such as charity casinos. A third type is "educational," such as seminars or motivational speeches.

"Donorship" is a form of fund-raising in which individuals and groups are encouraged to make gifts and endowments to the organization. This is often called "planned giving" and can include bequests in wills. Usually charitable organizations are the recipients, with official receipts being given for purposes of tax deductions.

Reiss (1992) described some unique fundraising techniques by events in Aspen, Colorado. The Dance Aspen summer festival partnered with the Aspen School District to raise money for a new theater at the elementary school. The event organizers get 25 years of summer use while the school benefits year round. The Aspen Music Festival benefits from a scheme in which local businesses donate goods and services that the festival resells using scrip in $5, $10, and $20 denominations. Supporters redeem the scrip at the same businesses, paying 80% of actual value—everyone wins.

Pitfalls of Fund-Raising

Similar to the principles of cost and revenue management, good fund-raisers minimize the risks and maximize the opportunities for profit. This translates into avoidance of cer tain types or large-scale projects, and favoring known winners. A conservative approach is usually best. Putting money up front is probably a common pitfall, as is overreliance on third parties as opposed to doing it yourself. Choosing the wrong fund-raiser can lead to public relations or even legal problems, not to mention losing money—that is why so many associations have professional event managers do their fund-raisers!

Principles for choosing fund raisers are suggested:

- stick to your distinctive competencies (if in the events business, why not use mini-events featuring elements of the festival or main event?);
- target them to your own stakeholders and known market segments;
- learn from the mistakes of others and avoid overused methods;
- try to get everything donated to fund-raisers;
- spread out the risks; avoid get-rich-quick schemes with high risk entailed;
- plan the fund-raiser with the same professionalism put into the main event;
- build on strengths and experience, as opposed to one-time efforts;
- schedule them so that cancellation can occur without penalty.

The Ethics of Fund-Raising

Professional fund-raisers have published their code of ethics (www.afpnet.org), and a number of general principles should be highlighted. First and foremost is the necessity to check and obey all pertinent laws. And it is essential to match actual deeds to promises made to the public. Money raised for charity must go to charity, and the amount allocated to fees or overheads should be kept to a minimum. This comes into play frequently when private fund-raising or merchandizing firms are retained to generate the needed revenue. Certain types of fund-raisers might be considered inappropriate or culturally offensive, including the sale of certain products and activities that are controversial. Environmentally responsible actions are important. Making decisions on what is appropriate is partly ethical and partly marketing.

Grants

"Grants" are generally made by public agencies and foundations to further some cause. They are often awarded on a competitive basis, or through a detailed application process, and increasingly they come with explicit conditions, making them more like sponsorship. Local governments often provide grants to events to foster the arts, create community spirit and cohesion, improve the quality of life, and meet urban renewal goals. Tourism agencies give grants to assist in marketing, and to make competent bids for events.

The manager's ability to secure grants for the event begins with a plan, similar to that for securing sponsors. The major elements of the plan should be:

- identify the goals of granting agencies you can meet;
- use philanthropy guides, government directories, and networking to identify potential sources of grants and application requirements;
- prioritize the options, reflecting your ability to deliver, the match between the event's goals and the source, the investment of time and money that might be required to prepare for and make the application, and ultimate accountability demands;
- prepare necessary application forms and backup material, such as the business plan or letters of support;
- have a plan to administer the grant (e.g., when does the money become avail-

able; what exactly can it be spent on; who in the organization is responsible for meeting all conditions?);

- keep detailed records of related actions and expenditures;
- prepare accounts as required;
- evaluate benefits and costs.

Advice given later on sponsorship is pertinent, especially when it comes to developing a good working relationship with grant-givers and in accountability for money received.

Merchandizing and Licensing

Events are natural merchandizing marts, and many events have retailing as their primary purpose. Products are sold on-site at most events, but increasingly licensing is being used to extend merchandizing efforts. "Licensing" is the legal tool used to obtain royalties, and protect the event's rights, when distributors and retailers are granted permission to sell event-related goods. To license products the event must have protection for its name, logo, or designs in the form of copyrights, trademarks, or other legal devices. Similar legal principles apply to the granting of sponsorship rights.

The event manager cannot assume, however, that everything with the event logo or design on it will sell—merchandizing requires a strategy and skill. B. Black (n.d.) advised organizers to leave merchandizing to the professionals, to reduce risks. Experienced retailers can turn production around very quickly and track sales; they know the customers and what products will move. To get the best deal, event managers should take bids, looking for a percentage of total sales and/or a guaranteed minimum return. Contracts are needed to specify other details, like how logos and event names can be used and types of merchandize permitted.

"Consignment" selling might work in some instances, as this strategy allows retailers to sell the goods with a fixed percentage going to the event, and return them if unsold. This practice is risky for the event, unless it has a way of disposing of surplus goods. However, it can be used to extend the reach of the event when retailers are otherwise reluctant to buy event goods outright.

Goals of the merchandizing strategy include:

- sell merchandise that benefits the event in terms of revenue, positive image, and long-term growth;
- partner with appropriate wholesalers and retailers in ways that maximize benefits to the event;
- license goods where the arrangement extends the reach of the event and secures revenue that could not otherwise be obtained;
- regulate all merchandizing on and off the site to assure quality and proper image projection.

Merchandise Lines

Was there ever an event that did not sell t-shirts? What about pins, buttons, and posters? But event merchandise lines have gradually become more and more sophisticated, offering a range of low-cost souvenirs alongside high-quality, high-profit items. As well, slapping the event name or logo on common products is being balanced with unique and exclusive products that might not be readily available elsewhere. When the event has a popular and respected name and/or logo it can use them to create its own line of "brand-name" merchandise.

Typical and not-so-usual products include the following general categories:

- clothing,
- pins and buttons,
- jewelry,
- toys and sports equipment,
- packaged foods and beverages,
- art works (including posters),
- unique souvenirs and collectibles.

Pricing the Goods

A cost-plus strategy can be used to obtain a predetermined rate of return to meet revenue targets. Of course, this rule often has to be modified by the reality of what people will pay, competition, and other considerations such as pre- and postevent discounting. The rights to sell merchandise at events can be put out to tender, looking for high bids, or sold at a fixed (say 10%) fee. Up-front cash guarantees are normal, to ensure the merchant delivers. The guarantee can be linked to projected sales, although this is risky to the merchant if there is no track record or conditions have substantially changed. Different categories of merchandise can be sold separately.

Food and Beverage Sales

Food and beverage sales are an essential service at most events, potentially a targeted benefit to attract specific market segments, and a major source of revenue. When planning this vital part of event operations, a number of key alternatives and principles must be considered.

The types, numbers, sizes, and products should be planned in harmony with revenue goals, site planning principles, and theming. A simple rule of thumb on the number of outlets required for festivals was proposed by Andera (1994), who suggested that 100,000 visitors need about 5000 servings, or 33 large outlets. Suppliers can sometimes provide information or advice on what volume of food and beverages is desirable, although they might be biased if the event is to pay up front. By monitoring attendance and food/beverage sales, managers can better forecast their needs next time around.

Costs and Profits

The "cost of sales" is an important calculation. It consists of direct costs (the amount paid for the product) plus indirect costs (overheads). Quigley (n.d., p. 88) advised that overheads should be kept to 7% of sale price, labor costs to 15%, and the cost of food or beverage to 30%. A rule of thumb is to make half of the cost of every sale in profit, or, expressed another way, to mark up the price of items by 100%.

Where contracted concessionaires are used, they can be charged rent for space, or a percentage of sales or profits can be taken by the organizers. Quigley (n.d., p. 88) referred to an IFEA survey, which revealed that 45% of members responding to their survey charged vendors a flat fee, 20% charged a percentage of sales, and 30% charged both.

Flakus (n.d., p. 96) reported that many events charge vendors 15–25% of gross food sales as rent, which is then applied against an up-front deposit. The exact rental fee or percentage figure can be fixed in advance, or negotiated individually. These amounts might have to be adjusted annually, especially if demand by vendors falters. Contracts will be required to specify the terms and mutual responsibilities, with an example being provided in IFEA's *Event Operations* manual (IFEA, n.d.).

Another practice to generate revenue and keep customers happy is that of specifying prices, or price minima and maxima, to vendors. Otherwise, there is the risk of either price gouging, which can dissatisfy customers, or discounting, which can harm revenue.

When there is a variety of sources, the organizers can arrange to place their outlets at the best locations, or perhaps these spaces could be offered to private concessionaires by auction or for premium rentals. Vendors with the best sales records and quality service can be given preferred sites.

Vendors might also be required to acquire all their food and beverages from a central commissary run for profit by the event organizers, or from an official supplier. Flakus (1995, p. 96) cautions that this practice can raise prices.

Other costs must be considered. The inventory of food and beverages plus related supplies can be very expensive, especially if the event organizers are responsible for costs whether supplies are used or not. It is preferable to carefully forecast needs and not secure more product than can be sold. Also, arrangements can be made with some suppliers to accept surplus goods, if they are not perishable. Other surplus inventory can be sold or given to staff and volunteers, or to charitable agencies.

Taxes on purchases and sales must be factored into the calculations. Are vendors or the organizers responsible for taxes? Does charitable status affect the organizers' legal obligations for collecting and forwarding taxes to different levels of government? Other considerations are: will service charges be levied on sales, or gratuities accepted? who gets the proceeds, the staff and volunteers or organizers?

Events that do their own food and beverage sales might want to follow Quigley's advice and stick to high-volume, high-profit, and low overhead items. This "keep it simple" strategy will involve the lowest risk and generate the highest positive income, but might also be boring and incompatible with the theme.

Food festivals, on the other hand, must put their theme first. All event managers should assess the environmental and health implications of their food and beverage policies.

Delivery Formats

A choice of delivery formats includes the following:

- formal restaurants or cafés,
- beer or beverage tents or enclosed areas (see Rizzo, 1991, for details on beer sales),
- booths with standing only,
- menus versus restricted offerings,
- specific eating times versus continuous availability.

Often food, beverages, and entertainment are provided together, with entertainment being the factor that generates extra length of stay and greater consumption. Food and beverage festivals typically select vendors through a more rigorous system to ensure quality and compatibility with the theme and ambience. If competition to participate is high, competitive bids or a lottery system can be used to make the initial screening, followed by tight control over the product, price, and quality.

Financial Control

The easiest payment system is cash based, but many event organizers prefer to use coupons or "scrip" of some kind. In this system patrons are required to buy "funny money" from the event and can only employ this scrip on the site. Its advantages are:

- security: money is handled at one or a few sites with tight controls possible;
- honesty and accuracy: if the organizers are entitled to a share of vendor sales, this system guarantees accuracy (vendors must exchange all their scrip for cash at the end of the event);

- some patrons might keep the coupons as souvenirs, which constitutes a clear profit for organizers;
- some users might spend more if they lose track of how many "festival francs," for example, equal $1 or 1 £.

Quigley (n.d.), however, feels that forcing customers to buy scrip is an inconvenience and might stymie impulse purchases. Some customers might buy a fixed amount of "funny money" and leave when it is spent.

If a cash system is used, vendors or staff might be tempted to cheat. "Secret shoppers" or spotters can be used to keep track of both service quality and the quantity sold, cash handling procedures (e.g., do all receipts go into a cash register?), and staff honesty. Organizers should keep careful track of attendance and sales, especially comparing results from year to year, to determine what the sales and profits levels should be under given circumstances. Daily cash register tabulations should be supplied by each vendor for tracking and comparative purposes.

"Smart cards" are likely to replace cash at many events. These will eliminate many security problems and permit detailed auditing of sales. Another potential problem area is that of free food and beverages for staff and volunteers. This is often viewed as a perk for workers, but it should be controlled. Providing each worker with coupons redeemable for specified amounts or types of food and beverage works well.

Health and Safety

Local health inspectors will have to be consulted to ensure that all applicable licenses are obtained, and fire marshals will advise on safety where cooking and heating are factors. Many event organizers require by contract that vendors obtain these licenses and insurance, and take responsibility for meeting all standards.

Alcohol Sales

The risks associated with alcohol service must be evaluated against the potential gains. Alcohol service can provide the bulk of revenue for organizers, is often expected by customers, and is a part of the theme at many festivals and special events. Quigley (n.d., p. 92) noted that 85% of his survey of IFEA members did serve alcohol at their events.

Hospitality Training

Numerous events employ service clubs and volunteer amateurs to provide food and beverages, and aside from being financially essential this is often part of the event's charm. But this strategy carries risks, such as health problems, inefficiencies, and financial losses.

At a minimum, all personnel involved with food and beverage preparation and sales should receive basic training in several areas:

- cleanliness and meeting health standards,
- personal and customer safety (e.g., use of gas appliances and fire),
- cash handling and control systems,
- service quality (remember: servers are part of the product).

The Price of Admission

Festivals put on by community groups and public agencies are typically "free." This is a basic part of the festival's attraction, especially to residents. As suggested in South Carolina's Festival Planning Handbook (South Carolina Department of Parks, Recreation and Tourism, 1982), "the broader your appeal, the less it should cost for visitors to participate. It is often more effective to cover your expenses or raise funds in other ways than admission charges"

(p. 1). The free or very inexpensive event also encourages last-minute decisions to attend, and spontaneous participation by tourists in the area. Such events contribute to the image that a destination always has something happening, and that a particular facility or setting is a people-place.

Yet charging an admission price can raise large amounts of money, and many events cannot survive without it. As well, there are good marketing reasons for charging admission, as discussed later in the book.

Pricing Structures

Events can choose from a range of price structures:

- single admission price for everyone, or differential pricing based on age, time, groups, etc.;
- free general admission, but with a price for specific attractions, or admission price plus charges for specific attractions;
- no admission price, but charge for extras like parking, reserved seating, programs, etc.;
- no charges, but with recommended "donations";
- no charges for those complying with special provisions such as the wearing of period costumes;
- sponsor-provided discounts readily available to offset the price;
- single admission, multivisit, or seasonal passes.

Setting the Price: Cost Recovery

Full cost recovery, or average cost pricing, sets the price to regain all variable and fixed costs of the event from the users. A margin for profit can then be added. Obviously, this might not be appropriate for events considered to be a public service. A second approach is to set a price to recover from consumers only the operating costs, or only a portion of fixed or capital costs. This makes sense for public service events that cannot survive without some revenue from users. It is also applicable to events having grants or sponsorships that can be used to reduce costs.

One-time special events have to face several complications. Most mega-events cannot hope to recover all their costs from admissions, given the enormous capital investments. Instead, they will probably set attendance and revenue targets that will lead to a pricing strategy. One important factor will be the desire to generate strong tourism demand, thereby favoring package deals. To encourage repeat visits by residents, many events presell passes. Over the duration of a longer event, pricing can be modified to reflect demand trends and public reaction to the product.

Break-Even Analysis

This is a tool to help in setting prices, and for cost–revenue management in general. The basic logic is that at some level of demand or sales, revenues will be sufficient to cover the event's costs. Figure 9.1, left side, shows the anticipated fixed cost of the event, and the sloping line indicates revenue from increasing sales or admissions. The question is: "how many paying customers do we need to break even?"

In this example the price (or average revenue) per customer is $10 and the event has fixed costs of $10,000. This situation can occur when a venue is rented and all supplies purchased in advance, the price is advertised, and the demand somewhat unknown. If nobody pays, the organizers lose their entire investment. At 1000 paid admissions the

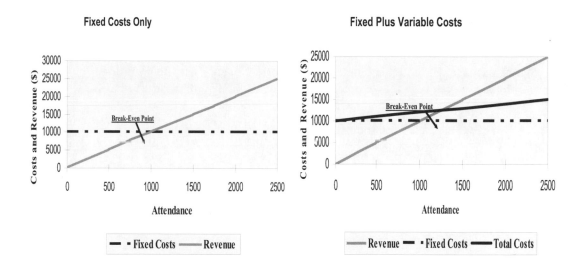

Figure 9.1. Break-even analysis.

break-even point is reached and every additional admission generates profit. Unless the manager can be assured of the minimal sales to break event, it is risky to produce the event. Sometimes grants, sponsorships, and other non-customer-driven revenue sources can be used to overcome anticipated revenue shortfalls.

More complex analysis must be undertaken to determine the break-even point when variable costs are incurred by increasing attendance. In Figure 9.1, right side, the organizer's problem is to identify the break-even point where rising attendance not only generates a predictable revenue per customer (at a given or average price) but also generates variable costs such as additional "free" programs, more staff, and utility or equipment charges. In these cases the "cost of sale" per customer must be considered, along with the "contribution" of each sale to meeting fixed costs. This is also called "cost-profit-volume analysis" (Livingstone, 1992, p. 33).

In the second example fixed costs are again $10,000 and the price remains at $10. But each paying customer engenders $2 of variable costs. This means that attendance of 1000 leads to $10,000 in fixed costs and $2,000 in additional variable costs. The formula for determining the break-even point (BEP) where both fixed and variable costs are applicable is: BEP (in terms of the number of paid admissions) = total fixed costs/price per unit – variable costs per unit.

The calculation "price per unit minus variable cost per unit" yields the "contribution" of each customer to meeting fixed costs. In our example the calculations are: BEP = $10,000/$10 – $2 $\doteq$ 10,000/8 = 1250. Therefore, paid attendance of 1250 is required to break even.

As a tool in pricing, the break-even point can be calculated for different price/revenue and cost assumptions. But several problems can arise:

- only experience can demonstrate the price elasticity of the event (i.e., the effect of increases or decreases on demand);
- factors affecting elasticity are not stable (e.g., disposable income; competition; nature of the event product; packaging);

- many costs are not stable or predictable;
- detailed cost accounting is necessary to identify fixed and variable costs.

Where experience with pricing is lacking, other events can be examined, or market research undertaken to evaluate potential customers' likely willingness to pay for the event at several levels of pricing.

Spreadsheet software can be used to test the cost–revenue relationships in constructing break-even graphs. This allows for quick evaluation of what happens when price is changed, which is a type of "sensitivity analysis." The break-even point is also sensitive to changes in costs, so if some costs are reducible or uncertain, the spreadsheet can demonstrate the implications of fluctuations while price is held constant.

Determining the Break-Even Price

A variation of break-even analysis (from Geier, 1993) is used when the object is to determine the break-even price. In these cases: BEP = total costs/maximum attendance. This calculation only works if total attendance can be fixed in advance, although estimates of the potential for selling tickets can be used in what-if scenarios. For example: if we sell 1000 tickets and our costs are $10,000 what do we have to charge to break even?

Profit Targets

If the event is supposed to make a profit or surplus, the following formula will work (from McDonald & Milnes, 1999): admissions needed to achieve profit target = profit target + total fixed costs/contribution margin per unit.

Remember from above that price per unit minus variable cost per unit yields the "contribution" of each customer (admission) to meeting fixed costs.

Backward Pricing

Sometimes the price is set without regard to costs (usually for political reasons), and the manager must determine the feasible level of service or program based on anticipated revenues at that price. Various attendance estimates can be tested to forecast total revenues.

Follow-the-Leader (Reference Pricing)

Many events simply use other events and attractions as reference points to determine a comparable price. The competition should always be scouted, of course, but this approach reduces a key marketing decision to a simplistic decision. The risk is that prices are similar but costs are different, leading to losses.

Prestige Pricing

This is a variation in which the price is deliberately set higher than the competition for positioning reasons, usually to suggest quality and attract higher-spending visitors. Any loss of demand must be compensated by higher prices and spending levels per visitor.

Market Penetration

Reduce the price to attract or retain customers in the face of higher competition or failing demand. Hopefully the new or retained audience will be loyal as prices go back up over time. If the discounts are substantial this strategy might be called "predatory," with the attempt to drive competition out of business. In some jurisdictions this tactic is illegal, but it also risks a price war that nobody wins.

Price Skimming

Events with strong competitive advantages, such as one-time mega-events with guaranteed high demand, can sometimes get away with charging high prices. This is analogous to "skimming" the cream off the milk. The downside is that high pricing risks a political and consumer backlash.

Demand Based

"What the market will bear" is often heard as the justification for prices. This is not sophisticated unless accompanied by research on willingness to pay, or price elasticity. Price can and should be used to increase demand when attendance is lagging and decrease it when crowding is a problem, but the potential implications should be carefully evaluated.

Yield or Profit Management

"Yield management" is popular with airlines and hotels, but seldom applied to events. It requires the manipulation of capacity and price to balance supply and demand and to achieve greater revenue or profit. When hotels or airlines anticipate lower demand they drop the price or add value to the package. Events can practice yield management in a number of ways.

According to the Center for Hospitality Research at Cornell University (2001), yield management is also useful for separating price-sensitive from price-insensitive customers, and this means that different segments or target markets can be attracted by manipulating the price. For example, it might be desirable to have free or inexpensive programming for families at one venue and high-price entertainment for tourists and others at another venue.

The timing of an event is one issue that can affect revenue potential, particularly where competition is involved. Also, remember that tourists will pay more than residents for many attractions and events. Events that include weekends and that offer tourist packages might do better financially as a consequence. Through research and experience events should find the peak times of year, month, week, and day when demand will be highest.

One goal is to maximize total revenue through timely manipulation of price. Sell unused capacity (such as tickets for different shows and venues), for example, by offering discounted prices. Packaging a number of features under one price, and offering passes for longer periods of time, are related ways to manage demand and maximize revenue.

"Duration management" is a related concept. Many restaurants, at peak demand periods, actively encourage a rapid turnover of "covers" in order to seat more customers. Events should be concerned about over-stays when it does not yield higher spending (usually longer stays mean more spending on food, souvenirs, etc.) or when the capacity of the venue/site is reached and others cannot get in. One solution is to introduce multiple, scheduled sessions for visits, and this can be combined with advanced bookings. Indirectly, parking costs can be manipulated to encourage shorter or longer stays. The presence of free entertainment will encourage longer stays.

Sponsorship

"Sponsorship," according to International Events Group (IEG, 1995) is "a cash and/or in-kind fee paid to a property (such as an event) in return for access to the exploitable commercial potential associated with that property." Others have stressed that sponsorship is more of an "affiliation" or "association" of events and corporations for their mutual benefit, although it generally involves payments for specific services rendered by the event.

It is therefore different from grants and donations, although the event manager always has to know what each resource supplier wants from the event.

To the event manager, a sponsor is any individual, agency, or group that provides resources in exchange for specified benefits or performance. From the sponsor's perspective, the term "event marketing" refers to the use of events to meet marketing goals (see the discussion in Cunningham & Taylor, 1995).

"Lifestyle marketing" stresses the linking of business to the attitudes and preferred lifestyles of customers. Events present a particularly effective way to reach people while at leisure, engaging in their preferred activities with friends and family, and in their home community or leisure environment. "Relationship marketing" links companies with communities or customers through causes of mutual interest. Companies and other sponsors working with events can position themselves as being proponents of popular causes. In general, people respond better to sponsorship than other advertising (IEG, 1995, p. 6), and think more positively of sponsors associated with causes and popular events.

Growth of Sponsorship

Catherwood and Van Kirk (1992) noted that the 1984 Los Angeles Olympic Games ushered in a new era. "It showed that sponsorships were potent marketing tools, and that companies could not only promote established products but introduce new ones through special events" (p. 11). Until that time sponsorship was often viewed as charity or advertising, while in recent years more integrated lifestyle and event marketing has come to the fore.

According to IEG (1995, p. 2), sponsorship has emerged as the fourth arm of marketing, alongside advertising, public relations, and sales promotions. The bulk of sponsorship investment has always gone to sports (IEG, 1995, p. 9) but sports' share of the pie has declined while arts, causes, festivals, other special events, and entertainment tours and attractions have gained. By 2000, sponsorship by North American companies totaled almost $9 billion, with sports taking about 70% (cited in Bennett, Henson, & Zhang, 2003).

Factors affecting the growth and significance of sponsorship have been identified (e.g., Catherwood & Van Kirk, 1992; Crompton, 1993; IEG, 1995; Skinner & Rukavina, 2003). Events have been forced to pursue corporate sponsors because of the diminishment of traditional funding sources and heightened competition, while corporations started in the 1990s to place a much greater focus on the bottom line—they want tangible results.

Media "noise" and the high cost of advertising favors more targeted marketing, and events provide an attractive vehicle. Keegan, Moriatry, Duncan, and Paliwoda (1995, p. 635) noted that advertising in media is more limited by government restrictions in Europe, giving rise to greater emphasis on event sponsorship to create large numbers of "consumer impressions." People are also reading newspapers less, especially the younger generation, and broadcast media are so fragmented that reaching target segments through traditional advertising has become difficult. Event sponsorship offers a respectable and more personal way to deliver the message or make the sale.

Skinner and Rukavina (2003), in their book *Event Sponsorship*, speak from experience in saying that sponsors since the 1990s are no longer content with signage and on-site hospitality; they want business-to-business marketing opportunities and measured results of their return on investment. Now website sponsorship partners are becoming common and technology will continue to have impacts on event marketing.

Benefits to Event Organizers

Most obviously, sponsorship yields resources that otherwise would not be available. This has not only fueled growth in the number and scale of events, but in their quality as well. It has boosted professionalism by allowing the retention of staff and development of management systems. In its *Official Guide to Sponsorship*, the International Festivals Association (IFA) (n.d.) noted that its membership growth had paralleled dramatic sponsorship expansion since the 1980s. This trend, according to Bruce Skinner, past-president of IFEA, has altered the basic structure of the community festival: "Events, especially new ones, are better because they are able to invest dollars into new and exciting programming" (IFA, n.d., preface).

Extending the marketing "reach" is another benefit of sponsorship. Through the sponsors' "augmentation" of their investment, additional advertising and public relations efforts are often made. And marketing advice can be obtained directly from many sponsors, given their interest in seeing the event become a success. Greater use of television and unusual product tie-ins (such as movie theater ads) is noticeable.

Potential benefits to the event include:

- revenue for administration and operations;
- increased marketing scope and reach through use of collateral promotions by the sponsor;
- growth of the event's constituencies (i.e., supporters and contacts);
- enhancement of the image of the event through association with a positive corporate image.

Success with sponsorship might also result in professional and human resource gains, through use of the sponsor's staff and expertise. Skinner and Rukavina (2003) claim that a well-sponsored event has a number of characteristics that set it apart, namely:

- outstanding staff;
- it is perceived as the best;
- gives added value to sponsors;
- stays in touch with sponsors;
- engages in networking, to open doors;
- sees through the eyes of sponsors;
- creates a good image;
- gives sponsors results.

Benefits to Sponsors

Public relations, charity, and community involvement are still important to many corporations, but marketing now prevails. Nor is it just advertising that motivates sponsors, because events reach smaller audiences than mass media. The terms "relationship marketing" and "lifestyle marketing" are more accurate descriptors of contemporary event marketing.

It is worth considering that small events in small communities will likely operate in quite a different environment from events in large cities that deal with major corporations. Mount and Niro (1995) studied event sponsorship in small communities and determined that local businesses might be just as motivated by civic duty as by marketing, and that promotional goals—while usually important—can be secondary to goodwill. Wicks (1995) also examined event sponsorship in a small town, concluding that local businesses were important in both sponsoring and organizing a major event. The sponsors were motivated by a desire to create a positive community image and a sense of pride among townsfolk. Congruity between event goals and dominant local values is important in these situations.

Skinner (in Skinner & Rukavina, 2003, p. 236) predicted that not only will sponsorship grow, especially outside the sport sector, but sponsors will want more exclusivity. This in turn will lead to fewer but larger sponsorship deals. Experiences rather than impressions will be more and more important, changing the way sponsorship is evaluated.

What benefits are sponsors looking for? There are many possibilities:

- heightened visibility (through various media);
- image enhancement of corporation or product through association with a popular event;
- to highlight product benefits or otherwise reinforce the public's perception of a product;
- shape consumer or public attitudes (either social marketing or corporate marketing);
- direct sales outlets at the event;
- relationships with customers and target segments;
- enhanced awareness of the corporation and its products/services;
- opportunities for entertaining the sponsor's business associates, staff, VIPs, etc.;
- internal marketing (involvement of staff in worthwhile events; team building, morale boosting);
- profitable linkages with other sponsors, suppliers, government officials, institutions, etc.;
- differentiation of the company or product from competitors;
- to demonstrate a tie or commitment to a particular market niche, such as an ethnic group or gay consumers;
- enhance the company's reputation for being community oriented or socially responsible;
- to test new products through sampling;
- to provide executives and key clients with entertainment or the opportunity to meet celebrities at the event;
- provide opportunities for firm-to-firm marketing through event operations (incentives for retailers, distributors etc.).

Meenaghan (2001a) summarized key theoretical considerations for sponsors who want to maximize their effectiveness. The first major consideration is that consumer goodwill can be earned (and lost) through sponsorship, and it is goodwill that separates sponsorship from mere advertising. The level of involvement that consumers have in an activity or event in large part determines their response to the sponsors, so the ideal sponsorship reaches those who are emotionally involved with the activity/event. This is the essence of "relationship" marketing, and the relationship should extend beyond event sponsorship and reach the consumers directly on an ongoing basis.

Sponsorship of events does result in a transfer of image (or co-branding), and in part this is determined by the consumer's perception of "congruence," or the fit between sponsor and event. It might be difficult, for example, for a beer company to gain a sophisticated image through sponsorship of fine arts, but this might work for wine. Timing is another issue, with Meenaghan (2001b) suggesting that early sponsors could reap more benefits because latecomers can be perceived as jumping on a bandwagon. Consumers also tend to think that companies that sponsor events in a big way are successful and large.

Costs and Risks of Sponsorship

Sponsorship will not always be obtained cheaply. With many events and causes seeking sponsors, the cost of research, preparing proposals, administering contracts, and serving sponsors—including accountability reports—can be substantial. Larger events will increasingly have full-time staff working on sponsorship.

There are potential risks as well, not the least of which is the possibility that organizers' goals get "displaced" by those of major sponsors, or that a commercial orientation will alter the event in subtle but profound ways. To avoid the risks, managers must have a sponsorship plan, know exactly what is needed and what can be exchanged for sponsorship, and be skilled in managing the process.

Both parties could face image problems arising from sponsorship, either through unforeseen incidents or a poor fit. Event failure, such as poor attendance or poor quality, might reflect badly on the sponsor's image. Media criticism or neglect is a risk to both parties. Conflicts over policy, program, and operations can occur, and the unexpected termination of a partnership can hurt.

Meenaghan (2001a) warned that sponsors have to earn goodwill, and that it can be lost or even converted into hostility if the relationship between sponsors, events, and consumers is abused. Termination of long-standing, successful sponsorships is therefore potentially risky. Meenaghan (2001b) also demonstrated through research that consumers might make specific complaints against sponsors:

- sponsors interfere in the event (such as timing for TV audiences, not fans);
- tickets go to sponsors rather than ordinary people;
- sponsors are only interested in high-profile events, not grass-roots events;
- sponsors sometimes get in the way of enjoying the event.

Ambush Marketing

A major concern of event marketers is the "ambush" (Ettore, 1993). "Ambush marketing" in general refers to a competitor attempting to grab media attention or other benefits away from an official sponsor. For example, in a number of events nonsponsors were able to gain public attention by hiring a blimp to fly over a stadium. Although usually used in a pejorative way, synonymous with cheating, "ambush marketing" is viewed by some as a legitimate and morally correct way to "intrude upon public consciousness surrounding an event" (Meenaghan, 1994, p. 79). But left unchecked it can cause consumer confusion and undermine all sponsorship benefits.

Organizers will increasingly be asked to provide a defense against ambush marketing. The Olympics have been particularly hard hit by ambushers over the years and have become aggressive in fighting them off. This is a high priority because of the enormous fees paid by the "top" global sponsors. Jensen (1995) explained the strategy employed by the IOC in defending the Atlanta Summer Olympics in 1996 against ambushers. Print campaigns were to paint ambushers in general as parasites, and the IOC announced it would directly respond to any unauthorized event marketing through its "sponsor protection unit" by public confrontation and, if necessary, legal action. This would be combined with public education and assistance to sponsors so they received full value.

Who Are the Best Sponsors?

Traditionally it was tobacco and alcohol companies that sponsored events, and mostly sport events at that. This has changed, partly because of legislation in some countries (e.g., Canada banned all tobacco advertising including a sponsorship presence at events, resulting in a substantial loss to the event sector). In small communities the choices for event sponsors can be quite limited. As noted earlier, local businesses tend to support events that are perceived to be good for the community, so every type of business is a prospect.

The "fit" between events and sponsors is an important consideration. The best sponsors are not just those that provide the most resources but those that ensure harmony, or a close fit between the goals, images, and programs of each. Events benefit from stable sponsorship relations. Resource flow is more predictable, the event program can be protected from sudden, unwanted changes at a new sponsor's request, and more effective marketing strategies can be implemented. "Partnership" goes beyond long-term contracts. It implies a meeting of the minds on what is best for the event and the sponsor—a good fit. Partners work out their goals together, and solve problems in a positive, nonconfrontational manner. Partners often compromise on details, but should avoid sacrificing basic principles to protect the partnership.

Many sponsors will pay more for collateral advertising and promotions (called "augmentation") by perhaps two or three times the actual sponsorship value. Some firms are better able to do this than others, so they might make the best sponsors for achieving maximum exposure. Organizers can also leverage a major sponsorship in the sense that obtaining one or more key sponsors will act as a magnet for others. This can occur either because of the sponsors' reputations, the scale of their sponsorship, or their ability to attract related businesses.

The proper commencement of sponsorship planning begins with a review of the mandate and goals of the organization. For some, dealing with the private sector might not fit. More likely, however, some kinds of sponsorship will be found to be appropriate and highly desirable. Some of the most likely sources of a misfit, however, include the following:

- tobacco and alcohol products generally do not fit with amateur and youth sports, health themes, and certain other events that want a "clean, family" image;
- environmentally friendly events do not want to associate with environmentally destructive corporations;
- cause-related events cannot associate with those representing the opposite position.

The best fits between events and sponsors often suggest themselves, such as sports and athletic equipment suppliers, but just as many good relationships will occur through careful analysis and smart approaches to potential sponsors. Many events find they must start with small sponsors in their own communities, many of whom feel some degree of obligation to help out. Gaining access to regional and national-level decision makers can be difficult, and the competition for attention is intense. Events with head offices in their area have an advantage, although local "champions" can often be found within corporations to take the application to higher levels. Either way, building on a solid local base of sponsors is a good strategy.

The Sponsorship Plan

Sponsorship has to fit the event and its culture, goals, and strategies. Most need sponsors, so they make adjustments and manage the relationships for mutual benefit. It helps to have a policy and a plan, otherwise mistakes can be made. Decide on your needs, goals, and priorities. You might not get sponsorship of everything, nor at the desired levels. The event might prefer to not pursue certain categories of corporation. Decide on whose responsibility it is to research and approach potential sponsors. In many events this is the shared responsibility of directors, the general manager, and professional fund-raisers.

Prepare a budget. It costs money to conduct research, prepare submissions and the support material, deliver on promises (such as signage), and then to service the relationship—including accountability research and reports. This has to be balanced against cash and in-kind value.

Develop sponsorship "platforms," as explained below, which are the rights and privileges that companies will pay for. This might require modification of your event, as many are not founded with sponsors' appeal in mind. Assign values (or cash and in-kind targets) for each platform.

Prepare a Sponsorship Proposal and select targets to approach; do your research and avoid wasting yours and their time; many companies post online sponsorship criteria or will provide their policy and requirements to you upon request. Be prepared to do research necessary for accountability and for evaluating your own position. Also prepare for sponsor servicing (building and maintaining relationships).

Creating Sponsorship Platforms

Events must be viewed and managed as marketable products to succeed at sponsorship. To the extent that it does not detract from meeting the organization's mandate and goals, management should maximize sales by increasing potential benefits to sponsors. This principle also covers events created solely as sponsorship vehicles, for-profit events that won't be profitable without major sponsors, and events that can only commence or grow if they offer the right sponsorship opportunities.

Brooks (1994) argued that sponsorship, from the sponsor's viewpoint, is a "medium that helps amplify and aim a message" (p. 173). As such, it is a form of communication, and has three dimensions. The first dimension relates to the sponsor's focus: the company, a product, or a brand. Second, the company can use sponsorship for strategic or tactical advantages. Strategic goals pertain to positioning (i.e., its place in the marketplace relative to competitors), and should lead to improvements in image, awareness, distribution, market expansion and relationships, and in combating competitors. Tactical goals are sales related, including stretching the advertising dollar and increasing sales in a measurable manner. The third dimension is the sponsorship platform, which, in terms of sports, involves the choice of athlete, event/competition, the sport as a whole, or a team.

Figure 9.2 illustrates a framework for understanding and developing event sponsorship. The "platforms" consist of one or more bases upon which sponsors can build on-site plus "augmented" programs. The usual platforms are the entire event and subcomponents, but the organization itself can be a platform—especially if it produces more than one event. Also, the participants—such as artists or athletes—can be sponsored through the event. Confusion often results, however, when the participants carry their own sponsorships, or the sport or art organizations involved in events bring their own sponsors. The result can be an event with a title sponsor different from the star athlete's, within a group of sponsorships attached to the sport governing body - compounded by different companies advertising on the televised broadcast and others attempting to ambush the event! When sponsorship gets so confusing that it ceases to offer opportunities for clear communications, sponsors will start to create their own events (Jones, 1993), and are increasingly doing so.

The figure also shows types of sponsorships, general benefits gained, and what sponsors provide to the event. This system must be balanced and mutually beneficial to sponsors, organizers, and participants or it will cause problems.

Event managers should systematically audit their organization and event(s) to identify and value platforms and potential benefits to offer, then target them to either general

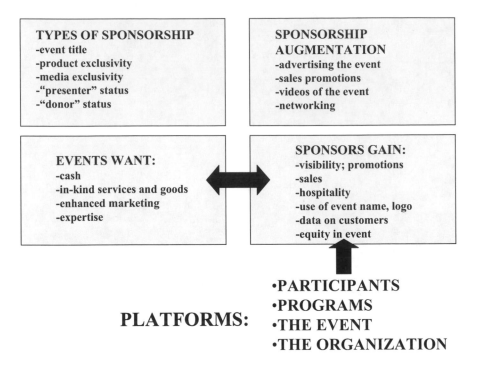

Figure 9.2. Event sponsorship framework.

types of sponsors or to specific companies. It will help to rank your platforms and "offers" in order of value to your key targets. The audit for a hypothetical music event might reveal the following:

Platforms: (1) one event, each of 2 days; (2) three styles of music, six popular entertainment groups, a star athlete; (3) two separate venues; (4) seven food and beverage items for sale; (5) all-year public relations exposure through community activities.

Offers: (1) one exclusive title sponsorship; (2) 2 days × 2 venues for signage and media coverage; (3) 7 × 2 (venues) for exclusive product categories; (4) 15 program element sponsorships; (5) exclusive media opportunities in 3 categories (for each music style); (6) all-year sponsorships in all categories.

Many events use a simple-to-develop hierarchical approach to sponsorship, each with fees and benefits differentiated:

- Title Sponsor (cost to sponsor: $100,000). Benefits: name the event; free tickets; prominent signage at all venues; hospitality tent; etc.
- Gold Sponsor ($50,000) (no limit on numbers). Benefits: less than those for the title sponsor.
- Silver ($25,000) (no limit).
- Bronze ($5–10,000) any number.

This will likely be in addition to product and media exclusivity categories. The greatest weakness of the above example is that it does not actually offer a product; rather, it stresses what the event wants, in the form of cash. Many potential sponsors will be more sophisticated in their needs and will want to purchase very tangible products. For them, the following system might work better:

- Title Sponsor: (one only; cost to be negotiated).
- Seven "Presenting Sponsors" for program elements or entertainment groups (the cost for each to be uniform).
- Five product exclusivity sponsors (e.g., the "Official supplier of . . .").
- Three Exclusive Media Sponsors.
- Donors: any number.

Potential sponsors will know exactly how many sponsors there are in each major category, at what cost, and with what benefits.

"Presenting Sponsor" is sometimes the top category, as in "this event is presented by . . ." However, Skinner and Rukavina (2003, p. 34) said it is not as valuable because the sponsor's name is often dropped from the title.

What Is it Worth (How Much to Charge?)

There are no magic numbers to guide managers in pricing their event's sponsorship products. Obviously, the more successful the event is in meeting sponsor goals, the more it should receive in exchange. The balance between cash and in-kind fees must also be considered, along with the competitive situation.

IEG (1995, p. 19) suggested that tangible sponsorship benefits, such as tickets and other things that can be given a monetary value, are not as important as more qualitative benefits. After all, how can you objectively value association with a prestige event? On the other hand, IEG has developed a sponsorship valuation service to quantify the value in dollars and cents, taking into account the following (from Skinner & Rukavina, 2003, p. 185):

- attendance or people reached by the sponsorship;
- signage and other displays of corporate logos/messages;
- visibility on the event's website;
- sponsor's visibility or related messages about the sponsor in all media coverage;
- inclusion in mailing lists;
- sampling opportunities;
- the value of tickets and other hospitality;
- advertising in media where results (such as audience size) can be measured.

Exclusivity and protection from ambush increase the value of sponsorship, as do audience loyalty and respect in the community.

As a rule of thumb, it is probably wise to value your products high, then negotiate downwards. Offering a range of opportunities by price will help match sponsors' abilities with your own needs. Costs should be considered when setting the price of sponsorship products. The time of paid staff is a factor, plus office overheads and direct costs from preparing and distributing sponsorship proposals.

Competition

All events are in competition with each other when it comes to acquiring resources. So it pays to know what "the competition" is doing, who are their sponsors, and what benefits they offer. This does not require industrial espionage, but some research is appropriate.

Successful sales people know that potential customers respond well to unique selling propositions (USP). The USP can be defined as the single-most important benefit you can offer a target segment, your greatest accomplishment (e.g., media coverage), or something completely unique about your event or organization. Sponsors will naturally be interested in any competitive advantage your event offers, compared with other events and marketing opportunities. This should emerge from your evaluation and research, or through creative brainstorming by your team!

Criteria Used by Sponsors to Assess Sponsorship Proposals

Crompton (1993) detailed major criteria used by corporations to decide on sponsorships, including the following:

- the match between the company and the event audience;
- exposure potential (all media);
- potential for integrated marketing (e.g., cross-promotions);
- competitive advantages to be gained;
- level of commitment and the costs involved;
- the event and its organization; its reputation.

Weppler and McCarville (1995) researched how corporations make decisions on sponsorship opportunities. Many units are often involved within the company, so proposals that meet a number of internal goals might stand a better chance. The quality of the proposal was considered to be important, reflecting on the professionalism of the applicant, and past performance of the event is an important factor.

Related research by Sunshine, Backman, and Backman (1995) concluded that applicants must understand by whom, and where in the organization, decisions are made. Delays and rejections might occur if sponsorship proposals are made, for example, to local rather than regional or national headquarters, or to public relations rather then marketing managers. Faxing or mailing a proposal might work with some sponsors, but might result in instant rejection by others, so the proper communication channel must be known in advance. And while some reviewers might prefer very short, concise proposals, the amount of competition for sponsorship dollars suggests that a thorough proposal is usually better.

Peterson and Crayton (1995) concluded that economic impact data can be an important factor in winning sponsorships. Such data can provide concrete evidence of the event's financial health and its ability to attract tourists or other target segments. When undertaken by a credible researcher or firm, the study adds credibility to the event itself.

The case study of Volvo, following this section, shows the importance of understanding corporate philosophy and goals.

The Sponsorship Proposal

Remember that you are proposing an investment opportunity that must meet the potential sponsor's marketing goals. Event government and nonprofit agencies that sponsor events want specific social marketing benefits.

An attractive, thorough, but concise proposal document should be customized for every important sponsorship target. A generic package is useful as a first effort, and will suffice for minor sponsorship targets. But when managers have done proper research and know what companies are the top targets, the proposal should precisely fit that sponsor's needs. That is an optimal situation, and it might never be fully realized—but it is worth pursuing.

A good proposal will have the following elements:

- introductory letter (personalized to the target) listing the key benefits of interest to the company and what is being requested from them;
- details of the platforms and benefits; sponsorship categories;
- background material about the event and its organization: origins, purpose, goals; key people associated with the event (short biographies or even pictures); program, photos, press releases; data on visitors, impacts, media coverage.
- endorsements from satisfied sponsors; listing of committed sponsors and partners;
- business or index card for easy reference.

The Approach and Making the Sale

Companies get numerous requests for funding and are unlikely to pay attention to one more standardized proposal. Personal contacts are good, especially if one of the event's organizers, staff, or friends can get directly to a senior company official. Many sponsors, especially those within the event's community, will want a face-to-face approach, and will hope for some personal satisfaction from the arrangement. Treating these sponsors as part of the event family will pay off.

A concise, professional presentation is preferable to informal chatting or simply handing the proposal to the target. This first impression made on the person handling the proposal might make all the difference when it comes to the company determining its priorities, especially if it is the only contact made.

Some sponsors have to be nurtured and brought along slowly. Invite potential sponsors to the event and treat them like special guests. Make certain they speak with satisfied sponsors. Show them the tangible benefits to their company, and the personal satisfaction that comes from being closely associated with the event and the people making it happen.

Indirect approaches can also work. Ask your major sponsors to approach their suppliers, buyers, and associates both on your behalf and to arrange joint promotions around the event.

The Contract

Sponsorship is usually thought of by both parties as a legally binding agreement, entailing mutual benefits and obligations. As such, it requires a contract and probably professional legal advice (see IFA and Argonne Productions, 1992; IEG, 1995).

Eric Martin, quoted in the book *Event Sponsorship* (Skinner & Rukavina, 2003, p. 134), explained the three types of sponsorship documentation: confirming letters (one party states what it believes the agreement covers); letters of agreement (easier to execute, but should legally carry the weight of a contract); and formal contracts.

With many sponsors, large amounts of money, and more impersonal relationships between events and corporations, most events and sponsors will actually prefer a contract specifying key points:

- purpose; term of the contract;
- schedule of actions and payments by both parties;
- definitions or explanations of actions required from both parties;

- specification and clarification of rights, such as whether or not the sponsor obtains exclusivity;
- liability (who is responsible; insurance requirements);
- use of trademarks, logos, patented processes—if applicable; ownership of broadcast rights;
- specification of retained rights (the event does not give up any permanent rights to its program, broadcast rights, etc.);
- future options (e.g., for renewal);
- termination and amendment procedures;
- assignments and subcontracting rights;
- what is NOT covered;
- compliance with appropriate laws;
- penalties for nonfulfillment;
- authority of the signatories.

Particularly important points to get legally binding include exclusivity (the only sponsor in a defined category), money and when it is to be paid, liability if things go wrong, terms of compliance, and accountability. Increasingly sponsors want protection against ambush marketing.

A trend that will disturb many event managers is for major sponsors to seek contractual performance guarantees. In other words, their payments will be contingent upon specified benefits being achieved, or penalties will apply if targets are not reached. Sponsors might want to protect against the following:

- attendance below projections;
- exposure not as promised (in various media, signs, etc.);
- lower than anticipated TV ratings;
- sales not up to forecasts;
- cancellation of the event, or reduction in its time or program;
- audience demographics not matching predictions.

From the event manager's point of view it would be better not to make such detailed promises, or if they are made to tie performance to an incentive or bonus system rather than to penalties.

Satisfying the Sponsor: Accountability

It is much easier and cheaper to keep your sponsors than to obtain new ones. Multiyear sponsorship deals are desirable, working to the advantage of both parties, so it is useful to speak in terms of partnerships in which both parties work together for mutual benefit. The manager, accordingly, deals with key sponsors on a permanent, friendly, and business-like basis.

Bill Charney (n.d.,a) gave advice on successfully renewing sponsorships. At a minimum, event managers will have an obligation to fulfill the contract or promises made to sponsors. If there was a problem, the manager must be able to prove to the sponsor that all efforts were made to meet the event's obligations. To do this will require a system of evaluation and control, especially over the benefits that are most important to sponsors. At larger events it might be essential to have a host and trouble-shooter assigned to sponsors.

Sue Twyford (n.d., p. 45) provided additional advice:

- give more than was promised;
- make sponsors look good at all times;
- communicate regularly; make them part of the event family;
- make it easy for them to sign up, get the most out of the event, enjoy themselves, and reenlist.

Skinner and Rukavina (2003, p. 177) recommended to events that they make sponsors feel like owners, especially by involving employees and getting a representative on the event's board of directors. Event managers are encouraged to be proactive in showing how sponsors can get more benefits, rather than simply responding to sponsor requests.

What research and data are required for evaluation and accountability? Negotiate who does what among the following activities (i.e., event or sponsor):

Attendance: Can an accurate count or reliable estimate of visitor numbers be provided? Differentiate between total gate (i.e., numbers of tickets sold, or total number of visits) and numbers of visitors (individuals attending, no matter how many times).

Visitor profiles: This will show sponsors if they are reaching their target market segments. Find out in advance how they define their targets (e.g., sociodemographic groups; is race/ethnicity important?).

Sponsor visibility: Produce photos or videos demonstrating the visibility of sponsors' signs, advertising messages, logos, booths, etc. Provide copies of all communications, press releases, etc. How many brochures were distributed? How much paid advertising was commissioned? Consider placements in the event brochure and souvenirs. Mentions in press releases are also important.

Sales: How much of the sponsor's product was sold? Related measures include the numbers of people reached by the sponsor's service, or the numbers of promotional coupons handed out. If sponsors provide free samples, a measure of the numbers who sampled the product or service will be desired.

Media coverage: For print media, clip all coverage and note its date, size (column inches), location (page 1 versus an article buried among the ads), and readership of the paper/magazine. For radio and television, document the stations' audience size and profile, length and types of spots (e.g., ads, talk-shows, public service announcements), and time of day.

Media contents: This is more difficult than documenting coverage, as it requires a content analysis of what was said or the images broadcast. Was it all favorable? Did the sponsors get prominent coverage? Providing sponsors with the actual copy will allow them to judge. Contents can be categorized in a number of ways, but the type of coverage is very important. "Editorial" coverage (i.e., commentary on a news item) can be very credible, if people respect the media or the writer. "Advertorials" are usually feature stories printed in magazines at the request of a client, and for a fee; the costs are less than full advertising rates but they might be better received than ads. News coverage of an event in which the sponsor's name is mentioned or their logo visible can be valuable, but broadcast news items are often fleeting.

Media value: Many events assign a dollar value to the "free" publicity they get. This is controversial, for several reasons. Valuing the coverage at the same price you would have to pay if it was advertising ignores the fact that advertising is targeted exactly to the desired audience, at the right time and in a manner the manager controls. At a minimum, "free" publicity must be discounted in value when compared with targeted advertising. Second, the contents of "free" publicity are often ignored. Should a dollar value be assigned to an unflattering or even critical commentary by the local news media? Only if you believe that all publicity is good. Third, measures of "potential audience reached" are of dubious value unless backed by reliable market area surveys of broadcasting and media audiences/readership.

Consumer awareness and response: Visitor surveys and interviews can be used to test consumer awareness of sponsorship and related messages at the event, or upon departure. Interactive displays are increasingly used to actually record data about consumers interested in a sponsor's products, but the same data can be obtained through forms completed to be eligible for a prize or special promotion. Many sponsors will value a mailing list of potential consumers, especially if it has been screened by some method that indicates interest and means to purchase.

Impacts: Data on the amount of visitor spending created by the events will interest the tourism and hospitality sectors, especially when it is demonstrated that event tourists stay overnight in commercial accommodation, eat at restaurants, and spend money on other entertainment and attractions. Negative social or environmental impacts will discourage some sponsors, but the manager is advised to be honest and deal with these problems effectively, rather than trying to hide or ignore them. Major sponsors are too sophisticated to be fooled, and they might be monitoring the event in ways unknown to the organizers.

Evaluation of Return on Investment for Sponsors

Kerstetter and Gitelson (1995) tested guests at an arts event to see if they could recall any of the event sponsors, but fully 70% could or would not name any. Even worse (from the sponsors' perspective) 40 companies were incorrectly named as sponsors, showing how difficult it is to get messages across. The researchers said results reflected the fact that many sponsors of the event were there for the first time, and that repetition would be necessary to increase awareness levels. Local businesses will also have a more difficult time in communicating with tourists than with residents.

Evaluating Your Sponsorship Efforts

Set your evaluation criteria in advance, or you will not know how to measure sponsorship effectiveness (i.e., meeting your targets) and efficiency (getting the most for your investment and efforts). As well, you have to beware of unanticipated outcomes such as goal displacement, where sponsors' influence becomes a negative force.

A number of strategic issues have to be evaluated periodically:

- what the return on your investment is (in terms of money and in-kind value versus effort and costs incurred in getting the sponsorship);
- cash versus in-kind ratio (cash is often better; can in-kind be converted to cash?);
- your sponsorship categories and price relative to other events (are you being short-changed?);
- can extra effort, investment, or a new position be justified in terms of generating substantially more revenue?

The life cycle of a sponsorship should be reviewed regularly. An ideal relationship is one that lasts, but most sponsors will not renew indefinitely. Can losses be anticipated and replacements brought quickly on board? Can former sponsors ever be brought back? Do you know exactly why sponsors left?

Sponsorship Evaluation Reports

Inform each sponsor of how their objectives were met, and what was done—or will be done—to correct any problems. Placing a value on the benefits to sponsors helps a lot, but raises the issue of valid and reliable ROI measures. A typical evaluation report will include:

- media coverage, audience estimates, content analysis;
- signage with photos; a video summary;
- attendance counts and visitor survey results (especially questions pertaining to sponsors);
- copies of all communications mentioning the sponsor;
- data on on-site exhibits, sampling, and sales by sponsors;
- itemization of benefits to sponsors' employees and business partners (hospitality, volunteering).

Case Study: Volvo Event Management

The corporate world is increasingly involved with events, mostly as sponsors, but in some cases—like Volvo—in their production. Sven Osterberg is manager of Volvo Event Management (VEM) in Gothenburg, Sweden, at the headquarters and home of Volvo cars. VEM was established in 1986 and is jointly owned by Volvo Car Company (owned by Ford Motors) and Volvo AB (the original company, still in Swedish ownership). It is overseen by a Board of Directors, with three directors from each of the two parent companies.

There are three groups within VEM, each with a different location and somewhat different functions. The headquarters is in Brussels where they have responsibility for internal communications and Volvo's golf events. In Southampton, England, the team directly manages the Volvo Ocean Race, including media management. The Gothenburg team looks after "utilization" of the race, which Sven defines as activities intended to maximize its branding benefits. This office also arranges VIP visits, oversees Volvo's sponsorship of golf in Sweden, and looks after the Volvo Baltic Race for which Volvo is title sponsor.

Although formed originally as an in-house events production company, VEM now only directly owns and manages golf and sailing events. According to Sven, it makes more sense to own an event outright, from a corporate branding perspective, but that is a very expensive proposition and good opportunities are rare. One such opportunity was to acquire the Whitbread Around the World Race.

Elsewhere in the world, national- and regional-level sport event sponsorship by Volvo varies a great deal. As the Volvo brand developed into a world leader, the sports it associates with have changed. Not only does it get more expensive to continuously sponsor a specific sport over time, but there is real value in associating with new sports—like sailing—that are directly associated with Volvo's core competencies (it has a large marine division) and also suggest innovation with positive lifestyle associations for its target markets.

Volvo's Event Sponsorship Philosophy and Strategy

Volvo is a famous, global brand, and the company recognizes that awareness of the brand is greater than its market share. To Volvo, the basic "brand proposition" rests on quality, safety, and environmental care.

Their sponsorship strategy stresses events rather than individuals, and cultivation of long-term partnerships. Specific sports are favored, including (to date): equestrian, skiing, tennis, motor racing, mountain-biking, golf, and sailing. Volvo cars appeal mostly to mature consumers, especially as in most market areas the cars are viewed as luxury products. Association with "lifestyle sports" that appeal to the mature market, especially sailing and golf, provides a close fit.

Profile: Volvo Ocean Race (www: volvooceanrace.org)

Twenty companies were interested in acquiring this global, round-the-word sailing event when Whitbread (an English beer company) put it up for sale. In 1997 it cost Volvo roughly US$7.5 million to purchase, with the tangible assets acquired (some staff and an office) being valued much less than the rights to continue and rebrand a well-established, global event. An additional $20 million was spent to produce the first Volvo Ocean Race held in 2001–2002, and a further $10–15 million was invested to leverage it for marketing purposes. As it is held every 4 years, there is a defined cycle of organization, investment, evaluation, and planning.

A race of this magnitude requires that syndicates form to organize and attain sponsorship for each competing yacht. In the first Volvo Ocean Race, eight teams competed, with their respective syndicates spending from US$12–20 million each. Syndicates might very well change with each race, and Volvo requires that interested parties approach them with a proposal. A video has been prepared to attract syndicate interest. To avoid any potential conflict among sponsors, Volvo retains a right to veto any proposal. Co-branding possibilities among Volvo and the team sponsors can also be developed.

The connection between event and tourism occurs mostly in the ports of call. The stopovers were largely inherited from the Whitbread days, but VEM intends to take a more commercial approach to selecting ports to reach a bigger audience, facilitate business-to-business hospitality, and generate revenue. Ports have to bid for the right to host part of the race, and that means they are looking for tourism and promotional benefits. In the first race, 10 ports spent from $1 to 1.5 million each on their own events and promotions.

Each port produces an onshore event. Volvo enters into contractual arrangement with the host city, and the more competition there is the better the deal will likely be for Volvo. In the eyes of Sven Osterberg, the event is "traveling theatre" for these host cities. VEM will evaluate the success of each city-hosted event before deciding on subsequent race routes and venues.

"Utilization" or "leveraging" of the Volvo Ocean Race aims to develop relationships, cultivate the media for positive exposure, and create new sales opportunities. Internal marketing is also a goal, through incentives to sales staff, motivational seminars given by the competing skippers, and educational programs. The idea is to create pride and passion about Volvo, and to unite a global company.

Relationship marketing drives the business-to-business hospitality surrounding the race. Volvo registered 12,000 visitors to its hospitality venues during the first event. These were mostly customers, some of whom won a race-themed trip as a prize. Establishment of an Ocean Race Club encouraged customers and other interested parties to get intimately involved.

Media relations encompass television, the Internet, print media, and radio. Specific tactics include advertising, signage, and product exhibitions at each port, promotions at automotive shows, use of a public relations boat, and merchandising a Volvo Ocean Race clothing collection produced by the Musto Company. Communications about the Ocean Race employ key words that suggest a good fit between sailing, the event, and the Volvo brand, including: adventure, excitement, team effort, endurance, motivation, leadership, technically advanced, clean environment, and man versus the elements. Volvo also likes to see this race portrayed as the Formula One for sailing boats.

After the first Volvo Ocean Race, an evaluation was undertaken. All media coverage was measured and assigned a monetary value equal to advertising costs for TV and print media. Effects on brand awareness and perceptions were also evaluated, through 2000 interviews in Europe, both pre- and postrace. Overall, Volvo was quite satisfied with the results, although they remain confidential. A bonus was the overtarget sales of a special-edition, Volvo Ocean Race car.

Photo 9.1. Volvo Ocean Race, Gothenburg Stopover (credit: Volvo Ocean Race/Rick Tomlinson).

The second Volvo Ocean Volvo race was scheduled for 2005–2006. In 2007 Volvo intends to launch the Volvo Pacific Race. The annual Volvo Baltic Race features the same boats that compete in the others, but only in Swedish and German waters and ports.

Sven Osterberg is 41 years old with a Bachelor of Science in Business Administration from Gothenburg University. He joined Volvo in 1988 and made a career within Treasury and Corporate Finance, living in Amsterdam and Geneva for 4 years. Since 1999 he has been General Manager for VEM Sweden. He is a keen sail racer and was involved in the acquisition of the Whitbread Round the World Race.

Financial Management

In the private sector the budget is a plan to achieve a target level of profitability. Many events, however, aim to break even. Some are organized and produced on faith alone, with the budget being more of a wish list than a financial planning tool! Such poorly planned and financed events use the budget to show where they hope money will come from, and how they will spend it—if it is obtained.

When the budget is properly conceived as a planning tool, the manager then appreciates the need for keeping it somewhat flexible. Conditions will change and the budget must be adapted accordingly. At some point in time, however, the cost side of the budget will become relatively fixed and all staff will thereafter be required to adhere to its cost and expenditure limits.

Given the nature of many events, which rely on gate revenue and sales at the event, costs might be controlled but revenues remain wildly unpredictable. This not only complicates the process and causes managers untold stress, but it leaves many events in the unenviable position of facing losses or even bankruptcy each and every year.

Goals of Cost–Revenue Management

"Cost–revenue management" is the process of identifying and managing all cost and revenue centers to ensure the financial health of the event organization.

The goals might be some or all of the following:

- secure long-term, predictable revenue sources that will meet basic organizational costs;
- tie program elements to specific revenue sources, such as sponsorships and grants;
- focus on revenue-generating activities;
- control and reduce cost centers;
- get other organizations to assume responsibility for financial risks, or at least to assist with covering any shortfalls.

The more sophisticated managers get at cost–revenue management and budgeting, the more business-like the event organization becomes. This raises an issue for those events that do not want to grow or professionalize, but for most events it represents an inevitable and desirable progression from amateur to professional management. Accordingly, several principles are offered:

- Events are businesses and should be managed as such.
- Event organizations should aim to make a profit (i.e., surplus revenue) to ensure financial self-sufficiency; without a surplus there will be no reserve fund and little possibility of capital investment for expansion.
- Events must establish a comprehensive financial planning and control system, including full cost–revenue management, budgeting, and standardized accounting and reporting.

Preparing the Budget

The "budget" is "a plan expressed in monetary terms" (Anthony & Young, 1984, p. 357). Managers use the budget to forecast their financial future, to help set priorities and plan the event, and to keep spending within limits. "Operating budgets" plan for one financial year of operations, "capital budgets" are prepared for capital acquisition, and "cash budgets" are used to summarize planned cash receipts and disbursements. Many event managers prepare only operating budgets.

One-time events often do not have their assets in place when they commence planning, and the revenue for many periodic events is not only uncertain but usually earned at the event itself, yet many expenditures must be made in advance. Budgeting for these conditions is quite different from a budget prepared in an organization that allocates a specific amount to the event.

Most event budgets will be of the "line item" type, in which the focus is on expense elements like labor, rentals, supplies, and entertainers, and revenues from admissions, sales, etc. But a "program budget" might also be appropriate, concentrating on the costs and revenues associated with each program element, venue, or subevent. Line item budgets naturally require more detail, whereas program budgets might require subbudgets from each program area.

Table 9.1 illustrates how both line item and program budgeting can be combined. For accounting purposes each program will require a code number, just like each line item. Program costs and revenues will be aggregated from the line items. In this budget antici-

Table 9.1. Hypothetical Event Operating Budget Combining Line Items and Programs

	Program				Line Item Totals
	A	B	C	D	
Expenditures					
Wages and salaries	$2,500	$3,000	$250	—	$5,750
Equipment rentals	$1,000	$500	—	$200	$1,700
Consumable supplies	$250	$100	$50	—	$400
Fees to performers	$3,000	—	—	—	$3,000
Advertising and promotions	$500	$1,000	—	—	$1,500
Share of overhead allocated to program	$4,000	$2,000	$50	$50	$6,100
Total program costs	$11,250	$6,600	$350	$250	$18,450
Undistributed overhead (administration)					$15,000
Total expenditures					$33,450
Revenues					
Admission fees	$22,000	$5,000	—	—	$27,000
Sponsorship fees	$10,000	$1,000	—	$800	$11,800
Rentals to vendors	$1,500	$500	—	—	$2,000
Merchandise sales	$3,000	$1,000	$800	$300	$5,100
Food and beverage (net profit)	$6,000	$3,000	$600	—	$9,600
Total program revenues	$42,500	$10,500	$1,400	$1,100	$55,500
Other revenue (sponsorship, grants, donations, investments)					$21,000
Total revenues					$76,500
Projected surplus ($76,500 – $33,450)					$43,050

This budget forecasts surplus revenue in each program area and in total. Food and beverage revenues are net (i.e., price of sales minus costs). Approximately one quarter of general overheads (administration, marketing, wages, etc.) has been allocated to specific programs.

pated costs and revenues are allocated among four programs. Any costs that cannot be fairly allocated to programs (or venues) are considered to be nonspecific, or "overhead." Similarly, there are revenue items that are not specific to programs. While this kind of simple budget reveals expected losses or surpluses, it does not consider capital expenditures nor debt charges.

The Budgeting Process

The budget will initially reflect the goals of the event and the organization producing it. There will be a big difference in budgets for events designed to make a profit versus those for which it is acceptable to break even or incur a loss.

Three normal steps in the process (Anthony & Young, 1984, p. 266) are:

- guidelines sent to operational managers or committee chairs, along with notification of constraints and guidelines for the area's budget proposal;

- estimates are submitted, including justification;
- review and approval; cost–benefit evaluation can be used to review new programs; ratios can be employed to compare areas or programs on their cost-effectiveness; negotiation might be part of the process.

Budgets for most events are annual, but businesses often employ monthly budget revisions to monitor progress and keep everyone on track. Senior managers sometimes prepare a draft budget, usually with input from all functional areas and the board of directors, if any, but not necessarily with estimates being submitted.

Budgets must be discussed, even hotly debated, because they set both financial goals and spending limits. The budget, for example, will allocate projected revenue among possible competing functional area managers, thereby determining their activities for the coming year. The budget will also prioritize (explicitly or implicitly) elements of the event program. This happens when "entertainment," as an example, is allocated X dollars, while "ceremonies and speakers" is allocated less.

If the budget is initially kept general and flexible, the program elements might be costed out at a later date. Thus, the program manager might first have to fight for a larger piece of the financial plan, then allocate the resources among competing program elements. In this way, budgeting and programming go hand in hand. The budget might also have to be prepared and revised in conjunction with the business plan, especially if sources of revenue are not fixed. The business plan, including a budget, is used in such cases to secure resources.

Managers must learn from past experience and use this knowledge to prepare ever-more realistic and accurate budgets. In this way, last year's financial statements become the starting point for the next budget. Two basic approaches are possible: "zero-based" budgeting, in which all functional areas and program elements start from scratch every year (i.e., they must freshly justify every budget item), and an "incremental" budgeting approach, in which managers build on last year's items and amounts. Most managers prefer to build, always looking for growth and/or improvements, but zero-based budgeting imposes a useful discipline on the process. It is more intimately tied to the annual evaluation process, whereby successes must be demonstrated, not assumed.

Controlling Costs

"Cost centers" are program or management areas, and "cost objects" are specific elements in each area. For example, entertainment is a major cost center for events, with specific cost objects including each performer, the equipment, staff, and venue rental.

"Direct costs" are those that can be allocated to specific programs, but budgeting must also consider "indirect costs," or "overheads" (i.e., the overall costs of management such as office rental, general manager's salary and insurance) and whether or not to allocate a portion to each cost center.

"Fixed costs" must be paid regardless of attendance at the event, and regardless of revenue. These can include capital costs (e.g., for buildings and equipment), rental of venues, commitments to entertainers and participants, and guaranteed prizes. Obviously, keeping fixed costs to a minimum is a goal of many event managers.

Many costs, however, are "variable: that is, they increase or decrease depending on attendance. This was previously examined in this chapter.

In the absence of experience, or when using zero-based budgeting, managers might develop their budget from general cost centers to more specific breakdowns of cost objects over a period of time. Some general principles of cost management can be stated (in addition to the preceding principles of cost–revenue management):

- Cost centers should have matching revenue sources, if at all possible.
- Every cost center and object should be controlled.
- Cost growth might be justifiable if it generates extra revenue.
- General overheads should be minimized; event failures are sometimes attributable to organizations and staff who consume too much of the resource base, relative to event production.
- Aim to minimize fixed costs and control variable costs.
- Many decisions about costs have to be made in advance (e.g., how many portable toilets to rent? how many security guards? how many programs? how much food and beverage?).
- Charge cost-recovery prices for variable costs.
- Analysis of variable costs might suggest attendance limits or some other form of capacity for the event, to avoid uncontrolled cost escalation.

Cash Flow Management

In order to adhere to the budget, and as a tool in setting and revising budgets, the event manager must be able to monitor and forecast cash flow. The budget might show that revenues will ultimately match costs, but this can easily give rise to a false sense of security. The costs might be ongoing, but the revenues are mostly coming from the event at the end of the budget year. Furthermore, many event-related costs are definite, but some revenues are uncertain.

The essence of cash flow management is to accurately forecast, for every month (or week, if necessary) of the budgeting period, all expenditures and revenues. Create a cash flow "calendar" showing the times at which expenditures must be made and revenue is to be realized. Potential shortfalls are thereby readily identifiable, although contingency plans are required to deal with unexpected variations.

Shortfalls are not necessarily fatal, and are often unavoidable, but the event manager must have a strategy for dealing with them. Perhaps some suppliers can be persuaded to hold off a while in their bill collecting, preferably until the event is over (this is called "back-ending"). A sponsor could be approached to advance some money. Friendly relations with a bank manager or grant-giving agency are highly desirable, as the line of credit is an important cash flow management tool. When a credit line is established the appropriate officials can withdraw cash or write checks against a preset limit, with payback according to an established and comfortable schedule. Some event managers will not commit to expenditures unless the revenue is guaranteed or the money is already in the bank.

At budget time, all managers must be required to identify not only anticipated costs and revenues, but to schedule them as accurately as possible. A grant has been applied for, but when exactly will the money be received? Will it be in installments or all at once? Is it conditional on performance? Are expenditures required before the event, or after?

This cost–revenue scheduling and forecasting will undoubtedly impact the budget itself. Some budgeted items might start to look very risky because expenditure will be required prior to anticipated revenue. Even if specific budget items look sound on the cash flow forecast, the overall cash flow picture might look bad, necessitating a rethinking of all items. Those budget items with short-term revenue potential might come out as higher priorities than those requiring short-term expenditures.

It is common to "discount" the value of money earned later, rather than sooner. Up-front revenue not only allows much greater flexibility and reduces risks, it is worth more to the organization because it does not have to be borrowed, it can be used to pay back loans, and it can earn money if invested.

MPI's (2003) textbook *Meetings and Conventions: A Planning Guide*, comes with a sample template for a cash flow statement. Revenues and expenses are shown on a monthly basis, resulting in calculations of "income over expense" and "cumulative cash flow" (positive or negative). The break-event point is revealed when (or if) at some point in the calendar cash flow becomes positive.

Accounting

Accounting is more than "keeping the books." Events with large budgets or paid staff must be professional about accounting, and that means having an expert on the board or staff, or retaining the services of an accounting firm.

"Financial accounting" involves the preparing and presenting of financial statements as required by law or other external responsibilities. In many jurisdictions it will be a requirement of law to file annual reports to satisfy the requirements of incorporation or not-for-profit status, and to file tax statements whether there is any profit or not. "Generally accepted accounting practices" (GAAP) are used by accountants to compile and present the reports, but these can vary between countries and between profit and not-for-profit organizations.

"Management accounting" involves the preparation and internal use of financial reports to assist in budgeting and forecasting. Solvency ratios are tools in management accounting.

Bookkeeping and Accounting

The starting point for financial control is "keeping the books" and adhering to sound accounting practices. The "books" might be a simple hand-written journal with periodic posting to ledgers for balancing and closing. In accordance with GAAP the numbers can be manually processed into the four main financial statements: income, balance sheet, cash flow, and retained earnings. But increasingly it is necessary to employ computerized information and accounting systems to handle the challenges of money management and accountability.

Forst (1992, p. 90) described the essential elements in such a system. It must record, classify, and summarize financial transactions so information can be used by managers, and for external accounting. An "audit trail" must be present, based on dates and unique codes for transactions, so that transactions can be traced backwards and forwards through source documents and financial statements. Analysis must be able to support budgeting, tax reporting, and financial analysis.

Various accounting system modules are available in modern software (from Forst, 1992, p. 91). The core module is a database that takes the place of the hand-calculated ledger and is built around a "chart of accounts," which provides details on six basic categories: assets, liabilities, equity, revenues, cost of goods sold (or of services), and operating expenses. A double-entry system is used to record debits and credit (in the jargon of accounting, assets are called "debits" and equity plus liabilities are called "credits"). This module can generate the main financial reports. Linked to the chart are optional modules that will prove invaluable to many event managers: accounts receivable and payable, payroll, inventory, fixed assets, job costing.

"Cash accounting" is what most individuals practice when they determine if they have money on hand to pay their bills! But organizations practice "accrual accounting," which recognizes revenue when it is committed to, earned, or is due, and recognizes expenses when committed. This system might confuse some people, but it allows for a complete picture of the event's or organization's financial health. Periodic reconciliations are required, to make certain that commitments become actual cash revenue or expenditures.

The Audit

External accountants are normally retained to provide an annual auditor's report of the organization's financial position. This report expresses the auditor's opinion on whether or not the financial statements conform to GAAP. Without such audits there might very well be suspicion that the organization is hiding something. Furthermore, the external audit is often required to get financing, or to meet incorporation requirements.

Accounting and the One-Time Event

According to McGrane (1995), one-time events are not considered to be "going concerns" and therefore are not subject to GAAP. Although mega-events will certainly employee professional accountants, smaller events might be tempted to ignore proper accounting and control systems.

For the 1996 Atlanta Olympic Games a volunteer audit team was assembled and their efforts could serve as a model for other event projects. They started with a thorough risk analysis and examined the experience of previous games. Experts on construction, royalties/licensing, and television broadcasting were recruited to cover these crucial financial areas. Standardized recording and reporting procedures were created to cover all aspects of the event project. Work before the Games also included establishment of a budget review process, a contracts audit, ticket sale controls, logistical planning audit, and technology capacity review.

During the Games the focus was placed on auditing services, including transportation, food, security and safety, emergency medical car, and cash disbursements. Ticket use was also controlled. Postevent accounting work covered contract termination, reconciliation of accounts, employee termination, and any litigation that emerged. As can be seen, the accounting function is intricately linked with all manner of financial controls.

The Key Financial Statements

Balance Sheet (or Statement of Financial Position)

The "balance sheet" shows assets versus claims on assets—which are called liabilities and equity—on a given date (Andrew & Schmidgall, 1993, p. 29). Both sides of the balance sheet must be kept equal, as in: assets = liabilities + equity.

In a balance sheet the event manager will itemize "current assets" including cash and other assets that will be used or turned into cash within 1 year, such as redeemable bonds. As well, "long-term assets" are listed, including equipment and land at their original cost minus any accumulated depreciation. Assets are not recorded at market value, so there can be a discrepancy between "market" and "book" value. Against these assets are listed all creditors' claims against the organization. "Current liabilities" are those to be repaid within 1 year, such as interest or principle payments on loans, and long-term liabilities, such as the balance of a mortgage or loan. "Equity" consists of the owners' claims, and so can be thought of as "owners equity"; it consists of the original investment, if any, plus "retained earnings." This latter category consists of revenue that has been reinvested in the organization.

The balance sheet demonstrates how all assets of the organization have been or are being paid for. The "worth" of the organization, consisting of its cash, bonds, land, equipment, or whatever, has been created through investments and earnings, plus (in many cases) borrowing.

A balance sheet does not show if any surplus revenues have been paid out as profit or dividends to investors, or invested in other projects. And as a measure of the organization's "worth," the list of tangible assets is misleading unless liabilities are subtracted.

The Income (Profit and Loss, Operations) Statement

"Income statements" summarize the results of operations at a given point in time—usually the end of the fiscal year, or when an audit is completed after the event. This statement tells the reader (e.g., the bank manager, sponsors, grant givers, and board of directors) how well management performed in financial terms. Did we make or lose money? Are we in a healthy position to launch our next event? The formula is: income = revenues – expenses.

"Expenses" occur when things are bought, when major assets are depreciated, or when things that were bought on credit are used. Revenues are matched against expenses whether or not a cash payment is made during the period of time covered by the statement. In the income statement for businesses selling products (including the sale of event admissions or merchandise), expenses represent the "cost of sales." "Income" includes all sales, by cash or credit (Fetters, 1992, 16).

Different formats can be used for the income statement. Many businesses like to show departmental costs and revenues, or these can be appended on separate, more detailed forms.

The "bottom line" of the income statement states the good or bad news in bold terms: profit or loss. The expression "keeping an eye on the bottom line" implies that the event manager is ever-conscious of the results of all decisions on this telling figure. To some, the connotation is that of a penny-pinching, profit-seeking manager, but that is too harsh a position. All managers must be conscious of their organization's current and future financial health.

Pliniussen (1994) said that the income statement for not-for-profit organizations shows revenues raised and expenses incurred, with the surplus or deficit on the bottom line measuring "the organization's ability to raise funds to meet its obligations, rather than the extent of its success or failure" (p. 55). In this context, the manager of an event with a deficit might still be deemed to have done a good job.

In more complex statements, line items from the budget, or departmental summaries are presented. This gives much more information because it shows the costs for every revenue source, and whether they yielded a surplus or loss. If detailed cost–revenue management and accounting procedures have been followed, this is the logical place to summarize the data.

Income (or "profits") from sales and operations can be put back into the organization to sustain and develop it. These "retained earnings" are an important source of equity and might very well be essential to ensure solvency.

The Statement of Cash Flow

This statement reflects sources and use of cash for a period of time, as opposed to the income flows shown on the income statement. It is worth repeating that a supposedly profitable operation (as judged by income) can go bankrupt because its cash flow is out of balance.

Nonoperating actions such as capital acquisitions and dividend payments show up on the cash flow statement. Also, the proceeds of sales are sometimes not collected, generating large amounts under "accounts receivable" that distort the bottom line on the income statement. It must also be noted that while depreciation affects the income statement it is not a cash flow (Andrew & Schmidgall, 1993, p. 35).

The cash flow statement can be used to forecast the organization's ability to generate future cash flows or to meet obligations, and the need for credit. The reasons for differences between net income and cash flows are demonstrated. Cash and noncash aspects of investing and financing are identified. Three main sections are shown in the statement:

investing activity covers capital expenditures or sales; financing activity includes issuing and repaying debt, or paying dividends; operating activities are the sales and related cash expenditures associated with running the event.

Statement of Retained Earnings

When the organizers or owners of the event retain surplus revenue for use in ongoing operations or the next event, these are retained earnings. Dividends paid to owners or investors are also considered to be "retained." Net income figures from the income statement are an integral part of this statement. Note that it reveals not only the total amount of retained earnings but the balances in the retained earnings account at the beginning and end of the year.

For not-for-profit organizations, all earnings (above costs) are "retained" as "net assets" or "fund balance" and thereby increase the organization's equity (Anthony & Young, 1994, p. 406).

Measures of Financial Performance

Solvency

Because many small organizations have cash flow problems it is useful to periodically calculate "solvency," or the ability to meet one's liabilities. Suppose a lender called in a "demand loan" (i.e., one that must be paid in full upon demand): can the organization pay up? The "current ratio" is a measure of solvency, expressed as: current assets/current liabilities.

"Current" means an asset available for disbursement within a year, and a current liability is one that must be paid within a year. For a picture of very short-term solvency (or "liquidity"), a "quick ratio" can be calculated by including only those assets readily convertible to cash. Inventory, such as unsold merchandise, can be included if its quick sale at known prices can be guaranteed. Unfortunately, inventory is often difficult to sell and might have to be heavily discounted. Obviously the current or quick ratio should be greater than 1 or there is no protection against sudden demands on assets. A current ratio of 2:1 or higher would normally be desired.

When current liabilities are subtracted from current assets the result will hopefully be a positive number. This is the "working capital" available to the organization. Many events get their working capital from loans, lines of credit, or grants and sponsorships, rather than from their own accumulated resources. This greatly limits their scope for development.

Return on Investment (ROI) and Return on Assets (ROA)

The term "return on investment" is often used as a short form to ask: "are we getting our money's worth?" In this context, the investor or manager might ask of any event, program, or project, "what is our ROI?". In fact, that is not a simple question to answer.   ROI is, strictly speaking, a ratio that measures financial performance over a specific period of time, expressed as: revenue/total investment.

"Revenue" includes income from sales, grants, sponsorships, or other sources. "Total investment" includes equity (i.e., the original investment), retained earnings (i.e., reinvested revenue), and debt. The goal, of course, is to achieve a high ratio of revenue to investment, at least in terms of traditional business practices. A similar but perhaps more appropriate ratio for not-for-profit events might be "return on assets" (ROA), expressed as: revenue/assets.

This ratio shows what revenue is earned relative to the total assets of the organization at a point in time. Given that all assets have potentially multiple uses (i.e., there is an opportunity cost for putting on an event), it is useful to compare projects or events on how well they use those assets. Of course, this is also a financial performance measure and fails to consider intangible value.

Net Worth

What is our net worth? The board or an owner might want to know this, and if accounts are computerized an instant answer should be possible. It is a calculation of assets minus liabilities, where:

$$assets = cash + accounts\ receivable + depreciated\ capital\ items$$

$$liabilities = accounts\ payable + debt$$

While this yields a measure of financial "worth" at a point in time, an event organization can be healthy even with small net worth if its debt is also small. On the other hand, if most of the "worth" is in capital items like property and equipment, cash flow problems could be imminent.

To the extent that the owner or manager can demonstrate sound financial performance, and a positive benefit to cost ratio in terms of both tangibles and intangibles, the perceived "worth" of the event will increase—and so support should follow. In the section on sponsorships it was also asked, how much is the event worth? The manager who can demonstrate the value of the event to sponsors is likely to gain more or better sponsorship support.

Benefit to Cost Ratio

When evaluating a proposed event, capital expenditure, or program element, the manager can perform an evaluation of all costs and benefits. If the resultant "benefit to cost ratio" is greater than 1, the expenditure might be worthwhile. However, this evaluation is complicated by the question of what to count as costs and benefits. Many intangible costs and benefits surround events, and these can be difficult to compare. As well, there are externalities and opportunity costs to consider.

Financial Controls

Managers must assure that everyone sticks to the agreed-upon budget, that money and resources are not consumed without proper authorization, and that revenues are secure and properly recorded. Control mechanisms are needed, and some of the challenges are rather unique to events. For example, the following situations can arise:

- Staff and volunteers don't share senior manager's concern for sticking to the budget. How can everyone be forced to comply? What happens when an "opportunity" arises that cannot be resisted?
- Cash is generated by on-site sales, attracting the close interest of criminals. How can security be maximized?
- Checks are being written by volunteers, unregulated by senior managers. Who has spending authority?
- Numerous staff and volunteers are raising money, some of which never gets into the event's bank account; most gets to the right place, but it becomes uncertain where it came from.
- Grant-giving agencies and sponsors want to know exactly where their contributions went, but the books don't allow for such detailed analysis.

Controls on Cash and Signing Authority

Cash can easily disappear; hence, a control system is critical. First determine who is allowed to access cash and bank accounts, and who is to be issued a credit card. Ideally, these key people will be bonded (insured) against loss and theft. As a precaution, two signatures of officers can be required on all checks and invoices. The question of who has "signing authority" must be decided by the board or owners.

A numbered receipt book is needed to keep track of cash disbursements. All expenditures should be followed by completion within 30 days of standard expenditure statements. Detailed records are required of all purchase orders and invoices in order to forecast cash flow and determine liabilities.

At many events large sums of cash can flow in an out, requiring very tight handling procedures. Steps can be taken to reduce cash, such as the use of scrip, or requiring credit cards and other forms of prepayment. A safe might be required on site, or frequent (but unpredictable) cash pickup by security guards.

Inventory Control

Keep video or photographic records, as well as detailed inventory lists, especially for expensive equipment. When items are rented or borrowed, extra responsibilities for protecting them should be assigned. All assets should be numbered and identified with tags or, where possible, indelible and unalterable engravings and markings.

During events, a great deal of equipment can become "mobile" and hard to track. This problem makes it necessary to assign specific responsibilities for the handling and disbursement of supplies. A formal system of signing receipts for equipment use might be required.

Reimbursements

Formulate a clear policy on what staff and volunteers can claim as expenses, getting the appropriate authorization, and procedures for reimbursement. Managers who incur an expenditure should be required to secure a second signature (e.g., the CEO or treasurer) to authorize reimbursement to themselves. Expenditures not covered by detailed budget forecasts can present problems, so all personnel must know their spending limitations.

Credit

Suppliers want to be paid within 30 or 60 days of delivery, and services often require payment on the spot. Because of the cash flow peculiarities of many events, this often creates a problem. One solution is to arrange for credit with suppliers and services, building up a trust relationship.

The need for control comes from the risk of runaway credit, late and otherwise unexpected invoices, or sudden demands for immediate payment. Senior managers must be on top of all credit arrangements and work the details into cash flow forecasts. Alternatively, paying for everything in cash by way of a single line of credit can simplify things greatly.

Ticketing

Events selling tickets should ensure that ticket stubs containing the same consecutive numbers are retained and that each sale gets recorded in a ledger (Geier, 1993). Unsold tickets must be saved for future tax audits.

Complimentary tickets must be tightly controlled, especially if they entail reserved seating or other benefits. Only key managers or directors should be authorized to distribute complimentary tickets, and each one should be recorded.

Procedures are also needed for reselling returned tickets and refunding the customer. When group sales are important, time and amount limits are imposed on refunds, which means that large numbers of tickets get returned as the event approaches. Computerized ticketing permits better control and auditing of sales.

Charitable Receipts

Registered charities can issue tax receipts for donations. If a part of a ticket price or purchases is considered to be a donation, this amount must be specified. Receipts will likely require authorized signatures. Is the event organizer required to charge sales, goods and services, or other taxes? Check all applicable laws regarding this important responsibility.

Contracts

"Contracts" are agreements enforceable by law, covering arrangements and commitments between two or more parties. Event managers will likely enter into contractual arrangements with many parties, including sponsors, suppliers, vendors, entertainers, insurance companies, lending institutions, and others. The absence of contracts can greatly increase risks of financial losses. Lawyers are not always required for preparing and implementing contracts, but in many cases it is wise to take legal advice and use standard (or approved) forms.

A contract can be said to exist when something is offered and accepted (in writing or verbally, with witnesses), its purpose and provisions are legal, terms are specified and clear, there is valuable consideration (payment in some form), its intention is understood, and both parties have the capacity to contract (i.e., parties know what they are doing and can deliver on promises).

Contracts are often based on negotiation, but events can offer take-it-or-leave-it contracts to vendors and suppliers if their bargaining power is great. Venues and suppliers might employ the same strategy with events! According to Catherwood and Van Kirk (1992), standard contract elements consist of:

- specification of the agreeing parties,
- purpose of the contract;
- duration of the contract;
- terms;
- signatures;
- witnesses and date signed.

The contract "terms" are the heart of the agreement. These are specifications of:

- responsibilities or obligations of the agreeing parties;
- considerations (financial or other) to be received by all parties;
- liability for risks, insurance coverage, etc.;
- rights to amend, extend, or terminate the agreement;
- penalties for noncompliance or cancellation compensation.

Study Questions

- Whose responsibility is it to generate revenue?
- What have ethics got to do with generating revenue?
- What are some of the potential costs and problems associated with fund raising, obtaining grants, and merchandizing?
- What are the various optional pricing strategies an event can use for admission?
- Define fixed and marginal costs and give examples for an event.
- Be able to calculate the break-even point for an event with fixed and variable costs.
- Why is sponsorship vital to most events? Who sponsors events, and why?
- What are sponsorship platforms?
- Describe the essential ingredients in sponsor management.
- Outline the Volvo philosophy and strategy for sponsorship of events.

- Why is the budget a planning tool?
- What are typical cash flow problems for events and how can they be managed?
- What must the event manager do to control costs and protect assets?

Advanced Study Questions

- Describe a comprehensive revenue plan for an event. What are the relative advantages and disadvantages of each potential source of revenue?
- Through research, determine the sponsorship criteria and application process of several potential sponsors for an event. Determine the "fit" between potential sponsors and the event.
- Develop a detailed sponsorship proposal for an event and test it on a real potential sponsor.
- For an existing event, show how cost centers can be matched by revenue streams. Use this in developing both a capital and operating budget.
- Examine the finances and develop an appropriate set of financial performance measures for an existing event.

Chapter 10

Safety, Health, Risk Management, and Security

Learning Objectives:

- Understand the unique risks associated with event planning and production.
- Be able to develop and implement comprehensive health and safety, and risk management plans.
- Know how to achieve effective security for events and venues.
- Be able to cope with emergencies through crisis management and contingency planning.
- Understand the nature and roles of legal contracts.

Special Hazards and Threats Associated With Events

The risks associated with event production are many, and potentially severe in their consequences. Consider the following serious risks:

- The audience at a rock concert surges toward the stage, crushing to death several young people.
- Football fans riot in the streets before and after the game, causing a great amount of property damage.
- a drunk patron causes a fatal car accident on the way home.
- Food from one supplier is contaminated, resulting in numerous illnesses.

Those examples focus on the event guest; but also think of all the health and safety hazards that staff and volunteers face, and include all the potential legal threats and financial losses an event organization could encounter. Finally, think of negative social and environmental impacts as risks. All these potential problems have to be anticipated and managed.

"Safety and health management" aims to ensure that all event participants and attendees, as well as those affected by an event, are protected from threats to their health and safety. It is people focused, and includes the very important crowd management and security tasks.

"Risk management" is closely related, and can be defined as the process of anticipating, preventing, or minimizing potential costs, losses, or problems for the event, organization, partners, and guests. Ask the question: "what is at risk?" Is it the loss of money, reputation, and survival of the event and its organizers, or personal safety and health?

Identification of "threats" or "hazards" is a necessary part of risk management. They can be thought of as something that can go wrong, cause an accident, or interfere with the event and its organization. For example, these are all hazards of threats or hazards: poisonous snakes, bad weather, dangerous equipment, overcrowding, inadequate financial controls, poorly trained staff, terrorist attacks, criminals, fire, disruption to essential services. The potential risks associated with weather, for example, include: cancellation and resultant financial losses, unhappy customers, lightning strikes, wind damage, flooding, and resulting lawsuits.

Risks can generally be identified through analysis and common sense, but there is a subjective element as well. Some managers or stakeholders might have quite different perspectives on what risks are important. There is also a big difference between hazards to life and property and those that threaten public relations and customer satisfaction, those that affect organizational viability (like a lawsuit), and those that result in mere inconveniences.

Furthermore, some risks are internal to the organization and some are external. A personal injury does not necessarily directly affect the organizers, but could result in a lawsuit and bad publicity. Noise, erosion, and pollution might be caused by an event but the costs are borne by the community at large.

Protests and Terrorism

Events are ever-popular targets for protesters and even terrorists who believe that gaining attention for their views is justification for disrupting or harming the lives and businesses of others. Some of the protesters are skilled at manipulating the media, creating an atmosphere that fosters civil disobedience, and provoking conflict with authorities. Others use their talents to foster peaceful and even festive demonstrations.

After September 11, 2001, people were afraid to assemble or even appear in public places. While that fear diminishes with time, all attraction and event managers had to adjust their thinking and develop better security systems. The bigger the event, and the more media coverage it receives, the more likely it is that it will be targeted by criminals, prostitutes, demonstrators, or terrorists.

Crowds and Traffic

Crowd behavior must be taken into account when planning the event and its setting. Large crowds in themselves are not necessarily problematic, but large crowds combined with certain management or site deficiencies can spell disaster. Security, health, and comfort problems are magnified greatly as the size of a crowd increases, particularly if the site and management systems were geared to a smaller crowd. Under certain conditions, crowd behavior can become unruly. Traffic increases with crowd size and presents a number of logistical, legal, and safety issues.

Celebration and Revelry

Whenever one group or community celebrates some aspect of its culture and value system, others might object and protest. In part this is a challenge for media and stakeholder relations, but it also can be a serious enough concern to require reconsideration of the event theme.

And celebration sometimes turns into revelry and lawlessness. There are from time to time events that are so closely associated with revelry that the host community decides to shut them down, or a major repositioning strategy might be necessitated.

Inexperienced Management and Volunteers

When training is inadequate, especially among volunteers recruited at the last minute, problems are simply waiting to happen. One-time events are very risky if the organizers are inexperienced and do not seek competent advice. Events promoted by outsiders can generate special risks for unwary communities—many have been suckered by promises of big revenues or instant tourist attractions. Security must be taken seriously, as inadequate security systems and personnel can actually cause problems, such as by improper responses to dangerous situations. Inadequate on-site communications poses special problems, especially to the security system but also to crowd control and customer satisfaction.

Activities

Competitive sports, rodeos, events serving alcohol, thrill rides, and other event-specific activities often carry their own special risks. Hazards to persons translate into potential financial risks for organizers, especially if organizers can be shown to have been negligent in identifying and preventing the hazards. Even sedate music festivals contain hidden risks, such as electrical shocks from sound systems. No event is immune, so a risk audit must always be undertaken.

Insurance—the cost or absence of it—increasingly dictates whether or not dangerous activities can be held at special events.

Animals

Whether they are on display (e.g., the circus or petting farms) or part of the event (the rodeo) there are inherent health and physical dangers to animals and humans plus the likelihood of animal-rights protests.

Health Hazards

Health hazards abound at many events. Fireworks present the risk of uncontrolled explosions, and the predictable nuisance or danger caused by smoke and noise. Health must be the primary concern with all food suppliers. Weather can be a challenge, with heat exhaustion and dehydration risks (water and cooling stations might be required).

Infectious diseases are a growing risk, given the extent of international travel. Infection might originate with water, food, animals, or the interaction of many humans. Common accidents can be anticipated, especially falling and scraping.

Crime

Theft from guests, suppliers, or the organizers must be considered, as well as theft by staff and volunteers. Sexual harassment and assault is an issue, especially in crowds where drinking or drugs are found. Barker, Page, and Meyer (2003) examined the link between crime and events, and conducted research on this topic at the America's Cup event in Auckland. They concluded that overseas event tourists are likely to have higher concerns about crime and safety, and that the presence of police is an important factor shaping visitor perceptions. Events can also cause a shift in criminal activities, related to the concentration of police and crowds in certain areas.

Financial Losses

Financial controls, discussed earlier, are essential to preventing losses. But many events cannot be produced without acceptance of some degree of financial risk. Mega-events in particular entail major financial risks, as witnessed by a number of spectacular financial failures.

Alcohol

Events featuring alcohol consumption can foster a feeling among some patrons that anything goes. Even when consumption is regulated and overindulgence is not a problem, events can still face lawsuits arising from uncontrolled underage drinking (see Emmets, 1995, p. 67). Consequently, every event serving alcohol (or likely to attract drinkers) needs an alcohol risk management system.

In British Columbia (British Columbia Ministry of Attorney General, 1992, p. 11) a public inquiry into problems at special events revealed that alcohol was the top public-raised issue, including the operation of beer gardens, underage drinking, the transport of alcohol, inadequate fines for violators, and unruly behavior due to drinking. Inadequate site control and the checking of cars and persons for liquor were also problems identified. Additional costs and risks associated with alcohol consumption include:

- personal injuries and criminal acts owing to drunkenness;
- additional insurance costs against the possibility of law suits (e.g., if the event is held partially or wholly responsible for an accident, injury, or criminal act by serving alcohol);
- additional security and clean-up costs;
- major financial losses arising from law suits;
- vandalism;
- image problems and resultant lost patronage;
- attracting the wrong types; repelling families and other segments.

Target Markets

Who is being attracted to the event? Sometimes a particular segment will cause problems because of their habits or expectations, whereas in other settings it is the combination of incompatible segments that leads to problems. Attracting tourists, especially those from different cultures, poses certain risks. Will information about health, safety, rules, and hazards be understood by all customers?

The Setting

Permanent facilities usually have the bugs worked out and risks are already identified, whereas temporary sites might contain hidden hazards. Assessment of location and site suitability must contain a thorough evaluation of potential risks. Knowing all building codes and standards is necessary to avoid site-related risks. Accessibility and capability to handle emergency responses of various kinds is a critical risk area. What happens if there is a fire, a riot, a heart attack?

Vulnerability to weather is a major factor when choosing locations and designing venues. Are there adequate provisions for bad weather? One music-in-the-park type of event had a contingency plan in case it threatened rain on the day of the event. Organizers that morning were in a quandary because the forecast was for rain, but it was not raining early in the morning. It was decided to move the main entertainment into the back-up facility, which was generally considered to be inadequate. The results: it did not rain; many customers were turned away due to capacity limits; beer sales soared because of heat and high humidity in the temporary structure. What else could have been done?

Quality Control

Quality control is often difficult owing to the occasional or one-time nature of many events. Poor quality poses financial risks and could exacerbate other problems, especially with regard to dissatisfied customers.

The Risk Manager

Risk management has to pervade the entire organization from top to bottom—every staff person, volunteer, and participant has responsibility. The event manager or CEO of the organization in charge has primary responsibility, but might designate specific risk management tasks to a professional. Often this person will have a security or law enforcement background, for the simple reason that they are trained and experienced in preventing crimes, coping with all kinds of emergencies, and handling difficult situations as they occur. Depending on the event, the appropriate risk manager might be less involved with security and more with health and safety issues, crowd control, or financial controls.

Event venues need permanent security and risk management personnel, including sport facilities, convention and exhibition centers, art and cultural centers. Every event held in the facility, as well as its ongoing security, requires conformity to overall policies and procedures. For example, certain types of events, exhibits, or acts might be precluded from the facility. The event risk manager can, to a degree, rely on permanent measures to ensure that individual events are safe and secure. But individual events will always present new challenges.

Peter Tarlow (2002, p. 34), author of the book *Event Risk Management and Safety*, advocated the application of "Gemba Kaizen" to the risk manager's job. This Japanese approach requires the manager to avoid routines that might lead to errors and instead to seek constant improvements.

A necessary starting point is information, specifically how it is obtained and processed. The risk manager requires detailed understanding of the event, and a constant flow of information about how it is being planned and produced. Direct observation will be required, plus established monitoring and reporting procedures. Tarlow also advocated an approach to risk management that views it not as a necessary evil but an integral part of event planning and management. Risk managers should not stifle innovation, but help foster creativity and even help market the event as safe and worry free.

The Health and Safety Plan

Responsibility for health and safety starts with the event owners or board of directors and extends through all management functions. In larger events, and at event venues, a specific manger or "safety officer" might be required. This work is closely related to risk management and security.

A very useful manual ("The Event Safety Guide," revised 1999) on health and safety planning for music events has been prepared in the UK by the Health and Safety Executive of their central government. In the UK and other jurisdictions it is requirement of law for many events and facilities to produce a policy and plan for health and safety, and there are government inspectors to ensure compliance with all pertinent laws and regulations.

Every type of event and event setting requires such a plan, and the general elements of the planning /management process include:

- commitment at all levels to health and safety (make it part of the event mission statement);

- ongoing risk assessment (what are the threats?);
- health a safety policy and procedures;
- management systems to implement the policy and procedures, including monitoring and enforcement mechanisms;
- evaluation and revision process.

Health and safety management must occur over the full "life cycle" of the event, starting with its concept stage and ending only with termination of the event organization. Consider the different issues that arise at each stage:

- Concept: does the event entail specific health and safety risks? Are they acceptable?
- Long-range planning: includes risk assessment.
- Site or facility development: construction and delivery hazards; competence of the contractors and the workforce; quality and reliability of the infrastructure; impacts on the environment and community.
- Staffing: hiring the right people; health and safety training for staff and volunteers.
- The event: supervision of food and beverage, sanitation, and other essential services; crowd and traffic management; security; emergency procedures; comfort and health stations and related personnel.
- Shut-down and termination: deconstruction and materials removal; residual site.
- Contamination and clean up; site security; final evaluations.

What Should A Health and Safety Plan Cover?

First identify all pertinent laws and regulations, in part through consultations with the authorities who issue permits or make inspections (e.g., police, fire, health, emergency response, building inspection). Advice from insurance companies can be invaluable, and do not forget staff, volunteers, and unions as sources of experience and ideas.

Specific concerns include:

- Site or facility design and infrastructure: site suitability; signage; crowd management; fencing and other barriers; safety and health hazards eliminated (congestion points, locked exits, electricity, equipment); food and water cleanliness and availability; vehicle–pedestrian segregation; design capacity; noise and light; electricity; drainage; separation of crowds from emergency and health facilities; observation points for monitoring the audience and site conditions; temporary versus permanent seating; fire hazards eliminated (chemicals, rags and garbage, wood); fire safety assured (test smoke detectors, sprinklers, water hydrants and hoses); fire lanes: kept open, and each structure is within easy access (50 meters); positioning of flammable materials and gases; food storage; waste disposal and recycling; -sanitation, water cleanliness.
- Temporary installations and services: as their supply and supervision are not always predictable, it is essential for all suppliers/contractors to be given contractual responsibilities and limits, and for the event or venue managers to supervise them.
- Comfort and health stations (and related information).
- Crowd management; behavioral rules and enforcement.
- Staff and volunteer training; communication of risks and hazards to employees

and volunteers, and to attendees and other participants; developing safe work procedures and habits.

- Accessibility and evacuation; emergency routes and exits; safe gathering places.
- Standards (targets and requirements).
- Availability of emergency services on site (e.g., fire-fighting equipment).
- Emergency broadcast warning system (adequacy for large, noisy crowds?).
- Keeping aisles and exits open at all times.

Monitoring and Evaluation

"Monitoring" has two distinct forms: active and reactive. Active monitoring consists of inspections and checking documents for breaches of laws or rules. Reactive monitoring occurs when there is a problem, so "incident reports" are a necessary part of this process. When the event is over, or at specific stages during a longer event, all the documentation from monitoring feeds into formal evaluations.

Design Capacity

Indoor venues will have an assigned capacity, with the maximum number of persons determined in advance by fire or other authorities. For outdoor concert sites, the Health and Safety Executive (1999) suggested 0.5 square meters be available per person. An additional technical factor is the ease of entry and exit. Flow rates for entrances and exits should be estimated, both for normal and emergency conditions, resulting in an estimate of the "minimum evacuation time." Additional consideration must be given to persons with special accessibility needs, such as those in wheelchairs or who must be carried (e.g., babies).

Technical risk factors will lead to designation of a safe capacity, and on this point it is undoubtedly better to err on the side of safety than to attempt to cram more people into a venue.

Beyond the technical risk considerations, organizers should also assure that the event experience is not diminished by overcrowding the site. For example, will everyone in a huge audience be able to see and hear performers? Will rubbing shoulders with other event-goers add to the atmosphere?

Absolute, predefined limits: Are there legal fire or safety limits to the facilities? Is seating reserved? Is access restricted to presold tickets?

Limits arising from accessibility: Hhow many convenient parking spaces are available? What is the maximum number of arrivals by way of public or specially provided transport?

Economic considerations: What is the break-even number? At what point will variable costs exceed profit margins (if applicable)?

Previous experience and similar events: expert opinion on maximum and optimum capacity; customer feedback and satisfaction levels; evaluation of incidents.

Judgments considering guest or participant comfort and safety: desired quality of experience; the anticipated audience (age, party composition, expectations).

Emergency Response

Johnson (n.d., p. 71) called for all events to have a written "emergency action plan" to ensure that staff and volunteers will respond promptly and adequately to both predictable and unusual problems. Instructions should be posted in all appropriate areas so that everyone has access to emergency telephone numbers and other procedures.

Training by police and fire departments can probably be arranged for most events. Fire marshals will in any event have to inspect most sites regularly for conformance to public safety codes. Also, get electricians and other technical experts to advise and train in other safety procedures. First aid training can be obtained from organizations like St. John's Ambulance, as this group is often found at events to provide emergency services.

A number of other important measures include:

- provision of smoke detectors and fire extinguishers;
- provision of first-aid kits, stretchers, and nursing stations;
- readily available communication devices;
- on-site or on-call police, fire, ambulance services;
- emergency lighting.

Emergency evacuation of an event is always a possibility and has to be planned for and rehearsed. Under what circumstances will organizers or officials order a crowd to evacuate? Any smell of smoke, or only a confirmed fire that cannot be extinguished immediately? A bomb threat? Violent incident? And how the evacuation occurs is important, or it could result in more harm than good. An uninformed crowd can quickly become a panicky mob.

Risk Management

This section outlines the risk management process and contents of a risk management plan.

Identification of Risk Fields

One of the foundations of risk management is "forseeability," and it is a key element in determining negligence (Ammon & Fried, 1998). Event and facility managers must draw on past experience, the experience of others, and systematic determination of possibility risks. They may occur in each of these major risk "fields":

Financial: loss of revenue sources, theft and loss of assets, including data, name, and logos; costs exceeding projections; law suits and other unanticipated costs.

Management: the risk of goal displacement, takeovers, or management failure.

Health and safety hazards for organizers, participants, guests, and the general public: accidents (at and outside the event), health problems, fire, crime, terrorism, social disturbances, and unanticipated emergencies.

Environmental: negative impacts on the environment, community, and economy; natural hazards (earthquakes, floods, etc.).

Identification of Specific Risks, and the Consequences, Within Each Field

The "task analysis" performed for project planning provides a starting point for managers and staff to identify and evaluate risks. Each task requires certain actions, sometimes physical and sometimes mental, which all have potential implications. As the event takes shape and more detail is added to the task breakdown and schedule, greater focus will be possible on risks.

Scenario-making is definitely useful, and can be done quite well at staff meetings. Start with known or possible problems and risks (e.g., what happened at other events?) and work backwards to see how they can be avoided. This exercise will help shape the task analysis, schedule, and program. Development of a risk evaluation form or spreadsheet for each event and subunit is recommended.

Assignment of the Probability of Risks Occurring

Evaluate the probability of occurrence. How likely is it that each risk will materialize? Group the risks into high, medium, and low probability categories, but do not assume that low probability hazards will not occur!

Estimation of the Potential Magnitude of Impacts

Not all risks will necessarily result in losses or problems, so try to anticipate the positive and negative outcomes of each potential circumstance and the magnitude of the consequence. Those with potential negative and severe consequences require special consideration. Within each risk field major disasters could occur, and they should be ranked according to potential magnitude, from multiple perspectives. Protecting the organization and its assets might come into conflict with protecting the environment or the public, so beware of bias in this assessment.

Ranking of Risks, From High to Low Priority

Which risks have to be dealt with? Combine the probability of occurrence with evaluation of the potential severity of each, especially those for which the organizers will likely be held responsible. High-priority risks have to be dealt with at once. Figure 10.1 illustrates a risk prioritization matrix.

Identification of Strategic Options to Deal With Risks and Selection of Appropriate Strategies

According to Berlonghi (1990) there are several generic strategies for events to follow.

Avoidance: Managers must seek to anticipate risks, determine their probability of occurrence, severity of their impacts, and ways to avoid or reduce them. Where risks are too great, or cannot be handled, the hazard (such as a program activity or venue) should be eliminated.

Reduction: Some hazards can be minimized or kept to an acceptable level through better management, training, or operations. In truth, most event managers live with certain risks, but this decision should not be taken without some form of ongoing assessment and reduction strategy being in place.

Probability / Severity of Impact	Almost Certain To Occur	Might Occur	Very Unlikely
Severe Impact	**HIGHEST PRIORITY**		
Moderate Impact			
Low Impact			**LOWEST PRIORITY**

Figure 10.1. Risk prioritization matrix.

Reduce the severity of damage or losses: Assuming that problems will occur, the manager must be prepared to cope. The event must have emergency response procedures. Thefts occur, but the number and severity can be minimized. Weather is unpredictable, so contingency plans are necessary.

Diffusion: Spreading risks among stakeholders or over time and space can be effective. For example, if sponsors or other organizations are involved, it is logical that risks should be spread among all parties, rather than being absorbed by the event organization alone. However, logic might not convince the other parties to accept a share of risks. Vendors and suppliers can usually be required to share in the risk management process and provide their own insurance.

Re-allocation: In some cases the risks can be re-allocated completely, as where a parent body or municipality absorbs risks for specific events. Any group under contract to the event can be required to absorb their own risks and take out independent or co-insurance.

Insurance: Insurance is necessary to protect against risks that materialize. Insurance companies increasingly demand that managers demonstrate that they have a risk management strategy in place, and these companies might even give appropriate advice. Liability laws and the need for types and amounts of insurance vary widely among countries and cannot be generalized. Event managers have an obligation to investigate their needs carefully, or to rely on government agencies or event associations to provide advice.

Rea (n.d.) advised that events need three basic types of insurance coverage. Liability covers the risks of being sued or otherwise held responsible for damage. General liability insurance is common, but other types might be required to protect the directors, staff and volunteers. Liability insurance is almost always required on vehicles. Property insurance is needed to protect against loss and theft. Many events also take out insurance to protect themselves financially, including insurance against bad weather, cancellation of the event, or other types of business interruption.

Wojcik (2003) advised that venue owners generally require those leasing a facility for an event to enter into hold harmless and indemnification agreements (to protect the owners), and to buy their own liability insurance, especially when alcohol is served. The amount of risk involved can determine the cost of this kind of insurance.

Consider the following items that might require special insurance:

- specific hazards (including bad weather and cancellation; third-party liquor liability);
- specified liabilities (e.g., loss of life, injury, financial loss);
- specified property (on site and off);
- specified persons and groups (e.g., staff, volunteers, participants, audience, bystanders);
- specified venues;
- bonding key employees (against the possibility of loss or theft);
- errors and omissions (for directors and professional staff);
- protection of intellectual property;
- for sports: antidoping; restraint of trade or status for athletes and teams;
- merchandizing.

Managers should consult insurance companies or brokers to make certain they understand issues related to insurance. Ask insurance companies what services are provided (e.g., risk assessment). Check the company's reliability and reputation, and discuss how the event's past history might limit coverage or increase rates.

Vigilance is demanded when obtaining insurance. Items might be covered, but under what circumstances? Does the event have to undertake certain preventative actions? Exactly what losses are covered? Note exclusions and policy limits. The time period of coverage must be stipulated, along with renewal procedures. Schachner (1994) advised that low-bid insurers might not do everything they promise, so check contracts carefully.

Costs to the insured can be high, so it is common practice to require vendors, performers, and other event participants to obtain their own insurance. But venue managers often require events leasing the premises to sign "hold harmless" clauses in their contracts, which passes the risk to the event. Suppliers are often required to insure the products they supply to the event as to quantity and quality specified and health and safety regarding the product's use. Co-insured "riders" can be demanded of all contractors to make certain the event is named in the contractor's insurance.

The IFA and Argonne Productions (1992) advised that events cannot be protected against their own negligence. But to transfer or remove liability a number of actions can be taken, including the hiring of insured professionals, liability insurance covering the event, and the use of waivers, release and consent forms (samples are provided in that publication) from everyone who can place the organizers at risk.

For example, participants in any risky activity can be asked to sign a form stating they understand and willingly accept responsibility for any resultant injury or loss. This will not necessarily protect the organization against a lawsuit based on negligence (i.e., where the organization did not take due care in protecting its customers or guests).

Implementation of Strategies and Evaluation of Results

Implement strategies by formulating an action plan, training appropriate staff and volunteers, and rehearsing crucial operations (e.g., emergency response). Establish a formal evaluation system for the event and assign responsibilities. Aim to constantly improve the process.

Synergistic and Cascading Risks (Worst-Case Scenarios)

Risk evaluators should pay particular attention to two special circumstances. When two or more incidents occur together their effect might be "synergistic" (i.e., much more problematic than if the incidents occurred separately). Consider a festival opening its gates to a rush of patrons anxious to obtain the best (nonreserved) seating. One person slips and is injured under someone else's feet. This problem should be manageable. But what happens when a barrier collapses from crowd pressure at the same time as the person falls, and now it is impossible to reach the injured party because the planned emergency routes are blocked? Two problems together spell much more serious consequences.

Now imagine an indoor exhibition hall full of customers when the power fails. Normally, a backup system cuts in immediately. Now consider what happens if a major water pipe breaks, first shorting out the main and backup power, then flooding the floor and causing numerous patrons (who are in the dark) to panic and flee the area! This "cascading" disaster scenario is worse than any one incident on its own.

Alcohol Risk Management

According to Emmets (1992, p. 68) the event must take responsibility for a patron's drinking, as the law (at least in the US) will generally place that burden on the event anyway. "Reasonable care" must be taken to ensure that, amongst other potential risks:

- no one is served a potentially dangerous amount of alcohol;
- no one under the legal age gets served;
- alcohol is not brought into the venue or consumed outside approved areas;
- drinking does not lead to crowd behavior problems;
- hazards are not created (such as broken glass);
- drinkers do not drive automobiles away from the event;
- drinkers leave the grounds safely.

As well, the manager wants to avoid having the event's image tarnished by alcohol-related problems while at the same time attaining revenue targets. A comprehensive "alcohol risk audit" should cover:

- the concessions or settings where drinking occurs;
- security and medical personnel and services as they relate to drinking;
- the servers (bartenders) and their training/professionalism;
- how the event is promoted; its image;
- crowd management and emergency response systems;
- admissions procedures;
- reaction to, and reporting of, incidents.

Techniques for Effective Alcohol Management (TEAM) was developed by the Public Health Foundation and is widely implemented. It has been endorsed and adopted by IAAM. Training for Intervention Procedures by Servers of Alcohol (TIPS) is an alternative and is available from the Miller Brewing Company.

Home Team is a project of the Public Health Foundation of Los Angeles County, California. They provide alcohol risk audits and training program for venues and events, wherever alcohol is served. As consultants, they review existing policies and procedures, interview key personnel and patrons, observe the event and its operations, prepare documentation, launch awareness and education campaigns, and undertake training. They can also determine the level of implementation of policies, determine liabilities, and advise on emergency preparedness and response. If this type of organization does not exist in your area, try to get one established.

A number of specific actions can be taken, based on the risk audit:

- instruct security in how to screen patrons, confiscate illegal substances of all kinds, and deal with the intoxicated ("detox" centers might be required where incbriated patrons can be given time and coffee/food for a period of time);
- require patrons to show proof of age;
- reduce the amount served per unit (e.g., smaller cups);
- limit the number of drinks any one patron can purchase;
- use only cash bars, no free drinks;
- reduce the hours of serving alcohol; quit early, well before the event ends;
- increase the waiting time for alcohol (e.g., restrict the number of outlets);
- train servers in how to recognize danger signals and when to refuse additional purchases;
- take car keys from the inebriated; provide an alternative means for getting home;
- employ a "designated driver" program in which one driver per group is encouraged to avoid alcohol; sponsors might be willing to provide free soft drinks;
- raise the price of alcoholic beverages to discourage overconsumption (also, do an analysis to determine if increased prices can generate more revenue);

- recover all glass and metal beverage containers for recycling or serve beverages only in plastic, recyclable cups;
- educate the public, and advise the patrons on site of all policies and regulations through obvious signs or other means;
- define the areas in which it is to be served (many jurisdictions require segregation);
- security assigned to beverage areas should be able to check for identification to prevent underage drinking, handle rowdy customers, and regulate the flow of people;
- have security patrols check parking lots and other areas where illegal consumption might be occurring;
- serve alcohol only with food (beware: salty snack food will encourage more drinking);
- employ marketing methods to position the event as a peaceful leisure opportunity and discourage unwanted segments.

To protect the event, its organizers, sponsors, participants, staff, and volunteers, written policies and procedures are required for all risk areas. Furthermore, policies are useless unless training is undertaken, evaluation completed, and the system constantly improved. Boese (n.d.) explained how the program called TIPS can be used to help reduce problems at events.

The Learning Organization and Risk Management

Event managers need to create a learning organization—one that learns from its mistakes as well as successes, and institutionalizes these lessons in its planning and management systems. In the context of risk management, O'Toole and Mikolaitis (2002, p. 137) refer to the "risk resilient" organization as one that is characterized by (among other things) recognition of the importance of having all staff members manage risk, and full integration of risk management in all aspects of event planning and management—including thorough documentation. They also suggest that "constructive insubordination" be encouraged to ensure that no one ignores a potential risk.

Crowd Management and Control

Crowds do not always listen to authority (Tarlow, 2002, p. 94). Once part of a mob, even ordinary, law-abiding people can be swept up in hooliganism or riots, having lost their sense of individualism and their normal inhibitions. Abbott and Geddie (2000) explained that "crowd management" is aimed at the facilitation and movement of crowds, whereas "crowd control" applies to actions taken when a crowd behaves badly or gets into trouble. Management involves planning, training, forming scenarios, and research; control includes decision-making processes based on situation models to react effectively to a variety of potential problems and risks.

The crowd control process involves three stages:

- precrisis or preevent: prevention and contingency planning;
- crisis stage: implement contingency plans; document situations and responses;
- postcrisis stage: evaluation.

There are a number of important considerations for event managers:

- effectiveness of all communications;
- ushering and security;
- assessing different event conditions (risks) including alcohol, drugs, noise, smoke, the venue, program;
- assessing different audiences (risks) including sport fans, and their behavior;
- hiring or training professional managers and legal counsel (on-site legal counsel recommended);
- festival seating versus reserved;
- queuing and ticketing; punctuality; time of day; staggered or all at once?;
- advance versus on-site ticketing; price of entry (avoid making change); separate wickets for cash sales and entry for those with tickets;
- exiting: all at once or staggered?;
- communications;
- signage and information; sound system;
- staffing: identification, placement, roles;
- lighting: emergency and mood;
- restricted areas and access badges; security.

Crowd Profile and Warning Signs

Is the mix of people, management, setting, and other environmental factors potentially dangerous? Tarlow (2002, p. 98) reported on results from a conference of representatives from beach communities that identified loss of control with a number of key factors: mainly young people, good weather, alcohol, boredom, inadequate security, and darkness. In other words, that is a recipe for trouble. Warning signs, according to Tarlow, include the following:

- emergence of a drinking-party atmosphere;
- introduction of alcohol or drugs into a crowd;
- loss of individualism and inhibitions;
- fire starting;
- division into opposing factions;
- the presence of weapons.

Security

To be effective in potentially difficult situations, security has to be visible in sufficient strength and acting with appropriate professionalism. At some events volunteers in T-shirts printed "staff" might suffice, but at others uniformed police officers might be required. In fact, both on- and off-duty police officers often serve as security at events. There are many security firms available, although not all specialize in events and crowd control. Appropriate ones will offer advice on event management to avoid problems, trained (and where necessary) bonded security staff, and appropriate vehicles and equipment.

Security Plan

The details of a comprehensive security plan are:

- Purpose: a clear statement of what the plan covers and intends to achieve.
- Objectives or performance standards: specifics targets (e.g., injury and illness prevention).
- Situation analysis: What have we learned from past experience at our event and

similar events? What are the risks (refer to risk management plan)? What resources are available (e.g., budget, personnel, outside help)?

- Organization: Is there a committee or group in charge of the plan?
- Authority and responsibility: Who has overall authority to make decisions and is responsible for the plan?
- Personnel and reporting: What are the staff and/or volunteer positions and their assignments? To whom does each person report?
- Preparation: training; rules and regulations.
- Tasks: see the security checklist (Table 10.1).
- Schedule: assignments and shifts.
- Communications and contingencies: what to do in case of emergencies; who to contact, and how.
- Evaluation and reporting: formal and informal evaluation of effectiveness and costs.
- Plan revisions (e.g., new performance standards, new resources, better training).

Communications

There are some very technical but potentially important communications issues:

- Do all staff, volunteers, participants, and emergency officials have access to and use a common communications channel? (Provide cell phones or walky-talkies.)
- Is nomenclature for site features and signs understood by everyone? (What have you called the safe, emergency assembly points where people go to in case of fire? What does it say or signal on those signs that are supposed to tell people where the toilets are?)
- How do individuals make and respond to onsite communications? (Establish a protocol to avoid any confusion or "noise" that could interfere with important messages.)
- Will all organizers and emergency officials agree on what exactly constitutes an emergency? (Establish a grading system, so that "condition red" means evacuation is necessary, based on predetermined criteria.)
- Are clearly interpreted maps of the site and emergency systems available to everyone in need?
- Do all workers understand exactly who to contact to make a report or seek information?
- Are staff clearly identified and always in positions where they can assist or cope with emergencies?
- Do you have backup power and communications systems, including switch-over protocols so that people know what to do? Is there an emergency, off-site control center?
- Will television cameras facilitate safety and security to the point that potential privacy considerations are secondary? Establish rules for their supervision and use.
- Are records or log entries kept of all important communications, to ensure that decisions are documented fully and information gaps exposed?

Legal Issues

Protecting the event and its various stakeholders from legal problems is an important risk management function. If possible, retain professional legal counsel or get a lawyer to

Table 10.1. Event Security Checklist

Preevent Preparations
  Security plan complete and approved
  Personnel duties and responsibilities assigned
  Reporting and communications channels established and understood by all personnel
  Training complete
  Schedule of event and security duties finalized
  Emergency plans and procedures established and understood by all personnel

Functional Assignments
  Official "stewards" or uniformed police for crowd control
  Parking and traffic control (including surveillance of vehicles)
  Entrance (visibility of security, ticketing, searching customers, checking credentials and
    for banned substances)
  Cash and valuables protection (including escorted money transfers)
  Equipment (lock-up and keys, storage areas, patrols)
  Stage/performer security (including accommodation and transport)
  Perimeter and after-hours patrols
  Customer safety and information (including information and fist-aid posts)
  Command post and communications
  Health and safety inspections (food, beverages, equipment, vehicles)
  Participant/competitor protection (including accommodation and transport)
  Media protection and facilitation (including special provisions for access to restricted ar-
    eas)
  Emergency response teams

Policies and Procedures Needed
  Ticketing or other admission process; guest identification
  Uniforms or other identification of security personnel
  Observation of guests and site (cameras, plain-clothes officers)
  Alcohol risk management
  Banned substances
  Crowd size, movement, and management (e.g., use of signs and barriers)
  Guest age restrictions, behavior, and dress
  Fireworks and lasers (as hazards)
  Evacuation process, signs and exits
  Emergency equipment accessibility
  Lighting and alarm systems
  Hours of operation
  Communication and emergency protocols
  Hazardous materials and systems
  Response to inclement or dangerous weather conditions
  Queuing (e.g., permissible length of line-ups)
  Seating (reserved vs. festival style)
  Ventilation
  Fire prevention

serve on the board or in a legal committee. A standing committee for legal matters is a good idea, with primary responsibilities including:

- know all pertinent laws and regulations, and ensure compliance;
- meet with all pertinent authorities and officials;
- disseminate important legal information;
- develop standard contracts and enforce them.

Contracts

Contracts make agreements and arrangements legally binding between the signatories. In a contract the responsibilities and risks assumed by each party must be specified. Events will often be asked to assume many risks when renting facilities, for example. Suppliers to events can be asked to take responsibility for certain risks such as health and safety arising from their delivery of food and beverage services. The most common types of contract used in the events sector include the following:

- rental of venues and equipment (e.g., audio-visual, tents, vehicles) by the event organizers;
- subcontracted services (e.g., sound technicians and fireworks companies) to the event;
- entertainment contracts (usually through their agents) for the event;
- rental of space and provision of services to exhibitors and meetings/conventions;
- contracts with co-producers or owners of the event;
- sponsorship contractors (made with corporations and agencies);
- advertising (through various media companies, some of whom might be sponsors);
- licensing (selling licensed products or licensing others to sell event-related merchandise);
- VIP or celebrity visits and endorsements.

When selling or buying services, or in renting a facility to others, several pricing options arise that become formal parts of contracts. These can be mixed as the occasion demands.

- Cost-plus: some or all costs of the service provider are absorbed by their clients, and then profit or wages are obtained at a fixed rate or a percentage of sales or revenue; detailed cost and labor audits might become necessary.
- Fixed price: all costs and wages/profits are included in a single price.
- Incentive or profit-sharing: parties agree to divide revenues on a sliding scale so that a larger attendance or greater sales yields a larger share (usually in addition to cost recovery).
- Contingency: additional payments are made when and if certain conditions arise, such as inflation in costs (the longer the planning period the more important this becomes) or where the nature of the service provided cannot be fully specified in advance.

Events or event companies that provide or use standardized services will want the pertinent contracts to be standardized, but in many situations negotiations take place. For highly technical services or agreements, there is no substitute for experience. When faced with unusual conditions, it is wise to bring in an expert for the negotiations, or to have professionals check draft agreements before signing them.

Many event-related contracts include detailed and often technical "specifications" of goods or services to be delivered. Costs will be tied to these specifications, so they have to be precise and well thought out. If an event specifies a mediocre sound system, or fails to state its precise needs in the contract, it is likely to be disappointed with the supplied system. Where an exact technical specification is unavailable or unknown, the contract can specify the level of service that is to be provided, or describe the desired end result in terms that make it clear what is needed. Sometimes it is best to let the suppliers recommend specifications, as they know their equipment and services best, but that embodies a risk of paying more than is necessary. If contracted services are to be "tendered" (i.e., put out for competitive bids), very precise specifications will be essential.

Contracts must be negotiated, written, legally signed, and deposited with all parties. Deviations from the specifications must be detected, and the contract enforced. Regular inspections and reports might be useful.

Waivers and Release Forms

It is usual for facility and recreation providers to require users to read a notice concerning liability and sometimes to sign a waiver. Event managers can use the same tools, especially for sports or any other risky activity. Forms can also cover consent for emergency medical treatment and transport. Expert legal opinion is required, as the law varies, but normally the event producers cannot free themselves of liability arising from negligence. In other words, due diligence is required to identify the risks to customers or participants, and measures must have been taken to eliminate or reduce them. Safety and behavior rules have to be communicated to customers and participants, who must agree to abide by them. For many activities the minimum physical and health conditions necessary to participate should be specified.

Incident Reports

An "incident" is every accident and any other occurrence that could result in loss, damage, injury, or lawsuit. Every incident, whether it looks serious or not, should generate an incident report prepared by a trained staff person or volunteer. These can not only help assess future risks, and help in training, but should reduce liability by documenting the causes and responses. They should include the following:

- date, time, and place;
- reporter(s) (who is writing the report);
- incident and its (possible/likely) causes;
- effects of incident (follow up afterwards);
- witnesses (their statements and contact details);
- actions taken (such as first aid; elimination of any obvious causes);
- evaluation (learn from mistakes; take preventative actions).

Negligence

Negligence should be tested, not assumed. Lawyers and insurance providers can provide expert opinion on what the event producers must do to avoid negligence. A common test is to ask what a reasonable, intelligent person would be expected to do to learn about risks and eliminate or reduce them. What would a patron or participant expect from facility providers and event producers to ensure their health and safety? A serious form of negligence is to cover up known problems. Not meeting lawful standards or codes of practice established by professional associations is another common form of negligence. Placing untrained staff or volunteers in positions where they can create risks, or fail to deal with them effectively, might be considered negligence. Allowing dangerous behavior or processes to continue could be negligent (see the discussion in Sawyer & Smith, 1999).

Study Questions

- What unique risks are associated with events, for organizers, participants, sponsors, guests, and the general public?
- Describe the main elements in a health and safety plan. Include a discussion of how site capacity is important and how it can be determined.
- Outline a risk management plan including generic strategies for dealing with risks.
- What are the main principles of alcohol risk management? What related training is needed for staff and volunteers?
- Describe an appropriate response be event organizers to a common emergency.
- Distinguish between crowd management and crowd control.
- How are communications and security linked?
- Describe the security manager's main responsibilities.
- Why is a legal committee needed?

Advanced Study Questions

- Conduct a health, safety, security, or risk audit of an existing event and make recommendations for improvements.
- What contributions can be made by social-psychology and environmental design to crowd management at events?
- Do you think alcohol should be sold at events? Consider all the pros and cons, and compare the risks to other risks faced by events.

Chapter 11

Marketing

Learning Objectives

- Be able to formulate and implement a comprehensive marketing plan for the organization and the event.
- Be able to use the full marketing mix, including product, place, price, promotions (communications), people, packaging, and programming in developing appropriate strategies.
- Be able to conduct marketing audits on events and destinations.
- Be able to forecast market potential (demand) for events.
- Be able to segment the market to determine appropriate and viable targets.
- Be able to provide the benefits desired by customers and guests.

The Marketing Concept and Marketing Mix

Some people mistakenly equate marketing with selling or promotions. Others define it by reference to the traditional "four Ps" of product, place, price and promotion, but this is not really a definition, just a description of basic marketing elements. Others have defined marketing as the interface between an organization and its environment, thereby stressing both the exchange process wherein consumers purchase products or services, and the need for constant market intelligence.

The notion of an "exchange process" is fundamental to all marketing. This exchange must be voluntary, both for producer and consumer, and mutually beneficial—otherwise the relationship fails. Events produce something of value for the audience, whether entertainment or education, while the audience either pays for the benefits or otherwise justifies and sustains the organization. Events also produce value for sponsors, governments, tourism agencies, and many other stakeholders, so those exchanges are also marketing. Keegan, Moriarty, Duncan, and Paliwoda (1995) stated that "Contemporary marketing is about building relationships. A product, service, brand, or corporation is successful only to the degree that it means something important to the people with whose lives it is linked" (p. xiv).

Many commentators have stressed that developing a customer orientation is the heart of marketing. "Customer orientation" can be defined as: *the process of continuously identifying and meeting the needs and wants of potential and existing customers and clients.*

The most important consequence of adhering to a customer orientation is the constant development of the event to satisfy target markets. But many event producers will object to this orientation if it is carried to an extreme. Many events are service oriented and based on the knowledge or assumption that the event "does good." In this context it is common to think of the audience as clients, and the community at large as the beneficiary. Nevertheless, event managers who ignore audience development and marketing risk serious problems.

Other events, such as meetings and conferences, are produced commercially for clients. The producer of this type of event has a primary relationship with the client and often views the attendees as guests, rather than customers. Principles of quality service management and customer satisfaction are still applicable, but the orientation is somewhat different.

Keegan (1995, p. 5) explained that a strategic approach to marketing emphasizes the management of mutually beneficial relationships and partnerships within the broad organizational environment. Profits, or revenues, are not the end goal but a reward for high performance. In this way marketing is at once (p. 7):

- a concept and philosophy;
- a set of actions (i.e., the marketing mix);
- a business process (i.e., market research and planning).

To Keegan (1995, p. 7), the three great principles of contemporary marketing are:

- create customer value greater than that of competitors;
- create competitive advantage through a more attractive "total offer";
- focus on customer needs and wants.

Based on the above discussion we can develop an appropriate definition of marketing for the events sector, encompassing the notion of a marketing orientation: *Marketing events is the process of employing the marketing mix to attain organizational goals through creating value for customers and other stakeholders. The organization must adopt a marketing orientation which stresses the building of mutually beneficial relationships and the maintenance of competitive advantages.*

This definition should not be confused with "event marketing," as that term is usually used by corporations to describe marketing through sponsorship or production of events. Marketing is always undertaken in the context of fulfilling the event's mandate and goals, whether public service or profit. The more comprehensive its goals, the more challenging marketing events becomes.

The "marketing mix" consists of those elements that the manager can manipulate or influence to achieve goals. Morrison (1995) said there are eight, each beginning with the letter P, and these have been adapted to events in Figure 11.1. The diagram also classifies the components as being "experiential" and "facilitative." This distinction highlights the fact that some marketing elements directly affect the customer's experience at the event.

Product

Many events suffer from a "product orientation"—that is, they try to sell their event with little or no regard for what potential customers need, want, and will pay for. Many event organizations fail to consider alternatives to their marketing mix because they are committed to a single product concept.

Place

This term refers first of all to the location and setting of the event, which can be a particular building, space, set of venues, or a general location such as "downtown." A major

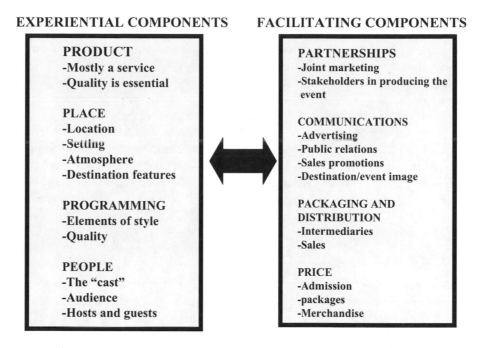

Figure 11.1. The marketing mix for events.

part of this component in the marketing mix is ambience, or atmosphere, and how it is created through design and programming.

"Place" also refers to the distribution of event products, or how they are sold to customers. This is mostly a facilitative component, but if done poorly can negatively affect the customer's enjoyment. In Figure 11.1 distribution is combined with packaging.

Programming

To a built attraction, resort, or community, events are a key programming element for animating the place. But programming within the event is also a marketing decision, especially by way of creating targeted benefits. Various "elements of style" are employed to create unique, attractive programs, and both program and service quality figure prominently in making the event a success.

People

People are an integral part of the marketing mix. First and foremost, the staff and volunteers are usually essential ingredients in making the event a success—they are literally part of the product and can be referred to as "the cast." This fact gives rise to the need for "internal marketing," which is the process of developing team spirit and a customer orientation among staff and volunteers. Customers are also part of the product in the sense that most events cannot take place without them! The interactions between customers, the setting, and the staff/volunteers constitute a large part of the event experience and so cannot be left to chance. We call the management of these processes "interactive marketing." In the context of a destination, host–guest relations in general are important. Whether at an event or external, the hospitality received by visitors directly shapes their experience.

Partnerships

Marketing, especially in the tourism field, often demands the formation of partnerships to engage in "joint marketing" initiatives. Single events often cannot, on their own, achieve their marketing goals. The most common partners will be tourist organizations, governmental agencies such as city promotional offices, and other events. Joint marketing will be different from single-event marketing. While event managers might want to promote their event above all else, joint initiatives will generally have to promote the destination first, and then multiple events. This does not have to replace communications by single events, but they can become more targeted. As well, when packages are jointly marketed, event managers might have to modify their price and even their products to make the packages more attractive. Partnerships are also important in the production of events, as many organizations require direct involvement from other groups. Partnerships and relationship marketing are obviously part of the same process.

Communications (Promotion)

Although "promotion" is a commonly used term, it is more accurate to speak of the "communications mix," which refers to the full range of communications tools including advertising, public relations, and sales promotions. Image building for the event and destination is a related element. There is a tendency to emphasize "promotions," or specific campaigns developed to publicize the event. But the communications mix requires ongoing management and relationship building, not just one-off efforts.

Packaging and Distribution

A package is any combination of elements offered for sale at a single price. Packaging seeks to make the event experience more attractive by lowering costs (compared to buying all the elements singly), maximizing convenience, or providing "value added" in the form of extra features that cannot be obtained otherwise. Destinations can package events with other attractions and services, or events can offer their own—either for a specific event or in conjunction with other events, attractions, and services. Tour companies market diverse packages, so event marketers can seek to influence them to promote specific events more effectively. When selling tickets and event packages the distribution network becomes important. Intermediaries of various types will be required, such as travel agents, tour companies, computerized ticketing agents, and others. Good relationships must be cultivated with packaging partners and intermediaries.

Price

Even events that are nominally "free" impose a price on customers in the form of time, travel costs, or lost opportunities. More specifically, event organizers usually have to set one or more prices for their products, including admission to the event, merchandise, vendor rentals, and sponsorship fees. These latter two categories do not impinge directly on the customer. The price of event-related packages will often be largely outside the control of the event organizers, and this could prove damaging.

Positioning and Branding

An event should have a positive and competitively strong image in the minds of target segments, or preferably the population at large. "Positioning" uses the entire marketing mix to establish the desired image and maintain it, relative to competitor events or other attractions. For example, a fine arts festival might want to be perceived as being not only sophisticated and international in quality (like all the others), but also fun and accessible to the general public.

To test the potential or effectiveness of a positioning strategy, the perceptions and responses of target markets must be researched. In this example, consumers and potential consumers would be asked a series of questions to determine if they do in fact perceive the festival as being just as sophisticated and more accessible than others of its kind. They could be asked to give a score out of 7 to the festival and to comparable events on each of these two dimensions, using a continuum from unsophisticated to very sophisticated and not accessible to very accessible. Results can be plotted on a multidimensional scaling diagram as shown in Figure 11.2. When the average (mean) scores are calculated, those events perceived to be both sophisticated and accessible should be placed in the upper-right quadrant. If your event is not there, a positioning challenge is evident.

"Branding" is a marketing concept based on the use of a name, symbol, or logo to identify a company or unique product. Probably one of the best known brands in the events world is the Olympics and its five-rings logo (owned by the International Olympic Committee). The brand should be an easily recognizable name plus symbol or logo, and in the minds of consumers or the public at large it should ideally stand for the qualities the event wants to be known for—especially those expressed in the positioning strategy for each target segment.

When a brand is fully developed it can be compared to other brands, so that an event like the Calgary Stampede, with a well-established brand, could be compared not only to other events but to other brands. Why is that useful? One practical application of brand

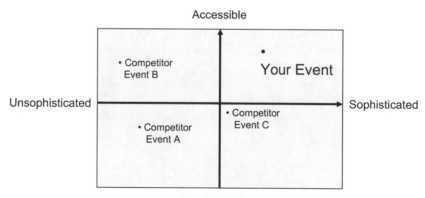

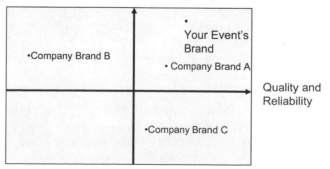

Figure 11.2. Positioning an event.

mapping (a comparison very similar in method to the multidimensional scaling illustrated in Figure 11.2) is to find sponsors that are very compatible to the event in terms of public or target market recognition and favor. Both event and sponsors, for example, would want to be perceived as embodying tradition, quality, reliability, and social/environmental responsibility. This kind of brand mapping is illustrated in an article by Green and Muller (2002).

"Brand extensions" are highly desirable for events, assuming the event itself is well received. The Olympic rings, as a case in point, are highly valued by corporations for co-branding and so the Olympic logo appears on many lines of merchandise (under licensing agreements of course). Events can create other events with the same brand, or get into totally different enterprises on the strength of their existing brand.

"Brand equity" is the value of the brand, both in terms of goodwill and tangible returns. In the corporate world it is common for companies to buy well-known brands to add to their portfolio, an example being that of large wine companies purchasing (and keeping) small family winery brands. The only way for an event to realize its equity in monetary terms is to offer itself for sale, but it can be realized over time in other important ways including increased sponsorship and grant revenue, public and political support, and ability to borrow money. In this way "brand equity" is similar to the concept of "institutionalization" or becoming a tradition.

The Marketing Audit

To prepare for marketing or to evaluate the organization's marketing efforts, an audit should be conducted. This is particularly important in a tourism context as there is little point in promoting events as tourist attractions if the events themselves are uninterested in tourists, do not engage in marketing, do not work effectively with the tour industry, or do not have an attractive product and high-quality services. A number of indicators can be used to determine if event organizations are marketing oriented:

- Is there a statement of mission, mandate, or vision related to the customer, guests, or clients? Does it mention tourism?
- Have specific marketing and tourism-related goals been formulated? Has a marketing plan been completed?
- What marketing research has been undertaken?
- Does the organization include a committee or person responsible for marketing? How does its activities impact on the program and the budget?
- Is there a strategic planning process, as opposed to last-minute, annual programming?
- What are the formal links with destination marketing and tourism planning agencies?
- Does the event belong to or work with the various tour associations (especially bus/coach tours)?
- Does the event have a presence, singly or jointly, in foreign or domestic travel trade fairs or consumer shows?
- Does the event have a visible presence at other events and attractions?
- Can event packages be bought through travel agents or foreign tour companies? Who packages the event?
- Can tickets be reserved? What is the pricing strategy?
- Does the event have a toll-free number?
- Are hosts or guides provided to tour groups?

Destination Audits

As part of strategic event tourism planning, each event should be encouraged to undertake a detailed marketing audit as described above. But a destination can undertake a modest event marketing audit by examining a number of indirect indicators, such as:

- evidence of event marketing in various published tourist magazines, brochures, and travel guides;
- availability of event-related packages;
- the distribution and quality of event calendars and brochures for specific events;
- media coverage of events;
- representation of the event sector at trade shows attended by the area tourist organization;
- contacts with travel agents, hoteliers, and tour companies to determine their level of interest and involvement in events;
- discussions with key event sources, such as a selection of event staff and volunteers, festival/event associations, or sponsors.

As well, a simple questionnaire can be sent to event organizers to determine their practices, needs, and priorities for marketing and management. This basic type of needs assessment might generate interest in collective action or cooperation with the tourism industry and marketing agencies.

Creating a Tourist Orientation for Events

Becoming a tourist-oriented event requires much more than adoption of the marketing concept, although that is a prerequisite. Because the needs and motives of tourists are likely to be different from those of residents, and the tourism and hospitality industry must be accommodated, becoming a tourist-oriented event is much more complex.

A publication by Tourism Canada (1994) entitled *Packaging and Marketing Festivals and Events for the Canadian Tourism Industry* outlines the basic elements of a tourist-oriented event, and similar advice was provided in *The Cultural Tourism Handbook* (Lord Cultural Resources Planning and Management, 1993). Key points are:

1. Identifying and meeting the needs of tourists for:
   - more information; in different languages; longer in advance; with easy booking and packaging;
   - assurances about the event and the packages bought;
   - special support services (transport, access, accommodation, food, comfort, communications);
   - a quality product worth the investment; a destination experience in addition to the event;
   - value, or increased perception of value for money;
   - convenience, security, and support in group travel.
2. Providing the essential visitor services:
   - preferably a toll-free number (for information and reservations);
   - reserved seating; a ticketing policy;
   - information kits available upon request and distributed to prospects (e.g., individuals and tour companies);
   - commitment from residents (as volunteers, participants, hosts, and accommodation or service providers);

- cooperation from the local industry (to ensure rooms are available, provide sponsorships, and discounts for packages, to promote the event);
- an easily accessible information, ticketing, and service office and on-site facility;
- decoration of the site and community; programming for visitor tastes; creation of the right ambience to attract and satisfy visitors;
- shuttle services to and among venues;
- hosts, guides, and hospitality for arriving tourists, both at the site, at gateways to the community, and at places of accommodation.

3. Packaging:
   - designed for target markets;
   - providing choice and added value.
4. Uniqueness and perceived special qualities.

Marketing Planning and Measuring Demand

The marketing planning process generates "marketing plans," which are typically prepared every year. The one-time event needs an initial marketing plan as early as the feasibility study, with periodic modifications as the project develops. Figure 11.3 illustrates the marketing planning process, which draws from the overall strategic planning process discussed in Chapter 3. Its main stages are discussed below.

The situation analysis includes future scanning and organizational audits. The major concerns for the marketing process, however, are factors affecting demand for the event or affecting the organization and its resources and capabilities.

At the most basic level, this assessment will be largely qualitative and based on readily available material (including studies of other events). More sophisticated organizations will undertake original research to quantify market potential, including segmentation studies. These key questions must be addressed by destinations and events:

- What is the existing and potential demand for special events of this type, in this area, based on past experience?

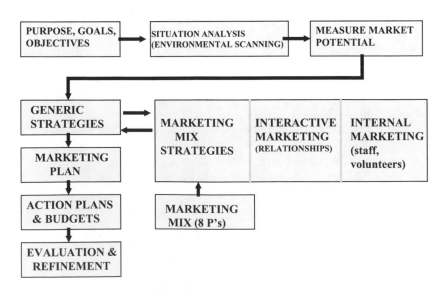

Figure 11.3. Marketing planning process.

- How many customers can be expected, including local, regional, and national/international origins?
- What types of person/group are most likely to be interested in this event, or can be most easily attracted?
- What are their needs and motives? What benefits will they get from the events?
- What are the anticipated spending patterns of visitors/customers? What will people pay for packages, admission, and merchandise?

Measuring Market Potential (Demand) for One-Time Events

The most difficult forecasting problem is faced by the one-time event. Mules and McDonald (1994) noted that forecasting the attendance or impacts of events is often difficult: "The data on which forecasts are based are often of doubtful quality and their applicability problematic" (p. 45). Furthermore, major events are all different and must be analyzed individually; drawing conclusions from other mega-events could be very misleading. Nevertheless, forecasts are essential for planning, especially when bids are made and mega-events won.

Dungan (1984) showed that expected attendance at one-time events could be based on an estimate of market penetration, with other events and comparable attractions, such as theme parks, used as guides. "Market penetration" is calculated as a percentage, so that if every resident in the local market area attended once, the penetration would be 100%; if every resident attended twice, the penetration rate would be 200%. Dungan reported that Expo '67 in Montreal achieved a local market penetration of 618% (i.e., over 6 visits per capita), whereas the 1964–65 World's Fair in New York achieved a low penetration of 82%. But all market areas and events are unique, and events are different from theme parks and other attractions, so direct comparisons have obvious weaknesses.

Market area surveys can be used to make better forecasts of market penetration. What is required are "tracking surveys" in the local, regional, and national or international target markets to measure awareness of the planned event, attitudes towards it, and respondents' assessment of their likelihood or actual intent to attend. These periodic samplings can also be used to gather valuable information on other elements in the marketing mix, especially price. Over time, a more refined forecast of attendance can be derived, and the event modified according to market preferences.

Calculating the Penetration Rate

The formula is: $R = P \times F$, where R = penetration rate; P = percentage of each origin market's population that will attend; F = the mean per capita frequency of visits.

If 40% of a city's 100,000 population visits an event at an average of 2.5 visits per capita, the penetration rate is $0.40 \times 2.5 = 1.00$. This means an attendance of 100,000, but it all comes from 40,000 individuals. If every resident came to the event once, the penetration rate is also 1.00. Thus, it is a measure of drawing power, which can only be based on past experience and/or original market research (such as by asking: Are you certain you will attend? If not, what is the probability you will attend? How many times?). Xie and Smith (2000) show how to use market penetration with particular emphasis on income effects.

Research Note

Xie, P., & Smith, S. (2000). Improving forecasts for world's fair attendance: Incorporating income effects. *Event Management, 6*(1), 15–23.

When applied to major events, such as a world's fair, it is normal to forecast penetration rates from a small number of zones based on proximity, such as: 1) residents of the host city; 2) residents of the day-trip zone; 3) residents of the overnight or vacation zone. The basic assumption, based on almost universal experience with events, is that close-in residents will attend the most, and most frequently. For example, much of the success of Vancouver's 1986 expo was attributed to selling affordable season's passes to residents who then used the expo frequently for dining and entertainment (and to external forces and good marketing). The authors noted that income is a major factor that has to be factored into attendance forecasts, particularly after the lower-than-predicted attendance at the New Orleans World's Fair in 1984, which was partly blamed on being too expensive for locals.

Blackorby, Ricard, and Slade (1986) undertook an interesting analysis of various world's fairs, using linear regression analysis to detect the key factors affecting attendance. They concluded that three factors—average price in US dollars, size of the site in acres, and the number of foreign pavilions—accounted for 93% of variation in attendance at the world's fairs they examined. Using this conclusion they predicted an attendance of 18 million paid visits to Vancouver's Expo '86, which can be compared with the official forecast of 13.5 million and the final count of 22.1 million site visits (Lee, 1987).

Another approach to forecasting attendance at a one-time event was conducted by Louviere and Hensher (1983), using choice theory. In this research survey respondents in one "experiment" were asked to select preferred mixes of event attractions, and those in another survey were required to rank choices by examining alternative locations, prices, types, and sizes of the event. From these data the researchers calculated probabilities of attendance for the population as a whole, specific to a number of event alternatives. Ideally this kind of analysis would be incorporated into a tracking survey.

Trend Extrapolation for Periodic Events

For established events, a trend extrapolation is the easiest way to forecast next year's attendance, but many factors (especially the weather and competition) can intervene. If reliable attendance estimates are available for a period of years, the growth or decline over a period of years can be projected to continue at the same rate, but only if it is assumed that prevailing conditions of supply and demand that affect the event will continue.

Comparisons

Comparison with other events is a reasonable starting point for new events wanting to make a demand forecast. Similar events have to be researched, particularly taking into account market area (e.g., distance to cities), competitive position (are there other events at the same time or in the same area?), and attractiveness (size, quality, and diversity of the proposed event compared to the others). The comparison will be more useful if the origins and growth of comparable events can be traced, focusing on their initial attendance and their promotional efforts.

Destination planners can assist in forecasting by collecting reliable data from many events and analyzing long-term trends. Total attendance at festivals and special events has grown in many regions, so a more refined assessment of demand specific to types of events, and geographic patterns of demand, will help a great deal.

It must be cautioned, however, that as the number of events within a market area increases the growth of new events might very well be impeded by established competition. Factors to consider are:

- New, unique events can tap "latent demand" (i.e., unmet demand for specific, new experiences).

- The emergence of multiple events can increase total demand (i.e., the size of the events "pie" gets bigger) through increasing publicity, word of mouth recommendations, and greater interest in the event sector.
- New events can achieve market penetration through "stealing" demand from established events, especially if the new ones are perceived to be better or different.
- Old events might be declining through lack of new programming, or poor management, giving new events a natural window of opportunity.

Causal Factors (Price and Income Elasticity)

More sophisticated techniques of demand forecasting, especially regression analysis (see S. Smith, 1995), require knowledge of "causal factors." For example, tourism demand forecasts consistently reveal that rising personal income leads to rapid growth in travel demand, and this can be used in a regression analysis to forecast demand between specific origins and destinations. Other factors, such as costs and exchange rates, will certainly intervene, and marketing efforts must also be considered. While the factors most responsible for demand changes in tourism are understood, there has been little analysis of event demand. Is it more or less price or income elastic than other tourism products?

"Price elasticity" refers to a predictable relationship between price and demand in which increased price results in corresponding decline in demand. "Income elasticity" is the relationship in which demand rises correspondingly as consumer income (or disposable income) rises. There is no reason to believe that demand for most events is not price and income elastic, but research on specific cases has been lacking. Some events, however, might have sufficient appeal to be considered preferred goods.

Under what circumstances might events be considered "preferred goods" for which residents or tourists will pay more than usual? Mega-events of a once-in-a-lifetime nature might very well encourage many people to spend whatever it takes to attend it, whereas annual events will not usually have this effect unless they contain specific elements of very high appeal. Some evidence from focus groups (Getz & Cheyne, 2002) suggested this is true. A number of respondents in New Zealand considered a possible trip to the Sydney Olympics in the year 2000 to be a once-in-a-lifetime opportunity that would be worth more to them than other desirable foreign, event-specific trips.

Sometimes raising prices and fostering a mystique around an event or program element can elevate them to the status of preferred goods. Snob appeal, exclusivity, and excellence will likely be required.

Qualitative Forecasting Methods

Because of the problems associated with statistical forecasting, a number of qualitative methods have been used in tourism studies. The most basic is "expert judgment," either by individuals or groups. Managers do this all the time in their own planning exercises, but more formal techniques can be applied. The "Delphi method" involves several rounds of structured consultations among a panel of experts with the usual purpose of identifying trends or future scenarios, and assigning probabilities and importance ratings to them.

A scenario, in the context of strategic planning, is a hypothetical description of circumstances at some point in the future. Planners formulate scenarios for one of two general reasons: to show what might happen and how it will affect the event or destination; to show a desired future state and draw inferences about how to achieve it. Trend analysis and understanding underlying causal factors are essential to good scenario making when the object is to predict a future state and its implications. Working backwards, the planner can then determine how to influence the various forces shaping trends that will likely lead to that future state: either to prevent it, modify it, or develop strategies to adapt to it.

In the second approach, imagination is required. Conjure up a desired future, say one in which your destination is blessed with a rich portfolio of attractive events, then determine how to achieve that goal. It sounds simple, but it is actually difficult. The ideal future state is easy enough to depict in a scenario, but realistically describing the pathways and actions needed to get there requires a considerable amount of real-world expertise.

Willingness to Pay

To an economist, "demand" is the amount of a good or service consumed (i.e., purchased) over a schedule of prices. In other words, what would the demand be for the event, in terms of total attendance, if the price was X? In the absence of direct experience in evaluating the change in demand that results from price changes, the potential customer's "willingness to pay" can be assessed.

Limited research on willingness to pay for events has been undertaken. In a major study of festivals in Canada's National Capital Region (Coopers & Lybrand Consulting Group, 1989) customers at five free-admission events were asked how much they would pay, while at two events with admission prices a sample was asked if the amount was too high, low, or just right. One useful result was the revelation that tourists would be willing to pay more than residents, which makes sense given that many traveled specifically to attend the event or were already on a pleasure trip.

About 20% of respondents at the free events said they would not pay anything. The consultants suggested that this represented a "contingency valuation" problem, as consumers would fear the introduction of a price. This author's personal experience with similar questions at events supports the conclusion that most consumers will say they are comfortable with prices similar to those already charged. Major increases are likely to be met with considerable negative reaction. This makes it difficult to determine what proportion of the audience might be lost if prices are introduced or raised, and it also suggests that it can be difficult to introduce a charge at free events. Several issues and problems with this technique must be considered:

- People are likely to underestimate what they would actually pay (they do not want to encourage increases!).
- Some segments will be able to afford more; increasing prices therefore becomes an "equity" issue for public services.
- Tourists, and those attracted specifically to the event, will likely pay more.

Segmentation and Selecting Target Markets

To better understand the event consumer, and for purposes of more effective marketing, it is necessary to segment the market. "Segmentation" methods normally employ research and analytical techniques to identify relatively homogeneous groups that can be targeted through marketing. An option is to segment people on the basis of their actual and often varying travel or consumption patterns; this is known as "occasion-based" segmentation (Morrison, 1995).

To be useful, a market segment must meet certain criteria (Mill & Morrison, 1985). The group of people being described as a "target market" or "segment" must have common characteristics (i.e., homogeneity). It must be a measurable group (how many are there?), and of a size or characteristics making them worthwhile of attention (e.g., small, wealthy, special interest groups can be important). Finally, the organizers must be able to effectively and affordably communicate with the group. Although the ways to identify target markets are many, and often overlapping, meeting these criteria ensures that target marketing does not get out of control. In practice, each event should focus on one or several easily defined groups. For events and event tourism the following criteria are also important:

- Segmentation must identify the groups most interested in attending and/or traveling to various types of events, including those who currently consume event-related products.
- Identify travelers with a secondary interest in attending events; pay particular attention to emerging or potential markets and segments.
- Determine the segments by reference to variables that can be used to enhance target marketing (discussed below).
- Describe the segments by reference to how they can be reached through the communications mix.
- Identify the highest "quality" visitors and event tourists.
- Consider the durability of segments (will they last?), their size and quality (are they worth the effort?), and the cost-effectiveness of attracting them relative to other targets.
- Consider the event's and destination's distinctive competencies and competitive advantages when establishing target segments.

S. Smith (1988) said that segmentation can also answer questions about the size of potential markets, spending patterns, price sensitivity, loyalty, response to changes in the marketing mix, and the potential effectiveness of promotions. Once the segmentation analysis is completed, the most promising groups are selected as target markets and the marketing mix should be oriented to these groups. In fact, the product and target markets must be continuously matched, as both are likely to change over time.

Below, the major segmentation variables are discussed. Depending on the circumstances, any one or combination of these variables might be used to delimit existing and target markets. However, geographic, demographic, and socioeconomic variables are almost always needed for events. Figure 11.4 depicts the variables grouped according to the main segmentation questions: From where will they come? Who exactly are they? What do they want? Under what conditions will they attend the event? How can we reach them? How often will they visit?

Geographic Variables

Most event visits will be generated within the local or regional market area. Surveys are needed to determine the existing and potential ratios of local, regional, and long-distance consumers, using criteria like distance traveled, name of the home community, or postal code address. A decision will have to be made on what constitutes a resident versus a tourist, and this is often made on the basis of an arbitrary distance traveled (say, 80 km or 50 miles) or by reference to local authority boundaries, census-defined metropolitan areas, or delineations of trading or commuting zones.

Telephone surveys in likely market areas can be used to test awareness and interest levels, advertising effectiveness, and other variables that correlate with distance, access, and other geographic factors. Remember that if only visitor surveys are used, no data are obtained on noncustomers.

Combining geographic data with other marketing facts through "encoding" is a valuable technique. For example, in many countries census data can be combined with postal code information to reveal patterns and potential applications such as:

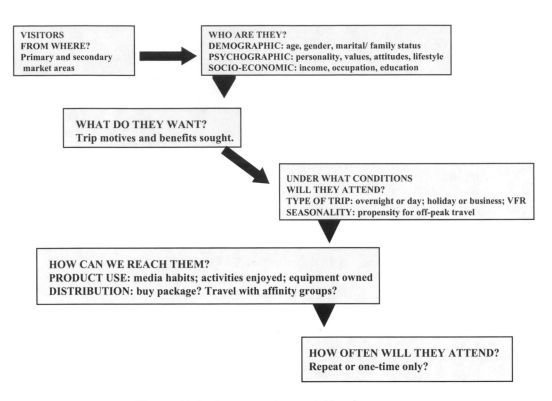

Figure 11.4. Segmentation variables for events.

- communities with high-income residents (the kind who travel most or to consume cultural products);
- areas with older residents (who might be most interested in group travel);
- concentrations of families (most likely to seek low-cost, accessible entertainment, and social outlets);
- ethnic neighborhoods (most interested in certain types of music);
- households with boats or other sporting equipment (potential sports show consumers);
- newly settled versus well-established areas (perhaps indicative of interest in local community-building events).

Demographic Variables

Age and gender are usually important factors affecting demand for events, along with marital and family status. Household type and size are potentially useful, such as the distinction between one- and two-parent families, and identification of nontraditional households. Race and ethnicity are becoming more important in many countries, reflecting the increasingly multicultural nature of the population.

Age, gender, family status, and other variables combine in the "life stage concept," which has important implications for all leisure activities and preferences. Young people before marriage have a set of values, desires, opportunities, and constraints that is quite different from that of married couples, "empty-nesters" (i.e., couples whose children have left home), and the elderly who are retired.

Sports and entertainment events are more likely to attract young males, whereas arts and cultural festivals have much stronger appeal to females. Community festivals and celebrations do attract more families, with a more balanced gender distribution. In Saskatchewan, for example, it was found that 60% of visitors at a range of events were with families (Derek Murray Consulting Associates Ltd., 1985). In Dickens on the Strand in Galveston, Texas, the research found that 35% of respondents to the on-site random survey were with a group of adults without children, while 21% were in a single family group with children. Females accounted for 53% of the sample (Ralston & Crompton, 1988a).

The setting, sponsors/organizers, and theme will probably have a marked bearing on attracting different racial or ethnic groups. Ethnic and multicultural festivals are often aimed directly at achieving intergroup mixing and fostering better communications and understanding, whereas it appears that different types of entertainment, cultural, and sporting events have distinct racial and ethnic appeal. For example, the Louisville Kentucky Bluegrass Music Festival (Kentucky Department of Travel Development, 1987) had an audience that was 96% white. Most surveys do not record this information, and it might be inappropriate to do so in direct interviewing or self-completion questionnaires. It is nevertheless a factor organizers should consider, and nonintrusive measures can be taken by direct observation to determine if certain groups are underrepresented in the audience.

Socioeconomic Variables

This group of variables pertains to an individual's or household's economic status (income, employment) and related factors such as educational attainment. Income is the greatest predictor of travel consumption and entertainment expenditure, although it certainly does not explain everything.

Surveys for Dickens on the Strand festival in Galveston (Ralston & Crompton, 1988a, 1988b) revealed its customers to be "up-market" in terms of age and income levels. Combined with other data, this revealed a segment of repeat adult visitors without children who traveled specifically for the event and spent a lot of money on accommodation, dining, etc. Sponsors and tourist authorities love these high-yield tourists. But it also suggested the need to appeal to other segments, including families.

Psychographic Variables

These are based on psychological or personal dimensions, such as personality traits, beliefs, values, attitudes, and lifestyle preferences, which can help explain motives and travel behavior. "Psychographic segmentation" has become popular in tourism research (see the discussion in Morrison, 1995), but some have found it to be of limited value if not combined with other segmentation variables.

Plog (1987) identified dimensions used commonly in psychographics-based tourist segmentation:

- adventuresomeness (the explorer types);
- pleasure seeking (related to the desire for luxury);
- impulsivity (will spend a lot, without planning);
- self-confidence (will travel alone);
- planfulness (wants package tours and bargains);
- masculinity (the action-oriented and outdoor groups);
- intellectualism (is lured by culture and history);
- people orientation (wants to be close to others).

Whatever the psychographic factors employed in segmentation, there will be the need to link these to one or more of the other segmentation methods. The psychographic dimensions of these ideal segments, expressed in terms of what event tourism marketers hope to find, could be:

- values, beliefs, and attitudes (e.g., belief in the centrality of arts in society; sports valued as character builders; belief that festivals are good for the community);
- personality traits (e.g., conservatives who will buy packages; adventurers and will seek out the authentic and unique);
- lifestyle (e.g., active in a variety or sports, arts, or within the community; already a consumer of similar products).

Benefits Sought

Consumers can usually identify what they want from an attraction or travel experience, such as: to enjoy social and family relationships; to learn about cultures; to have fun or be entertained; to compete or achieve. If asked what benefits visitors derived from an event experience, they are attaching meanings to it, such as: "we had an authentic cultural experience"; "I enjoyed the time spent with others." A great deal can be learned through focus groups or interviews about how people perceive the event experience (Getz & Cheyne, 2002).

Depending on the product, benefits can be defined and consumers or potential visitors can be asked to rank those which interest them most. Segments based on stated benefits will have to be correlated with other factors, especially demographics. Older adults with high incomes, for example, are less likely to seek thrills.

Type of Trip

Are your event visitors most likely to be on an informal day-trip, family touring vacation, visiting friends and relatives, staying at a second home, on business, or traveling primarily because of the event? A number of other segmentation variables can be combined to form useful trip-type segments. For example, the business traveler is often difficult to segment on demographic and geographic variables, but many of them will display common patterns of activity when in a destination. How easy will it be to attract them to an event and add a day to their trip? Events can also be packaged with conferences, and possibly provide an incentive to bring families with the business traveler.

Seasonality

This is an often-ignored segmentation variable, but has particular relevance to events. Some groups are easier to attract in the off season, while the largest market potential is likely to be in the summer holiday and tourist season. Another way to look at this method is to ask what would happen to an event's markets if it moved seasons?

To be useful, other segmentation variables must be attached to seasonality. Older, retired people are generally easier to attract in spring and autumn. Busy professionals want to take short getaway trips throughout the year.

Repeat Visits

Numerous festival surveys have detected a loyal group of return visitors, obviously including a high proportion of area residents. But this important group also includes a segment with strong "brand loyalty" to particular events, returning again and again, and a segment that takes in many different events. Music festivals in particular seem to attract a mobile audience, and sports have dedicated traveling fans.

Research by Plant (1985) found that approximately 48% of the visitors to the Elmira (Ontario) Maple Syrup Festival were repeaters, with an average number of 4.55 previous visits. Of the first-time customers, one half had never been to the Elmira area previously, showing that the event was a key to enhancing awareness of the whole region. Repeaters tended to be middle aged, married, and well educated, with fewer students, young people, and seniors.

Product-Related Variables

Those with likely interest in sport events can be identified by the equipment they own, magazines they read, and their recreational activities. An event can also concentrate on persons who are frequent users of certain facilities, and clubs with specialized product demands (e.g., antique car hobbyists). The object is to identify products or services linked to the target segment and the event.

Distribution Channel Variables

Another approach is to identify target groups by the ways in which the event can be linked to potential customers. Tourists might be most easily reached through specialized tour wholesalers who do their own marketing. Links with parks and recreation departments in nearby cities can pay off, as they might organize senior citizen excursions to events. In both cases, the target groups are defined by the way in which they are reached.

Problems and Limitations of Segmentation

Many of the segmentation variables discussed above can be, on their own, misleading or misinterpreted. Often a number of factors must be understood, such as the age, gender, lifestyle, and attitudes of a person, before their demand for events can be predicted. Segments are often not as homogeneous as they might seem, because the cluster or factor analysis used in their formation is subject to manipulation to achieve a certain number of segments.

The biggest failure of segmentation, as currently practiced, is its almost total lack of consistency. Each new study seems to invent new methods and terms, based on different sampling, and based on often untested theory. This criticism is not applicable to simple studies, but is typical of multidimensional and psychographic segmentation. The result is a confusing array of segment labels and an inability to directly compare or combine results.

Because of the confusion, and the need of many event managers to undertake marketing with small budgets, a practical market segmentation framework is outlined later in this chapter.

A Benefits Model for Target Marketing

Figure 11.5 is a conceptual model to assist in understanding the nature of event products relative to target marketing. The essence of the concept is to market specific benefits to desired segments, while providing essential services and generic benefits to everyone.

Essential Services

These are necessary to undertake any event or operate any permanent attraction. They cannot normally be considered as benefits, but the absence or inadequacy of any of them

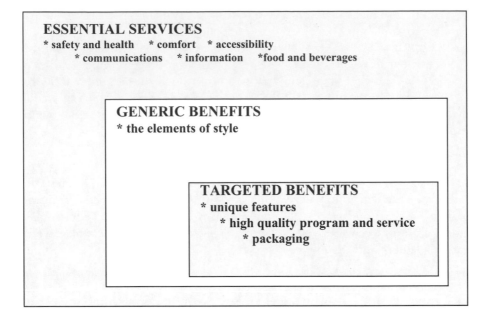

Figure 11.5. Benefits model for targeted marketing.

will cause visitor dissatisfaction. A formal evaluation system must be put in place to ensure high quality and the meeting of performance criteria for each essential service, and customers should be asked to give their opinions on adequacy.

Generic Benefits

People attend special events expecting a different kind of experience from other types of attraction. To the extent that most or all of these benefits can be provided, the appeal of the event will be maximized. When we examined programming, generic benefits were described as "elements of style."

Targeted Benefits

Residents, day-trippers, and tourists in the area might attend an event out of curiosity or on impulse, as a recreational outing. They will expect certain generic benefits and basic services. To attract tourists specifically to travel to an event, however, something extra is usually required. The first step is to strive for uniqueness.

"Uniqueness" has several dimensions related to events (Getz & Cheyne, 2002). First, it can be a function of rarity. Something that occurs infrequently (Olympics, world's fair, America's Cup) or in very few places or only one place (Indy 500, Cannes Film Festival) has special appeal. The presence of celebrities, or a higher than usual quality of artists, performers, or players can also contribute to a perception of uniqueness. Some of it is "mystique," and therefore partially fabricated through promotions. Small festivals and events can try to develop this mystique by emphasizing rarity, combined with image building based on quality, cost, or some other competitive advantage.

Almost any component of the event production can become a "feature" or "specialty" that can differentiate the product from competitors. Entertainment, visitor activities, and merchandise can all be targeted to special interest segments. Food and drink are essential to most events, but specialty food, wine, beer, and bake-off events attract gourmets, competitors, and those curious about ethnic products.

High quality in programming and service delivery can differentiate events and attract target markets. While many food and beverage events exist, a few can position themselves to be the best. Sometimes snob appeal, through pricing and promotions, can be used to lure high-spending visitors.

Packaging is also a tool for targeting events. A carefully crafted and promoted package can greatly enhance the appeal of an event relative to those without similar convenience. Certain target segments, including affinity groups and many seniors, will respond better to packaging and group tours.

Targeting Through Theming

An event's "theme" communicates its benefits and can be used as a target marketing tool. All festivals are themed, by definition. They celebrate or commemorate something of importance to the community, such as its heritage or way of life. But the theme is more than the mere object of celebration. As noted by Korza and Magie (1989), the theme unifies an event or festival: "By permeating every aspect of a festival . . . a theme can provide programmatic direction and coherence and provide a hook which is readily understood by the media and audiences" (p. 10). In other words, the object of the celebration suggests a theme, but the realization of a theme is a function of coherent programming and image making.

Uniqueness of theme is getting harder to create. Creativity and even a sense of humor have helped some communities find a theme that both expresses local heritage and is bound to capture attention. For example, Queenan (1989) asked: "In a state where annual festivals celebrate everything from antique stoves to zucchini, why not long underwear?" (p. 13). She was referring to Piqua, Ohio and its annual Great Outdoor Underwear Festival.

Event themes can be linked to destination area themes for mutual advantage. In some cases the regional theme is strong, giving rise to events that take advantage of, and reinforce, the destination image. Some regions have based their image making and theme on the success of one or more special events. There is no need to try to link all events into a coherent destination theme, however; diversity is to be valued. Rather, packages and tours can be employed to highlight and link the events that most strongly develop the destination image or theme.

Other special events almost always have a specific theme based on the nature of the event, such as a sport or recreation activity. But special events do not always develop a theme fully or integrate it well in promotions. Kreag (1988) advised that all the important elements of an event have to be synthesized "into a cohesive message or statement of purpose" to ensure effective communications. Themes can be expressed in a number of ways:

- in the name of the event;
- through logos and mascots;
- in the setting/design;
- in the activities and attractions;
- in food and beverages;
- in merchandise for sale;
- in consistent advertising format and style;
- by stressing specified (targeted) benefits.

A Practical Segmentation and Marketing Strategy

Segmentation and marketing can be carried to illogical extremes, producing more confusion than anything. It can also be a complex and expensive process, requiring extensive market research and analytical expertise. Consequently, a more practical approach to segmentation is needed, and this is provided in Figure 11.6.

The Local Market Area

The basic premise of the strategy is that most events are dependent on local and day-trip (regional) markets. Mega-events will draw a higher number and proportion of overnight tourists than small events, and meetings or conventions can have exceptional tourist draw. But distance will almost always be an important factor in shaping demand.

Key target segments in the local market include the obvious: participants; competitors; special interest groups related to the event theme; known users of related events or attractions; and repeat visitors. Add the segments known to frequent festivals and special events, such as families and seniors for festivals, young males for sports, and educated females for arts. Residents in the most immediate neighborhood of a festival and family-oriented events are primary segments. It does not take much research to identify these basic target segments, nor will it require unusual effort to reach them.

The key marketing needs for these local target groups are shown in Figure 11.6. Because the community should be interested in all local events, it is possible and highly desirable to keep the population aware of the event all year, relying mostly on free publicity and word-of-mouth contacts. A sense of community involvement and ownership could pay better dividends than advertising. This can be accomplished through open management, a theme meaningful to the residents, taking the planning and the event itself into the community, a good volunteer recruitment and reward system, and wide, interorganizational networking.

MARKET AREA

	LOCAL (Residents)	REGIONAL (mostly day visitors)	OVERNIGHT & LONG DISTANCE TOURISTS
KEY TARGET SEGMENTS	-event participants -related interest groups -known repeat visitors -immediate neighbours -families and general audiences	-motorists up to 100 miles -bus tour groups -related interest groups -known repeat visitors -event participants	-those staying in area -passers-through -second home and seasonal residents -related interest groups -event participants
MARKETING NEEDS	-free publicity -all-year public relations -community "ownership" -local sponsors -free events or price discounts -newspaper and radio ads	-cultivate group tours -targeted ads in all media -predictable date and venue -linkage to other events and attractions -cooperative promotions -compatibility with destination themes -visitor information -competitive pricing	-cooperative promotions -media coverage -destination promotions -enlist residents to bring visitors -develop Hallmark Event status -price/package to encourage longer stays

Figure 11.6. Practical segmentation and marketing strategy.

Local sponsors can provide most of the necessary advertising, with emphasis on last-minute reminders (residents can and will engage in impulse event-going). Ensuring that the event program and directions to get there are readily available (e.g., in the local newspaper the day before the event) will facilitate impulse attendance. Residents will also know all about traffic and parking problems, and they might fear extra congestion near events, so you must overcome this barrier through well-publicized transportation and parking solutions. Finally, ensuring high visibility for the event (e.g., through parades, main street locations, banners and posters) can be a lure for impulse attendance.

The Regional Market

An event's main regional market, geographically, is within an easy day-trip and preferably no more than a 2-hour drive, one way. Nearby cities, particularly those with quick road access, are the prime targets. Surveys have found that a 50–100 mile-radius is about the maximum market area for most small to medium-sized events, but a visitor survey or even casual conversations with visitors can define the main market area.

Segments in this day-trip zone will be similar to the local target groups, but with emphasis on repeat visitors (get a list of addresses!) and bus tours. Seniors' clubs are frequent day-trippers by bus, and many special interest groups can be encouraged to hire a bus or use special shuttle transport. They can be reached through community-group directories, parks and recreation departments, and other readily available public sources. Organizers should not forget that participants, as in sports tournaments, are also target markets.

Charter bus companies and tour wholesalers should be approached to organize tours, and these groups should be afforded special reception and services. A shuttle service that is cheap and reliable can be important. Marketing to these regional segments should emphasize all-year cultivation of tour companies and special interest groups, with seasonal awareness and reinforcement messages in paid advertising. There is probably little value to most events in trying to maintain an all-year visibility throughout a regional market. Many events put on a publicity drive, gaining momentum in the months and days before the event. Publicity stunts and numerous press releases are used to attract media attention.

Predictability is important to the regional market, especially to encourage repeat visits, and where organizers rely on word-of-mouth promotions. Holding the event on the same date (e.g., first weekend in April) and at the same place will eventually pay off in developing local and regional markets. It is not so important in other tourist markets, where last-minute trip decisions are less likely. If consumers know that an annual event (or events put on by certain organizers) is always of high quality, repeat visits from a distance are more likely.

The regional market requires special communications channels and information sources. Develop linkages with other attractions and events to maximize impact. Cooperative promotions can go a lot farther than the promotion of a single event, especially if a coherent destination theme can be developed that features events. Ensure that the information available to out-of-town visitors is adequate to their special needs.

People traveling a distance will be more willing to pay an admission price, but not if it is out of line with similar events and attractions. Special interest target markets, such as persons interested in certain types of music, or in antiques, might prefer paying an admission to events (or elements of the event) if higher quality or exclusiveness is thereby ensured.

Tourist Markets

In this context the "tourist" is an overnight visitor or long-distance traveler. Some will travel relatively short distances within the day-trip zone, but they want an overnight experience. Others—mainly segments attracted to targeted benefits—might travel great distances for the event.

Marketers should not forget long-distance travelers who are just passing through, and those who are in the area for business or visiting friends and relatives. Residents can be used as distribution agents to get information about events into the hands of potential visiting friends and relatives; residents should believe the event is a worthwhile experience for their visitors. Finally, second-home owners constitute a tourist market for events located in resort areas.

The most likely target for long-distance travel to the event (as the main trip purpose) are participants, especially in sports, and persons with a known special interest in the event theme or program (such as arts or music club members). Membership lists of clubs and associations can be a powerful marketing tool, and local clubs and associations can be used to promote the event to their wider memberships.

Joint marketing, linking events to regional and national campaigns, will be necessitated to reach some long-distance tourists. More than likely, the general-purpose tourist (such as those on a touring trip or package) will only be lured to a small event if it is included in a preplanned itinerary, brought to the visitor's attention early in the visit, or it is occurring in a place convenient to the tourist. Promotion of the destination itself is essential, and event organizers should take the lead in ensuring that events are promoted at the same level as other attractions and services.

Mega-events rely on a "must-see" image linked to their uniqueness, but lesser events can stress unique features as well, thereby catching the eye of casual tourists. If there are several events in a touring area, the tourist might be lured by the "biggest," "best," or "only" one of its kind. But organizers have to weigh the potential advantages of exaggeration and gimmicky image making against the need to inspire resident confidence in the event, and the thoughtful tourist's desire to experience authentic cultural festivities. Creation of "hallmark" status is the long-term goal.

Finally, pricing for tourists has to include package deals and other incentives, such as long-stay discounts, to encourage overnight visits. Wholesalers might have to be offered special prices linked to the volume of tourists they bring to the event. The economic benefits will be magnified greatly as the number of overnight tourists increases.

Generic Marketing Strategies

According to Porter (1980), competitive advantage can be gained through three generic marketing strategies: differentiation, market focus, and cost leadership. The application of these to events is discussed below, followed by other strategies.

Differentiation

To Porter (1980), only product differentiation assures sustainable competitive advantage. Events must cultivate uniqueness in program, theme, and targeted benefits, and use the marketing mix to gain a position of strength relative to competitors. Stressing value is more important than competing on price. Events that imitate others are not differentiated. If there are others just like it in the same market area, some will likely not succeed.

Market Focus (Niche Marketing)

Pursuing one target market segment above all others can be an effective strategy for some events, especially if it is a high-yield segment. The goal is to out-compete all other events for this segment. Events with refined themes and highly targeted benefits can employ this strategy, but not something-for-everyone festivals.

Cost Leadership

If costs can be kept low through subsidies, economies of scale, or more efficient operations, products can compete through cost leadership. Lower prices, in this strategy, should result in higher demand than competitors, while keeping prices the same as competitors should result in higher relative profit margins.

Many events have no direct competition with other events, or are free, and so cost leadership is not applicable. Adding value to the event experience is more likely to be a sustainable strategy, although all managers should strive for greater efficiency.

Market Penetration

This strategy is one of attracting more users to the same event, without necessarily changing the types of users or the market area. Managers of static attractions and resorts can use special events to get patrons returning more frequently, but the challenge for annual events is quite different. It can be accomplished through better promotions, price discounting, better sales to special interest groups, or giving better value for money.

Aggressive marketers might take aim at luring customers from the nearby competition, through direct comparison and boasting of advantages. This has limited possibilities for one-time events, and for community festivals without obvious competition. The uniqueness of events should be a fact, not a promotional fantasy! Another technique is to use visitor and market surveys to identify nonusers within established market segments (organizers should have already identified customer needs and desired benefits) and promote to them more aggressively, such as through direct sales.

Product Reformulation

If established audiences are losing interest, modifying the program or other fundamental elements of the product (e.g., the setting) can stimulate repeat visits. Just as theme parks add new rides or special events regularly, annual festivals can adopt a long-range plan to keep adding new and appealing features. Arts festivals do the same when they upgrade the quality of performances or attract "big-name" headliners. If the product improvements are consistent in theme, the same market segments can be lured back. Care must be taken to not drastically alter the event program to the point where returning customers are both surprised and disappointed with the changes.

Market Development

This strategy seeks out new target markets for the same product, often in geographical terms or by benefit-defined segments. For annual events, it means tapping the day-tripping market and then going after tours and independent travelers from farther afield. Cooperative efforts with tourist organizations and regional/national promotional bodies are necessary. Most special events find that direct marketing to bus tours is an excellent way to break into new tourist markets. See the research paper by Walle (2003) for a practical application.

Research Note

Walle, A. (2003). Building a diverse attendance at cultural festivals: Embracing oral history/folklore in strategic ways. *Event Management, 8*(2), 73–82.

Walle discussed how to broaden the market for events, in this case a "serious arts" festival that had become overly narrow in its appeal. The Erie Summer Festival of the Arts wanted to broaden its community appeal, and so it introduced an oral history/folklore program to attract new segments. Walle concluded that there are a number of generic strategies events can use to expand their audience: working with new partners (to bring in new ideas/resources, or to enhance credibility); selecting new programs/activities/attractions that broaden the appeal but do not undermine the established theme; bring in an expert for advice (related to the new ideas) and as facilitator; prepublicity for innovations (get the media interested); promoting the event all year makes innovations easier; make the market-broadening campaign a multiyear project.

Product Development

An alternative is to develop new products, such as offering variations of the event, aimed at the same market. For example, an arts festival can add different types of performance throughout the year. Some events have winter and summer versions, catering to different tourist markets, while others have multiple sites.

Diversification

This is the most radical marketing strategy, and is seldom used by event organizers. The aim is to create new products for new markets. It will also require planned organizational change.

Case Study: Generation Y and Action Sports

In the 1990s and early 2000s there has been tremendous interest on the part of corporations and the media in action sports that appeal mostly to Generation Y, and specifically to teenage males (Bennett et al., 2003). ESPN has its X Games (see below) and NBC had its Gravity Games, with a clear link existing between television coverage, information available on the Internet, participation in these sports, and attendance at "media-driven sporting festivals."

Not everyone is enthused about action sports, as they appeal more to teenage males, and less to African Americans as opposed to whites, Hispanics, and Asians. Perhaps surprisingly, these young males also prefer soccer over other traditional American sports.

While Gen Y values product quality and "coolness," and no doubt defines "cool" in part as anything not liked by their parents, companies value the enormous spending power of this target audience. It is not just television that drives action sports, as there exists an Internet-based community of interest to bring the like-minded together. Computer ownership or access is extremely high among Gen Y, and Internet use is a daily pastime for most of them.

What Are Action Sports?

The main sports in this category are skateboarding and snowboarding. According to the National Sporting Goods Association these two sports had the highest growth in participation for those aged 7–17, between 1997 and 2002. Another sources, American Sports Data (2003), "action sports" account for five of the most popular in the US, namely: in-line skating (ranked first), followed by skateboarding (second), snowboarding (fourth), BMX biking (eighth), and wakeboarding (ninth). These are sports for youth and young adults; for example, nearly half of all wakeboarders are between the ages of 12 and 24. ESPN's polls (2002) revealed that 70% of youngsters are action sport fans.

Action sports are closely associated with television and Internet media. ESPN reported that the X Games VIII in 2002 attracted almost 63 million viewers, while Winter X VII also set TV viewing records.

Tony Hawk (www.tonyhawk.com) is a superstar with action sport fans. By age 12, Tony was sponsored by Dogtown skateboards, by 14 he was pro, and by age 16 Tony Hawk was the best skateboarder in the world. In the ensuing 17 years, Hawk has entered an estimated 103 pro contests. He won 73 of them, and placed second in 19, by far the best record in skateboarding's history. In 1999 Activision and Tony created Tony Hawk's Pro Skater video game for PlayStation. The next year, Tony Hawk's Pro Skater 2 was released and jumped to the number one position for over a month. Since then, the THPS series has become one of the best-selling video game franchises of all time. In 2002, Tony launched the Boom Boom HuckJam, a 24-city arena tour featuring the world's best skateboarders, BMX bike riders, and Motocross lunatics performing choreographed routines on a million-dollar ramp system, while a big-name band (such as The Offspring, Good Charlotte, and Social Distortion) plays live on an adjacent stage. The hugely successful (and massively publicized) HuckJam tour sold out arenas across the country.

What Are the X Games?

ESPN (www.expn.com) first introduced its X Games franchise in 1995, and it has evolved into the premier brand in "action sports." In addition to being a form of television programming for ESPN the annual X Games and Winter X Games are known as the premiere sport competitions for professional action sport athletes. X Games IX were held in August of 2003 in Los Angeles, showcasing over 300 of the world's best action sport athletes who competed for medals and prize money of over $1 million. The sport competitions were Aggressive In-Line Skate, Bike Stunt, Downhill BMX, Moto X, Skateboard, Surfing, and Wakeboard.

Southern California is the action sports hub, and it has been estimated that it will generate over 10,000 room nights for hotels and generate $50 million (annually) for the city's economy. As well, worldwide media coverage of the event focuses attention on the downtown and major sport venues in central Los Angeles.

International X Games started in 1998 with the Asian X Games, with more recent additions being Latin X Games and European X Games.

Photo 11.1. Massive crowds attend X Games X at Staples Center, Los Angeles (credit: Shazamm/ESPN).

X Games Global Championship was held for the first time in 2003, with the unique concept that winter and summer sports were held and telecast simultaneously: winter action sports from Whistler Blackcomb, Canada, and summer sports from San Antonio, Texas. The event will take place every other year.

X Games skateparks have been constructed in a number of US locations since 2001, through a partnership with the Mills Corporation. These public sport venues provide for skateboarding, bike stunt riding, and in-line skating, plus a lounge, observation deck, retail outlet, and large-screen television.

Winter X Games VIII were held in Aspen in January, 2004 and involved over 250 athletes in Moto X, ski, snowboard, and snowmobile. Over 65,000 spectators attended the 4-day event.

How They Are Organized

ESPN formed its Event Creation and Management department in 1995 to further develop its owned and operated events. Today, renamed as ESPN Original Entertainment Events group (EOE), the department is responsible for the creation and execution of several annual ESPN events across the globe, including the X Games, Winter X Games, X Games Global Championship, Asian X Games, and Latin X Games. The group also assists with the production of the ESPY Awards and Great Outdoor Games. This event programming provides increasing value to ESPN's cable TV partners, while creating valuable proprietary programming that can be utilized across many different media including television, video on demand, Internet, film, DVD, radio, and more.

Due to the dedicated resources of the EOE Events team, the X Games brand has grown to include EXPN.com, EXPN Radio, the large-format film *ESPN's Ultimate X*, X Games skateparks, and various X Games branded products.

Photo 11.2. Winter X Games VII (credit: shazamm/ESPN).

EOE is organized as follows:

- Public Relations (media relations, crisis communications, athlete relations for publicity).
- Marketing (local and regional promotions, collateral materials, school programs, grassroots marketing, affiliate relations).
- Business Administration (contracts, uniforms, accounting, housing, travel, risk/safety management).
- Sports and Competition (sport organizations, courses, athlete relations, and athlete registration).
- Event Production (volunteers, event staging, credentialing).
- Medical (spectator and athlete medical services).

Other departments of ESPN also work on the X Games, including TV Production, Sponsorship Marketing and Promotions, Consumer Marketing (national campaign), Legal, Corporate Communications, Affiliate Sales and Marketing, ESPN Enterprises, ESPN Research, EXPN.com, ESPN The Magazine, and ESPN.com.

X Games Community Relations and Cause Marketing Programs

X Games partners with a number of causes, including:

- Boarding for Breast Cancer
- School programs
- Make a Wish Foundation
- Hospital visits
- Boys and Girls Clubs of America

Study Questions

- What is "customer orientation" and how is it applicable to events?
- Explain the differences between experiential and facilitating elements in the event marketing mix.
- How do events position themselves in the marketplace, and why?
- What is branding and how is it applied to events?
- Why is it so difficult to predict demand for many events? What methods are available?
- Describe the main segmentation variables for events.
- What are generic and targeted benefits?
- Which of the common marketing strategies would work best for a one-time as opposed to periodic event? Explain your reasons.
- Why do day-trippers and tourists require different marketing from locals?

Advanced Study Questions

- Conduct a marketing audit of an event, including its tourism orientation. Make recommendations for more effective marketing.
- Test consumers on their perceptions of events in the same marketplace, using multidimensional scaling.
- Outline separate marketing strategies for local, regional, and long-distance target markets for an event in your community. Compare your ideas to what the organizers actually do. Can you offer them any useful advice?

Chapter 12

Market Research: Understanding the Event Customer

Learning Objectives

- Be able to conduct market research to support event marketing efforts.
- Be able to conduct consumer research including visitor and market area surveys.
- Be able to plan, design, implement, and analyze a visitor survey.
- Be able to estimate attendance at events.
- Understand the importance of reliability and validity in research methods, and especially the challenges of sampling.
- Understand motivations for attending events within the context of the consumer decision-making process.
- Learn from available research on event tourists and consumers.
- Know how events can meet diverse needs and motives, and how to provide and promote these.

Why Do People Attend Events?

Marketers must understand the needs, motives, and expectations of potential customers to influence decisions and satisfy patrons. But according to research undertaken by Mayfield and Crompton (1995), many festival organizers do not undertake thorough customer-oriented research, believing in their own ability to know what their customers want, or lacking the resources to do it. The culture of organizations often leads to product orientation, rather than a marketing orientation, in which case market research is undervalued.

Needs, Motives, and Benefits

Figure 12.1 presents three main categories of needs (drawing from Maslow, 1954), specific motives arising from each need that can generate visits to events, and corresponding benefits offered by events. For any type of event, in any setting, some combination of these generic benefits will attract visitors. The addition of highly targeted benefits (to specific market segments) will strengthen the pull of events, which is discussed a bit later.

To define "motive" we defer to Iso-Ahola (1980), who said: "A motive is an internal factor that arouses, directs and integrates a person's behavior" (p. 230). The event-goer wants to satisfy one or more needs through attendance or participation in the event, so event-related motivational studies must address not merely the reasons given for being at an event but also the underlying benefits sought. "Behavior" in this context refers to more

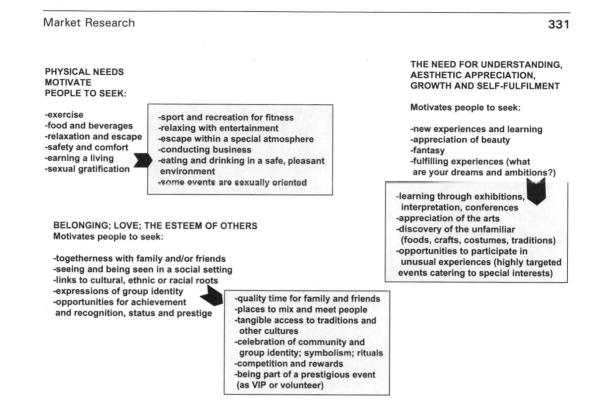

Figure 12.1. Needs, motives, and benefits offered by events.

than superficial activities at events, it also refers to the meanings attached to those actions. For example, having a party is generally fun, but is also likely to involve social bonding or cultural celebration.

A widely accepted leisure and travel motivation theory has been put forward by Iso-Ahola (1983) and Mannell and Iso-Ahola (1987), who argued that leisure and travel behavior is stimulated by both a desire to escape undesirable conditions and, simultaneously, to realize desired experiences (Figure 12.2). Underlying this concept is the belief that people

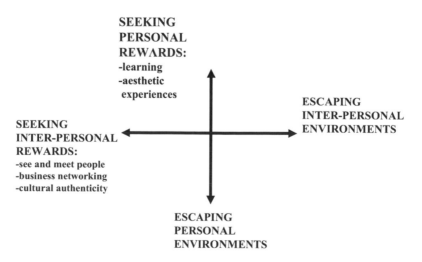

Figure 12.2. Seeking and escaping motivational theory.

seek levels of "optimal arousal," or a balance between under- and overstimulation in their environments and personal lives.

This seeking–escaping behavior operates within both personal and interpersonal dimensions. It can therefore be said that a trip to an event is motivated both by the desire to escape and the desire to seek out new experiences, relative to the person's interpersonal and personal needs. Marketing people often refer to "push and pull" factors (i.e., motivators to get away from and attractions to move towards), but it is wrong to think of them as acting independently.

An inherent part of the seeking–escaping theory is that of "intrinsic" motivation: that is, an activity or behavior motivated by one's own values and needs, not by reference to what others want. By contrast, "extrinsic" motivation occurs when a behavior or activity is done to please someone else, meet obligations, or for a reward. Attending an event might be done for reasons of personal development (e.g., to learn something new; for aesthetic enjoyment), or because the family or friends expect it. Often a combination of internal and external motives will be found. Asking people to explain their motives, however, might encounter a number of problems: dishonesty, recall problems, inability to articulate motives, or the expression of motives in terms of what the respondent thinks is socially acceptable or desired by the interviewer.

In Figure 12.3 is a conceptual framework for examining motives. Some are intrinsic, stemming from personal needs including seeking and escaping. Some are extrinsic, arising from the influence of others. Together these help explain why a lot of people attend events without strong interest in the theme or program. The third category consists of event-specific motives that translate into the marketing concept of targeted benefits.

Consumer Decision-Making Process

Figure 12.4 conceptualizes the consumer decision-making process for events. Underlying the desire to travel, pursue a leisure activity, or specifically attend an event are basic human needs that lead to behavioral motivations. People expect that certain activities or experiences will provide the desired benefits to meet their needs and wants, but of course many choices are available. Events must compete with other forms of leisure and other

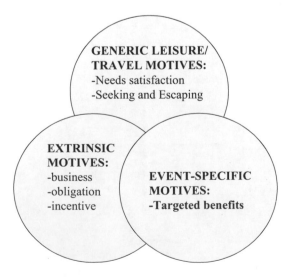

Figure 12.3. Framework for evaluating event motivations and behavior.

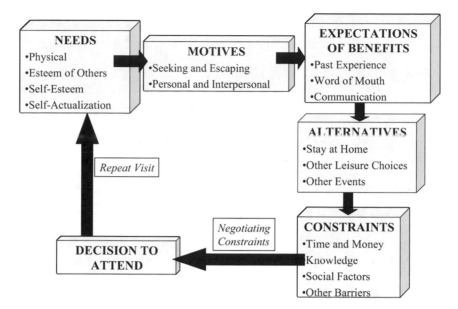

Figure 12.4. Consumer decision-making process for events.

events. As well, there are many barriers to possible participation, some personal (time, money, social influences) and some related to the event (location, accessibility, cost). Even if the consumer decides to attend an event, there can be good reasons why the desired experience never occurs.

To some researchers a key point is that motivations and travel behavior evolve, leading to the formulation of a "travel career ladder" (Pearce, 1993; Pearce & Caltabiano, 1983). This concept combines basic notions from the needs hierarchy, but is dynamic in that persons are presumed to change their motivations over time or across different situations. Also, people may hold more than one motive at a time, although usually one type tends to be dominant. Situational factors, such as time, money, and family, can strongly influence movement up the ladder, from a concern with biological needs through safety and security, relationship development, and finally to fulfillment or self-actualization. Some people retire from the ladder or do not travel at all.

Serious Leisure and Involvement

For many people attending events is more than just entertainment, it is an integral part of their lifestyle and a major component of sure pursuits. "Serious leisure" is a term coined by Robert Stebbins (1982, 1992) to describe life-long interests typified by the acquisition of specific knowledge and skills, perseverance, amateurism, searching for durable benefits or self-actualization, enhancement of self-image, and self-gratification. Serious leisure often encompasses one's entire social world, and this description certainly applies to many people who take sports and hobbies seriously enough to attend or compete in many events or to volunteer for events that match their interests, often resulting in travel over great distances.

A related concept is "involvement." Studies of leisure and recreation involvement (e.g., Havitz & Dimanche, 1999) suggest that those who are highly involved with a particular leisure interest can be expected to value participation in related events as a central part of their lifestyle, and to exhibit behaviors such as joining clubs. McGehee, Yoon, and Cardenas (2003) applied this concept to runners.

Research Note

McGehee, N., Yoon, Y., & Cardenas, D. (2003). Involvement and travel for recreational runners in North Carolina. *Journal of Sport Management, 17*(3), 305–324.

Using accepted scales to measure leisure involvement, these researchers studied the travel-related effects of higher involvement (i.e., running is more central to their lifestyle). Highly involved runners were found to take more overnight trips to races, they spent more, and attended more than less-involved runners. Higher involvement also led to more interest in evaluating brands of related merchandise (e.g., running shoes) and can result in strong brand loyalty, which is important for sponsors. The highly involved runners also were more active in seeking information about races and the places in which they were held.

Consumer Research on Events

Research on Festival Motivations

The anthropological and sociological literature (e.g., Abrahams, 1987; Falassi, 1987; MacAloon, 1984; Manning, 1983; Turner, 1982) is rich in its descriptions and interpreted meanings of festivals and other cultural productions or rituals. Such events are universal and ancient, forming an integral part of human civilization. In many respects, participation in events is play and the participant finds release from daily routine and/or reaffirmation of cultural values.

C. Lee, Lee, and Wicks (2004) provided a useful review of literature on festival motivation studies (including Crompton & McKay, 1997; Formica & Uysal, 1998; Scott, 1996; Uysal, Gahan, & Martin, 1993), concluding that there is a clear core set of motives for attendance, although it does vary somewhat with the type of event. These researchers also concluded that demographic variables did not explain as much difference in motives as did participation-related variables.

Research Note

Lee, C., Lee, Y., & Wicks, B. (2004). Segmentation of festival motivation by nationality and satisfaction. *Tourism Management, 25*(1), 61–70.

Using a factor analysis of data obtained from visitors to a Korean "Culture Expo," the researchers identified six motivational dimensions: cultural exploration, family togetherness, novelty, escape, event attractions, and socialization. These were consistent with other festival motivation studies reported in the literature. A cluster analysis performed on the six motivational dimensions identified four consumer segments, of which the "multipurpose seekers" were the most numerous and, perhaps because they had the broadest range of motives, were most satisfied. Domestic visitors and foreign visitors responded to different promotions, with foreigners more influenced by friends and travel agencies and domestic visitors more responsive to radio and television advertising. Foreigners were found to be more satisfied, overall.

Formica and Uysal (1998) examined cultural authenticity as a motivator to attend the Spoleto Festival, and other events that combined cultural and historical elements. Ethnic events have been associated with cultural identity, pride, and promotion (Carlson, 1998). Similarly, gay and lesbian event-related travel has been linked to the need for group identity and bonding (Pitts, 1999). Specific to sport events, Bale (1989) suggested that travel to mega-events was symbolic, or "collective rituals," like a pilgrimage. Green and Chalip (1998) concluded from a study of a women's sport event that participants valued the opportunity "to come together to celebrate the subculture they share as women football players" (p. 277).

Motivation to Attend Sport Events

A number of studies of sport events suggest that this market is quite different from cultural tourism. Leibold and Van Zyl (1994) noted that sport enthusiasts attending the Los Angeles Olympics in 1984 came primarily to see the Games but generated very little revenue in dining and sightseeing. They concluded that sport tourists might be less affluent and spend less on entertainment than average travelers.

Nogawa, Yamaguchi, and Hogi (1996) studied two "sport for all" events in Japan, where the emphasis was on the joy of participation and health or fitness, not on winning. They found that regardless of travel duration, the health/fitness and challenge motivators were paramount among participants.

Gillis and Ditton (1998) compared tournament and nontournament recreational billfish anglers as to their motives. This sport attracts mostly the wealthy elite and they are highly sought-after tourists. The researchers found the respondents to be mostly interested in the challenge of sport fishing, and the experience of catching large specimens.

Raybould (1998) also studied motives for participating in a fishing event, this one a week long in a remote, Australian location. His found that "social stimulation" and "escaping" motives were rated highest, contrary to the competitive aspects and extrinsic rewards stressed by organizers. Most respondents were male, so "family togetherness" ranked lowest. The statement "because the event was unique" achieved the highest individual mean response, and it was included in the "social stimulation" factor. The researcher's conclusion was that organizers should emphasize the social and relaxation benefits and make less of the extrinsic rewards (i.e., prizes) and competitive elements.

Nicholls, Laskey, and Roslow (1992) studied several events in Florida and found that visitors at a car race were very likely (75%) to participate in sport themselves, and many attended other racing events. Few, however, (15%) had attended a ballet or classical concert. This audience drank lots of beer and ate plenty of fast food. Not unexpectedly, males outnumbered females by about two to one.

Motivations for Attending Conventions and Meetings

It might be assumed that people attend meetings and conventions because they have to, but this is certainly not the case for many attending association meetings. Price (1993) found that education, networking, career path, and leadership enhancement were major factors influencing association members to attend conferences and conventions.

Oppermann and Chon (1997) modeled the decision-making process for convention attendees, concentrating on personal and business factors, the event itself, and its location. One of the major motivational factors they discussed was the level of commitment to an association, as that would influence its value to the participant. Hearing experts in a field, keeping up with developments, learning new skills, and developing valuable new relationships are other specific motives. Destination image is important, but locational inhibitors such as cost and accessibility can counter that attractor.

Ngamsom and Beck (2000) found that opportunities for travel overseas, outdoor recreation, business or political activities, a change of pace, networking, and education were all important motivators for association members. Inhibitors were found to include perceived safety and security risks, inconvenience, unfamiliarity with destinations, time, money, and personal health problems. Deals on travel packages, opportunities to do things with family, and costs covered by employers were all important factors facilitating attendance at international conferences.

Visitor Surveys

Whether by self-completed questionnaire, direct interview, or logbooks, visitor surveys provide essential information for marketing and evaluation of events and event tourism. They are relatively easy and inexpensive to undertake and analyze, at least at a basic level, but they do present challenges of design, sampling, and interpretation.

It is now quite easy to get access to event surveys and professionals capable of advising organizers or tourism officials on how to implement them. But experience in conducting and reviewing numerous surveys has convinced this author that it is a mistake to use somebody else's questionnaire, or to fit bits and pieces from surveys together and call it your own. Instead, it is essential that each visitor survey be formulated for specific purposes, and in such a way that the evaluators or planners get exactly the information they need. The following steps provide a simple guide to this process of custom designing the survey. Table 12.1 provides a large number of sample questions that can be incorporated into visitor surveys, with appropriate adaptation to the circumstances.

State the General Purposes of the Survey

Different purposes require different methods and measures. It is efficient to accommodate multiple purposes, but only with the resources to do it properly. Joint ventures among event organizers, tourist agencies, and other stakeholder should be pursued for these reasons. A visitor survey can be an excellent, and in many cases essential, method for obtaining data to:

- determine visitor needs, motives, and benefits sought;
- permit market segmentation and targeting;
- assess the effectiveness of communications and sponsorship;
- evaluate customer service and program quality;
- determine visitor spending and tourism impacts;
- obtain ideas for product and market development.

Determine the Specific, Ultimate Uses of Data

The worst mistake is to try to do too much, and that unfortunate outcome often occurs when a committee designs a survey! If a committee is in charge of research, a smaller subcommittee can be established to work out the options and design and test the survey. Include at least one experienced survey methodologist, and try to get representation from the tourism industry.

To avoid becoming overambitious, the evaluators must carefully specify who exactly wants the data, and in what ways the data will be used. The interests of tourism and the arts community will coincide in some areas, but conflicting needs are likely. So the group must prioritize the possibilities, and a good way to do that is to ask each stakeholder to rank their key objectives or questions. If there still remain too many questions after accommodating all the top priorities, it might be necessary to launch more than one survey. A master survey can be formulated with inserts of questions (to meet different needs) randomly mixed in, or a short on-site survey can be augmented by a longer take-home form.

List Key Data Requirements, Measures, and Alternative Data Collection Methods

Any goal or question can be converted into specific data requirements. For example, to evaluate the effectiveness of promotions it will be desirable to ask visitors how they heard about the event, or what information sources they consulted. The objective of determining economic impacts requires data on visitor spending. The measures must be developed next. Visitor spending can be measured in a number of ways: on- or off-site; by place; type of expenditure; by time of day or day of week. The unit of measurement is normally monetary in nature, and can be aggregated by party or kept at the individual level.

To collect each type of data might require different methods, and the visitor survey might not be best for all of them. Logbooks have been used to measure tourist spending, but they would require very special expertise to attempt at a special event because visitors might only stay a short time and may be difficult to contact in advance. Direct interviews on the site or at exit points will work, as will self-completed questionnaires. An interesting alternative is the conducting of a postevent, random telephone survey in the market area. Each method has merit, and limitations, but the intent at this stage is to screen all the options and determine the list of measures to be covered in the visitor survey.

Assess Feasibility of Methods

Which method will be most cost-effective in obtaining the data needed? Can the organization provide the human resources, funds, and technical expertise necessary to do the job right? It might be a matter of cost or convenience that determines the choice of survey methods. And the comfort and convenience of visitors must not be forgotten. There is no point in giving them self-completion questionnaires without pencils, or forms hard to write on, or that take an hour to read and complete. Are there convenient places to sit and write, or in which to be interviewed? Will questionnaires be picked up, or are there places at exits for drop-offs?

Selecting the sampling method is a crucial decision, and will be an important factor in determining feasibility. Options are presented later, and each has implications for cost, timing, personnel, and ultimate use of the collected data. "Quick and dirty" surveys, without random sampling, do yield useful insights for minimal cost, but cannot be used to measure impacts or convince sponsors of success.

Another factor to weigh is the need for support data. A random survey of visitors is meaningless without accurate attendance counts or estimates. Logbooks cannot be used for reliable estimates unless the participants are known to proportionately represent all event-goers.

Survey Design

Some creativity is involved in formulating the questions and formatting the survey, but all designs and questions should be pilot tested. The best tests are at events, but for many organizers that is impossible. Instead, a sample of ordinary people, the organization committee, and some experts could all be asked for feedback. Revisions will likely be in order, and if they are major ones, another test should be attempted. Finally, arrangements for production, personnel, and equipment can be made.

The Sampling Method

This section is concerned with getting a valid and reliable sample of visitors or consumers. Of course, if you are able to question the entire population of event guests there is no need for a sampling method.

Table 12.1. Sample Visitor Survey Questions

Visit/Trip Characteristics

These initial questions identify the true tourist from the resident, and give useful information on party and trip characteristics that can be cross-tabulated with other information. Attendance estimates require knowledge of the average number of days each visitor attended (for multiday events). How many times the average person entered the event area is also important.

Is this the first year you have attended this event?

How many years have you been here previously?

Is this the first day of this event you have attended?

How many days have you been to the event?

Is this your only trip to the event today? How many trips to the event have you made today?

Where is your permanent home?

Where did you travel from today (to get to the event)? How far away is that?

How did you travel to the event (private car, train, etc.)?

Are you staying in this area/city over night? For how many nights?

How many nights in total are you away from home this trip?

Where are you staying? (specify type of commercial accommodation versus staying with friends or relatives)

Did you come to this event alone, or with a group? What kind of group? (family, friends, tour group, etc.) How many adults are in your group? How many children?

How long have you been here so far? How much longer are you planning to stay? Option for take-home questionnaires: How many hours/minutes were you at the event in total? For multiday events, ask how many days the respondent came to the event?

Motivations and Information Sources

This is an important group of questions for marketing and impact assessment.

Are you in this area/city mainly to attend this event? If there is another reason, how important was the event in taking this trip, on a scale of 10 (10 being highest, and equivalent to 100%)? Option: Please indicate how important this event was in your decision to travel to this area/city: not at all; somewhat important; very important; the only reason.

Why did you come to this event? (open-ended, or provide possible reasons, such as: for the music, the food, a family outing). Option: Which of these things attracted you to this event? (list the main features)

How did you find out about this event? (open-ended, or provide a list of sources, including friends/family, and don't remember) Option: Do you remember hearing about this event from the following sources? (list advertising/promotion sources)

Have you been to a similar event recently? Which ones?

Economic Impact

More accurate and complete information on expenditures can be obtained from logbooks and postevent surveys. If it is an on-site survey, all that can be requested is an estimate of what the respondent will likely spend. The idea is to calculate average visitor spending at the event, in the area, and on the trip. Tourist expenditure must be separated from that of residents.

Please record all the expenditures you have made at this event (list all possible categories).

And what else did you spend while in this area/city, this trip? (include accommodations, transport, eating out, shopping, other attractions and entertainment)

Finally, what else did you spend on this trip? (i.e., getting here and returning home)

Activity Patterns

It is very useful to know what visitors actually see, do, and spend money on while at the event. Relying on memory will produce errors, so it is best to provide a list (if space and time permit) of all the possible activities, then let the respondent check off those completed or attended, and possibly those that are planned. For multisite or multiperformance events it is

Table 12.1 continued.

very important to know how many visitors went to each one, just as it is important to know how many days each person attended, otherwise accurate attendance and spending estimates are impossible.

What have you done or visited at the event? Please check off all those things listed below. Anything else? What else do you plan to do before you leave?

What else have you done or visited in this area?

Consumer Evaluation

At the simplest level are open-ended questions asking visitors to state likes, dislikes, problems, and suggestions. Try to corroborate the answers by means of direct observation and staff evaluations.

Importance–Performance Measures

Please tell us about any problems you have experienced at the event (in the area).

What did you particularly like about the event?

What did you particularly dislike?

Any suggestions for improving the event?

What else would you like the event to offer in the future?

Was the event exactly what you expected? What was different?

Do you plan to return in the future?

Would you recommend the event to someone else?

Please indicate how satisfied you were with all the following activities/events/attractions. (Respondents can be asked to rank them in order of satisfaction, or to indicate from 1 to 5 their degree of satisfaction with each; be sure to have the same items measured in terms of their importance)

Personal Data

Each question can be modified to obtain data on the whole group.

Please tell us/write in your age, in years (or age categories can be used).

Are you male or female?

Are you married? Do you have children?

What is your occupation/type of employment (including student, homemaker, retired, unemployed)?

What is your highest level of completed education (show categories)?

What is your annual income (probably best to use broad categories)?

Please describe the group you came with today (number, age, gender, relationship).

Be sure to thank, and if possible reward, all respondents. Remember that a survey can be a public relations tool, as well as an evaluation device.

Turnstile "Intercept" Sampling

In the "turnstile sample" every *n*th person (say, 1 of every 10 or 100) through the gate can be given a questionnaire or interviewed. This should ensure randomness, assuming that each person has an equal chance of being selected and that no person is covered twice. It must also be decided if only adults are to be surveyed, or if one member of each family or party is to be covered.

It is possible to estimate statistical levels of confidence for the sample only if it is known what proportion of the total attendance was sampled, and then only if there was no response bias (such as only certain types of people completing the forms). An interviewer can generally get a higher response rate, but they are restricted by the number of available interviewers. At peak times the turnstile interview sample might break down due to the sheer volume of arrivals.

A two-stage survey design has been highly recommended for events, such as combining a short, on-site questionnaire with a subsequent telephone interview with the same respondents. Pol and Pak (1994) argued that this method improves the quality of data, enables a broader range of questions to be asked, and permits follow-up on specific points. It is clearly a more costly research method per response, but can reduce the number of contacts needed to obtain reliable and detailed information.

On-Site "Intercept" Sampling

An alternative to the turnstile method is to intercept visitors as they move about an open site, or where they congregate on the site. Wherever people line up, surveyors have a good chance to systematically select every nth person. It is important to avoid arbitrary selection of respondents or a selection bias can occur (i.e., there might be a natural tendency to approach people of a certain type). Line-ups are particularly good because the people are waiting anyway, and might not mind filling out a form. The alternative is to select every nth person past a given point, such as the entrance to a building or area.

Personal questions present a problem, however, so verbal interviews should be concerned with general matters only, unless privacy can be assured. A combination of interview and self-completed questionnaire is a possible solution, with personal matters relegated to self-completion.

The big problem is to ensure that the whole site and all activities are covered, over the duration of the whole event. Keep in mind that the composition of the crowd will vary over time and over the site, depending on the attraction, services, and accessibility. To overcome this problem requires "stratification" of the sample, in terms of:

- time sampling: instruct interviewers to conduct the survey during specified times throughout the event;
- spatial sampling: ensure that surveyors are assigned specific sectors that cover the whole site.

Because these on-site intercept methods do not ensure a truly random sample, but do apply strict selection criteria, they are called "systematic." In terms of reliability they are not as good as random samples, but can potentially be better than quota samples.

Quota Sampling

If 200 respondents are desired, interviewers can be told to collect 10 or 20 each, subject to getting a balance between the genders and a good age spread. Other characteristics such as race or ethnicity might be important to specific events, and can be incorporated in the quotas. While this is a simple and useful approach, there is no basis for estimating the characteristics of the whole crowd from a quota sample. Of course, none of the nonrandom methods can be used for estimating the characteristics of the whole crowd, at least according to strict statistical practices. The evaluator must try to get the most representative sample possible, then qualify the final estimates by noting the limitations of the sample and resulting biases.

Other Survey Problems

A special problem in tourism surveys is that of selection bias attributable to length of stay in the area, or at the event. Those who are in the area or on the grounds longest will have the greatest chance of being intercepted for questioning. Turnstile sampling avoids this problem, assuming that repeat visitors are not covered twice. Approaching visitors as they leave the site or area also overcomes this problem, assuming a random or systematic sampling frame. If an on-site quota sample is used, the length-of-stay bias cannot easily be avoided.

According to Robinson and Carpenter (2002), the demographics of a 4-day professional golf event were substantially different each day, leading the researchers to conclude that it was really four events in one! This fact not only affects sampling, but also sponsorship and the entire marketing mix.

If self-completion questionnaires are used, the respondents must be provided with suitable places and the means to complete the forms and get them back to the evaluators. Some events invite respondents to visit a central place and provide a reward for those who comply. Others provide drop-off points at exits (don't use receptacles that look like waste bins!). If possible, you could ask for the address of everyone given a form, then write to them if they don't return it in time. This might be viewed as a breach of confidentiality, however. The best approach might be to use a short interview or questionnaire that can be completed in the presence of the interviewer. An alternative is to collect names and addresses of those willing to be mailed a questionnaire after the event, as this can lead to higher response rates.

The possibility of selection and interview biases have already been mentioned. Once a sampling frame has been selected, the interviewers (or those selecting questionnaire recipients) must follow the system. If a quota sample is used, there is a lot of room for selection bias, even though the quota might stipulate an even number of males and females and age groups. What about race or party type? Self-completed questionnaires can fail if their design or format suffer from any of the following:

- print too small to read by some recipients;
- language or words not understood by some visitors;
- too much detail; a format that appears too complicated;
- questions that are too personal;
- no pencil or pen provided;
- flimsy paper that is hard to write on;
- unattractive design, color, or print.

Design of a survey is in part determined by the purpose, number of questions, and intended recipients. In part it is an art, helped by trial and error and examination of other surveys. As a general rule, the shorter and simpler the questionnaire, the better and more accurate the responses will be. If an incentive can be offered to complete and return the questionnaire, that is desirable. Another good rule of thumb is to commence with easy, descriptive questions and leave personal questions to the end. Restrict write-in (open-ended) questions to the minimum, otherwise the forms can get messy and coding will be complicated. People in a hurry often ignore write-in questions.

Personal interviews can eliminate or reduce some of the problems associated with self-completion questionnaires. Skilled interviewers can shift the order of questions, probe where necessary, and double-check key points. Unless the interview is done in private, however, personal questions should be self-completed. The survey form must therefore be well organized and easy to use for both interviewer and respondent.

Reliability and Validity

Faulkner and Raybould (1995) noted common sources of visitor survey errors. The sample size must be large enough to permit estimation of the margin of error, and must be random or representative to avoid selection bias. If large numbers of people fail to respond, there is a real risk that the sample will not be representative. Errors in responses can occur, and in recording the answers if by interview. Processing and analytical errors are a final threat to achieving valid and reliable information.

Proper sampling methods must be followed to ensure results that are "reliable": that is, the same results (within limits of probability that all sampling entails) could be achieved if the survey was replicated on the same population. Sampling that is neither random nor systematic will produce major errors, and it will be impossible to determine the type or size of the errors by doing another, similar survey.

"Validity" means that the data obtained by the survey are theoretically sound; you obtained true information about the object of your investigation. Through poor wording or improperly conducted interviews it is possible to introduce all kinds of biases that will yield misleading results. For example, "interviewer bias" could result in leading questions and false responses. Poorly worded questions result in ambiguous answers.

How many visitors should be sampled? Burgan and Mules (2000) said that more is better, especially where distinct groups like tourists and residents are likely to have quite different characteristics (such as their spending). A stratified sample is useful in such cases to make sure you get enough tourists (or other minority group) to make reliable estimates. A usual problem is that the mean tourist expenditure is subject to bias by outliers (a few who spend a lot or hardly anything). They give examples from a festival and motorsport events.

Logbooks

An alternative to on-site questionnaires and take-home surveys is the use of logbooks. In this method a random or systematic sample of event visitors is provided upon arrival or in advance with a structured logbook. Any question can be asked, but the method is particularly useful for gathering more detailed and accurate information about activities and spending. At the end of each day of the event and the related trip, for example, a detailed sheet on types and amounts of expenditure would be completed.

Logbooks can be combined with questionnaire surveys, either by splitting the population to compare results on the same questions, or separating the population into two groups with spending covered only in the logbook sample. Faulkner and Raybould (1995) tested the cost-effectiveness and accuracy of logbooks versus questionnaires at a major sport event in Brisbane, Australia. Their results suggest that logbooks yield better expenditure data, but the response rate will be much lower (in their case, 97% vs. 23%). The challenge for researchers, therefore, is to obtain a committed sample and provide sufficient motivation for them to fully complete and return the books, such as a cash reward.

Attendance Counts and Estimates

Without reliable numbers, organizers cannot estimate total spending, nor can tourism planners calculate the impacts; the proportion of repeat visitors cannot be determined, nor can market segments be estimated; trends cannot be established and forecasting is hindered. Political problems also arise from inadequate or controversial attendance estimates. Organizers of some events want to demonstrate the size of their constituency or make a statement about support for a cause.

Burgan and Mules (2000) discussed the different methods available for attendance estimation. Obtaining box office data is sometimes possible, and the authors show how to make the attendance estimate when some of the sample attended free events and some attended ticketed shows. Estimates can be based on the known capacity of venues, hotel occupancy, revenue information (e.g., concession sales), or aerial survey (which must be supplemented by data on average length of stay or turnover). They also show how to deal with attendance bias where multievent-goers have a higher probability of being sampled.

Visitors and Visitation

As a general rule, events with gates and ticketed admissions have little trouble calculating total paid attendance, which can also be called "the gate" or "total visitation." But they might have more difficulty knowing how many individuals attended, because visitors are likely to attend more than one activity (at multisite events) or on more than one day. If only total visitation is known, organizers will be unable to estimate total tourist spending, which can only be calculated by multiplying the average spending of all visitors by the total number of visitors.

To illustrate this problem, consider a 2-day event that had a total attendance of 10,000 each day (as measured by paid admissions). A random visitor survey on the second day found that 50% of the sample had actually attended on both days, so 5000 of the second-day crowd were repeaters, and the total number of individual "visitors" was not 10,000 but only 7500 (5000 the first day plus 2500 new visitors on the second day). If average visitor spending of the sample was $10 (covering both days), then the total visitor spending was $10 × 7500, *NOT* $10 × 10,000! Of course, this problem could be avoided by taking separate random surveys each day, and calculating separate estimates of average visitor spending per day.

With a multiday event, or an event with multiple sites, the estimation of average and total visitor spending can get quite complicated. Not only will a complex sampling frame be required, but a statistician is needed! Researchers conducting an impact assessment of the Barossa Vintage Festival described a sampling and weighting procedure for use in multievent, multivenue festivals (Denton & Furse, 1993).

Benchmarks and Indicators

A "benchmark" is the initial attendance count or estimate against which future counts/ estimates are compared, to establish trends. Other "indicators" of attendance can be linked to this one-time attendance figure, and the indicators monitored to make future estimates. One common indicator is that of total sales, based on the assumption that if X number of visitors generated Y amount of sales, then any growth in future sales indicates that attendance has increased proportionately.

The best indicators will be those thought to be directly dependent on the size of the crowd, such as: total receipts; number of items consumed; attendance at one easily measured activity or site. Over time it is probable that the linkages between total attendance and these indicators will change, so if they are used it must be with caution and with monitoring of the factors that might cause divergence. For example, total sales or receipts will certainly vary with gross attendance, but might also rise or fall with promotion, accessibility to the outlets, competition from new items in other events, or even the weather.

Parade Counts

The simplest approach is to determine the depth of the crowd at a point (e.g., five deep) and apply this figure to the parade length (e.g., five persons per meter × 2 kilometers). Big errors are likely, however, if any of the following occur:

- people bunch together in clusters because some points on the route are highly favored or viewing is impossible;

- attendance peaks just as the parade passes;
- viewers move along with the parade.

Static Crowds

Where a crowd occupies a space, and there is no significant coming and going, a simple grid sampling can be used to make a reliable estimate of attendance. Divide the space into equal cells by fixing reference points along the perimeters. It does not matter much that the site is irregular, so long as there are cells covering all places where visitors will stand/sit. Again, sample at least 30. If the cells are small, there is no need to worry about clustering, because the differences between cell occupancies will be small. If clustering is a problem you must separately count the cells where bunching occurs or where occupancy is abnormally low. The estimate is then derived the same way as for parades, by multiplying the average cell occupancy by the total number of cells included, then adding the counts from separated cells.

If you can take an aerial photo of the site, a complete count might be possible, or grid lines can be drawn onto the photo. Be careful about the angle, as a low oblique shot might not reveal people behind various objects. Raybould, Mules, Fredline, and Tomljenovic (2000) describe an application of this technique.

Research Note

Raybould, M., Mules, T., Fredline, E., & Tomljenovic, R. (2000). Counting the herd: Using aerial photography to estimate attendance at open events. *Event Management, 6*(1), 25–32.

The researchers document how they used aerial photography to make an attendance estimate at a festival where a large, outdoor crowd assembled. On other estimation methods, they said "tag and recapture" was often unsuitable as many special events are too complex in terms of people movements to make it accurate (e.g., clustering around a stage; high turnover rate). They criticized the parade count method as being complex and requiring too many observers. Aerial photography can be used to estimate peak attendance when everyone is outdoors. For all open events a good understanding of the event, crowd dynamics, and venue is required to decide on the best estimation method. Photography is not labor intensive and is potentially very cost-effective.

Where movement is unrestricted, as in main street events, the grid sampling technique can be used to estimate the peak attendance, or several counts can be taken to determine general trends. But for most open events this will be impractical owing to site arrangements. Besides, an estimate of total attendance is desired. The main problem is "turnover" — the fact that the people in the crowd are constantly changing as some enter and others leave. Three techniques can be used in these situations: vehicle counts, pedestrian counts, and market area surveys.

Vehicle Counts

In some cases it might be possible to count all vehicles arriving at the site(s). Buses, boats, trains, or planes would be counted separately, so that total arrivals by these modes are known. For cars, an average number of passengers must be estimated by counting the number in every *n*th (say, every 20th) car. The average is then multiplied by the total number of cars. To make this work will require one or more observers to count all arrivals, and all entrances must be covered.

But some vehicles might make multiple visits. The only way to take this into account is to somehow mark all arrivals, as with window or bumper stickers, or to give first-time arrivals a parking ticket to show upon return. But returning vehicles might bring back different people! The only way to find out is to ask. Also, what do you do about pedestrians and bicyclists? They must be counted separately, but this will be impractical unless all entrances can be observed.

A third complication, particularly acute for main street festivals, is local traffic unrelated to the event. One way to separate visitors from locals (or normal business travel) is to stop all arrivals at road entrances and issue visitor stickers, and/or channel visitors to designated parking lots. General traffic surveys can also be used to estimate normal local volumes, which can be subtracted from total counts on the day of the event, but there will be errors attributable to normal fluctuations in local traffic.

Counting Moving Pedestrians

Like vehicles, pedestrians can also be counted as they enter or leave the event area, even if there are no gates. In this system observers must cover all entrances and either count all arrivals/departures or take sample counts regularly. For example, over an 8-hour event a 1-minute sample every 15 minutes would yield 32 counts. Much like the parade segments and crowd cell counts, the average count for the 32 sample minutes is multiplied by the total number of minutes in 8 hours (480) to get the estimate of arrivals. And like those other methods, blocks of time known to have very high or very low arrivals should be isolated and counted separately.

A similar system, called the "police method" (Indiana Department of Commerce and Indiana State Festival, 1988), is to count people in a defined area (e.g., 10 square meters) three times over the event's duration. This should be done in the peak flow area, and not at entrances. The total of the three counts are summed and divided by 3 to yield the average count. This average is multiplied by the total number of cells in the entire event area through which people are moving, and finally this figure is multiplied by the number of hours of pedestrian flow.

Both techniques yield very rough estimates, and neither one copes with the problem of some people being counted more than once. They are actually measures of total flow, rather than total attendance, and can be heavily influenced by site design.

Tag and Recapture

This method has been described by Brothers and Brantley (1993). It was borrowed from wildlife estimation techniques and involves the "tagging" of randomly selected visitors as they enter (at least 10% of them), followed by subsequent random selection of visitors on site to determine what proportion of them were tagged. A number of conditions have to be met and statistical estimation techniques are required.

Attendance Estimates From Market Area Surveys

If the primary market area is known (from visitor surveys), a postevent random household survey, most easily undertaken by telephone, can be used to estimate total attendance. Selected respondents must be asked who in the household attended what events, when, and how many times. The problems are twofold: long-distance tourists will have to be ignored, or estimated by some other means; telephone-based sample frames contain errors because of unlisted numbers, households that have no phones, and potentially high nonresponse rates.

What Attendance Data Are Really Needed?

It is clear that estimating attendance at open events is difficult. No 100% reliable count is possible unless there is complete control of entrances and exits, and statistically reliable estimates are only possible when random samples can be taken. For most open events, only a rough estimate can be obtained, and even then the evaluations must take into account the problems of multiple entrances, turnover, and counting procedures.

Given the problems, the manager should determine the most important attendance data. Where accurate counts and estimates are not possible, consider employing the following measures:

- peak attendance (the highest number present at one time);
- paid attendance (ignore the unpaid);
- attendance at key venues or activities.

Perhaps the real measure of success is sales or revenue, rather than how many people attended. But if any kind of tourism analysis is desired, it will be essential to conduct visitor surveys and attendance counts.

Triangulation

Where there is uncertainty about the attendance, using two or preferably three independent methods is recommended; this is called "triangulation". Either the results of separate estimates can be averaged, or they can yield high and low bounds. An example is at an open event where peak crowd size is estimated by way of a grid/cell count and total attendance is estimated by way of vehicular counts and a market area survey.

Conducting Market Area Surveys

When only visitors are surveyed the event manager learns nothing about why people do not attend, nor about the potential for attracting new segments. There are several basic approaches to market area survey and examples have already been presented. The various foreign pleasure market surveys conducted by Canada, the US, and many other countries are the most ambitious type and clearly beyond the capability of most event managers. Hopefully more destinations will develop event-related questions in this type of foreign research.

In a unique piece of contract research, Wicks and Fesenmaier (1995) attempted to measure the market potential for events within a 5-hour driving radius of an Illinois town. This "catchment area," or area of demand potential, contains over 30 million residents, and this population was found to be very active in traveling for events; 94% of respondents had taken at least one vacation trip within 300 miles of home during the previous year, and 74% had made an overnight trip. Fully 57% of all pleasure trips had included a festival or special event, and 31% of them had traveled more than 50 miles for an event; 55% had included an event in an overnight trip. These and other data enabled the researchers to estimate there were 50 million event attendances in the region annually!

The survey by Wicks and Fesenmaier (1995) is an excellent example of event-related market area research that is within the capability of most destination organizations such as visitor and convention bureaus. Through telephone or mail-outs, a random sample within the target zone can be asked a series of questions regarding event preferences, visits to events and related trip details, and awareness and interest in specific events. Consultants for the major evaluation of eight festivals in Canada's National Capital region used local telephone surveys to help estimate attendance at events. Two other pertinent surveys have been reported: by Verhoven et al. (1998) for a single event and Yoon, Spencer, Holecek, and Kim (2000) for Michigan's event tourism market.

Research Note

Verhoven, P., Wall, D., & Cottrell, S. (1998). Application of desktop mapping as a marketing tool for special events planning and evaluation: A case study of the Newport News Celebration in Lights. *Festival Management & Event Tourism, 5*(3), 123–130.

Declining attendance over 4 years at this holiday event was attributed to increased competition and decreasing novelty. The authors recommended that new attractions be added each year to bring people back. Their mapping technique identified the primary "catchment area" and proved that a "distance-decay function" explained much of the travel to this event. In other words, advertising beyond the primary catchment area would not be cost-effective in increasing attendance. Income was apparently a factor in determining the exact catchment area, as lower income households could presumably less afford the admission charge or did not have private cars. Offering lower cost packages with public transport would possibly help overcome this barrier.

Research Note

Yoon, S., Spencer, D., Holecek, D., & Kim, D.-K. (2000). A profile of Michigan's festival and special event tourism market. *Event Management, 6*(1), 33–44.

Data were obtained from selected questions contained in a market-area household telephone survey funded by Tourism Michigan and Michigan State University. Respondents in Michigan and surrounding states plus Ontario, Canada, were asked about pleasure trips taken to/within Michigan and the included activities. Results showed that 28% of those who had taken such a trip in the previous 12 months had included an event, and these event-inclusive trips were primarily in the summer months. Forty-three percent of the event-inclusive trips were by residents of Michigan, and the primary motive for all pleasure trips taken to/within Michigan was visiting friends and relatives. Those persons including festivals and events were much more action oriented and participated in many different forms of recreation and entertainment, plus their trips involved more nights in the state, thereby resulting in higher expenditures.

Many destinations conduct "exit surveys," which interview departing visitors. The logistics are difficult and the costs high, but extremely valuable data can be collected on activities, expenditures, likes and dislikes, etc., of visitors to the area. Unfortunately, many exit surveys do not include sufficient data on events. Ideally, all major travel-related surveys should include the following basic data:

- Have respondents traveled specifically/mainly for an event? If yes, what kinds? Where and when?
- Have respondents attended events while on trips for other purposes? If yes, what kinds? Where and when?
- What types of activities and benefits do travelers seek (that could be manifested through events)?
- How important are certain types of events in motivating travel or in selecting a destination?
- What specific benefits are desired from events of various kinds?

Case Study: Marketing the Calgary Stampede

Background

For over a century, the Calgary Exhibition & Stampede (CE&S) has hosted agricultural, commercial, educational, and entertainment activities year-round. This unique community organization is best known for presenting the Calgary Stampede, a 10-day cultural phenomenon recognized as one of the world's most successful annual events.

The Calgary Stampede is a blend of professional rodeo, agricultural fair, international tourist attraction, and community celebration that preserves and promotes Western heritage and values. A focal point for civic pride, the Stampede both reflects and involves the Calgary community. Its roots reach back to Calgary's earliest days as a ranching and agricultural center, and Calgarians salute their heritage by dressing Western and decorating their offices and businesses during Stampede.

The Calgary Stampede is one of Canada's most important tourism attractions, and research by Tourism Calgary places the Stampede second only to the Rocky Mountains as an internationally recognized Canadian icon.

Attendance grew rapidly and steadily starting in the 1960s, and reached an all-time high in 2004. Extensive market research into guest satisfaction, as well as strategic planning for achieving a wide range of benchmarks, have helped the CE&S to maximize the potential of its historic site and to reinforce the Stampede's relevance to the community.

Ownership and Organization

The CE&S is a not-for-profit, volunteer-driven organization that generates almost $80 million in revenue each year. That revenue is reinvested into the community through year-round public programming and through improvements and additions to Stampede Park and its facilities. Located in downtown Calgary, Stampede Park has been home to the CE&S since the 1880s. The Park covers 138 acres and houses one of Alberta's largest collections of exhibition halls, sports venues, and meeting facilities. The CE&S leases the Park and its facilities from the City of Calgary. Provincial funding through the Alberta Lottery Fund also enables the CE&S to offer programs and undertake facility enhancements.

The organization's Board of Directors consists of 25 directors elected from shareholders, three directors appointed by the City of Calgary, one appointed by the Province of Alberta, and the immediate past President and Chairman of the Board. Directors are not paid for their service. Shareholders are volunteers who cannot receive compensation or dividends. Shares cannot appreciate in value, cannot be sold, and cannot be held by non-Albertans.

The CE&S Chief Operating Officer supervises a permanent staff of 300 year round, plus 1200 part-time employees and 3500 staff who are hired specifically for the 10 days of Stampede. With more than 2100 volunteers, the CE&S boasts one of Canada's largest volunteer programs. Over 50 volunteer committees are dedicated to organizing events and promoting agriculture, Western heritage and the Stampede throughout the year.

In late 2002, the Calgary Exhibition and Stampede's Board of Directors initiated a major strategic evaluation of the organization's role in the community. This included extensive market research with Stampede volunteers, employees, stakeholders, and community leaders. The research confirmed that the purpose of the CE&S is to preserve and promote Western heritage and values, which were defined as including friendliness, neighborliness, entrepreneurship, and hard work.

The research also identified four key areas as business priorities: year-round operations, agriculture, Western heritage and values, and the 10-day festival (the Calgary Stampede). In 2003, the CE&S began a reorganization of its senior management team and staff to support these four priority areas.

Site Planning and Expansion Plans

In 2004, the CE&S unveiled its Master Plan to expand and redevelop Stampede Park. The Master Plan takes into account changing social, economic, and demographic realities. The plan is informed by nearly 15 years of extensive community consultation and by interviews conducted in 2003 with a wide cross section of Calgarians. This research found that the community supports both the CE&S's focus on promoting Alberta's Western heritage and values, and its role in linking rural and urban Alberta.

Photo 12.1. Stampede site, Calgary (credit: Calgary Exhibition and Stampede).

The Master Plan encompasses a 20-year vision for Park development that will transform Stampede Park into a 193-acre, multiuse community park. The plan will be implemented in several phases, and has an approximate price tag of $550 million. The CE&S intends to finance this expansion internally and through the exploration of new funding and investment opportunities with private, public, and community partners.

A 2001 survey of nonvisitors to the Stampede provided many insights into attitudes towards the Stampede, and suggested that the CE&S consider refreshing a number of elements including its agricultural exhibits. Early phases of the Master Plan include building an Agricultural Education Pavilion to replace the current agriculture building.

As well, research undertaken to identify potential target markets suggested that features such as parks, historic walkways and gardens, heritage attractions, exhibition facilities for festivals and Western-themed events, and a retail/entertainment zone would appeal to out-of-town visitors, year-round. One of the first priorities of the Master Plan is the implementation of a Greening Initiative to add landscaped courtyards, gardens, and plazas to Stampede Park and to help create a network of urban parks.

Visual design is always an important part of the event experience, and Stampede Park will be themed around the CE&S's core purpose of preserving and promoting Western heritage and values. The new site plan includes clear entry points and highly visible directional landmarks that can be easily understood by domestic and international visitors. Five themed Activity Zones will be created to help visitor orientation. Each zone will have a distinct visual profile that will identify and support the experiences people can have there, such as remembering, creating, celebrating, experiencing, or playing.

Stampede Marketing

Two CE&S divisions work in tandem to market the annual Calgary Stampede. Stampede Programming undertakes marketing research, advertising, and guest services, and is responsible for on-stage entertainment at the Coca Cola Stage and Nashville North, the evening Grandstand Show, the Stampede Showband, and CSTV. This division is also responsible for programming three special themed days during Stampede as well as one-off promotional events presented in conjunction with external partners. Sales Development undertakes promotions, creates and maintains a Stampede website that goes on-line during the festival's 10 days, oversees the box office and merchandising, handles tourism and group sales, and offers corporate hosting opportunities. The Corporate Communications and Stakeholder Relations division handles media relations and oversees year-round messaging on the CE&S's place in the community.

The CE&S has three objectives in marketing the annual Stampede:

- to increase paid gate attendance (includes prepurchased tickets for the afternoon rodeo and for the Evening Show, which features the chuckwagon races and the Grandstand Show);
- to increase awareness of and purchases of additional entertainment and experiences at Stampede Park such as Midway rides, food and beverages, lottery tickets, etc.;
- to increase awareness of the CE&S's core purpose of preserving and promoting Western heritage and values.

One marketing initiative has seen the successful introduction of corporate hosting packages. These packages are geared to CEOs, VPs, and Directors; business owners; and office, sales, and account managers who want to host their clients, employees, suppliers, or business partners at the afternoon Rodeo. A wide range of high-end options are available, ranging from packages with infield seats and meals at Ranahans (an exclusive hosting venue in the Grandstand that features dining areas, lounges, and viewing areas), to a Sales Manager Rodeo Package that includes a half-day seminar for sales teams on networking and selling during the 10 days of Stampede. In 2004, a new package called 30X was developed to provide quality corporate hosting opportunities at a midlevel price point.

CSTV and Stampede Entertainment Inc. (SEI)

CSTV (Calgary Stampede Television) distributes highlight packages of rodeo events and the chuckwagon races to local, national, and international media. In 2004, the CE&S joined with other partners to form Stampede Entertainment Inc. (SEI). This new venture is designed to enhance entertainment programming with "bigger" acts that will draw additional patrons to the Calgary Stampede each July.

Media Relations

The CE&S works closely with local, national, and international media throughout the year, providing news items, story ideas, and background information on the Stampede through media releases and articles as well as by facilitating interviews and photo opportunities.

The media is seen as a key community stakeholder. The media is invited to the annual Stampede Kick-Off, an event held in advance of each Stampede to showcase highlights of that year's 10-day festival. As well, a comprehensive Media Guide is produced annually that provides an overview of Stampede attractions and events, quick facts, and lists of key contacts. Media releases are posted on the CE&S website.

Both news and travel media come from all over the world to cover the Calgary Stampede. Calgary's major print media set up temporary bureaus on Stampede Park and encourage readers and the public to visit them. Several television and radio stations broadcast live from the Park throughout the 10 days. The CE&S also partners with local media to present events (such as concerts) or promotions (such as contests) that have a strong appeal to their target audiences. These sponsorships add value to the visitor experience at Stampede Park, while driving attendance for the CE&S and boosting the profile of the media partner.

Tourism Sales

The CE&S sells directly to consumers in their primary markets in North America and utilizes indirect selling to the travel trade in the Americas and internationally. By selling directly to the travel trade through wholesalers, receptive operators, tour operators, airlines, and travel agents, the Stampede encourages and educates sales agents to sell the Calgary Stampede directly in-market.

The CE&S also collaborates on programs, promotions, and advertising with DMOs (Tourism Calgary), PMOs (Travel Alberta), and the Canadian Tourism Commission. Travel Alberta's GSAs (General Sales Agents) in-market such as Japan, UK, Germany, and Australia are kept up to date on new products and hosted on familiarization tours during the 10 days of Stampede.

Net rates (10% off retail) on tickets and packages are available exclusively to the travel trade. The CE&S's block space policy is very user friendly to the industry, as a deposit is not required to hold tickets. Tickets can be held from September to reconciliation in mid-June.

Every year, CE&S staff attend major Canadian travel trade shows such as Rendezvous and Canada's West Marketplace, as well as the National Tour Association, American Bus Association, and Canada's Media Marketplace in the US; Spotlight Canada in the UK; Corroboree in Australia; and Canada Calls in New Zealand. Recently, Kanata in Japan has been added to sell in-market to encourage tour operators to add Stampede product to their itineraries.

At the consumer level, awareness of the Stampede is created through Travel and Leisure Shows in selected markets such as California, Texas, the Pacific Northwest, Ontario, Quebec, and Western Canada. As well, the CE&S spearheads a consortium of select tourism attraction partners that maximizes representation at consumer shows in these markets. At these shows, a display booth is set up, collateral sales material such as brochures and flatsheets are distributed, and a contest is offered to encourage visitation to both the booth and the destination. Contest entry forms are used to create a consumer database but, due to new privacy laws, only the names of consumers who have indicated their permission on the ballot are retained.

Pricing

Admission to the Park during Stampede provides access to a wide range of free agricultural events, cultural exhibitions, and live performances. These are funded in part by revenue from gate admissions. Gate price in 2004 was $11.00. Once in the Park, guests can also buy: tickets for midway rides, snacks and meals ranging from fast food to fine dining; tickets for the afternoon Rodeo; and tickets for the Evening Show, which includes the Chuckwagon Races and the Grandstand Show.

Reserved seating is sold for the Rodeo and for the Evening Show. In 2004, the Calgary Stampede introduced a new rodeo pay out structure that awarded over a million dollars in prizes. From a marketing perspective, the million dollars places the Stampede second only to the National Finals Rodeo for prize money, boosts the Rodeo's profile, attracts the best cowboys to compete, and increases rodeo ticket sales. These tickets include Park admission. Rodeo ticket prices range from $26.00 to $50.00.

Tickets for the Evening Show range from $33.00 to $63.00. These tickets include the Chuckwagon Races, a 90-minute Grandstand Show featuring performances by singers, dancers, acrobats, and musicians on the TransAlta stage (which is valued in excess of $6 million), and a fireworks display.

The CE&S offers special programs and themed days that provide value for visitors and opportunities for everyone to enjoy the Stampede. On the night before Stampede starts, Sneak-a-Peak provides everyone an opportunity to enter the Park at a reduced admission. Three days are programmed with a range of themed activities and entertainment options that target specific audiences. ENMAX Family Day offers a free breakfast and stage show, plus free Park admission for families who arrive before 9 a.m. Western Heritage Day is geared towards seniors and includes special morning exhibits and performances (with complimentary coffee and donuts) plus free rush Rodeo and Evening Show tickets, free bingo, and free rides on the Skyride. Admission is free for adults 65 and over all day long. Kids' Day includes a free breakfast and stage show, interactive displays, free admission to children 12 and under entering the Park before 9 a.m., and the opportunity to purchase discounted prices on midway rides.

The Stampede also partners with sponsors to provide attractive discounts and promotions that offer additional value for locals and visitors. For example, Canada Safeway sells an Advance Midway Deal that offers unlimited weekday rides for $20.00. Calgary Wal-Mart stores offer the chance to purchase three gate admissions for the price of two. Guests can bring four Dentyne Ice outer package gum wrappers to receive $2.00 off regular gate admission.

Internet Marketing and Packaging

The CE&S website (www.calgarystampede.com) has become one of its most important marketing and revenue tools. The website provides one-stop shopping for tickets, travel packages, and Stampede merchandise.

In 2004, a new on-line ticketing system was introduced that allows real-time seat reservations and enabled customers to print their own tickets at home. During Stampede, a featured called "My Day" makes it easy for guests to view the schedule of events for each of the 10 days and plan a visit.

The CE&S has created 10 popular travel packages that are generating new revenue streams while enhancing visitor experience with added elements such as horseback riding, white water rafting, camping, shopping, and dining. Packages are available on the CE&S website and can be booked on-line or by calling a toll-free number.

The core package is the Two Day Thrill Package, which appeals directly to the international visitor and encourages visitation over 2 days. It offers premium seating at the Rodeo and Grandstand Show as well as added value such as coupons. This package is the most common component for tour operators to include in their tour itineraries, and all 10 packages are available to the travel trade at net rates. Other packages include additional components from tourism partners and attractions throughout Alberta. Some offer exclusive elements. Each package can be customized by adding accommodation, RV or car rentals.

Purchases made by travel agents and tour wholesalers are commissionable at varying rates depending upon volume, and organized groups are offered a 10% discount on tickets for groups of 50 or more.

Sponsorship

The Calgary Stampede is an ideal event sponsorship medium. Event sponsorship holds many advantages over traditional media: direct contact with over 1 million person-visits at the Stampede; on-site and community-wide joint promotions with the CE&S; high exposure to the media (each year media from around the world are accredited to cover the Stampede, plus Calgary Stampede Television distributes highlights packages). Consumer research is available to show sponsors the target audiences.

Sponsorship programs are designed for integrated marketing: to provide signage and collateral visibility on site (e.g., in 750,000 copies of the daily events schedule), media exposure, corporate hosting, employee involvement and other benefits (such as an employee night at the Stampede, volunteering and ticket specials), and leveraging (i.e., sponsors' brands are aligned with the Stampede as much as possible, enabling sponsors to use, for example, Stampede logos and images).

The Sponsorship Department builds sponsor relationships that offer enhanced product to Stampede patrons while providing value for sponsor companies. The Department develops sponsorship packages that will meet a company's needs for comprehensive marketing programs with product agreements and sales overlays.

There are currently five categories for sponsors: "Stockmen's Club" ($100,000+); "Ranchman" ($40,000–99,999); "Cattle Baron" ($10,000–39,999); "Trail Boss" ($2,500–9,999), and "Wrangler" ($1,000–2,499). In early 2005, the CE&S will be realigning these levels and introducing a sixth category, the Stampede Champion, for the organization's largest sponsors.

Benefit packages correspond to the level of investment each organization makes with the Stampede. Portfolios can include: "ownership" or entitlement rights of specific events or prop-

Photo 12.2. Stampede Chuchwagon Race (credit: Calgary Exhibition and Stampede).

erties; promotional rights; product supply/category exclusivity; employee involvement; pre ferred supplier status; signage; collateral advertising opportunities and exclusive access. Long-term sponsorship relationships are particularly encouraged, yielding more stable revenue sources for the CE&S and greater marketing opportunities for the sponsor within the community.

A particularly successful Stampede sponsorship vehicle (literally!) is the ever-popular Chuckwagon racing. It is referred to as the GMC Rangeland Derby, and each year since 1923 companies have bid for the rights to "own" 1 of 36 chuckwagon canvasses where their logo or message can be displayed. The racing teams compete for over $800,000 in prizes, and top teams attract the highest bids. The Grandstand attracts 18,000 spectators nightly, and the races are broadcast on television to a national and international audience. As well, the chuckwagons are displayed throughout Calgary during the 10-day festivities, and some are randomly selected to appear in the Stampede parade.

Target Markets

The criteria used by the CE&S to select target geomarkets are: geographic breakdown of Stampede ticket sales; in-house tracking of requests for information via e-mail, a toll-free information line, and questions submitted to the CE&S website; external exit surveys; statistics generated by Statistics Canada; airline lift and connections; proximity; population; demographics and psychographics.

The CE&S also targets markets that have been identified and established by the Canadian Tourism Commission, Travel Alberta, and Tourism Calgary.

Each geographic market is well established and has a proven affinity or interest in the Stampede. The markets are as follows:

Local and corporate: Calgary and Regional
Canada short haul: British Columbia, Alberta, Saskatchewan, Manitoba
Canada long haul: Ontario, Quebec
US short haul: Pacific Northwest states
US long haul: California, Texas
International: UK, Australia/New Zealand, Germanic Europe, Japan

Market Research

Research immediately bore out the obvious following the events of September 11, 2001: the travelers of the world would be staying at home. The CE&S addressed this new global reality by adjusting their marketing strategies to focus on more regional markets. Although the international traveler remains an important target for Stampede marketing, research has shown that the 10-day event attracts repeat visits from residents in regional markets. Regional residents have easier access to the Stampede because they can choose to either fly or travel by car, and because they need less travel time than visitors coming from overseas. The new regional emphasis has been effective in encouraging return visits over multiple years by regional visitors.

Tourism market research (i.e., knowing the customer) is an important element of the CE&S' marketing plan, which also tracks demographics and visitor psychographics.

On-site visitor surveys are conducted annually, including a tracking of visitor profiles, activities, and satisfaction levels. As well, telephone surveys have been undertaken periodically among Calgarians and other southern Albertans.

On-site interviews are spread over the 10-day event, at different times and places. The consultant, Ipsos Reid, estimated the survey results were accurate within ±2.98%, 19 times out of 20.

The follow data are from the Ipsos Reid 2004 Stampede Exit Survey.

Visitor Attendance and Origins. A large majority of attendees every year are Calgarians. In 2004, 70% were from Calgary, 8% came from another country, 12% were from other parts of Canada, and 11% were from other parts of Alberta. Visitor surveys do not include staff, volunteers, and Stampede participants.

Visitor Motivations. Annual visitor surveys track the proportion of people who come to "look around" versus those with specific motivations. In 2004, 55% of visitors were "lookers" and 44% of visitors came for something specific. Of the specific attractions mentioned, the most popular are the rodeo (36%), the Grandstand Show (15%), chuckwagon races (15%), and animals (8%). "Midway" rides and entertainment appeal more to younger attendees, while the rodeo attracts an older audience.

Visitor Satisfaction. Overall satisfaction with the 2004 Calgary Stampede was very high, with 95% rating their experience as "excellent" or "good," up 2 percentage points from 2003 and a 10 percentage point increase over 2002. Almost half (49%) rated their experience as "excellent" and 46% rated it as "good"; 60% said the event met their expectations and 36% said it exceeded their expectations.

Nonuser Research. The CE&S has surveyed nonusers since 2001. Objectives are to examine barriers to attendance and to measure the appeal of current elements of the Stampede.

This focused market research has provided many insights into attitudes toward the Stampede. Like all market research conducted by the CE&S, it has been a catalyst for new approaches to programming and marketing the Stampede. For example, when research suggested that the Stampede consider refreshing the Midway, the CE&S responded by incorporating new standards for exhibitor and concession booths; ensuring more open space by relocating elements of the Midway; and creating a new layout that improved traffic flow. By 2004, 65% of attendees at the Stampede visited the Midway during their stay at the Park, an increase of 10% over 2003.

Study Questions

- What basic human needs can be met by events? How?
- Explain how event customers might be both seeking and escaping.
- What is serious leisure and how does it relate to event attendance and volunteering?
- Why are people who are highly involved in a sport or activity likely to become event tourists?
- Why is it important to understand the benefits people seek from events?
- How are intrinsic and extrinsic motives different? Why are some people attracted for generic reasons and other for event-specific reasons?
- Describe the steps in designing and implementing a visitor survey.
- What is the best way to sample guests at closed (e.g., a theater with reserved seats) and open (e.g., a street festival) events?
- Why is it essential to have a good attendance estimate? What are the possible methods?
- Explain how the Calgary Stampede conducts and uses market research.
- Why are visitor and market area surveys both useful?

Advanced Study Questions

- How can the related theories of serious leisure and involvement be applied to gain a better understanding of motives to attend and volunteer at events?
- Describe a research project designed to test the link between involvement in a particular hobby or sport and travel for related events, leading to a marketing strategy for that type of event (e.g., marathon running, wine making, arts and crafts, jazz).
- Use the consumer decision-making process for events to explain how event marketers can identify and help overcome constraints to attend.

Chapter 13

Communications and Sales

Learning Objectives

- Be able to employ the full communications mix to effectively promote the event and establish and maintain relationships.
- Be able to develop and implement an effective, ethical advertising campaign.
- Be able to use appropriate media to promote events at the destination level.
- Be able to sell events through packaging and intermediaries, as well as sales promotions.
- Be able to cultivate an attractive image of the event, and use events to enhance destination imagery.
- Be able to package events for maximum tourist appeal.
- Be able to work with the tour industry to achieve marketing goals.
- Be able to evaluate communications' effectiveness and efficiency.

The Communications Mix

Although many managers use the term "promotion," it is but one of several forms of communication. The "communications mix" consists of all the methods by which the event communicates with its various constituencies and markets, including advertising, sales promotions, and public relations. Sponsorship is considered to be a fourth arm of communications, from the sponsor's perspective (IEG, 1995).

According to Crompton and Lamb (1986), a marketing strategy must include the communications tasks necessary to influence the consumer buying process: informing, educating, persuading, reminding. Public relations has the added function of fostering community support and sponsorships, but that too is part of ensuring demand for the event. All communications must be coordinated to achieve marketing goals. Event managers have a number of special challenges to consider:

- There is often a need for intense, short-term promotion of the upcoming event.
- One-time events must manage communications very carefully to achieve early awareness and ensure a peaking of demand as the event nears.
- During long events, such as world's fairs, communications can continue during the event and partially make up for earlier weaknesses.
- The communications budget is often inadequate, being of secondary importance to getting the event produced.
- Many constituencies must be involved (e.g., grant-givers, sponsors, suppliers, par-

ticipants, politicians, target markets, volunteers) in event communications.

- Sponsorship has the potential to greatly enhance the quality and extend the scope of communications.
- Events are often very attractive to the media, especially television.
- Many events are mostly media oriented, with the explicit goal of generating substantial coverage and image enhancement for organizers and destinations.
- Maintaining good public relations within the host community can be essential to long-term development of the event.

Advertising

The essence of "advertising" is not just that it usually costs money, but that specific messages are delivered in a predictable, often repetitive, manner over (usually) mass media. The messages can be visual, verbal, written, or auditory, and are intended to accomplish one or more of the following goals:

- create or increase awareness of the event (or the organization, cause, program elements, sponsors);
- create or enhance a positive image;
- position the event relative to competition;
- inform targets (of dates, places, cost, program, etc.);
- generate a need or want for the event (persuade);
- convert demand into sales;
- remind target segments of the event or how to purchase.

A common mistake is to advertise indiscriminately, rather than in a focused, goals-oriented manner. Without target marketing and a comprehensive communications strategy, a lot of advertising can be wasted. Furthermore, because it is often difficult to evaluate results, effectiveness might be taken for granted rather than tested and refined.

Advertising Media

The basic choices consist of print media (newspapers, magazines, flyers, direct mail, billboards, etc.), broadcast media (television, radio), or electronic media (movies, Internet, video, etc.). The term "broadcast media" refers to the use of public airwaves. Radio and TV are increasingly engaging in 'narrowcasting" (i.e., aiming at specific target segments) facilitated by cable and satellite systems.

Relative advantages and disadvantages of employing the various media are summarized in Table 13.1. In general, it can be concluded the TV is the most powerful medium, but also the most expensive. Catherwood and Van Kirk (1992, p. 157) said that TV coverage gives credibility to events and can boost impulse attendance, although news coverage can also achieve these objectives. Small events will find it difficult to pay for television time and so must seek out media sponsors, other sponsors who will advertise the event on TV, or rely on news and public service announcements.

Radio has certain advantages. It is better targeted to certain demographic and lifestyle or cultural groups, and to specific music tastes. Young people listen to radio more than they read. Events and radio stations make excellent partners, especially when music is involved. Radio is more useful to generate wide awareness of the event, and detailed information immediately prior to it. Audible imagery can be used effectively to convey the feeling of celebration and excitement, or to provide a sample of musical specialties. Contests with event-related prizes work well on radio, and may attract sponsors. In large urban areas with multiple stations it is possible to target market using radio, especially with

Table 13.1. Advantages and Disadvantages of Advertising Media for Events

The Medium	Advantages	Disadvantages
Television	Conveys the sights and sounds of events to more people Can increase spontaneous attendance Lends credibility to event	Expensive to produce messages Expensive to buy time Might lack targeting
Radio	Can be targeted to lifestyle and music tastes Frequent repetition possible Short lead time to produce Can be inexpensive	Low reach on certain stations Low attention levels in audience No visuals
Magazines	High quality; color Can be highly targeted Longer life; many readers	Long lead time Some have low reach Costly production
Newspapers	Timely; short lead time Local; good for details Low production costs Good first-time reach Good for information details	Not targeted Misses youth and language groups Poor reproduction Builds Reach slowly
Direct mail	Most selective of media Fast response Flexible formats Can be personalized Good for coupon redemptions	Most expensive per impression Must compete with junk mail clutter
Flyers	Cheap per unit Easy to distribute Convey essential information in easy to read format	Disposable and often thrown away Must be delivered
Posters	Easily placed in key locations Catch the eye Can be sold as art	Must secure cooperation to post Can be ripped off
Billboards	Potentially large reach Strategic locations possible Grabs attention	Can be expensive Easily tuned out after first exposure
Brochures	Wide dispersal is possible Low per-unit cost Easy distribution Tourist oriented	Lots of wastage Not very targeted

regard to the big differences between rock, country, alternative, ethnic, and middle-of-the-road programming.

Many cities and regions have their own magazines, often with an entertainment and "what's on" emphasis. These can be used much like newspapers, although their production deadlines will require extra lead time. Care is needed to check on when and how they are distributed, and who will get them. National newsstand and subscription magazines will not be affordable to small events, but they do offer an excellent way to reach special interest groups and targeted socioeconomic segments. The marketer must check circulation numbers and geographic distribution, determine the magazine's coverage of desired segments, and estimate costs compared with other media options. Sports and hobby magazines are often targeted precisely, but not all readers will be interested in travel. And there are numerous travel-themed magazines—their readers are largely in the upper socioeconomic classes and travel frequently.

Newspapers are an important media outlet for events, especially because of the ability to reach local and regional audiences with detailed information in a timely fashion.

Magazines are less frequently used, are more expensive, and require higher quality production, and are best when highly targeted. Getting events covered in travel magazines through the hosting of travel writers (offer them free familiarization tours in partnership with other attractions) is a good way to reach potential tourists.

Direct mail has its uses, but few events employ this medium. It works best to reach specific audiences through geocoding, and of course your loyal, repeat visitors. Specially prepared flyers or brochures can be distributed through the mail (which can be expensive) or by employing door-to-door delivery.

Events typically use flyers and posters, which can be mass produced at low per-unit costs and widely circulated locally. It is difficult to assess their effectiveness, but posters in particular can serve the double-purpose of being art to sell.

Brochures require special consideration in their design and circulation, and are discussed later in the chapter, along with event programs. Other possibilities for events include:

- listings in event calendars published by commercial firms or tourist agencies, cultural groups, etc.;
- home page on the Internet;
- movie and video ads;
- banners on streets and buildings.

Communicating on the Internet

Internet functions are evolving, and with the introduction of interactive capabilities there is great scope for innovation. Key functions, beginning with the simplest, include:

- being listed within a directory of events, types of event, or as part of a destination's attractions inventory;
- providing consumers with detailed information about the event and its program, including photographs;
- being linked to other events, attractions, packages, and related information sources;
- inviting and responding to dialogue; developing a database of potential and real customers;
- making sales (tickets and merchandise);
- providing forms (e.g., to volunteer) and audience/market surveys;
- press releases;
- providing sample, virtual experiences of the event.

The event marketer should seek to maximize creative "hyper-links" (i.e., to ensure that the event can be reached by a simple click of the mouse from many other home pages). For example, the marketer of a jazz festival will obviously want to be listed under festival and jazz directories, but why not also develop links to nearby resorts and hotels, other festivals, to venues, and to discussion groups for music lovers.

Increasing sophistication in the use of Internet capabilities, both by consumers and suppliers, will result in greater innovations and possibly unexpected opportunities for marketing and virtual reality sampling. The downside is that it is getting harder and harder to find what you want on the Internet because of all the "noise," the ambush marketing (e.g., nasty pop-ups!), and confusion over "official" sites. Constant monitoring of how actual consumers find and use your website is vital.

Advertising Campaigns

To get professional advice and best results a professional advertising agency could be employed for the campaign. Managers who must, or want to, do it themselves need to plan the campaign carefully. A starting point is the budget, which will dictate to a large extent what media can be used, how frequently, and in what market areas. The usual situation is that not enough money is spent on advertising, or it is left to the whims of whatever media sponsor can be signed up. How much is enough? There is no rule of thumb specific to events, but there should be a direct connection between the total event budget and the advertising expenditure. It is not just that bigger events can afford the advertising, but that they need it more—to generate the demand.

Up front, performance objectives must be set. Otherwise, the expenditure cannot ultimately be justified nor the advertising improved. Specific criteria can include the following:

- Reach: how many people in the target areas or segments will receive the messages within the campaign period?
- Frequency: average number of times the message is received.
- Accuracy (aim for minimal mistakes in the messages delivered).
- Recall: do people remember the messages?
- Comprehension: degree to which recipients understand the message.
- Impact: measures of actual behavioral change, especially sales or attendance at event; before the event, measure willingness to pay and intent to attend.

Selection of the media should be based on an evaluation of advantages and disadvantages related to the needs of the event. At the same time, media sponsorship must be solicited to extend, not replace, the paid advertising. Most commercial media companies will be willing to offer discounts or two-for-one deals to the events they sponsor, but not give advertising away. Contracts will be required, both for sponsorship and advertising buys. Prices can often be negotiated. Joint communications should be used to maximum advantage. Join with other events or attractions, related services, sponsors, and tourist organizations to extend the campaign.

A timeline is essential. Use the event's critical path to establish the flow of advertising, critical dates at which key information must be provided, and the balance between media types as the campaign matures. For annual events, there is little point in paying for ads throughout the year, but there is much to gain by obtaining free publicity in the local papers as often as possible. Ads placed close to the event time should have a combination or alternating focus on attention-grabbing visual effects, in keeping with the theme, and detailed information about location, schedules, attractions, and costs. Coupons for price discounts and other incentives can be used, and event programs circulated. Sunday might be the best day to promote certain events, especially as many decisions to attend will be relatively spontaneous. Sunday is the day for leisure, and the noise from other advertisers is reduced.

Repetition of advertising is essential, and the frequency of ads should increase as the event nears. As well, attractive imagery should be highlighted in the early stage of the campaign, to arouse interest, whereas full information is required at the time of ticketing and when the event arrives.

An advertising budget is difficult to devise without the benefit of experience or professional advice. Many event managers take what Morrison (1995) calls the "affordable" approach—we spend whatever we can afford! Many businesses base their marketing budget on a percentage of sales, but this might not be applicable to nonprofit events. If there is a profit motive, however, it is not unreasonable to allocate 5% of total expected (or last year's) sales revenue.

The recommended approach is to work back from goals, attendance or sales performance objectives, targeting strategies to ensure that there are sufficient resources to be successful. Paid advertising will then likely be viewed not as a luxury, but as an essential component in the communications mix. Always evaluate advertising effectiveness to improve the next campaign.

Legal, Ethical, and Values Considerations

Advertising and other communications present considerable scope for creativity, but also for misleading, false, or offensive messages. The manager has an obligation to adhere to appropriate laws, as many jurisdictions have both advertising codes and consumer protection laws. Ethics is a trickier matter, with ambiguities to plague even the most thoughtful manager. Judgments must also be made about the possibility of offending someone's values, especially when it is unknown who might be offended and why.

General principles can be applied to alleviate or avoid these problems (based on the Canadian Code of Advertising Standards as reproduced in Keegan et al., 1995, p. 598):

- be accurate; no deceptions, especially on price and benefits to be received for payments;
- be clear; avoid ambiguous messages;
- avoid negative comparisons;
- be able to deliver what is promised;
- specify any warranties and guarantees;
- consider community decency and the values of others;
- do not employ false testimonials or claims;
- do not play on fears;
- avoid appeals to children.

Sales Promotions

A "sales promotion" is a nonrecurrent action intended to generate sales or increase attendance. The promotion can be aimed directly at consumers, the travel industry, or intermediaries who can influence sales. The most common forms are:

- price related (discounts, two-for-ones, coupons);
- cross-promotions (involving one more sponsors or products);
- gifts (in return for sales);
- donations (a portion of the price goes to charity);
- group sales;
- contests;
- sampling;
- incentives and commissions;
- frequent customer benefits.

The sales promotion seeks to add value to the decision to purchase or attend, and to convey a sense of excitement and urgency (Keegan et al., 1995, p. 571). Sales promotions can also stimulate a first visit, encourage repeat visits, and generate positive word-of-mouth discussion. Sponsors can be found to create the promotions or participate in those invented by the event marketer.

Very common event promotions include coupons redeemable on site for a gift or free/reduced admission, free sampling on site, and group discounts and benefits. Sponsors frequently put together cross-promotions around event platforms.

There are costs and risks, of course, such as the possibility that regular admission or sales prices will be undermined. Customers come to expect discounts and extras if they are offered frequently. Also, because of the number of sales promotions facing consumers, it might be difficult or expensive to find one that is more effective than average.

Public Relations

"Public relations" (PR) can be defined as the actions and communications of the organization that are aimed at fostering awareness, understanding, and positive attitude toward the organization and its operations. As observed by Kudrle and Sandler (1995, p. 4), the results of good, bad, or nonexistent PR efforts can be seen in the public's perceptions of the organization (or the event) resulting from all communication sources.

It is also useful to think of PR as one aspect of relationship marketing: the fostering of mutually beneficial relationships with customers and other stakeholders or publics. PR efforts can directly target customers, or grant-givers, lenders, subsidizers, sponsors, and other groups upon which the event is dependent. As well, the media is an important focus of PR, because they can often deliver the messages more widely and effectively—especially to the general public. Managers might also see their internal marketing efforts in the context of PR.

In contrast with advertising, PR messages are likely to be received with higher credibility, especially if they appear to be news or are in the form of positive editorials. Costs can be kept low, and sometimes "free" publicity can be received, but PR value is not created without planning and effort. It will also be difficult to evaluate PR success unless performance objectives are set out in advance.

A variety of communications channels can be employed, but most require the identification and cooperation of "gatekeepers"—the persons who accept or reject PR messages or programming. This is particularly important when events approach the media, all of which are bombarded with requests. Getting to know the local station and newspaper personnel will therefore pay off when it comes to getting your communications accepted.

The main methods of PR management are summarized in Table 13.2, along with event-specific advice. Below, greater detail is given to the media kit, which features prominently in all event communication strategies.

The Media Kit

The object is to ensure that anyone requesting information, especially the media and tour companies, gets timely and positive information about the event. Typical contents include:

- background to the event and its organization;
- past successes; a fact sheet;
- the event program and specific features;
- detailed schedule;
- list of sponsors and profiles of major supporters;
- contact names and addresses;
- photos for reprinting; audio and video tapes, if available.

Table 13.2. Public Relations and Communications Tools for Events

The media kit
Provides basic information and positive features

Videos
Supplement media kits with videos for broadcast media
Get sponsors to prepare and distribute videos; sell them
Videos can have multiple uses: general broadcast; news items; recruiting and thanking sponsors; appealing to volunteers; trade show exhibits; direct sales to tour companies

Press releases
Timely, concise messages for general media use (e.g., announcement of the event program and its features; summary of the event's successes and impacts)

News conferences
Bring media together for major announcements
Usually combined with a special event to attract maximum media presence and foster more personal relationships

News reporting
Foster good relations with reporters

Calendar listings
Get into all the event listings

Posters and banners
Not just at the event

Audio visual material for borrowing and sales
A slide library; videos; tapes of musicians

VIP visits and celebrities
To attract media coverage and obtain explicit or implicit endorsement

Hospitality
At the event, news conferences, or other
To foster personal relationships: with writers, broadcasters, other stakeholders

Speeches
Managers or volunteer spokespersons spread the message

Ambassadors
Many events have competitions to appoint official ambassadors, often in combination with the wearing of costumes or entertainment

Appreciation rewards
Formal thanks to volunteers, media, other stakeholders
Combine with a social event

Familiarization tours
Invite travel writers or other media to the event and/or destination, leading to feature stories
Commission writers/photographers to do features

Newsletters
Keep everyone informed regularly

Charitable donations
Get publicity for all worthwhile deeds

Personal calls
Telephone three key contacts every day

Formal briefings
To financial stakeholders and sponsors
To lobby governments and officials

Publicity stunts
Often event performers can arrange a stunt prior to or at the event to attract extra attention

Public Relations Events

Event managers should have no trouble thinking up and executing effective PR events! Kudrle and Sandler (1995) discuss PR events for the hospitality industry, and many of their ideas will work for the events sector. Some of the common events or functions that can attract positive media coverage and/or public and stakeholder involvement include:

- celebration of the organization's or event's anniversaries;
- launching new events, programs, or attractions;
- awards (for volunteers, staff, participants, art etc.);
- celebrations when awards are given to the event;
- donations to charities (e.g., presentation of the check);
- groundbreaking for new developments;
- celebrity and VIP visits (great photo-ops);
- fund-raiser galas (invite plenty of local opinion leaders and media personalities);
- contests.

Managing the News

PR efforts are mostly proactive, designed to get favorable attention. But when something bad happens to the organization, such as accidents or other incidents at the event, managers must be ready to react. All too often when an accident happens at an attraction or public venue the media find personnel or officials who all too easily "put their feet in their mouths" and make a bad situation worse. Elsewhere we discuss how to deal with negative imagery, but in the context of public relations it is necessary to stress that every staff person and volunteer has a role to play, both in the positive and negative contexts. Based in part on Kudrle and Sandler (1995, p. 166), here is some advice for reacting to bad news:

- Every staff person and volunteer should know that only the senior manager or president of the organization is authorized to make public statements; everyone else must refer all inquiries to the designated spokesperson.
- The organization's spokesperson(s) must receive training in how to handle the media, both for positive and negative events.
- Always tell the truth, but do not release confidential information to the media; get the facts before talking; speculation as to what went wrong or whose fault it was is almost always counterproductive.
- Try to get the facts out to the media before they hear and report rumors.
- Stress the positive response of staff to any incident, if possible; heroes are always popular.

Press Releases and News Conferences

These forms of communication are essential tools for most event managers, especially those that must maximize free media coverage and reporting. Martinez and Weiner (1979) advised that nonprofit organizations should use the press release to announce events, solicit coverage, issue statements, and provide background information. Working from the key points first to more general background information provides the media with the essence of the news up front.

When really important news is to be announced, the news conference is appropriate. The trick, of course, is to ensure that the media come out and don't just ask for the press release to be faxed! Throwing a theme party usually works, especially if announcements about the program and entertainment can be combined with live demonstrations. Television coverage of the news conference is highly desirable, so the venue and announcements must be attractive and interesting. Resist the temptation to have lengthy or many speeches, yet have key officials, supporters, sponsors, entertainers, and others available for interviews. Highlight that which is new and exciting. If the news conference is not useful to the media they won't come back and it can turn into a damaging venture.

Gordon (2003) advised that each type of media has different requirements when it comes to lead times (e.g., 3–5 months for magazines), and different interests. Magazines and the trade press prefer advance features on noteworthy industry events and stories about celebrities or causes, while your local newspapers and radio stations are likely to prefer local angles. Getting radio personalities involved in the event will increase their coverage! Television wants action, so they probably will not cover a speaker unless there is urgent news; instead arrange a highly visual publicity event. Gordon suggested holding publicity events during the week when more TV crews are available, and scheduling them between 9 a.m. and 3 p.m. for maximum impact.

Public Service Announcements

Public service announcements (PSAs) are made by television, radio, and cablevision companies free of charge to charities and nonprofits. In some jurisdictions it is a condition of their license, although most media believe that PSAs are good for community relations.

Event mangers can increase the number and effectiveness of PSA communications about the event or the organization by preparing their own. Usually short announcements of between 10 and 60 seconds are required for radio, and they can be taped in advance. Alternatively, a press release might be read over the air.

Brochures

Enter most travel centers, hotels, and attractions and you will be confronted by racks of brochures promoting every type of attraction and service. Visitors often browse these displays looking for things to do, or to find interesting souvenirs. In this author's experience, events are universally underrepresented and often poorly presented by the quantity and quality of brochures offered to the traveling public.

Whatever the reason for this dearth of tourist-oriented material, event managers should realize there are benefits to developing and widely circulating an annual brochure or—if the event is predictable in terms of time and venue—a longer lasting brochure.

Wicks and Schuett (1993) concluded from research that travel brochures are used to help plan travel, and are references used on the trip and in the destination. Accordingly, they must be available through the mail, along the road, and at transport terminals. They do not necessarily motivate a trip, but can make the difference for an event being visited or not.

Getz and Sailor (1993) examined attraction-specific brochures and drew conclusions about their design and distribution. Conventional wisdom calls for a design based on the AIDA principle: attract Attention; sustain Interest; develop a Desire; and make a call to Action. This is a sound starting point in brochure design, and the research found that unusual shapes and formats, rather than the standard rectangular, fold-out brochure, worked well to attract interest. This can be crucial to get browsers to pick it up. Through focus groups, it was found that brochure aesthetics were important, and that clear information and maps were vital. Descriptions and photos should convey the event's benefits to target audiences. Older consumers are likely to have different ways of evaluating brochures, it was found, so it might be desirable to have separate brochures for the major target segments. And residents of an area do not want the same material as visitors; locals can use more information because they are able to keep useful communications handy for later use.

Destination Event Calendars

A review of event calendars and travel guides for numerous destinations reveals a generally unsophisticated approach to event promotion and coordination. The prevailing mode is that of an annual or seasonal event calendar, standing alone or as part of a more comprehensive guide, which merely lists events without a description of their characteristics and without any theming or packaging. These enable event-goers to confirm dates in advance, but are usually not very informative or appealing.

Presumably many tourist organizations look upon the calendars mostly as a cheap way to assist the events, but this attitude is shortsighted. Attractive formats, photos, and feature stories are far better ways to communicate and promote the excitement and diversity of events. Even if only a small proportion of the listed events can be featured in each issue, all the others are likely to benefit from increased consumer interest in the publication. Better still would be a series of attractive event calendars for each region or theme, each including more detailed descriptions of all the listed events.

Jago and Shaw (1995) evaluated special event calendars produced by the Australian state and territory tourism organizations. They concluded that there is confusion surrounding the target markets for such publications, and little had been done to assess their cost-effectiveness. Because the public has different needs than the travel trade, the same event calendar is unlikely to satisfy both groups.

One good example was produced by Special Events New South Wales, Australia (1995). Their 1995 Autumn Events Calendar had an attractive color cover and provided information on dates, prices, and venues. Color photos were used to highlight a selection of events. The introduction promised: "New South Wales offers a feast of events and experiences, for all tastes, all year round. As the seasons change so does the nature of things to see and do. In Autumn NSW celebrates its rich rural life by staging agricultural shows across the state, with Sydney's world renowned Royal Easter Show in April."

Three types of events were classified in this calendar: arts and entertainment, Australian culture, and sports. It was clearly aimed at the tourist and contained a listing of state travel centers. Travel agents were advised on how to make bookings by fax, and consumers were told how to make telephone orders.

General Travel Guides

The all-purpose destination travel guide is a common publication, and they often contain event sections or calendars. A major problem with them is that the event calendar can easily get lost among the detail or the advertisements. A key opportunity, on the other hand, is to feature festivals and events, or photos of events, to enhance overall attractiveness and create a sense of excitement. After all, how many pictures of nice scenery and outdoor recreation will the average reader pay attention to? It is probable that the imagery of group activity at special events has stronger appeal than photos with no people and no activity in them.

According to Vogt, Fesenmaier, and MacKay (1993), personal experience and word of mouth are the most important sources for vacation decision making. But information and the information-seeking process are important. Based on research in the American Midwest, focusing on weekend getaways, these researchers found that 63.4% of their sample asked for information in advance to learn about unique events that would occur during the planned visit. The travel guide and supporting information about events are therefore valuable in shaping getaway destinations and itineraries. People want to use their time efficiently, so all the data on schedules and prices of events must be supplied well in advance. To make the destination attractive and event-going easy, toll-free numbers should be provided and perhaps coupons used as lures.

Sales

Marketing efforts must ultimately result in sales, measured variously as total event attendance, number of paid admissions, revenues from merchandizing and the gate, or other revenue generated. Communications are intended to create demand, but the manager cannot usually afford to sit back and wait for that demand to translate into sales all by itself.

Few events employ professional sales forces, but the larger ones, and one-time mega-events in particular, cannot afford to be without salespersons. Sometimes volunteers can be employed, and often it is the manager who must make the sales pitch, especially to major sponsors and tour companies. Below we discuss the most important customer-oriented sales methods and provide some pertinent advice for the event manager.

"Retailing" is the most universal sales method, involving a passive store display or some other system where the customer comes to the ticket or package seller. Events can and do establish their own stores and ticket offices, and many use sponsors such as banks and grocery stores to get into their big retail system.

A popular, indirect retailing method is that of telephone or fax ticketing through commercial reservation operators. These often entail high commissions, but are valuable for events wanting the assurance of widespread ticket availability. Customers like the convenience of phoning and using credit cards. Regional or national reservation systems offer the considerable advantage of providing up-to-date information on numerous events, which is particularly applicable to tourists in a new destination.

A more recent innovation is the use of the Internet for sales. Events can place information about how to order, include forms to download and fax, or create interactive e-mail information and ticketing processes.

"Wholesaling" involves the selling of blocks of tickets or packages to other companies who in turn retail them to their customers at a profit. The Calgary Stampede, for example, places large blocks of tickets to its rodeo and evening shows in the hands of tour companies. As the event approaches, unsold tickets can be returned. This approach fosters tourist demand, but requires considerable effort in dealing with the retailers.

"Direct Sales" involves making an appeal directly to individuals or groups. This can be done through mail-outs (the most common technique), or telephoning and door-to-door canvassing. Customers might also be reached at other events and attractions, and through corporate sponsors who canvass their staff. "Personal sales" employs salespersons to make calls "in the flesh." This will be most cost-effective for wholesaling and group sales in particular, as it requires a lot of time and skill.

"Telemarketing" is a form of direct sales that is become enormously successful in North America, especially when combined with television "infomercials" or all-retail cable channels. Events can use volunteers or commercial companies to call households and businesses for sales. The downside is that consumers are increasingly annoyed with telephone solicitations. It is better to use the event's database to make more selective sales calls.

"Database marketing," in which the event maintains a permanent database and mailing/ phoning lists to reach target individuals or groups, has become well established. Event managers can purchase lists, but it is best and cheapest to compile your own. As well, sponsors will want your database of qualified customers. Not only existing and potential customers should be included, but also tour companies, sponsors and grant-givers, suppliers, participants, volunteers, and anyone else of possible importance. Several common techniques for developing databases are:

- ask customers to provide detailed information about themselves (on ticket forms or through contests and free gift promotions);
- require all volunteers, participants, suppliers, and media to fill out registration cards;
- ask sponsors, volunteers, participants, and others to provide their own lists.

Be sure to ensure the confidentiality and security of personal data, and check to see if there is legislation regarding privacy and data collection.

Word of Mouth

Research has proved the importance of personal selling for festivals and special events. Word-of-mouth recommendations account for a large proportion of responses whenever event patrons are asked to name the main source of information about the event or to name the reason for attending. This is informal personal selling, but it can also be helped along by several simple techniques:

- interorganizational networking (the more organizations involved, the wider the potential circle of communications);
- maximizing volunteer participation (similar to above);
- participants, visitors, and performers can be given information and promotional merchandise to take home;
- recruitment incentives: give residents incentives to bring visiting friends and relatives; give first-time visitors discounts for a return visit with new customers.

General awareness and PR campaigns in the host community can also pay off by fostering a sense of pride and community ownership, which ensures free promotion. Paid employees must also be a part of the personal selling process, and this can be encouraged through training.

Word of mouth will have its best impact in the local and regional audience, but there is definitely potential for the tourist market as well. Event marketers can focus on people with second homes in the area, as they will have a greater personal interest in the event. Invite them to the event and encourage them to spread the message to their home communities. Expatriates are another group worth cultivating. Having occasional "homecomings" can get events in touch with these former residents, and they can become long-distance ambassadors.

Developing and Communicating a Positive Image

Crompton (1979) defined destination images as "the sum of beliefs, ideas and impressions that a person has of a destination" (p. 18). Hunt (1975) emphasized that a person's image of an area might have more to do with how the media projects the area or its attractions than with its tangible resources, and Goodall (1988) stressed that a destination image is conditioned by available information. People develop "preferential images" of ideal holidays or experiences, according to Goodall, and this determines how they react to actual experiences.

Gartner (1993) explained that images are formed by means of several agents. "Organic" image formation occurs through personal experiences, and particularly previous visits. This phenomenon is closely linked to word-of-mouth recommendations, wherein someone else's images affect your own. Advertising and information requested by people are "overt" agents that obviously try to convey the destination or event in the best possible light. Accordingly, consumers might be skeptical. More "covert" methods include the use of celebrities or other spokespersons to give credibility to the messages. Similarly, the use of "advertorials," familiarization tours, and media relations are all designed to generate favorable images and messages. Fully autonomous sources, such as news reports, probably carry the most authority, but might not reach intended markets. Gartner commented (1993): "If the event reported is of major importance the opportunity for image change, in a relatively short period of time, is present" (p. 201). Hence, reports of violence against visitors can quickly lead to negative images and trip cancellations.

Images are not static. They change with new information, particularly news of disasters and other bad publicity, and also in response to the first-hand reports of friends and relatives. Much of the image is based on perceptions of the destination or attraction, not reality. Accordingly, Goodall (1988) said that "Personal images can therefore not only be influenced by, but can be manipulated, even created by forces external to the individual" (p. 10).

How is this accomplished? Both supply and demand factors have to be considered: creating an image to satisfy the needs or desired benefits of the target markets, and creating an image to highlight the best attributes of the event or destination. Uzzell (1984) advised that the image be constructed in a form that appeals to the potential consumer's emotions and desires: "It is an image of something he wants to be, to have, to experience, or to achieve" (p. 84). In this way, both the push (need) and pull (attraction) factors must be addressed in image making. The tension between wanting to get away from the ordinary or the bad, and finding the extraordinary and the good, can be exploited.

Actual mechanisms of image making are part science and part art. The science is in researching the needs, motives, and perceptual processes of potential customers. The art is in producing an event or products to meet the needs and in effectively communicating the strengths of the attraction.

Image Making for One-Time and Recurring Events

Every event "purchase" should be a special experience in the life of the visitor, and it might be a once-in-a-lifetime spectacular. The image of a one-time event has to be constructed in such a way as to make it a "must see" attraction. Emphasizing its uniqueness is essential, but there must be more. After all, many types of events have imitators and television makes it possible to stay at home and witness something unique from anywhere in the world. So the image must combine uniqueness and the rewards that only "being there, being part of it" can bring.

For recurring events, it is essential to make the experience so attractive and complete that repeat visits are assured and word-of-mouth promotions will be strong. Thus, the event itself is part of the image-making process. The integrated theme, high-quality goods, services, and entertainment, the setting, the staff and volunteers, are all instruments of image making. Similarly, each and every event is an integral part of the destination region's image enhancement. If the one event attended by the overseas visitor is a bad experience, the entire region suffers the consequences.

Targeted benefits, aimed at the special interests of key market segments, are important for creating "brand loyalty." Those visitors who find exactly what they are after will likely return. The image of the event or destination area should also employ the strengths of festivals and events to establish the image of a sophisticated, exciting place to come back to.

Evaluating Communications Effectiveness and Efficiency

The old marketing adage always applies: if you want to know the value of advertising, stop doing it. On the other hand, if you want to improve its effectiveness and do it more efficiently (i.e., better results for less money), you must evaluate results. "Conversion studies" are widely used to determine the effectiveness of specific communications. For example, when people call for (or receive by mail) a specific event promotion, subsequent telephone calls can be made to determine what proportion (and their characteristics) bought an event ticket. Conversion rates can only be calculated for targeted messages and promotions, not broadcasting, although market area research can at least determine who heard a given message. The basic validity problem in conversion studies is the assumption that it was the targeted promotion or message that resulted in a sale, whereas in realty many possible factors influence a customer's decision to attend.

Research by Shibli and the Sport Industry Research Centre (2002) illustrates methods for estimating the value of media exposure for an event and the host community.

Research Note

Shibli, S., and the Sport Industry Research Centre. (2002). *The 2002 Embassy World Snooker Championship, an evaluation of the economic impact, place marketing effects, and visitors' perceptions of Sheffield.* Prepared for Sheffield City Council.

A sample of television viewers in the UK provided data on the average and peak size of the live broadcast audience for the snooker championship, as well as the television rating (the percentage of all viewers watching a single program). Television coverage extended over 17 days, consecutively yielding almost 100 hours. A total cumulative audience of over 94 million was exposed to the event and to messages about Sheffield, although it was estimated that 18 million different people constituted this audience. The event's highest television rating (8.2%) was achieved at the final session. The data revealed that viewer interest grew as the event progressed towards the final. More males watched this sport event (57%), and they tended to be aged 55 and older (57%). The volume of clearly visible or audible exposure for sponsors' logos or messages was calculated using specially trained observers and software, then a cash equivalent value was calculated based on how much it would cost to purchase television advertising in the form of 30-second messages. The same was done for messages about Sheffield. The study emphasizes that there is no guarantee that such media exposure is effective.

Packaging

Events are themselves packages—of activities, venues, and experiences that cannot otherwise be enjoyed. The first principle of packaging, therefore, is to combine elements for the consumer that otherwise are difficult to acquire, or that contain value-added features. The extra value can come from a package price (cheaper than buying the elements separately) or the inclusion of features not available to those not buying the package. Convenience should be maximized through packaging, effectively removing barriers to making the purchase. Assurance or security, the feeling that the trip will be safer and the experience guaranteed, is another key benefit to the customer.

The goals of packaging for events are related both to the event's marketing strategy and the destination:

- attract tourists off-season through event packages;
- reach specific, high-yield market segments;
- generate additional revenue and improve the cash flow through advance bookings;
- enhance the event's image (through related promotions);
- encourage visitation outside the peaks (e.g., weekdays);
- develop partnerships with sponsors, tour companies, etc.;
- combat competitors.

Although the main focus of packaging is likely to be tourism, every event can develop and sell packages. Some ideas follow:

- two or more events for one price;
- two or more elements of the event for one price, or a discounted price;
- the event plus other attractions;
- sponsors' products included in the admission price.

Packaging for Tourists

The group tour business (in which everyone buys the same tour) provides volume, whereas packages purchased by individuals can serve to attract specific segments. Packages can be "all-inclusive" in nature, assembling everything the tourist needs and wants for one price, or provide limited benefits as when visitors must separately arrange for their own meals or transport.

Events can form the "core product" (i.e., the major attraction) of the tour package, or can be an added element to give value to other packages and other events, as illustrated in Figure 13.1. Independent travelers should be able to purchase the event package easily and prior to arrival in the area. Group tours will usually be wholesaled to tour companies from outside the area, but local destination management companies can be valuable partners in selling packages. Events are logical and appealing add-ons to incentive tours and meetings.

Targeting packages is preferable to simply offering one or two for general consumption. They can be customized through market research and cooperation with the tour and hos-

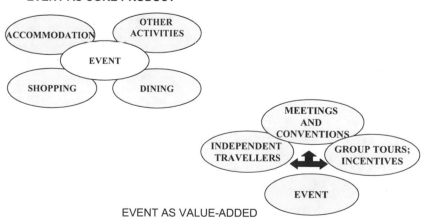

Figure 13.1. Event tourism packaging.

pitality industries. Figure 13.2 provides a framework that can be used as a starting point for event packaging. Across the top are the elements that can be combined in many ways for a good package: accommodation, dining, other activities (attractions and entertainment), and shopping. Transportation will often be added, but this depends on the segments being targeted. In some events the form of transportation can actually be part of the themed experience.

Figure 13.2 shows several event types, each of which will likely attract different market segments. Research will be needed to provide profiles of existing and potential customers. For example, the sport event is more likely to attract younger males whose interests are focused on the event itself. Their accommodation and dining preferences might very well be lower cost. Any add-on activities should fit their profile—possibly nightlife, adventures, or amusements. As to shopping, sport souvenirs will probably be popular.

The up-market cultural tourists attending a performing arts event can be expected to differ substantially from the sport traveler. Accommodations should be of higher quality, and fine dining can be featured. Cultural tourists tend to combine events with visits to galleries, museums, and other cultural attractions.

When it comes to shopping, packages can include "free" souvenirs (costed into the total price), shopping at the event itself, and excursions arranged through merchants or shopping centers. Similarly, dining can be included, at the event or elsewhere.

Managers should also remember that many events contain elements that will appeal to multiple segments, so that more than one package is likely to be needed. For example, the Olympics appeal to sports fans, but also to cultural tourists, because all Olympics contain arts festivals. A community festival might have a sufficiently diverse program to attract music lovers of different types, athletes for participatory events, and sophisticated urbanites interested in acquiring antiques and sampling down-home cooking.

Caution is required for several reasons. Not all packages might be viable, so reliance on the tour industry is important. Also, trying to attract too many different segments could result in user conflicts and programming headaches. Events can put together and sell their own packages, but this might be risky and difficult. Tourist organizations like visitor and convention bureaus can assist, or actually market the packages. A third option is to work

EVENT TYPES	ACCOMMO-DATION	DINING	OTHER ACTIVITIES	SHOPPING
SPORTS	All types; Urban and Resort	Basic eating	Nightlife; Adventure; Amusement	Sports souvenirs
ETHNIC	All Types; Urban and small towns	Ethnic food; Themed restaurants	Ethnic areas	Authentic arts/crafts
LIFESTYLE; FOOD/WINE	All Types; Urban and small towns	Themed; specialty dining; wines	Nightlife; Wineries; Country tours	Wines; Specialist products
PERFORMING ARTS	Mostly Urban Upscale Hotels	Fine restaurants	Theatres; Museums; Galleries	Arts, crafts; Fashion
SMALL-TOWN FESTIVALS, FAIRS	B+B; Inns; Farms, Motels	Festival food; Cafes	Sightseeing; Historic sites	Local produce; Crafts
ECO-EVENTS	Camping; Budget class	Festival food	Wilderness; Adventure	Eco-friendly products

Figure 13.2. Framework for targeted event packaging.

with tour companies to encourage and help them to create and sell packages featuring the event.

Bus Tours

As observed by McConkey (1986), bus tours have many advantages but also tend to be highly price sensitive and often consist of seniors who require extra care and might not be high spenders. Also, the bus tour market is very competitive and committed marketing is needed to secure and keep tours coming.

Getting involved in the bus associations and their marketplaces is a starting point, and offering familiarization tours for operators is often necessary. Destination tourist organizations will do this for events, or at least assist them. Familiarization tours can be used to get the wholesaler to the event, or at least to the setting at a different time.

The wholesalers will typically look for certain elements of attractiveness, from their perspective, including how well the tourists and escorts will be received. Other criteria in selecting events could include:

- distance from their markets;
- cleanliness and safety;
- uniqueness of the event;
- its established reputation;
- suitability of the event and its setting for their markets;
- value for price (to the tourists and to the wholesaler);
- available information, and its quality; promotions by the event itself.

McConkey (1986) said that establishing personal relationships with tour wholesalers and other intermediaries is critical for success in attracting tour groups. The event's marketing people have to work to get to know the intermediaries and their needs or preferences. The attitude of event staff might be as important as the product in maintaining good relations.

Benefits and Costs of Packaging

Events can increase tourist numbers and revenue, both off and on the site, through packaging. Specific target markets can be attracted, and a better match realized between product and visitor demands. For example, group tours provide the opportunity for selling meals or souvenirs in larger quantity under ideal merchandizing conditions, to assemble higher quality entertainment, and to broaden the program. Sponsors might also be easier to cultivate when the numbers and characteristics of tourists present attractive marketing opportunities. Destinations can enhance their overall attractiveness by including events in general packages or making events the focus.

In return, events will usually have to make specific changes to cater to packages (all of which are likely to include reserved tickets) and group tours in particular. In addition to the points listed earlier, events might have to:

- expand the event's duration to accommodate more tourists and a preference for weekend visits;
- change dates to meet tour company demand;
- move or expand the venue to accommodate increased numbers;
- control access and reserve seating/viewing areas;
- add facilities (such as bus parking, more toilets, or reception areas);

- develop ticketing, reservation, and refund systems;
- schedule for group tour arrivals; ensure punctuality within the program;
- work closely with the industry;
- develop a pricing strategy;
- plan and produce programs at least 1 year in advance (so that tour companies can adequately market their packages);
- consider the impacts of, and manage, larger number of visitors with specific expectations and needs;
- provide photographs and other promotional material for tour companies to use in their marketing.

Creating a Package

Packages, aimed at target segments, can accomplish different goals. Determine in advance if the aim is to build attendance, generate revenue, expand market share, provide benefits for sponsors, or boost tourism to the destination. Any combination of these goals is possible.

Market research, and especially segmentation, is necessary. Sometimes this can be done by examining existing data, as described earlier, or by consulting the tourist organizations and tour operators. They know the marketplace. In particular, examples of successful packages to the destination and its events should be examined. The event's own visitor surveys can also reveal segments suitable for target packaging. A package concept should next be formulated, with creativity to make it interesting. Give it a catchy name.

A Tourism Canada publication (1994) provides a form to evaluate packaging ideas. Elements of the package (e.g., type of accommodation, additional entertainment, meals) are evaluated for their relationship to the theme and whether they are essential or optional to the package. It is important to ask what the unique selling proposition will be, or what gives the package added value. How unique is it? What kind of image will it convey about the event? Will it afford a competitive advantage?

Presumably the event will have a clear theme that is expressed through the package, such as heritage, the arts, or sports. Alternatively, program elements, especially entertainment and spectacle, can provide an effective event package theme. This theme should be used when combining the event experience with other opportunities in the area.

Feasibility must be assessed, including the price and ability to deliver the product at high and consistent standards. Setting the price will likely involve negotiations with suppliers, such as accommodation establishments and bus companies; this also helps determine the marketability of the product. One test is to see if a tour company will be interested in taking over the package. Another test is to compare it directly with existing successful packages.

In the Tourism Canada (1994) publication detailed advice is given on setting the price. This involves determining fixed costs per customer (e.g., rental of one bus and driver, one host/guide) and variable costs (e.g., per meal or reserved seat at the event). Add overhead costs, like marketing and staff time, and determine the break-even point. Add a profit margin, but also allow for contingencies. Other considerations include discounts for large groups, whether or not drivers and guides get free product, and special prices for seniors or youth.

Remember that in selling the package through intermediaries, commissions of 10–15% or higher will normally have to be paid. These can be negotiated, but many travel agents and tour retailers will not touch a package without adequate commission rates.

Hosting Tour Groups

The tourist is an honored guest of the event and the host community, and must be made to feel as such. To enhance the tourist's experience a number of additional benefits can be offered:

- a welcome and departure ceremony that is distinct from that given to other customers;
- easier accessibility, parking, and related directions;
- more detailed and better quality information, including souvenir programs;
- small gifts or "free" extras;
- arrangements with local accommodations, restaurants, entertainment places, etc., to offer discounts, other inducements, and better service;
- emergency and amenity services aimed at the special needs of strangers (e.g., rest areas, food and beverages, medical);
- some tourists will appreciate being identified as guests, while others might prefer anonymity while enjoying the event—give tourists a choice;
- on-site tours or guides; a look at the "backstage" and meetings with performers, organizers, celebrities, etc.

The tour wholesaler, bus driver, or travel agent involved in the packaging process should also be afforded some degree of special attention. An example is the treatment given bus tours by Winnipeg's Folklorama, one of Canada's major multicultural or ethnic festivals. Folklorama prepares special group tour booking forms, offers packages for one or more nights of attendance and food, beverages, and entertainment at different ethnic pavilions, and assistance in arranging accommodations (Folklorama, n.d.). One of their main target markets is the nearby American states, and especially Minneapolis/St. Paul, where links with bus tour companies have been cultivated. Participating bus tours are given special access, reserved seating, and escorted pavilion tours. The wholesaler is provided with information kits for each tourist, itineraries, and complimentary packages for drivers and escorts.

Tour operators commonly ask for 25% discounts off regular prices, plus free admission for drivers and escorts, in order to generate a profit margin and make the package price attractive.

Creating Destination Tours Involving Events

Tours and packages in event tourism can be categorized as follows:

- by theme (e.g., a tour of food festivals);
- by area and theme (cultural events of "Scottish Country");
- by season (fall fair tour);
- by circuits (linking gateway cities to hinterland events);
- piggybacking (linking minor events to major event attractions).

With imagination, festivals can also be constructed of package tours, such as a touring festival of winter carnivals or village fetes. Similarly, a festival of castles, markets, country towns, or cowboy heritage can be organized to consist of a package tour to special events in each setting.

More Advice on Event Packaging and Group Tour Servicing

- Price the package to allow adequate profit for the event and the tour operators; check out the competition.

- Allow for visitors with special needs; be flexible where practical and important to the customer; otherwise, packages are standardized. (e.g., allow for wheelchair seating and special diets).
- Vouchers are generally issued to tour companies, who reissue them to customers; voucher redemption at the event, hotels, etc., must be prearranged.
- Accommodation establishments must be able to reserve blocks of rooms for event patrons.
- Inform all visitors and tour companies of special requirements (e.g., if visas are needed; currency exchange facilities; prices—especially what is NOT included in packages; what is subject to cancellation or replacement in the package or in the event program).
- Exceed customer expectations by providing a bonus (e.g., a welcome gift or goodbye souvenir; meet a VIP or performer).
- Establish a refund policy and procedures (e.g., accept cancellations without penalty up to 30 days before the event).
- Advise the customer whether taxes are included or extra.

Evaluating Packaging

A "conversion rate" can be calculated on the basis of how many people receiving specific information about the package (e.g., in a mail-out or in response to telephone/Internet inquiries) purchased the event package. Package customers should be surveyed to learn about any problems and to measure satisfaction levels. Participating tour companies, hotels, etc., have to be asked for feedback on how the packages could be improved for their target markets. A customer complaint system is needed at the event organization.

Study Questions

- Which elements of the communications mix are suitable for marketing events?
- Discuss the advantages and disadvantages of advertising media, for different types of events.
- What should a good event website include?
- How are ethics related to advertising?
- What public relations tools do you think will work best for a festival? For a one-time sport event?
- Explain the value of word-of-mouth promotion.
- How is the marketing of events connected to destination marketing?
- State the main advantages of packaging to events, and the main consumer benefits.
- Why do event packages have to be different depending on the event?
- What are the special challenges involved in attracting and hosting group tours?

Advanced Study Questions

- Search the Internet and conduct a systematic comparison of event websites; specifically evaluate their value as general marketing tools, for making sales, and in promoting the destination or host community.
- How are the principles of advertising related to sponsorship? Give specific examples of how event organizers and sponsors can maximize co-promotions, sales, and branding.
- Construct a suitable package to help sell an event, with specific attention to its tourism value and the detailed implications for event management.

Chapter 14

Evaluation and Impact Assessment

Learning Objectives

- Be able to integrate evaluation within the organization and the event to achieve a learning organization.
- Be able to evaluate the effectiveness and efficiency of the event and the organization.
- Be able to undertake the necessary research to conduct evaluation and impact assessment.
- Be able to employ observational techniques, as well as evaluative checklists and surveys.
- Be able to measure and evaluate the economic impacts of events, including cost–benefit evaluation.
- Be able to maximize the local economic benefits of events through understanding of the multiplier concept.

Evaluation Concepts and Methods

Evaluation steers the entire planning and marketing process. It is the way to constantly "learn" more about the organization's environment, the intended and unintended outcomes of events, and ways in which to improve management. Very practical reasons for evaluation can be simply stated:

- to identify and solve problems;
- find ways to improve management;
- determine the worth of the event or its programs;
- measure success or failure;
- identify and measure impacts (costs and benefits) of the event;
- satisfy sponsors and other stakeholders (accountability);
- gain acceptance/credibility/support.

Probably the most unique aspect of event evaluation is the complexity of addressing all the perspectives on events—even the smallest have to consider their impact on the community and environment. As well, the volunteer base imposes special evaluation demands, as does the sponsorship dimension. In a tourism context, evaluation issues multiply, often requiring complex economic impact assessment techniques to determine worth.

"Evaluation" means the subjective determination of worth—to place a value on something—yet it often employs quantitative measures and techniques. In the end, however, simple or complicated the process, the manager must reach a decision based on part science and part wisdom. Was the event a success? Should the program be scrapped? Did the sponsors get their money's worth?

The science of evaluation begins with realization that this is how organizations (and managers) learn. Without evaluation we do not know if our actions achieve desired results, and therefore we do not know what actions cause what effects. To grow and achieve sustainability, or adapt to change, organizations must institutionalize the learning process. Three basic types of evaluation occur.

"Formative evaluations" are undertaken during feasibility studies and preplanning of events, or as part of strategic planning; they include needs assessments, learning about tourist and resident markets, creating attractive products, setting up effective organizations and new product or marketing ideas. Generating and testing programming ideas is also "formative."

"Process evaluations" can be applied to the organization as a whole (by way of a management audit) to help improve effectiveness, and during the operation of an event, such as through observation and quality control techniques, or during the implementation of a plan. The idea is to determine if the plan or event is being implemented as intended, and otherwise to take corrective action; sometimes improvements can quickly be put in place. Regular internal evaluations of all the management functions (e.g., marketing effectiveness) fits into this category.

"Outcome" or "summative evaluations" are conducted after the event or at the end of a program or planning period to evaluate its impacts and overall value; results are fed into the planning process. Many stakeholders want accountability, and they stress specific outcomes and impacts of most interest to them. This includes return on investment calculations for sponsors, and environmental audits for the community. A broad and complex outcome evaluation question is "what is this event worth," and it can only be answered by referring to the mandate and goals of the organization and the interests of all key stakeholders.

Determination of Cause and Effect

Sometimes evaluators want to prove that their event or program was the cause of a desired outcome, such as the creation of jobs (a tangible benefit) or more intangible social and cultural benefits. To do this requires more sophisticated evaluation methods, often employing experimental designs with control groups. The determination of economic impacts of events is a special case, because it does not require an experiment with a control group—nor could that easily be arranged. Rather, it is sufficient to demonstrate through research that "new money" came into the study area because of the event. This is not a simple task, however, as will be shown later in this chapter.

It is often satisfactory to simply determine what the outcomes are and to use this information to do better the next time. For example, the point of inquiring about visitor satisfaction is to improve event quality, not necessarily to prove what exactly leads to satisfaction. In such cases evaluation asks quite different questions from cause–effect research.

Action Research

"Action research" is very useful in the events field. The manager puts into place a course of action (such as a program or fund-raising initiative) and then evaluates how well it works while it is running. It is different from "process evaluation" in that the program or initiative is ongoing and is continuously improved. The program manager is the evaluator. For more information on this approach, see this university website: www.scu.edu.au/schools/gcm/ar/arhome.html.

Effectiveness and Efficiency

These terms are used frequently in evaluation. "Effectiveness" is a measure of goal attainment, or how well did we do in reaching our objectives? Efficiency is a measure of resource use, as implied in the questions: Did we waste money? What is the optimal use of our resources?

Measures of effectiveness are required for impact assessment or any summative evaluation. Internally, measures of effectiveness are needed to evaluate the contribution of each person and committee in attaining the goals. Sometimes intangible goals, such as fostering appreciation of the arts or contributing to community development, resist precise measurement. In business, revenue generation is the most common measure.

Approaches to evaluating effectiveness were identified by Tzelepi and Quick (2002):

- Goal attainment: achieving the desired output (but goals are not always clear, and attainment of goals might not make the organization effective in other ways).
- Systems resource approach: open systems approach in which resource acquisition determines outputs; the focus is on measuring outputs, so organizations can be compared without reference to goals; obtaining resources indicates that the outputs are valued.
- Internal process approach: internal processes such as information flow and coordination determine effectiveness (this approach is heavy on human resource evaluation, but different processes can still achieve the same ends).
- Competing values: internal goals might be in conflict (goals might be set and effectiveness measured by reference to dominant power blocks, or as an amalgam of individual preferences).
- Strategic constituencies: takes into account critical stakeholders, internal and external, asking how satisfied are each?

To evaluate efficiency, managers will examine the resources consumed to produce a given unit of output, then determine if more can be achieved for less, or if increased inputs can produce a lot more desired output. For example, the event manager must ask if the monetary investment in souvenirs generates enough revenue to warrant the expenditure, and how the revenue might be increased. Perhaps more spending on merchandise will achieve far greater profits. The problem arises when the desired output is an intangible, such as "fostering the arts." What level of expenditure is reasonable to achieve this kind of social goal?

Return on Investment (ROI)

The economic impact assessment described in detail in the next section is often used to come up with ROI measures, such as: for every $1 of public investment in this event the local/state/national economy realized $3 in economic benefit. An example of this approach is given, namely the cost–benefit evaluation of the Adelaide Grand Prix.

There is a tendency to try to calculate an economic ROI in dollars and cents, but that is not always possible. Other measures of value have been suggested in previous chapters, including tourism value (e.g., market share and growth potential) and social service value (e.g., number of targeted people served, or changes in attitude). ROI cannot realistically be calculated without objectives and measures being specified in advance. This is something to clarify or even negotiate with sponsors and grant-givers, as it could become crucial in satisfying and retaining them.

Accountability for sponsorship and grant money often leads the event manager to search for ROI measures. It is simple to do in a situation where an owner calculates the profit realized from an investment (or a return on assets), but not so simple when one organization has to report to another about how cash donations and in-kind support were used to generate desired benefits. Coughlan and Mules (2002) provided an example of research into the effectiveness of event sponsorship.

Research Note

Coughlan, D., & Mules, T. (2002). Sponsorship awareness and recognition at Canberra's Floriade festival. *Event Management, 7*(1), 1–9.

Researchers at a number of events have found that patrons often do not know, or incorrectly name, sponsors. When presented with a list of sponsors and nonsponsors, people often select well-known brands because of their prominence in the marketplace, regardless of involvement with the event in question. Face-to-face interviews with on-site visitors queried recall of sponsors at this floral festival. When asked if they knew the main sponsor of the event, 82% said they thought they did, but then only 70% correctly named the sponsor (overall, 58% knew the main sponsor). Respondents were also asked to name up to three sponsors, unprompted (at the exits, where no signage was visible), and the maximum any sponsor achieved (there were 19) was 38% of respondents; all sponsors received more than one mention. Fifty-four percent of those asked did name one or more sponsors, of which only 12% named one incorrectly. Because 51% of attendees were tourists, recognition of local sponsors, as opposed to national brands, was reduced. Tourists in general did better than locals in recognizing event sponsors, but residents did better with the local sponsors—presumably because they were repeat sponsors of this event. The authors concluded with advice: the fewer the number of sponsors, the more likely they will be recognized; sponsors should be highly visible on the event site; be a long-term presence at the event; use integrated marketing at and surrounding the event.

Evaluating the Impacts of Events on Place Marketing

Contributing to the formulation of a positive image of a city or destination (or its repositioning) is one of the economic roles of events, but it is difficult to evaluate. This is a special case of ROI calculation, as illustrated by Shibli and the Sport Industry Research Centre (2002).

Research Note

Shibli, S., and the Sport Industry Research Centre. (2002). *The 2002 Embassy World Snooker Championship, an evaluation of the economic impact, place marketing effects, and visitors' perceptions of Sheffield.* Prepared for Sheffield City Council.

One part of the evaluation was an estimate of the value of media coverage. The cumulative audience of the televised snooker championship within the UK was estimated to be 95 million viewers (i.e., about 18 million individuals watching multiple times), over 17 consecutive days and 100 hours of broadcast. Just over 1% of the television coverage was devoted to human and place interest stories that included "postcard" images of Sheffield, for which a monetary value was calculated based on the commercial cost of the equivalent broadcast time. In total 44 postcards yielding 79 minutes of coverage were broadcast. However, analysis showed that too much of this "postcard" exposure featured competitors, or buildings that only residents would recognize. A second dimension of the evaluation was a survey of spectator perceptions of the city, from which it was determined that snooker tourists (mostly males) rated Sheffield highly as a place to visit. The problem is that the profiles of the television audience, spectators, and typical visitors to Sheffield are all different, raising the question of how best to promote the city.

Making Evaluation a Permanent Part of the Organization

The "learning organization" requires a permanent approach to evaluation, and so does the "accountable organization." Evaluation results often get filed and forgotten, especially if they are negative! But nobody learns, and nothing progresses without open and honest evaluation, so the evaluator must try to maximize the usefulness of research and analysis in both practical and political ways. To maximize the effectiveness of all evaluations, the entire process must be firmly institutionalized. In other words, evaluation must not be viewed as an occasional job for solving problems or generating new ideas. It must be a permanent and important responsibility of senior managers.

Key principles should be followed:

- Set up an evaluation committee, or assign the specific responsibility for evaluation to the main planning committee.
- All committees must have an evaluation task which inputs to the main evaluation committee.
- Establish clear goals and objectives, with measurable performance standards each year.
- Start the planning of each event through evaluation of the previous one.
- Train all volunteers in observation and evaluation techniques; every volunteer and staff person has an evaluation role to play.
- Evaluate with all stakeholders in the event, including the public at large.
- Never cover up problems or minimize costs, it always comes back as a problem or scandal! Gain credibility and support by meeting problems head on.
- Start out with modest evaluation exercises and work slowly toward more complicated research and evaluation; consult research experts and get advice from event associations.
- At a minimum, get a one-time grant or sponsorship to conduct a benchmark visitor survey and impact assessment; it can be updated periodically.

Misuses of Evaluation

Negative performance evaluations are sometimes used to terminate a person's employment, and it is certainly possible to "rig the results" to justify the decision. Similarly, unpopular programs can be "proved" to be too costly or ineffective. Bad performance can sometimes be covered up by evaluations that show positive results in some other area. And managers have been known to conduct time-consuming and expensive evaluations to reinforce or increase their importance. And when results are not shared, there is often the suspicion that results are being "managed" to further someone's ambitions.

Basic Data Needs, Measures, and Methods

The major types of data needed to conduct comprehensive event and event tourism evaluations, specific measures used, and an indication of the methods generally required to obtain the data are shown in Table 14.1. For example, the most basic piece of information needed is the attendance at events. This can be broken down into several types of

Table 14.1. Basic Data Needs and Methods for Event Evaluation

Data Types	Specific Measures	Methods
Attendance		
Total event attendance	Total number of customers	Ticket sales
Attendance at subevents	Number of visitations	Turnstile counts
	Turnover rate	Vehicle counts
	Peak attendance	Crowd estimates
		Market area surveys
Visitor Provile		
Profile of each visitor	Age in years	Visitor survey
	Male or female	Market area survey
	Employment status	Direct observation
	Educational level	
	Income level	
Type of party	Family only	
	Family and friends	
	Friends only	
	Alone	
	Tour group	
	Tour group plus family/friends	
Size of party	Number of visitors traveling together	
Market Area and Trip Type		
Home address	country, state, city, or town	Visitor survey
Origin of trip	Origin on day of survey	
	Stops on the trip	
	Accommodation used	
Type of trip	Number of nights	
	Packages used	
Mode	Type of vehicle	Observation
Marketing and Quality Management		
Information sources	Media consulted	Visitor survey
	Importance of word of mouth	
Reasons for trip	Reasons for trip to the area and to the event	
	Importance of event in motivating the trip	
Benefits sought	Desired experiences, activities, good, and services	
Satisfaction	Things that pleased or displeased	Suggestion box
	Suggestions	
	Intent to return	
	Willingness to recommend the event	
Quality of program and service	Importance–performance measures	Participant observation
	Service quality failures	
Activities and Spending		
Activities at the event	Attendance at specific event activities or venues	Visitor survey
		Turnstile count
Activities outside the event	Activities on the trip and elsewhere in host community	Observation
		Business survey
Expenditures	Spending on: travel (car, etc.), accommodation, purchased meals, groceries, entertainment, other events or attractions, other shopping	Financial records

Table 14.1 continued.

Data Types	Specific Measures	Methods
Economic Impacts (Area)		
Benefits for the area attributable to the event	Average visitor spending	Visitor survey
	Total incremental visitor expenditure in the area (attributable to the event)	Local market area survey
		Attendance counts/ estimates
	Direct, indirect, and induced income or value added (i.e., macroeconomic impact)	Accommodation occupancy survey
		Business survey
	Tax and employment benefits	Multipliers or econometric models
Business Impacts (Event)		
Profit or loss	Cash flow	Financial audit
Financial reserves or debt	Assets and liabilities	
Return on Investment		
For sponsors and grant givers	Sponsor recognition by visitors; attitudes and images held	Visitor survey
		Media audit
	Behavior of visitors (sales, etc.)	On-site sales records
Other Impacts		
Ecological	Impacts on wildlife	Observation
Environmental	Pollution caused	Audit of environmental practices and outcomes
Social	Waste generated	
Cultural	Amenity loss (privacy, noise)	Stakeholder inputs
	Aesthetics	Community resident survey
	Traffic delays	
	Accidents/injuries	Visitor survey
	Social problems (behavior)	Police, fire, environmental service records
	Cultural change	
	Positive educational and behavioral effects	
Cost–Benefit Evaluation		
Tangible costs and benefits	Ratio of tangible benefits to tangible costs	Expert analysis
Intangible costs and benefits	Evaluation of intangibles	Stakeholder input
	Evaluation of net value	
Distribution of costs and benefits		

data, namely tourists versus residents, total attendance, attendance at individual sites and attractions, turnover rate, and peak attendance. The measures can be of visitors, visitor parties, total gate, or number of visitations. Methods used to obtain these measures include gate counts, crowd estimates, vehicle counts, and market area surveys.

Observation Techniques and Applications

Using standard checklists, event staff and volunteers can gain a great deal of quantitative information as well as an enhanced subjective evaluation of the event. For some organizers, observational research might be a necessary substitute for visitor and market surveys. It should be a formal part of all evaluation strategies. Observations have several advantages over surveys:

- All staff and volunteers can participate, each contributing their own unique perspective on the event, the customers, and the impacts.
- Customer behavior is sometimes a better indicator of problems, preferences, and attitudes than are formal responses to surveys.
- Key elements of the event product can only be evaluated by means of direct observation: how people behave under different circumstances; how transport and movement controls actually work; the quality of the experience actually delivered (including food and entertainment); the quality of service delivered by staff/volunteers as measured against management criteria; the use of information or directional material and signs; the effectiveness of waste, litter, and pollution controls.
- The atmosphere or ambience of the event, which is a vital but intangible element of the product, can be evaluated best by a combination of direct observation and visitor comments; everyone associated with the event will likely have a valuable opinion on the overall effectiveness of the atmosphere, or at least on specific factors that create atmosphere.

It is a mistake, however, to rely too heavily on casual comments and unsubstantiated observations. Use of an evaluation checklist is recommended, covering several types of measurement:

- items that are present or absent, adequate or inadequate (determined by performance criteria, not subjective opinion); for example, are there enough litter bins, and are they emptied frequently enough to avoid spillage?
- items judged to be good or bad, such as the quality of food;
- items requiring lengthy observation and analysis, such as the behavior of visitors under specific circumstances; for example, what was the effect of signposting on pedestrian flows?
- items requiring a summary conclusion, such as the overall quality and visitor satisfaction with entertainment, as determined by observation of visitor reactions and comments.

Some checklists can be completed during the event, though not by all workers, while every volunteer and staff person should complete a form after the event.

Secret Shoppers and Participant Observation

An alternative, or additional step, is to have "secret shoppers" on staff for the sole purpose of making observations. Fast-food chains use shoppers to secretly evaluate food, service, and facility quality, and event managers can do the same. These people should ideally be trained observers, and there are advantages and disadvantages in using known observers as opposed to those who will be strangers to other staff and volunteers.

A major consideration is ethics. Some forms of secret observation can be violations of human privacy or dignity, so observers should be told the limits of their assignments. On the other hand, casual and unobtrusive observers can fit into the crowd without any influence whatsoever. And if staff evaluations are included, there is merit in making them open and obvious so that staff know they are being observed. Everyone subject to evaluation should, of course, have advance knowledge of the criteria being used, and should not be expected to perform duties they are not trained and qualified to handle.

An example of how participant observation can be used in evaluation and quality management has already been provided in Chapter 6, regarding service mapping. The purpose is to have trained evaluators experience the event as much as possible like any other guest or customer, but to take detailed notes of any potential problems or service failures.

Economic Impact Measurement and Evaluation

In this section we examine in detail the concepts and methods of economic impact measurement and evaluation for events. As a starting point, it can be noted that Carlsen, Getz, and Soutar (2000) reviewed the literature and practice of economic impact evaluation in Australia, then used a Delphi research technique to determine what research directions were needed. They found that some agencies do not make evaluation results public, but release the most favorable findings selectively. Other agencies do not debate validity or reliability, leaving that to consultants who use "black-box" methods to estimate economic benefits.

Pressure was building among event development agencies for standardized methods because the results of impact studies were being compared (like methodological apples and oranges), resulting in political questions about why X did better than Y. Important pre- and postevent evaluation criteria were revealed. Before the event it is a matter of forecasting impacts and reaching a decision on bidding, support, or program. Risk assessment and the probability of success are important issues, and both relate in part to the event organizer's competence and track record. After the event, it is a matter of goal attainment and comparing costs with benefits. Problem-free operations and financial results are two important measures.

Misleading Presumptions About Event Impacts

A number of misleading presumptions persist about event impacts, presumably because of the immaturity of event-related research. An article by Crompton and McKay (1994) also explored this issue, documenting seven errors encountered in event impact assessments. These are incorporated into the ensuing discussion of presumptions and use of the multiplier.

Presumption 1: To Justify Events, or to Obtain Grants, it is Necessary to "Prove" Their Economic Benefits

Organizers and supporters of festivals and special events want to obtain grants from public agencies, and they feel that development-minded officials must have "proof" that events create economic benefits. Crompton and McKay (1994) noted: "A scarcity of tax dollars has led to increasing public scrutiny of their allocation. In this environment, producing an economic impact study to demonstrate that economic returns to a community will exceed investment has become almost a *de rigeur* requirement for event organizers. Often these studies are not conducted impartially or objectively," but are done "to legitimize the event's public support by endowing it with an aura of substantial economic benefits" (p. 33).

Presumption 2: All Festivals and Special Events Create Economic Benefits

The evidence strongly suggests that many events have little direct economic impact on their community or region, largely because they cater mostly to residents. When events attract out-of-region visitors, grants, or sponsorships, they start to create directly measurable economic benefits. Events can also have a significant cumulative impact by improving the destination's image and overall attractiveness, which can be evaluated through studies of perception and trip motivation within target market areas.

The "attribution problem" relates to this question: How much of the spending of event-goers can be attributed as economic impact of the event? To the event organizers the total expenditure of all their customers is an important financial statistic, but in a tourism context the expenditure of visitors who came to the area because of the event is much more important than total revenue. The spending of tourists who travel to an area because of an event is considered to be "new" or "incremental," and therefore is equivalent to the earnings of an export industry.

Presumption 3: Construction of New Facilities for Mega-Events Is a Benefit

For mega-events like world's fairs and Olympics, and sometimes smaller special events, new facilities or community infrastructure is required. Proponents of the event might claim these additions as benefits to the community, but they are usually costs. The benefit would exist only if capital for the construction is new money to the area, such as one-time grants from central governments.

Also, once the facilities are built—especially cultural and recreational ones—operating costs must be taken into account. Even if the new facilities are considered to be benefits, the permanent operating costs are borne by the host community. But some of these costs can be discounted if the facilities are able to attract new events and new tourist expenditure in the future.

Murray (1991) advised that impacts are realized in stages, commencing with planning and bidding, and proceeding through construction, production, and wrap-up stages. Some impacts might not become apparent for years, while others will be extremely difficult to measure.

Presumption 4: Festivals Are for Everyone; All Visitors Are Alike

Many event organizers like to believe this, especially if they have a mandate to promote community development and foster leisure or the arts. However, numerous event visitor surveys have revealed that event customers, and particularly event tourists, are a highly segmented market. This has major implications for event impact evaluation and related demand forecasting or feasibility studies. Some events attract more and higher spending tourists than others, and as reported for the Adelaide Festival (Centre for South Australian Economic Studies, 1990) event tourists spent more per day than average tourists, even when excluding festival ticket sales. The attraction of high-yield tourists, defined in the context of tourism goals for the area, should take higher priority than mass marketing and complex impact measurements.

Presumption 5: Events Create Lots of Employment

Another unfortunate consequence of the use of multipliers and econometric models is the frequent estimate of employment generated by events. The assumption made by using multipliers or other impact models is that so many units of "new" or "incremental" income, created by tourist expenditure, will in turn create employment. Usually this supposed benefit is expressed as full-time job equivalents (FTEs). Crompton, Lee, and Shuster (2001) warned that although the IMPLAN model they used for estimating the economic impacts of an event estimated creation of many jobs, in reality, festivals and special events create few full-time jobs and there is available capacity in the workforce to absorb the short-term increase in labor demands.

Successful event organizations typically have small numbers of all-year or part-time staff and most labor at events is done by volunteers. Economists are very reluctant to assign an economic benefit to the contribution of volunteers (Sports Economics, 1991, pp. 2–3) because they create no new income for the area. Under some circumstances volunteer labor might even be considered a cost, such as a case where people work on events for free instead of taking paid employment.

As to the income generated by tourist expenditure, it will usually be dispersed widely among suppliers, accommodation and dining establishments, retail shops, etc. It helps sustain jobs, and that is very important, but the assumption that tourist expenditure at small events can create new jobs is largely wishful thinking.

Presumption 6: All the Expenditure of All Event-Goers Can Be Counted as Economic Benefits

This can be called the "attribution problem": of all the money spent by event-goers, how much can be attributed validly to the event as its economic benefit to the area? It is a very complex question to answer, and there is no consensus among experts as to exactly what can be counted as benefits. The major questions to be addressed are: (a) Should expenditure of area residents be counted as benefits, or is it simply money that would otherwise be spent locally on other things? (b) Can tourist expenditure be counted as a benefit if the tourist would have visited the area regardless of the event? (c) Do events have cumulative and intangible impacts?

To determine how much of the spending at events and on event-related trips can be considered "incremental" (i.e., new money for the area), a number of assumptions are typically made concerning the appropriate portion of resident and tourist expenditure. Some economists argue that only the expenditure of true tourists should be counted, while residents' spending must be ignored, yet frequently studies include a percentage of resident spending on the assumption that the events acted to retain money that would otherwise be spent elsewhere, or generated resident spending over and above normal levels.

In the study of eight festivals in Canada's Capital Region (Coopers and Lybrand, 1989), the consultants asked area residents if they spent more than usual during the time of the events they attended, leading them to include a proportion of residents' expenditure. In a study of the Adelaide Festival (Centre for South Australian Economic Studies, 1990) residents attending the festival were asked if they stayed at home, rather than taking a vacation out of the state, because of the event. Researchers in Adelaide concluded that 10.3% of resident visitors were "holidaying at home" and 75% of those would have otherwise traveled outside the state. They also concluded that another 7000 residents would have traveled outside South Australia more, if it was not for the festival. Accordingly, a proportion of resident expenditure was counted as a benefit for the state.

Researchers who decide to include resident expenditure in the calculation of incremental income should think very carefully about the validity of this practice. First, inclusion of any resident spending is considered to be invalid by most experts (e.g., Sports Economics, 1992, p. 2, recommends against it), and the author of this book believes all resident expenditure to be merely an internal transfer—like taking in each other's laundry. The opportunity costs occur because spending at an event likely decreases resident spending elsewhere in the area. It is also difficult to measure, requiring a separate survey or set of questions just for residents, resulting in higher research costs and more complex methods of survey and analysis. Respondents cannot be expected to give reliable answers to such questions as "did you holiday at home because of the event?" or "did you spend more than usual because of the festival?"

Most importantly, the object of all such impact evaluation should be visitor oriented. The key questions pertain to the event's ability to attract outsiders and to generate revenue from tourism. The value of an event as a leisure or cultural phenomenon (i.e., having "social benefits") is legitimate, but is an entirely different field of inquiry. As an example, Ellis (1990) conducted an evaluation of the Halifax, Nova Scotia, Buskers Festival and concluded that it had a great return on investment for the city because of the large entertainment value generated for residents. Coopers and Lybrand (1989) estimated the "social worth" of festivals by asking respondents about their willingness to pay for free events or to pay more for events having a charge. Burns et al. (1986) described a technique to estimate the "psychic benefit" of an event by assigning monetary value to estimated costs of noise and disruption that residents were willing to bear. These are all useful methods to be included in cost–benefit evaluation, but they have little to do with event tourism.

Tourists visiting an area because of an event (or any other kind of attraction) typically spend money getting there and back, some of which is within the destination area being studied, as well as at the event itself. It is tempting to consider all tourist expenditure at the event (usually admission fees, tickets to performances, parking, shopping, dining, and drinking) as a benefit to the area—minus, of course, the amounts lost to the area, such as: the costs of all goods and services that were imported; costs of bringing in talent or staff from outside; organizational and marketing expenditure outside the area. But to do so ignores several issues.

What should be done about the expenditure of a tourist who happened to be in town for a convention and incidentally spent money at a festival? It is quite possible that the tourist would have spent money somewhere else, if the event was not occurring, so that all the convention-goer's spending in town should be counted as a benefit of the meeting, not the festival. Attributing the expenditure to both the conference and the event would be double counting, so some sort of allocation is required. The best way to determine the allocation is by asking all visitors a set of questions about their reasons for visiting the destination.

The types of questions commonly employed to solve the attribution problem are two-fold: What proportion of your trip to this area is attributable to the event? Would you say that this event was the only (or main, an important, somewhat important, not at all important) reason for your trip here? From the answers, the proportion of tourist expenditure attributed to a given event or attraction can be estimated. In the example of Winterlude in Canada's Capital region (Coopers and Lybrand, 1989) respondents were asked to give the proportion of their trip motivated by the festival, leading to an estimate that 75% of tourist expenditure could be considered incremental. In contrast, the Festival of Arts attracted only 8% of tourists in attendance, and it was deemed to have no incremental benefit at all (partly because residents attending it said they spent less than normal). Because Winterlude was the dominant tourist attraction of all eight festivals studied, it accounted for $40.6 million of the total $61 million in contribution to the region's gross domestic product.

For the Adelaide Festival (Centre for South Australian Economic Studies, 1990) it was estimated that 900 tourists extended their stay because of the festival, and only the portion of their spending that occurred during the extended stay was included as incremental.

There is a certain arbitrariness in these attribution procedures that might best be handled by doing a "sensitivity" analysis. Such an approach was taken in the study of nine festivals in Edinburgh (Scotinform Ltd., 1991), where the consultants used different attribution weightings (e.g., from 79% to 100% of the expenditure of residents and from 10% to 27% of day-tripper expenditure was excluded) before concluding that the results were not effected in a major way.

"Time switching" (Burns et al., 1986) is another complication. Some tourists attending events might have simply rescheduled a planned visit to the area, while others might have stayed away because of perceived congestion or expense associated with an event. As well, some residents might actually be tempted to leave town while a major event is held, thereby generating an economic loss for the area. Researchers will find it difficult to take these considerations into account, but at a minimum visitors should be asked if their visit to the area would have been made at another time (say, within a 12-month surrounding period) and had merely been rescheduled to take in the event. The expenditure of time-switchers should be deleted completely from calculations of incremental income.

It can be argued that because events enhance the tourist image of an area there is a "background" economic benefit attributable to events from tourists attracted by this enhanced image. An earlier study of Winterlude (EKOS Research Associates Inc., 1985) found that tourists believed their visit to the event heightened their image of the capital region. This image-enhancing factor could have long-term, positive effects on tourism, but actual measurement of benefits would be very difficult. Some researchers have asked if event-goers plan to return to an area, or would recommend the event or the area to others.

A related line of questioning would be to assess the value of media coverage, either in qualitative terms or by assigning monetary value to free publicity. Even more subjective is the notion that special events make residents feel proud (confirmed by Burns et al., 1986, in their study of the Adelaide Grand Prix), and that heightened civic spirit will have tangible benefits for the area.

Presumption 7: Multipliers and/or Econometric Models Must Be Used to Estimate the "Secondary" Impacts of Events

Although accurate multiplier analysis can add to the evaluation process, multipliers have been greatly abused in economic impact assessments, usually by misappropriating multipliers intended for quite different purposes, larger regions, or other areas (Archer, 1982; Fleming & Toepper, 1990; Murray, 1991). Tourism-specific multipliers do not exist, and they are not generally calculated for local areas, so researchers are tempted to apply a general income multiplier for a country or a region without actually measuring the direct and indirect local/regional impacts of incremental spending generated by events. To overcome this problem some researchers have employed econometric models, as with the Coopers and Lybrand (1989) study, but these also have limitations.

Unfortunately, it appears that the use of multipliers or other models in calculating secondary benefits is often for the purpose of exaggerating the estimate of economic benefits. Multipliers are really intended for use in comparing the economic performance of various sectors of the economy (Archer, 1982). Because of the importance of this topic, and the confusion surrounding multipliers, the ensuing section provides a detailed examination of the applications and pitfalls researchers will encounter.

Multipliers

Economic impact assessments often include a "multiplier" calculation to demonstrate that incremental tourist expenditure has "direct," "indirect," and "induced" benefits for the local economy. The idea is that "new" or "incremental" money ripples through the economy, changing hands many times, thereby having a cumulative impact greater than the initial amount of tourist expenditure.

Figure 14.1 illustrates the multiplier concept for events. The "direct" income for the area comes from tourists attracted specifically by the event (spending both at the event and on other goods and services such as accommodation and shopping), plus any new money received from outside by the organization (mostly grants and sponsorships), and other incremental revenue tied to the event, such as money for new infrastructure received from a higher level of government. Keep in mind that tourists spend a lot of money on the trip itself that never reaches the local area, which is why it is important to define the study area boundary. Also remember that not all the new money received by the event organizers circulates in the local economy. Anything they pay for prize money, taxes to higher levels of government, or to import goods and services (including entertainment) cannot be counted in the multiplier calculations—they are "leakages." When looking at the organization's budget it is important to consider exactly where their money comes from and where it is spent.

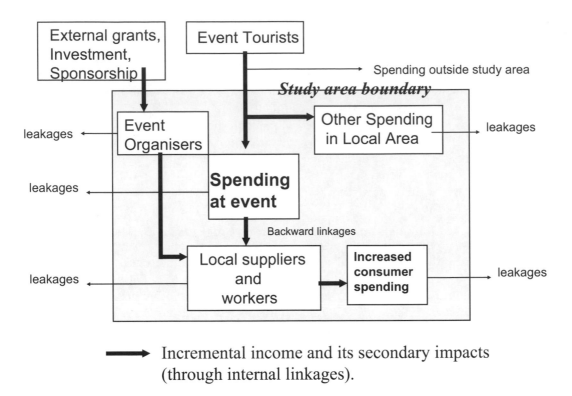

Incremental income and its secondary impacts (through internal linkages).

Figure 14.1. The event income multiplier.

Most of the economic benefits of events occur at the level of "direct" income, because once the money starts to circulate there are many "leakages." The organizers, as well as other businesses in the local area that receive money from tourists, do business with both local and external suppliers. The money spent on local suppliers is called a "backward linkage," and it creates local profits, taxes, and wages. The overall effect on the economy beyond these first two rounds of monetary flow is called the "induced" income, and is mostly related to higher consumer spending because of increased profits and wages. Indirect and induced income is often lumped together and called "secondary" local area income.

In general, it is desirable to maximize incremental income (new money), maximize internal business linkages, and minimize leakages. Later we examine specific points for increasing the local economic benefits from events.

Types of Multipliers

A source of much confusion is the use of different types of multiplier and different ways of expressing them. It also appears that some tourism and event boosters use multipliers incorrectly, to exaggerate the benefits. Archer (1982) examined the misuse of multipliers, and his article is essential reading for those who want to use the technique in impact assessment.

The "multiplier" usually used in tourism impact studies is the "income multiplier," which "is basically a coefficient which expresses the amount of income generated in an area by an additional unit of tourist spending" (Archer, 1982, p. 236). For example, if a festival attracts tourists to an area and they spend $100,000 (this is considered to be "new" or "incremental" income for the area), and this spending is found to generate $50,000 of income for the area (after subtracting leakages), then the income multiplier is 0.5.

Archer (1982) cited a number of income multipliers from various studies: for small island countries they ranged from 0.58 to 1.30; for counties and states in the US they were 0.88 to 1.30; for counties in the US they ranged from 0.39 to 1.30. Small town, county, and regional tourism income multipliers in Great Britain ranged from 0.18 to 0.47. A University of Missouri study in 1986 (quoted in Crompton & McKay, 1994) concluded that 90–95% of US county income multipliers fall in the range of 0.4–0.8, with somewhat higher coefficients for cities. These examples show clearly that the size of the area is an important factor in shaping the multiplier. The same applies for underdeveloped economies—a great deal of leakage occurs owing to imports and other outbound monetary flows.

The "value-added" multiplier, similar to the income multiplier, is preferred by some economists. It represents the wages, profits, and salaries of all the producers in the chain of production begun by incremental tourist expenditure. It cannot exceed a value of 1.0 unless induced consumption is included, and then can have a value up to 1.5 (Burns et al., 1986, p. 14).

Other multipliers are based on the effects of incremental tourist spending on economic activity (sales, transactions, outputs, gross domestic product) rather than income to residents. These can have high values that can be misused to exaggerate the true value of tourism to a local area. Archer (1982, p. 239) gives the example of a small town which was calculated to have a "sales multiplier" of 1.46 and an income multiplier of 0.36 in its hotel sector. This meant that an incremental tourist expenditure of $100, in a hotel, would generate $146 of sales activity in the area, but only $36 of local income! Another important point from this example is that sectors of the economy have different multipliers.

Employment multipliers are also commonly cited in tourism studies, and can be expressed as the number of jobs created per unit of tourist expenditure (e.g., one job created for every $100,000), or as the ratio of jobs created indirectly by tourist spending to the jobs created directly in the tourism sector. All multipliers are linked, because they all measure the effects of incremental tourist expenditure. And income is what creates jobs, although how many jobs depends on other factors beside the total amount of tourist spending. Tourist expenditure in commercial accommodation creates many service sector jobs, but tourists staying with friends and relatives, and day-trippers, have a much smaller impact.

Examples of multipliers for events have been provided by Vaughan (1979) regarding impacts on Edinburgh and Hatten (1987) on the impacts of the 1986 World's Fair on Vancouver and British Columbia. This type of study is complex, and not without problems. Multipliers for cities are usually not available and have to be estimated. Multipliers for regions and countries can be applied to local areas only by making big assumptions.

Multipliers for Various Economic Sectors

As mentioned, there is no such thing as a tourism multiplier; rather, incremental spending in different economic sectors will have different multiplier coefficients. Crompton and McKay (1994) illustrated this fact for their study of a City X event, using the metropolitan trading area as the unit for estimating impact. Their income multipliers for various sectors were: food and beverage (1.26), admission fees (1.07), entertainment (1.08), retail (1.12), lodging (1.05), automobile (0.69), commercial transport (0.81), other (1.12).

A number of factors directly determine the multiplier, the most important of which are: amount of leakage/imports (e.g., gasoline for autos is seldom produced locally); backward linkages into the local economy (e.g., how integrated is it? can all supplies and raw materials be obtained in the area?); ownership (which affects the retention or expatriation of profits); labor versus capital intensity (e.g., visitor spending in hotels creates more jobs than in bed and breakfast, but B&B is locally owned and uses mostly local supplies); source of labor (immigrant workers might repatriate wages). These factors have to be considered on a case by case basis.

Maximizing Local Income Benefits From Events

A coordinated event tourism strategy that seeks to maximize local economic benefits should strive to meet the following objectives:

- attract more tourists to the area specifically for the event;
- attract more external grants and sponsorships;
- make it easier for the visitor to get to the area using local suppliers (e.g., work with local transport companies to package the event) so that more of their total expenditure comes into the area;
- make the event long enough and attractive enough to encourage overnight stays in the host community;
- ensure sufficient accessibility and accommodation so that both tours and individual travelers are able to make convenient overnight stopovers specifically for the event;
- encourage residents to invite guests to stay with them during the event, and to take guests to the events;
- provide sufficient merchandizing to attract visitor spending at the event;
- coordinate events and other attractions to build a "critical mass" sufficient to attract and hold visitors in the area;
- research is necessary to identify and measure the linkages and leakages, and where exactly gains can be realized;
- the event should employ mostly local people for staff and performers;
- require the licensing of merchants/vendors/exhibitors so that locals can be given priority, or a share of profits kept locally;
- make purchases from local suppliers;
- put profits back into community projects;
- make sure that all visitor needs are provided for at the event, or locally (i.e., food, entertainment, souvenirs, accommodation, gasoline).

A few guidelines on types of visitors can also be stated. For creation of local income, the ideal event visitor meets these characteristics:

- stays at least 1 night in the area, preferably at serviced commercial accommodation;
- comes in a group, all of whom spend money;
- consumes merchandise, food, and beverages at the event and in the community;
- prefers local produce, crafts, arts, etc., over imports;
- spends a substantial part of the travel costs locally (gasoline, bus fares, etc.).

Case Study: Canadian Tulip Festival

In 2003 a major event research study was undertaken by the Research and Information Section of the Ottawa Tourism and Convention Authority (called Ottawa Tourism: www.ottawatourism.ca). Martin Winges, Director of Research and Information for Ottawa Tourism, was kept busy overseeing studies of 21 events in the city—surely one of the most ambitious event-related research projects ever conducted. Results, including the methodology, are intended to benefit all events across the country by encouraging a standardized approach.

The primary sources of data were an on-site visitor survey at various festival venues. This was necessary to randomly sample tourists and estimate the proportion of tourists versus locals. For the Tulip Festival, 2968 attendees aged 15 and older were intercepted on 18 of the 19 festival days, and interviews were conducted with 2777. To find out how many residents attended the various summertime events a telephone survey was conducted once a month over the summer, resulting in 1003 interviews. A detailed look at the Tulip Festival follows.

Attendance and Tourist Numbers at the Tulip Festival

In 2003 this festival attracted up to 1.1 million visits by almost 500,000 persons, including an estimated 180,346 tourists (i.e., 36.5% were nonlocal visitors who lived at least 80 kilometers or 50 miles beyond the city of Ottawa). There was also a group who were not city residents but lived within 80 kilometers or 50 miles, and some of their spending was attributable to the event because they made trips into the city for festival activities.

Local festival-goers attended 2.78 days on average, while tourists attended 1.69 days on average. However, the true tourists stayed in the Capital Region an average of 3.45 nights, with 78.2% staying at least 1 night. It can be concluded that the festival was a major factor in attracting and extending tourists' stays in the area, as the typical summertime tourists spend much less time in the area. Tourists also had the largest party sizes, and many were in groups—but they had fewer children with them. These festival tourists were primarily wealthier and older than the attending residents (average 48.7 years), and there were more females (56%) than males. The percentage of tourists staying in commercial accommodation was 44.5%, with another 27.3% staying with friends and relatives.

The Attribution of Spending

Economic benefits were estimated for the city of Ottawa. Respondents were asked to specify the percentage of their decision to visit Ottawa that they attributed to the festival. Of the tourists from beyond 50 miles (80 km), 46.7% stated that the festival accounted for 100% of their decision to visit the city, while only 17% said it had no influence. Overall, it was determined that 65.3% of nonresident visitor spending could be attributed to the festival. This is very high, and likely due to the fact that it is a well-publicized spring event, well outside the regular tourist season when many more attendees would have been traveling regardless of the event.

Expenditures

When estimating economic impacts, the analysts included three categories of spending: (1) the proportion of tourist spending in Ottawa that could be attributable to the event; (2) the portion of residents' spending on friends and relatives who had come to the city because of the event (9.3% of locals claimed attributable spending for friends and relatives); (3) the portion of "fringe" residents' spending (those who lived outside the city of Ottawa but within 50 miles/80 km) that could be attributed to the event.

Tourists, on average, spent $218.78 per person per trip, with accommodation being the biggest category (at $80.10), followed by restaurants ($61.02). By comparison, visitors from the 'fringe' (within 50 miles) spent on average only $23.77 per person per trip, most of which was spent at the event itself. Residents who spent money on visiting friends and relatives spent it mostly on groceries and at restaurants.

It was estimated the festival was responsible for generating $24.8 million Canadian dollars in new spending in Ottawa, of which fully 93% was attributed to real tourists (i.e., $23.1 million). Incremental tourist spending ("new money" attributed to the event) has widespread impact in Ottawa. Of the $23.1 million, the largest amounts went to the following: the commercial accommodation sector ($8.9 million), restaurants ($6.6 million), admission to the festival ($1 million), other entertainment ($1 million), retail clothing ($1 million).

The study author used an econometric model called TEAM (Tourism Economic Assessment Model, developed by the Canadian Tourism Research Institute of the Conference Board of Canada) to estimate the event's economic impacts. It is customized to simulate the inputs, outputs, and tax structure of specific local economies, measuring spin-off effects of tourism spending on various sectors based on known industry linkages. Capital expenditures and daily operating expenditures were not included.

Taking into account the portion of their spending that could validly be attributed to the Tulip Festival, tourists generated $24.8 million of direct, incremental spending, of which $21.3 million remained as a contribution to the local gross domestic product (this was called the "net economic impact" and refers to "value added" or the profit generated for the area). The "total economic activity" in Ottawa attributable to the festival was estimated to be $40.7 million (this figure represents total industry output, or the total of all direct, indirect, and induced impacts of all goods and services produced within the economy). Table 14.2 shows a comparison between 1997 and 2003. Note that the festival reports the "total economic activity" figure, calling it "gross economic impact." The 2003 event was twice as long and methods were not identical.

In terms of employment, the study estimated that the equivalent of 495 full-year jobs were sustained by this level of tourist expenditure, most of which were in the service and retail sectors. Benefits included $2.4 million in taxes for the city, $5.3 million for the province of Ontario, and $6.2 million for the federal government.

Financial Issues for Canadian Tulip Festival Organizers

Unfortunately, growth and the creation of substantial economic benefits does not always equal financial success for event organizers. In 2003 attendance at its Major's Hill Park site (with paid admission) was down 8% from the previous year—a decline attributed to the

Table 14.2. Canadian Tulip Festival Visitor Profile, and Impacts

	2003	1997
Attendance		
Person-visits	1,154,257	542,095
People	494,524	222,170
Avg. person-visits	2.3	2.4
Gender		
Female	57%	62%
Male	43%	38%
Age		
15–24	8%	15%
25–44	45%	46%
45–64	37%	28%
Over 65	10%	11%
Origin		
Local	63% (314,199)	73% (161,517)
Tourists	37% (180,346)	27% (60,653)
Other		
Families	26% had children	30% had children
Economic Impact		
Gross economic impact	$40.6 million	$15.4 million
Total visitor spending	$24.8 million	$10.6 million
Employment (from visitor spending)	495 person-years	221 person-years
Taxes generated/supported	$13.8 million	$4.6 million

Source: Ottawa Tourism and Convention Authority.

negative effects of the Iraq war and short-lived SARS outbreak (an infectious respiratory disease) on travel. This resulted in a deficit of over $220,000 on a budget of $4 million.

"While we create millions of dollars in economic activity for the community and the tourism industry, we only get the price of an admission ticket and some concession sales from the visitors—about $15, and this only from Major's Hill Park which caters to less than 10% of our total clientele" said Michel Gauthier, Executive Director. The shortfall led to cuts in overhead expenses, revised arrangements with creditors, staff losses, and a search for new revenue sources. A financial stability strategy was then developed to ensure continuity, according to Joan O'Neill, President of the festival society.

Economic Impact Evaluation Process

There has been a great deal of experience in conducting valid economic impact assessments of events, including many published papers about methods and issues. Crompton's (1999) report for the National Parks and Recreation Association, including results from economic impact assessments of sport events across the US, is an excellent reference. Published journal articles by Dwyer et al. (2000a, 2000b) show how to validly conduct impact assessments for a variety of events including conferences, festivals, and sports.

There are still points of contention among theorists, and differences in methods being employed. This author finds little justification for using multipliers, as explained elsewhere, but they are commonly employed by consultants. As well, there are some who believe that a portion of resident expenditure at events can be considered an economic benefit of the event, whereas I think there is no sound rationale for this inclusion. The biggest concern is that deliberate exaggerations of benefits are frequently made, while cost and negative impacts are frequently ignored or downplayed, so economic impact studies should be models of transparency and restraint.

The following steps cover the whole process, including the optional use of multipliers.

Step 1: Formulate Precise Research Goals

Care in formulating research goals will help in avoiding many of the problems and pitfalls discussed above. The researcher or manager must first decide what is of principal interest: for example, knowing that the event attracted a high proportion of out-of-region tourists is extremely important to most event organizers, but estimating regional income and employment benefits is likely to be of interest mainly to tourism agencies.

Rules

- Define the study area within which costs and benefits are to be calculated.
- Delimit the scope of the evaluation (which costs and benefits to measure; quantitative and qualitative evaluation techniques to be used).
- Define tourists and residents.
- Set criteria for attribution of incremental expenditure (i.e., should resident spending be included?).
- Formulate precise research and evaluation questions.

Recommendations

A great deal of trouble and expense can be saved by avoiding multipliers and other models, and by keeping the whole evaluation process as simple as possible.

- Aim the research at determining the number and types of tourists attracted to

the area, with emphasis on high yield; if necessary, and a reliable methodology is available, estimate incremental expenditure.
- Exclude the spending of area residents.

Step 2: Determine Data Needs and Appropriate Methods
Rules

- Specify types of data needed to answer the research questions; determine the measures needed and the appropriate methods to collect and analyze the data.

Step 3: Determine Attendance at the Event; Calculate Total Number of Tourists and Tourist-Visits
Rules

- Whenever possible, use controlled access and/or ticket sales to estimate attendance.
- For open events, use a systematic observation method which avoids double counting by applying weightings derived from visitor surveys (asking: how many visits have you made, on how many days?).
- Take into account the difference between total number of visitors and total person-visits, and between tourist and resident visits (feasible only if a visitor survey is undertaken)

Recommendations

Avoid estimates based on casual observation.

Step 4: Conduct Visitor Surveys

To obtain event visitor expenditure data both diary and questionnaire methods have been used. With diaries a sample of visitors is asked to complete a daily record of activities and expenditures. The nonresponse bias of diary methods (i.e., a higher drop-out rate) was found not to be a problem by Faulkner and Raybould (1995) and Breen, Bull and Walo (2001). However, in both those research studies it was found that questionnaire responses tended to underestimate expenditure, owing to memory lapses, and both found significant differences between males and females. It was suggested by Faulkner and Raybould that males are more likely susceptible to the "social bravado" bias whereupon they report more spending on items influenced by peer pressure (e.g., drinking, entertainment). The Bree et al. analysis also found no significant differences in data obtained by those who handed in questionnaires at the end of a multiday sporting event and those who mailed it back later.

Rules

- An on-site visitor survey is necessary for estimating the number and proportion of tourists at events; their motivations, spending patterns, and whether or not visits were extended or expenditure increased due to the event.
- Ensure that a systematic sample of individuals is taken.
- Include performers, officials, competitors, etc.
- Stratify the sample by applicable factors such as venue, time, and day; use weightings to reflect the true distribution of attendance.
- Guard against sampling bias caused by length of stay and multiple site visits by

ensuring that individuals are not mistakenly counted twice; make estimates of average length of stay and number of visits and "weight" the results to reduce the effect of length of stay bias.

- Use past experience or educated guesses to derive a sample size that will yield high confidence limits for statistical analysis, especially ensuring a large enough sample of tourists.

Recommendations

Avoid recall bias by conducting surveys on-site or combining on-site with take-home surveys. Diaries are likely to yield more accurate expenditure estimates. Offer incentives to obtain higher response rates.

Step 5: Conduct Surveys of Other Event Visitors

Tyrrell and Johnston (2001) advised that economic impact studies must include the spending of all categories of event visitor: spectators, participants, sponsors and their guests, officials, the media, volunteers, exhibitors and vendors. Theses researchers found that the largest share of economic impacts at certain sport events came from spending by sponsors. Solberg, Andersson, and Shibli (2002) determined that the media covering international sport events generated the largest per-person impacts (i.e., they generated the highest "yield").

Instead of random samples of event visitors, a complete census of all the special groups might be possible and necessary. For example, in team sports, some might be very heavy spenders and others might get their ways paid by local organizers.

Step 6: Estimate Total Visitor Expenditure (by Tourists and Others)

Frechtling (1994) mentioned eight different ways to make estimates of tourist expenditure, most of which are not applicable to events. Direct observation could be used at event sites, such as recording sales, admissions, and service fees, but this tells nothing of off-site expenditure. Postevent household surveys could measure event-related expenditure, but only in sampled market areas and with the added problem of recall bias. Whatever technique is used, the researchers must pay particular attention to the business traveler who might not know all related trip expenses, and to the package tourist who might not be able to assign the accurate portion of trip expenses to the study area. For these special cases a number of additional questions are needed, or special subsamples will have to be taken to probe more deeply.

Regardless of the survey technique or sample frame, recall bias is a major problem. A number of studies have demonstrated that tourists often underestimate their expenditure, especially after some time has passed (Howard, Lankford, & Havitz, 1991; Sheldon, 1990). Consequently, on-site and exit surveys are likely to yield the best estimates of daily expenditure, and measurement of expenditure for the entire trip is best taken immediately upon completion of the visit. A combination of on-site interviews and self-completed, take-home questionnaires can also be used to good effect (Ralston & Crompton, 1988a, 1988b). As discussed earlier, log books are an alternative for collecting detailed expenditure data.

For the purposes of estimating tourist expenditure, an average amount per tourist-visit can be calculated, then multiplied by an estimate of total tourist-visits. Or an average amount per tourist can be estimated and multiplied by the estimated number of tourists. In the case of a study of the Barossa Wine Festival (Tourism South Australia, 1991) respondents were asked to itemize their spending on the day of the interviews only. Daily expenditure was then divided by the number of adults covered in the sample, then multiplied by the total number of planned visitor-days. This yielded an estimate of visitor spending per adult.

Sports Economics (1991, p. 4) warned of the problems of using mean versus median tourist expenditure visits. If the sample is random and sufficiently large there is no worry, but in inadequate samples a few large outliers will distort the estimate to total incremental expenditure. Use of medians will result in bias, but lower statistical error. If the outliers are a characteristic of the population as a whole, as well as the sample, use of the mean is proper. Otherwise, the median should be used to enumerate from the sample, but with outlier values added separately.

A special problem occurs when more than one event occurs simultaneously, as in the case of Edinburgh's festival season every August. The researchers (Scotinform Ltd., 1991) found that many tourists and residents went to several events during their stay, giving rise to a serious risk of double counting. To overcome this problem they invented a separate category for the "multiple event visitor" and avoided attribution of their expenditure to specific events.

Normal expenditure categories are: food and beverage, recreation and entertainment, travel, accommodation, retail shopping, admission fees. These should be disaggregated geographically (i.e., on-site, off-site within area, outside the subject area) and possibly by time (before, during, and after the event). If sector-specific multipliers are going to be applied, the expenditure categories must match the definitions of each sector.

Rules

- Determine average spending per visitor-day, separating on site from off site, and within the study area from outside the study area (if total trip expenditure is estimated, the on-site, within-area amounts must be distinguished).
- Include spending by performers, officials, etc., but also account for wages, profits, etc., they remove from the area.
- Avoid double counting when events overlap; create a multiple-event category of visitor.
- In small, nonrandom samples, avoid using expenditure means if large outliers occur.
- Use expenditure categories that match available classes of multiplier.
- Take into account the special estimation problems associated with package tours (what portion to allocate to the area?) and business or related trips (the traveler might not have paid).
- Minimize recall bias by conducting surveys on site or as soon after the event as possible.

Recommendations

Use a combination of on-site exit interviews, logbooks, and take-home questionnaires to get reliable estimates of expenditure per day and for the whole trip.

Step 7: Estimate Expenditure "Attributable" to Tourists

From questions on trip motivation, timing, and spending, an estimate can be made of "new" or "incremental" income derived from all event visitors. Only the spending of persons who traveled because of the event and who would not have visited the region otherwise can be counted totally. The spending of time-switchers has to be eliminated, as that of multiple-purpose travelers must be discounted. For those staying longer or spending more because of the event, a portion of their expenditure can be included. With regard to event visitors who had other reasons for traveling but definitely planned to attend an event, Yu and Turco (2000) argued that their event-specific spending should be considered new money and included in economic impact estimates. The inclusion of any amount of resident spending is controversial, but could only be justified if was demonstrated that the event prevented residents from spending money on travel outside the area (and this is extremely difficult to prove).

Rules

- Determine the importance of the event in motivating the trip, an extended stay, or increased spending.
- Subtract time-switchers, who would have visited the area anyway (say, during the same year).
- Do not confuse total incremental expenditure with economic impact.

Recommendations

Ask several motivational questions to obtain a valid measure of the importance of the event.

Step 8: Calculate Net Income and Macroeconomic Impacts

Rules

- Gross visitor expenditure attributed to the event does not equal net income for the area, because of leakage and the multiplier effect.
- Apply a value-added or income multiplier to account for all the direct and secondary effects of incremental expenditure.
- An econometric model can be used instead of multipliers to account for macroimpacts over time.
- Government revenue, in the form of taxes at all levels, is usually taken into account when value-added multipliers are applied; otherwise it must be estimated separately.

Recommendations

"Yield" should be emphasized rather than macroimpacts, by examining the number and types of tourists attracted and their activity and spending patterns.

Step 9: Do a Cost–Benefit Evaluation

Cost–benefit analysis has the added advantage of being able to draw conclusions about the net benefit of the event after costs have been subtracted, and of incorporating intangibles and noneconomic measures.

Evaluation of Costs and Benefits

There is a tendency to use the multiplier to demonstrate only macroeconomic benefits, without consideration of economic costs, and without evaluation of intangibles and noneconomic items. That makes the multiplier a tool for generating misleading conclusions. Cost–benefit analysis has the added advantage of being able to draw conclusions about the net benefit of the event after costs have been subtracted, and of incorporating intangibles and noneconomic measures. It can be used in postevent evaluations, or in feasibility studies to help determine the overall worthiness of a proposal. It is not a method without difficulties. Several general problems always arise:

- how to measure or compare tangibles, such as revenue, with intangibles, such psychological benefits;

- how to subtract intangible costs from tangible benefits;
- determining the parameters of the calculations (what area to cover? what time period?);
- measure benefits and costs for the whole community or just the public sector?

In addition, events give rise to special problems. A landmark study of the Adelaide (Australia) Grand Prix by the Centre for South Australian Economic Studies (Burns et al., 1986) highlighted these issues:

- Demand is primarily for related services, not the event itself; therefore, data acquisition must be broad.
- Peaking of demand is typical of short-term and occasional events; the impacts might therefore be difficult to isolate from general trends.
- Peaking also affects the level and distribution of benefits.
- Special attention must be given to the reallocation ("switching") of funds locally, which is not a real benefit.
- The benefits of events might occur over a long time period (e.g., heightened tourism image leading to increased travel), but investments will often be short-term; therefore, the "discounted present value" of benefits must be compared with costs.
- Justification of costs for event infrastructure might have to be made by considering future use (e.g., the facility legacy).
- Major beneficiaries of events are both the customers and, potentially, the entire host community; therefore, "externalities" are of major interest.

The methods used in the Australian Grand Prix cost–benefit analysis provide a good model, although circumstances and resources will be important factors in shaping methods for different events. One final product of the analysis was a chart (see Table 14.3) showing an upper and lower estimate of the benefit to cost ratio, from the State of South Australia's perspective. Two ratios for tangible economic benefits and costs are shown: an upper estimate of 3.8:1 and a lower estimate of 3.1:1. These ratios can be interpreted as

Table 14.3. Benefit–Cost Ratios for the 1985 Grand Prix in Adelaide, South Australia (Tangible Economic Benefits and Costs Only)

Upper Estimate		Lower Estimate	
Benefits		**Benefits**	
Visitor expenditure (including multiplier effects)	$9,865,000	Visitor expenditure	$6,571,000
Event and construction costs funded from outside the state, including multiplier effects	$14,941,000	Event and construction	$13,765,000
Total benefits	$24,806,000	Total benefits	$23,630,000
Costs		**Costs**	
Event and capital costs funded within the state	$6,571,000	Event and capital costs	$7,520,000
Benefit to cost ratio	3.8:1	**Benefit to cost ratio**	3.1:1

follows: for every dollar of cost (or investment in the event), between 3.1 and 3.8 dollars of benefit to the state of South Australia were realized. Intangibles were treated separately.

Tangible Costs

The Grand Prix researchers (Burns et al., 1986) had to wrestle with the very definition of costs, as applicable to an event like the Grand Prix. Typical of many "mega-events," different levels of government were involved. Grants from the Commonwealth of Australia were counted as benefits, as they were new revenue made available only because of the event. But grants by the state to the event were counted as costs, because that money could have been used for other state purposes (i.e., it had an "opportunity cost"). If the city of Adelaide had been the area for which the cost–benefit evaluation was undertaken, then state grants might have been considered benefits—if they were not simply diverted from some other payments to the city.

The Grand Prix costs were of the following types:

- grants from within the state that could have been used for other purposes;
- construction and demolition expenditure (minus applicable grants);
- amounts written off as depreciation;
- planning, marketing, and operating costs (minus applicable grants);
- cost of borrowing (interest payments);
- externalities: costs to other government agencies (police, fire, health, transport, waste disposal, etc.), which can be attributed to the event as being above and beyond the norm; costs of damage to private property caused by the event; economic losses to businesses adversely impacted by the event.

One could also include the costs of crime associated with events, inflationary costs to housing, property, food etc., if caused by the event and related development.

Tangible Benefits

External grants are benefits to the region only if they constitute new, and not diverted, sources of funds. Spending by residents is mostly a redistribution of local wealth and not a benefit. The Australian Grand Prix researchers (Van der Lee & Williams, 1986) concluded: "The once in a lifetime character of the first Grand Prix and the relatively limited time to change consumption and savings habits leads to the suggestion that it was likely that some increased expenditure was financed from existing savings, thereby providing some additional economic stimulus in the short term" (p. 46). But they did not include any resident spending in their calculations of tangible benefits, yielding conservative estimates.

Benefits of the Grand Prix attributed to the state of South Australia included:

- grants received from outside the area to construction or event operations;
- private investment attracted by the event (most events by themselves lack the ability to attract new hotels, etc., but might have the effect of accelerating developments; any development "boom" might also result in a subsequent "glut" with weaker businesses experiencing actual losses);
- tourist expenditure attributable to the event; the value-added multiplier was used to estimate total impact on the state.

Multipliers derived from state input–output tables for various industry sectors were used. These ranged from 1.109 for expenditure in the food sector to 1.212 for transport, with a weighted average for all sectors of 1.192.This approach is more accurate than using a gross regional or national multiplier.

Employment

Most events generate little in the way of permanent employment, although the larger annual ones require at least a small full-time staff. Mega-events requiring a lengthy planning, operating, and shut-down period can have a more substantial impact, particularly if major construction projects are necessitated. Hatten (1987) reported that Expo '86 in Vancouver generated 29,000 on-site jobs over the 6-month event and increased employment 7.6% overall in the metropolitan area.

The income created by small events, regardless of direct job creation, does create support jobs, both in tourism and in other sectors as well. The "employment multiplier" is often used to estimate the number of jobs created for every direct job in tourism or, more appropriately for events, the number of jobs created per unit of tourist spending. These jobs are expressed as person-years of employment, or "full-time equivalents" (FTEs), as many of the jobs are temporary (e.g., site construction and site staff) or part-time. For example, the study of eight events in Canada's National Capital Region estimated that tourist income from the events generated 1881 person-years of employment in the region, including only 20 full-time jobs (Coopers and Lybrand, 1989). In the Edinburgh events study it was estimated that 1319 FTE jobs were created in the region, and 3034 in Scotland.

Estimates made with multipliers must be treated with extreme caution, as the FTE jobs they "measure" do not really exist—they are mostly bits of existing jobs. It is highly probable that tourist expenditure at events (except the largest ones) will be mostly absorbed by existing labor (i.e., through overtime and more part-time work) rather than through creation of new jobs.

Taxes and Other Public Sector Revenues

Many event impact assessments include an estimate of the tax benefits accruing to government from tourist expenditure at events and related travel. Additional indirect impacts can be created through local property taxes or corporate and income taxes.

One example was given by Taylor and Gratton (1988), who reported that public authorities gained an income of $125 million from the 1984 Los Angeles Olympics. A Coopers and Lybrand study (1989) found that of the $61 million contribution of eight festivals and events to Canada's National Capital Region, $8.8 million was direct tax income to governments.

Turco (1995) provided data on the economic impacts of the 1993 Kodak Albuquerque International Balloon Fiesta. It was estimated that both the city and the state gained substantially from tourist expenditure, as follows: city revenue from lodging taxes, $987,277; city revenue from sales taxes, $1,234,443; state revenue from sales taxes, $1,323,237; state revenue from gasoline taxes, $900,041.

When estimating public revenue from taxes it is essential to consider a number of qualifiers. If local taxes are based on property values alone, then events will contribute little. It is through lodging/hotel taxes that the greatest benefit can accrue, but only when it can be demonstrated that the event attracted tourists who would not otherwise have visited the area, or they stayed longer and in commercial accommodation because of the event. Local business taxes might also increase through the added volume of event tourism, but this will often be difficult to demonstrate.

From the perspective of senior levels of government the tax revenue question is more difficult to evaluate. Travel within a state or country does not generate incremental benefits; only inbound travelers should be counted. It must usually be assumed that events are simply one of a range of leisure opportunities and that any related travel is a substitute for other internal travel. Senior levels of government might, however, be interested in altering the regional pattern of travel to bolster the economies of depressed areas.

Events that stimulate tourist spending on highly taxed goods and services obviously generate high public sector revenues, so the presence of room and sales taxes is an important variable, as is the nature of the event attractions and spending outlets. Andersson and Samuelson's work (2000) can be consulted for additional insights and methodological details.

Research Note

Andersson, T., & Samuelson, L. (2000). Financial effects of events on the public sector. In L. Mossberg (Ed.), *Evaluation of events: Scandinavian experiences* (pp. 86–103). New York: Cognizant Communication Corp.

These authors provided a model for assessing public sector benefits, including taxes and social security payments at various levels, and related costs such as police and infrastructure. "Opportunity costs" are assessed in the context of asking what else could or would have been funded by public agencies if the event was not held. Benefits are increased if employment is generated, both through additional income taxes and social security payments, and a reduction in unemployment insurance payments.

Intangible Costs and Benefits

Intangibles (things not measurable in dollars or other comparable units) can be dealt with in two ways: analyze them subjectively, and separately from the items measured in dollars, or attempt to give them a surrogate monetary value. Some items might actually contain elements that can be treated quantitatively or subjectively. For example, events can have an impact on local housing. The inflation of rents or property values can be measured in dollars, which makes it a tangible cost. But human costs associated with eviction, reduced choice, homelessness, or despair require either a surrogate measure (e.g., try to give a dollar value to time spent homeless), or must be treated in a purely qualitative way.

Several intangible costs were dealt with in the Australian Grand Prix research. Traffic congestion and parking problems experienced by the general population were at times serious. A household survey of residents attempted to measure time lost by residents, and a monetary value was given to this time. Noise disturbances from the races were actually measured (in decibels), and the household surveys determined the degree of public inconvenience caused by noise in several zones around the racecourse. The public was also asked to measure their level of inconvenience arising from crowding. The most interesting intangible cost of the races was that of motor accidents. The researchers analyzed trends in road accidents in the Adelaide area and determined that the Grand Prix did have a psychological impact that led to an increase in accidents and injuries, over and above that which could be attributed to increases in traffic volume alone. Dollar values were assigned to deaths and injuries, but this measurement will be offensive to some and meaningless to others.

Giving surrogate monetary value to the intangible costs is useful, but fraught with problems. It is also hard to argue that intangible costs are sufficient to neutralize the economic benefits. This line of cost–benefit assessment can only be done in a political forum where values are explicitly stated and weighted. For example, can a motor race be justified if it leads to riots, crime, accidents, or deaths?

Some potential long-term benefits associated with events are very difficult to measure. In the Adelaide case, researchers looked at possible advantages accruing to the region and concluded that the races might have increased local entrepreneurial activity and interest in investment, and an improved attitude of residents toward local products. The analysts concluded: "Perhaps the major long term benefit would be an attitude change on the part of local businessmen and workers, the development of confidence and pride in one's ability" (Burns et al., 1986, p. 28). In this way events can be an "enabling mechanism" for broader and more ambitious changes. Other mega-events have been seen in this light, and even small community festivals could achieve similar improvements in attitude, resulting in real gains for the viability of the economic and social community. Such gains are not easily quantifiable.

Other intangible costs and benefits have been cited in the tourism and event literature, and any of these could be important under certain circumstances. Costs might include an increase in crime and prostitution, which are almost always associated with large crowds. The "demonstration effect" might also come into play, as residents of the host community adopt the values or consumer habits of richer tourists. Or actual hostility for tourists might arise where residents feel they are being exploited.

"Psychic Benefits" and "Consumer Surplus"

Event proponents often talk about intangible benefits like increased civic pride, social cohesion, cultural significance, happiness, or having a special experience. Do these have any economic value? Can they be included in a cost-benefit evaluation? Andersson and Samuelson (2000) argued that these constitute a "consumer surplus" when people would willingly spend more than the actual cost of the event. Similarly, it was argued by Burns et al. (1986), who attempted to provide surrogate dollar values on a number of intangible costs and benefits associated with the fist Australian Grand Prix in Adelaide, that there was a consumer surplus because residents recognized many intangible costs of the event but still supported it enthusiastically.

The "contingent valuation method" has been used to examine people's willingness to pay for events, and this also gets at the notion of psychic benefits. It is usually found that tourists are willing to pay much more than residents, no doubt because for them the event is either the object of their trip or a special experience, whereas residents can presumably enjoy it some other time or have better options for using their disposable income. Capturing higher prices and other economic benefits from event tourists returns some or all of their consumer surplus to the host community.

When support for the arts or cultural events is argued, it is important to consider the psychic and social benefits, even if they are intangibles and hard to fit into a cost–benefit evaluation. Some would argue that sports have a great psychic impact because they reach more people than many forms of the arts, but that is missing an important point. Sports are mostly viable within the private sector, especially professional sports, whereas many arts and cultural events cannot exist as private enterprise and must receive subsidies. This issue is also examined in the section of Chapter 6 that looks at the value of programs.

Resident Perceptions and Attitudes

Much of the progress made in evaluating the social and cultural impacts of events has been in the form of community or resident surveys, based on the belief that those affected by events know best what the impacts are and whether or not they are positive or negative. Concepts and methods have been documented in papers by Delamere, Wankel, and Hinch (2001), Delamere (2001), and by Fredline and Faulkner (2002a, 2002b).

Research Note

Delamere, T., Wankel, L., & Hinch, T. (2001). Development of a scale to measure resident attitudes toward the social impacts of community festivals, part I: Item generation and purification of the measure. *Event Management,* 7(1), 11-24.

Delamere, T. (2001). Development of a scale to measure resident attitudes toward the social impacts of community festivals, part 2: Verification of the scale. *Event Management,* 7(1), 25-38.

In these back-to-back articles the researchers develop and test a scale to measure resident attitudes to social impacts of community festivals. The authors believe that economic and social goals must be balanced to ensure sustainable events. Reliable and valid attitude scales can be an important tool in evaluating events and event development or bidding programs. Their scale was tested on residents of one community in Edmonton, Canada, in the context of local impacts of the annual folk festival, and results were plotted on two expectancy-value grids (similar to importance-performance analysis). The grids graphically reveal the costs and benefits that hold high value for respondents, along with their assessment of the likelihood that each will be achieved (benefits) or inflicted (costs). Respondents were found to be largely expecting positive social benefits, although a number of costs were rated moderate both in terms of value and expectancy: disruption of normal routines, intrusions into their lives, reduced privacy, overcrowding, too much traffic, and unacceptable noise levels. These are clearly concerns that have to be addressed by event organizers and the city. Also of interest is the researchers' recommendation that community expectations of costs and benefits be managed, as people's expectations might be out of line with reality.

Research Note

Fredline, E., & Faulkner, B. (2002). Residents' reactions to the staging of major motorsport events within their communities: A cluster analysis. *Event Management,* 7(2), 103-114.

Fredline, E., & Faulkner, B. (2002). Variations in residents' reactions to major motorsport events: Why residents perceive the impacts of events differently. *Event Management,* 7(2), 115-125.

In these two articles the researchers examine host community reactions to major motorsport events in Melbourne and Gold Coast Australia. In the first article a cluster analysis was performed that identified the issues of greatest importance to five groups whose attitudes ranged from most negative through ambivalent to most positive about the impacts of the races. By statistically weighting data from the two city samples, it was estimated that 65% of the populations favored continuation of the races in their current venues. The most negative group (11% of the sample) were older, lived closest to the race areas, were the best educated, were not motorsport fans, and were least likely to work in tourism. In contrast, the most positive group (13%) lived some distance from the events, were the youngest, more interested in motorsports, and more likely to work in tourism. In the second article additional analysis was undertaken regarding the cluster memberships, with results emphasizing that identification with the event theme (racing plus ancillary activities) was the most important factor separating negative from positive perceptions and attitudes. A number of important issues were considered: relocating the races to permanent venues, involving residents in decision making, ameliorating negatives, and compensating affected people.

The Distribution of Costs and Benefits

The question of WHO benefits and WHO pays the costs is often more important than determining and measuring the actual costs and benefits. It is partially an issue of scale, as tourism is often promoted by senior levels of government and by the industry, with local governments and communities picking up many of the costs. And it is an issue of values, as in the case where the severity of some costs is seen to outweigh anticipated benefits.

Unfortunately, these distributional questions are often not asked in impact assessments or in feasibility studies that forecast the costs and benefits of a proposal.

Regarding events, we have already listed some of the key distributional issues in the earlier discussion of the multiplier concept. There it was argued that the multiplier is a planning tool, to be used to help maximize benefits to the host community. By tracing the linkages and leakages that determine the multiplier, the evaluator can learn where the costs and benefits lie, and then take measures to correct problems or realize opportunities. The goal should be to modify the event or its organization to achieve widespread benefits for the community and to minimize costs and disruptions.

Externalities are the most difficult problem. Is it justifiable for event organizers to attain their goals/profits at the expense of property damage, noise, traffic congestion, or other disruptions to uninvolved residents? And can ecological damage or pollution be accepted? What about changes in the social fabric of a community, as a result of annual exposure to large influxes of tourists? The tourism industry gains, but the community is forced or encouraged to change. These are not easy issues to resolve, but they should be considered and debated.

Impacts Specific to Types of Events

Different types of events, in their unique settings, will have different impacts. Each type presents the researcher with somewhat different challenges.

Meetings and Conventions

Conventions generate huge tourism impacts. An average attendee is worth $1,200 a visit in local spending, according to *Tradeshow Week*. IACVB determined that the average delegate's expenditures were mostly on hotel rooms (46.8%), followed by nonhotel restaurants (12.4%), retail stores (11.8%), and hotel restaurants (11.8%) (cited in The 2002 Travel and Leisure Market Research Handbook, p. 305).

Dwyer (2002), writing about convention tourism impacts in the book *Convention Tourism* (Weber & Chon, 2002), noted the following key facts:

- Substantial numbers of people accompany convention-goers (in Australia the accompanying tourists add 15–20% to convention-related expenditures).
- Convention tourists are likely to spend more than other types of visitor (in Singapore, about three times as much! See: SCEB, 2000).
- International convention tourists stay longer and spend more than domestic visitors.
- Corporate and medical conferences generate the highest visitor expenditure.
- Longer conventions generate more spending in total.
- Pre- and postmeeting tours add considerably to the economic impacts (in one study, up to 50% of total spending by international convention-goers was on tours).
- Substantial economic benefits can also accrue from spending by organizers, associations, and sponsors (if it is "new money" to the area).
- International convention tourists (at least in Australia) spend most of their money in capital cities and tourist "gateways," while interstate visitors spend equally in urban and nonurban areas.

Conventions and conferences tend to attract mostly tourists who would not otherwise have traveled to the host city and therefore inject mostly new money into its economy. They also tend to be higher yield visitors, as they mostly stay in hotels, especially if someone else is paying for the trip. When a convention center evaluates its impact on a city it has to specify the number of events that attract mostly local residents for meetings, as these generate little if any new money for the city; they might be justifiable on the grounds that the facility has surplus capacity and needs to generate cash flow. Events though convention centers typically have a tourism-oriented mandate. Research by Grado, Strauss, and Lord (1998) sheds light on the impacts of this sector in a rural region.

Research Note

Grado, S., Strauss, C., & Lord, B. (1998). Economic impacts of conferences and conventions. *Journal of Convention and Exhibition Management, 1*(1), 19–33.

The researchers assessed the impacts of conventions and conferences in a rural, nine-county portion of Pennsylvania. They determined that a majority of attendees were nonresidents and they injected substantial economic benefits. Moreover, their spending was equal to or greater than other types of tourists in this area, including recreationists, and this sector had a high income multiplier because convention-related spending generated high levels of local employment and used local supplies.

Sport Events

Many sport events attract a variety of tourists, each with different spending patterns. Athletes might get paid to attend, or win prize money; therefore, leakages to the area occur. Spectators, including the friends and relatives of participants, are valuable tourists who will likely stay in commercial accommodation. Officials might also get paid and therefore take money out of the local economy. Media covering sport events usually inject a lot of new money.

Sport facilities are permanent event venues and constitute a tourism resource for the host community, but if they are purpose-built for an event they represent a cost, or at least an investment that has to be amortized over many events. Similar to a convention center, managers of sport facilities can claim tourism-related economic benefits to the community based on the number of tourists who traveled specifically for events.

As a tourism strategy, creating and bidding on participation sport events has proven to be very successful—so much so that destinations are very competitive in this sector. See the research paper by Solberg et al. (2002) for a focused look at sport event impacts.

Research Note

Solberg, H., Andersson, T., & Shibli, S. (2002). An exploration of the direct economic impacts from business travelers at world championships. *Event Management, 7*(3), 151–164.

Impacts of various types of sport event tourists were examined by studying two events in Norway and two in the UK. The focus was placed on nonparticipants and nonspectators, or the "business" tourists that accompany major sport events. This category included team officials and officials from governing bodies, staff working for organizers, media workers, sponsors and their guests, and a variety of Very Important Persons such as politicians and celebrities. It was found that visitors from the media were a very small proportion of all travelers at the events, but the media at the two Norwegian events stayed the longest and spent the most money. In the UK the media were of a different type, being mostly freelancers, and they were not big spenders, so international coverage of a sport event makes a big difference. The authors also concluded that sports with a large following in the host country will attract many more tourists.

Festivals

Research conducted for the British Arts Festivals Association (2003) proved they constitute a major wealth-creator for the nation; 137 festivals spent 37.4 million pounds sterling in a year, stimulating a total of 90 million or more pounds elsewhere in the UK economy. These festivals employed over 3000 staff, plus created income for numerous performers and technicians. Of course, these figures show that arts festivals are big business, but do not say anything about tourism-related impacts.

Our case study of the Canadian Tulip Festival showed very high economic impacts are obtainable by festivals that attract tourists, especially in the nonpeak travel season. Festivals also tend to attract lots of visiting friends and relatives who do not use commercial accommodation and who might have visited anyway. However, these and other "casual" visitors to festivals might extend their length of stay or increase their spending because of the event, so it is legitimate to attribute that portion of their local expenditure to the event.

Many community festivals have diverse programs that include specific events that attract real tourists, such as participants in sport events. This is an excellent strategy for adding economic value to a resident-dominated festival. One-day festivals are common, and they do not encourage people to stay overnight, even if they attract tourists. Festivals that extend over two weekends are also common, and at these events there is often a big difference between weekend visitors (more tourists staying overnight) and weekday attendees (more residents). Festivals that attract vendors, such as art and craft sales, can generate substantial economic impacts through their expenditure in the area, but it has to be remembered that they also take money home with them.

Surveys such as that undertaken by Crompton, Lee, and Shuster (2001) are needed to determine the net impact for the area.

Research Note

Crompton, J., Lee, S., & Shuster, T. (2001). A guide for undertaking economic impact studies: The Springfest example. *Journal of Travel Research, 40*, 79–87.

This article provides specific guidelines for conducting economic impact studies of events, as illustrated by an evaluation of Springfest in Ocean City, Maryland. Their interviews revealed a large number of genuine event tourists, time-switchers who had changed their plans to accommodate the festival, and casual visitors who had not traveled because of the event. They also found that a portion of "casuals" did extend their visit owing to attendance at Springfest. In total, they estimated that time-switchers and casuals constituted 49% of all visitors.

Trade and Consumer Shows

Most of these events are also associated with specific venues that can claim tourism benefits for their community, based on the tourists their events attracted and related spending. Trade shows in general are likely to have a greater economic impact, as companies often send their exhibits and delegates a long way to participate (see our case study of the Orange County Convention Center). Consumer shows, on the other hand, are largely attended by residents and some or all of the exhibitors might be local as well. Furthermore, association conferences are often accompanied by trade shows, generating potentially even greater impacts because of the visiting exhibitors.

Art and Museum Exhibitions

When galleries or museums host major touring exhibitions they are often promoted as tourist attractions. The more unique they are the more they can attract cultural tourists from outside the host community. Similar to festivals, they also tend to attract a lot of residents, casual visitors, and time-switchers. A study by Mihalik and Wing-Vogelbacker (1992) is one of the few to document the impacts of this type of event.

Research Note

Mihalik, B., & Wing-Vogelbacker, A. (1992). Traveling art expositions as a tourism event: A market research analysis of Ramesses the Great. *Journal of Travel and Tourism Marketing, 1*(3), 25–41.

A study of this "itinerant event" emphasized that its value could be measured in terms of educational value, cultural understanding, promoting scientific, or technical trade, encouraging tourism, and contributing to place marketing. Museums use them to build community support and memberships as well as their profile. The Ramesses the Great Exhibition at the Mint Museum of Charlotte, North Carolina, was a success in that it generated over 600,000 ticket sales and resulted in museum membership jumping from 3000 to 9000. Exit surveys determined that about 73% of visitors came from the defined "secondary market" beyond metropolitan Charlotte and within 150 miles.

Study Questions

- What are the main reasons for conducting evaluations of the event and the organization?
- Describe the three general types of evaluation.
- Define effectiveness and efficiency and give event-related measures of each.
- What are the pros and cons of using each of these evaluation measures: secret shoppers; staff meetings; participant observation; visitor surveys?
- How are evaluation reports used and misused?
- Describe the basic data needs and methods appropriate for evaluating event quality.
- What is return on investment and why is its measurement increasingly important?
- Do events create jobs? How?
- What kind of multiplier is best for estimating economic impacts of events?
- What is the attribution problem?
- Give examples of linkages and leakages related to the economic impacts of events.
- Why should a cost–benefit evaluation be conducted? What are tangibles and intangibles?

Advanced Questions

- How would you justify an event in terms of "psychic benefits"? What research is needed to examine the "consumer surplus"? Explain these terms and give examples.
- Show how to construct and implement the research for a valid economic impact assessment, including attendance, visitor spending, the attribution question, and calculation of incremental income.
- Discuss evaluation processes and methods in the context of the event management system, specifically to diagnose management problems.
- Link stakeholder theory to evaluation, specifically with regard to determining the overall value of an event.
- Compare and assess the various methods of collecting visitor expenditure data, for these types of events: participant sports; conference; exhibition; festival.
- Develop new ROI measures for an event sponsor, local government, and the regional tourism marketing organization. How would the data be obtained and the calculations be made?

Bibliography

Abbott, J., & Geddie, M. (2000). Event and venue management: Minimizing liability through effective crowd management techniques. *Event Management, 6*(4), 259-270.

Abrahams, R. (1987). An American vocabulary of celebrations. In A. Falassi (Ed.), *Time out of time, essays on the festival* (pp. 173-183). Albuquerque: University of New Mexico Press.

Ahmed, Z. (1991). Marketing your community: Correcting a negative image. *Cornell Quarterly, 31*(4), 24-27.

AIEST. (1987). *The role and impact of mega-events and attractions on regional and national tourism* (Vol. 28). St. Gallen, Switzerland: Author.

Allen, J. (2003). *Event planning ethics and etiquette: A principled approach to the business of special event management.* New York: John Wiley.

Allen, J., O'Toole, W., McDonnell, I., & Harris, R. (2002). *Festival and special event management* (2nd ed.). Milton: Wiley.

American Sport Education Program. (1996). *Event management for sport directors.* Champaign IL: Human Kinetics.

American Sports Data. (2003). *Superstudy of sports participation.* www.americansportsdata.com

Ammon, R., & Fried, G. (1998). Crowd management practices. *Journal of Convention and Exhibition Management, 1*(2/3), 119-150.

Andera, J. (1994). Food and beverage concessions. Reproduced in *Fundamentals of arts festival management.* National Assembly of Local Arts Agencies.

Anderson, C., & Anthony, R. (1992). Making key strategic decisions. In J. Livingstone (ed.), *The portable MBA in finance and accounting.* New York: John Wiley.

Andersson, T., & Samuelson, L. (2000). Financial effects of events on the public sector. In L. Mossberg (Ed.), *Evaluation of events: Scandinavian experiences* (pp. 86-103). New York: Cognizant Communication Corp.

Andrew, W., & Schmidgall, R. (1993). *Financial management for the hospitality industry.* East Lansing, MI: American Hotel and Motel Association Education Institute.

Angus Reid Group. (1989). *Calgary Stampede 1989 visitor profile and market potential research study.* Calgary: Author.

Angus Reid Group. (1991). *Examining the profile, behaviour and motivations of 1991 Calgary Stampede visitors.* Calgary: Author.

Angus Reid Group. (1995). *1995 Exhibition and Stampede visitor survey.* Calgary: Author.

Anthony, R., & Young, D. (1984). *Management control in nonprofit organizations* (3rd ed.). Homewood, IL: Richard D. Irwin Inc.

Anthony, R., & Young, D. (1994). Accounting and financial management. In R. Herman (ed.), *The Jossey-Bass handbook of nonprofit leadership and management* (pp. 403-443). San Francisco: Jossey-Bass.

Archer, B. (1982). The value of multipliers and their policy implications. *Tourism Manage-*

ment, 3(4), 236-241.

Archer, B. (1989). Trends in international tourism. In S. Witt & L. Moutinho (Eds.), *Tourism marketing and management handbook* (pp. 593-597). New York: Prentice Hall.

Arcodia, C., & Reid, S. (2003). Goals and objectives of event management associations. *Journal of Convention and Exhibition Management, 5*(1), 57-75.

Argyris, C., & Schon, D. (1978). *Organizational learning.* Reading, MA: Addison-Wesley.

Armstrong, J. (1985). International events: The real tourism impact. In *Conference Proceedings of the Canada Chapter, Travel and Tourism Research Association* (pp. 9-37). Edmonton.

Backman, K., Backman, S., Uysal, M., & Sunshine, K. (1995). Event tourism: An examination of motivations and activities. *Festival Management & Event Tourism, 3*(1), 15-24.

Baker, D., & Crompton, J. (2000). Quality, satisfaction and behavioral intentions. *Annals of Tourism Research, 27*(2), 785-804.

Bale, J. (1989). *Sports geography.* London: E. & F. N. Spon Ltd.

Baloglu, S., & Love, C. (2003). Association meeting planners' perceived performance of Las Vegas: An importance-performance analysis. *Journal of Convention and Exhibition Management, 5*(1), 13-27.

Barker, M., Page, S., & Meyer, D. (2003). Urban visitor perceptions of safety during a special event. *Journal of Travel Research, 41*, 355-361.

Bateson, J. (1989). *Managing services marketing: Text and readings.* Chicago: The Dryden Press.

Baum, J. (1996). Organizational ecology. In S. R. Clegg, C. Hardy, & W. R. Nord (Eds.), *Handbook of organization studies* (pp. 77-114). Beverly Hills, CA: Sage Publications.

Baxter, M. (2001). Let's put on a show: Special events and live entertainment at waterparks can make the difference between an average season and an exceptional one. *Aquatics International, 13*(8), 42.

Benedict, B. (1983). *The anthropology of world's fairs.* Berkeley: Scolar Press.

Bennett, G., Henson, R., & Zhang, J. (2003). Generation Y's perceptions of the action sports industry segment. *Journal of Sport Management, 17*, 95-115.

Berlonghi, A. (1990). *The special event risk management manual.* Self-published by A. Berlonghi, P.O. Box 3454 Dana Point, CA 92629.

Berry, L., & Parasuraman, A. (1991). *Marketing services: Competing through quality.* New York: The Free Press.

Beverland, M., Hoffman, D., & Rasmussen, M. (2001). The evolution of events in the Australasian wine sector. *Tourism Recreation Research, 26*(2), 35-44.

Bharadia, G. (1986). *Why do people volunteer?* Volunteers and Volunteerism in Calgary Series, No. 7, Research Unit for Public Policy Studies, University of Calgary.

Bitner, M. (1993). Managing the evidence of service. In E. Scheuing & W. Christopher (Eds.), *The service quality handbook* (pp. 358-370). New York: Amacom.

Bitner, M., Booms, J., & Tetreault, B. (1990). The service encounter: Diagnosing favorable and unfavorable incidents. *Journal of Marketing, 54*, 71-84.

Black, B. (n.d). Licensing. In *Money-making ideas for your event* (pp. 37-38). Port Angeles, WA: International Festivals Association.

Black, J. (1995, January). Understanding liability insurance. *Association Management*, L53-L55.

Blackorby, C., Ricard, R., & Slade, M. (1986). The macroeconomic consequences of Expo '86'. In R. Anderson & E. Wachtel (Eds.), *The expo story.* Madeira Park: Harbour Publishing.

Boella, M. (1992). *Human resource management in the hospitality industry* (5th ed.).

Cheltenham: Stanley Thornes.

Boese, D. (n.d.) Celebrate responsibly. In *Event trends in the 90's* (pp. 87-91). Port Angeles, WA: International Festivals Association.

Bohlin, M. (2000). Traveling to events. In L. Mossberg (Ed.), *Evaluation of events: Scandinavian experiences* (pp. 13-29). New York: Cognizant Communication Corp.

Boissevan, J. (1979). Impact of tourism on a dependent island: Gozo, Malta. *Annals of Tourism Research, 6,* 76-90.

Boorstin, D. (1961) *The image: A guide to pseudo-events in America*. New York: Harper and Row.

Bos, H. (1994). The importance of mega-events in the development of tourism demand. *Festival Management & Event Tourism, 2*(1), 55-58.

Bos, H., van der Kamp, C., & Zom, A. (1987). Events in Holland. *Revue de Tourisme, 4,* 16-19.

Bourdin, G., & Church, I. (2000). *Customer satisfaction and quality costs: Towards a pragmatic approach for event management.* Paper presented at Events Beyond 2000—Setting the Agenda, Australian Centre for Event Management, University of Technology Sydney.

Breen, H., Bull, A., & Walo, M. (2001). A comparison of survey methods to estimate visitor expenditure at a local event. *Tourism Management, 22,* 473-479

British Arts Festival Association. (2003). *Festivals mean business.* London: Author.

British Columbia Ministry of Attorney General. (1992). *Report of the Task Force on Public Order.* Victoria: Author.

Brooks, C. (1994). *Sports marketing.* Englewood Cliffs, NJ: Prentice Hall.

Brothers, G., & Brantley, V. (1993). Tag and recapture: Testing an attendance estimation technique for an open access special event. *Festival Management & Event Tourism, 1*(4), 143-146.

Brown, G. (2002). Taking the pulse of Olympic sponsorship. *Event Management, 7*(3), 187-196.

Brown, G., Chalip, L., Jago, L., & Mules, T. (2001). The Sydney Olympics and brand Australia. In N. Morgan, A. Pritchard, & R. Pride (Eds.), *Destination branding: Creating the unique destination proposition* (pp. 163-185). Boston; Butterworth-Heinemann.

Bryant, S., & Gaiko, S. (1999). Determining skills necessary for meeting planners. In W. Roehl (Ed.), *Proceedings, The Convention/Expo Summit VII,* Las Vegas, Department of Tourism and Convention Administration, William F. Harrah College of Hotel Administration, University of Nevada at Las Vegas.

Burgan, B., & Mules, T. (1992). Economic impact of sporting events. *Annals of Tourism Research, 19*(4), 700-710.

Burgan, B., & Mules, T. (2000). Sampling frame issues in identifying event-related expenditures. *Event Management, 6*(1), 223-230.

Burns, J., Hatch, J., & Mules, T. (Eds.). (1986). *The Adelaide Grand Prix: The impact of a special event.* Adelaide: Centre for South Australian Economic Studies.

Butler, R., & Grigg, J. (1987). The hallmark event that got away: The case of the 1991 Pan American Games in London, Ontario. In *PAPER 87, People and Physical Environment Research Conference.* Perth: University of Western Australia.

Calgary Exhibition and Stampede. (1991a). *The new horizon 2000 vision: The case for expansion.* Calgary: Author.

Calgary Exhibition and Stampede. (1991). *1991 annual report.* Calgary: Author.

Calgary Exhibition and Stampede. (1995). *The year in review 1995.* Calgary: Author.

Cameron, C. (1989). Cultural tourism and urban revitalization. *Tourism Recreation Re-*

search, 14(1), 23-32.

Carlsen, J. (2000). Events industry accreditation in Australia. *Event Management, 6*(2), 117-121.

Carlsen, J., Getz, D., & Soutar, G. (2000). Event evaluation research. *Event Management, 6*(4), 247-257.

Carlsen, J., & Taylor, A. (2003). Mega-events and urban renewal: The case of the Manchester 2002 Commonwealth Games. *Event Management, 8*(1), 15-22.

Carlson, A. (1998). America's growing observance of Cinco de Mayo. *Journal of American Culture, 21*(2), 7-16.

Carver, J. (1990). *Boards that make a difference.* San Francisco: Jossey-Bass.

Catherwood, D., & Van Kirk, R. (1992). *The complete guide to special event management.* New York: John Wiley.

Cavalcanti, M. (2001). The Amazonian Ox Dance Festival: An anthropological account. *Cultural Analysis, 2.*

Center for Hospitality Research at Cornell University. (2001). *Yield management.* Ithaca, NY: Author.

Center for Exhibition Industry Research. (2003, March 26). News release.

Centre for South Australian Economic Studies. (1990). *The 1990 Adelaide Festival: The economic impact (Vol. 1: Summary; Vol. 2: Methodology and Results: Details).* Adelaide: Author.

Cetron, M., & Davies, O. (2001a, March/April). Trends now changing the world: Technology, the workplace, management, and institutions. *The Futurist.*

Cetron, M., & Davies, O. (2001b, January/February). Trends now changing the world: Economics and society, values and concerns, energy and environment. *The Futurist.*

Chalip, L., & Leyns, A. (2002). Local business leveraging of a sport event: Managing an event for economic benefit. *Journal of Sport Management, 16,* 132-158.

Charney, B. (n.d.a). Sponsor renewal: How to keep them coming back. In *IFA's official guide to sponsorship* (pp. 53-58). Port Angeles, WA: International Festivals Association.

Charney, B. (n.d.b). The arts and sponsorship: creative opportunities. In *Money-making ideas for your event* (pp. 48-49). Port Angeles, WA: International Festivals Association.

Charney, B. (n.d.c). Working with a board as a paid executive. In *Event operations* (pp. 51-54). Port Angeles, WA: International Festivals and Events Association.

Chernushenko, D. (1994). *Greening our games: Running sports events and facilities that won't cost the earth.* Ottawa: Centurion.

Cherry Creek Arts Festival and Comoco. (n.d.). *Environmental blueprint.* Denver: Author.

Cheska, A. (1981). *Antigonish Highland Games: An ethnic case study.* Paper presented at the North American Society of Sport History, ninth annual convention, Hamilton.

Citrine, K. (n.d.). Site planning for events. In *Event operations* (pp. 17-19). Port Angeles, WA: International Festivals and Events Association.

Coopers & Lybrand Consulting Group. (1989). *NCR 1988 festivals study final report* (Vol. 1). Report for the Ottawa-Carleton Board of Trade. Ottawa: Author.

Coopers and Lybrand Consulting Group. (1992). *Evaluation of the Canadian Tulip Festival.* Ottawa: Author.

Coughlan, D., & Mules, T. (2002). Sponsorship awareness and recognition at Canberra's Floriade festival. *Event Management, 7*(1), 1-9.

Coyne, B., & Coyne, E. (2001). Getting, keeping and caring for unpaid volunteers for professional golf tournament events. *Human Resources Development International, 4*(2), 199-214.

Crompton, J. (1979). An assessment of the image of Mexico as a vacation destination and the influence of geographical location upon that image. *Journal of Travel Research, 17*(4), 18–23.

Crompton. J. (1993). Understanding a business organization's approach to entering a sponsorship partnership. *Festival Management & Event Tourism, 1*(3), 98–109.

Crompton, J. (1995). Factors that have stimulated the growth of sponsorship of major events. *Festival Management & Event Tourism, 3*(2), 97–101.

Crompton, J. (1999). *Measuring the economic impact of visitors to sports tournaments and special events.* Ashburn, VA: Division of Professional Services, National Recreation and Park Association.

Crompton, J. (2003). Adapting Herzberg: A conceptualization of the effects of hygiene and motivator attributes on perceptions of event quality. *Journal of Travel Research, 41*(3), 305.

Crompton, J., & Lamb, C. (1986). *Marketing government and social services.* New York: John Wiley.

Crompton, J., Lee, S., & Shuster, T. (2001). A guide for undertaking economic impact studies: The Springfest example. *Journal of Travel Research, 40*(1), 79–87.

Crompton, J., & Love, L. (1995). The predictive validity of alternative approaches to evaluating quality of a festival. *Journal of Travel Research, 34*(1), 11–24.

Crompton, J., & McKay, S. (1994). Measuring the economic impact of festivals and events: Some myths, misapplications and ethical dilemmas. *Festival Management & Event Tourism, 2*(1), 33–43.

Crompton, J., & McKay, S. (1997). Motives of visitors attending festival events. *Annals of Tourism Research, 24*(2), 425–439.

Cunneen, C., & Lynch, R. (1988). The social meanings of conflict in riots at the Australian Grand Prix motorcycle races. *Leisure Studies, 7*(1), 1–19.

Cunningham, M., & Taylor, S. (1995). Event marketing: State of the industry and research agenda. *Festival Management & Event Tourism, 2*(3/4), 123–137.

Darcy, S., & Harris, R. (2003). Inclusive and accessible special events planning: An Australian perspective. *Event Management, 8*(1), 39–47.

Dean, L. (1985, Winter). Learning about volunteer burnout. *Voluntary Action Leadership.*

Delamere, T. (2001). Development of a scale to measure resident attitudes toward the social impacts of community festivals: Part 2: Verification of the scale. *Event Management, 7*(1), 25–38.

Delamere, T., Wankel, L., & Hinch, T. (2001). Development of a scale to measure resident attitudes toward the social impacts of community festivals: Part1: Item generation and purification of the measure. *Event Management, 7*(1), 11–24.

Denton, S., & Furse, B. (1993). Visitation to the 1991 Barossa Valley Vintage Festival. *Festival Management & Event Tourism, 1*(2), 51–56.

Derek Murray Consulting Associates Ltd. (1985). *A study to determine the impact of events on local economies.* Report for Saskatchewan Tourism and Small Business. Regina: Author.

Dimanche, F. (1996). Special events legacy: The 1984 Louisiana World Fair in New Orleans. *Festival Management & Event Tourism, 4*(1), 49–54.

Dungan, T. (1984). How cities plan special events. *The Cornell Hotel and Restaurant Administration Quarterly, May*, 83–89.

Dwyer, L. (2002). Economic contribution of convention tourism: Conceptual and empirical issues. In K. Weber & K. Chon (Eds.), *Convention tourism: International research and industry perspectives* (pp. 21–35). New York: Haworth.

Dwyer, L., Mellor, R., Mistillis, N., & Mules, T. (2000a). A framework for assessing "tangible" and "intangible" impacts of events and conventions. *Event Management, 6*(3), 175–189.

Dwyer, L., Mellor, R., Mistillis, N., & Mules, T. (2000b). Forecasting the economic impacts of events and conventions. *Event Management, 6*(3), 191–204.

Economic Planning Group and Lord Cultural Resources. (1992). *Strategic directions for the planning, development, and marketing of Ontario's attractions, festivals, and events.* Toronto: Ministry of Culture, Tourism, and Recreation.

Edosomwan, J. (1993). *Customer and market-driven quality management.* Milwaukee WI: ASQC Quality Press.

EKOS Research Associates Inc. (1985). *EKOS report on Winterlude: Executive summary.* Report for the National Capital Commission. Ottawa: Author.

Ellis, J. (1990). *The application of cost-benefit analysis: The 1987 Busker Festival—a case study.* Master's thesis in Development Economics, Dalhousie University, Halifax.

Elstad, B. (2003). Continuance commitment and reasons to quit: A study of volunteers at a jazz festival. *Event Management, 8*(2), 99–108.

Emery, P. (2001). Bidding to host a major sports event. In, C. Gratton & I. Henry (Eds.), *Sport in the city: The role of sport in economic and social regeneration* (pp. 91–108). London: Routledge.

Emmets, C. (1992). Alcohol management: Maximizing profits while minimizing problems. *Fair Dealer* (reprinted by Home Team).

Ettore, B. (1993). Ambush marketing. *Management Review, 82*(3), 53–57.

Falassi, A. (Ed.). (1987). *Time out of time: Essays on the festival.* Albuquerque: University of New Mexico Press.

Farber, C. (1983). High, healthy and happy: Ontario mythology on parade. In F. Manning (Ed.), *Celebration of society: Perspectives on contemporary cultural performance* (pp. 33–50). Bowling Green: Bowling Green Popular Press.

Farrell, J., Johnston, M., & Twynam, D. (1998). Volunteer motivation, satisfaction, and management at an elite sporting competition. *Journal of Sport Management, 12*, 288–300.

Faulkner, B., & Raybould, M. (1995). Monitoring visitor expenditure associated with attendance at sporting events: An experimental assessment of the diary and recall methods. *Festival Management & Event Tourism, 3*(2), 73–81.

Faulkner, B., Chalip, L., Brown, G., Jago, L., March, R., & Woodside, A. (2000). Monitoring the tourism impacts of the Sydney 2000 Olympics. *Event Management, 6*(4), 231–246.

Fetters, M. (1992). Understanding and analyzing financial statements. In J. Livingstone (Ed.), *The portable MBA in finance and accounting.* New York: John Wiley.

Fidler, M. (1995, January). Leading the association. *Association Management,* L41–L42.

Flakus, G. (n.d.). Important trends in food concessions management. In *Event operations* (pp. 95–97). Port Angeles, WA: International Festivals and Events Association.

Fleck, S. (1996, March). Events without barriers: Customer service is a key in complying with the Americans With Disabilities Act. *Festivals,* 34–35.

Fleming, W., & Toepper, L. (1990). Economic impact studies: Relating the positive and negative impacts to tourism development. *Journal of Travel Research, 29*(1), 35–42.

Folklorama. (n.d.). Book your world tour (brochure).

Formica, S. (1998). The development of festivals and special events studies. *Festival Management & Event Tourism, 5*(3), 131–137.

Formica, S., & Murrmann, S. (1998). The effects of group membership and motivation on attendance: An international festival case. *Tourism Analysis, 3*(3/4), 197–207.

Formica, S., & Uysal, M. (1998). Market segmentation of an international cultural-historical event in Italy. *Journal of Travel Research, 36*(4), 16–24.

Forst, B. (1992). Using the computer in finance and accounting. In J. Livingstone (Ed.), *The portable MBA in finance and accounting*. New York: John Wiley.

Frechtling, D. (1994). Assessing the impacts of travel and tourism. In B. Ritchie & C. Goeldner (Eds.), *Travel, tourism and hospitality research* (2nd ed., pp. 359-402). New York: John Wiley.

Fredline, E., & Faulkner, B. (2002a). Residents' reactions to the staging of major motorsport events within their communities: A cluster analysis. *Event Management, 7*(2), 103-114.

Fredline, E., & Faulkner, B. (2002b) Variations in residents' reactions to major motorsport events: Why residents perceive the impacts of events differently. *Event Management, 7*(2), 115-125.

Fredline, L., Jago, L., & Deery, M. (2003). The development of a generic scale to measure the social impacts of events. *Event Management, 8*(1), 23-37.

Freeman, R. (1984). *Strategic management: A stakeholder approach*. Boston: Pitman.

Frisby, W., & Getz, D. (1989). Festival management: A case study perspective. *Journal of Travel Research, 28*(1), 7-11.

Gartner, W. (1993). Image formation process. In M. Uysal & D. Fesenmaier (Eds.), *Communication and channel systems in tourism marketing* (pp. 191-215). New York: Haworth Press.

Geier, T. (1993). *Make your events special: How to plan and organize successful special events programs for nonprofit organizations* (2nd ed.). New York: Cause Effective Nonprofit Resource Development Center.

Getz, D. (1983). Capacity to absorb tourism: Concepts and implications for strategic planning. *Annals of Tourism Research, 10*, 239-263.

Getz, D. (1991). *Festivals, special events, and tourism*. New York: Van Nostrand Reinhold.

Getz, D. (1993a). Event tourism: Evaluating the impacts. In B. Ritchie & C. Goeldner (Eds.), *Travel, tourism and hospitality research: A handbook for managers and researchers* (2nd ed., pp. 437-450). New York: John Wiley.

Getz, D. (1993b). Corporate culture in not-for-profit festival organizations. *Festival Management & Event Tourism, 1*(1), 11-17.

Getz, D. (1997). *Event management & event tourism*. New York: Cognizant Communication Corp.

Getz, D. (1998a). Event tourism and the authenticity dilemma. In W. Theobald (Ed.), *Global tourism* (2nd ed., pp. 409-427). Oxford: Butterworth-Heinemann.

Getz, D. (1998b). Information sharing among festival managers. *Festival Management & Event Tourism, 5*(1/2), 33-50.

Getz, D. (1999). The impacts of mega events on tourism: Strategies for destinations. In T. Andersson, C. Persson, B. Sahlberg, & L. Strom (Eds.), *The impact of mega events* (pp. 5-32). Ostersund, Sweden: European Tourism Research Institute.

Getz, D. (2000). Festivals and special events: Life-cycle and saturation issues. In W. Garter & D. Lime (Eds.), *Trends in outdoor recreation, leisure and tourism*. Wallingford, UK: CABI.

Getz, D. (2001). Festival places: A comparison of Europe and North America. *Tourism, 49*(1), 3-18.

Getz, D. (2002a). Event studies and event management: On becoming an academic discipline. *Journal of Hospitality and Tourism Management, 9*(1), 12-23.

Getz, D. (2002b). Why festivals fail. *Event Management, 7*(4), 209-219.

Getz, D. (2003). Sport event tourism. In S. Hudson (Ed.), *Sport and adventure tourism* (pp. 49-88). Binghamton, NY: The Haworth Press.

Getz, D. (2004a). Bidding on events: Critical success factors. *Journal of Convention and*

Exhibition Management, 5(2).

Getz, D. (2004b). Geographic perspectives on event tourism. In A. Lew, M. Hall, & A. Williams (Eds.), *A companion to tourism* (pp. 410–422). Oxford: Blackwell Publishing.

Getz, D., & Carlsen, J. (2005). Quality management for events. In B. Prideaux, G. Moscardo, & E. Laws (Eds.), *Managing tourism and hospitality services: Theory and international applications.* Wallingford, UK: CABI.

Getz, D., & Cheyne, J. (2002). Special event motives and behaviour. In C. Ryan (Ed.), *The tourist experience* (2nd ed., pp. 137–155). London: Continuum.

Getz, D., & Fairley, S. (2004). Media management at sport events for destination promotion. *Event Management, 8*(3), 127–139.

Getz, D., & Frisby, W. (1988). Evaluating management effectiveness in community-run festivals. *Journal of Travel Research, 27*(1), 22–27.

Getz, D., & Frisby, W. (1991). Developing a municipal policy for festivals and special events. *Recreation Canada, 49*(4), 38–44.

Getz, D., O'Neil, M., & Carlsen, J. (2001). Service quality evaluation at events through service mapping. *Journal of Travel Research, 39*(4), 380–390.

Getz, D., & Sailor, L. (1993). Design of destination and attraction-specific brochures. *Journal of Travel and Tourism Marketing, 2*(2/3), 111–113.

Getz, D., & Wicks, B. (1994). Professionalism and certification for festival and event practitioners: Trends and issues. *Festival Management & Event Tourism, 2*(2), 103–109.

Gibson, H. (1998). Active sport tourism: Who participates? *Leisure Studies, 17*(2), 155–170.

Gillis, K., & Ditton, R. (1998). Comparing tournament and nontournament recreational billfish anglers to examine the efficacy of hosting competitive billfish angling events in Southern Baja, Mexico. *Festival Management & Event Tourism, 5*(3), 147–158.

Gitelson, R., Kerstetter, D., & Kiernan, N. (1995). Evaluating the educational objectives of a short-term event. *Festival Management & Event Tourism, 3*(1), 9–14.

Gleick, J. (2000). *Faster: The acceleration of just about everything*. New York: Vintage Books.

Goldblatt, J. (1990). *Special events: The art and science of celebration.* New York: Van Nostrand Reinhold.

Goldblatt, J. (1994). *An exploratory study of event tourism management-related training issues for second tier U.S. cities*. Unpublished thesis, George Washington University.

Goldblatt, J. (2002). *Special events* (3rd ed.). New York: John Wiley.

Goldblatt, J., & Nelson, K. E. (2001). *The international dictionary of event management* (2nd ed.). New York: John Wiley.

Goodall, B. (1988). How tourists choose their holidays: An analytic framework. In B. Goodall & G. Ashworth (Eds.), *Marketing in the tourism industry: The promotion of destination regions* (pp. 1–17). London: Croom Helm.

Gordon, K. (2003). Making a scene: Your special event won't be so special if nobody hears about it. *Entrepreneur, 31*(5), 79.

Grado, S., Strauss, C., & Lord, B. (1998). Economic impacts of conferences and conventions. *Journal of Convention and Exhibition Management, 1*(1), 19–33.

Graham, S., Goldblatt, J., & Delpy, L. (1995). *The ultimate guide to sport event management and marketing*. Chicago: Irwin.

Gratton, C., & Kokolakakis, T. (1997). Financial games. *Leisure Management, 17*(7), 13–15.

Gray, B. (1989). *Collaborating.* San Francisco: Jossey-Bass Publishers.

Green, B., & Chalip, L. (1998). Sport tourism as the celebration of subculture. *Annals of Tourism Research, 25*(2), 275–291.

Green, C., & Chalip, L. (2004). Paths to volunteer commitment: Lessons from the Sydney Olympic Games. In R. Stebbins & M. Graham (Eds.), *Volunteering as leisure/leisure as volunteering:An international assessment.*Wallingford, UK: CABI.

Green, C., & Muller,T. (2002). Positioning a youth sport camp:A brand mapping exercise. *Sport Management Review, 5*(2), 179–200.

Green and Gold Inc.(1999).*Environmental management and monitoring for sport events and facilities.* For the Department of Canadian Heritage, Sport Canada (www.greengold.on.ca/)

Greenwood, D.(1972).Tourism as an agent of change:A Spanish Basque case study. *Ethnology, 11,*80–91.

Gregson, B. (1992). *Reinventing celebration: The art of planning public events.* Orange, CT: Shannon Press.

Hall, M. (1992). *Hallmark tourist events: Impacts, management and planning.* London: Belhaven.

Hall, M. (1994a). *Tourism and politics: Policy, power and place.* Chichester: John Wiley.

Hall, M. (1994b). Mega-events and their legacies. In P. Murphy (Ed.), *Quality Management in Urban Tourism: Balancing Business and Environment Proceedings* (pp. 109–123). University of Victoria.

Hanlon, C., & Cuskelly, G. (2002). Pulsating major sport event organizations:A framework for inducting managerial personnel. *Event Management, 7*(4), 231–243.

Hannan, M., & Freeman,J.(1977).The population ecology of organizations.*American Journal of Sociology, 82,*929–964.

Harris, R., Jago, L.,Allen,J., & Huyskens, M. (2001).Towards an Australian event research agenda: First steps. *Event Management, 6*(4), 213–221.

Harvie, J. (1986). *The participation of women in the voluntary sector.* Volunteers and Volunteerism in Calgary Series, No. 5, Research Unit for Public Policy Studies, University of Calgary.

Hatten, A. (1987). *Economic impact of Expo '86.* Victoria, British Columbia: Ministry of Finance and Corporate Relations.

Havitz, M., & Dimanche, F. (1999). Leisure involvement revisited: Drive properties and paradoxes.*Journal of Leisure Research, 31*(2), 122–149.

Herzberg, F. (1966). *Work and the nature of man.* Cleveland:World Publishing Co.

Higham,J., & Ritchie, B. (2002).The evolution of festivals and other events in rural southern New Zealand. *Event Management, 7*(1), 39–49.

Higgins, C., & Duxbury, L. (2001). *National work–life conflict study for Halth Canada, final report.* Ottawa.

Hiller, H. (2000). Mega-events, urban boosterism and growth strategies:An analysis of the objectives and legitimations of the Cape Town 2004 Olympic bid. *International Journal of Urban and Regional Research, 24*(2), 439–458.

Howard, D., Lankford, S., & Havitz, M. (1991).A method for authenticating pleasure travel expenditures.*Journal of Travel Research, 29*(4), 19–23.

Howell,A.(1986). *Why do volunteers burnout and dropout?*Volunteers andVolunteerism in Calgary series, No. 8, Research Unit for Public Policy Studies, University of Calgary.

Huffadine, M. (1993). *Project management in hotel and resort development.* New York: McGraw-Hill Inc.

Hunt, J. (1975). Image as a factor in tourism development. *Journal of Travel Research, 13*(3), 1–7.

Indiana Department of Commerce and Indiana State Festival Association.(1988).*Indiana's how to of festivals and events.* Indianapolis:Author.

Institute for Volunteering Research for the England Volunteering Forum. (2003). Online at www.ivr.org.uk. Research conducted by Katharine Gaskin.

International Events Group. (1995). *IEG's complete guide to sponsorship*. Chicago: Author.

International Festivals Association. (n.d.). *IFA's official guide to sponsorship*. Port Angeles, WA: Author.

International Festivals Association and Argonne Productions. (1992). *Festival sponsorship legal issues*.

International Festivals and Events Association. (n.d.). *Event operations*. Port Angeles, WA: Author.

Iso-Ahola, S. (1980). *The social psychology of leisure and recreation*. Dubuque, IA: Brown.

Iso-Ahola, S. (1983). Towards a social psychology of recreational travel. *Leisure Studies, 2*(1), 45-57.

Jacobs, J., & Gerson, K. (1991). Overworked individuals or overworked families? Explaining trends in work, leisure, and family time. *Work and Occupations, 28*(1), 40-63.

Jago, L., Chalip, L., Brown, G., Mules, T., & Shameem, A. (2003). Building events into destination branding: Insights from experts. *Event Management, 8*(1), 3-14.

Jago, L., & Shaw, R. (1995). Special event calendars: Some exploratory research. *Festival Management & Event Tourism, 3*(2), 49-58.

Jago, L., & Shaw, R. (1999). Consumer perceptions of special events: A multi-stimulus validation. *Journal of Travel and Tourism Marketing, 8*(4), 1-24.

Jamal, T., & Getz, D. (1995). Collaboration theory and community tourism planning. *Annals of Tourism Research, 22*(1), 186-204.

Janiskee, R. (1980). South Carolina's harvest festivals: Rural delights for day tripping urbanites. *Journal of Cultural Geography, October*, 96-104.

Janiskee, R. (1985). *Community-sponsored rural festivals in South Carolina: A decade of growth and change*. Paper presented to the Association of American Geographers, Detroit.

Janiskee, R. (1991). Rural festivals in South Carolina. *Journal of Cultural Geography, 11*(2), 31-43.

Janiskee, R. (1994). Some macroscale growth trends in America's community festival industry. *Festival Management & Event Tourism, 2*(1), 10-14.

Janiskee, R. (1996a). The temporal distribution of America's community festivals. *Festival Management & Event Tourism, 3*(3), 129-137.

Janiskee, R. (1996b). Oktoberfest—American style. *Festival Management & Event Tourism, 3*(4), 197-199.

Janiskee, R. (1996c). Historic houses and special events. *Annals of Tourism Research, 23*(2), 398-414.

Janiskee, R.. (2003). Oktoberfest in America. In M. Hall, L. Sharples, R. Mitchell, N. Macionis, & B. Cambourne (Eds.), *Food tourism around the world* (pp. 331-335). Oxford: Butterworth-Heinemann.

Janiskee, R., & Drews, P. (1998). Rural festivals and community reimaging. In R. Butler, M. Hall, & J. Jenkins (Eds.), *Tourism and recreation in rural areas* (pp. 157-175). Chichester: John Wiley.

Jawahar, I., & McLaughlin, G. (2001). Toward a descriptive stakeholder theory: An organizational life cycle approach. *Academy of Management Review, 26*(3), 397-414.

Jensen, J. (1995). Olympic goal: Global truce. *Advertising Age, 66*(28), 1, 6.

Johnson, D. (n.d.). Festival risk management: Success with safety. In *Event operations* (pp. 71-73). Port Angeles, WA: International Festivals and Events Association.

Jones, H. (1993). Pop goes the festival. *Marketing Week, 16*(23), 24-27.

Jordan, J. (1980). The summer people and the natives: Some effects of tourism in a Vermont vacation village. *Annals of Tourism Research, 7*(1), 34-55.

Kang, Y., & Perdue, R. (1994). Long term impact of a mega-event on international tourism to the host country: A conceptual model and the case of the 1988 Seoul Olympics. In M. Uysal (Ed.), *Global tourist behavior* (pp. 205-225). Binghamton, NY: International Business Press.

Katz, A. (1981). Self help and mutual aid: An emerging social movement. *Annual Review of Sociology,* 129-155

Keegan, W. (1995). *Global marketing management* (5th ed.). Englewood Cliffs, NJ: Prentice Hall.

Keegan, W., Moriarty, S., Duncan, T., & Paliwoda, S. (1995). *Marketing: Canadian edition*. Scarborough: Prentice Hall.

Kelly, J. (1985). *Recreation business*. New York: Macmillan.

Kentucky Department of Travel Development. (1987). *Market and economic analysis of the 1987 Bluegrass Music Festival.* Tourism Research Series, No. 39. Frankfort: Author.

Kerstetter, D., & Gitelson, R. (1995). Perceptions of sponsorship contributors to a regional arts festival. *Festival Management & Event Tourism, 2*(3/4), 203-209.

Klop, A. (1994). Event management. In L. Trenberth & C. Collins (Eds.), *Sport management in New Zealand: An introduction* (pp. 229-242). Palmerston North, New Zealand: Dunmore Press.

Korza, P., & Magie, D. (1989). *The arts festival work kit.* Amherst, MA: University of Massachusetts Arts Extension Service.

Kotler, P., Bowen, J., & Makens, J. (1996). *Marketing for hospitality and tourism.* Upper Saddle River, NJ: Prentice-Hall.

Kotler, P., Haider, D., & Rein, I. (1993). *Marketing places.* New York: The Free Press.

Kraus, R. (2000). *Leisure in a changing America: Trends and issues for the 21st century* (2nd ed.). Boston: Allyn & Bacon.

Kreag, G. (1988). *Festival, fair and event marketing*. Paper presented at Festivals and Events Seminar, University of Minnesota.

Kudrle, A., & Sandler, M. (1995). *Public relations for hospitality managers: Communicating for greater profits*. New York: John Wiley.

Laermer, R. (2002). *Trendspotting: Think forward, get ahead, and cash in on the future*. New York: The Berkley Publishing Group.

Larson, M. (2002). A political approach to relationship marketing: Case study of the Storsjoyran Festival. *International Journal of Tourism Research, 4,* 119-143.

Lee, C., Lee, Y., & Wicks, B. (2004). Segmentation of festival motivation by nationality and satisfaction. *Tourism Management, 25*(1), 61-70.

Lee, H., Kerstetter, D., Graefe, A., & Confer, J. (1997). Crowding at an arts festival: A replication and extension of the outdoor recreation crowding model. In W. Kuentzel (Ed.), *Proceedings of the 1966 Northeastern Recreation Research Symposium* (USDA Forest Service Gen. Tech. Rep. NE-232, pp. 198-204). Radnor, PA: Northeastern Forest Experiment Station.

Lee, J. (1987). The impact of Expo '86 on British Columbia markets. In P. Williams, J. Hall, & M. Hunter (Eds.), *Tourism: Where is the client?* Conference papers of the Travel and Tourism Research Association, Canada Chapter.

Lee, S., & Crompton, J. (2003). The attraction power and spending impact of three festivals in Ocean City, Maryland. *Event Management, 8*(2), 109-112.

Leibold, M., & van Zyl, C. (1994). The Summer Olympic Games and its tourism marketing— city tourism marketing experiences and challenges with specific reference to Cape Town,

South Africa. In P. Murphy (Ed.), *Quality Management in Urban Tourism: Balancing Business and the Environment Proceedings* (pp. 135-151). University of Victoria

Light, D. (1995). Heritage as informal education. In D. Herbert (Ed.), *Heritage, tourism and society* (pp. 146-169). London: Mansell.

Livingstone, J. (Ed.). (1992). *The portable MBA in finance and accounting*. New York: John Wiley.

Long, P. (2000). After the event: Perspectives on organizational partnerships in the management of a themed festival year. *Event Management, 6*(1), 45-59.

Lord Cultural Resources Planning and Management. (1993). *The cultural tourism handbook*. For Province of Ontario. Toronto: Author.

Louviere, J., & Hensher, D. (1983). Using discrete choice models with experimental data to forecast consumer demand for a unique event. *Journal of Consumer Research, 10*(3), 348-361.

Lynch, K. (1960). *The image of the city*. Cambridge, MA: MIT Press.

MacAloon, J. (1984). Olympic Games and the theory of spectacle in modern societies. In J. MacAloon (Ed.), *Rite, drama, festival, spectacle: Rehearsals towards a theory of cultural performance* (pp. 241-280). Philadelphia: Institute for the Study of Human Issues.

MacCannell, D. (1976). *The tourist: A new theory of the leisure class*. New York: Schocken Books.

MacMillan, I. (1983). Competitive strategies for not-for-profit agencies. *Advances in Strategic Management, 1*, 61-68.

Macnaught, T. (1982). Mass tourism and the dilemmas of modernization in Pacific island communities. *Annals of Tourism Research, 9*, 359-381.

Mannel, R., & Iso-Ahola, S. (1987). Psychological nature of leisure and tourist experiences. *Annals of Tourism Research, 14*, 314-331.

Manning, F. (Ed.). (1983). *The celebration of society: Perspectives on contemporary cultural performance*. Bowling Green: Bowling Green Popular Press.

Marris, T. (1987). The role and impact of mega-events and attractions on regional and national tourism development: Resolutions of the 37th Congress of the AIEST, Calgary. *Revue de Tourisme, 4*, 3-12.

Martin, C., & Tulgan, B. (2001). *Managing generation Y.* Amherst, MA: HRD Press.

Martinez, B., & Weiner, R. (1979). Guide to public relations for nonprofit organizations and public agencies. The Grantsmanship Center (reprinted in *Fundamentals of Arts Festivals Management*, 1994).

Maslow, A. (1954). *Motivation and personality*. New York: Harper and Row.

Mayfield, T., & Crompton, J. (1995). The status of the marketing concept among festival organizers. *Journal of Travel Research, Spring*, 14-22.

McCabe, V., Poole, B., Weeks, P., & Leiper, N. (2000). *The business and management of conventions.* Brisbane: Wiley.

McConkey, R. (1986). *Attracting tours to special events*. Paper presented to the Annual Conference of the Canadian Association of Festivals and Events, Hamilton.

McDonald, M., & Milne, G. (1999). *Cases in sport marketing*. Sudbury, MA: Jones and Bartlett.

McGrane, T. (1995). Olympic auditing. *Internal Auditor, 52*(4), 64-66.

McGregor, D. (1960). *The human side of enterprise*. New York: McGraw Hill.

McGehee, N., Yoon, Y., & Cardenas, D. (2003). Involvement and travel for recreational runners in North Carolina. *Journal of Sport Management, 17*(3), 305-324.

McLaurin, D., & Wykes, T. (2003). *Meetings and conventions: A planning guide*. Mississauga, Canada: Meeting Professionals International Foundation.

Meenaghan, T. (1994). Point of view: Ambush marketing—immoral or imaginative practice? *Journal of Advertising Research, 34*(5), 77–88.

Meenaghen, T. (2001a). Understanding sponsorship effects. *Psychology and Marketing, 18*(2), 95.

Meenaghan, T. (2001b). Sponsorship and advertising: A comparison of consumer perceptions. *Psychology and Marketing, 18*(2,) 191.

Meeting Professionals International. (2003). *Meetings and conventions: A planning guide.* Mississauga, Canada: Author.

Mendell, R., MacBeth, J., & Solomon, A. (1983). The 1982 world's fair—a synopsis. *Leisure Today, Journal of Physical Education, Recreation and Dance, April,* 48–49.

Meredith, G., & Schewe, C. (1994). The power of cohorts. *American Demographics, 16*(120), 22–31.

Mihalik, B. (1994). Mega-event legacies of the 1996 Atlanta Olympics. In P. Murphy (Ed.), *Quality Management in Urban Tourism: Balancing Business and Environment Proceedings* (pp. 151–162). University of Victoria.

Mihalik, B., & Wing-Vogelbacher, A. (1992). Travelling art expositions as a tourism event: A market research analysis for Ramesses the Great. *Journal of Travel and Tourism Marketing, 1*(3), 25–41.

Mill, R., & Morrison, A. (1985). *The tourism system, an introductory text.* Englewood Cliffs, NJ: Prentice-Hall.

Mintzberg, H. (1994). *The rise and fall of strategic planning.* New York: The Free Press.

Mitchell, S. (2000). *American generations: Who they are: How they live: What they think* (2nd. ed.) New York: New Strategist Publications Inc.

Mohr, K., Backman, K., Gahan, L., & Backman, S. (1993). An investigation of festival motivations and event satisfaction by visitor type. *Festival Management & Event Tourism, 1*(3), 89–97.

Morrison, A. (1995). *Hospitality and travel marketing* (2nd ed.). Albany NY: Delmar.

Morrow, S. (1997). *The art of the show.* Dallas: Education Foundation, International Association for Exposition Management.

Moses, E. (2000). *The $100 billion allowance: Accessing the global teen market.* New York: John Wiley.

Mount, J., & Niro, B. (1995). Sponsorship: An empirical study of its application to local business in a small town setting. *Festival Management & Event Tourism, 2*(3/4), 167–175).

Mowen, A., Vogelsong, H., & Graefe, A. (2003). Perceived crowding and its relationship to crowd management practices at park and recreation events. *Event Management, 8*(2), 63–72.

Mules, T., & Faulkner, W. (1996). An economic perspective on special events. *Tourism Economics, 2,* 107–117.

Mules, T., & McDonald, S. (1994). The economic impact of special events: The use of forecasts. *Festival Management & Event Tourism, 2*(1), 45–53.

Murray, J., (1991). Applied tourism economic impact analysis: Pitfalls and practicalities. In *Building Credibility for a Credible Industry, Proceedings of the TTRA 23d annual conference* (pp. 19–31). Long Beach California.

National Endowment for the Arts. (2002). *Survey of public participation in the arts.* http://www.arts.gov/pub/ResearchNotes.html

Ngamsom, B., & Beck, J. (2000). A pilot study of motivations, inhibitors, and facilitators of association members in attending international conferences. *Journal of Convention and Exhibition Management, 2*(2/3), 97–111.

Nicholls, J., Laskey, H., & Roslow, S. (1992). A comparison of audiences at selected hallmark events in the United States. *International Journal of Advertising, 11*(3), 215-225.

Nogawa, H., Yamaguchi, Y., & Hagi, Y. (1996). An empirical reserach study on Japanese sport tourism in sport-for-all events: Case studies of a single-night event and a multiple-night event. *Journal of Travel Research, 35*(2), 46-54.

Noronha, R. (1977). Paradise reviewed: Tourism in Bali. In E. de Kadt (Ed.), *Tourism: Passport to development?* (pp. 177-204). Oxford: Oxford University Press.

Oakley, E., & Krug, D. (1991). *Enlightened leadership: Getting to the heart of change.* New York: Simon and Schuster.

O'Brien, E., & Shaw, M. (2002). Independent meeting planners: A Canadian perspective. *Journal of Convention and Exhibition Management, 3*(4), 37-68.

Oppermann, M., & Chon, K. (1997). Convention participation decision-making process. *Annals of Tourism Research, 24*(1), 178-191.

O'Toole, W. (2000). The integration of event management best practice by the project management process. *Australian Parks and Leisure, 3*(1), 4-8.

O'Toole, W., & Mikolaitis, P. (2002). *Corporate event project management.* New York: John Wiley.

Parasuraman, A., Zeithaml, V., & Berry, L. (1985). A conceptual model of service quality and its implications for future research. *Journal of Marketing, 49*, 41-50.

Pearce, P. (1993) Fundamentals of tourist motivation. In D. Pearce & R. Butler (Eds.), *Tourism research: Critiques and challenges.* New York: Routledge.

Pearce, P., & Caltabiano, M. (1983). Inferring travel motivation from travellers' experiences. *Journal of Travel Research, 2*, 16-20.

Pennington-Gray, L., & Holdnak, A. (2002). Out of the stands and into the community: Using sports events to promote a destination. *Event Management, 7*(3), 177-186.

Perry, H., & Kelly, R. (1988). *Association management: Perspectives, practices, and procedures for the management of non-profit organizations.* Owen Sound: Big Bay Publishing Inc.

Peterson, K., & Crayton, C. (1995). The effect of an economic impact study on sponsorship development for a festival. *Festival Management & Event Tourism, 2*(3/4), 185-190.

Pfeffer, J., & Salanick, G. (1978). *The external control of organizations.* New York: Harper & Row.

Pine, B., & Gilmore, J. (1999). *The experience economy: Work is theatre and every business a stage.* Boston: Harvard Business School Press.

Pitts, B. (1999). Sports tourism and niche markets: Identification and analysis of the growing lesbian and gay sports tourism industry. *Journal of Vacation Marketing, 5*(1), 31-50.

Plant, B. (1985). *Visitor profile analysis 1985 Elmira Maple Syrup Festival.* Bachelor's thesis, Department of Recreation and Leisure Studies, University of Waterloo.

Pliniussen, J. (1994). *Introduction to Canadian business management.* Toronto: McGraw Hill Ryerson Ltd.

Plog, S. (1987). Understanding psychographics in tourism research. In J. Ritchie & C. Goeldner (Eds.), *Travel, tourism and hospitality research* (pp. 302-213). New York: John Wiley.

Pol, L., & Pak, S. (1994). The use of a two-stage survey design in collecting data from those who have attended periodic or special events. *Journal of the Market Research Society, 36*(4), 315-326.

Porter, M. (1980). *Competitive strategy: Techniques for analyzing industries and competitors.* New York: The Free Press.

Preda, P., & Watts, T. (2003). Improving the efficiency of sporting venues through capacity management: The case of the Sydney (Australia) Cricket Ground Trust. *Event Management, 8*(2), 83–89.

Price, C. (1993). *An empirical study of the value of professional association meetings from the perspective of attendees.* Unpublished doctoral dissertation. Virginia Polytechnic and State University, Blacksburg.

Queenan, L. (1989, August). *Ohioana,* 13–15.

Queensland Events Corporation. (1991). *QEC corporate plan: 1991 and beyond.* Brisbane: Author.

Queensland Events Corporation. (2003). *Queensland events: The year in review 2003.* Brisbane: Author.

Quigley, T. (n.d). Enhancing your festival's food and beverage operations. In *Event operations* (pp. 87–92). Port Angeles, WA: International Festivals and Events Association.

Ralston, L., & Crompton, J. (1988a). *Profile of visitors to the 1987 Dickens on the Strand emerging from a mail back survey.* Report #2 for the Galveston Historical Foundation.

Ralston, L., & Crompton, J. (1988b). *Motivations, service quality and economic impact of visitors to the 1987 Dickens on the Strand emerging from a mail back survey.* Report #3 for the Galveston Historical Foundation.

Raybould, M. (1998). Participant motivation in a remote fishing event. *Festival Management & Event Tourism, 5*(4), 324–241.

Raybould, M., Mules, T., Fredline, E., & Tomljenovic, R. (2000). Counting the herd: Using aerial photography to estimate attendance at open events. *Event Management, 6*(1), 25–32.

Rea, M. (n.d.). Managing the insurance process. In *Event trends in the 90's* (pp. 57–61). Port Angeles, WA: International Festivals Association.

Redding, J. (1997). Fast cycle organization development: Analysis and assessment from an organizational learning perspective. *Organization Development Journal, 15*(1), 82–91.

Reiss, A. (1992). Festival boosts audiences and funding by linking tourism to the arts. *Fund Raising Management, May,* 52, 54.

Ritchie, B. (1984). Assessing the impacts of hallmark events: Conceptual and research issues. *Journal of Travel Research, 23*(1), 2–11.

Ritchie, B. (2000). Turning 16 days into 16 years through Olympic legacies. *Event Management, 6*(2), 155–165.

Ritchie, B., & Crouch, C. (2003). *The competitive destination: A sustainable tourism perspective.* Wallingford: CABI.

Ritchie, B., & Smith, B. (1991). The impact of a mega-event on host region awareness: A longitudinal study. *Journal of Travel Research, 30*(1), 3–10.

Ritchie, K. (1995). Marketing to generation X. *American Demographics, 17*(4), 34–39.

Rizzo, L. (1991). *The key to success in running an outdoor festival.*

Robinson, M., & Carpenter, R. (2002). The day of week's impact on selected socio-demographic characteristics and consumption patterns of spectators at a Ladies Professional Golf Association event. *Sport Marketing Quarterly, 11*(4), 242–247.

Robinson, M., Hums, M., Crow, R., & Philips, D. (2001). *Profiles of sport industry professionals: The people who make the games happen.* Gaithersburg, MD: Aspen Publishers.

Rogers, T. (1998). *Conferences: A twenty-first century industry.* Harlow: Addison Wesley Longman.

Rogers, A., & Slinn, J. (1993). *Tourism: Management of facilities.* London: Longman, the M and E Handbook Series.

Rosenbaum, B. (1982). *How to motivate today's workers: Motivational models for man-*

agers and supervisors. New York: McGraw Hill.

Rozin, S. (2000, April 10). The amateurs who saved Indianapolis. *Business Week,* 126, 130.

Rutley, J. (n.d.). Security. In *Event operations* (pp. 75-83). Port Angeles, WA: International Festivals and Events Association.

Ryan, C., & Bates, C. (1995). A rose by any other name: The motivations of those opening their gardens for a festival. *Festival Management & Event Tourism, 3*(2), 59-71.

Ryan, C., & Lockyer, T. (2002). Masters' Games—the nature of competitors' involvement and requirements. *Event Management, 7*(4), 259-270.

Saayman, M. (Ed.). (2001). *An introduction to sports tourism and event management.* Potchefstroom, South Africa: Institute for Tourism and Leisure Studies.

Saleh, F., & Ryan, C. (1993). Jazz and knitwear: Factors that attract tourists to festivals. *Tourism Management, 14*(4), 289-297.

Sawyer, T., & Smith, O. (1999). *The management of clubs, recreation, and sport: Concepts and applications.* Champaign, IL: Sagamore Publishing.

Schachner, M. (1994). Special events require planning, experts say. *Business Insurance, 28*(8), 2, 32.

Schein, E. (1985). *Organizational culture and leadership.* San Francisco: Jossey-Bass.

Schlegel, J. (1995a, January). Structuring a board meeting. *Association Management,* L45-L46.

Schlegel, J. (1995b, January). Managing the meeting. *Association Management,* L46-L47.

Schmader, S. (n.d). From the flow chart to action. In *Event operations* (pp. 7-14). Port Angeles, WA: International Festivals and Events Association.

Scotinform Ltd. (1991). *Edinburgh Festivals Study 1990-91: Visitor survey and economic impact assessment, final report.* Edinburgh: Scottish Tourist Board.

Scott, D. (1996). A comparison of visitors' motivations to attend three urban festivals. *Festival Management & Event Tourism, 3*(3), 121-128.

Senge, P. (1990). *The fifth discipline: The art and practice of the learning organization.* New York: Doubleday.

Senge, P., Roberts, C., Ross, R., Smith, B., & Kleiner, A. (1994). *The fifth discipline fieldbook: Strategies and tools for building a learning organization.* New York: Doubleday.

Shackley, M. (2001). Sacred world heritage sites: Balancing meaning with management. *Tourism Recreation Research, 26*(1), 5-10.

Sheehan, A., Hubbard, S., & Popovich, P. (2000). Profiling the hotel and conference center meeting planner: A preliminary study. *Journal of Convention and Exhibition Management, 2*(2/3), 11-25.

Sheldon, P. (1990). A review of tourism expenditure research. In C. Cooper (Ed.), *Progress in tourism, recreation and hospitality management* (Vol. 2). London: University of Surrey and Belhaven Press.

Shibli, S., & the Sport Industry Research Centre. (2002). *The 2002 Embassy World Snooker Championship, an evaluation of the economic impact, place marketing effects, and visitors' perceptions of Sheffield.* For Sheffield City Council.

Shone, A., & Parry B. (2001). *Successful event management.* London: Continuum.

Sigelman, L. (1981). Bureaucratization and organizational effectiveness, a double-dip hypothesis. *Administration and Society, 13*(3), 251-264.

Simonson, L. (1995, January). Parliamentary pointers. *Association Management,* L48-L50.

Skinner, B. (1938). *The behavior of organisms.* New York: Appleton-Century-Crofts.

Skinner, B. (1974). *About behavior.* New York: Knopf.

Skinner, B., & Rukavina, V. (2003). *Event sponsorship.* New York: John Wiley.

Smith, S. (1988, November). The festival visitor: It may not be who you think it is. *Feed-*

back, the Official Publication of the Waterloo (Ontario) Chamber of Commerce, 1.

Smith, S. (1995). *Tourism analysis: A handbook* (2nd ed.). Harlow, England: Longman.

Smith, V. (Ed.) (1977). *Hosts and guests: The anthropology of tourism*. Philadelphia: University of Pennsylvania Press.

Sofield, T. (1991). Sustainable ethnic tourism in the South Pacific: Some principles. *Journal of Tourism Studies, 1*(3), 56–72.

Sofield, T., & Li, F. (1998). Historical methodology and sustainability: An 800-year-old festival from China *Journal of Sustainable Tourism, 6*(4), 267–292.

Solberg, H., Andersson, T., & Shibli, S. (2002). An exploration of the direct economic impacts from business travelers at world championships. *Event Management, 7*(3), 151–164.

Solomon, J. (2002). *An insider's guide to managing sporting events*. Champaign, IL: Human Kinetics.

South Carolina Department of Parks, Recreation and Tourism and the South Carolina Festivals Association. (1982). *Festival planning handbook* (2nd ed).

Special Events New South Wales. (1995). *1995 autumn events calendar*.

Spiller, J. (2002). History of convention tourism. In K. Weber & K. Chon (Eds.), *Convention tourism: International research and industry perspectives* (pp. 3–20). Binghamton, NY: Haworth Hospitality Press.

Spilling, O. (1998). Beyond intermezzo? On the long-term industrial impacts of mega-events: The case of Lillehammer 1994. *Festival Management & Event Tourism, 5*(3), 101–122.

Sports Business Market Research Inc. (2000). *Sports Business Market Research handbook*. Norcross, GA: Author.

Sports Economics. Published by The Centre For South Australian Economic Studies, Adelaide, No. 2, 1991; No. 3, 1992.

Statistics Canada. *1998/99 national population health survey.*

Stebbins, R. (1982). Serious leisure: A conceptual statement. *Pacific Sociological Review, 25*(2).

Stebbins, R. (1992). *Amateurs, professionals and serious leisure*. Montreal: McGill University Press.

Steers, R. (1991). *Introduction to organizational behavior* (4th ed.). New York: Harper Collins.

Stiernstrand, O. (1997). Servicekvalitet inom evenemangsturism. Ostersund, Sweden: ETOUR.

Stone, T., & Meltz, N. (1988). *Human resource management in Canada* (2nd ed.). Toronto: Holt, Rinehart and Winston.

Sunshine, K., Backman, K., & Backman, S. (1995). An examination of sponsorship proposals in relation to corporate objectives. *Festival Management & Event Tourism, 2*(3/4), 159–166.

Sutherland, A., & Thompson, B. (2003). *Kidfluence: The marketer's guide to understanding and reaching generation Y—kids, tweens and teens*. New York: McGraw-Hill.

Swarbrooke, J. (1995). *The development and management of visitor attractions*. Oxford: Butterworth-Heinemann.

Tanke, M. (1990). *Human resources management for the hospitality industry*. Albany, NY: Delmar.

Tarlow, P. (2002). *Event risk management and safety*. New York: John Wiley.

Tassiopoulos, D. (Ed.). (2000). *Event management: A professional and developmental approach*. Lansdowne: Juta Education.

Taylor, P., & Gratton, C. (1988). The Olympic Games: An economic analysis. *Leisure Management, 8*(3), 32–34.

Teigland, J. (1996). *Impacts on tourism from mega-events: The case of the Winter Olympic Games.* Sogndal, Norway: Western Norway Research Institute.

Testa, B. (2002). Web warriors. *The Meeting Professional, 22*(3).

The 2002 travel and leisure market research handbook. (2002). New York: Richard K. Miller & Associates.

Thrane, C. (2002). Music quality, satisfaction, and behavioral intentions within a jazz festival context. *Event Management, 7*(3), 143-150.

Tomlinson, G. (1986). *The staging of rural food festivals: some problems with the concept of liminoid performances.* Paper presented to the Qualitative Research Conference on Ethnographic Research, University of Waterloo.

Tourism Canada. (1994). *Packaging and marketing festivals and events for the Canadian tourism industry.* Prepared by MGB Tourfest Inc., and The Economic Planning Group of Canada, Ottawa.

Tourism South Australia. (1991, April). *Barossa Valley Vintage Festival visitor survey.* Adelaide.

Travel Industry Association of America. (2001). *Partners in tourism 2001.*

Travel Industry Association of America. (2003). *Domestic travel market report 2003.* Washington, DC: Author.

Turco, D. (1995). Measuring the tax impacts of an international festival: Justification for government sponsorship. *Festival Management & Event Tourism, 2*(3/4), 191-195.

Turner, V. (Ed.). (1982). *Celebration: Studies in festivity and ritual.* Washington: Smithsonian Institution Press.

Twyford, S. (n.d.). Sponsor servicing. In *IFA's official guide to sponsorship* (pp. 45-48). Port Angeles, WA: International Festivals Association.

Tyrrell, T., & Johnston, R. (2001). A framework for assessing direct economic impacts of tourist events: Distinguishing origins, destinations, and causes of expenditures. *Journal of Travel Research, 40*, 94-100.

Tzelepi, M., & Quick, S. (2002). The Sydney Organizing Committee for the Olympic Games (SOCOG) "Event Leadership" training course—an effectiveness evaluation. *Event Management, 7*(4), 245-257.

UK Sport. (n.d.). *Major sport events: The guide.* www.uksport.gov.uk.

U.S. Travel Data Center. (1989). *Discover America 2000.* Washington, DC: Travel Industry Association of America.

U.S. Travel Data Center. (1993). *1994 Outlook for Travel and Tourism, Proceedings of the Nineteenth Annual Travel Outlook Forum.* Washington.

Uysal, M., Gahan, L., & Martin, B. (1993). An examination of event motivations: A case study. *Festival Management & Event Tourism, 1*(1), 5-10.

Uzzell, D. (1984). An alternative structuralist approach to the psychology of tourism marketing. *Annals of Tourism Research, 11*, 79-99.

Van der Lee, P., & Williams, J. (1986). The grand prix and tourism. In J. Burns, J. Hatch, & T. Mules (Eds.), *The Adelaide Grand Prix—the impact of a special event* (pp. 39-57). Adelaide: Centre for South Australian Economic Studies.

Van der Wagen, L. (2001). *Event management for tourism, cultural, business and sporting events.* Melbourne: Hospitality Press.

Vancouver's Cultural Tourism Initiative. (2001, January). *Visiting audiences: A tourism guide for cultural organizations.*

Vanhove, D., & Witt, S. (1987). Report of the English-speaking group on the conference theme. *Revue de Tourisme, 4*, 10-12.

Vaughan, R. (1979). *Does a festival pay? A case study of the Edinburgh Festival in 1976.*

Tourism Recreation Research Unit, Working Paper 5, University of Edinburgh.

Verhoven, P., Wall, D., & Cottrell, S. (1998). Application of desktop mapping as a marketing tool for special events planning and evaluation: A case study of the Newport News Celebration in Lights. *Festival Management & Event Tourism, 5*(3), 123-130.

Vogt, C., Fesenmaier, D., & Mackay, K. (1993). Functional and aesthetic information needs underlying the pleasure travel experience. In M. Uysal & D. Fesenmaier (Eds.), *Communication and channel systems in tourism marketing* (pp. 133-146). New York: Haworth Press.

Vroom, V. (1964). *Work and motivation*. New York: John Wiley.

Walle, A. (2003). Building a diverse attendance at cultural festivals: Embracing oral history/ folklore in strategic ways. *Event Management, 8*(2), 73-82.

Wang, P., & Gitelson, R. (1988, August). Economic limitations of festivals & other hallmark events. *Leisure Industry Report*, 4-5.

Waters, H. (1939). *History of fairs and expositions.* London, Canada: Reid Brothers & Co. Ltd.

Watson, G. (1993). *Strategic benchmarking*. New York: Wiley.

Weber, K., & Chon, K. (Eds.). (2002). *Convention tourism: International research and industry perspectives*. New York: Haworth.

Webster, G. (1995, January). Meeting your fiduciary responsibilities. *Association Management*, L50-L53.

Wellner, A. (2003). The next 25 years. *American Demographics, 25*(3), 24-27.

Weppler, K., & McCarville, R. (1995). Understanding organizational buying behavior to secure sponsorship. *Festival Management & Event Tourism, 2*(3/4), 139-148.

Whitson, D., & Macintosh, D. (1996). The global circus: International sport, tourism, and the marketing of cities. *Journal of Sport and Social Issues, 20*(3), 278-295.

Wickham, T., & Kerstetter, D. (2000). The relationship between place attachment and crowding in an event setting. *Event Management, 6*(3), 167-174.

Wicks, B. (1995). The business sector's reaction to a community special event in a small town: A case study of the Autumn on Parade Festival. *Festival Management & Event Tourism, 2*(3/4), 177-183.

Wicks, B., & Fesenmaier, D. (1993). A comparison of visitor and vendor perceptions of service quality at a special event. *Festival Management & Event Tourism, 1*(1), 19-26.

Wicks, B., & Fesenmaier, D. (1995). Market potential for special events: A midwestern case study. *Festival Management & Event Tourism, 3*(1), 25-31.

Wicks, B., & Schuett, M. (1993) Using travel brochures to target frequent travellers and 'big spenders.' In M. Uysal & D. Fesenmaier (Eds.), *Communication and channel systems in tourism marketing* (pp. 3-19). New York: The Haworth Press.

Williams, P., Dossa, K., & Tompkins, L. (1995). Volunteerism and special event management: A case study of Whistler's Men's World Cup of Skiing. *Festival Management & Event Tourism, 3*(2), 83-95.

Williams, P., & Harrison, L. (1988). *A framework for marketing ethnocultural communities and festivals*. Unpublished report to the Secretary of State Multiculturalism Ottawa.

Wilson, J., & Udall, L. (1982). *Folk festivals: A handbook for organization and management*. Knoxville: The University of Tennessee Press.

Wojcik, J. (2003). Public entities seek to cut event liability; hold-harmless pacts, cover common. *Business Insurance, 37*(20): 28.

World Tourism Organization. (1999). *Changes in leisure time*. Madrid: Author.

Wyman, K. (1989). *Guide to special event fundraising*. Ottawa: Canadian Department of the Secretary of State, Voluntary Action Directorate.

Xie, P., & Smith, S. (2000). Improving forecasts for world's fair attendance: Incorporating income effects. *Event Management, 6*(1), 15–23.

Yoon, S., Spencer, D., Holecek, D., & Kim, D. (2000). A profile of Michigan's festival and special event tourism market. *Event Management, 6*(1), 33–44.

Yu, Y., & Turco, D. (2000). Issues in tourism event economic impact studies: The case of Albuquerque International Balloon Fiesta. *Current Issues in Tourism, 3*(2), 138–149.

Zeithaml, V., Parasuraman, A., & Berry, L. (1990). *Delivering quality service: Balancing customer perceptions and expectations*. New York: The Free Press.

Index